MONICA PATEL
NOV '17.

The Institute of Chartered Accountants in England and Wales

STRATEGIC BUSINESS MANAGEMENT

database hacked ⊗ — cyber security 337

Edition 4

Question Bank

ICAEW

www.icaew.com

Strategic Business Management
The Institute of Chartered Accountants in England and Wales

ISBN: 978-1-78363-488-0
Previous ISBN: 978-1-78363-233-6

First edition 2014
Fourth edition 2017

The content of this publication is intended to prepare students for the ICAEW examinations, and should not be used as professional advice.

British Library Cataloguing-in-Publication Data
A catalogue record for this book is available from the British Library

Originally printed in the United Kingdom by Wheatons Exeter Ltd on paper obtained from traceable, sustainable sources.

Wheatons Exeter Ltd
Hennock Road
Marsh Barton
Exeter
EX2 8RP

Contents

The following questions are exam-standard. Unless told otherwise, these questions reflect the style, content and format that you can expect in your exam.

July 2017.

Marking – Technical Knowledge and Skills

Marks are awarded in the Strategic Business Management (SBM) paper for both technical knowledge and professional skills.

Technical knowledge and understanding

Technical knowledge and understanding will include the information in the SBM learning materials texts for business strategy, financial management, financial reporting, assurance and ethics. It may also include brought forward knowledge from professional level. Marks will be awarded for displaying this knowledge in the context of the questions. The emphasis is on the use of knowledge, rather than repetition of knowledge. Consequently, technical knowledge needs to be applied to complex scenarios in light of the specific commercial and environmental conditions in the question, and taking account of client requirements.

Professional skills

Marks will also be awarded for exercising professional skills. (For a full list of these skills, with examples, you should refer to the skills grid in the Study Guide.) These skills are classified under four headings:

- Assimilating and using information
- Structuring problems and solutions
- Applying judgement
- Drawing conclusions and making recommendations

Each question will require different skills. Also, the balance of marks for technical knowledge and skills is likely to vary between questions. The balance is specific to each question, hence it is difficult to generalise. However, for example, if an organisation is considering a change to its organisational structure, 'Technical' marks will be available for explaining the implications of the different structures being considered. 'Skills' marks will then be available for evaluating the main advantages and disadvantages of the structures being considered, directly in the context of the organisation being considered in the scenario.

Similarly, if the question requires you to evaluate the strategic and operational risks an organisation faces in undertaking a particular strategy, 'Technical' marks will be available for correctly identifying and analysing the risks highlighted by the scenario. 'Skills' marks will then be available for assimilating the qualitative and quantitative information provided in the scenario in order to identify and prioritise the key risks which the organisation faces.

Equally, a question which requires financial analysis skills in valuing a company is likely to have a high proportion of skills marks with a lower level of technical knowledge.

Finally, ethical skills will demand more than the straightforward implementation of ethical rules. Rather, they are likely to require ethical judgement to be exercised in complex scenarios, where the appropriate ethical stance may be unclear.

421 - supply chain Mgmt. ✓

423 - Interest Rate Parity ✓

~~424~~ - PFI (Assurance report).

440 - Brand valuation. ✓

435 - Financial performance comparison.

441 - DD definition
+ procedures /key risks

445 - Disposal group /Held for sale ✓

307 - Operating segments. ✓

Question Bank

256 - Hedging techniques ✓

258 - Accounting for Hedging ✓

259 - PPP. ✓

265 - Pension Plan
acc/ng treatment + explanation. ✓

446 - Interest rates futures contract ✓

236 - Branding strategy. ✓

248 - Risks of franchising ✓

249 - CRM + Big Data. ✓

251 - Mgmt control

411 - Liquidation ✓

293 - Joint Arrangements ✓

295 - Assurance
↳ Joint Arrangements. ✓

246 - Due Diligence on each item of FS. ✓

242 - EPS + DEPS ✓

461 - Big Data Analytics ✓

462 Corp. Gov. ✓

463 - sustainability (Defn)

269 - CSR (defn)
+ explanation.

Your exam will consist of:

2 questions   100 marks

Pass mark

Exam length   3.5 hours

The ACA student area of our website includes the latest information, guidance and exclusive resources to help you progress through the ACA, Find everything you need, from exam webinars, past papers, marks plans, errata sheets and the syllabus to advice from the examiners at icaew.com/exams

275 - Foreign Ex Risk

302 - Provision.

318 - Collar.

ICAEW

1

1 Hobart plc

Hobart plc ('Hobart') is a small listed company which operates a chain of 40 motor car retail outlets. All the outlets sell both new cars and previously owned (ie used) cars.

Potential purchase of Tasman Ltd

Tasman Ltd ('Tasman') is a small motor retailer with 20 outlets. It has performed poorly in recent years and has entered administration in the past few days. The administrator is attempting to sell the business as a going concern and has been in discussion with Hobart as a potential purchaser. A key issue that has arisen is the valuation that Hobart should place on the Tasman business. In this context, the board of Hobart has approached the firm in which you are a senior, for advisory work with respect to the valuation and also in respect of financial and commercial assurance on the potential deal.

The meeting with the finance director

The finance director of Hobart, James Lafon, called a meeting on 1 December 20X6 with the assignment partner, Helen Dunn, and summarised the situation as follows:

'We have looked at some of the details and Tasman looks like it could be a useful strategic addition to our group. It has a good reputation for customer service, well-trained staff, and some modern showrooms, which are in good locations that are not covered by our existing network. A major problem, however, is that Tasman has been tied into a long-term contract with a single motor manufacturer, Rex plc ('Rex'). The contract was originally for six years and it had three years left to run. Unfortunately, the contract with Rex had an exclusivity clause that had prevented Tasman acting as a franchisee for any other motor manufacturer.

Basically, the Rex contract has been a disaster. Rex cars have proved to be unreliable according to recent surveys. There have been several recalls due to manufacturing faults and the reputation of its cars has fallen dramatically in the past few years in all car market surveys. As a consequence, nobody wants to buy them unless they are heavily discounted from retail list prices. Tasman has therefore had difficulty making sales targets and has not achieved sufficient sales volumes to receive bonus payments from Rex under the terms of the contract. As a result, Tasman has made losses in the past two years forcing significant downsizing and then, last week, it entered administration.

Our problem is how do we value a loss making business in order to make an offer? The administrator wants to sell the business as a going concern and he is clearly looking for a premium over the asset values. What I require from your firm is a range of values as the basis on which to make an offer, and around which we can negotiate. I need some justification for these figures as, if we are the only potential buyer we need to negotiate with the administrator. However, I also need an estimate of the maximum price that we should pay if there are other buyers and we need to bid. I know the information is a bit limited at the moment, so please indicate any reservations about the information that you have.

In addition, I am concerned about the risks that may be involved. The administrator has agreed to see me for a day next week, so I can go through the financial records and view the assets. I would like you to come with me and I require some preliminary briefing notes. Therefore, please provide an outline of the key commercial and financial issues that you would wish to consider in order to provide an assurance report on the information underlying the valuation. I also need an explanation of the key risks for other members of the board.

I have provided you with some background information (**Exhibit 1**); an indication of the Hobart directors' strategy for Tasman (**Exhibit 2**); and forecast financial statements for Tasman. (**Exhibit 3**).

On a related issue I have been asked by my chairman to show you a memo he has received from our Senior Independent Director expressing some concerns with regard to the proposed acquisition of Tasman (**Exhibit 4**). For information I am also giving you summary financial statements for Hobart in 20X5 (**Exhibit 5**). We would like you to provide your professional opinion on two matters:

(1) The concerns raised in the memo

(2) Implications for corporate governance that the chairman should consider in view of the memo and its contents

The assignment partner's instructions

Following the meeting with the Finance Director the assignment partner calls you into her office. She explains the details of the meeting with James Lafon and then she provides you with the following instructions:

'I would like you to act as senior on the Hobart assignment. Using the information on Tasman provided by James, the finance director, I would like you to prepare a memorandum which sets out and explains the required valuations. Assume a tax rate of 23% in your valuation calculations, and for this purpose please ignore the memo from the Senior Independent Director.

Please also provide a risk assessment and the assurance notes required by James for the meeting with the administrator. I will ask somebody else to look at the tax issues so ignore these for now.

Finally please provide an assessment of the issues raised by the Senior Independent Director and also the potential implications for corporate governance in Hobart. This should be provided in draft as a separate memorandum to the chairman, which he needs to help him with his preparations for the board meeting where the proposed acquisition of Tasman will be discussed.'

Requirement

Prepare the memorandum and the draft memorandum required by the assignment partner.

Total: 55 marks

Exhibit 1 – Background information on Tasman

The Tasman business was set up over 50 years ago and continues to have a good reputation for service. In December 20X3, Tasman signed a six-year contract with Rex to become a franchised dealer. Prior to the agreement, Tasman had not been franchised to any car manufacturer and had thus sold only used cars.

In 20X4 an offer was made to acquire the Tasman brand name for £2m by an international car dealer. The offer was given serious consideration, but was ultimately refused. *Rex = major creditor + customer*

Tasman sells both new cars (all manufactured by Rex) and used cars. The used cars are made by a variety of manufacturers and are mainly the trade-in vehicles of customers buying new Rex cars.

In 20X4, Tasman acquired Darwin Ltd, a small car dealer with one garage. This garage is still being operated, but now trades under the Tasman brand name.

Marketing evidence provided by Tasman suggests that the total revenue of the company would continue to fall by around 10% per year if the Rex franchise contract remained in force.

In 20X5, a car sold by Tasman crashed due to brake failure, injuring the occupants. As a consequence Tasman is being sued for a substantial sum, which may be as much as £5m. The case is not expected to be settled until 20X8.

The tax written down value of Hobart's plant and machinery at 31 December 20X6 is expected to be £7m.

A consultant advising Tasman had recently estimated its annual cost of equity as 10%.

Exhibit 2 – Hobart's intended strategy for Tasman

Due to the litigation against Tasman, the directors of Hobart would prefer to acquire the Tasman business as a whole (including all the tangible and intangible assets), but not to acquire its shares.

Hobart's strategic plan for Tasman is to re-launch the business selling used cars and also, if possible, operate an alternative manufacturer's franchise by taking advantage of existing relationships. There would be immediate disengagement from the Rex franchise.

Forecast annual results under this new strategy – assuming that a new franchise arrangement can be set up – include a 100% increase in revenues in 20X7 with the same gross profit margin percentage as for 20X6. Administrative and distribution costs are fixed costs, but synergistic savings of £400,000 should be achieved in 20X7 arising from the acquisition. Thereafter, annual profits should be constant. Annual capital expenditure to sustain the business should be around £500,000. This mainly relates to property and none of this expenditure is expected to be allowable for tax.

Exhibit 3 – Forecast financial statements for Tasman Ltd

Statement of profit or loss for the year ended 31 December

	Unaudited forecast 20X6 £'000	Actual 20X5 £'000
Revenue	23,000	27,600
Cost of sales (Note 2)	(20,000)	(24,000)
Gross/profit	3,000	3,600
Exceptional item (Note 1)	(1,500)	(200)
Administrative and distribution costs (Note 2)	(2,800)	(2,800)
(Loss)/profit from operations	(1,300)	600
Finance costs	(900)	(500)
(Loss)/profit before tax	(2,200)	100
Income tax expense	nil	nil
(Loss)/profit for period	(2,200)	100

Note
Retained earnings at 1 January	2,600	2,500
Retained earnings at 31 December	400	2,600

Summary statement of financial position at 31 December

	Unaudited forecast 20X6 £'000	Actual 20X5 £'000
Assets		
Non-current assets		
Goodwill (Note 1)	500	2,000
Property, plant and equipment (Note 3)	14,000	16,200
	14,500	18,200
Current assets		
Inventories (Note 4)	11,000	9,200
Receivables	500	800
	11,500	10,000
Total assets	26,000	28,200
Equity and liabilities		
Issued capital	5,000	5,000
Revaluation reserve	1,000	1,000
Retained earnings	400	2,600
	6,400	8,600
Non-current liabilities – loans (Note 5)	14,600	14,000
Current liabilities	5,000	5,600
Total equity and liabilities	26,000	28,200

Notes

1   The exceptional item relates to the impairment of goodwill in Darwin Ltd.

2   Cost of sales consists almost entirely of variable costs. Administration and distribution costs are nearly all fixed costs.

3   The estimated fair value of property, plant and equipment at 31 December 20X6 is £22m, of which £15m relates to property. Costs of selling the property, plant and equipment would be £500,000. There have been no acquisitions or disposals of property, plant and equipment during 20X6.

4   Inventories at 31 December 20X6 consist of £4m of used cars and £7m of new Rex cars. (There is currently some uncertainty, but about £4m of these inventories are consignment stock from Rex.) The administrator is claiming that the total estimated net realisable values at full retail list price are £4.5m and £8.5m respectively at 31 December 20X6. However, they may take some time to sell and discounts, or other incentives, would be needed to sell the new Rex cars, perhaps amounting to £750,000.

5   The non-current liabilities include bank loans of £11.6m secured by a fixed charge over property and a floating charge. The other non-current liabilities consist of subordinated loans from Rex of £3m with a second floating charge over assets.

[handwritten annotations: "Stock doesn't belong to Tasman", "£4 + (£7 - £4) = £7m"]

Exhibit 4 – Memorandum from Senior Independent Director

To: Edward Springer, Chairman Hobart plc
From: Senior Independent Director
Date: 26 November 20X6
Subject: Acquisition of Tasman

Chairman

As you know, I have some concerns about the proposed acquisition of Tasman and how it fits in with the board's current growth strategy. My main concern is that the business risk may be greater than the board should be prepared to accept, unless a suitably low acquisition price can be obtained.

I do not know what offer price may be under consideration, but there will clearly be implications for shareholder value. Presumably James Lafon has looked into the ways of financing an acquisition, but I would expect that the company will be able to obtain the finance it requires. I should like to question, however, the potential implications for our cost of capital and share price.

Hobart should not be pursuing an acquisition strategy simply for the purpose of creating a larger business, and I worry that this proposal is being championed by our executive director colleagues against the inclination of most of the board non-executives.

I should like to suggest that the concerns I have raised in this memo will be discussed when the board meets to consider the Tasman acquisition.

Garfield Hanks

Senior Independent Director

Exhibit 5 – Hobart summary financial statements

Statement of profit or loss for the year ended 31 December 20X5

	£m
Revenue	176.9
Cost of sales	(132.5)
Gross profit	44.4
Administrative and distribution costs	(19.4)
Profit from operations	25.0
Finance costs	(9.0)
Profit before tax	16.0
Income tax expense	(3.7)
Profit for the period	12.3

Summary statement of financial position at 31 December 20X5

	£m	£m
Assets		
Non-current assets		210
Current assets		
Inventory	42	
Receivables	28	
Cash	15	
		85
Total assets		295
Equity and liabilities		
Issued share capital (50m shares)		50
Other reserves		37
Retained earnings		53
		140
Non-current liabilities – loans		115
Current liabilities		40
Total equity and liabilities		295

Notes

1 Dividend payments in the year to 31 December 20X5 were £9.6m.
2 The current market value of Hobart's equity is about £200m.
3 Non-current liabilities have remained unchanged since the end of 20X5.

2 Knowhow plc   RTQ

* Acquiring 80% of shares not 100%

You are an adviser to the finance director of Knowhow plc. Knowhow plc is a listed company which operates three international airports in the UK and a further two airports in Germany. The company serves long-established regional airlines and services both domestic and international, mainly European, routes.

Knowhow's mission statement is 'To become the most successful airport group in Europe, by focusing on our customers' needs and safety, and providing them with a superior airport experience.'

The directors of Knowhow plc have been approached by the board of Flyzone Ltd, an unlisted company that owns and operates an international airport in the UK. All five of the directors of Flyzone Ltd are approaching retirement age. Between them, they own 80% of their company's share capital. They wish to realise their investment and have identified that Knowhow plc might be interested in acquiring their shares.

The directors of Knowhow intend to discuss the approach at their next meeting. The directors have already agreed the importance of undertaking financial due diligence in relation to any potential acquisition. However, the finance director believes it is crucial that the due diligence process includes commercial and operational aspects as well as financial due diligence.

The finance director has asked you to prepare the following sections to be included in her report to the board of Knowhow plc:

(1) Calculations of three ratios that concern the directors of Knowhow plc (earnings per share, gearing and non-current asset turnover) as at the end of 20X9 with brief comments on the results under each of the following circumstances:

  ① • Knowhow plc does not invest in Flyzone Ltd.
  ② • Knowhow plc acquires 80% of Flyzone Ltd in the manner described in **Exhibit 1**.
  ② • Knowhow plc acquires 40% of Flyzone Ltd in the manner described in **Exhibit 1**.

  Ignore the effects, if any, of the proposed share option scheme to be offered to the incoming directors of Flyzone Ltd. Assume that the values given in the attached statements of financial position are substantially the same as the fair values of the assets and that non-controlling interests will be measured as a share of identifiable net assets.

BV = FV.

(2) For each of the scenarios associated with the investment in Flyzone Ltd, a discussion of the issues associated with these actions in relation to how they impact on Knowhow plc's shareholders.

(3) A discussion of the implications of the share option scheme for the accounting figures of the Knowhow Group. (You do not need to consider the accounting treatment in the individual accounts of Knowhow plc and Flyzone Ltd.)

(4) A discussion of the advantages and disadvantages of the two alternative offers to invest to the present directors of Flyzone Ltd.

(5) A discussion of the implications of the differences in the approach to corporate responsibility of Knowhow and Flyzone.

(6) An evaluation of whether the proposed acquisition is an appropriate strategic option for Knowhow.

(7) A discussion of the benefits of undertaking commercial due diligence as well as financial due diligence.

You have been provided with some notes prepared by the finance director (**Exhibit 1**), and notes from the most recent management meeting (**Exhibit 2**). You have also been provided with sets of projected financial statements for Knowhow plc and Flyzone Ltd (**Exhibit 3**).

Requirement

Prepare the report extracts requested by the finance director.

Total: 55 marks

Exhibit 1

[margin note: new market]

Flyzone Ltd's airport does not compete directly with any of those owned by Knowhow plc. Most of the flights operating to or from the airport are short-haul, but there are two flights per day departing to the USA. Most of the airlines using the airport are 'low-cost' airlines. *[margin note: new market]* *[margin note: reputational damage]*

[margin note: reliant on mgmt team]

The directors of Knowhow plc are intrigued by this approach because Flyzone Ltd's management team, none of whom are presently on the board, can offer expertise that could be useful to them. Knowhow plc's existing airports are generally viewed as destinations in themselves. If they could attract transatlantic flights then they would be better positioned to offer connecting flights to transit passengers. Airlines would start to use their airports as intercontinental hubs. To date, one of the biggest problems in entering this market has been the airlines' reluctance to work with a company that has no experience of this market.

In relation to the 'low-cost' airlines, this is also a market that requires a different type of management expertise. Knowhow plc has again found it difficult to attract such business.

One significant difference in the way that the two companies are managed in practice is the attitude to corporate responsibility. Knowhow's corporate responsibility report clearly demonstrates that the directors view its ethical responsibilities seriously. Staff at its airports are paid more than staff in equivalent roles at other airports in the same country. In return they are expected to provide a high standard of service to passengers and to minimise delays as far as possible. Knowhow also has a biodiversity programme that has been developed in discussion with environmental charities, and has promoted the environmental awareness of its staff through tailored training programmes. By contrast Flyzone has never sought to do more than fulfil its legal responsibilities and is in a long running dispute *[margin note: reputation]* with local community groups over noise at its airport. A significant proportion of its staff are migrants paid only the minimum wage, and Flyzone has faced a number of claims for wrongful dismissal in recent years from UK staff. Consumer websites rate Flyzone's airport some way below all of Knowhow's airports for comfort and ease of passenger experience. *[margin note: mission]*

Even though an investment in Flyzone Ltd could be an important strategic investment for Knowhow plc, the directors are concerned about the impact this transaction might have on the company's share price. They do not wish to proceed with an investment unless their key accounting ratios (earnings per share, gearing (defined as book value of debt compared to book value of debt plus book value of equity) and non-current asset turnover) will remain within acceptable limits.

The directors of Knowhow plc are considering making two alternative offers to the directors of Flyzone Ltd (both of which would require the directors of Flyzone Ltd to stand down from the board after the transaction): *[margin note: expertise]* *[margin note: 1 or 2]*

(1) They might purchase the directors' 80% of the share capital by exchanging one new share in Knowhow plc in return for every two shares held by the directors. At present, Knowhow plc's share price is £8.50 per £1 share. *[margin note: mv]*

(2) They might purchase a 40% stake in Flyzone Ltd (ie 50% of the shares held by the five directors) by exchanging one new share in Knowhow plc for every three shares purchased from the directors. *[margin note: 1 to 3]* Under this arrangement, both Knowhow plc and the retiring directors would each appoint a single individual to the board of Flyzone Ltd. *[margin note: 5 members]*

As part of the negotiations surrounding Knowhow plc's interest in Flyzone Ltd, three of Flyzone Ltd's present senior management team have agreed to accept places on the board of Flyzone Ltd with effect from the retirement of the existing board members. Two of these managers were selected on the basis of their expertise in the transatlantic market and the third for her expertise in negotiating with low-cost airlines. The current directors of Flyzone Ltd have agreed to sign a contract to provide Knowhow plc with advice and consultancy support in return for a nominal management fee should either of the above offers go ahead. *[margin note: clauses?]*

Flyzone Ltd's three new directors will receive options to buy a substantial number of shares in Knowhow plc directly from the company at a price of £8.90 per share on the third anniversary of them joining the board of Flyzone Ltd. These options will be given in return for advising the directors of Knowhow plc on matters of business strategy.

Exhibit 2 – Notes from management meeting

Service delivery – Knowhow has continued to focus on improving service delivery and passengers' experience of its airports. These are key performance measures, and Knowhow continuously seeks to improve the quality of its processes and services, while keeping costs under control. The directors have always felt such an approach will enable Knowhow to improve the competitiveness and profitability of its airports. _Differentiation strategy_

The group also continues to invest in its airports in order to improve passengers' experience further; on the basis that this should increase passengers' propensity to spend in the airports' retail outlets and catering facilities.

There has been clear progress in improving service standards in the last 12 months, with overall passenger satisfaction scores reaching a record level.

A recent survey of European air passengers (conducted at a range of airports across the continent) found that the airport environment was a big factor in the choice of airport for business and first class passengers. Factors which contributed to this 'environment' were: leading airlines operating from the airport, not low-cost airlines; luxury passenger lounges; and the quality and variety of restaurants and shops.

Low-cost airlines – The Chief Executive has expressed concern about the impact that the growth of 'low-cost' airlines in recent years will have on airports. His concern is that the 'low-cost' model has led to airlines and passengers putting increased emphasis on lower costs and lower prices, rather than quality. In this context, Knowhow will not be as competitive as some of its rivals, and this may be another reason why Knowhow has found it difficult to attract business from low-cost airlines.

Quality or cost – The Operations Director noted that Knowhow has always sought to compete on the basis of the quality of the services it offers its customers. If it starts hosting more low-cost airlines, and changes its focus to minimising costs rather than upholding quality, this could change the whole culture of the organisation.

Exhibit 3

The following projected financial statements have been prepared in support of the negotiations between Knowhow plc and the directors of Flyzone Ltd. They do not take into account Knowhow plc's proposed investment in Flyzone Ltd. The Knowhow Group includes several 100% subsidiaries but no associates.

If the investment proceeds then it will take place on 1 January 20X9.

Projected statements of comprehensive income for the year ended 31 December 20X9

window dressing ↓ sale

	Knowhow Group £m	Flyzone Ltd £m
Revenue	285	86
All expenses including tax expense	(146)	(48)
Profit attributable to equity holders	139	38

Projected statements of financial position as at 31 December 20X8

	Knowhow Group £m	Flyzone Ltd £m
Non-current assets	1,440	561
Current assets	20	8
	1,460	569
Share capital (£1 shares, fully paid)	800	200
Share premium	200	80
Retained earnings	210	70
	1,210	350
Non-current liabilities	240	210
Current liabilities	10	9
	1,460	569

Projected statements of financial position as at 31 December 20X9

	Knowhow Group £m	Flyzone Ltd £m
Non-current assets	1,578	604
Current assets	23	11
	1,601	615
Share capital (£1 shares, fully paid)	800	200
Share premium	200	80
Retained earnings	349	108
	1,349	388
Non-current liabilities	240	220
Current liabilities	12	7
	1,601	615

3 Fowler Ltd

You (Robert O'Hara) are the audit senior in charge on a client, Fowler Limited. Your manager is Janet Hales and you have just received the following memo from her.

MEMO

To: Robert O'Hara
From: Janet Hales
Subject: Fowler Ltd – meeting with Chief Executive, 10 July 20X8

I have been requested to attend a meeting next Friday with Archie Millinchamp, the recently appointed Chief Executive of Fowler Ltd.

The topics for the meeting are as follows:

(1) The costing systems are in need of improvement. This became a matter of concern during last year's audit. We recommended that a thorough review be made of the costing of all products to ensure that overhead allocations are appropriate, as well as any related effects. The FD, Oliver Bradford, has completed his investigation into the costing systems and Archie sees this as the main subject matter for Friday's meeting.

(2) Profitability has declined since last year and Archie wishes to discuss this. I would also like a description of the analytical procedures that we shall need to carry out on the financial information available.

(3) In order to meet the profitability targets set by the parent company, King plc (King), Fowler's managers were asked to make suggestions for limiting costs. Archie has supplied notes of a recent managers' meeting (please note these are confidential). He believes that the suggestions are quite imaginative, but doubts whether all of them are ethical. As an ICAEW Chartered Accountant, he acknowledges that he has to adhere to ICAEW's ethical guidance.

(4) Operations management and cost reduction: responding to possible strategic initiatives proposed by King.

I need you to prepare briefing notes for my use in Friday's meeting. I enclose background information on Fowler Ltd for your information (**Exhibit 1**) and copies of Oliver's work on the costing system (**Exhibit 2**). I also enclose the summarised management accounting statements of profit or loss for the nine months to 30 June 20X8 (**Exhibit 3**) and the notes supplied by Archie of a recent managers' meeting (**Exhibit 4**).

I have also enclosed my notes from a phone conversation with Archie (**Exhibit 5**) about operations management and cost reduction at Fowler. Archie has indicated he wants to talk about this in more detail at our meeting. Again, please remember these are highly confidential, but please can you include in your notes an assessment of the main issues arising from King's idea to split Fowler's operation into two parts.

Do not include detailed background points on Fowler Ltd, as I have been involved with Fowler for some time.

Janet

Requirement

You are required to prepare briefing notes for Janet's meeting with Archie Millinchamp covering the proposed costing system and the reasons for the profitability deterioration for the 9 months to 30 June 20X8.

Total: 55 marks

Exhibit 1

Background notes – Fowler Limited

Fowler Ltd manufactures and supplies oil seals and other fluid seals. The company manufactures a wide range of such products ranging from the relatively simple single-lip rubber seal to complex seals with hydrodynamic aids allowing sealing alternatively in both directions.

Its principal markets include the appliance, heating, chemical, oil refining, defence, motor and general engineering industries. It manufactures the products in runs of between 50 and 12,000 units.

King plc acquired Fowler towards the end of 20X5 as a means of entering new markets. Prior to the acquisition of Fowler, the new Chief Executive of King had attracted considerable publicity when he implemented a Total Quality Management programme aimed at 'making high quality, low cost products which are delivered on time to our customers'.

At that time Fowler had also suffered a downturn in its market share and margins. It was therefore no surprise when immediately after the takeover, King had insisted that Fowler should maintain its prices and aim to recapture market share by providing a high quality product with a high level of customer service. The immediate consequence of this policy had been a further fall in sales volume and margins.

The situation reached a crisis in late 20X7 when Fowler submitted its quotes for a wide range of products to be sold to the Ministry of Defence. The tender was to supply up to sixty different seal products ranging from the simple to the complex, and for volumes ranging from 1,000 to 50,000 units. Despite the intense competition, Fowler had expected to win most of the orders for the more complex devices and several of the high volume orders. The management was shocked to learn that the company had been awarded only eight contracts. These contracts were mainly for simple and low volume products. The directors resolved to investigate the reasons for the failure to win orders for which the company was well suited and they asked the Finance Director to begin by reviewing the company's pricing policies.

Since the date Fowler was acquired by King, the marketing and sales department was encouraged to search aggressively for new business and new markets in order to use the spare capacity brought about by the loss of volume in the traditional markets. They soon discovered a new and potentially very profitable market, that of producing plastic mouldings manufactured to close tolerances and to → established individual customer specification. The market existed in the UK and the rest of Western Europe. This competition new product and market provided Fowler with significant competitive advantages over its low-cost competitors. Fowler's proximity to its customers, the emphasis on quality and customer service rather than on price, and the more complex manufacturing process all gave the company a competitive advantage. It quickly built up a significant market share. ⟩ distinguishing on this (differentiation)

By the end of the third quarter of the year to 30 September 20X8 Fowler's total sales were not far short of budget and the company was beginning to see the impact of the switch to the higher margin products. However, the directors are concerned about the increase in overhead expenses. They had anticipated some increase in overhead costs as a result of implementing King's directives on TQM but the results were still disappointing. The directors are particularly keen to achieve the profit target set by King plc. They concluded that, at this late stage, the only option available to them was to ask the company's managers to cut back on their discretionary expenditure in the final quarter.

Exhibit 2

MEMO

To: Archie Millinchamp
From: Oliver Bradford
Date: 30 June 20X8
Subject: Review of Costing System

Following Holmes Thomson's management letter comments and your suggestion to research into the company's costing system, price setting and other aspects of profitability, I enclose the summarised results of my review.

(1) **Costing and pricing system at December 20X7**

Fowler Ltd has traditionally priced its products at cost plus, where cost is computed using a total absorption costing system.

I have initially reviewed costing for two of the products for which we tendered last Autumn. The costings under our current system were as follows:

Product:	A7 Rubber seal	C4 Water pump seal
Category:	Complex	Simple
Volume:	20,000	2,000
	£	£
Materials	7.72	6.44
Materials o/h (10%)	0.77	0.64
Direct labour @ £6.30 per hour	2.65	1.13
Direct labour o/h (205%)	5.43	2.32
Machine overheads @ £27.56 per hour	66.14	8.54
Total cost	82.71	19.07
Tender price (Cost + 30%)	107.52	24.80

Fowler was awarded the contract for supply of C4, but not A7. We have since learnt that our tender price for A7 was 20% higher than that of the competitor who won the contract.

(2) **Alternative costing and pricing**

I am becoming increasingly concerned about the company's cost plus pricing system when allocated overheads can comprise between 60% – 90% of the total cost of a product. I am not confident that the costing system reflects the increased automation in the factory or that it adequately costs automated production processes.

In my investigation into the system I focused attention on the product flow in the factory and concluded that most of the overheads could be explained by distinct support activities. After reviewing each overhead account together with the functional managers, I have identified an appropriate overhead rate for each activity. However for general, administrative, marketing and selling overhead it was very difficult to attribute to individual products or even product groups. Further analysis is required in this area.

Using the results of this analysis it was possible to 're-cost' products A7 and C4 as follows:

Product:	A7 Rubber seal	C4 Water pump seal
Category:	Complex	Simple
Volume:	20,000	2,000
	£	£
Materials	7.72	6.44
Direct labour @ £6.30 per hour	2.65	1.13
Overheads:		
Direct labour (111%)	2.94	1.25
Machine hours @ £15.20 per hour	36.48	4.71
Set-up	2.53	6.33
Production ordering costs	1.70	8.50
Material handling	0.83	4.14
Product number administration	1.19	11.89
General	10.68	8.39
Total cost	66.72	52.78
Tender price (Cost + 30%)	86.74	68.61

The differences between the costings are significant – I now intend to re-cost most of the other products for which we tendered last year.

As a start, the costings for one of our plastic moulds, the P8, are as follows:

Original costing

Product:	Plastic moulding P8 (per 100 units)
Category:	Complex
Volume:	10,000
	£
Materials	5.60
Materials o/h (10%)	0.56
Direct labour @ £6.30 per hour	4.47
Direct labour o/h (205%)	9.17
Machine overheads @ £27.56 per hour	46.85
Total cost	66.65
Tender price (cost + 30%)	86.65

ABC costing

	£
Materials	5.60
Direct labour @ £6.30 per hour	4.47
Overhead:	
Direct labour (111%)	4.96
Machine hours @ £15.20 per hour	25.84
Set-up	15.82
Production ordering costs	8.50
Material handling	4.14
Product number administration	2.38
General	14.61
Total cost	86.32
Tender price (cost + 30%)	112.22

Exhibit 3

Fowler Ltd – Management accounts – executive summary

Statement of profit or loss summary – 9 months to 30 June 20X8

	Actual £'000	%	Budget £'000	%
Sales	16,920	100	18,110	100
Cost of sales				
Materials	(3,785)	22	(4,068)	22
Labour	(1,602)	9	(1,724)	10
Production overheads	(7,759)	46	(6,875)	38
Total	(13,146)	78	(12,667)	70
Gross profit	3,774	22	5,443	30
Marketing, selling, general and admin costs	(1,400)	8	(1,200)	7
Trading profit	2,374	14	4,243	23
Interest	(320)	2	(360)	2
Profit on sale of non-current assets	200	1	–	0
Profit before taxation	2,254	13	3,883	21
Income tax expense	(902)	5	(1,281)	7
Profit after taxation	1,352	8	2,602	14
Dividend	(2,000)	12	(2,000)	11

Fowler Ltd

Actual – 9 months to 30 June 20X8

	Rubber & leather seals	Water pump seals	Plastic moulds	Total
Sales volume (100 units)	150,000	65,000	50,000	265,000
	£	£	£	£
Sales revenue	6,900,000	7,020,000	3,000,000	16,920,000
Raw materials	1,350,000	1,755,000	680,000	3,785,000
Direct labour	600,000	845,000	157,400	1,602,400
Overheads	3,502,620	3,582,358	673,496	7,758,474
Profit	1,447,380	837,642	1,489,104	3,774,126
Profit margin %	21%	12%	50%	22%
Profit	1,447,380	837,642	1,489,104	3,774,126
Marketing, selling, general and admin costs	570,000	580,000	250,000	1,400,000
	877,380	257,642	1,239,104	2,374,126
				14%

Fowler Ltd

Budget – 9 months to 30 June 20X8

	Rubber & leather seals	Water pump seals	Plastic moulds	Total
Sales volume (100 units)	200,000	70,000	30,000	300,000
	£	£	£	£
Sales revenue	9,200,000	7,560,000	1,350,000	18,110,000
Raw materials	1,800,000	1,890,000	377,500	4,067,500
Direct labour	800,000	810,000	114,200	1,724,200
Overheads	3,488,240	3,190,836	196,122	6,875,198
Profit	3,111,760	1,669,164	662,178	5,443,102
Profit margin %	34%	22%	49%	30%
Profit	3,111,760	1,669,164	662,178	5,443,102
Marketing, selling, general and admin costs	600,000	500,000	100,000	1,200,000
	2,511,760	1,169,164	562,178	4,243,102
				23%

Exhibit 4

Notes on a recent managers' meeting

Suggestions for reducing costs

(1) **Reduce staff head count while avoiding redundancy payouts.** Suggestions included telling staff they faced only a temporary lay-off when there was no prospect of their being re-employed, thus saving redundancy pay and compensation in lieu of notice.

(2) **Limit bonuses.** Where possible, mark staff down in their appraisals, so that they fail to reach the performance levels required to qualify for a bonus.

(3) **Reduce training costs.** Scrapping the company's induction programme and reducing severely the amount of time staff spend on training each year.

(4) **Terminate Fowler's apprenticeship scheme.** Under the terms of the scheme Fowler pays 25% of the apprentices' wages and the school/university or state pays the remainder. The scheme lasts two years; in this time the apprentices can gain sufficient experience and knowledge to increase their employment opportunities. The scheme could be terminated immediately as apprentices are not given contracts of employment and Fowler has no legal obligations to provide them with assistance should the scheme be discontinued.

Exhibit 5

Notes from phone conversation with Archie Millinchamp

King plc are becoming increasingly unhappy about the level of overhead expenses in the business. Aside from the short-term measures which Fowler's managers have discussed in the management meeting, King are looking at longer-term strategies for reducing costs, and are particularly interested in the way supply chain management and operations management techniques could be applied in order to help reduce costs.

One idea King are considering involves splitting Fowler's operations into two parts: one making simple products (in particular, simple seals), and the other making complex products (such as the new mouldings). King's management team believe that the process for making simple seals is basically a 'commodity' and so cost and price are crucial in determining competitive advantage for these. By contrast, the competitive advantage of the more complex products comes from quality and customer service.

King want to discuss the implications of these differences on Fowler's supply chain, and the way the two groups of products can best add value to Fowler's business.

4 Archen plc

A Today
|
M

Archen plc is listed on the London Stock Exchange. It manufactures office furniture. The company has *outbound* been very successful in the UK, and in a couple of other Western European countries, but has not expanded beyond these countries.

Potential acquisition

You are a senior working for the auditors and business advisors of Archen. The current date is 31 March 20X9. The engagement partner called you into a meeting this morning and came straight to the point.

As part of its strategy for expansion, the Archen board has identified the possible acquisition of a company, Merry Ltd, which manufactures carpets, curtains and other home furnishings. The majority of its trade is overseas. Merry has had a reputation for producing high-quality furnishings and, as a result, it exports to all parts of Europe, to the US and to Asia. *New market, related diversification*

Negotiations are only at a preliminary stage at the moment and information is therefore limited, but the finance director of Archen, Toby Timmins, would like some help. He believes that Merry would be a good strategic acquisition as it would open up a new market for Archen in home furnishings and would also significantly enhance Archen's geographical presence. He is, however, concerned about the financial information provided by Merry, particularly as this information may form the basis of initial → *"window dressing"* take-over valuation discussions. He would therefore like us to evaluate Merry's financial performance.

Also, if the negotiations proceed further, we will probably be asked by Toby to do the financial due diligence work. He would like some idea now of what we would consider to be the key issues were we to undertake the due diligence work.

Archen's board believes that the acquisition of Merry will compel it to undertake a major review of its risk management systems, in order to comply with corporate governance best practice. We will need to consider the areas on which this review should concentrate. ↑ *as new market*

corp gov'

A further aspect of the review will be an analysis of how Archen's risk profile will change as a result of the acquisition, considering particularly the group's much wider international presence. In relation to this, we need to identify the key risks that the board needs to consider.

I have provided you with draft statements of profit or loss of Archen for the year ended 31 December 20X8 and of Merry for the years ended 31 December 20X7 and 20X8, together with some notes to these draft statements of profit or loss (**Exhibit 1**). I have also provided brief notes from the Archen finance director including his assumptions (**Exhibit 2**) and an email from the chairman of Merry (**Exhibit 3**).

Performance management

Balanced Scorecard

During my discussions with Toby, he has indicated that, if the acquisition of Merry goes ahead, it could provide him with an opportunity to introduce some changes to the management reports which are currently produced at Archen. Although the Board have got used to the reports they receive, Toby is concerned that they focus too narrowly on internal, financial performance information. In particular, he feels this will not be sufficient to understand and manage Merry's performance satisfactorily. He would like key non-financial performance measures to be introduced into the Board reports, as well as some strategic management accounting information.

Tony believes the Board will be resistant to the changes he would like to make to the Board reports, and so has asked us for our thoughts on the potential benefits of his proposals.

After the meeting, the partner sent you an email, requesting that you prepare the following:

(1) An evaluation of Merry's financial performance in the year ended 31 December 20X8 compared to the year ended 31 December 20X7. *X7 ∨ X8*

(2) Identify the key issues to be addressed in the financial due diligence, based upon your analysis of the draft financial statements of Merry and the supporting notes (Exhibit 1). Please also state the due diligence work we should carry out in respect of these issues, assuming we will be given open access to the financial records of Merry.

(3) Highlight the areas on which Archen's review of its risk management system should concentrate. Please also identify the key risks facing Merry which Archen's board need to consider in relation to the acquisition, and how Archen's risk profile will change as a result of the acquisition.

(4) A discussion of the reasons why it would be useful for Archen to include non-financial performance measures alongside financial ones in its performance management system, and advice on how strategic management accounting could help the directors manage the performance of the group.

Requirement

Respond to the requests in the engagement partner's email.

Total: 45 marks

31 mar x9

GP 120   150
GPM 33.3%   37.5%

Exhibit 1

Draft summary statements of profit or loss for the years ended 31 December

	Notes	Archen 20X8 Draft unaudited £'000	Merry 20X8 Draft unaudited £'000	Merry 20X7 Final £'000
Revenue	1	840,000	360,000	400,000
Cost of sales	2	(560,000)	(240,000)	(250,000)
Depreciation	3	(80,000)	(40,000)	(50,000)
Administration costs	4	(110,000)	(30,000)	(32,000)
Impairment	5	–	–	(5,000) *– for ?*
Provision	6	–	–	(28,000)
Write-back of unutilised provision	6	–	14,000	–
Financing income/(costs)	7	4,000	(18,000)	(12,000) *↓? repay?*
Profit before tax		94,000	46,000	23,000
Tax (at 23%)		(21,620)	(10,580)	(5,290)
Profit after tax		72,380	35,420	17,710

↑ 100%

Notes

1   Due to competitive conditions Merry has not changed the selling prices of its products since 1 January 20X7 and it has no plans to do so in the foreseeable future. *cut off? why increase?*

2   Cost of sales for Merry consists of approximately: 60% variable costs; and 40% fixed costs. *↓ Rev 11% COS 4%*

3   Merry reviewed the useful lives of its non-current assets during the year to 31 December 20X8. As a result of this review, it extended the remaining lives of these assets substantially. Had it not changed the asset lives, the depreciation charge for the year to 31 December 20X8 would have been £50m.

4   Administration costs are all fixed costs. *↓ 6.2%*

5   The impairment in the year to 31 December 20X7 related to a major non-current asset. *impairment but lives ↑.*

6   The provision in the year to 31 December 20X7 related to legal claims against Merry for poor workmanship. Lawyers for Merry are fighting these claims. By early 20X8, the directors of Merry believed that, on reassessment, some of the provisions were no longer required, although the legal cases were still outstanding. *– understated? – correspondence w/ lawyers. – reassessment?*

7   Archen has on deposit £80m cash earning 5% per annum.

Exhibit 2

Information and working assumptions from the Archen finance director

Matters are rather unclear at the moment so I have made some working assumptions. These include:

(a)   The consideration for the acquisition would be: one Archen ordinary share plus £3 in cash for every two Merry shares. Archen currently has 500m £1 ordinary shares in issue. Merry has 200m £1 ordinary shares in issue, of which 25% are currently owned by its directors.

(b)   We aim to acquire 90% of the ordinary share capital of Merry and leave 10% in the hands of its directors to give them incentives. *180m   60% reduction.* *– expertise & experience*

(c)   I am assuming that we would make the acquisition of Merry on 31 May 20X9 if the deal goes ahead. *↓ provision?* *– Directors may not be happy with it.*

↓ 100 Archen shares   geaning ratio will improve
300 cash

Exhibit 3

Secure email

From:	Harry.Harrison@Merry.com
To:	Toby.Timmins@Archen.com
Date:	22 March 20X9
Subject:	Potential take-over: confidential

[handwritten: window dressing]

Merry would be a good acquisition for Archen. The company is really going places. The year to 31 December 20X7 was great for us, but we have doubled profit in the year to 31 December 20X8 so there is a very high growth rate and we would expect this to be reflected in the price paid in any acquisition.

Confidentiality prevents us disclosing too much at the moment, but I have provided a draft statement of profit or loss for the year to 31 December 20X8 and some draft notes (included in **Exhibit 1**) – although our auditors are yet to make their main audit visit. Unfortunately, our auditors are taking their time and I would like to get on and complete this deal rather than wait for them to report.

Harry Harrison

Chairman – Merry Ltd

[handwritten: why in such a hurry?]

5 Pickering Packaging Ltd

[handwritten: ethics]

You, Lindsey Cotton, a senior with Bright and Spencer, ICAEW Chartered Accountants, have recently undertaken the audit of Pickering Packaging Limited ('PPL') for the year ended 30 April 20X9. The partner responsible for the audit is Max Spencer.

[handwritten: MBO]

[handwritten: 85k g=100k]

PPL is a parent company with two trading subsidiaries operating in a highly competitive sector with more than twenty major competitors, some of whom are listed. The PPL Group was subject to a management buy-out from a listed company, Paper Board plc, in 20X1 and continues to be owned and managed by the four man buy-out team. The major shareholder is Bob Graham (managing director) who, with his family, owns 85% of the 100,000 £1 ordinary shares of the group. The group has succeeded in doubling annual revenue from the date of the MBO to the current year.

PPL has historically been located on a large, relatively under-utilised site. The site was purchased from Paper Board's property company by PPL at the time of the MBO. During the year ended 30 April 20X9 part of the site, which was surplus to requirements and housed part of the factory, was sold to Food Corporation. This resulted in a substantial profit on sale. *[handwritten: "profit on disposal"]*

You have received the following memo from Max Spencer.

MEMO

Lindsey

As you'll recall from discussions during the last audit of Pickering Packaging, Bob Graham is currently considering ways to realise his investment in the group in order to raise money for other personal investment opportunities. Bob is keen to ensure that he does not undermine the ability of the company to grow when he realises his investment. At the moment he appears to want to retain control of the business, but it is possible he may change his mind depending on the possibilities. *[handwritten: ①]*

[handwritten: if minority SH, worth even less?]

There a number of issues which concern Bob, though. The first issue is what method Bob should use to realise his investment. He also wants an indication of how much his holding in the group may be worth.

[handwritten: business valn]

Another thing which Bob is concerned about, if he does relinquish control, is the impact that a change of ownership may have on staff. The staff base has grown substantially since 20X1 and there are now some very highly motivated managers in the business. Bob wants our views on what the problems might be if new owners acquired a majority shareholding. *[handwritten: ② culture]*

[handwritten: impact on accounts]

To keep his management team happy, Bob is keen to introduce a share option scheme as part of his managers' remuneration package in order to incentivise them, and he would like us to consider whether this is feasible. He is concerned as to how the issue of such options will impact on the accounts of the business and the work we need to undertake in our annual audits.

Finally, although this is not directly related to Bob's decision to realise his investment, he has indicated that he thinks the issue of sustainability needs to be given greater importance at Pickering Packaging, and he has saved extracts from several newspaper articles on the topic (**Exhibit 2**). He feels that the other three shareholders are rather dismissive of it though, and they think that the success of Pickering *[handwritten: – not just financial perspective]* Packaging should only be judged in terms of its annual revenue and profit growth. He has asked us for any comments we have on the importance of sustainability for businesses.

I am keen to respond to Bob as soon as possible in relation to all of his concerns. Please can you draft a letter which covers the following points:

(1) A discussion of the possible options available to Bob for realising his investment.

(2) Using the information in the information pack (**Exhibit 1**), estimate the value of Bob's holding, using at least three different valuation models.

> You can ignore the tax issues which may arise if Bob realises his investment, because I have already spoken to the tax department and they are going to provide us with the relevant information and advice relating to Bob's situation.

(3) Identify the problems which might arise if new owners acquire a majority shareholding in the group. *[handwritten: (i)]*

(4) Evaluate the proposal to introduce a share option scheme as part of the managers' remuneration package, and briefly discuss the impact which issuing share options will have on the accounts and the work required in the annual audit. *[handwritten: (iii)]* *[handwritten: (ii)]*

(5) Using the information from the newspaper articles (**Exhibit 2**) as appropriate, explain the importance of sustainability to Pickering Packaging.

Requirement

Draft the letter to Bob Graham that Max Spencer has asked you to prepare.

Total: 42 marks

Exhibit 1

Pickering Packaging Group

Information pack – year ended 30 April 20X9

[handwritten diagram: PPL 100% / \ 100% PFP PCL]

(1) **Group structure**

Pickering Packaging Limited ('PPL') is a parent company with two trading subsidiaries:

- Pickering Flexible Packaging Limited ('PFP')
- Pickering Cartons Limited ('PCL')

(2) **Principal activities**

[handwritten: differentiation strategy]

The principal activities of the two subsidiaries are the manufacture of high quality, added value flexible packaging and cartons for the food industry.

(3) **History**

The group was the subject of a management buy-out from Paper Board plc in 20X1 and continues to be owned and managed by the four man buy-out team. The share ownership structure is as follows:

R A J Graham and Family	85%
B J B Smith	5%
R J C Long	5%
A G H Cutts	5%

[handwritten: PPL group]

[handwritten: over 8 years, a 100% growth rate.]

The group has succeeded in almost doubling annual revenue from the date of the MBO to the current year.

(4) **Possible flotation**

The possibility of PPL floating is currently being discussed. The flotation will enable the shareholder directors to realise some of their investment in the group and provide access to capital markets to finance future acquisitions.

100,000 shares

(5) Competitors

PPL operates in a highly competitive sector in which there are more than 20 UK rivals, including listed companies. The sector is diverse in activity; the companies which most closely resemble PPL are Coral and Cradley.

(6) Management

The flexible packaging (PFP) and cartons (PCL) businesses are operated as two mainly independent corporate entities. They are managed at an operational level by three of the shareholder directors. The fourth, and majority, shareholder director is the group's managing director who provides strategic management to the group.

The group has approximately 500 employees and is considering implementing a share option scheme for senior management following any flotation.

(7) Capital expenditure

PPL recognises the need to replace existing plant over the next few years due to normal wearing and also the need to maintain its competitive advantage by employing the latest technology.

(8) Summary trading results

The impact of investment and the benefit of productivity improvements have resulted in a reduction in employee numbers while continuing to increase output. Sales, profit and staff number growth have been as follows:

	20X3/4	20X4/5	20X5/6	20X6/7	20X7/8	20X8/9
	£'000	£'000	£'000	£'000	£'000	£'000
Sales	34,200	35,188	37,905	39,534	41,741	41,797
Cost of sales	24,179	25,124	26,685	26,527	26,758	26,771
Gross profit	10,021	10,064	11,220	13,007	14,983	15,026
Operating costs	6,546	6,471	7,369	8,549	10,689	10,721
Operating profit	3,475	3,593	3,851	4,458	4,294	4,305
Profit on disposal of property	–	–	–	–	–	13,384
Profit before interest	3,475	3,593	3,851	4,458	4,294	17,689
Interest etc	(850)	(650)	(960)	(980)	(620)	599
Profit before tax	2,625	2,943	2,891	3,478	3,674	18,288
Tax	600	965	983	1,220	1,289	5,536
Profit after tax	2,025	1,978	1,908	2,258	2,385	12,752
Dividends	820	850	888	922	960	1,000
Staff numbers	522	515	511	502	494	490
Gross profit margin	29.3%	28.6%	29.6%	32.9%	35.9%	36.0%

↑ but slowing down
income?
Dividend DM growth rate

Following the property disposal in this most recent year, Pickering Packaging has £17.6m of cash on its statement of financial position.

(9) Forecast figures 20X9/Y0 – 20Y3/Y4

FCF

- Sales and gross profits to rise by 10% each year.

- Other operating costs excluding depreciation to rise by 3% per annum.

- Depreciation for 20X9/Y0 to remain at the 20X8/9 figure of £2m; the only change in the period 20X9/Y4 is a rise to £2.6m from 20Y2/Y3 due to acquisition of new assets.

- Significant expenditure of £6m on non-current assets in 20Y2/Y3. Other non-current asset acquisitions and disposals to cancel out each year.

- Interest over 20X9/Y4 is to remain at 20X8/X9 levels.

- Working capital levels to increase at the start of each year to be 10% of that year's predicted sales.

- Tax to be charged at 23% of taxable profits over 20X9-20Y4. Depreciation is fully tax allowable against profits.

CAPM

(10) Sector and market information

The current risk-free interest rate is 5%. The following market and sector information is provided.

	Market	Sector
P/E	12.3	9.625
Beta	1.0	0.67
Expected return	8%	N/A

Exhibit 2

Extracts from press articles about sustainable packaging

'The increased awareness of economic and environmental concerns in this day and age has led manufacturers to develop consistently improved beverage cartons that contribute to a better environment.'

- recycling
- renewable.

↗competitor

'The packaging company, Cradley, has recently launched several new design concepts which, as well as being easier to open, are designed to keep plastics use and costs to a minimum. Another key player in the carton industry, Coral, has introduced a new design which is fully-recyclable and lightweight. It will significantly reduce the company's carbon footprint, as well as saving costs on raw materials.'

'Consumers are demanding more renewable materials and environmental labelling on the products they buy. Many rate cartons as the most eco-friendly packaging type. And 35% of consumers said they regularly search for environmental labels and logos on food packaging.'

'According to Cradley's CEO, 'The findings [of a survey] reinforce the importance of putting environmental issues at the heart of the company's agenda… We have no illusions about the challenges we face, but by finding new ways to package food and to deal with waste we will make a difference for the future'.'

6 Zaltan plc

Zaltan plc is a listed company which manufactures copper piping for commercial and industrial use in transporting water and gas. Zaltan was established fifty years ago as a family company and the Zaltan family still own 40% of the ordinary share capital.

Possible acquisition of Cupro Ltd

You work as an accountant in the finance department of Zaltan. The newly appointed finance director, Hugo Hughes, has asked you to attend a meeting with some of the other directors to consider the implications of a possible acquisition. Hugo commenced the meeting:

'I have been in discussion with the board of Cupro Ltd to investigate the possibility of acquiring their entire ordinary share capital. We are still at a preliminary stage, but there may be significant benefits from the acquisition. There is no price agreed yet, but we estimate a bid price of about £20m, so assume this is approximately the level of finance that we need to raise.

A.Matrix
"market development"
new product·market ↘new product Diversification

Cupro is much smaller than Zaltan. It manufactures copper piping for the domestic household market, producing much smaller diameter pipes than Zaltan, but it also makes piping from other metals, which we do not currently do. It has three large, profitable, long-term contracts with house-building companies which make up 70% of its sales. These three contracts currently have two to four years remaining. Any acquisition would take place around 1 January 20X4. *← heavily dependent on those.*

My two major concerns are firstly, business risks from the acquisition and secondly, financing the acquisition. We have not made an acquisition before, so I am unclear what the business risks would be or how we would manage them. *Acqⁿ business risks*

In terms of financing, the board has made it clear that no new equity funding will be available in the foreseeable future as the Zaltan family are unable to subscribe for new shares and they do not wish to dilute their interests. Therefore we need to finance the acquisition in some other way and I have set out some proposals (**Exhibit 1**). In addition, we need some new general funding, in order to reduce the overdraft. I have provided a proposal for consideration (**Exhibit 2**). I do not have much information from Cupro at the moment, but I have set out extracts from its draft financial statements, and our own financial statements for comparison purposes (**Exhibit 3**).'

should an acqⁿ be happening

The chairman, Nigel Zaltan, who is an engineer, was unsure: 'I like the idea of the acquisition, and I agree that we cannot raise new equity, but I am not keen to raise new debt as this would increase gearing and financial risk. I would prefer to finance it out of our £19m retained earnings. We could raise the remaining cash of £1m by increasing the overdraft.'

The chairman continued, 'Again, although I like the idea of the acquisition, I am a bit concerned about the employment issues which Cupro appear to be having at the moment (**Exhibit 4**). I don't want an acquisition which makes sense financially to be undermined by human resources issues, and therefore I think we need to give careful consideration to the 'people' side of the acquisition as well as the 'numbers' aspects of it. It also seems that the security of their IT systems could be a cause for concern. I am worried about the implications for Zaltan if the acquisition goes ahead. With the merging of our IT systems likely to take place following acquisition, what should we be asking our IT people to do to ensure the security of our data?'

Finance director's instructions

Following the meeting, Hugo asked you to come to see him on 21 July 20X3. He came straight to the point:

'I would like you to draft briefing notes for a board meeting as follows:

- In respect of the possible acquisition of Cupro:

    - assess the business risks that are likely to arise from the acquisition; and

    - describe how the process of due diligence could reduce risk in the specific circumstances of this potential acquisition. I do not require a list of due diligence tests.

    I have provided some background notes on Cupro (**Exhibit 4**). Ignore the method of financing the acquisition.

- For the debt factoring (or invoice discounting) arrangement in **Exhibit 2**:

    - determine and explain how the interim financial statements of Zaltan for the three months to 30 September 20X3 would be affected; and

    - provide advice on whether you think this particular arrangement would be an appropriate source of new general funding to supplement any finance we may need for the acquisition.

- Using the information in **Exhibit 1** and other information available:

    - explain, with supporting calculations, how the financial statements for Zaltan for the years ending 30 June 20X4 and 30 June 20X5 would be affected by the loan notes (Proposal 1) and the bank loan (Proposal 2); and

    - provide a reasoned recommendation, advising which of these two debt instruments you would choose to finance the potential acquisition.

- Draft a written reply, in non-technical language, to Nigel Zaltan addressing the comments he made at the meeting.

- Draft a written response to Nigel Zaltan about the role that human resources should play in the acquisition process.

- Draft a response in light of the incident at Cupro (**Exhibit 4**), addressing the issues that Zaltan should consider with respect to the security of its data systems. Make recommendations regarding any actions it should take.

You are not required to consider tax or deferred tax.'

Requirement

Respond to the finance director's instructions.

Total: 60 marks

1 Jan X4 - post - acqn

Exhibit 1 – Financing proposals for the acquisition

Proposal 1 – Loan notes

0.8 p.a.

In order to finance the potential acquisition of Cupro, Zaltan has been advised by its investment bankers that it could issue to the public £20m of 4% nominal loan notes at par on 1 January 20X4 with interest paid annually in arrears. The loan notes would be redeemable on 31 December 20X7 at a premium of 28%.   *4 yrs*

The loan notes would require a fixed and floating charge over the assets of Zaltan and Cupro. There would be some covenants in the loan notes.

Proposal 2 – Bank loan

An alternative source of financing the potential acquisition of Cupro is from Zaltan's relationship bank. It has offered a £20m variable interest rate loan based on LIBOR plus a risk premium. Interest is payable half yearly in arrears and the rate then reset for the next six months. The initial interest rate is expected to be 9% per annum based on current debt market conditions. The loan would be available from 1 January 20X4 and the £20m would be repayable in full on 31 December 20X9. *6 yrs.*

The loan would also require a fixed and floating charge over the assets of Zaltan and Cupro. There would be extensive covenants in the loan agreement. *Risk of breach.*

Exhibit 2 – Proposal for new general funding – debt factoring (or invoice discounting)

We have unusually high trade receivables at the moment with a carrying amount of £20m. Of this figure, about £8m is due to be received between two and four months and could therefore be sold to a debt factor to improve our cash position. The terms offered are for 90% of the £8m receivables to be paid to us immediately on completion of the agreement with the debt factor (which should be around 1 August 20X3). This amount would be without recourse and so is not repayable by Zaltan.

A one-off credit protection insurance premium of 3% of gross receivables sold would be payable. There would also be interest payable of 1.5% per month on the amounts advanced, net of any cash received from the receivables by the debt factor. After three months all remaining amounts would be paid by the debt factor and any further responsibility for late payment or bad debts would belong to the debt factor.   *30 sep X3.*

Exhibit 3 – Extract from draft financial statements

Statement of profit or loss and other comprehensive income for the year ended 30 June 20X3

	Zaltan £m	Cupro £m
Revenue	96	30
Cost of sales	(50)	(20)
Gross profit	46	10
Operating expenses	(31)	(8)
Reorganisation costs	–	(5)
Profit from operations	15	(3)
Finance costs	(5)	(2)
Profit before tax	10	(5)

Statement of financial position at 30 June 20X3

	Zaltan £m	Cupro £m
Non-current assets		
Property, plant and equipment	140	50
Current assets		
Inventories	8	4
Trade receivables	20	3
Cash and cash equivalents	–	2
Total assets	168	59
Capital and reserves		
Issued capital – £1 shares	70	25
Revaluation reserve	–	5
Retained earnings	19	(2)

	Zaltan	Cupro
	£m	£m
Equity	89	28
Non-current liabilities		
Loans and provisions	60	25
Current liabilities		
Payables	12	6
Overdraft	7	–
Total equity and liabilities	168	59

Exhibit 4 – Cupro background information

For some years Cupro has been making losses. Following new investment in the latest technology, costs have been reduced (as redundancies were made following the introduction of new capital intensive production methods) but not to the extent that management expected. Losses are therefore expected to continue in future. There are ongoing employment disputes in response to the new technology and proposed further changes to working practices. *↳ legal claims?*

A new information technology system was introduced at Cupro towards the end of 20X2 which recently encountered some security problems. Cyber security is something that Zaltan's board has always expected the IT department to manage internally, but Cupro has recently had an external review of its cyber security by a firm of IT consultants, who evaluated the controls in place to protect Cupro's hardware and software. This review was commissioned after a virus infected Cupro's systems, apparently as a result of an employee browsing an unauthorised social networking site. The virus infected the company's key contract management data systems, which are linked with those of its customers. The system was down for several days, which caused significant business disruption, and the employee concerned has since been dismissed. *↳ legal claims*

the three
LT contract ←
↳ renewed?

↳ dependence?

We have asked them for more information, but Cupro's management has not shared the consultants' findings yet. They do however assure us that remedial work has now taken place following the consultants' advice, and Cupro's IT systems are now secure, and free from viruses.

↳ why not shared?

7 Hottentot Hotels Ltd

Hottentot Hotels Ltd (HH) operates a chain of business and leisure hotels in two separate divisions. You have just started working for HH as an assistant to the financial controller, Christine Constance, who is an ICAEW Chartered Accountant.

Christine called you into her office on your first day. 'As the business is expanding, we need to control that expansion and monitor performance better than we have in the past. I have provided you with some background information about the company (**Exhibit 1**) and some financial and other data (**Exhibit 2**).

for the
charts

I am concerned that we are not measuring performance appropriately. In particular, we need to be able to measure the performance of each of the divisions and each of the hotels in order to take the right decisions, including those about viability. We also need appropriate information on the value of our assets and how they are being used in the business.

More generally, I am concerned that we are focusing predominantly on financial aspects of performance, and are not paying enough attention to non-financial aspects – in particular 'customer service' aspects of performance.

Balanced
Scorecard.

I have included some notes I made at a recent meeting I attended with the divisional managers, at which we discussed the key areas which determine the success of Hottentot's hotels (**Exhibit 3**).

The marketing director has also told me that he believes we need to make better use of data in order to maintain our competitive position. In particular, he thinks we need to make use of Big Data analytics (**Exhibit 4**), but we will need additional resources in order for us to do this. The hotels marketing strategy as a whole is going to be discussed at the next board meeting, but I think the extent to which we leverage Big Data could be a significant part of the discussion, because the board will need to approve any associated spending – for example, recruiting data analysts or purchasing analytics software.

More immediately, an opportunity has arisen for us to expand into a new sector of the hotel market while, at the same time, selling some of our existing hotels to reduce the level of debt. I have provided details of this new proposal (**Exhibit 5**).

I need to report to the board next week and I would therefore like you to:

(1) Prepare an analysis of the performance of each of the two divisions for the year ended 30 June 20X1. In so doing, calculate and comment on the performance measures currently used by HH. Explain, with supporting calculations, alternative financial measures that would provide a more comprehensive analysis of performance. Using your alternative measures, assess whether the Leisure Division is currently viable.

(2) Explain the importance of measuring non-financial performance at HH as well as financial performance, and recommend a suitable framework for HH's performance measurement systems in relation to the issues discussed in the managers' meeting (**Exhibit 3**). Your recommendation should include suggestions for identifying critical success factors (CSFs) and key performance indicators (KPIs) for non-financial aspects of performance.

Please focus specifically on the issues discussed in the managers' meeting here, and do not discuss the implications of using Big Data.

(3) Set out an evaluation of the new proposal (**Exhibit 5**) – specifically:

- give advice, with supporting calculations, explaining whether HH should accept the new proposal; and

- explain the financial reporting implications of the new lease agreement.

(4) In respect of the fraud described in **Exhibit 6**:

- make recommendations as to how the specific internal control deficiency should be addressed; and

- explain how we should act in respect of the ethical issues arising.

In addition, I know you are more familiar with Big Data analytics than either me or the Finance Director, so please could you provide us with an evaluation of the main ways in which it could help to improve HH's performance in relation to the areas the Marketing Director has identified (**Exhibit 4**).

As a general point, please ignore any tax or deferred tax issues in your assessments of the company's performance or future proposals.'

Requirement

Respond to the instructions of the financial controller.

Total: 55 marks

Exhibit 1 – Background information

Company history

HH was established 15 years ago following a buy-out of the Prestige Division of an international hotel group. At that time, HH consisted of 32 hotels. All of these were 5-star hotels based in major UK cities, excluding London, and were primarily focused on the business market. ⤳ luxury

The hotels have been successful in attracting business customers through individual bookings and conferences, partly because of the general expansion of the economy at that time and partly because of the shortage of such hotels in some cities.

The amount of new finance available has been limited by the high levels of debt following the buy-out. Operating cash flows have been reinvested in the business and no dividends have been paid.

Establishing the Leisure Division

There was limited scope to expand further in UK cities in the business market, so the board took a decision, immediately after the buy-out, to expand into the leisure market and set up a separate division for this purpose. The Leisure Division targets families taking holidays and short breaks in popular rural and coastal locations. All the Leisure Division hotels are 4-star and they are smaller and lower priced than the Business Division hotels.

Expansion of the Leisure Division was slow due to financing constraints but, despite modest performance, one hotel was acquired each year. More recently, however, the Leisure Division has started to make operating losses and its performance is being scrutinised by the board to decide whether it should be sold.

Pricing and performance

HH's business model is to advertise a standard price for hotel rooms at around the sector average for each division's hotels, but to offer discounts selectively in order to obtain bookings from more price-sensitive customers. This might involve reducing selling prices for regular customers, offering lower prices at times when occupancy is expected to be low, and keeping a database of customers to assess their buying habits and their price resistance in order to tailor discounts to individuals.

Each hotel manager has discretion to offer discounts of up to 30% below standard prices, but they can also increase prices on a temporary basis (eg if there is a popular local event). Overall, managers are expected to award an average discount of 10% on revenues from rooms.

Standard prices are the same within each division for all its hotels, irrespective of location. All rooms within each division are a standard size and specification.

In addition to room bookings, revenue is generated from other activities such as restaurants, bars and conferences. These other sources of revenue normally amount to 30% of the gross revenue from room bookings (ie before any discounts). No discounts are offered on these other revenues.

The performance of divisions is measured according to three metrics:

- Room utilisation (ie % of rooms occupied)
- Gross room revenue generated per hotel
- Return on assets (operating profit divided by year-end total assets) based on the financial statement carrying amounts

Hotels are open 360 days a year.

Finance

The bank has written several letters to HH about the high level of debt of the company. It has urged that steps should be taken to reduce the level of the £30m loan outstanding.

Exhibit 2 – Financial and other data

	Business	Leisure
Standard room price (per night)	£150	£100
Number of hotels	32	16
Average number of rooms per hotel	100	50
Average annual room occupancy	75%	50%
Average fair value per hotel building	£4m	£1m

Management accounts

Draft statement of profit or loss for the year ended 30 June 20X1

	Business £'000	Leisure £'000
Revenue		
Rooms at standard price	129,600	14,400
Less room discounts	(12,960)	(1,440)
Other (food, drink, conferences)	38,880	4,320
Total revenue	155,520	17,280
Fixed costs	(98,400)	(13,600)
Variable costs	(42,120)	(4,680)
Operating profit/(loss)	15,000	(1,000)

Variable costs are 25% of total revenues before discounts.

Total fixed costs of the company consist equally of: (1) head office costs (these include administration, finance, human resources, purchasing and marketing and are allocated between the two divisions on the basis of revenue generated); and (2) fixed costs incurred in the operations of each individual hotel.

Extracts from draft statement of financial position at 30 June 20X1

	£'000	£'000
Property, plant and equipment		
Business hotels		
Cost	64,000	
Depreciation	(32,000)	32,000
Leisure hotels		
Cost	16,000	
Depreciation	(4,000)	12,000
Other PPE		10,000
Net current assets		1,000
Total assets		55,000
Share capital		10,000
Retained earnings		15,000
8% bank loan		30,000
		55,000

All hotel buildings are currently owned by HH and are recognised using the cost model and HH does not intend to change this accounting policy. Depreciation on hotel buildings is on a straight line basis and has been charged over a useful life of 40 years with a zero residual value. However, on 1 July 20X0, a survey of the properties showed that all hotels had a remaining useful life of around 50 years at that date. HH intends to revise the useful lives of these assets in accordance with IFRS, in the draft management accounts for the year ended 30 June 20X1, to determine the depreciation charge. However, no entries for depreciation of property for the year have yet been made.

The head office and all land are held on operating leases.

'Other PPE' is recognised at their carrying amounts and consist of fixtures and fittings. About 90% of the £10m relates to the Business Division.

Exhibit 3 – Managers' notes on factors which determine hotels' performance

Four key areas define the success of our hotels: financial performance, the team (staff), the customer, and the business processes in place for satisfying customer needs.

Financial performance is the core around which everything else rotates, because ultimately the company exists in order to make money. However, it can only do this by satisfying its customers, through the efforts of its staff and its business processes.

The divisional managers pointed out that the company's mission statement refers to the aim of enhancing guests' experience by providing excellent hospitality, including a good night's sleep, an enjoyable dining experience or a productive meeting. The managers stressed that the quality of a guest's experience will influence not only customer satisfaction levels but also the likelihood of repeat bookings. At the end of their stay, all customers are asked to complete a short survey, expressing how satisfied they are with their stay.

The managers acknowledge that their staff play a key role in shaping guests' impressions of their hotel. Because HH is offering 4 and 5-star hotels, guests expect high quality service and customer care from the staff. Achieving a combination of efficiency and care is one of the key elements of achieving customer satisfaction.

The staff also need to be supported by the hotels' systems and processes. In particular, the managers highlighted that having an efficient and easy-to-use reservations system is vital to maximising room occupancy rates.

However, several managers noted that customers have commented that the check-in/check-out procedures at the front-desk should be made more efficient to prevent queues forming at busy times. Currently, each staff member has their own specific tasks, but one suggestion is that if staff had a wider range of skills across the hotel operation, this would provide greater flexibility to cope with peaks in demand.

On the other hand, e-commerce has become increasingly important in allowing the managers to use dynamic pricing – increasing or decreasing prices at short notice to reflect levels of demand and the number of rooms still available.

Finally, the managers said that while hotels are a service business, they are not wholly people-based services. The physical product remains important in terms of both guest accommodation and food and beverages. The Managing Director of the Prestige Division has argued that ensuring a consistently high quality of food is served to guests, and ensuring consistently high levels of room cleanliness are two critical success factors for the hotels in the division.

Exhibit 4 – Marketing information

Hottentot's marketing director has joined the company relatively recently, having previously worked at another hotel group. The director believes that Hottentot should be making better use of Big Data analytics, in particular in relation to room pricing and customer relationship management.

At the moment, a weekly forecast for both divisions is generated from the company's management information systems showing the current level of bookings for that week (confirmed occupancy as a % of capacity) and the average price for rooms still available. (Figure 1 below shows an example of the weekly forecast report).

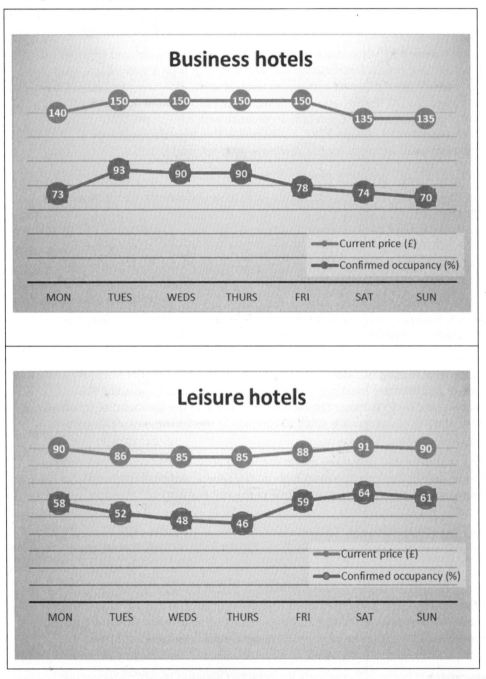

Figure 1 – example weekly forecast report

The marketing director has argued that, although these weekly reports are a useful high level summary, they have limited value as a decision-making tool for hotel managers. When the hotel managers apply their discretionary changes to prices, they do so on the basis of their awareness of local market conditions and the expected occupancy rates for their individual hotel.

[handwritten: vary prices based on location]

Similarly, the marketing director believes that although customer satisfaction surveys can provide some useful data, Hottentot should also be analysing customer feedback via social media forums (such as online travel review sites).

Exhibit 5 – A new proposal

[handwritten: Business available?]

Five newly-constructed, small hotel properties could be acquired on 1 January 20X2, under 30-year leases. These leases include not only the building, but also the fixtures and fittings. They would be 3-star, modern style hotels on the edge of cities where land is much cheaper than in city centres.

[handwritten: quality? reputation?]

[handwritten: 5 x 2 = £10m]

The business model is that these hotels would be designed to attract business customers travelling by car and who do not want to drive into city centres or who wish to arrange out-of-town meetings. The cost of constructing each hotel, including fixtures and fittings, would be £2m. There would be no *[handwritten: → revenue]* restaurant. Conference rooms are offered, without charge, to groups of residents, so the only source of revenue is individual room bookings.

A professional surveyor believes that the buildings will have a useful life of about 40 years but he emphasised that this was only a rough estimate. He refused to give a residual value for the hotels after 30 years stating: 'Look, who knows what the condition of the hotels will be in 30 years, it depends on so many factors such as maintenance and usage. They could be worth more than the £2m each it cost to build them or they could be worthless. It would just be guesswork.'

As part of this proposal, HH would sell all the Leisure Division hotels at their fair value and use the proceeds generated to reduce the amount of the loan outstanding to the bank.

Data for the new proposal are as follows:

Standard room price per night	£120
Number of hotels	5
Average number of rooms per hotel	40
Expected average annual occupancy	90%
Average fair value per hotel	£2m

No discounts are to be offered. Variable costs are expected to be 30% of revenues generated.

The fixed cost per year for each hotel is £400,000 (excluding head office costs, depreciation and lease rentals). Lease rentals are initially £300,000 per annum for each hotel, but are subject to rent reviews every three years.

[handwritten: most likely will increase.]

Exhibit 6 – Notes on internal control issue – prepared by the former assistant financial controller

A fraud was discovered in one of the Leisure Division hotels. The hotel manager had been encouraging customers to pay in cash by authorising a small discount of around 5% to 10% for doing so. He was then recording the transaction at the maximum 30% discount and retaining the difference for himself. His wife worked on the front desk of the hotel, accepting the money from the customers and she provided false invoices to customers. They have both been dismissed, but it is not clear how much they stole in this way or what internal controls should be implemented to prevent this happening again.

[handwritten: – Husband/wife]
[handwritten: – small amount]
[handwritten: – already dismissed]

In addition, I am not sure of the ethical position, but if we report the fraud to the police, this would make the problem known outside the company.

8 Zappo plc

You are Tish Hope, a newly qualified accountant at a medium-sized firm, which has just been engaged as adviser to Zappo plc, a small listed company which runs a chain of retail stores that sell games software for computers and consoles. Zappo has a year end of 31 December. You have just been emailed by Ab Potts, the managing partner of your office, to brief you about a meeting he has just had with Fran Simmons, the Finance Director of Zappo.

To: Tish Hope
From: Ab Potts
Date: 4 May 20X5
Subject: Zappo

Tish

I had a very useful meeting with Fran Simmons yesterday, at which we discussed Zappo's current situation. Zappo's board believes that it needs to take drastic action if it is to reverse a recent decline in its business, and therefore requires our advice. The board is most concerned with the number of people entering its stores ('footfall'); they regard this as the most important factor in the industry and the board believes it needs to update its image to improve this. I am seeing Fran again next week just before Zappo's next board meeting, and I need you to prepare briefing notes for my meeting with Fran.

[handwritten: CSF]

[handwritten: Brand/reputation]

I attach notes from the last board meeting (**Exhibit 1**) – please note that these are confidential.

I gather that the Zappo board thought that the acquisition of GameStar could be a very good idea. At the next board meeting the directors will discuss how much they would be prepared to pay for GameStar.

Fran Simmons also gave me a copy of a memo she prepared for the Zappo board (**Exhibit 2**). I understand that the board members have all received a copy. The memo indicates to me that there are a number of operational issues that Zappo need to address in connection with their proposed purchase of GameStar. I have my doubts about the wisdom of circulating it in advance of their board meeting.

[handwritten: ethics?]

So here's what I would like you to do.

(1) I would like you to look at the proposals under consideration by the Zappo board and let me know what you consider to be the strategic advantages and disadvantages of acquiring GameStar and developing LeagueStar. *[circled 2]* *[circled 1]*

(2) I need you to calculate a valuation for GameStar using the data in **Exhibit 3.** As well as carrying out the calculation, I need you to explain the limitations of the method you've used and give an overview of the issues that due diligence work we would do on the acquisition would cover. You should know that Zappo's cost of equity is 12%. Both GameStar and Zappo are financed entirely by equity. *[circled 3]* *[circled 5]*

[handwritten: Ke. no debt!]

(3) You will see from the notes of the board meeting, the directors are considering two possible methods of financing the investments. Please can you comment on the impact of the two alternative methods of financing. *[circled 6]*

(4) I have a few concerns about operational issues for Zappo if the purchase of GameStar goes ahead, and I would appreciate your comments about the issues that Zappo faces with regard to:

- the management of the company's brand, with suggestions about how the company might develop a branding strategy. *[circled 7]*
- obtaining information about footfall. *[circled 8]*
- merging the operations of the two companies. *[circled 9]*

Requirement

Respond to Ab Potts's email.

Total: 60 marks

Exhibit 1

Notes from the Zappo board meeting

The directors made three suggestions for improving Zappo's profitability.

(1) **Acquire GameStar business and combine Zappo and GameStar** *[handwritten: Horizontal]*

[handwritten: Synergies surplus cash (sale of asset)]

GameStar is a UK company in the same industry as Zappo and has a good geographical fit (ie there are few instances of GameStar and Zappo stores being co-located and therefore in direct competition). GameStar has enjoyed much more successful advertising than Zappo in recent years and, therefore, is much more popular with the game-buying public, and more profitable.

[handwritten: reputation/brand.]

GameStar is currently owned by Citrus Holdings plc and would be Zappo's first acquisition if the board decided to purchase it. The proposal would be for Zappo to acquire all of GameStar's share capital.

Post integration issues

Given that the GameStar brand is stronger than Zappo's, if GameStar is acquired the two businesses would be merged immediately post-acquisition by 'hiving down' the trade and assets of Zappo into GameStar. At that time GameStar would be Zappo's wholly owned subsidiary. The two businesses would then both be operated under the more profitable 'GameStar' brand name. The acquisition would take place on 31 December 20X5.

HIVING DOWN

(2)   Launch of LeagueStar

↳ DB/S but not P/L.
↳ Ddepn

LeagueStar is a new system comprising fixed plant and machinery installed into each shop to allow live gaming competitions to be held. Members of the public may therefore come into the shops to play games in national leagues. The idea is that this will increase footfall into the stores, and therefore improve profitability significantly. Additionally, buyers will want to purchase games chosen to be used for LeagueStar in order to practise at home, which will allow Zappo to work with the suppliers of those games to run promotions on those specific games. The LeagueStar system will cost £35m, and it is expected that the system will have a useful life of ten years.

£3.5m depn.

(3)   Sell unproductive assets

This relates to Olde Towers, Zappo's office building in central London, which was acquired for £20m ten years ago and, due to the subsequent strength of the property market, is now expected to be sold for around £70m. It has been too large for Zappo's requirements and now, given Zappo's financial predicament, there seems to be good reason for selling it.

Zappo would relocate to GameStar's head office, a smaller building much more suitable to its needs. GameStar currently leases this from Citrus Holdings, but the freehold will be transferred to GameStar before the acquisition for its market value of £22m. Its original cost was £10m.

Financing the acquisition

70m
(24)
(8)
38

Zappo's majority shareholder owns 60% of its ordinary share capital and he has already agreed to invest £24m of new equity in the form of a rights issue. It is believed that the non-controlling (minority) shareholders will subscribe at least a further £8m. It is anticipated that the balance of the funding requirements for the acquisition and the investment in LeagueStar will be met from the sale of Olde Towers.

Zappo has agreed with its bankers that, in the event of a shortfall of funding, the bank will make a loan available for the amount of the shortfall at an annual interest rate of 6%. The company currently has no debt in its capital structure.

Exhibit 2

Fran Simmons' memo to Zappo board

To: Zappo Board
From: Fran Simmons

30 April 20X5

Issues relating to the proposed purchase of GameStar

As you probably know, I am in favour of the purchase of GameStar. This memo sets out some of the reasons behind my thinking on this matter.

Brand image

I have concerns about the Zappo brand image. The Zappo brand name is rather tired, and recent feedback from some of our stores suggests that we have a 'down-market' image. GameStar does not have the same image problem, and I am convinced that purchasing GameStar and re-branding the existing Zappo stores will improve the image of our stores and help to increase footfall.

The computer games industry

I also have concern about the changing nature of the market for selling electronic games. All retail stores selling electronic games have been facing a challenge from downloaded games. Many games users prefer to download games from the Internet rather than visit stores to buy them; and among users of smartphones and tablets there is a view that games should be available free or for very little charge.

A current advantage that retail stores have is that downloading large games can take a long time, so there is still motivation for customers to visit a games store. Downloading large games will become easier in time, for example through cloud computing, so the challenge to games stores could become more intense.

It is also reassuring that although smartphone and tablet users make extensive use of electronic games, there are many consumers who like to buy games consoles and the games that go with them.

I also think that our retail stores have a strong response to competition from downloading of games.

(a) I believe that our planned investment in LeagueStar will attract more visitors to our stores.

(b) The success and profitability of our stores is based on the ability of customers to bring back used games to obtain a refund or credit. Given a choice between buying a game online for £15 and buying one from a Zappo store for £40 but getting a refund of £30 or more for taking it back within two weeks, there is a lot to be said for buying from a games store.

[handwritten left margin: not that much of a difference - comfort - convenience]

If you are not aware of our returns policy, if a customer buys a new game, he can obtain a cash refund or a credit for returning the game at any time, provided that the game is still in working condition. The amount of the refund depends on the length of time since the game was purchased. Returned games are then re-sold, but at a lower price; and customers can return these too and get a refund. Downloading doesn't allow customers the same opportunity. *[handwritten: Refunds ✓ Most like to keep games]*

Profit margins

As you know, profit margins at games stores depend on the amount of footfall. Profitability at our stores may be low, but I believe that we can boost profits by increasing footfall. I asked the managers of two stores recently to measure footfall over a seven-day period. One store manager told me that in the week, there were 1,850 visitors to the store and sales turnover was £13,250. The other store reported a footfall of just 1,200 visitors in the week, but revenue was £12,600. There is a lot we can work on to improve performance. *[handwritten: £10.5]*

*[handwritten left margin: *Footfall may not always work]*

[handwritten: 77.2]

Operational issues and the purchase of GameStar

Some of my colleagues have expressed concerns about the practical aspects of the acquisition of GameStar. I consider these concerns to be excessive. Zappo stores have a fairly high labour turnover: most of our stores staff are unskilled and opportunities for career development are very limited. These staff are unlikely to show hostility to a merger of operations with GameStar. I have already decided that after the purchase, we should switch to using the GameStar IT systems, which appear to be better than the systems we use in Zappo. *[handwritten: → training   transferring data]*

Conclusion *[handwritten: — culture clash remuneration]*

The purchase of GameStar will stimulate change and improvement for Zappo, and will provide us with added competitive advantage over our competitors. I shall be arguing strongly in favour of the proposed purchase at the next board meeting.

Exhibit 3

GameStar financial data: Profits after tax

Years ended 31 December	20X3 £'000	7%	20X4 £'000	11%	Forecast 20X5 £'000
Profit after tax	1,590	→	1,701	→	1,888

[handwritten left margin: g distributed →]

For the last three years, GameStar has distributed all its profits as dividends to its parent.

The above numbers were prepared without taking into account the proposed acquisition by Zappo.

9 Safetex plc

It is now November 20X8.

Safetex plc (Safetex) is an AIM listed company which imports, installs and maintains security and safety equipment in the UK domestic household market. Its major products include burglar alarm systems, smoke alarms, security cameras and fire extinguishers. 75% of its ordinary shares are held by John Rawlings, the chairman, with the remainder being widely held.

You are a senior in the business advisory department of the firm of accountants acting for Safetex. The chief executive of Safetex, Jason Yontton, and a manager in your firm, Saeed Shah, recently had a meeting to which you were invited.

Meeting with the chief executive of Safetex

Jason commenced the meeting: 'The Safetex board has recently undertaken a business review to assess the company's performance and we have come up with some ideas to expand and move forward. Our main product has been burglar alarms which we have sold throughout the UK. We have focussed on the upper end of the household market, with fairly high profit margins, selling mainly to customers in high socioeconomic groups living in large houses. The problem is that this end of the market has become saturated with most of this sector now having alarms. We have therefore become too dependent on revenue from annual maintenance and servicing visits to existing customers and on selling other smaller products to customers during these visits. As a result, the vast majority of our sales are to existing customers, and the company is not expanding its customer base.

We have therefore identified two possible expansion strategies. We do not have either the financial or the non-financial resources to do both, so we will need to choose between them. I have provided some background details of Safetex (**Exhibit 1**) and I have described the expansion strategies for you in a summary of our business review (**Exhibit 2**) but, in essence, one plan is to set up a separate division under a new brand name, offering low price alarms at the lower end of the domestic household market, where most of the growth in the industry is occurring. The other plan is to enter the commercial alarms sector through the acquisition of Commercial Alarms Ltd (CAL), which installs alarms for industrial customers.

I have provided some financial details for these two possible expansion strategies, as well as some details for Safetex (**Exhibit 3**) and some working assumptions for you (**Exhibit 4**). What I would like from your firm is the following:

(1) An evaluation and comparison of the two proposed expansion strategies, so far as the current information permits. This should include consideration of strategic risk and other possible business strategies for growth. We do not have an acquisition price for CAL yet, so any conclusions will be provisional.

(2) Please include any implications for John Rawlings as the majority shareholder and any other governance implications that would arise from an acquisition of CAL.

(3) The board is keen to know how the proposed expansion strategies will affect earnings per share. I would therefore like you to determine the expected EPS (and, if appropriate, any diluted EPS) of the company for the year ending 31 December 20X9, for each of the two strategic options on the basis of the working assumptions I have set out for you (Exhibit 4).

(4) I would like you to determine an estimated valuation of CAL on which we could base a bid to acquire its entire ordinary share capital. In so doing, use a working assumption of 10% as the weighted average cost of capital for the annual discount rate.

(5) Please comment on the financing arrangements for the proposed acquisition of CAL. The board is aware of the importance of the share price of Safetex in the current proposals.

(6) Please comment also on the implications of a takeover of CAL for remuneration policy and HRM issues generally (**Exhibit 5**).

(7) I would like you to review the financial statements provided (Exhibit 3) and set out the necessary financial due diligence work for CAL that we would carry out for each of the items within these financial statements. Assume we will be given open access to the financial records of CAL at some stage.'

Manager's instructions

Following the meeting, Saeed spoke to you. 'This is a really exciting client. If we perform well on these instructions there is a good chance that we will also be awarded the acquisition work. I would therefore like you to prepare a draft response to Jason containing the information required by him.'

Requirement

Carry out the instructions of the manager, Saeed Shah.

Where appropriate, assume a tax rate of 23%.

Total: 60 marks

Exhibit 1 – Safetex business background

Safetex was established around 40 years ago and grew rapidly, with branches located throughout the UK. The company obtained an AIM listing in 20X1. From 20X3 onwards, sales growth began to slow down due to market saturation. As a consequence, revenues and profits have been constant for the past few years and, in the absence of a new strategy, this is expected to continue.

Safety and security devices in their basic form are imported. The company then makes minor amendments (eg casings) and installs the equipment in customers' houses.

The company has a good reputation and, unlike most competitors, gives a three-year guarantee with all its installations.

Exhibit 2 – Expansion strategies

Strategy 1 – Set up a new division

This strategy involves setting up a separate division under a new brand name to enter the low price sector of the domestic household alarm market. The policy would be one of price penetration to establish high sales volumes and market recognition of the new brand. Prices would therefore be lower than those charged to our existing upmarket customers. Outwardly the products might be different designs, but the cost and substance would be the same as existing products. Our policy is to be inwardly and operationally the same as the existing business, but for the alarms to appear different to customers in order to minimise reputational damage to our existing business. The initial incremental investment and reorganisation costs will total to about £3m.

If this venture is agreed we could act quickly and commence trading by 1 January 20X9.

Strategy 2 – Acquisition of CAL

This strategy involves entering the commercial sector of the market by acquiring CAL, which supplies alarms to businesses. In this case, the product would need to protect larger premises and would thus need to be more sophisticated than the existing products. The profit margins are likely to be greater than Safetex's existing business as there is less price resistance in this market, with greater emphasis on quality.

The parent company of CAL, Hogsmood plc, is a large manufacturing company which, along with many other products, makes alarm systems. Hogsmood has decided to focus on manufacturing and therefore wishes to sell CAL. Preliminary sale negotiations have already commenced. Currently, all CAL's products are manufactured by Hogsmood and, given their specialist nature, they would continue to be sourced from Hogsmood after an acquisition. However, the skills needed for installation and maintenance exist within the Safetex workforce.

If the deal is agreed in the next few weeks, we could complete the takeover by 1 January 20X9.

Exhibit 3 – Financial data

Draft, forecast statements of profit or loss and other comprehensive income for the year ending 31 December 20X8

	Notes	Safetex £'000	CAL £'000
Revenue		24,000	12,000
Cost of sales	1	(18,000)	(6,000)
Gross profit		6,000	6,000
Operating expenses	2	(1,500)	(2,000)
Profit from operations		4,500	4,000
Finance costs		(1,500)	(360) — 1.44%?
Profit before tax		3,000	3,640
Tax (23%)		(690)	(835)
Profit for the year		2,310	2,805

Note: There was no other comprehensive income forecast for the year.

Draft, forecast statements of financial position at 31 December 20X8

	Notes	Safetex £'000	CAL £'000
Non-current assets			
Property, plant and equipment	3	40,000	20,000
Current assets			
Inventories	4	3,000	6,000
Trade receivables		500	4,000
Cash and cash equivalents		3,000	2,500
Total assets		46,500	32,500
Capital and reserves			
Issued capital – £1 shares		6,000	1,000
Reserves	5	11,000	3,640
Equity		17,000	4,640
Non-current liabilities			
Loans and provisions		28,000	–
Intra-group balance owing to Hogsmood	6	–	25,000
Current liabilities		1,500	2,860
Total equity and liabilities		46,500	32,500

Handwritten annotations: Hogsmood may demand it back ⊛

Notes

1   Hogsmood transfers alarm systems to CAL on a full cost plus basis according to group policy. On average, this transfer price is about 80% of the fair value of the price that would need to be paid following an acquisition. *(Handwritten: costs ↑ post acq^n → none after acq^n (replaced by safetex 'mgmt chg))*

2   Operating expenses of CAL include management charges from Hogsmood for central services such as IT, finance, legal, and marketing. Such costs are allocated to subsidiaries based on the number of employees. Operating expenses of CAL also include depreciation of £1m. *(Handwritten: depn is too high)*

3   CAL uses historical cost to measure property, plant and equipment. Their fair value is currently £40m.

4   The Hogsmood Group policy requires CAL to take delivery and hold the inventories once the goods have been manufactured. The inventories are held on a sale or return basis, but all such inventories are recognised in the financial statements of CAL.

5   CAL pays out all profits after tax as dividend to Hogsmood.

6   The intra group balance is repayable on demand.

Other notes

The revenue and costs of Safetex's existing business are unlikely to change in the immediate future if CAL is acquired.

[handwritten left margin: Consideration {]

The consideration for the acquisition would be: two newly issued Safetex ordinary shares plus cash for every one CAL share. The amount of the residual cash payment will be determined by the agreed valuation of CAL. Safetex ordinary shares are currently trading at £6 each.

Hogsmood will not continue to extend the intra-group loan beyond 1 January 20X9 if the acquisition takes place. As a consequence, Safetex has approached an investment bank to identify a method of CAL refinancing this debt. The only feasible refinancing identified is £25m 4% convertible bonds issued at par, which would also be their fair value. These bonds would be issued by Safetex. Interest would be payable annually in arrears. Each £100 of bonds would be convertible into 15 Safetex shares at any time up to maturity on 31 December 20Y1. The annual rate of interest for similar bonds without conversion rights is 7%.

Exhibit 4 – Working assumptions

Strategy 1 – Set up a new division

[handwritten left margin: Buy same quality @ b price]

The key working assumption with this strategy is that revenues for the new division in 20X9 would be £3m, but these revenues would double in each of the next two years before stabilising indefinitely at the 20Y1 level. Sales would generate an overall margin of 5% after tax. There would be minimal incremental fixed costs given the close operational fit with our existing business. We think we would lose revenues from the existing Safetex business of about £1m per year as a result of customers buying products from the new division instead of from Safetex.

Strategy 2 – Acquisition of CAL

Under Safetex management, the sales volumes of CAL would be expected to grow at 4% per annum indefinitely. In order to achieve this sales volume growth, however, expenditure on non-current assets would need to be £1.2m per annum and CAL would need to spend an additional £0.3m per annum on marketing. Ignore inflation. *[handwritten: ↳ CAPEX]*

[handwritten left margin: wcap]

Cost of sales for both Safetex and CAL consists entirely of variable costs. Other operating costs consist entirely of fixed costs.

Interest on corporate bonds for companies in the risk class of CAL is 7% per annum. CAL's annual weighted average cost of capital is 10%.

Exhibit 5 – HRM issues

Safetex is based in London, where it has its head office operations. It also rents space in regional centres, where installation and maintenance engineers are based. CAL is based in Birmingham, where it has its head office not far from the manufacturing site of its parent company Hogsmood. All CAL marketing staff and installation and maintenance engineers are located in the same premises as head office.

About 60% of the cost of sales and operating expenses in Safetex and 40% in CAL consist of labour costs.

Safetex does not operate a bonus scheme for its staff or management, but it has a fairly generous defined contribution pension scheme. CAL has a much less generous pension scheme for its staff, but management, marketing staff and engineers are all eligible for annual bonuses, depending on the company's sales turnover and success in winning new customers in the year.

[handwritten: ® performance oriented. motivation etc.]

10 Coopers Coffee Company Ltd

It is now July 20X9.

Coopers Coffee Company Ltd (CCC) operates a chain of coffee bars serving high-quality coffees. It also serves other drinks and snacks.

Meeting with the finance director

You are a senior in the firm which has recently been appointed as auditors and business advisers for *Ethics?* CCC. The finance director of CCC, Jack Johnson, contacted the engagement partner.

'We are in a period of rapid expansion and I have some concerns regarding our business strategy, customer relationship management, control and risk management. I have provided you with background notes from our business plan (**Exhibit 1**) and I would like your firm to accept an engagement to review the matters which I have outlined for you in my assignment briefing notes.'

Assignment briefing notes

(1) Business strategy and risk management

We have been expanding rapidly simply to compete in our market. If we don't open new outlets, *↗ competition* our competitors will. However we have huge concerns about the quality of service provided by franchisees and the level of customer service. We try to monitor franchisees, but this is difficult when we have so many individual franchisees spread all round the country.

The board needs to review its expansion strategy, because there is too much risk in what we are doing at the moment.

I have set out some basic data with respect to CCC outlets (**Exhibit 2**).

I would like your firm to provide an analysis of the risks for CCC associated with a policy of expansion by franchising, compared to expanding using our own outlets.

(2) Customer Relationship Management (CRM)

We know that our main competitors use market research to obtain insight into their customers' attitudes. We see effective customer relationship management as a key requirement for successful expansion.

At a marketing conference recently, our marketing director was talking to his counterpart from 'Café 2 Go' (which is the second largest operator in the coffee bar market, behind Best Bean).

In order to get a more detailed understanding of what its customers think about it, and are saying *very important* about it, Café 2 Go monitors the scores its outlets are given in online customer review forums (such as 'TripAdvisor') and analyses the comments people are posting about its outlets on social media networks (such as Twitter). This analysis of customers comments is referred to as 'sentiment analysis'.

Café 2 Go now has its own social media monitoring department, to analyse what customers are saying about the company, on the basis that this can help identify new opportunities and areas for improvement in its existing relationships with its customers.

Café 2 Go's marketing director gave our marketing director a copy of one of the reports produced by the social media monitoring department (**Exhibit 3**) as an illustration.

I would like your thoughts about how we should be monitoring our customers and developing a more effective CRM policy.

(3) Franchise fees

↗ manipulation   *customer service*

As part of our business plan we commenced franchising this year by setting up (10) franchise relationships and, frankly, they have not performed as well as we expected. A summary of the standard terms for a franchise agreement is set out in my notes (**Exhibit 4**) and the key issue in this context is that franchisees are required to pay us 10% of all revenue.

I would like advice to help me decide how much we should be charging franchisees for the CCC franchise. In the first instance, I need to determine by how much the revenue of an independent café (such as Hoole Café – **Exhibit 5**) would need to increase, as a result of being a CCC franchisee, in order to justify the current franchise fee. My working assumption is that independent, good quality, coffee bars, such as Hoole Café, charge the same prices as CCC, but would have more customers if they used the CCC brand name.

If we change the franchise fee, are there any other aspects of our franchising policy that we should consider changing?

(4) **Management control**

I should appreciate your views about management control over our outlets. As the business expands, control will get much more difficult, and we need to consider ways of ensuring that we achieve satisfactory profit levels, quality and service levels and revenue growth across the company.

I would like your opinions about the planning and control systems we might apply.

Partner's instructions

The engagement partner sent you the following note.

I have agreed to accept the assignment requested by CCC. I would like you to read the assignment briefing notes provided by Jack Johnson and, in response to these, prepare a memorandum addressing each of the following.

(1) Assess the strategy of expanding through a combination of the equity business model (opening CCC-owned outlets) and franchising. *outlets v franchise 5*

(2) Compare the risks for CCC associated with a policy of expansion by franchising new outlets and a policy of opening new outlets directly owned by CCC.

(3) Suggest alternative approaches to a rapid expansion strategy that CCC might pursue.

(2) CCC's board believes that they need to invest more in customer relationship management initiatives, in order to attract and retain customers. Can you do two things for me here:

(4) First can you explain the main issues the company should consider when developing a CRM policy?

(5) Second, please can you evaluate the potential benefits from using Big Data analytics in a similar way to Café 2 Go?

(3) Using Jack Johnson's working assumptions, determine and explain the additional amount of sales revenue per annum that would need to be generated by an independent café applying for a franchise in order to cover the franchise fees in present value terms. Use the figures for the Hoole Café Ltd (**Exhibit 5**) as a numerical example. Use a 10% annual discount rate. Also, assume the operating cash flows occur at year ends, but that the initial franchise fee is paid at the start of the franchise. *(6) assumptions*

(4) Provide some initial recommendations about how control systems can be made effective within the company. In particular, can you address a concern that Jack Johnson has expressed about the risk of understatement of income by franchisees? He suspects that there may be understatement of cash by employees and also that franchisees may find ways of under-stating their income in order to boost their own profits at the expense of CCC, and avoid paying part of the 10% franchise fee. *(7)*

(5) Where our firm accepts additional work for an existing audit client, I need to provide information for the ethics partner. Please provide draft notes which explain for each of the issues raised by Jack Johnson in his 'assignment briefing notes' either:

- any ethical issues that arise, and appropriate safeguards we intend to take, in carrying out the assignment; or

- why there are no significant ethical issues in accepting the particular type of non-audit work for this audit client. *advice? not implementing?*

Requirement

Respond to the engagement partner's instructions.

Total: 45 marks

Exhibit 1 – Business plan: background notes

The UK coffee bar market

The UK coffee bar market is dominated by three large companies (the 'big three') which jointly have a 70% market share. 'Coffee bars' are cafés which are branded primarily as selling a range of high quality coffees, but also sell other drinks and some food. The UK industry has grown up from almost nothing in the mid-1990s to over 10,000 outlets in 20X9, and it continues to expand.

The leading companies in the market have saturation cover in the UK for coffee bars, but are continuing to look for new ways to expand their business. They have grown in the past through a mixture of opening outlets that they own themselves and establishing franchises. Although they have offered individual franchises in the past, they now agree only corporate franchises with ten or more outlets. Return on capital employed in the industry, measured as operating profit to net assets employed, is over 40% per coffee bar outlet.

Op profit / net assets

CCC's operations

CCC is an independent business owned by a private equity company. At 30 June 20X8, it had 300 outlets which were owned, controlled and operated directly by CCC. *3% of total outlets*

The business plan includes an objective to expand the number of outlets by 10% per annum for the next five years. However, the cost of opening new outlets and the availability of finance, are becoming constraints on further expansion. As a consequence, for the year ended 30 June 20X9, the business plan adopted a policy of expanding by franchising ten new outlets, and this objective was achieved.

CCC did not previously have any franchise arrangements and does not have any outlets outside the UK. → alternative

The board of CCC is concerned that they are adopting franchising as a strategy at a time when other companies in the industry are limiting new franchising arrangements and also appear to be terminating some existing franchises. ↳ *entering market with strategy in decline*

Exhibit 2 – Basic data

An outlet of average size (ie seating capacity of 60 seats) and performance owned directly by CCC (ie not franchised) would typically expect the following results:

	Notes	£'000	
Revenue		360	
Cost of sales	1	(240)	GPM 33%
Gross profit		120	
Administrative expenses and other costs	2	(10)	
Allocated head office costs	3	(40)	OPM 58·3%
Operating profit		70	

Notes

1 **Cost of sales**

   15% × 120 = 18   *mark up of 3.*   *15% × 240 = 36*   *mark up of 6*

   Cost of sales includes the costs of the coffee beans, drinks, foods and tableware, which are charged to all outlets, owned and franchised, at the same price. About 15% of variable costs relate to these items, which are provided to outlets by CCC head office at a mark-up of 20% on costs.

   Also included are property rentals, staff costs and other operating costs directly associated with providing the product and service to the customer. Overall, about 50% of costs of sales are fixed costs and the remainder are variable costs.   *FC 120   VC 120*

2 **Administrative expenses and other costs**

   These relate to administration and other costs incurred at the individual outlets. These are all fixed costs.

3 **Allocated head office costs**

   Head office costs are not allocated to franchisees as these outlets are expected to carry out their own administration at local level. Any other costs incurred centrally by CCC such as marketing are recovered within the normal franchise fees.

Exhibit 3 – Café 2 Go: Social media analysis

Customer response analysis & review ratings

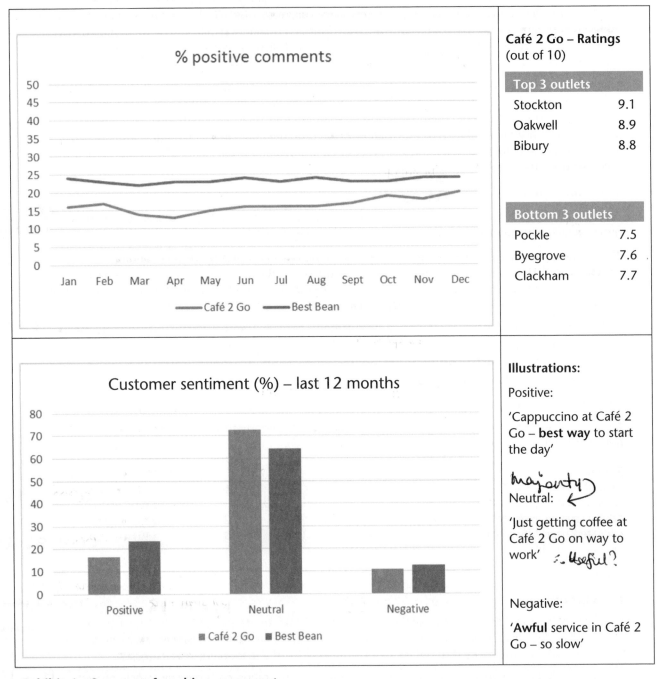

Café 2 Go – Ratings
(out of 10)

Top 3 outlets	
Stockton	9.1
Oakwell	8.9
Bibury	8.8

Bottom 3 outlets	
Pockle	7.5
Byegrove	7.6
Clackham	7.7

Illustrations:

Positive:

'Cappuccino at Café 2 Go – **best way** to start the day'

Neutral:

'Just getting coffee at Café 2 Go on way to work'

Negative:

'**Awful** service in Café 2 Go – so slow'

Exhibit 4 – Summary franchise agreement

CCC charges franchisees an initial, fixed fee and an annual franchise fee of 10% of the franchisee's total annual revenue. In return the franchisee is allowed to operate using the CCC brand name and to benefit from advertising and operational support for five years. After five years the franchise agreement can be renegotiated on new terms, but either party then has the option to terminate the arrangement.

Franchisees are given exclusivity within a distance of two kilometres from their outlet. The initial franchise fee, which averages £100,000, depends on the size and location of the outlet, the number of interested bidders and on a process of negotiation. Franchisees normally need to borrow most of the money to pay this fee.

The franchisee benefits from a brand name which has high levels of recognition throughout the UK. Consumer surveys have shown that the CCC brand is associated with good quality and customer loyalty. Compared to an independent coffee shop with similar operating characteristics, the CCC brand appears to enhance sales volumes significantly. However customer relationship management is an area where the CCC board believes that further improvements can be made.

Franchisees are required to abide by the terms of the franchise arrangement so CCC can protect its reputation. Franchisees are also required to purchase all coffee beans, food and other drink products from CCC in order to maintain the consistency of the product across owned and franchised outlets. The prices and products served are also uniform across all branches of CCC whether owned or franchised.

The size of each outlet varies from a seating capacity of 40 up to 100 people. The average seating capacity is 60.

Some potential franchisees have been deterred by the high initial charge of £100,000 to acquire a CCC franchise.

Exhibit 5 – Hoole Café Ltd application for a franchise

Hoole Café Ltd has one outlet and it has applied for a CCC franchise. For the year ended 30 June 20X9 it provided the following summary information.

	Notes	£'000	
Revenue		240	
Cost of sales	1	(180)	
Gross profit		60	GPM 25%
Administrative expenses and other costs	2	(50)	
Operating profit		10	OPM 4.2%

Notes

1 **Cost of sales**

   Overall about 50% of cost of sales are fixed and the remainder variable.

   90 FC
   90 VR

2 **Expenses**

   Administrative expenses and other costs are fixed. The Hoole Café has seating for 50 people. *Below average.*

11 Delta plc

Delta plc is a construction company (with a number of UK trading subsidiaries) quoted on the London Stock Exchange. The group specialises in the construction of out-of-town supermarkets and has enjoyed considerable growth over the last ten years. However, after pressure from the Green Lobby, the UK government has decided to stop issuing planning permissions for out-of-town shopping centres for the next five years. The company has a 31 December year end. Assume that now is 31 December 20X7.

Diversification strategy

↗ cash ↓

With limited investment opportunities and cash available, the board of Delta has decided to diversify into other areas. As part of this diversification strategy, Delta bought a 10% share in Lambda plc, another listed company, on 30 September 20X7. The investment took the form of 20m shares, at £9 per *£180m* share. Lambda plc has recently applied for planning permission to build a series of golf courses around Britain and there is a high chance of the company obtaining the necessary permissions. Delta expects Lambda's shares to appreciate significantly once permission for the development of the golf courses is granted.

As a further diversification, Delta bought a large plot of land in France for €90m on the same date. The purchase of the land on the outskirts of Paris was from a French company, and Delta plans to develop a shopping centre there. The French government has no plans to limit development of out-of-town shopping centres as there are generally not the same space restrictions in France compared to the UK. Delta is committed to make the payment for the land in full and is being allowed to pay on 30 June 20X8 due to some short-term cash flow issues. The French company has agreed to wait for the payment. *6 months* *↳ liquidity*

Review of strategy and risk

In the last board meeting of the year, on 17 December 20X7, the board of directors of Delta reviewed the strategic position of the group and a number of the directors were apprehensive about the exposure to market and currency risk. As a result of this meeting, the Group Finance Director has summoned you, the Group Financial Controller, into his office. You hope that he hasn't got anything significant on his mind as you have a New Year's Eve party to go to this evening.

'I'm really pleased that the investment we made in Lambda has been doing so well. The share price of Lambda had hit £10 when I looked just now and as a result we are sitting on an unrealised profit of £20m. The longer-term prospects for Lambda continue to look good as it is still highly likely that the planning permission for the golf courses will be granted. The board is very keen to hold on to the shares, but we are worried that the stock market performance in the next 12 months may weaken. We can't guarantee that Lambda's share price will stay buoyant if all other shares are going down, in spite of its excellent long-term prospects.

We want to protect the value of the shares and need to explore ways of hedging our position in order to protect the profits we have achieved so far. The board is also worried that the continuing devaluation of the pound against the euro will increase the cost of the French investment which may prove to be unprofitable.

I shall be making a presentation to the board, straight after New Year, on our exposure to market and exchange rate risks and their possible impact on our financial statements. I would like you to help me with some thoughts about the possible impact on our profits and reserves of movements in both the euro/sterling exchange rate and share prices. In addition, I would appreciate your thoughts about other significant risks in the two investments the company has made.

I would also like you to outline the risk management strategies you think we could employ, indicating the strengths or weaknesses of each.

For hedging strategies for currency risk, could you give me some idea of the financial reporting implications.

Potential acquisition in Australia

An unforeseen opportunity has arisen, through business contacts, to acquire a construction company in Western Australia, Boolonga Construction Pty Ltd ('BC'). The company is available at a price of 60 million Australian dollars for 100% of the equity.

I have done some initial research into the investment and its expected returns (**Exhibit 2**) and I think that it could be a very interesting and valuable acquisition that fits in well with our diversification strategy.

Please can you prepare briefing notes, including numerical illustrations where possible, to help me explain the relevant points to the board. I have just heard from Stephen Currant from Grafton Financial Research who I asked to produce some predictions on the stock market, exchange and interest rates over the next year (**Exhibit 1**). You should use his predictions as working assumptions in your calculations. For the purposes of this briefing you can assume that the time value of money would have no material effect on the payment to be made on 30 June 20X8.

Can you also include in your briefing notes a financial, strategic and risk assessment of the potential acquisition in Australia.'

Requirement

Prepare the briefing notes requested.

Total: 55 marks

Exhibit 1

Grafton Financial Research

Email

To: Jonathan Hubert of Delta plc
From: Stephen Currant
Date: 31 December 20X7
Subject: Forecasts

As requested in our conversation this morning, please find the forecasts for the stock market, the euro/sterling exchange rate and interest rates over the next 12 months.

(1) Share prices

We have considered a wide range of predictions from commentators as well as the output from our own model. In general terms we are pessimistic about the prospects for the market as a whole over the next year. The share price predictions below for Lambda plc have been derived from forecasts for the market as a whole and the beta of Lambda. Based on these predictions and suitable assumptions relating to volatility and interest rates we have also calculated the value of a put option on those dates.

Our forecast for Lambda's share price at half yearly intervals and the values of put options with a £10 exercise price during the next year are shown in the table below.

	31/12/20X7	30/6/20X8	31/12/20X8
	£	£	£
Price per share	10	9.5	8.5
Value of put option exercisable on 31/12/X8	0.745	0.812	1.5
Intrinsic value	0	0.5	1.5
Time value	0.745	0.312	0

(2) Exchange rates

	Spot rate	Forward contract dated 30 Jun 20X8
	€/£	€/£
1/10/20X7	1.3594	No longer available
31/12/20X7	1.3034	1.3051
30/6/20X8	1.2534	1.2534

(3) Interest rates

Annual interest rates as of today are quoted at:

	Sterling	Euro
6 month maturity	5.495% – 5.505% pa	5.945% – 5.955% pa
9 month maturity	5.595% – 5.605% pa	5.995% – 6.005% pa

Exhibit 2

Boolonga Construction (BC) is a private construction company in Western Australia, that has grown over the past 15 years since its incorporation. The purchase price for 100% of the company's equity would be A$60m. Delta would finance this with an Australian dollar loan of A$30m and £20m in cash. (The current exchange rate is A$1.50 = £1.)

[handwritten: r = 40%]

[handwritten: g = rb.]

The expected profits after tax for the company in 20X7 are A$9.0m. BC's policy in recent years has been to retain 40% of earnings within the business, to finance business growth. If this rate of earnings retention continues in the future, we would expect earnings to continue rising by 5% per annum. *[handwritten: →]* *[handwritten: →]*

If Delta acquires BC, we would be inclined to continue with this earnings retention and growth strategy, and to remit all dividends to the UK. *[handwritten: 60% for uk divis.]*

Economic predictions are inevitably uncertain, but our best estimates are that inflation in the UK will average 2% per annum for the foreseeable future and the annual rate of inflation in Australia will average 3.5%. *[handwritten: PPP?]*

We may need to review the appropriate cost of capital to apply to evaluation of this acquisition, but for the purpose of analysis a cost of capital of 12% should be assumed.

A decision to acquire BC must be taken quickly, because the family owners are planning to retire and want to finalise the sale of their business within the next three months.

12 Rafford plc

Tilliam Well is a successful entrepreneur who regularly seeks advice from the firm of ICAEW Chartered Accountants in which you are working as a trainee ICAEW Chartered Accountant. Len Littleton, your manager, has passed on to you an email from Tilliam Well which reads:

Email from Tilliam Well

I have been searching for a construction company in which I could take a substantial stake and join the management team. I have been looking at companies with a market capitalisation of around £200m and have come across Rafford plc which has a market capitalisation of about this amount.

I have reviewed the 20X7 financial statements of Rafford (**Exhibit 1**), which show the revenues have significantly increased, from £851m to £1,410m, but there are that many things going into profit and therefore I can't actually work out what this increase means in terms of net results. On the face of it, a market value of only 15% of revenues seems very low. In comparison, Otnes plc, another company I've come across (**Exhibit 2**), has revenue of £142m and a market capitalisation of around £220m. In each case, the net assets of the company seem to bear no resemblance to the share price, and I understand that not all assets are included in the accounts, but I thought at least I would be able to identify a minimum value from the net assets figure.

Asset based valⁿ

One thing in particular which I don't understand is the accounting treatment of the pension schemes that these companies operate. From the notes to the financial statements, I see that both companies are making some adjustments to the pension expense, which they refer to as 'remeasurement or actuarial gains and losses'. But Otnes includes these in profit or loss, whereas Rafford classifies them as other comprehensive income. Not only do I not understand what these adjustments actually mean, but I don't understand how to make the results of the two companies comparable. So, could you please give me an explanation of the accounting treatment that these two companies have followed as well as an explanation of how the present value of the liability has been calculated – with everything I've read about pensions recently I am concerned that these liabilities might not be the whole story.

Other P/L

Rafford OCI

It would be useful to me if you could produce some calculations and notes on these two companies. I would particularly like:

(1)　an overall review of the financial performance of Rafford;

(2)　an explanation of its market value, looking at both total profits and dividends, as well as some pointers as to any other information I could use;　*DCF, DVM, PE*

(3)　an overall comparison of Rafford's value with that of Otnes; and

(4)　an explanation of what the pension expenses and liabilities mean.

Regards

Tilliam

Len Littleton had allocated this work to Bart Lakey, a colleague of yours, but part way through he got called away to another client. Tilliam Well is pressing for a response so Len Littleton has told you to do the best you can from the summarised information that Bart Lakey managed to put together.

Requirement

Prepare notes which address the requests of Tilliam Well.

Total: 40 marks

Exhibit 1 – Summarised information – Rafford plc

Rafford plc employs 3,900 people and is organised into two operating segments:

Op-segments

Construction: comprehensive range of construction services and a leading infrastructure contractor

House building: individually designed homes and bespoke developments, specialising in 'brownfield' sites and affordable housing

Rafford – Statements of profit or loss and other comprehensive income for the year ending 31 December

	20X7 £m	20X6 £m
Revenue	1,410	851
Cost of sales	(1,278)	(765)
Gross profit	132	86
Administrative expenses	(69)	(50)
Profit from operations	63	36
Finance cost	(8)	(5)
Profit before tax	55	31
Tax	(11)	(6)
Profit for the year	44	25
Other comprehensive income:		
Revaluation of available-for-sale investment	3	–
Gains/losses on re-measurement of retirement benefit obligations	3	(2)
Total comprehensive income for the year	50	23

Rafford – Statements of changes in equity for the year ending 31 December

	Share capital £m	Share premium £m	Retained earnings £m	Total £m
Balance at 1 January 20X6	11	8	36	55
Changes in equity for 20X6				
Issue of share capital	3	44		47
Dividends			(5)	(5)
Total comprehensive income for the year			23	23
Balance at 31 December 20X6	14	52	54	120
Changes in equity for 20X7				
Issue of share capital	5	139		144
Dividends			(7)	(7)
Total comprehensive income for the year			50	50
Balance at 31 December 20X7	19	191	97	307

SP↑sig?.

Rafford – Statements of financial position as at 31 December

	20X7 £m	20X7 £m	20X6 £m	20X6 £m
Assets				
Non-current assets				
Goodwill		109		57
Acquired intangibles		12		2
Property, plant and equipment		6		7
Available for sale investments		25		22
		152		88
Current assets				
Land held for development	548		209	
Developments in progress	157		75	
Trade and other receivables	279		184	
Cash and cash equivalents	40		22	
		1,024		490
Total assets		1,176		578
Equity and liabilities				
Capital and reserves				
Ordinary share capital – 5p shares		19		14
Share premium		191		52
Retained earnings		97		54
Equity		307		120
Non-current liabilities				
Retirement benefits	25		47	
Borrowings	88		2	
Other	45		56	
		158		105
Current liabilities				
Trade and other payables	653		344	
Taxation	8		5	
Borrowings	50		4	
		711		353
Total equity and liabilities		1,176		578

The notes to the financial statements include the following.

(1) **Segment results**

	Revenue 20X7 £m	Profit from operations 20X7 £m	Revenue 20X6 £m	Profit from operations 20X6 £m
Construction	1,069	17	626	11
House building	340	39	224	31
Central	1	7	1	(6)
	1,410	63	851	36

(2) **Profit from operations is after crediting/(charging)**

	20X7 £m	20X6 £m
Employee benefit expenses	(161)	(104)
Operating lease rentals	(10)	(6)
Development costs recognised as an expense	(293)	(181)
Profit on sale and leaseback	4	4
Restructuring costs	(2)	(2)
Gain in curtailment resulting from closure of final salary pension scheme to future service accrual	15	–

(3) **Acquisitions**

During 20X7 an acquisition was made in the Construction segment which generated revenue of £66m and profit from operations of £3m in the post-acquisition period. If the acquisition had been made at the start of the financial year, revenue would have been increased by a further £175m and profit from operations by a further £10m. The consideration was £111m and the fair value of the net assets acquired was £59m.

During 20X6 acquisitions were made which generated the following in the 20X6 post-acquisition period:

	Revenue £m	Profit from operations £m
Construction	91	1
House building	9	1

If the acquisitions had been made at the start of the financial year, the further increases to revenue and profit from operations would have been:

	Revenue £m	Profit from operations £m
Construction	249	3
House building	29	3

The total consideration was £101m and the fair value of the net assets acquired was £44m.

Other information

The weighted average number of shares in issue for 20X7 was 305m (20X6: 235m) and the number in issue at the year-end was 380m (20X6: 280m).

The total dividend per share for 20X7 was 3p (20X6: 2.7p). 11.1% ↑

Share price (average over last month) 53p.

Exhibit 2 – Summarised information – Otnes plc

Otnes plc employs 481 people and is organised into two operating segments:

- Property and land: property development and brownfield and greenfield land development for landowners and local authorities

- Construction: civil engineering projects, local authority flats and houses and commercial buildings

Otnes – Statements of profit or loss and other comprehensive income for the year ending 31 December

	20X7 £m	20X6 £m
Revenue	142	100
Cost of sales	(96)	(65)
Gross profit	46	35
Administrative expenses	(15)	(10)
Increase in fair value of investment property	3	5
Profit on sale of investment property	2	–
Profit from operations	36	30
Finance cost	(1)	–
Profit before tax	35	30
Tax	(7)	(6)
Profit for the year	28	24
Other comprehensive income	–	–
Total comprehensive income for the year	28	24

Otnes – Statements of changes in equity for the year ending 31 December

	Share capital £m	Revaluation reserve £m	Retained earnings £m	Total £m
Balance at 1 January 20X6	15	3	78	96
Changes in equity for 20X6				
Dividends			(4)	(4)
Total comprehensive income for the year			24	24
Balance at 31 December 20X6	15	3	98	116
Changes in equity for 20X7				
Dividends			(5)	(5)
Total comprehensive income for the year			28	28
Balance at 31 December 20X7	15	3	121	139

Otnes – Statements of financial position as at 31 December

	20X7 £m	20X7 £m	20X6 £m	20X6 £m
Assets				
Non-current assets				
Goodwill		4		4
Investment properties		30		41
Property, plant and equipment		100		71
Deferred tax		9		13
		143		129
Current assets				
Land held for development	50		38	
Developments in progress	45		50	
Trade and other receivables	17		19	
Cash and cash equivalents	15		3	
		127		110
Total assets		270		239
Equity and liabilities				
Capital and reserves				
Ordinary share capital – 10p shares		15		15
Revaluation reserve		3		3
Retained earnings		121		98
Equity		139		116
Non-current liabilities				
Retirement benefits	38		43	
Borrowings	28		20	
Other	6		6	
		72		69
Current liabilities				
Trade and other payables	44		42	
Taxation	12		8	
Borrowings	3		4	
		59		54
Total equity and liabilities		270		239

The notes to the financial statements include the following.

(1) **Segment results**

	Revenue 20X7 £m	Profit from operations 20X7 £m	Revenue 20X6 £m	Profit from operations 20X6 £m
Property and land	81	35	43	29
Construction	61	6	57	6
Central	–	(5)	–	(5)
	142	36	100	30

(2) **Profit from operations is after crediting/(charging)**

	20X7 £m	20X6 £m
Employee benefit expenses	(19)	(17)
Depreciation of property, plant and equipment	(5)	(5)
Development costs recognised as an expense	(39)	(14)
Gains on re-measurement of net defined benefit pension obligation	7	5

(3) Property, plant and equipment includes property in the course of construction with a carrying amount of £70m (20X6: £38m).

Other information

The number of shares in issue at the year-end and the weighted average for 20X7 was 150m (20X6: 150m).

The total dividend per share for 20X7 was 3.3p (20X6: 2.7p). *22. 2%*

Share price (average over last month) 149p.

13 Connor Construction plc

Connor Construction plc (CC) is an international civil engineering company with operations throughout the world. You are employed by CC as an assistant to the finance director, Kate Matkin.

Kate resigned last week in order to join a rival company. The chief executive, Alf Ragg, made Kate clear her desk immediately and asked her to leave the premises. *] harsh!*

Instructions from the chief executive

The following day, Alf called you into his office and came to the point:

'We are likely to be without a finance director for some months while we search for the right person to take up this important role. A lot of responsibility will fall on you during this period.

I have one immediate task for you. We have been approached by the Muldovian government to build a 15 kilometre section of highway. Before she resigned, Kate set out some basic details of the potential contract and I will make these available to you (**Exhibit 1**).

I have a board meeting next week which will discuss whether we wish to accept this contract. I am worried about the impact of exchange rate fluctuations and other risks. I am also concerned about the fact that we may not be able to recognise any profit until the end of the contract when we receive a large proportion of the total fee.

In addition, I think it is important that we consider the potential corporate social responsibility (CSR) issues arising from the contract before we accept it. Kate had begun looking at some of these before she resigned and I will pass on her notes to you (**Exhibit 2**).

I need you to help me by preparing the following:

- A schedule showing the impact of the potential Muldovian contract on CC's expected financial reporting profit after tax in £s for each year of the contract. For this purpose assume a constant exchange rate of £1 = M$2. Please explain your calculations.

- Calculations showing the expected net present value of the contract at 1 January 20X2. In this case, please consider the possible future variations in the exchange rate.

- Briefing notes explaining the financial and operating risks that would arise for CC from acceptance of this contract and describing how these risks should be managed.

- An evaluation of the corporate social responsibility issues associated with the contract.

- Advice regarding the viability of the contract from our perspective, explaining, with reasons, whether or not we should accept it. *⟹ conclude.*

- Notes for me to use at a meeting with Steve Verdy which set out the tax implications for him of relocating to Muldovia (**Exhibit 3**). Muldovia has a flat rate of income tax of 10%, with no personal allowance.'

Requirement

Respond to the chief executive's instructions.

Total: 40 marks

Exhibit 1 – Notes on the potential Muldovian highway contract (prepared by Kate Matkin)

Background

→ delays, problems, safety

The government of Muldovia has approached us to build 15 kilometres of highway, which includes one section through difficult mountainous terrain.

p covenants

As Muldovia is a developing nation, the project is being partly financed by the World Bank, which has imposed some conditions on the Muldovian government and on the construction company carrying out the contract. The World Bank has agreed that the financing it provides is to be determined in Muldovian dollars (M$) and the cash will be made available gradually over the period of the contract. This has affected the timing of the stage payments that CC would receive.

↓ currency risk?
notalig?
↳ liquidity?

Operations

A decision on the contract needs to be made very soon or it will be offered to a competitor.

The contract will commence on 1 January 20X2 and is expected to last for four years. In each of the first two years, five kilometres of highway will be constructed. The final five kilometres of highway, however, are to be built through more difficult terrain and this will take the remaining two years of the contract to complete. The Muldovian government has recognised this issue and has allowed for the expected difficulties in setting the overall price.

Terms of proposed contract

The contract is at a fixed price and is denominated in M$. The total price is M$88m. Payments would be made to CC by the Muldovian government as follows:

31 December 20X2	M$18m
31 December 20X3	M$18m
31 December 20X4	M$18m
31 December 20X5	M$34m

The final payment would be made on condition that all the construction work has been satisfactorily completed.

Cash received is to be remitted to the UK. CC would convert the M$ received into £s immediately on receipt. CC has a 31 December accounting year end.

Costs

The equipment for the contract would be acquired on 1 January 20X2 at a cost of M$12m. It will have a zero residual value at the end of the contract.

The annual operating costs (excluding depreciation) are equal in each year of the four-year contract. They will be incurred partly in M$ (amounting to M$11m per annum) and partly in £s (amounting to £2m per annum).

While operating costs accrue evenly over each year, it can be assumed that cash flows arising in respect of these costs occur at the end of the year to which they relate.

Tax

The Muldovian tax rate is 30% and is payable on all profits earned on projects in Muldovia. Financial reporting profit according to IFRS is subject to tax. Depreciation on the initial cost of the equipment is allowable for tax in Muldovia. The taxable profit on this contract will be computed after deducting all costs attributable to the contract incurred in both Muldovia and the UK.

Tax is paid at the end of the year to which it relates.

Exchange rates

The exchange rate for the Muldovian currency is expected to be £1 = M$2 at 1 January 20X2. There is to be a general election in Muldovia in early 20X2 and it is very uncertain which party will win. If the Democratic Party wins the M$ is expected to stay at £1 = M$2 over the life of the contract. If, however, the Republican Party wins, the M$ is expected to depreciate against the £ at 10% a year over the life of the contract. According to opinion polls there is an equal probability of each party winning.

The functional and the presentation currency of CC is the £.

Discount rates

Projects of similar operational risk in the UK are discounted at 10% per annum.

Exhibit 2 – Background environmental information relating to the potential Muldovian highway contract (prepared by Kate Matkin)

In our Corporate Social Responsibility Report last year we stated 'Connor is built upon the values of conducting business in a socially responsible and ethical manner. This means we use sustainable business practices, and bring benefits to the communities in which we work.'

When working on international projects, Connor's policy is to work with local contractors and suppliers from the host country wherever possible, and to ensure that the environmental impact and social disruption caused by the construction process is minimised. *↳ mountains → building HW*

The construction of the highway should have major benefits to the economy of Muldovia, because it will provide a link between two industrial towns, which are separated by the mountainous region. *(+)*

However, the route of the highway will pass through several remotes villages which will be destroyed! *⊗* The Muldovian government plans to offer minimal compensation to the villagers for the loss of their homes. *↳ unethical & not socially responsible*

The surrounding natural environment will also be damaged. The Muldovian government believes that this damage is less important to Muldovia than developing its economy, and the government believes the road is vital to sustain Muldovia's economic growth. However, the mountainous region is home to several rare plant species and contains a site of archaeological interest. Local opposition groups have been campaining against the construction of the road, and their campaigns have attracted the attention of the international media. *→ sustainability?* *↳ reputational damage ↳ direct assoc.*

Muldovia has been enjoying significant growth recently, and this has led to something of a construction boom at the moment. As a result, some of the local firms are employing workers with inadequate experience or insufficient training in order to keep pace with demand. Health and safety regulations are much less strict in Muldovia than in the UK. Last year, workers from another UK civil engineering company refused to work at another site in Muldovia where there had been a number of accidents caused by sub-contractors. *even legal proceedings.*

Exhibit 3 – Relocation of Steve Verdy to Muldovia

The board has asked me to approach Steve Verdy, who would be the project manager for the potential Muldovian contract, to ask him to relocate to Muldovia on a 15-month contract. It is proposed that his Muldovian contract of employment will commence on either 1 January 20X2 or 1 July 20X2. Steve owns a house in West London which I am sure he will be able to rent out while he is living in Muldovia. Of course, there is always the possibility that he will want to stay longer in Muldovia. Steve is a UK resident and has a Muldovian girlfriend, so I suspect that he will be very happy to be based in Muldovia. *ties? tax period? PPP?*

14 Optica Scientific Instruments Ltd

You (Francis Banks) are a senior, working for Grapeseed, Miley & Co, ICAEW Chartered Accountants. Your firm has a client called Optica Scientific Instruments Limited (Optica) whose business consists of the design and manufacture of a variety of precision instruments for scientific and industrial use.

The CEO of the company is Percy Toone, a UK citizen aged 55 who is an experienced businessman with a background in scientific instrument technology. He is a major shareholder, although there are a number of other shareholder interests to be taken into account. In addition to Optica, Percy has various other business interests around the world.

Optica was established many years ago (it is now July 20X8) and is currently a leading player in the area of scientific instruments. Its major product is the AA Spectrophotometer which accounts for 48% of sales. Currently, the company has no subsidiaries and all the trading activities are run through Optica itself, with all its senior management and administrative functions based in its head office. The company currently exports some of its products to North and South America, which are very large potential markets. However, at the present time, it is finding it difficult to compete effectively with manufacturers in the USA and South America because of the logistics of shipping its products and the high costs of manufacture in the UK. In addition, Optica exports a small number of units to various European countries and perceives this to be a growth area of some potential. No real market penetration has been achieved in either market to date for the AA Spectrophotometer.

In essence, Percy has decided that he would like to expand the business by opening a subsidiary overseas. He has selected two countries as possible locations for this expansion and these are:

- Westland – as a base for the Westland and North American markets where costs will be denominated in New Pesos (N$).

- Eastland – as a base for new expansion into Central and Eastern Europe where costs will be denominated in Eastland Forints (EAF).

Optica has managed to secure some funding from the operating cash flows of the business and a sterling loan from bankers. Unfortunately, Optica does not have sufficient resources or borrowing power to cover both projects and must therefore choose which of these two markets to select. Its board feels the deciding factor will be which of the two will maximise after tax sterling income of the company over the next three years and would like help in making this evaluation.

Percy has recently written to the audit partner of Grapeseed, Miley & Co, Mrs Vivienne Justice, asking her to assist in the evaluation of the options regarding some of his current business plans and to ask for her views on any other factors she believes he should consider with respect to these plans. Mrs Justice has asked you to assist her in advising Percy Toone.

Partner instructions

Francis,

We have to prepare a report to the board of directors at Optica, and I need you to draft some of the parts of this report. The work is mostly connected with Optica's proposed expansion overseas.

(1) First, I need you to use the attached data (**Exhibit 1**) as a basis for preparing financial data that will help the board make the investment decision. You should work on the basis that Optica is trying to maximise its sterling income. Your calculations should be to the nearest £1,000.

(2) Second, I need you to explain to the board whether the maximisation of after-tax sterling income is an appropriate method of judging the suitability of the investment. If there is a more suitable method of investment appraisal, please can you identify it and explain why it is better. I also would like you to analyse briefly the wider strategic issues surrounding the expansion.

[handwritten left margin: established competitor - expansion (LT) Demand for such product? Differentiating on? Remittance of profits]

(3) A couple of members of Optica's board have raised doubts about the practical aspects of the expansion. They feel that there are likely to be many potential difficulties, but are unsure what the problems might be. Please can you identify the possible practical issues that may be relevant if a new subsidiary is established. *[handwritten: suppliers - quality, skilled labour / workforce, mgmt control over operations, ^]*

(4) Last, investment in either country will mean that Optica's foreign currency risk profile could change substantially. I need you to explain the various exchange risks that Optica will face if it invests in either Eastland or Westland, and how Optica can manage the risks you identify. I also need you to describe the assurance work that we shall need to carry out to verify Optica's treatment of foreign exchange risk.

[handwritten: → remittance of profits, translation risk]

Vivienne

Requirement

Respond to the instructions of the audit partner, Vivienne Justice.

Total: 40 marks

Exhibit 1 – Financial data in relation to the proposed expansion

Summary of the overall demand for AA Spectrophotometers

	Westland production	Eastland production
Total market size (units)	16,000	1,500
Optica's estimated market share (%)		
Year 1	1.625	16
Year 3	2.5	28

Market sizes are expected to remain constant over the next 3 years. Anticipated selling prices are stated below expressed in sterling based on the expected exchange rates (see Note 3 below). Sales will actually be priced in the local currency of the market in which the sale is made.

	Westland £	Eastland £
Year 1	25,500	32,000
Year 3	27,000	36,000

Year 2 sales units and sterling revenues are expected to be an average of Year 1 and Year 3.

Direct costs

The costing structure of one unit of the AA spectrophotometer as manufactured in the UK (for the export to North America or Europe) together with the anticipated equivalent figures for the Americas and European markets, if manufactured locally, is as follows (in Year 1 prices).

	UK £	Westland N$	Eastland EAF
Unit selling price	32,500	422,500	11,200,000
Direct cost per unit	(22,750)	(173,225)	(3,981,250)
Gross profit per unit	9,750 _30%_	249,275 _59%_	7,218,750 _64.5%_

Revenue figures are based on sales in the market local to where the items are produced at Year 1 exchange rates. They show that Optica can achieve a much better margin by selling into Westland or Eastland using a local manufacturing base. However against this they would have the costs of setting up and running a local facility.

Cost inflation is running at 9% in Westland and 17% in Eastland (and is expected to continue to be these figures for the next couple of years at least).

Notes

1 **Labour** – Precision instruments require an element of skilled labour, which in turn requires high levels of training. Optica currently sends its skilled workers on a specialised course to achieve this training level.

2 **Taxation** – Assume that the taxable profits will be the same as the profits for financial reporting purposes. Rates of tax in the two proposed locations are:

Westland: 34%

Eastland: 36% (plus a tax incentive for a new business of a 60% reduction in the tax payable during the first five years)

3 **Exchange rates** – According to the long term economic review by the International Trade Association, it is likely that the exchange rates in Year 1 through to Year 3 will be as follows:

	N$ to £	EAF to £
Year 1	13.00	350
Year 2	12.50	425
Year 3	12.00	500

better   _worse_

4 **Cost of manufacturing facility**

The Eastland government has agreed in principle to make a grant of 30% towards the cost of the actual building itself, as long as local contractors and materials are used. Provisional costings are as follows: _CSR_

		Westland N$ (000's)	Eastland EAF (m)
Cost of land		10,000	320
Building cost	_769_	20,000	1,500
Less grant → _must amortise the grant._		–	(450)
		30,000	1,370
Equipment including transportation/installation		52,000	1,960
	_6,308_	82,000	3,330 _9,514_

Buildings will last no more than 20 years for Westland and 30 years for Eastland and the equipment eight and ten years respectively. Corporate policy is to depreciate assets on a straight-line basis.

5 **General overheads**

For Year 1 it is estimated that these will be as follows:

	Westland N$ (000's)	Eastland EAF (m)
General overheads	21,103	1,907.35

15　Hyper-Thin Glass Ltd

The chief executive of Hyper-Thin Glass Ltd (HTG), David Ridd, was not happy. The board has been unable to agree on the action to take regarding one of the directors who needs to sell his shares in the company.

In order to resolve the stalemate, David decided to obtain some independent advice to help guide the board in this matter. He therefore approached the company's business advisers, Jensen, James and Joplin LLP (JJJ). You work for JJJ as a senior. Terry Jensen, the engagement partner, took you along to a meeting with David.

Background information

In advance of the meeting, David sent to you the following background information about HTG.

HTG was formed as a management buy-out in 20X2 from an international glass manufacturing *[handwritten: MBO]* company, Rowdean plc. 'Hyper-Thin Glass' was a special project making narrow-width, high performance, self-cleaning glass. Rowdean decided to abandon its plans for 'Hyper-Thin Glass', but the four senior managers working on the project formed HTG to acquire the assets from Rowdean at their carrying amount. The four managers were able to raise enough equity, each acquiring 25% of the share capital. However, significant loan finance was also needed by HTG, which was provided by Rowdean in the form of a £4m bond. *[handwritten: Debt + equity]*

[handwritten margin: unique product]

The four managers became directors. The HTG board consists of Angela (responsible for the glass manufacturing division and also research and development), Barry (responsible for the double glazing division and also company finance director), Sophie (marketing director and human resources) and David (chief executive). There are about 100 other staff.

[handwritten margin: small co.]

The operations of the business are conducted through two divisions: Division A which manufactures high performance glass; and Division B which manufactures and retails double glazing units using glass from Division A.

An offer of £2m was recently made by a large glass manufacturing company to buy all rights to use the 'Hyper-Thin Glass' name for the next ten years. This was considered, but rejected, by the HTG board.

[handwritten margin: Benchmark for am dep Amortisation — £200k p.a.]

The meeting with the chief executive

David opened the meeting: 'The original business plan was to obtain an AIM listing by the end of 20X9, thereby enabling each director to take advantage of the listing to sell shares as an exit route when appropriate. The recent conflict has been caused by Barry who is going through a divorce and needs cash for his shares in early 20X7 as part of the divorce settlement.

[handwritten margin: Barry = FD (double glazing)]

'He would like to sell his shares to the other three directors at an agreed price. If this is not possible, he was planning to sell his holding to somebody outside the company for whatever price he could obtain. The problem is that he cannot find a suitable outside buyer and we, the other three directors, cannot agree on a price for his shares. Barry thinks we may try to exploit his difficult personal financial position by offering a low price, so that we can make a profit when we go for an initial public offering on AIM in a few years.

[handwritten margin: in no position to negotiate]

[handwritten: → minority shareholding.]

'Even if we could determine the value of the company as a whole I am not convinced that a quarter of the shares would be worth a quarter of the value of the overall share capital. We did not enter into a shareholder agreement when we formed the company, so there is no valuation formula to bind us.

'At yesterday's board meeting a set of instructions was drafted for your firm in respect of this matter (**Exhibit 1**). I have also provided you with the forecast draft financial statements for the year to 31 December 20X6 and some notes (**Exhibit 2**). You may also like to speak to Barry on this matter to ensure you have all sides of the story.'

The meeting with Barry

You accompany Terry to a meeting with Barry.

Barry opened the meeting. 'I have no wish to sell my shares, but I am being forced into it by my personal circumstances. I helped to form this company and I want to continue to be part of it as a director, even if I cannot continue to be a shareholder. However, as directors and shareholders, we all agreed that we would pay a small directors' remuneration to leave cash in the business and take capital gains later. If I am no longer a shareholder, then I will need my remuneration as a director doubled to a fair market rate.

[handwritten: Fv = 2x rate.]

As a possible alternative to buying my shares for cash, I have suggested to the board that I could take ownership of Division B, for which I am responsible, as payment for my shares. This would involve the transfer to me of all assets, contracts and rights currently relating to Division B in return for transferring my shares to HTG. I would then be able to raise cash from these assets to settle my divorce. In this case, I would no longer be a director of HTG.'

[handwritten: noreeeth for Barry but we work for HTG]

Partner's instructions

On returning to your office Terry provided you with some instructions: 'I would like you to prepare notes addressing all the issues raised by the board (Exhibit 1).

'I would also like you to provide notes for me concerning the ethical issues for the firm in respect of whom we should be acting for in providing this advice and whether it is appropriate to advise on all of the matters that have been requested. *[handwritten: ETHICS 6]*

There are quite a few things that concern me about this client. I am not altogether convinced that the board is realistic about its prospects for achieving an AIM listing in the next three years or so, and they may have ignored or under-estimated the risks and problems they face. They have not asked for our advice on this matter, but I should like to have a quiet word with them if I can. So I would like you to give me an assessment of the potential risks to a successful launch on AIM by the end of 20X9, from the *[handwritten: 8]* information we already have available. And can you make any comments about the corporate governance arrangements with a view to an AIM listing too, please.

There is one additional concern. As you are aware Rowdean is an important audit client of JJJ. Yesterday I *[handwritten: self-interest]* had a voicemail from the JJJ audit senior on the Rowdean audit who is currently assessing the recoverability of the loan to HTG and has asked us for any relevant information. The potential changes *[handwritten: 7]* in HTG's shareholdings may have a material impact on the fair value of the loan. Please make some notes for me setting out the ethical implications for JJJ.' *[handwritten: → confidentiality]*

Requirement

Respond to the partner's instructions.

Total: 60 marks

Exhibit 1 – The board's instructions to JJJ

The board is sympathetic to Barry's situation, but the other shareholders would have to borrow funds personally in order to raise enough cash to buy his shares.

The board has therefore developed two proposals for consideration, but these are not firm offers and the advice of JJJ is required.

Proposal 1 – the other three directors (Angela, Sophie and David) to purchase Barry's shares

The other three directors would buy equal amounts of Barry's shares. For this purpose HTG would obtain advice from JJJ on a valuation of HTG's equity.

We would like JJJ to provide the following with respect to Proposal 1:

(a) A value for the entire share capital of HTG applying a multiple of 5 times EBITDA (earnings before interest, tax, depreciation and amortisation) for the year ending 31 December 20X6. For this *[handwritten: 1]* purpose, use amounts from the draft forecast financial statements for the year ending 31 December 20X6 without further adjustments (**Exhibit 2**). *[handwritten: ✓]*

(b) An explanation of the extent to which a formula based on EBITDA can provide an appropriate *[handwritten: 2]* value for HTG's equity. *[handwritten: ✓]*

(c) An alternative valuation for the entire share capital of HTG, using an earnings-based valuation *[handwritten: 3]* method. Make any adjustments to reported earnings that you believe would be reasonable for the purpose of making this valuation. Assume your adjusted earnings figure for the year ending 31 December 20X6 will continue for the foreseeable future (ie there will be zero growth). Use 8% *[handwritten: assumptions (+ critique)]* per annum as the cost of equity to discount earnings. Briefly justify your valuation calculation.

(d) A calculation and explanation of how a 25% holding in HTG may be valued. *[handwritten: 4]*

[handwritten: minority SH.]

Proposal 2 – Transfer of Division B assets to Barry by HTG in return for all his shares

This alternative proposal would require a transfer to Barry of all Division B's assets, contracts and rights. Barry would not take on any of HTG's debt. In return, Barry's shares in HTG would be transferred to HTG. The shares would be cancelled after they are transferred. Barry would continue to trade with HTG, but on an arm's length basis.

(e) We would like JJJ to provide advice on the impact for the other three directors of Proposal 2 compared to Proposal 1. Include and explain supporting calculations.

Exhibit 2 – Draft forecast financial statements

Forecast statement of financial position at 31 December 20X6

	Notes	Division A £'000	Division B £'000	Total £'000
Non-current assets				
Property, plant and equipment	1	5,700	1,750	7,450
Current assets		300	250	550
Total assets		6,000	2,000	8,000
Capital and reserves				
Issued capital – £1 shares				1,000
Retained earnings				2,750
Equity				3,750
Non-current liabilities				
Loan from Rowdean				4,000
Current liabilities				250
Total equity and liabilities				8,000

Forecast summary statement of profit or loss for year ending 31 December 20X6

	Notes	Division A £'000	Division B £'000	Total £'000
Revenue	2, 3	42,800	4,000	
Cost of sales	2	(38,800)	(2,000)	
Total depreciation		(1,000)	(500)	
Administrative and other operating costs	4	(1,400)	(750)	
Operating profit		1,600	750	2,350
Finance costs				(200)
Profit before tax				2,150
Tax 23%				(495)
Profit after tax				1,655

Notes

1 The fair value of property, plant and equipment is currently £6.84m in Division A and £1.925m in Division B. There are no assets shared by the two divisions.

2 Revenue and cost of sales include transfers between the divisions. About half of the cost of sales of Division B represents purchases from Division A. The glass is transferred at full cost plus 25%. Sales to third parties by Division A are made at market rates which are normally about 10% above full cost.

3 A major contract was signed in August 20X6 by Division B to deliver 1,000 large double glazed units to a building company, Jegg plc. The total price of the contract was £1m and the cost of manufacture was £600,000, including glass transferred from Division A at £300,000. A deposit of £300,000 was received in September 20X6 from Jegg in respect of the contract. On 1 November 20X6, 600 units were delivered and a payment of £420,000 in respect of these units was also received.

By 31 December 20X6 manufacture of all the units should be completed and the final payment of £280,000 will, according to the contract, be due. The forecast financial statements for the year ending 31 December 20X6 therefore recognise the £1m revenue in full, along with the £600,000 cost of manufacture under cost of sales. The remaining 400 units will be delivered to Jegg in January 20X7.

Jegg is likely to make similar orders in future years.

ICAEW

4   Administrative and other operating costs include directors' salaries totalling £300,000. All directors are paid equally. Only Barry's remuneration is charged to Division B.

5   The company has a small overdraft and no cash is held at the bank.

6   No dividends have been paid since the company was formed.

16   Raul plc

It is now December 20X3.

Raul plc is an AIM listed company which manufactures central heating boilers for use in domestic households. It operates in a competitive market, and although its products have a reputation for good quality, larger manufacturers with a strong brand name are winning most of the growth in the market.

You are a senior working for Raul's auditors and business advisers, Roecastle and Rand LLP (RR), and you have been asked to accompany the engagement manager, Helen Higgs, to a meeting with Raul's finance director, Charles Chou.

Meeting with finance director

Charles commenced the meeting somewhat pessimistically: 'I'll be honest with you both, the company is facing a major financing crisis. However, I firmly believe we can pull through and return to profitability. I just wish I could make the bank believe that.

Raul has suffered poor financial results in the economic downturn, as demand has fallen and we have lost some major customers. Cash flow has been poor and our overdraft has increased substantially. The board has made some mistakes, but there is now a new chief executive and we have a plan for recovery.

When we prepared our management accounts for the period ended 30 September 20X3 we were in breach of a loan covenant. We knew this, but our bank, Lockington plc, is taking a much harder line with us than we envisaged. It is reluctant to continue the overdraft and the existing loan and, as a result, we may need to enter into administration.

Lockington is considering a refinancing package for both the current loan and the overdraft, if it can be convinced about the strength of our recovery. The financing package of £20m would be a new fixed term, variable rate loan. This would be for six years from 1 January 20X4 at a variable annual rate of interest linked to LIBOR, which would currently cost us 15%. We consider this to be a punitive interest rate. The principal amount of the loan would be repayable on 31 December 20X9. Our existing overdraft and loan are both at an annual interest rate of 10%.

One of the additional problems with the new loan is that there will be very challenging covenants. The bank would also require an assurance report from our auditors to support our forecasts, which is why I have asked to see you. I have prepared summary financial forecasts based on the existing financing arrangements (**Exhibit 1**) but I will need your help to adjust these for any new financing arrangements. What I am not clear about is what assurance you can give us, as the figures used are forecasts rather than the historical financial information that you normally audit.'

Helen interrupted Charles at this point. 'We did include a going concern disclosure in our 20X2 audit report in an emphasis of matter paragraph, but I had not anticipated the bank taking such a tough position. Have you searched for alternative forms of finance?'

Charles sighed. 'This has proved very difficult. None of our traditional sources of finance wanted anything to do with us. Eventually we did find a rich financier, Walter Baffet, who is considering offering Raul the following financing package:

- A loan for four years from 1 January 20X4. The terms are a fixed-interest loan of £10m with interest at 10% per annum. The principal is repayable on 31 December 20X7;

- A sale and leaseback arrangement for the company's main factory (**Exhibit 2**) which would generate a further £10m; and

- The issue of options to Walter on 1 January 20X4 to allow him to acquire 2m of Raul's ordinary shares at £5 per share at any time up to 31 December 20X7.

The share price is currently £4.50 per share, but it reached a high of £15.07 in August 20X0. However, the industry is very different now.

Under the terms of the financing package with Walter, Raul would not be allowed to pay any dividends before 20X8. There are some covenants, but these are not onerous.

What I would like from RR is the following:

(1) A draft forecast of profit before tax for each of the four years ending 31 December 20X4 to 20X7 with the adjustments for each of the alternative proposals:

- Lockington's loan
- Walter's financing package

(2) A forecast of operating and financing cash flows for each of the four years ending 31 December 20X4 to 20X7 and the expected cash balance at the end of each year, with the adjustments for each of the alternative proposals:

- Lockington's loan
- Walter's financing package

(3) A comparison of the two financing proposals with reasoned advice as to which one Raul should select, including an assessment of the risks associated with the proposals and any alternative arrangement we may need to consider for the company's future

(4) A summary of the nature of the assurance procedures to support the forecasts and the report that you could provide for the bank

I will of course take responsibility for the final versions of the forecasts. I just need some figures to help me that include the new financing arrangements. Please make clear any assumptions that you make in your calculations.'

Engagement manager's instructions

Following the meeting, Helen called you into her office. 'I am concerned about the future viability of this company and the alternative financing arrangements available need to be considered urgently.
I would therefore like you to do two things:

(1) Prepare a draft of the documents requested by Charles, to be on my desk today.

(2) I would like your views about the risk in Raul's plans for the next few years. I am concerned that management is over-optimistic about the future. So, can you please provide me with a memo about the risk that Raul's plan for survival will not work. You may find useful a summary of Raul's results for the 11 months to 30 November 20X3 **(Exhibit 3)**.'

Requirement

Respond to the instructions from the engagement manager.

Total: 55 marks

Exhibit 1 – Summary financial forecasts

Forecast summary statement of financial position at 31 December 20X3

	Notes	£'000
Non-current assets		
Property, plant and equipment	1	20,000
Current assets		
Inventories		3,000
Trade receivables		3,000
Cash		1,000
Total assets		27,000
Capital and reserves		
Share capital (Ordinary £1 shares)		5,000
Reserves		1,000
Equity		6,000
Non-current liabilities		
10% bank loan		10,000
Current liabilities		
Overdraft		10,000
Other current liabilities		1,000
Total equity and liabilities		27,000

Forecast summary statements of comprehensive income to 31 December

The company does not expect to experience any growth over the next few years and therefore the annual statements of comprehensive income for each of the years 20X4 to 20X7 are forecast to be identical as follows:

	Notes	£'000
Revenue	5	12,000
Operating costs	1, 2	(8,000)
Operating profit		4,000
Finance costs	3	(2,000)
Profit before tax		2,000
Tax	4	–
Profit for period		2,000

(handwritten: 33⅓%)

Notes

1   Depreciation amounts to £1m per annum and is included within operating costs. The cost model is used. The fair value of property, plant and equipment is £30m.

2   Operating costs comprise 50% fixed costs (including depreciation) and 50% variable costs.

3   The forecast does not take account of any refinancing of the loan and is therefore based on the existing annual interest rate of 10% on the bank loan and overdraft.

4   The company has substantial brought forward trading losses and capital losses and does not therefore expect any tax liability over the period 20X4–20X7.

5   There is a risk of losing a major customer in early 20X4 when a long term contract is due for renewal. This customer accounts for 10% of our revenue. The above forecasts assume that the customer will be retained. *(handwritten: Risk⊛ ↳ how likely?)*

Exhibit 2 – Proposed sale and leaseback arrangement

The main factory would be subject to a 10-year sale and leaseback agreement under Walter Baffet's financing package. At 31 December 20X3 the fair value of the factory is estimated to be £8m and its carrying amount £5m. The factory originally cost £7m.

The factory has a remaining useful life of 20 years and is being depreciated at £250,000 per annum.

Under the terms of the sale and leaseback agreement, Walter would pay cash of £10m for the factory on 1 January 20X4. Lease rentals would be £1.3m per annum for 10 years, payable annually in arrears. Market rentals for similar properties are about £1m per annum. Walter would take ownership of the factory at the end of the lease period at which time it is expected to have a fair value of about £8.25m.

(handwritten: rent > MV of rent)

The implicit annual interest rate of the sale and leaseback arrangement is 12%.

Exhibit 3 – Summary of financial results for the 11 months to 30 November 20X3

	Actual		Budget	
	£'000	£'000	£'000	£'000
Revenue		10,280		11,000
Materials	2,860		2,640	
Labour	2,380		2,053	
Other operating costs	2,890		2,640	
Total operating costs		8,130		7,333
Operating profit		2,150		3,667

(handwritten: 33.3%)

(handwritten: 20.9)

50% of labour costs are variable costs. Actual sales prices for the company's boilers were very close to budgeted sales prices. *(handwritten: ∴ sales volume is factor)*

17 Geo Carbon Engineering plc

Geo Carbon Engineering plc (GCE) is the listed parent of a group of companies manufacturing high technology, heavy engineering equipment for the oil industry. The group currently has three manufacturing plants in the UK, Norway and Kuwait.

You are a senior, working in the London office of a large global firm of ICAEW Chartered Accountants. A manager in your firm has invited you to accompany him to a meeting with Oliver Ohlson, the finance director of GCE, which is a new client.

Meeting with the finance director

Oliver commenced the meeting: 'We are considering entering into a joint arrangement and we would like your firm to help us through this process, both as our business adviser and to provide assurance services in respect of the venture. We have not asked our auditors to do this work as we believe it may compromise their independence, but they are fully aware of the situation.

The GCE board has been trying to enter into the South American market for some years. However, it has proved difficult to do this alone due to local regulations and the lack of a production site in the region, so we have been seeking to establish a strategic alliance with a partner already located in the region. The potential joint arrangement partner we found is Moddo Inc, which is a company resident in Muldovia in South America. Moddo wants to use GCE's expertise to help it to produce more technologically advanced equipment.

One of our major concerns is a lack of reliable information about Moddo. We will therefore require your firm to provide assurance over Moddo's systems, operations and processes, not just a financial audit. This is quite a wide remit and you may need to identify where external expert assistance will be required. I expect you to travel to Muldovia to complete part of your work.

I have provided you with background information for the project (**Exhibit 1**) and details of some issues in respect of the joint arrangement (**Exhibit 2**) which summarise the negotiations to date. I have also provided financial statement extracts comparing GCE with the relevant division of Moddo, which is PetroEng (**Exhibit 3**).

I have some concerns about the investment risk in this project, and am worried that the investment will fail to provide the return that GCE will require. This is partly because I think the cash flow estimates may be too optimistic and there are quite a number of potentially significant risks (**Exhibit 4**).

I would like the following from your firm:

- Notes explaining the two alternative ways in which the joint arrangement could be structured (**Exhibit 2**), indicating the benefits and problems of each. Include advice regarding the preferred structure of the joint arrangement for GCE. Ignore financial reporting and tax considerations for this purpose.

- An explanation and reasoned recommendation, with supporting calculations, as to which method of finance GCE should use for its initial cash contribution of £15m (**Exhibit 2**).

- Notes describing the assurance services that your firm could provide for GCE with respect to: (1) the initial set-up of the joint arrangement; and (2) continuing assurance over the four-year period.

- I have done my own DCF estimates for the investment, and I would like your independent views, based on the information available, about whether the investment will achieve the 15% DCF return we shall require and the investment risks. I would like to compare your assessment with those that I have already made myself.' (**Exhibit 4**)

After the meeting, your manager asks you to prepare notes responding to Oliver's request.

Requirement

Respond to the instructions of your manager.

Total: 40 marks

Exhibit 1 – Background information

Muldovia

Muldovia commenced moving towards being an open economy only five years ago. Prior to this, it operated as a closed economy with little international trade. It is now expanding rapidly, but the infrastructure is poor and the workforce lacks skills and technical expertise. There are still some trade barriers and some exchange controls are still in place. The Muldovian corporate tax rate is 40%.

The economic environment within Muldovia is uncertain. The currency is the Muldovian dollar (M$) which is readily exchangeable on international money markets following a decision by the Muldovian central bank last year to float the currency. The current exchange rate is £1 = M$2 and this is not expected to change before 31 December 20X1. However, the financial markets expect the M$ to depreciate against £ sterling by 5% per annum over the four years from 1 January 20X2 due to differences in rates of inflation. Inflation in the UK is expected to be insignificant. *→ what does that mean? no time value?*

The Muldovian government is keen to introduce expertise from developed nations into its economy to assist growth.

sending profits back up group (distribution) –losses?

Moddo Inc

Before being recently privatised, Moddo had been a state-owned, engineering company. One division of Moddo, PetroEng, makes heavy engineering equipment for the oil industry in Muldovia, where it has a monopoly as a result of a lack of local competition and protective trade barriers preventing imports.

The PetroEng equipment uses basic and old technology. There are currently no exports by PetroEng as the equipment is not of sufficient quality to compete in international markets.

Moddo has a single large factory from which a number of divisions operate, including PetroEng. The PetroEng equipment currently takes an average of nine months to manufacture. Other divisions make entirely different engineering products. *9m →*

The Moddo board hopes that, by forming a strategic alliance with GCE, it can use GCE's technology and expertise to develop improved products and increase PetroEng's production efficiency. As a consequence, PetroEng hopes to be able to update its product range and sell within Muldovia at a higher price, and also to begin to export to other countries in South America.

establish competition? ↑ competition + barriers to entry.

Exhibit 2 – Joint arrangement issues

After initial discussions between GCE and Moddo, the following has been proposed:

Heads of agreement

- The joint arrangement will be for an initial period of four years from 1 January 20X2, after which it will be dissolved or a new agreement made.

- An initial cash contribution of £15m will be made by each of the parties on 1 January 20X2 to finance working capital.

- In addition to their initial cash contributions:

  - Moddo, through its PetroEng division, will provide a substantial part of its existing factory. It will also provide unskilled labour and pay general expenses.

  - GCE will provide plant and equipment, engineers and management grade labour. It will also make available to PetroEng its engineering know-how. *} alot being provided!*

GCE will not sell any of the products currently being produced in its existing factories to customers in the oil industry in South America for the duration of the venture agreement.

- The activities of the joint arrangement are restricted to developing and producing engineering equipment for the oil industry in South America and exclude other operating activities of both companies.

- Revenues earned by the sale of engineering equipment under the new venture to customers in the oil industry will be shared equally between the venturers.

Structuring of the joint arrangement

Two alternative joint arrangement structures are being considered:

- ① Forming a separate entity for the joint arrangement; or

- ② Entering into a contract to control operations jointly. Each venturer will provide assets and contribute to costs in accordance with the agreement, but without creating a separate entity.

Financing

The initial cash contribution to the venture by GCE of £15m will need to be financed by borrowing. The Muldovian government has offered GCE a M$30m, 12% loan repayable on 31 December 20X5.

Alternatively, GCE could borrow £15m at 8% per annum from a UK bank, also repayable on 31 December 20X5.

Interest would be payable annually in arrears on either loan.

Exhibit 3 – Extracts from financial statements

Extracts from statements of profit or loss for the year ended 31 October 20X1

	GCE	PetroEng
	£'000	M$'000
Revenue	200,000	24,000
Operating profit	30,000	2,000

Extracts from statements of financial position at 31 October 20X1

	GCE	PetroEng
	£'000	M$'000
Non-current assets		
Property, plant and equipment	120,000	30,000
Current assets	20,000	10,000
Total assets	140,000	40,000
Equity	90,000	28,000
Non-current liabilities		
Loan 5% euro loan notes 20X5	20,000	–
Loan 6% sterling loan 20X8	25,000	–
Muldovian government loan 10%	–	10,000
Current liabilities		
Trade and other payables	5,000	2,000
Total equity and liabilities	140,000	40,000

Exhibit 4 – Investment appraisal data

For investment projects of this nature, GCE would require a minimum DCF return on investment of 15%.

It should be assumed that the initial investment of M$30m will be recovered at the end of the four-year period.

Oliver Ohlson, the finance director of GCE, has made his assessment by calculating the minimum annual cash flow that would be required, in Muldovian dollars, to provide a constant annual cash flow in £ to GCE to obtain a DCF return of 15%. He has assumed that the joint venture will remit all its after-tax profits to the joint venture partners each year and that there will be no exchange controls restricting the conversion of Muldovian dollars into sterling or their remittance to the UK.

His working assumptions are that there will be no inflation in the UK, inflation in Muldovia will be 5% each year and the Muldovian dollar/sterling exchange rate will move each year to reflect the differing rates of inflation in the two countries.

Assumptions

The currency of revenues and expenditures for the joint venture operations should be assumed to consist entirely of Muldovian dollars.

18 Krown Jools plc

'There are two key questions outstanding: first, what price should we offer for the acquisition of Gubb plc; and second, how should we finance this acquisition?'

Ranjit Roberts, the chief executive of Krown Jools plc (KJ), was summarising the outcomes of an important board meeting at which the potential acquisition of Gubb had been discussed. The meeting ended with agreement to make an offer for the entire ordinary share capital of Gubb.

KJ had no previous experience of making acquisitions. As a result, before making any offer for Gubb, it had been decided that KJ would obtain advice from Denton, Davies & Drew (DDD), the firm of accountants and business advisers for which you work as a senior. KJ is not audited by DDD.

Meeting

Ranjit asked Holly Harte, a DDD partner, to attend a meeting to discuss the potential acquisition of Gubb. Ranjit opened the meeting:

'Thanks for coming along, Holly. We have made some progress in discussions with the Gubb board, but there are still some crucial outstanding issues on which I would like your firm's advice. We particularly need your help at the moment, as we have not yet replaced our finance director, who resigned last month.

I realise that you have not acted for KJ previously, so I have provided some background information about the company (**Exhibit 1**). I have also set out the board's thoughts on the acquisition (**Exhibit 2**) and provided forecast individual company financial statements, for both KJ and Gubb, along with some working assumptions (**Exhibit 3**).

One of the major motivations in proposing this acquisition is to enhance KJ's earnings per share, as I believe this is a crucial Stock Market indicator for us. However, I have two issues which may create ethical concerns.

↑ EPS

First, I think that market analysts' forecasts of KJ's profits for the year ending 31 December 20X2 are too optimistic. The KJ board has not encouraged them to believe this, but neither have we corrected their overestimates. As a result of analysts' optimism, I believe that the KJ share price is overvalued at the moment and that it will fall when actual earnings are announced for the year ending 31 December 20X2. I am therefore going to recommend that we should move quickly with the acquisition of Gubb if we are to finance it by means of a share-for-share exchange, as the inflated KJ share price would make the terms favourable to KJ shareholders.

not ethical Gubb should do its own DD.

Second, the board has taken a firm decision to reorganise parts of KJ's operations. The reorganisation was intended to be in November 20X2, but I do not want to have to make a provision in the year ending 31 December 20X2, which would reduce profit. I will therefore delay the reorganisation until 20X3.

manipulation?

The KJ board has identified the following five tasks which it would like DDD to undertake:

(1) Calculate the maximum amount we should offer to acquire the entire ordinary share capital of Gubb. Use the discounted free cash flow method and apply the working assumptions in Exhibit 3. Assume for this purpose that the share-for-share exchange method of financing is used. Please explain any concerns that you have with this calculation. Include any additional information you require.

(2) Assuming that the acquisition takes place on 1 January 20X3, determine the forecast, consolidated earnings per share for the KJ group for the year ending 31 December 20X3 under each of the three suggested financing methods. Explain the likely impact of the change in EPS from 20X2 to 20X3 on the KJ share price.

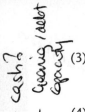

cash? gearing / debt gpacity

(3) Explain the issues the KJ board should consider before deciding whether to finance the acquisition using: (1) a share-for-share exchange; (2) borrowing; or (3) part share-for-share exchange and part loan notes.

(4) Explain any ethical concerns for the KJ board that may arise in respect of the two issues raised by me.

(5) Prepare preliminary notes which assess the strategic and operating risks of the acquisition. Ignore the method of finance for this purpose. A more detailed assessment of risks will ultimately be needed from DDD as part of commercial and operating due diligence reports but, at this stage, the board only needs notes based on the information currently available.'

Partner's instructions

Following the meeting, Holly called you into her office and, having explained what happened at the meeting, asked you to prepare notes for her, addressing each of the five tasks required of DDD by the KJ board.

Requirement

Respond to the partner's instructions.

Total: 40 marks

Exhibit 1 – Background information on Krown Jools plc

KJ is listed on the London Stock Exchange. It is a jewellery retailer which operates a chain of 90 shops throughout the UK. It has expanded by reinvesting its operating cash flows in new stores. KJ sells from shops located in prime positions in town and city centres. All shops are held under rental agreements.

KJ sells mid-market jewellery made from moderate grades of precious stones (eg diamonds and sapphires) and precious metals (eg silver and gold). Its customer base is mainly middle-income consumers. It does not sell low-quality fashion jewellery.

 EPS

The KJ board expects the company's profit after tax to continue to grow at an average rate of 4% per annum for the foreseeable future if it makes no acquisitions.

Exhibit 2 – Potential acquisition of Gubb

Negotiations

Preliminary discussions have taken place between the boards of KJ and Gubb. The KJ board has declared to the Gubb board its desire to make an offer to acquire the entire ordinary share capital of Gubb, subject to satisfactory due diligence and agreement on price.

Background information on Gubb

Gubb's shares are not listed. All its shares are owned by members of the Gubb family, who are also directors.

Gubb sells low-quality fashion jewellery and, rather than using precious metals and stones, it tends to use steel and synthetic stones. Its customer base is mainly young, fashion-conscious consumers on low incomes.

The company operates a chain of 40 shops located in cities throughout the UK. All shops are held under operating leases.

Gubb has made reasonable profits over many years but, more recently, profit has been at a fairly constant level and there is little prospect of future profit growth, unless Gubb is acquired by another company.

Acquisition strategy for KJ

KJ has reached saturation point with its shops in the UK as most major towns and cities already have a KJ outlet. KJ has identified the fashion jewellery market as a potential option for expansion. The acquisition of Gubb would give KJ a quick entry into this market.

For management purposes, KJ would maintain Gubb as an autonomous operating unit, but central administration would be merged. However, there would be no major changes to Gubb in the year ending 31 December 20X3, as KJ's management would use this time to gain a better understanding of the fashion jewellery industry and markets.

ICAEW

Methods of financing the acquisition

Three possible methods of financing the acquisition have been identified:

(1) A share-for-share exchange (ie paper-for-paper). The exchange would be in an agreed ratio based on: (1) a valuation of Gubb shares, determined for the purpose of the acquisition; and (2) the market price of KJ shares at the acquisition date. New shares in KJ would be issued to Gubb shareholders for this purpose; or

(2) A cash offer to Gubb shareholders for their shares, based on a valuation determined for the purpose of the acquisition. The cash required to make the acquisition would be borrowed in its entirety from KJ's bank at a fixed annual interest rate of 9%.

(3) As there is some uncertainty about the ability of KJ to raise a bank loan to finance the purchase, KJ may be able to persuade the owners of Gubb to accept 50% of the purchase price in the form of a share exchange and the remaining 50% in the form of loan notes with interest at 10%. The loan notes would mature after five years, when their holders would have the choice between redemption at par or conversion of the notes into KJ shares at the rate of 20 shares for every £100 of loan notes. The share-for-share exchange would be on an agreed ratio, similar to the method in (1) above.

The total acquisition price for Gubb shares would be the same under all three financing methods.

Gubb dividends and directors' remuneration

Gubb directors currently pay themselves a low salary, but the company historically has paid high dividends. KJ pays low dividends. Following the acquisition, the Gubb board will be unchanged. The Gubb directors have pointed out that they would need a higher salary to compensate for the loss of dividend income. It has been agreed that the increase in salaries would be £500,000 per year in total, and that the Gubb board members would each continue to serve as board directors for at least three more years. *corp gov.*   *extra salary*

Exhibit 3 – Forecast financial statements and working assumptions

Forecast statement of comprehensive income for year ending 31 December 20X2

	KJ £m	Gubb £m
Revenue	94.0	30.0
Cost of sales	(50.0)	(14.0)
Gross profit	44.0	16.0
Operating expenses	(35.0)	(11.2)
Operating profit	9.0	4.8
Finance costs	(2.5)	(1.0)
Profit before tax	6.5	3.8
Tax	(1.6)	(0.9)
Profit for the year	4.9	2.9

Forecast statement of financial position at 31 December 20X2

	KJ £m	Gubb £m
Non-current assets		
Property, plant and equipment	55.0	20.0
Current assets	22.0	11.0
Total assets	77.0	31.0
Equity		
Issued capital – £1 shares	20.0	10.0
Retained earnings	19.0	9.0
	39.0	19.0
Non-current liabilities		
Loans	20.0	9.0
Current liabilities		
Payables	18.0	3.0
Total equity and liabilities	77.0	31.0

The above forecast financial statements have been prepared in accordance with IFRS. Both companies use the cost model for non-current assets.

The carrying amounts for the assets of both companies are similar to their fair values except for the following:

- The fair value of KJ's property, plant and equipment is currently £110m and this is not expected to change in the near future.

- The head office building of Gubb was acquired for £6m on 1 January 20W3 (ie ten years ago) and is being depreciated over 50 years from that date, with a zero residual value. It is estimated that it will have a fair value of £10m at 31 December 20X2.

Working assumptions

The following working assumptions are to be made with respect to the potential acquisition of Gubb:

- The acquisition will take place on 1 January 20X3.

- Operating profit for the year ending 31 December 20X3 for Gubb will be the same as that for the year ending 31 December 20X2 as few changes will be made in the first year after acquisition.

- From 1 January 20X4 until 31 December 20X6, Gubb's operating profit will grow at 5% per annum through efficiency gains arising from merging the administrative activities of the two companies. Operating profit from 1 January 20X7 onwards will remain constant indefinitely at its 20X6 level.

- Gubb's capital expenditure (CAPEX) in cash terms will equate approximately to historical cost depreciation.

- Operating cash flows occur at the end of each year.

- Surplus land held by KJ will be sold for its carrying amount of £2.1m on 1 January 20X4 as a consequence of merging the operations of the two companies. There are no tax effects arising from this sale.

- The annual discount rate after tax for free cash flow is 12%.

- KJ's current share price is £3.95 per share. The shares will remain at this price until 1 January 20X3.

- There will be no change in working capital requirements for either KJ or Gubb as a consequence of the acquisition.

- Future corporation tax rates will be 24% for all relevant years.

19 Coriander plc

You are Paulina Constantine, the assistant Finance Director of Coriander plc and it is now early in the year 20X8.

Cortège is a French restaurant chain with outlets in eight major areas throughout London, the South East, the South West, the North West, North East, Midlands, Wales and Scotland. The company offers quality lunches at reasonable prices and has a strong customer base. Each major area of operation has a number of restaurants and for historical reasons each area is incorporated as an individual company with Cortège owning 100% of the share capital. The North of England operations were a relatively recent expansion away from the group's stronghold in the more southern parts of the country. During the last 5 years, since start up, the North East has been doing well but for some reason the North West company (Cortège NW Limited) has not kept pace. Louise Peters, Cortège's CEO, has had enough and is seeking to sell off this group of restaurants.

Cortège NW Limited (CNW) had revenues of roughly £1.5m in the most recent financial year, as compared to the other locations with similar numbers of restaurants that each generated revenues of at least £2.5m. CNW has failed to exploit the brand value of Cortège and create a stable customer base, and has experienced great difficulty in recruiting and retaining good quality staff. Successive managers have failed to control costs under the poor overall control of a general manager who has had significant bouts of ill-health. As a result, the best CNW has managed is to break even.

Upon hearing rumours that Cortège is contemplating the sale of CNW, Mark Jones, the CEO of the AIM listed company Coriander plc (Coriander), a rival company specialising in Indian food, approached Louise Peters to discuss the possibility of purchasing CNW. Given Coriander's background in the industry and their strategy of diversifying their revenue sources, Mark Jones and the Board of Coriander think that this is a good opportunity and feel confident that they can increase CNW's revenues through additional marketing and further improve profitability through efficient management and cost cutting initiatives. Cortège has offered to sell CNW for a price of £2,000,000. *— benchmark offer price*

very different to french!

Mark Jones agreed, in principle, on the price, having received an estimated value of the properties of about the same amount.

Mark Jones believes that Coriander will be able to increase CNW's sales by 25% within twelve months. He also believes that by the end of the second year CNW will be generating a profit of £300,000 which can be sustained at that level for the foreseeable future. He expects to accomplish this through increased advertising and promotional offers that will cost an additional £50,000 per year. *} assumption*

In addition, he believes that in the first year he will be able to reduce the cost of sales from 35% of revenue to 30% by more assertive negotiation with suppliers, better cost control and inventory management, and by changing the working routines and pay structure of staff. Mark has suggested making life uncomfortable for the existing junior managers so that they decide to leave voluntarily. The average cost of sales figure for the industry as a whole is about 33% of revenue. *→ unethical?*

→ difficult to achieve below average

Mark Jones contacted Alex Davis, the Finance Director of Coriander, who has extensive experience in negotiating deals and has worked on mergers and acquisitions before. Alex has serious reservations about the viability of the proposal. Firstly, he thinks that Mark's assumptions on sales growth and cost economies need to be substantiated. Secondly, he is not sure how the acquisition will affect the short-term performance of Coriander. Thirdly he wants to check that the price that Mark has agreed in principle is the right one. Finally, he is not confident that the advice provided by Theta Bank about financing the acquisition is practicable and whether Coriander would be able to raise the money in the ways that Theta Bank is suggesting. *planning to do A LOT*

Alex had a further meeting with his opposite number at Cortège and has collected more information about CNW's operation, performance and customer base. He sends you an email explaining what he wants from you as follows:

Email

From: Alex Davis
To: Paulina Constantine
Subject: Proposed Acquisition of Cortège NW Ltd

Further to our conversation this morning, and following my meeting with Dennis Gascoigne at Cortège, I attach the financial statements (statement of profit or loss and statement of financial position) for CNW (**Exhibit 1**).

I would like you to look at the following issues:

(1) Assess the robustness of Mark's assumptions about the performance that can be achieved and suggest how they might be corroborated. For comparison, I attach some performance ratios for CNW, the rest of Cortège and for Coriander which should assist you (**Exhibit 2**).

(2) If the purchase goes ahead, we may fund the deal from the proceeds of the issue of a convertible bond. We have been advised by our investment bank that we would be able to reduce funding costs through such an issue. I attach Theta Bank's advice on the issue (**Exhibit 3**). Although such an issue may result in lower funding costs I am worried about the potential dilutive effect on the earnings per share. I would therefore like you to indicate what your views are on the accounting treatment of such a bond and the impact on earnings.

Please use the attached information on Coriander to help here (**Exhibit 4**). *→ out of market?*

(3) We don't currently have very much in the way of restaurants in the North West of England. Please indicate what aspects you will need to consider in order to determine whether this purchase would lead to the relevant information from this business being reported in our financial statements under IFRS 8. As you know we attempt to minimise the amount of information about segments in the public domain.

(4)   Please produce a valuation of CNW to estimate the value of the business to be acquired and decide whether Mark was right to agree in principle. Please produce a valuation using (1) net asset values and (2) a suitable earnings multiple.

(5)   Please respond to my concerns about the practicality of raising the acquisition finance in the way that Theta Bank has suggested.

Requirement

Write a memo to Alex Davis addressing his concerns.

Total: 45 marks

Exhibit 1 – Financial information for CNW provided by Cortège

Statements of profit or loss for the years ending 31 December

	20X7 Draft	20X6
	£	£
Revenue	1,510,000	1,400,000
Cost of sales	(528,500)	(490,000)
Gross profit	981,500	910,000
Operating expenses	(700,000)	(650,000)
Profit from operations	281,500	260,000
Finance costs	(280,000)	(250,000)
Profit before tax	1,500	10,000
Tax	(300)	(2,000)
Profit for the period	1,200	8,000

Statements of financial position as at 31 December

	20X7 Draft	20X6
	£	£
Non-current assets		
Property, plant and equipment	6,200,000	6,100,000
Current assets	100,000	100,000
Total assets	6,300,000	6,200,000
Equity		
Issued capital	1,000,000	1,000,000
Retained earnings	300,000	300,000
Total equity	1,300,000	1,300,000
Non-current liabilities		
Loans	4,500,000	4,400,000
Current liabilities	500,000	500,000
Total equity and liabilities	6,300,000	6,200,000

The market value of the non-current assets owned by CNW has been estimated at the end of 20X7 as:

	£
Owned premises	5,900,000
Fixtures and fittings	1,000,000

Exhibit 2 – Performance indicators

	Coriander	Cortège	Cortège North West	Industry average
Cost of sales/sales	31%	32%	35%	33%
Break even level of sales	£1m	£1.1m	£0.75m	£1.05m
Expected sales growth (analyst estimates)	15%	12%		13%

Exhibit 3 – Theta Bank's advice

I suggest that you issue 1,000 convertible bonds with a three-year maturity and face value of £1,000 per bond. The interest will be paid annually in arrears and the nominal interest rate will be 7%

ICAEW

(ie £70,000 per annum). Each bond is convertible into 125 shares at any time until maturity. The prevailing market interest rate for a similar bond but without the conversion option is 10%. The above information is given on the understanding that any remaining funding required for the investment is through a new equity issue. You remain confident that you will be able to raise equity finance in three years' time should some or all of the bonds not be converted.

Exhibit 4 – Statement of profit or loss and other financial information for Coriander

The statement of profit or loss for the year ending 31 December 20X7 and the forecast for 20X8 are given below.

	20X8 (forecast) £	20X7 £
Revenue	10,390,000	9,620,000
Cost of sales	3,220,900	2,982,200
Gross profit	7,169,100	6,637,800
Operating expenses	1,700,000	1,697,000
Profit from operations	5,469,100	4,940,800
Finance costs	280,000	260,000
Profit before tax	5,189,100	4,680,800
Tax	1,037,820	936,160
Profit for the period	4,151,280	3,744,640

The effective tax rate for Coriander is consistently approximately 20%. As the forecast above shows, Coriander is predicting profits of just over £4m for the year 20X8.

Coriander has issued share capital of 3m ordinary shares of £1 nominal value each. The current share price is £10.00 (the annual dividend has recently been paid).

20 Luminum plc

Assume that now is January 20X5.

Luminum plc is an AIM-listed company that manufactures a range of detergents, soaps and other hygiene products, and distributes them to major retailers and independent customers in the UK. The board of directors are developing two projects to expand the company's business into mainland Europe, but their plans have been thrown into some confusion by the unexpected illness of the finance director. They want to make decisions about the two projects soon, before the finance director is expected to return to work, and they have asked for your assistance in providing them with information.

Karen Carter, the CEO, explains the issues to you as follows.

'At the moment all our sales are within the UK. One project we have in mind is to start exporting to customers in Northern France. We know that starting an export operation will have implications for our working capital requirements, and we want to have some idea of how much additional capital we might need. I shall supply with you with relevant information about this (see **Exhibit 1**). In addition, we haven't made a decision yet about whether to invoice our French customers in sterling or in euros.

Our current policy is to finance any increases in working capital by means of medium-term loans, even though this will often result in short-term cash surpluses. There are occasional cash deficits too, and we finance these by overdraft or by negotiating delayed payments with suppliers. We think that if we start exporting to France, it might be more sensible to finance the increase in working capital with short-term financing rather than medium-term loans.

We have another, bigger, project in mind. This is to establish a new distribution centre in Germany, for selling to customers in Germany and surrounding Eurozone countries. We will probably make the decision to invest, but we have not yet given enough thought to the method of financing the investment. I shall give you information about the investment and the financing options (see **Exhibit 2**).

The decision to invest in Germany will be based on DCF analysis of the estimates we have produced (see **Exhibit 4**).

There is another issue that I think my board should discuss. The future of our industry will depend on sustainability issues. Although our business is currently restricted to the UK, with plans for expansion into other parts of Europe, in the long run we must be able to compete globally with our competitors in all countries of the world, including developing countries in Africa and Asia. We will never succeed in becoming a successful listed company unless we can develop our business for global markets. I am aware that competitors are already showing concern about sustainability issues, such as disposal of toxic wastes, efficient use of scarce water, emissions to air and fuel consumption. I have read a lot about corporate social responsibility, but I think that sustainability is a lot more than just CSR and environmental policy. I would like a brief explanation of what sustainability is about and how it will affect our industry.'

At the end of your meeting with Karen Carter, you agree to provide information about the following matters in a memo.

(1) Calculate the effect on the working capital operating cycle of the company if it goes ahead with the project to export goods to France, and explain the main reasons for the change in working capital. Assume a full year's trading in your analysis and that sales will be spread evenly through the year. Ignore the proposed investment in Germany.

(2) Explain the benefits and risks of invoicing the French customers in euros and explain what methods are available to help minimise the risks. *Hedging*

(3) Explain the advantages and disadvantages of financing net current assets with medium-term loans, compared with short-term financing.

(4) For the proposed investment in Germany, evaluate each of the three suggested financing alternatives, and recommend the most appropriate form of financing. Assume that the German operation will be established as a separate subsidiary, and support your discussion of each financing option with a summary forecast consolidated statement of financial position at 31 December 20X5, and calculations of gearing at this date using book values and assuming an exchange rate of (1) £1/€1.20 and (2) £1/€1.30. For the purpose of this analysis, ignore the proposal to export to France.

(5) Also, for the proposed investment in Germany, can you provide me with the DCF analysis using the information I am giving you (Exhibit 4), and let me know your views about the project risk and the preference that may be indicated for a sterling or a euro loan to finance it.

(6) Provide me with a summary of the main aspects of business sustainability, and the connection between business sustainability and corporate social responsibility. In addition, please explain the key sustainability issues which are likely to affect our industry in the future, particularly in developing countries of the world.

Requirement

Respond to Karen Carter's request.

Total: 55 marks

Exhibit 1

Forecast financial outcomes, assuming no exports to France.

12 months to 31 December 20X5	£'000
Revenue	23,260
Cost of goods sold	13,959
Purchases	9,306
As at 31 December 20X5	
Accounts receivable (58.2 days)	3,339
Accounts payable, trade creditors (76.7 days)	1,956
Inventory	4,055

(47% raw materials, 20% WIP, 33% finished goods)

Operating cycle: 111 days

Terms of trade for 90% of sales are 30 days' credit. The remaining amounts are paid by credit card: credit card payments are considered the equivalent of cash.

If the company begins exporting to France from January 20X5, annual sales will depend on economic conditions in the Eurozone, but the finance director of Luminum had estimated a 60% probability that sales in 20X5 would be €6.75m and a 40% probability that sales would be €8.5m. Assume even sales throughout the year. All sales will be on credit, and invoiced in euros. Accounts receivable for French customers are expected to be 20% of revenue on average.

Total inventory figures for Luminum are expected to be as follows, to accommodate the exports to France.

As at 31 December 20X5	£'000
Raw materials	2,441
WIP	1,041
Finished goods	1,984

Exhibit 2

A summary of total assets, equity and liabilities of Luminum as at 1 January 20X5 is as follows, before taking into account the investment in Germany.

	£'000
Total assets	28,050
Equity	15,600
Long-term borrowings (there are no other long-term liabilities)	9,350
Current liabilities	3,100

When translated at the current exchange rate of €1.20/£1, the proposed investment in Germany would cost £4.5m for the distribution centre and £1.75m for delivery trucks. All the assets to establish the German operation would be purchased in Germany.

Three financing options are under consideration:

(a) A sterling medium-term bank loan, or possibly a sterling bond issue.
(b) A euro-denominated medium-term bank loan.
(c) A new share issue.

Exhibit 3

Other information

£ strengthens, € weakens.

Assume the exchange rate at 1 January 20X5 is €1.20/£1, but that the exchange rate will change to €1.30/£1 by the end of 20X5. Assume a gradual change in the exchange rate through the course of the year.

Exhibit 4

More details of the proposed investment in Germany

If the company makes the initial investment, we estimate that this will be sufficient to sustain the business for the first five years before additional financing is required.

Estimated profits before interest and tax for the first five years are as follows.

Year	€m
1 (20X5)	0.5
2	1.0
3	2.0
4	3.0
5	3.0

The tax rate will be 20% of these profits, and there will be no further tax implications for remittances of dividends to the UK.

The distribution centre will be depreciated over 20 years and the delivery trucks over five years, both in a straight line to zero value. The trucks are expected to have negligible value after five years, but the market value of the distribution centre is expected to be the same at the end of Year 5 as at the beginning of Year 1.

A cost of capital of 10% should be applied, regardless of whether the loan is arranged in sterling or euros.

b) if in £, risk ↑.

Df should ↑

For the purpose of the DCF analysis, different assumptions should be used about the exchange rate. Assume that the rate will be 1.22 at the end of the first year, then 1.24, 1.26, 1.28 and 1.30 at the end of the second, third, fourth and fifth years respectively.

21 Horora plc

It is now February 20X6.

You are acting as a member of a small team of financial advisers to Horora plc, a UK-based company with a London stock market listing. The company has a number of commercial interests worldwide, but its main specialisation is the manufacture of specialist lighting equipment. It has a long-established business, but its rate of profit growth had been low until a new CEO was appointed in 20X1. Since that time the business has been turned round: non-performing subsidiaries have been sold off and sales and profits growth have picked up, partly through improved performance in existing operational units and partly through a number of well-judged acquisitions.

Horora now has the largest share of the market for specialist lighting equipment in Europe, and the board has agreed the following financial objectives for the next five-year business plan:

- To grow earnings per share by at least 5% annually

- To keep the financial gearing level, measured as the market value of long-term debt to the market value of equity, below 30%

- To maintain a price/earnings ratio for its shares at no less than the industry average

Proposed merger

Horora is currently in detailed negotiations about a merger with a US company, Blaze Inc. Blaze Inc is listed on NASDAQ and is similar in size to Horora – although somewhat smaller in terms of annual revenues and net assets. Its main line of business is lighting equipment, which explains the attraction of a merger for the board of Horora.

The recent financial performance of Blaze has not been as good as that of Horora and as a result the market capitalisation of Horora is much higher than that of Blaze. So although the management of Horora talk about 'merger' in discussions with the management of Blaze, a combination of the two companies would effectively be a takeover of Blaze by Horora.

Blaze holds some patents that it has not exploited as fully commercially as the Horora management think should have been possible, but the CEO of Horora thinks that in the event of a takeover/merger, they could be sold for about £125m. The group would have no commercial use themselves for the patents, so there would appear to be no reason for holding on to them.

Both companies think that a combination of their businesses would benefit both sides, both commercially and financially. The board of Horora think however that their company has a stronger bargaining hand and that they can negotiate the more favourable terms. They also think that they can convince investors that in the event of a merger/takeover, Horora will be able to apply its recent growth rate to the future earnings of Blaze and the merged company should be able to maintain Horora's current price/earnings ratio for its shares.

A summary of relevant financial data for the proposed merger is given in **Exhibit 1**.

New project

The central research laboratory of Horora has just developed a new type of underground and undersea lighting device, and the board must decide whether to develop the new product commercially. Commercial development would require an investment of £150m, which would be provided entirely by debt capital with a maturity of five years. The Finance Director does not think that this money could be raised as fixed interest debt, and that a bank loan, possibly a syndicated bank loan, would be required. The expected rate of interest would be LIBOR plus 1%.

The percentage profit margin on the new product would be small, due to the existence of an alternative product supplied by a rival group, but sales volumes could be extremely high, making up for the narrow profit margin.

The interest rate on borrowing could therefore be a critical factor in the profitability of the new product and the board has been informed that the cost of borrowing should not be allowed to exceed 6.5% per year.

The current rate of six-month LIBOR is 5.25%. ⟹ 6.25%

The current US dollar/sterling exchange rate is US$1.50/£1.

The CEO of Horora has asked you to prepare a memo that deals with the following requirements.

(1) Explain, with supporting calculations, how the estimates of post-merger values have been derived by the Horora Finance Director and the company's professional advisers.

(2) Comment briefly on the likely impact on share price and market capitalisation for each of Horora and Blaze if a merger is agreed on the terms proposed by the Horora board. Make appropriate assumptions based on the information given in Exhibit 1.

(3) If the board of Blaze rejects the terms offered, calculate the maximum total amount and price per stock unit that Horora might agree to offer to acquire the stock of Blaze, without reducing the wealth of Horora's current shareholders.

(4) Indicate how the merger might contribute to the achievement of Horora's stated financial objectives.

(5) Suggest ways in which the company may be able to ensure that the cost of borrowing for the new product development will not exceed 6.5% per year for the five-year borrowing term. } IR swap.

Requirement

Prepare the memo required by the Horora CEO.

Total: 40 marks

Exhibit 1

Extracts from the Statements of consolidated income for the year ended 31 December 20X5:

	Horora	Blaze
	£m	$m
Revenue	1,960	2,300
Operating profit	686	690
Earnings for ordinary shareholders	346	276

Extracts from the Statements of financial position as at 31 December 20X5:

	Horora	Blaze
	£m	$m
Total net assets	2,000	2,100
Total equity	850	1,550
Total long-term debt (bonds)	1,150	550

Other data

	Horora	Blaze
Ordinary shares of £0.10	450m shares	
Common stock of $1		400m units
Current share price	£7.00	$5.06
Share price high/low over past 12 months	£7.90/£5.75	$5.70/$3.15
Industry average P/E	9.2	
Current market value of debt	102.50	101.80

Five-year revenue and earnings record

	Horora		Blaze	
	Revenue	Earnings	Revenue	Earnings
Year	£m	£m	$m	$m
20X1	1,330	285	1,750	232
20X2	1,410	293	1,890	243
20X3	1,560	310	2,031	254
20X4	1,750	327	2,165	265
20X5	1,950	346	2,300	276

Economic data

Horora's economists have provided forecast rates of interest and inflation in the two main areas of operations for the next 12 months as follows:

	Annual interest rate Forecast %	Annual inflation rate Forecast %
UK/Europe	4.5	2.0
US	2.5	1.5

mmH?

Terms of the merger

Horora intends to persuade the board of Blaze to accept terms for combining their businesses on the basis of a merger through share exchange, with Horora issuing one new share to acquire two stock units in Blaze.

I share → 2 units

The Finance Director of Horora, assisted by the company's professional advisors, have made the following forecasts for the combined entity after the merger/acquisition.

- The market value of the combined entity is predicted to reach £5,300m.
- The expected earnings per share in the first year post-merger will be 81.5p.

They believe this is a 'conservative' estimate as it excludes the estimated value of the software licences owned by Blaze.

A cash offer as an alternative to a share exchange is unlikely, although the board of Horora have not ruled out this possibility should the bid turn hostile. However, a hostile bid would require substantial new borrowing by Horora.

Except for the potential profit on the sale of the licences, no savings or synergies from the merger have yet been identified.

22 Puller plc

Puller plc ('Puller'), which was incorporated over 30 years ago, is a listed company which owns a chain of hotels located throughout Europe.

Assume it is now the end of 20X8.

Recent performance

Since new management was appointed a number of years ago, Puller has been successful in increasing its revenues and controlling costs. It has a room utilisation (ie rooms occupied as a percentage of rooms available) of 85%, compared to an industry average of around 75%.

A strategic review in 20X7 identified a key objective as the expansion of the business. Unfortunately, there has been unwillingness by local governments to give planning permission for building new hotels, particularly in the most desirable in-town locations. This has created a barrier to expansion for Puller, as it has not been possible to open new hotels as it has wished. As a consequence, the Puller board has spent some time trying to identify smaller chains of hotels which it might acquire and it is currently considering a small privately-owned hotel chain, Rantz Ltd ('Rantz').

Potential acquisition of Rantz Ltd

Rantz operates 15 hotels, all in the UK. Ten of these hotels are large, in-town, four-star hotels, the freeholds of which are owned by Rantz. The other five hotels are smaller out-of-town two-star hotels which are held under leases.

Rantz Ltd shareholdings are:

	£1 ordinary shares
Jeff Rantz (chairman and chief executive)	45% 0.9m
Charles Fang (finance director)	35% 0.7m
Managers and other employees	20% 0.4m

The Puller board of directors has made an initial approach to the board of Rantz, suggesting that it might wish to make an offer. The Rantz board of directors has suggested that it might be willing to recommend a sale if an appropriate offer was made and it indicated that it would be willing to make some limited, non-public, information available to Puller in order to enable an initial bid to be made.

At this stage, the Puller board of directors remains undecided about how best to integrate the Rantz hotels into the existing Puller business model if their bid ultimately proves successful. The majority of Puller's existing hotels have earned four-star ratings, and have established a favourable reputation for their clean, contemporary style, and accessories (such as free Wi-fi access in every room). These characteristics have made Puller's hotels particularly popular with business travellers.

[handwritten: shorter stay -]

Valuation and performance

You are an assistant to the group accountant of Puller, Emma Woodward.

Rantz has provided financial statement data (**Exhibit 1**) and some additional data (**Exhibit 2**). Emma has also provided some additional notes to guide you based on a recent meeting with the Rantz board, together with some post acquisition performance assumptions made by Emma (**Exhibit 3**).

Emma has asked you to prepare a draft report which addresses each of the following requests: *[handwritten: - Asset based]*

- Make an estimate of the amount we should offer as an initial bid for Rantz Ltd. I know the information is incomplete at the moment, but I would like your best estimates. It is up to you to decide the most appropriate methods of valuation, but please give explanations of your approach, *[handwritten: constant growth figures]* including any weaknesses and the factors affecting the valuation. I suggest you initially use, where appropriate, a working assumption of 10% as the cost of equity for the annual discount rate, but please set out a section in your report as to whether you think this is reasonable.
  [handwritten: mix of stars/hotels → not app for package?]

- Explain any concerns you have with the financial reporting and other data provided by Rantz that you would like our auditors to look at during the due diligence process – I don't want a long list of all the usual items, just focus on anything that specifically arises from the information currently available in this case.

- Briefly evaluate the risks of the acquisition. *[handwritten: reputation; different strategies (cost saving for 2* hotels) different types of customers, level of customer service, services offered (wifi free in in room).]*
- Indicate the effect on the profit after tax of the Puller group for 20X9 arising from the acquisition, as our chairman is very keen that any acquisition would not damage our good record of earnings growth. *[handwritten: EPS]* *[handwritten: supply chain occ-rate length of stay]*

- Assuming that Puller makes a successful bid for Rantz, explain and evaluate the choices available to Puller in respect of the post-acquisition integration and marketing of Rantz, being either to maintain them as Rantz hotels or to rebrand them as Puller hotels. *[handwritten: establish, consistent message of product (4* and 2*)]*

Emma has indicated that she does not require any executive summary, contents page etc. She just wants you to prepare the above sections of the report.

Requirement

Prepare the sections of the report requested by the group accountant, Emma Woodward.

Total: 55 marks

Exhibit 1 – Financial information provided by Rantz

Statement of profit or loss and other comprehensive income for the years ending 31 December

[handwritten: → fall - volume? price?] *[handwritten: GPM↓]*

	Notes	20X8 Draft £'000	20X7 £'000
Revenue		45,900	47,600
Cost of sales *[handwritten: - ↑ why? prices gone up]*		(34,400)	(32,700)
Gross profit		11,500	14,900
Operating expenses	1	(6,000)	(5,000)
Profit from operations		5,500	9,900
Finance costs		(4,000)	(4,000)
Profit before tax		1,500	5,900
Tax		(420)	(1,652)
Profit for the year from continuing operations		1,080	4,248
Discontinued operation	2	500	600
Profit for the year		1,580	4,848

[handwritten: what? why? twice in a year?]

Statement of financial position at 31 December

	Notes	20X8 Draft £'000	20X7 £'000
Non-current assets			
Property, plant and equipment *[related to discontinued operations?]*	3	44,000	46,000
Current assets *[receivables?]*	4	8,000	5,000
Total assets *[cash?]*		52,000	51,000
Capital and reserves			
Issued capital		2,000	2,000
Retained earnings		6,400	4,820
Equity		8,400	6,820
Non-current liabilities			
Loans *[but no charge to finance cost?]*		28,000 ↑	26,000
Finance leases *[discontinued → 2* hotel?]*		13,000	14,000
Provision *[for what?]*		1,000	–
Current liabilities		1,600	4,180
Total equity and liabilities *[↓ payables? cash?]*		52,000	51,000

Notes

1 During 20X8 a charge of £1m was made as a provision for a claim against Rantz following the collapse of part of a hotel that injured several guests. *[investigation into why? other hotels?]* *[legal claims? compensation/detail?]*

2 The discontinued operation related to a major warehousing and office unit which was sold in late June 20X8 for £4m cash, which was equal to its carrying amount at that date. This facility had been used to store foods and other goods for Rantz, but it also generated a significant revenue stream as cold storage space was rented out to third parties. The contract to sell the facility had been signed in December 20X7. *[→ why? storage now?]*

3 Property, plant and equipment consists of ten hotel buildings which are owned and four which are held under finance leases. One further hotel operated by Rantz is held under an operating lease. All non-current assets are stated at historic cost less depreciation as follows:

	Owned properties £'000	Properties held under finance leases £'000	Fixtures and fittings £'000	Total £'000
Cost at 1/1/20X8	45,000	20,000	5,000	70,000
Additions	1,000	–	1,000	2,000
Cost at 31/12/20X8	46,000	20,000 *[5m]*	6,000	72,000
Accumulated depreciation at 1/1/20X8	15,000	6,000	3,000	24,000
Charge for the year	1,000	2,000	1,000	4,000
Accumulated depreciation at 31/12/20X8	16,000	8,000	4,000	28,000
Carrying amount at 31/12/20X8	30,000	12,000	2,000	44,000

[each 1.5m 4.6]

4 In 20X8, current assets include cash of £4m from the sale of the storage facility. The asset was presented as held for sale at 31 December 20X7. *[separate line showing this.]*

5 The company has not made any dividend payments.

Exhibit 2 – Other information

The business

[45% JR]

Rantz Ltd was established by Jeff Rantz 31 years ago. Jeff is now 65 and looking to retire, but the other shareholders have insufficient funds to buy out his shareholding. Charles Fang is only 50 and would like to continue working in the business even if there is a take-over. Directors' remuneration is £400,000 per year which is probably double the market rate for salaried executives for this type of company.

The only other member of the board is Jane Wilson a non-executive who has no shareholding.

The lack of substantial new funds has meant that only essential repairs and maintenance have been carried out in recent years and there has been little expansion. No new hotels have been acquired for several years.

Financial reporting

All property, plant and equipment are depreciated to a zero residual value over their estimated useful lives.

- Buildings

    - Owned buildings 50 years
    - Finance leases – unexpired term of leases (which average ten years from 31 Dec 20X8)

- Fixtures, fittings and equipment – 3 to 25 years

All depreciation is charged on a straight line basis.

The hotels which are owned have an estimated total fair value at 31 December 20X8 of £52m. It is estimated that the fair value of the benefits of the four finance lease agreements at 31 December 20X7, if the rights were to be sold to a third party, would be £11m (excluding any lease obligations).

The operating lease for the one remaining hotel will expire on 31 December 20X9. There is no option to renew the contract. *then what?*

Exhibit 3 – Additional notes

From the meeting between Emma and the Rantz board

Assume that the acquisition would occur on 1 January 20X9 and that future corporation tax rates will be 23%.

All in-town four-star hotels generate similar revenue and profit. Similarly all the out-of-town two-star hotels generate similar revenue and profit.

Data for the year to 31 December 20X8 is as follows:

DCF ↑FCF

	Four-star	*10%*	Two-star
Average room rate per night	£150	*165*	£75 *82.5*
Current occupancy	70%	*80%*	70%
Rooms per hotel	100		50
Days open per year	360	*Rev 4,752*	360

There is a working assumption that cost of sales is all variable cost, whereas operating costs are all fixed costs, and that variable costs increase in proportion to revenue.

Post acquisition performance assumptions

@75% CoS (3,564)   *Add back dep'n / Director salary / CAPEX   200 / 3,000 (before tax)*

Average room rates per night will increase at 10% per annum compound for two years then they will be constant.

It is anticipated that variable costs will increase by 10% per annum compound for two years then they will be constant, before any occupancy changes are taken into account.

Occupancy would increase to 80% immediately after a take-over for all hotels, partly as a result of £500,000 a year extra advertising spend. Also, due to a lack of capital expenditure, some of the hotels are in poor condition internally and externally. Capital expenditure (CAPEX) will therefore need to increase to £3m per year to achieve the revised occupancy levels. However, most of this expenditure is on hotel buildings, which is not allowable for tax.

↑ longer stays

The majority of Rantz's guests are currently leisure travellers. Although capital expenditure is needed to improve the condition of the buildings, many of Rantz's guests choose to stay there because they have a period charm which isn't found in many contemporary hotel designs.

23 Quanta

Assume that now is December 20X5.

Quanta is a UK listed company which operates in the eyewear business. It designs, manufactures and distributes lenses and frames for glasses and also contact lenses ('eyewear'), mainly in Europe and Asia.

After qualifying recently, you decided to move from the firm where you were working to take up a position as assistant to Caroline Dunn, the financial controller of Quanta. As part of your induction, Caroline gave you some background notes on the eyewear industry and Quanta. (**Exhibit 1**)

The tasks

You are meeting with Caroline Dunn to discuss the tasks that she would like you to carry out.

She tells you that the board of directors and senior management all share the view that the company has come well through the financial crisis and economic downturn, and that revenues will begin to pick up in 20X6. Quanta is one of the smaller global competitors in the eyewear industry and the board feels that the company needs to develop in order to compete more successfully. Now could be a very good time to expand the business, both geographically and also possibly by acquiring a chain of retail opticians stores to create a fully vertically-integrated business.

In order to finance any strategic expansion of the business, Quanta will need to raise new capital to create a 'war chest'[1] for acquisitions. The Quanta board considers that about £50m in new funds would be appropriate for this purpose. In view of the low prevailing interest rates, the board would prefer to borrow rather than raise new equity, possibly at an interest rate as low as 5% per annum. The finance director is aware, however, that the company should not breach the loan covenants on its existing bank loans. The most significant of these are a maximum ratio of debt to equity (at book value) of 100% and a minimum interest cover ratio of 5 times. (For the purpose of these covenants, debt consists of long-term and short-term loans; and the interest cover ratio is the ratio of operating profit to net interest expense.)

Caroline tells you that a draft forecast of the company's profitability has been prepared, together with other data, to be used in an application by the company to a bank that may be willing to organise the provision of a syndicated medium-term loan. (**Exhibit 2**)

She goes on to say that the board of directors has become aware that a retail opticians chain in Europe, Lorgnetta, may be available for sale. Lorgnetta, which is 100 per cent-owned by a family trust, has 105 outlets and made a profit after tax of €60,000 in its most recent financial year to 30 September 20X5. Financial information relating to Lorgnetta is summarised in **Exhibit 3**. Initial discussions have already taken place with Lorgnetta's owners: the biggest obstacle to a deal is likely to be reaching agreement on price.

'I have been speaking with Andy Kemp, our finance director, and we agree that we should make every effort to acquire Lorgnetta, because we should be able to buy it for a good price in view of its low profitability at the moment. If we can assume that annual sales growth will be 4% for the next five years and that we should be able to achieve savings from cost synergies of, say, €1m a year, we can probably recommend a price to the board that Lorgnetta's owners will accept.'

'Another issue to consider is pensions,' Caroline continues. 'As you know, Quanta provides a defined contributions pension scheme to its employees, and we would propose to offer similar arrangements to any new employees joining Lorgnetta if we were to acquire it. However Lorgnetta's existing employees have a defined benefits scheme and the pension fund is currently in deficit. I would like to know what business or financial risks will arise from this if the takeover goes ahead.

The board believes that Quanta needs to extend its physical presence globally, but we all know that ecommerce is growing at a rapid pace. At the moment, we sell contact lenses online, but nothing else. Our competitors are not much further down the line to establishing a business for online sales. I have been asked to submit a paper on the strategic issues involved in this form of expansion.

---

[1]: A war chest is a reserve of cash set aside in order to enable a company to take advantage of unexpected opportunities.

In confidence, I want to tell you about another problem that I have been asked to advise on. One of our non-executive directors has been asking questions about writing off inventories of glasses frames in our accounts. She thinks that the cost of writing off inventory is higher than it should be and that there must be some weaknesses in inventory management. This has led to a response from the marketing director. Here is an exchange of emails that I have been given by the CEO, who wants to sort out the problem which he thinks is an argument about finance.' (**Exhibit 4**)

Caroline concludes the meeting by saying that there are several things she would like you to do in the next few days, to help her in preparing papers for a board meeting that has been called for the following week. Her requirements are set out in **Exhibit 5**.

Requirement

Prepare the sections of the board papers as requested by Caroline.

Total: 50 marks

Exhibit 1

Background information on the eyewear industry and Quanta

The eyewear industry is for the design, manufacture and sale of glasses and contact lenses. The main product lines are prescription glasses, contact lenses, sunglasses and protective glasses for sports. The market is global and is dominated by four or five major players, which design, manufacture and sell both frames and lenses. The largest market is North America, followed by Europe and Asia.

For all types of glasses there is strong market segment for 'fashion brands'. An eyewear company may establish its own brands, and manufacture glasses under its brand name. In addition, a company may enter into a licensing agreement with top fashion houses and make and sell 'designer' glasses under the brand name of the fashion house. Licences are normally for between three and twelve years. The eyewear company pays a commission to the fashion house for each unit of sale.

~training

Eyewear with prescription lenses is sold largely through retail outlets, where customers are able to take an eye test so that a prescription for their glasses can be prepared. Customers usually buy new frames with new prescription lenses. Sunglasses and glasses for sports are sold through a wider range of retail outlets. Contact lenses are now mainly sold online.

Some eyewear companies operate their own chain (or chains) of retail outlets, but they sell their products through both their own outlets and also through other retail chains and department stores. Sales of frames to other retail chains are made wholesale through central purchasing departments.

Prescription lenses are made to order, and eyewear companies enter into a supply agreement with the stores through which they sell their frames.

Growth in the eyewear industry has been attributable largely to fashion and technological improvements: innovation helps to sustain product sales. Many users treat their glasses as fashion items and will often change their frames fairly regularly in order to keep up with the current fashionable 'look'. There have been continual technological improvements in both frames and lenses, prompting further sales.

IT/
R&D
= crucial

It is expected that in future, the size of the market will increase, due to an ageing population, the need for glasses to read smartphone and tablet screens, and relatively untapped demand in emerging economies. There may also be a large market in the future for 'smart' digital eyewear.

Quanta

Quanta was incorporated in the UK nearly 40 years ago. Its original owners were two opthalmologists (specialists in the diagnosis and treatment of eye diseases) who began by manufacturing prescription lenses for a local market. Over time the business has expanded and the company's activities now include the design, manufacture and distribution of a wide product range. The company does not own a retail chain of opticians stores and it sells most of its products through independent retail chains in many countries in Europe and Asia. More recently it secured an agreement for selling glasses through a retailer in Australia.

established competition

Quanta has a web site for selling its Quanta CL contact lenses online. It does not sell glasses online.

The company was not as quick as some of its competitors to identify the growth potential of the eyewear industry, and the largest market for eyewear, North America, is dominated by two or three other global companies. These companies have also secured licensing deals with most of the world's most well-known fashion houses, although licences are re-negotiated at the end of each licence agreement period. Quanta has gained a foothold in the fashion segment of the eyewear market by entering agreements with up-and-coming 'names' in fashion design, rather than with already-established brands.

Quanta makes its frames at two large manufacturing sites, one in the UK and the other in South Korea. Lenses are added to frames at the company's major distribution centres, in the UK, South Korea and Australia.

The company obtained a listing in 20X2.

Exhibit 2 – Quanta: Summary financial results and projections

Quanta
Summary statement of profit or loss for the year to 31 December

	20X4 Actual £m	20X5 Expected £m	20X6 Forecast £m
Sales	702.0	719.6	752.0
Cost of sales	(251.6)	(256.9)	(268.0)
Gross profit	450.4	462.7	484.0
Selling costs	(261.3)	(267.9)	(270.0)
Royalties	(2.8)	(2.9)	(3.0)
Advertising	(46.1)	(47.5)	(49.0)
General administrative costs and other expenses	(93.2)	(93.8)	(94.5)
Operating profit	47.0	50.6	67.5
Interest	(5.6)	(5.8)	(5.8)
Profit before tax	41.4	44.8	61.7
Taxation	(8.7)	(9.0)	(12.3)
Profit after tax	32.7	35.8	49.4
Depreciation and amortisation	25.3	25.6	26.0

Quanta
Summary statement of financial position as at 31 December 20X5

	£m	Expected £m
Non-current assets		
Property, plant and equipment		120.6
Goodwill		15.2
Other intangible assets		48.7
		184.5
Current assets		
Inventory	76.3	
Trade receivables	81.6	
Other	21.6	
Cash	10.2	
Total current assets		189.7
Total assets		374.2
Equity		
Share capital (160m shares)		40.0
Reserves		113.5
Total equity		153.5
Non-current liabilities		
Loans	73.5	
Other	21.3	
		94.8
Current liabilities		
Short term loans	23.3	
Trade payables	75.6	
Other	27.0	
		125.9
Total equity and liabilities		374.2

Other information
Sales in 20X5:

Europe	70%
Asia	25%
Australia	5%

[handwritten: very small, yet dist centre?]

Currency movements

[handwritten: → ↑ sk won for £]

20X5: UK £ appreciated in value against the South Korean won by 3% and fell in value by 3% against the euro during the same period.

[handwritten: ↳ less € for £]

Current share price for Quanta's shares   £3.20

Dividends. No dividends have yet been paid out of 20X5 profits, but the Quanta board is likely to propose an annual dividend of £12m for the year, payable during 20X6 – an increase of 2.5% on the 20X4 dividend.

[handwritten: g = 2.5%]

Exhibit 3 – Lorgnetta

Lorgnetta
Summary statement of profit or loss for the year to 30 September 20X5

	€'000
Sales	69,700
Cost of sales	(49,800)
Gross profit	19,900
Rental of premises	(4,650)
Labour costs	(10,420)
Other operating costs	(3,010)
Operating profit	1,820
Interest	(1,750)
Profit before tax	70
Taxation	(10)
Profit after tax	60

Other information

Number of outlets, all in Europe	105
Units sold in 20X5	61,500,000
Depreciation charge in 20X5	€870,000
Loans outstanding at 30 September 20X5	€25m
Equity at 30 September 20X5	€35m

[handwritten: £1.130 per unit]

Exhibit 4 – Inventory write-offs

To:	Martin Frobisher, Chairman, Quanta plc
From:	Susan Turner, Non-executive director
Date:	12 November 20X5

Martin

As agreed at the recent board meeting, I am sending you my thoughts about the large inventory write-off. The company is expecting to have inventory of £76.3m at the end of this year, consisting of:

	£m
Raw materials	17.9
Work in progress	3.9
Finished goods	71.2
	93.0
Provision for writing off finished goods inventory	16.7
	76.3

Although I can understand that some write-offs may be necessary, it seems beyond belief that they are so high at over 46% of our expected annual profit. It would seem to me that inventory management is woeful and inept, and the managers responsible should be reprimanded and corrective measures taken and profitability increased through improvements in system efficiency.

To: Martin Frobisher, Chairman, Quanta plc
From: Donna West, Marketing Director
Date: 14 November 20X5

Chairman

I have been sent a copy of the recent email from Susan Turner, the non-executive director, and have been asked to provide a response.

I consider her criticisms to be unwarranted and based on ignorance of our business. Quanta sells all its glasses through retail outlets of other organisations, and we supply them on a sale or return basis. We also hold inventories at our three regional warehouses, to meet any new sales orders from our customers. Our production facilities are not capable of producing small quantities to order, and batch production makes some inventory holding unavoidable.

About 50% of eyewear sales *[handwritten: 34,850]* are sales of fashion 'branded' glasses, and fashions change regularly. We get high volumes of returns whenever new models are introduced. Customers don't like to buy yesterday's model.

For these reasons, it is generally accepted that large write-offs of inventory are unavoidable if the company is to pursue its chosen business model.

Exhibit 5

I would like you to carry out the following tasks:

[handwritten margin: gearing to 78%? breach of IC covenants?]

(1) Review and comment on the forecast for revenue, costs and profits of Quanta that has been prepared for 20X6 and that is set out in Exhibit 2.

(2) Comment on the proposal to establish a 'war chest' for future acquisitions, in view of Quanta's current financial position. *[handwritten: ↑gearing, ↑financial risk, breaching covenants]*

(3) Using the information available about Lorgnetta, determine and justify a suitable offer price from Quanta for its shares. *[handwritten: earnings based as minimum? g=28% so DVM? or P/E?]*

(4) Explain how, in the event of acquiring Lorgnetta, business and financial risks for Quanta may be affected by Lorgnetta's defined benefits pension scheme. *[handwritten: e'ees not happy w/ other scheme — ↑er guarantees pension + bears risk/rewards]*

(5) Draft an assessment of the differing arguments of the non-executive director and the marketing director about the write-off of finished goods inventory and recommend a measure or measures that should be taken to resolve the disagreement. *[handwritten: 50% = 34,850   47.9% of this is w/off. NRV falls]*

(6) Provide a brief assessment of the strategic option to sell more products online. *[handwritten: — expand customer base - ↑ dist costs (↑ tricky to transport glasses than lenses)]*

24   Galaxy Travel plc

Assume that now is December 20X5.

You are recently qualified and have just been assigned to the business advisory and assurance section of Farrar Wood, a firm of ICAEW Chartered Accountants.

Your manager, Colin Lee, has asked you to attend a meeting with Sarah Timmins, the financial controller of Galaxy Travel plc (Galaxy). Galaxy is a UK listed company that sells holidays and operates a small airline for package holiday customers. Farrar Wood carries out advisory and assurance services for Galaxy, but is not the company's auditor.

Sarah Timmins has only recently joined Galaxy, having been appointed following the unexpected departure of her predecessor. To help with your preparation for the meeting, Colin has given some background information about Galaxy (**Exhibit 1**).

The meeting

Sarah begins the meeting by explaining the reason for assistance from Farrar Wood. Since she joined Galaxy, she has had extensive discussions with her colleagues and members of her department about a range of different issues, and she has listened to their views and opinions. However, she is still learning as much as she can about the company's business and she thinks it would be useful to compare their opinions with an independent view from a firm of ICAEW Chartered Accountants.

'So what I want from you is a report that comments briefly on a number of different issues. I shall use the comments in your report in my ongoing discussions with my colleagues. Let me go through the items I want you to consider.'

State of the company

'In our last annual report, the board of directors expressed confidence about the strength of the company's business and made an optimistic prediction about steady growth in the business in the future. I can give you summary information about the company's recent financial performance (**Exhibits 2 and 3**), and obviously you can obtain more details from our report and accounts. I want to know whether you think that the board's optimism is well founded.'

Strategic key performance indicators

'The board has been reviewing the company's long-term business plan. It has identified six key strategic drivers for our business, and it wants to identify suitable key performance indicators for each of them, to monitor actual performance over the period of the business plan. I can give you a list of the strategic drivers that the board has approved (**Exhibit 4**). We have some ideas, but would appreciate your advice about KPIs that might be appropriate for each of them.

'One of the strategic drivers is people. Galaxy needs to attract, train and retain top quality talent. The skills we need from our employees are also changing: our people need to be much more competent in IT. In the past we have tried to recruit and train graduates from top universities but the travel industry does not seem to attract as many good people as we need. Many graduates find it difficult to envisage a career with us. So as part of our strategy review, we shall be including proposals for a talent management strategy. I know that this may seem to be a policy issue for the Human Resources Department to sort out, but there are important financial implications too.'

[handwritten margin notes: – Grad scheme? – qualification – Internship?]

Proposed investment

'The board wants to develop its involvement in tourism between Germany and the USA, which it thinks is an area of the market that is under-developed but has huge growth potential. Our management team has come up with a proposal to invest in a start-up operation that will involve selling tailored holidays in the USA to German customers and selling holidays in Germany to customers in the US. To achieve the scale of operations that we have in mind, we will have to buy a dedicated aeroplane for transporting most of our customers between Europe and the USA. We won't need a large plane, but even the cost of a relatively small one is quite high. Galaxy already has a well-established operation in New York, to handle the US side of the business, but it will need to make a fairly large investment in Germany. Our management accountant has prepared a DCF analysis of the proposed investment, which shows a strong positive NPV (**Exhibit 5**). I know from experience, though, that financial estimates for new investments are often over-optimistic, and I would like to see a critical review of the figures and assumptions.'

Project management of investment if it goes ahead

'If the project is approved by the board, we will be working to a deadline to have the operation up and running in June 20X7, so time will be very tight. The biggest problem will be to establish our operations and systems in Germany, but there will be work to do in the USA as well. Galaxy will appoint a project manager with responsibility for implementing the project on time and on budget. I would expect to be the chairperson for the committee with supervisory oversight of the project. In my view, project management would be critical to the success or failure of this project and I want to make sure that we have an effective system for monitoring progress and performance of the project. I would like you to give me some preliminary ideas about this, with a view to establishing a monitoring system if the board gives the project its approval.'

Currency and fuel price risk management

'We hold most of our cash in sterling, but a large proportion of our expenditures are in euros, US dollars and other currencies. That's because we have to pay for hotels and other costs in the holiday destination countries. So we have large exposures to currency risk throughout the year. Fuel prices are another big concern: we have to buy fuel for our air fleet, but prices have been very volatile. At one time we thought that oil prices could only go one way – up – but that's not the case any more. Fuel prices recently have been lower than for many years, and we don't know which way they will go in the future. Hedging risks is an important part of the work of our Treasury department, but some members of the board find it difficult to comprehend. I would like to show you a memo that came to me from the company chairman yesterday (**Exhibit 6**). I want to provide a quick response to his questions. The company treasurer is away at the moment, so can you draft something for me please.'

Recent security breach of Galaxy's customer database

'You may be aware from the media coverage (**Exhibit 7**) that Galaxy's customer database was recently breached by hackers. Confidential financial and personal details of many of Galaxy's customers were stolen, but at this stage none of our customers have suffered any losses. The board wants to know what measures Galaxy needs to put in place to try to ensure that such an attack on our systems cannot happen again.'

Conclusion of the meeting

The meeting concludes with Sarah saying that she will set out in an email what she would like to see in a report from Farrar Wood.

Requirement

You are required to draft a report that responds to Sarah's requests (**Exhibit 8**).

Total: 60 marks

Exhibit 1

Galaxy Travel is a travel company, selling holidays to customers. It operates in a number of European countries, but most of its customers and sales offices are in the UK, the Netherlands and Scandinavia. It also operates a small fleet of aircraft in the UK, which it uses for transporting package holiday customers.

Although business was set back by the financial crisis and subsequent weak economic conditions, Galaxy came through the turmoil successfully, and has reported a profit in every year of its operation. It now expects annual growth in revenues of 3% for at least the next five years. Operations in the Netherlands have been an exception to the general success story. Galaxy has struggled to build up its business here, and in the year to 30 September 20X5 the Netherlands division reported an operating loss of £3m.

A strategic aim of the company is to build its online sales systems, so that over time it can reduce its reliance on its networks of sales offices. In the most recent financial year (to 30 September 20X5) 33% of total sales were online. The company plans to invest heavily in its online operation, and to improve its web sites so that customers find it easy to book holidays through this channel. Most online sales are through its own web sites, but Galaxy also uses external companies for selling 'late holidays' online.

Originally, Galaxy restricted its sales to standard package holidays, but over time it has built up a business selling 'unique' holidays that are tailored to the specific requirements of the individual customer. In the most recent financial year, about two-thirds of sales revenue came from tailored holidays and only one-third from package holidays. The board would like to increase still further the proportion of tailored holidays in total sales. This is because customers buying tailored holidays spend more and usually book (and pay for) their holidays earlier than buyers of package holidays.

The profitability of package holidays is continually under pressure due to competition. Customers are able to use the internet to compare the prices of rival tour operators, and many opt for the cheapest price available.

Exhibit 2 – Summary financial statements for Galaxy Travel plc

Summary statement of profit or loss for the year to 30 September

	20X5 £m	20X4 £m
Revenue	2,472	2,410
Cost of sales	(2,220)	(2,161)
Gross profit	252	249
Administrative expenses	(199)	(196)
Operating profit	53	53
Net interest costs	(18)	(17)
Profit before tax	35	36
Taxation	(7)	(7)
Profit after tax	28	29

The operating profit on a constant currency basis in 20X5 was £55m.

Summary statement of financial position as at 30 September 20X5

	£m	£m
Non-current assets		
Goodwill		185
Property, plant and equipment		254
Other		100
Total non-current assets		539
Current assets		
Inventory	10	
Trade receivables and prepayments	231	
Cash and cash equivalents	301	
Total current assets		542
Total assets		1,081
Equity		
40m ordinary shares of £0.50 each		20
Reserves		182
Total equity		202
Non-current liabilities		
Loans	172	
Other	109	
		281
Current liabilities		
Loans	99	
Trade payables and accruals	446	
Other	53	
		598
Total equity and liabilities		1,081

Exhibit 3 – Sundry information about Galaxy Travel plc

Current share price	£4.35
Dividends paid in year to 30 September 20X5	£24m

	£m
Property, plant and equipment	
Land and buildings	51
Aircraft	136
Advance payments on new aircraft	32
Computers and other equipment	35
	254

Segmental information, year to 30 September 20X5

Source of revenue	Number of customers	Revenue	Operating profit
	000's	£m	£m
UK	803	744	29
Netherlands	462	244	(3)
Scandinavia	1,047	799	12
Other (all in Europe)	877	685	15
	3,189	2,472	53

Working capital

The cash conversion cycle for companies in the travel and tourism business is somewhat unusual. Many customers book their holiday well in advance, paying either a deposit or the cost of the holiday in full when they do so. The company in turn makes reservations with hotels, car hire companies and transport companies: it pays some of them in advance but does not pay others until a time closer to the holiday dates. As a result, companies such as Galaxy have large cash balances, made up largely of customer deposits, and also large amounts of prepayments and also short-term creditors.

Exhibit 4 – Strategy drivers and business risk

At a recent board meeting, the board agreed that the company needed to focus clearly on a limited number of 'strategy drivers' – aspects of the business that should drive the company's strategy in the future. They identified drivers for the business:

(1) Becoming an online business   —% sales from online
(2) Selling tailored holidays   —% of tailored holidays
(3) Selling the Galaxy brand   — survey
(4) Exploiting technology and Big Data   — use of online reviews / social media
(5) Geographical expansion   — ~~£~~ countries sales made in
(6) Developing the company's people   — level of training provided

Many of the strategic risks for Galaxy are that competitors will drive their businesses in similar ways, but more successfully. Risks from political volatility and natural catastrophes seem unavoidable but need to be managed.

The board has asked the Chief Executive Officer to set performance targets for each of the strategic drivers, with an appropriate number of key performance indicators (KPIs) for each.

Exhibit 5 – Proposed investment

The proposed investment will require an initial capital investment of €62.5m. In the first year, total revenue from the operations (in euros and US dollars) is expected to amount to a sterling equivalent of £220m and 225,000 customers will buy holidays.

Assumptions

Cost of capital: 9%

Annual rates of inflation years 1 – 5 (and 0% from Year 6 onwards)

UK	2%
Eurozone	0.5%
USA	3%

Exchange rates

	Current	Year 1	Year 2	Year 3	Year 4	Year 5 onwards
€/£1	1.25	1.23	1.21	1.20	1.18	1.16
US$/£1	1.60	1.62	1.63	1.65	1.66	1.68

Annual sales and operational cash flows will increase by 3% per year for 5 years, and will be constant thereafter.

Year	Net operational cash flows after tax in euros		Net operational cash flows after tax in dollars	
	€m	£m	$m	£m
1	3.00	2.44	4.50	2.78
2	3.09	2.55	4.64	2.85
3	3.18	2.65	4.77	2.89
4	3.28	2.78	4.92	2.96
5	3.38	2.91	5.06	3.01
6 onwards	3.38	2.91	5.06	3.01

Capital allowances

	Year 1	Year 2	Year 3	Year 4
In euros: € m	3.125	3.125	3.125	3.125
In sterling: £ m	2.54	2.58	2.60	2.65

DCF analysis

Closing value of business at end of year 5 = PV of future net operational cash flows in perpetuity
= (in £m): $[(2.91 + 3.01)/0.09] \times (1/(1.09)^5) = £65.78 \times 0.6499 = £42.75m$

	Year 0 £m	Year 1 £m	Year 2 £m	Year 3 £m	Year 4 £m	Year 5 £m	Year 6 onwards £m
Outlay	(50.0)						
Capital allowance		2.54	2.58	2.60	2.65		
€ operational cash flows		2.44	2.55	2.65	2.78	2.91	
$ operational cash flows		2.78	2.85	2.89	2.96	3.01	
Value at end of Year 5							65.78
Total cash flow	(50.0)	7.76	7.98	8.14	8.39	5.92	65.78
Discount factor at 9%	1.0	0.9174	0.8417	0.7722	0.7084	0.6499	0.6499
Present value	(50.0)	7.12	6.72	6.29	5.94	3.85	42.75

NPV = + £22.67m

Exhibit 6 – Hedging risks

From: Victor Manson, Chairman
To: Sarah Timmins, Financial Controller

10 December 20X5

Sarah

I would like the board to review our policy for hedging exposures to currency risk and fuel price risk, but I am struggling to understand a few aspects of hedging. I have been given the following figures by the Treasury department, but I do not know what to make of them.

Hedged fuel and currency exposures

As at 6 December 20X5	Winter 20X5/X6	Summer 20X6
Euro	93%	77%
US dollar	95%	89%
Jet fuel	87%	72%

Can you tell me what these figures mean? Why are we not hedged 100% in anything, and why have we hedged less for summer 20X6 than for this coming winter period?

The Treasury department also tells me that we hedge our currency risks with a mixture of forward contracts and currency futures. Why do we need both?

If fuel prices are so low, do we need to hedge them at all?

One more question. I would like to know the financial reporting consequences of hedging currency risk. For example, if at the end of our financial year there are forward contracts or futures with a settlement date after the year end, could this expose the company to the risk of having to report losses on our hedged positions?

I should be grateful if you could get someone to give me an answer to these questions.

Exhibit 7 – Extract from a recent newspaper article

The database of holiday company Galaxy Travel has been hacked, with the details of thousands of customers stolen by unknown perpetrators. Account details, including names, addresses and bank account details of up to 3,000 individuals were taken. The breach was identified when a Galaxy employee noticed that large amounts of customer data were missing from the company's online bookings system. Initial indications point to the hackers accessing the Galaxy database through one of the external companies that Galaxy uses for offering late deals online, which has systems linked with those of Galaxy.

A number of the company's customers have told this newspaper that they are very concerned about the data breach, but so far nobody has reported any losses. Banks and other financial institutions have been alerted and are watching out for suspicious activity on the accounts of affected individuals.

The authority which monitors the use of personal data stored by commercial entities has said that it will investigate. In the past, significant fines have been issued to companies that fail to sufficiently protect personal data as a result of poor security measures.

Exhibit 8 – The client's requirements

The next day, Colin Lee shows you the following email that he has just received from Sarah Timmins. He tells you that he would like to draft a response to each of the requests in the email. He says that Sarah has asked for a quick reply, and he would like your help to do this. 'We don't have time to do much additional research,' he tells you. 'I have told Sarah that we shall give our views on the basis of the limited information that we have.'

From: Sarah Timmins
To: Colin Lee
Subject: List of requests

Colin

Can you please provide me with a brief report in the next day or so to the following requirements.

(1)   On the basis of the information available, please provide me with an assessment of the financial position and prospects of Galaxy.

(2)   Suggest suitable Key Performance Indicators for each of the strategic drivers in the board's draft business plan.

(3)   Provide a critical analysis of the DCF appraisal provided by our management accountant.

(4)   Recommend a framework for monitoring the project to implement this new investment, if it goes ahead.

(5)   Provide a response to the chairman's questions about treasury operations, risk management and financial reporting.

(6)   Provide advice on the actions that Galaxy should take to protect the security of its data systems in the future.

I apologise for asking you to provide a quick reply.

Sarah

25   Latchkey Ltd

Assume that now is early January 20X5.

You have recently started a new job with Gammon Limited (Gammon), a company that manages a fund specialising in investments in restructuring arrangements for companies in financial difficulty. The Operations Director of Gammon, Pat O'Driscoll, has called a meeting to discuss a possible investment in Latchkey Limited, a specialist construction company.

The meeting and possible investment

Pat began the meeting with an explanation of the investment under consideration.

'Gammon has entered into discussions with a private company, Latchkey Limited. I have prepared a memo describing the company and its operations which you can read through. (See **Exhibit 1**.)

Briefly, Latchkey's business is to build and sell retirement homes for couples or individuals aged over 60. It also manages some of the homes that it sells and then runs as care homes for elderly people no longer able fully to look after themselves.

The market for sales of retirement homes and care homes is expanding fast as the number of people in the UK reaching retirement age increases. Latchkey has been operating for about five years, but has struggled financially and operationally in the past two years. Its board of directors had been hoping to achieve a stock market listing for the company, but this objective has been shelved for the time being. There are several reasons for its difficulties, but I need to tell you that other companies in the same market for building and selling retirement homes appear to be doing well. Latchkey seems to be having difficulties due to a fall in property prices and also a high level of debt.

Latchkey was originally a family-owned and family-run company, and its two founders are both still executive directors. One of them is the Chief Executive Officer (CEO) and the other is the Operations Director (OD). There is a Finance Director and two independent non-executive directors, but we think that the founder-directors are still the driving forces behind the business. They also own about 30% of the equity. The rest is held by several venture capital funds. The company has been able to borrow a substantial amount of money from two banks: it needs the money to invest in buying land for development as well as to fund homes in the course of construction.

The company made a loss in its most recent financial year to 31 December 20X4, and only a small profit in the year before that. Two years ago it renegotiated its loans with the two banks, which agreed to extend the maturity date for the loans and also to change the main financial covenants. In spite of this, Latchkey is in breach of its covenants. The banks are getting fed up and we think that Gammon will be able to buy the loans from them for about 70% of their face value. We think that the banks will prefer this exit route for their lending rather than putting the company into administration for breach of covenant.

This creates a refinancing opportunity for Gammon. We have sufficient cash in our fund to provide additional financing if required, as well as to buy the loans from the banks. We would also want to take an equity stake.

I can give you some financial information about Latchkey (**Exhibit 2**).

If Latchkey is able to recover and continue in business, we would expect to be able to earn a good return on our investment – the high yield that our own investors expect from us. Its directors have given us some information about their recovery plan. (See **Exhibit 3**.) However as you can imagine we have some questions about the reliability of these forecasts.

If we invest in Latchkey we will want to ensure that the management of its operations improves. The company's board of directors has given us a list of the major risk areas for their business. They have also given us their views about why the company is in difficulties and not performing as well as competitors. (See **Exhibit 4**.)

There is one other issue which has me slightly concerned. Latchkey has just introduced a share option scheme for its senior executives and I do not see that we can simply cancel the scheme if we invest in the company. My concern is that this scheme could be expensive and affect the company's profitability, and the return that Gammon might hope to make on its investment. I have given some details about the scheme in my overview of the company (**Exhibit 1**).

Conclusion

Pat O'Driscoll concluded the meeting by saying that he wanted some views and information about Latchkey and a proposed refinancing and restructuring. He asks you to carry out a number of tasks and to report back to him. The list of tasks is shown in **Exhibit 5**.

Requirement

Draft a response to Pat O'Driscoll covering all the points he has asked you to report on.

Total: 60 marks

Exhibit 1 – Latchkey Ltd and its business

Latchkey Limited is a company that specialises in building and selling specially-designed retirement homes (one- and two-bedroomed apartments) in the UK. Some of these homes are designed as care homes, which elderly people buy and which Latchkey then manages. Although most of the company's revenues come from selling homes, there is a certain amount of income from care homes management. The company was established five years ago.

There are a number of other companies operating in the same market. Building and selling retirement homes is a niche market in the building and construction industry. The properties are especially-designed to meet the practical needs of older people. Homes are built in small apartment blocks: the housing density is higher than for traditional apartment blocks and there is a lower ratio of parking space to residential space, since many older people no longer own and drive cars. Homes are invariably located close to amenities and public transport routes.

Analysts believe that there is great potential in this market niche. The number of people in the UK aged 65 or over is expected to increase by 50% in the next 20 years, and many older people reaching retirement age want to 'downsize' by selling their family home and moving into something smaller.

Latchkey's main business involves buying land with potential for development and building retirement homes. Most of the land purchased for a land bank does not have planning permission at the time of purchase, and even though the authorities look favourably on the building of new homes for retired people, it can take a long time to obtain the necessary planning permission to build.

When planning permission has been obtained, the company can decide when to start new building. Each new building project has its project manager, who is responsible for obtaining all necessary resources – materials, labour and hired equipment – through local purchasing and hiring. The company's policy is to have a stock of completed homes or homes in the course of construction sufficient to meet sales demand for at least 18 months.

When a new building project begins, the sales department is responsible for selling the properties. Customers are encouraged to buy homes before completion, and to secure the sale by paying a deposit in advance. However most selling does not occur until after building work has been completed. The sales division has two regional sales offices, and also advertises properties on the company's web site.

For the first three years after it began operations, the company benefited from rising property prices. In the past two years, however, UK property prices have fallen by about 5% each year.

Brand strategy

The directors of Latchkey are optimistic about the longer-term future. They are aware that barriers to entry into the market for building retirement homes may not be high for established building construction companies, but they have a strategic objective of establishing Latchkey as a powerful brand within its sector of the market. The directors believe that by creating a strong brand, the company will be able to win and maintain a good share of its market niche.

Share option scheme

Latchkey, although a private company, has just introduced a share option scheme for its senior executives. The scheme gives its participants the right to subscribe for new shares at a price of £0.30 per £0.25 share. If all the executives participating in the scheme exercise their options, the total equity in the company would increase by an amount equal to 6% of the current number of shares in issue.

Exhibit 2 – Latchkey Ltd summary financial statements

Latchkey Ltd
Statement of profit or loss for the year to 31 December

	20X4	20X3
	£m	£m
Turnover: sale of homes	103.6	115.3
Cost of sales	(81.4)	(86.2)
Gross profit	22.2	29.1
Income from care home management	3.2	2.8
	25.4	31.9
Administrative expenses	(15.7)	(15.2)
Other operating expenses	(3.2)	(2.6)
Operating profit	6.5	14.1
Interest payable	(10.5)	(10.3)
Profit/(loss) before taxation	(4.0)	3.8
Taxation	–	(0.7)
Profit/(loss) after taxation	(4.0)	3.1

The company has not paid any dividend since its incorporation.
Interest on the company's bank loans is charged at a rate of six-month Libor plus 7.5%.

Latchkey Ltd
Summary statement of financial position as at 31 December 20X4

	£m	£m
Property, plant and equipment		2.9
Current assets		
Inventory (see Note 1)	230.7	
Receivables (see Note 2)	14.8	
Cash	1.2	
		246.7
Total assets		249.6
Short-term payables (see Note 3)		(94.1)
Total assets less current liabilities		155.5
Bank loans (see Note 4)		(120.0)
Net current assets		35.5
Share capital (ordinary shares of £1 each)		15.0
Reserves		20.5
		35.5

Notes

1 **Inventory**

	£m
Land for development	104.8
Sites in course of construction	62.5
Finished housing stock	63.4
	230.7

2 **Receivables**

Receivables are shared equity receivables. These arise from sales incentives whereby the company will receive a proportion of the resale proceeds from certain residential home apartments. Although shown here as current assets, these receivables are in fact long-term in nature, and will not be realised as cash until the relevant properties are sold. The company's equity share in these apartments is protected by a registered entry in the title for the property.

3 **Short-term payables**

Most short-term payables are conditional creditors, representing unpaid purchase consideration for land, where the purchase is conditional on certain contractual conditions being met. If these conditions are not met, payments to the creditors will not become due.

4 **Loans and loan covenants**

The company's loans are interest-only loans. The loan capital will be repaid in full at maturity date. The loans have maturity dates ranging between five and ten years.

Although the company has borrowed from two banks, the loan covenants attached to the loans are similar. The main financial covenants are a debt/equity covenant and an interest cover ratio covenant. These covenants were negotiated two years ago, when the company found itself in continual breach of its previous existing covenants. The banks were willing to extend the maturity date for the loan and amend the covenants, in the expectation that the company's financial position would improve.

The loan covenants currently in place are that the company's debt: equity ratio (measured by book values) should not exceed 300% and the interest cover ratio (ratio of operating profit to interest costs) must not fall below 2.0 times.

Exhibit 3 – Latchkey Ltd recovery plan for 20X5

The directors of Latchkey Ltd are projecting the following recovery in 20X5.

Assumptions

(1) Property prices will recover and selling prices of retirement homes will increase by 4% above 20X4 levels.

(2) The volume of sales of retirement homes will increase by 2% above the 20X4 level.

(3) Income from managing care homes will increase by 5%.

(4) The cost of sales per home and administrative and other operating costs will increase by 1%.

Forecast operating profit for the year to 31 December 20X5

	£m
Turnover: sale of homes	109.9
Cost of sales	(83.9)
Gross profit	26.0
Income from care home management	3.4
	29.4
Administrative expenses	(15.9)
Other operating expenses	(3.2)
Operating profit	10.3

Exhibit 4 – Latchkey Ltd: main risks and reasons for financial difficulty

The directors of Latchkey Ltd state in their annual report that there are seven major risks in the company's business:

(1) General economic conditions.

(2) Land acquisition: the risk of being unable to acquire a sufficient land bank for development.

(3) Development cycle: the risk of delays between acquiring land and obtaining permission for building construction.

(4) Build programmes. The risk of delays in start times and completion times for building projects, and also the cost of over-running budgeted construction costs.

(5) Risks of accidents during construction work (health and safety risks).

(6) Risks of poor sales performance by the sales division.

(7) Reputational risks linked to the quality of homes built and customer satisfaction.

The directors of Latchkey have told Gammon executives that in their opinion, the financial difficulties of the company are attributable to various factors, which include:

(1) Delays in the property development cycles, especially in starting times and completion times for building projects, but also longer average times for obtaining planning permission on purchased land.

(2) Falling property prices in the last two years.

(3) High interest charges on the bank loans.

(4) Overstaffing, and high health and safety costs.

Exhibit 5 – Requirements

Pat O'Driscoll asks you to perform the following tasks.

I would like your views on a number of different issues. There are two reasons for this. I want to see how familiar you are with financial reconstructions, so I have a few technical questions for you. Second, there are some issues about which I am unsure, and I would appreciate your views.

So here's my list of tasks:

(1) Views on reconstruction and exit route. As you know, I have some doubts about the recovery plan of the Latchkey board, and I want to consider how a reconstruction arrangement might work, based on the historical data that we have about the company and its business. First, I want you to

give me your thoughts about how a reconstruction deal might be arranged, and what are the prospects for its success. You should assume that Gammon will purchase the company's debts from its banks and that it will also be willing to provide additional financing if this is required. As part of your analysis, give your views on what makes the building of retirement homes such a special niche in the construction market. I would also like to hear your thoughts about corporate governance arrangements if a restructuring deal is agreed.

(2) How to assess the recovery plan. I am going to have to respond to the board of Latchkey about their recovery plan for next year. I want to know if their figures add up and how we can assess the assumptions they are making for the plan.

(3) I agree with the board of Latchkey that to create a successful business over the long term, Latchkey will have to develop a strong brand identity in order to compete in the market. Let me have your thoughts on what the company's strategy will have to be for building up a strong brand.

(4) How to turn round the company. If we are going to make a success of investing in this company, we are going to have to make sure that the company improves its operational performance. Let me have your ideas about where performance needs to be improved, and why.

(5) Can you suggest how we should deal with the share option scheme in proposals for a reconstruction scheme and refinancing the company? I am reluctant to offer generous terms, but we do not want to alienate Latchkey's senior management. For the reconstruction to work successfully, we may need their full support.

26 Plumbrite plc

Plumbrite plc is a listed company, based in the UK. It employs over 35,000 people worldwide and is one of the world's leading distributors of plumbing, heating and building materials. As well as operating its own retail outlets, Plumbrite also sells directly to building and plumbing contractors and merchants through its external direct sales units.

You are a senior working for Rice and Hughes (RH), a firm of ICAEW Chartered Accountants and business advisers. Plumbrite is a business client of RH's, but RH does not carry out the audit of Plumbrite.

You received the following email from the engagement partner, Lee Weller:

To: A Senior
From: Lee Weller
Date: 8 December 20X4

Welcome to the team. I know you are new to this client, so I have provided you with some background information (**Exhibit 1**).

Plumbrite's management are keen to benchmark performance in different countries in order to improve operating efficiency. As an initial pilot exercise, they have collated some performance data for the Building Materials (BM) division in UK and Taiwan (**Exhibits 2 and 3**), and I know they would like us to identify any performance issues which the data highlights. The management team are also interested in potential performance measures which they could use to evaluate the success of staff training activities within the division (**Exhibit 4**).

The management team have also been discussing some issues around the number of suppliers Plumbrite works with (**Exhibits 5 and 6**) and the need to improve the consistency of the company's retail branding (**Exhibit 7**).

I have a meeting at Plumbrite shortly and I need you to prepare some notes which:

- compare and contrast the annual performance for the BM Division in UK and Taiwan for the year ended 31 December 20X3, identifying any areas where additional information would also be useful.

- recommend two critical success factors for the UK and two for Taiwan which BM could apply in respect of the operation of its retail outlets in these countries. (Please base the critical success factors you recommend on the issues arising from your comparative performance analysis, as well as any other considerations you think are relevant.)

- recommend three performance measures which BM could use to evaluate the success of its staff training and development activities.

- evaluate the proposal to reduce the number of suppliers and to revise the terms of the 'preferred supplier' status contracts.

- briefly evaluate the proposal to rebrand the retail outlets as the marketing director has suggested, and discuss what assurance Rice & Hughes could provide in relation to the marketing director's projections. (I do not need a detailed list of assurance procedures though.)

- explain the financial reporting implications of the rebranding programme, if it proceeds on the basis the marketing director has suggested.

Requirement

Prepare the notes requested by Lee Weller.

Total: 55 marks

Exhibit 1 – Plumbrite: Background information

Plumbrite plc was founded in the early 20th Century as a plumbing and building materials manufacturing business and enjoyed very rapid growth in the 1970s and 1980s. In 1985, Plumbrite was listed on the UK stock exchange and at this time it also expanded into the USA by acquiring a building materials distribution company based in New Jersey.

In 1990, Plumbrite acquired a building supplies business in the UK and, later in that decade, made acquisitions of other European based plumbing and heating and building materials distribution companies.

In the early years of the 21st Century, Plumbrite sold off all its manufacturing business units and concentrated solely on being a distributor and retailer of plumbing, heating and building materials.

Corporate values

Plumbrite is proud of its history and traditions of distributing and retailing good quality products in locations which are convenient to its customers. It has developed a series of core values which are:

- trading fairly and honestly;

- being responsive to customer needs and market changes and not being satisfied with standing still, but seeking to continuously improve;

- employing committed people and providing training opportunities to develop their skills; and

- having respect for cultural diversity across all the company's stakeholders.

Strategic objectives

Plumbrite's Board of Directors has identified three strategic objectives for the company which all combine with the aim of improving shareholder value. The three strategic objectives are:

(1) to be the market leader in the regions of the world in which it operates;

(2) to deleverage the company by disposing of business units or individual retail outlets which do not contribute sufficiently to the aim of Plumbrite becoming market leader or are failing to meet minimum performance targets; and

(3) to continuously strive to improve its products and customer services.

Corporate responsibility aims

Plumbrite aims to provide excellent customer service across its two divisions. This excellence in customer service is underpinned by its:

- provision of high levels of staff training and development, with strong concentration on safety management;

- adherence to the highest ethical standards both internally and with respect to supplier relationships;

- concern to cause the least environmental damage possible within its operations in terms of emissions, waste management and recycling activities by employing environmental performance management methods; and

- promotion of product integrity through selling only safe and reliable products which are of the required standard of quality and partnering with key suppliers.

Strategic developments

Plumbrite aims to increase its market share by making repeat sales through its external direct sales units and retail outlets to existing customers and attracting new customers away from competitors. It places customer service as its key critical success factor.

The Board of Directors is constantly seeking improvements in the company's logistics, particularly in sourcing products and their delivery to its external direct sales units and retail outlets, wherever they are in the world. It is actively considering acquiring logistic resources in parts of the world where Plumbrite does not own warehousing and distribution facilities at present. All of Plumbrite's products are currently supplied from warehouses in the UK and the USA (see **Exhibit 5** for more details).

Business operations

Plumbrite has two operating divisions: Plumbing and heating; and Building materials.

Plumbing and Heating (PH)	Products:
	Baths, showers, toilets, sinks, heating systems, general plumbing parts such as taps, pipes and drainage systems.
Building Materials (BM)	Products:
	Concrete building blocks, bricks, tiles, flooring products, roofing materials, UPVC products such as doors and window frames.

The operating arrangements in both divisions are similar. Each division has two distribution warehouses, one each in the UK and the USA. Each division uses these warehouses to fulfil sales orders placed by its external direct sales units and retail outlets.

The external direct sales units sell to building contractors, plumbing contractors and merchants who supply small building and plumbing companies with materials and parts.

Plumbrite's retail outlets sell directly to the public and to the building and plumbing trades. Some of these retail sales outlets were set up, or acquired, as chains of retail outlets each with a common trading name, and these have been retained as separate business units. Where Plumbrite acquires a trade name, it amortises this over 20 years in its financial statements. All acquired chains of retail outlets were acquired as business combinations, and their trading names could be sold separately.

The retail outlets that have been acquired continue to operate under their own trading names so that Plumbrite can retain the benefit of the goodwill those retail outlets developed prior to acquisition. Each has a specific line of business, such as the sale of complete bathrooms and kitchens through chains of showrooms.

In some cases, acquired businesses have underperformed and have not met Plumbrite's profit expectations. In these cases, some impairment of goodwill has been necessary.

The plumbing and heating division carries out its retail operations through established chains of showrooms. These showrooms sell products to local tradesmen and also directly to the public. The building materials division's retail activities are carried out through small-scale retail outlets which are usually located on industrial estates and those that have been acquired retain their local building supply trading names.

Overall, Plumbrite has in excess of 90,000 suppliers and sells to over 1.2m customers across the world. Each of the two divisions operates its own large logistics and distribution network. They operate their own fleet of road transport vehicles to distribute products in Europe and the USA and use rail, sea and air networks for distribution to their external direct sales units and retail outlets in other parts of the world.

Divisional performance

The divisions measure performance at external direct sales unit and individual retail outlet level. Where retail outlets are organised into business units under a common trading name, then the performance of the retail units is consolidated enabling performance to be measured at the business unit level. The summary operating performance of the divisions for the financial year 20X3 is as follows:

	Plumbing and heating £m	Building materials £m	Plumbrite plc £m
Revenue	7,050	6,843	13,893
Operating profit	236	214	450

Exhibit 2 – Building Materials (BM) division

The Building Materials (BM) division operates a network of retail outlets and external sales units throughout the world.

BM analyses its sales in terms of the type of market sector. An analysis of each type of market sector for the year ending 31 December 20X3 is presented below.

(1) **Repairs and Maintenance sector (RM) – 60% of total BM sales revenue**

The repairs and maintenance sector products are largely purchased by independent builders, local tradesmen and individual Do-It-Yourself (DIY) customers. The demand for repairs and maintenance products in most countries is largely influenced by the age of the houses and buildings.

In the last five years there has been an increase in BM's sales revenues from this market sector compared to the other sectors. BM believes this increase has been driven by global economic factors. Competition in this sector is high with many businesses offering similar products at a comparable price and giving customers a range of incentives. BM aims to be the market leader in this sector in all of the countries in which it operates, through providing the widest range of products and offering the highest level of customer service in comparison with its competitors. Customer loyalty to BM in this sector is strong due to its focus on excellence in customer service and responsiveness to customer needs.

(2) **New construction sector (NC) – 35% of total BM sales revenue**

The new construction sector products are mainly purchased by building construction companies, normally for use in large infrastructure projects and housing developments. Demand in this sector is driven largely by economic cycles and by demographic trends such as the increasing average age of the population and fewer people per household. BM has identified that in some countries, in particular in northern Europe, revenue earned from the NC sector has fallen dramatically in the last five years.

However, in other markets, notably Asia and the Middle East, revenues earned from the NC sector have increased. NC sector customers expect prompt and accurate delivery of high quality products. Competition is less intense in this sector than in the RM sector but BM believes that this will change, as economic growth and population increases occur in its key markets of the world. BM aims to be the market leader in this sector in all of the countries in which it operates.

(3) **Sustainable building development sector (SB) – 5% of total BM sales revenue**

Sustainable building development is a relatively new sector for BM. In the last decade there has been an increasing demand across the world for sustainable new building development and the preservation and renovation of existing buildings. Examples of sustainable building products include solar panels and sustainably grown and sourced timber products. New building technologies and developments in sustainable building materials have resulted in a greater focus upon discovering ways to construct and maintain environmentally sustainable buildings. However, sales revenues are currently low in this sector and only a few of BM's retail outlets and external sales units sell sustainable building products. However, BM is confident that this area of business will continue to grow with the increasing environmental awareness of customers and governments around the world. There are currently only a few competitors to BM in this market sector.

Exhibit 3 – Comparative information for BM division in the UK and in Taiwan

UK

BM has operated in the UK since the Plumbrite company was founded over 100 years ago.

The UK has a well-established residential housing stock, with over 60% of residential property being over 40 years old. A large proportion of the population own their own homes.

However, industrial and residential new construction projects have slowed down in the last 10 years. Currently, most of BM's customers in the UK are small independent builders and tradesmen who value the wide choice of products offered and the high levels of customer service the company provides. BM's employees in the UK are well trained and dedicated employees, with considerable local knowledge.

There has also been a significant increase in the number of domestic home improvement ('DIY') sales in the UK over the last 15 years. The UK Government has been actively promoting the development of sustainable building projects and investment in large scale regeneration of derelict residential housing.

Taiwan

BM has operated in Taiwan for the last 10 years.

Taiwan has a developing economy which has achieved steady growth in the last five years. A large proportion of the population live in rented accommodation. There are many new residential and non-residential building projects underway in the country.

Most of BM's revenues in Taiwan are generated through sales to large building contractors, working on large scale building projects. BM faces strong competition from two large nationally based building materials suppliers, which provide locally sourced, highly competitively priced products. In particular, new construction (NC) market customers in Taiwan demand prompt and accurate delivery of high quality products. All of the products sold by BM's retail outlets located in Taiwan are supplied from BM's warehouses which are located in the UK and the USA.

Year ended 31 December 20X3	UK £m	Taiwan £m
Financial information		
Sales revenue	490.0	255.0
Gross profit	147.0	55.9
Operating profit	17.3	11.3
Capital employed	141.0	80.0
Other information		
Number of stores	105	40
Employees (full time equivalents)	1,370	605
Training days	19,150	6,075
Staff turnover (%)	1.0	3.5
Product returns (% of revenue)	0.4	2.2
On time deliveries (% of total deliveries made in the country)	97.6	92.4

Analysis per market sector in 20X3

	UK			Taiwan		
	RM	NC	SB	RM	NC	SB
% of sales revenue from sector	75	17	8	29	69	2
Cost of sales (£m)	267.8	50.9	24.3	63.4	130.8	5.0
Customer satisfaction rating (*)	97.2	96.4	98.5	94.2	95.7	90.1
Market position	1	2	3	2	2	n/a
Market share (%)	38	20	9	20	17	n/a
Market share of largest competitor (%)	23	30	14	24	19	n/a

(*): The Directors have set a target for customer satisfaction of 96% in all countries in which BM operates.

Exhibit 4 – Staff Training and Development in BM

One of the key aspects of Plumbrite's Corporate Responsibility aims is the provision of high levels of staff training and development.

BM considers that the skill development and the retention of its employees who deliver excellent customer service is fundamental to its business strategy and long-term success. BM provides skills training for all front-line employees. In 20X3, BM launched its 'Culture of Customer Service Excellence' training programme, which it intends to extend to all employees before the end of 20X4.

As part of a customer service and employee development drive, an online training academy has been set up in the UK. The academy offers a broad range of training modules and qualifications. All employees receive a detailed annual performance review and feedback from their manager. The results of these reviews will affect each individual's development plans and objectives for the next year. BM also conducts engagement surveys with each member of its staff in its retail outlets to assess the level of employee job satisfaction.

Exhibit 5 – Supply chain and sources of products

Plumbrite prides itself on operating an efficient supply chain and developing strong relationships with a wide range of suppliers across the world which offer quality products. It enters into long-term supply contracts with its suppliers where possible, and grants preferred supplier status to most of its suppliers. (This 'preferred supplier' status means that Plumbrite's legal and procurement teams have approved a supplier for use, and therefore orders can be placed with them without the need for any further checks on the supplier.)

All Plumbrite's external direct sales units and retail outlets are supplied from its warehouses in the UK or the USA. This means that some of its products which are sourced from Asia and Africa are shipped to the company's warehouses in the UK and the USA. External direct sales units and retail outlets in Asia and Africa then receive shipments from the company's warehouses. This means that some products, which Plumbrite sources from suppliers located in Asia and Africa, cross the world, are stored in the central warehouses, and then cross the world again to be delivered to their destinations in Asia and Africa.

Exhibit 6 – Possible supplier rationalisation in the Plumbing and Heating Division

The chief procurement officer (CPO) in the Plumbing and Heating Division was appointed five years ago and has been instrumental in increasing the number of suppliers which Plumbrite uses from 45,000 to approximately 65,000 now. This has resulted in an increase of 29% in the number of product lines stocked over the last five years. The CPO sees this as a source of competitive advantage, because Plumbrite now offers one of the largest product portfolios amongst its competitors.

Rationalisation of suppliers

However, at a recent Board meeting, Plumbrite's Logistics Director raised concerns that the growth in the number of suppliers has put considerable strain on the company's warehousing capacity, particularly in the Plumbing and Heating Division. (The BM and PH Divisions both have their own, separate warehouses.)

The Logistics Director has therefore suggested that Plumbrite should consider a complete rationalisation of its suppliers in order to increase efficiencies within logistics and to speed up delivery times. This rationalisation would mean cutting the number of suppliers by one third, based on a standard set of criteria for evaluating the current suppliers.

Plumbrite's current 'preferred supplier' contract terms also grant suppliers a three year contract with guaranteed minimum order quantities over that three year period.

The Logistics Director has proposed that the maximum term of all supply contracts be revised to one year, although they can be renewed on an annual basis. The Logistics Director has also proposed that the contractual minimum order guarantees be scrapped.

The Procurement Director disagreed with this strategy claiming that 'Plumbrite's success is as a result of the unrivalled product range we stock and the fantastic relationship we have with suppliers, all of which gives our customers the widest choice of products in the market place'.

Exhibit 7 – Retail branding

The Marketing Director reported that he recently saw three advertisements, all in the same magazine which is widely distributed throughout the UK, by three separate SBUs within the Plumbrite plc group. All three of the adverts were advertising bathrooms to the UK domestic market under different trade names. The Marketing Director has therefore done some preliminary analysis with a view to rebranding all of Plumbrite's retail outlets (in both divisions), starting with those in the UK as a pilot scheme. If the

UK rebranding exercise proves to be financially successful, then it would be rolled out as a rebranding strategy worldwide.

The trading names which generate the most turnover within the Plumbing and Heating Division and the Building Division respectively are 'Tubs 'n Taps' and 'Bricks 'n Build.' Therefore the Marketing Director believes that all the other retail outlets should adopt these trade names going forward. There will, however, be considerable costs incurred in rebranding the retail outlets. These will include refitting the retail outlets and changing the shop-front signage to reflect the new brand.

It has been estimated that the cost of refitting and rebranding a store will be £125,000 per retail outlet. Across the UK, Plumbrite has 580 retail outlets, of which 80% will need rebranding. Plumbrite's basic policy is to refurbish its stores on a five year rolling cycle.

In his business case to support the rebranding programme, the Marketing Director has estimated that UK revenues will increase by 5% per annum over the next three years, before remaining flat thereafter. He has also estimated that the operating profit margin earned on UK sales will increase by 0.25% due to the increased operating economies of scale.

One-off advertising costs to accompany the rebranding are estimated to be £1.75m. All Plumbrite's stores are already linked to the group's management information and inventory management systems so there will be no additional information systems costs associated with the rebranding.

Using Plumbrite's standard investment appraisal criteria (10% cost of capital, over a five year life), the business case shows a positive net present value for the programme of £5.2m.

27   Liebitz & Luber plc

Liebitz & Luber plc (LL) is a global company, manufacturing and selling chemical-based products worldwide. The company's products include: cleaning products, paints, adhesives, and fertilisers. LL is listed on the London Stock Exchange and its head office and board are located in the UK.

You are Zara Harris, and you work in the business advisory and assurance section of ICAEW Chartered Accountants, Raul & Roberts LLP (RR). RR does not audit LL. One of the managers in your department, Andrew Andover, asked you to accompany him to a meeting with the LL chairman, Martyn James.

A meeting with the LL chairman

Martyn opened the meeting: 'Thanks for coming to see me. I would like RR to help us review our risk management procedures at all levels. These have not been adequate in the past and we have suffered losses recently from not managing our risks appropriately.

The LL board has already carried out an initial review of risk management from the top down, including a reappraisal of our corporate governance structures and risk reporting procedures. As a consequence, we have decided to set up a risk committee as a separate committee of the board to ensure there is high-level responsibility for all risk management. The risk committee will comprise myself, as chairman, a non-executive director and two executive directors. Responsibility for strategic and operating risk management currently belongs to the audit committee, but this has not been satisfactory.

I realise that you have no previous experience of LL, so I have provided some background information about the company (**Exhibit 1**) and our current risk management procedures (**Exhibit 2**).

We need RR to help us identify and manage high-level risks, but I also have concerns about managing some specific financial risks (**Exhibit 3**) and health and safety risks from ammonia spillages (**Exhibit 4**).

A number of our major institutional shareholders have not been happy with the way the LL board has dealt with some key risks. Once we have completed redesigning our risk management procedures and internal controls, I would like RR to consider accepting a risk assurance assignment attesting to their effectiveness. I would hope that your report and conclusions could be published in our annual report and accounts.

Our review of risk management procedures and internal controls has also prompted the board to review the way we measure and report on performance (**Exhibit 5**) and the effectiveness of LL's information systems in providing us with the information we need for decision-making and control purposes (**Exhibit 6**).

As a preliminary step, the LL board has asked for the following from RR:

- An explanation of the financial risks associated with the issues set out in Exhibit 3 and an assessment of a suitable approach to managing these risks.

- An explanation of the financial reporting treatment of the planned purchase of ammonia in Exhibit 3 and for possible hedging arrangements. I do not require detailed calculations, but I do require comprehensive and clear explanations of how the relevant planned transactions should be treated in LL's financial statements.

- A briefing note which, using the information in Exhibit 4, provides advice to the LL board, on whether LL should insure against spillage risks or accept these risks. Prepare supporting calculations.

- An explanation and justification of the level of assurance that RR could provide in attesting to the effectiveness of LL's risk management procedures. Also, explain the benefits arising to LL from this risk assurance assignment. I do not need a list of assurance procedures.

- An evaluation of the potential benefits to LL from adopting integrated reporting, and an explanation of the potential value for LL's shareholders in reports measuring performance in respect of social capital and manufactured capital.

- An evaluation of the potential impact which introducing the new executive information system could have on performance management at LL.'

Immediately after the meeting Andrew asked you to draft a response to these requests from the LL board.

Assume the current date is July 20X4.

Requirement

Draft the response requested by Andrew.

Total: 45 marks

Exhibit 1 – Background information about LL

LL has three factories in the UK, one factory in China and one factory in Japan. All of these are approximately equal in size, but they manufacture different types of products. Some of the factory output is in the form of partially finished products, which are transferred to one of the other LL factories for completion.

Total external sales amounted to £900m for the year ended 31 December 20X3. There were a further £200m of internal sales in the year. External sales for the year ended 31 December 20X3 were geographically distributed as follows:

UK	40%
US	15%
Europe (eurozone)	25%
Asia	10%
Australia	10%

Operating profit for the year ended 31 December 20X3 was £62m.

Raw materials are one of the largest operating costs. Many of the raw material chemicals that LL uses are hazardous to individuals and there is also a significant risk of major fires and explosions. LL relies on a small number of key suppliers in order to obtain quantity discounts from bulk transport by ship or train, which is sometimes over long distances.

Some adverse events have affected profitability in recent years. Our factory in Japan was damaged by a tsunami and, as a result, we could not supply our Japanese customers for two months thereafter. We just did not have the appropriate business continuity procedures in place.

We have also suffered from exchange rate movements and commodity price movements, but in other periods we have benefited from such price movements. The global economic downturn has also caused us major problems.

LL has long-term gearing of approximately 40%, with debt comprising mainly variable interest rate loans.

LL has a 31 December accounting year end.

Exhibit 2 – LL's current risk management procedures

Financial risk management

The company's activities expose it to a variety of financial risks, including those arising from: foreign currency exchange rates, interest rates and commodity prices. The treasury department seeks to manage the potential adverse effects of these risks on the financial performance of the company. The treasury department reports on financial risk management to the board.

Strategic and operating risk management

The audit committee is currently responsible for strategic and operating risk management. It examines key risk events that have occurred and, in light of these, reviews risk procedures and policies. Every year it reviews the key risks of the business and reports to the board.

Exhibit 3 – Specific financial risks

One of the raw material chemicals that we use in our products is ammonia. This is a basic commodity, in other words it is the same, no matter where we buy it. It is traded on global commodity markets, therefore derivatives and other financial instruments are available based on its market price.

There are three issues for LL. First, ammonia is a dangerous substance therefore we would not want to hold too much of it in inventory; second, the price of ammonia as a commodity is volatile; and third, trading ammonia as a commodity is denominated in US$, whereas the functional currency of LL is £ sterling.

As a specific example, LL has a firm plan that it will require, in five months (ie on, or around, 22 December 20X4) the purchase of 2,000 tonnes of ammonia at the spot price on that date. The current spot price is US$500 per tonne, but LL does not want to make the purchase now, because of the costs and risks of storing ammonia for such a long period. Nevertheless, the LL head of treasury is concerned that there may be financial risks from fluctuations in the ammonia commodity price and in the £/$ exchange rate.

He therefore plans to hedge these risks, but is unsure how best to do this. He is also concerned about the impact on the financial statements of hedging arrangements for commodity price changes and currency fluctuations.

A futures contract for ammonia for delivery on 22 December 20X4 is currently US$520 per tonne, although it has fallen from a price of nearly US$530 per tonne in the past week.

The £/US$ exchange rates are:

Current spot:	£1 = US$1.55
5-month forward rate:	£1 = US$1.60

Exhibit 4 – Health and safety risks – chemical spillages

Concern has been raised by some directors about the risks that arise as a consequence of a possible spillage of chemicals, causing health and safety problems with associated costs. Some board members are also concerned, however, that the cost of insuring such risks has become excessive.

Management has collected the following data to support the board's decision making on this matter.

Number of spillages to occur in any one year	0	1	2	3
Probability	90%	5%	3%	2%

The probability of more than three spillages occurring in any one year is insignificant.

There are two types of spillage: major and minor. The costs per spillage and the probabilities (of any one spillage being major or minor) are as follows:

	Probability	Cost
Major	7%	£150m
Minor	93%	£10m

The annual insurance premium to cover the identifiable costs of all spillages in a year is £4m. However, the maximum payout for any one spillage is limited to £100m.

Exhibit 5

Although the audit committee reviews the key risks the business is facing, the performance measures which are reported in the monthly board papers are primarily financial. Similarly, LL's annual report and accounts focus primarily on short-term financial performance.

The audit committee has previously recommended that LL should give greater importance to non-financial performance measures, because these can play an important part in LL's strategic success and its ability to create value in the longer term. In particular, in the light of the dangerous nature of some of the chemicals that LL uses to manufacture its products, the audit committee has recommended that LL's performance measures should include measures focusing on environmental performance as well as health and safety. However, LL's performance measures have not yet been changed.

The Chairman of the audit committee has also suggested that LL should adopt an integrated reporting approach, but several of the directors said they were unconvinced by the concept of integrated reporting. They were aware of the six capitals for integrated and sustainability reporting, but were sceptical that measures of social capital and manufactured capital for example would be of any value to the company's shareholders.

Exhibit 6

The board is considering making a change to the information systems at LL.

Currently, each of the five factories has its own systems, and within this, each function (production, inventory management, sales, customer service, finance, and human resources) also has its own systems.

Reports are submitted by each function and then integrated at head office in order to provide summary information for the board papers which form LL's main strategic information system.

However, the board is considering the implementation of a new system based on an integrated, single database that would be accessible at any of LL's five factories, as well as at head office.

The company network would be upgraded to allow real-time input and updating of the database, although access rights will be restricted so that staff can only enter or amend data relating to their own function or site.

The database would support a detailed management information system and a high-level executive information system.

28 Textiles with Care plc

Textiles with Care plc (TC) is a listed company which manufactures clothes and household textile products in a number of factories throughout Europe, although most costs and revenues arise in the UK. TC also owns a chain of retail shops which sell the clothes made in TC's own factories, alongside those of other clothing manufacturers.

A new chief executive officer (CEO) of TC, Steve Gavinson, was appointed in July 20X5. After spending some time reviewing the business, Steve came to the preliminary conclusion that a reorganisation is needed. This would involve the closure of some business units.

Before making any final decisions, Steve decided to take external advice from Smith & West LLP (SW), a firm of ICAEW Chartered Accountants. You are a senior working for SW. You and the engagement manager, Kirsty Hall, meet with Steve.

The meeting

Steve opened the meeting: 'I want to reorganise TC and close down some of the underperforming business units. I am concerned, however, about the impact on the financial statements if I decide to close these units. I have provided you with some details (**Exhibit 1**).

'TC needs to raise finance to support the reorganisation and to expand the business. I would appreciate your advice regarding which of the alternative methods of finance we should select and I have provided details (**Exhibit 2**).

'Whichever of the alternative methods of finance is used, the finance provider will require profit forecasts to support the request for finance. It will also require an assurance report relating to these forecasts and I would like SW to provide this. I need to understand this process, so please explain the key assurance procedures that would be performed.

'I expect you to maintain absolute confidentiality in this assignment, as the reorganisation announcement may increase the TC share price. As part of my remuneration package, I am due to receive a fixed value of shares in TC. I want to receive these shares at a lower price before announcing the reorganisation which will increase the share price.

[handwritten right margin: unethical; insider trading?]

'Despite the need to reorganise some parts of TC, the textiles units are performing well, and the company has been looking at potential ways of increasing supply for its bed linen and kitchen linen products. We are considering a deal with a new supplier in Asia (**Exhibit 3**), but would appreciate your advice about the issues for TC to consider before we make any decisions about this.

'I have prepared supporting notes, in which I have set out what I require of SW .'

Instructions

After the meeting with Steve, you accompany Kirsty back to the office where she explains what you will be required to do on this engagement: 'I would like you to draft a response to the list of tasks that Steve has asked SW to carry out (**Exhibit 4**).

'Also, please draft a briefing note for me that sets out any ethical issues for SW and explains any actions that the firm should take.'

Requirement

Respond to the instructions of the engagement manager, Kirsty Hall.

Assume it is now November 20X5.   **Total: 40 marks**

Exhibit 1: Underperforming business units – prepared by Steve Gavinson

(1) **The Chester factory**

The Chester factory makes children's clothes and is treated as a profit centre. It has performed poorly and I am convinced it should be closed. For me, the question is when, not if, this closure should happen.   *[handwritten: announced   – provision – NCA held for sale.]*

It is my intention to prepare a formal plan and announce the closure, both publicly and to individual employees, before the 31 December 20X5 year end; then everyone understands their position. If we recognise losses in 20X5 as a result of the proposed closure, I do not mind too much, as they will be seen by shareholders as part of the previous CEO's tenure or part of the turnaround. The closure is planned to take place in March 20X6; however, I do not want closure costs recognised in 20X6, thereby affecting my first full year's profit as CEO.

If the Chester factory were to stay open, I estimate it would make an after-tax profit of only £200,000 per year for the foreseeable future. If we sold off the assets now, a recent valuation has indicated that we would obtain £8 million, after settling all liabilities, but before any closure costs.

Request for financial reporting advice

The following closure costs have been identified. Assuming that the announcement is made before 31 December 20X5, please determine the amount of the provision we can make in the financial statements for the year ended on that date.

	£'000
Statutory redundancy costs	220
Discretionary redundancy costs	340
Retraining of staff redeployed to other sites	200
Legal costs of solicitors for redundancies	22
Impairment of assets to be sold off	64
Expected profit on sale of patent rights	(150)
Penalty to exit a contract with a supplier as a result of the closure	88
Operating losses between date of announcement and date of closure	29
	813

(2) **Kidz Kitz Ltd**

The Kidz Kitz (KK) business unit is a separate subsidiary that operates a store selling children's clothing. The trade and assets of KK, including the brand name, were acquired from a rival company five years ago. KK is treated as a profit centre by TC and its cash flows are independent of the remainder of the group. CGU ⊛

The lease on the building, which is being occupied by the store, expires on 31 December 20X9 and the lessor will take possession of the building on that date. I have therefore decided that KK will cease to trade no later than 31 December 20X9. There will be no surplus assets as the lease will have expired, and closure costs will be approximately equal to the cash generated from the sale of other assets.

However, consideration is being given to immediate closure of KK if a suitable buyer can be found for the assets and a fair price agreed.

The carrying amounts of the assets attributable to KK are expected to be as follows at 31 December 20X5:

	£'000
Property, plant and equipment	1,600
Purchased goodwill	300
Brand name	460
Trade receivables	20
Inventories	380
	2,760

The finance director has prepared the following budgeted cash flows for KK for each of the four years to 31 December 20X9:

	20X6 £'000	20X7 £'000	20X8 £'000	20X9 £'000
Cash receipts from sales	5,200	6,400	6,600	6,300
Cash payments for inventories	(3,680)	(3,760)	(3,840)	(3,580)
Salary payments	(620)	(620)	(620)	(620)
Overhead payments	(900)	(900)	(900)	(900)
Interest payments on loan	(30)	(30)	(30)	(30)
Tax payments	–	(224)	(248)	(240)

disposal group ← It is estimated that the trade and assets of KK, including intangibles, could be sold as a single business for £2.2 million at 31 December 20X5, net of selling costs (which include the lease termination costs). If sold separately at 31 December 20X5, the property, plant and equipment would realise £1.2 million and the brand name could be sold for £220,000.

PPE (impairment)

Assume that operating cash flows occur on the last day of each year and that a tax rate of 20% will apply for the foreseeable future.

Annual discount rates based on a risk-adjusted weighted average cost of capital for KK are as follows:

Before-tax discount rate	7%
After-tax discount rate	6%

Request for financial reporting advice

No impairment losses have previously been recognised in respect of KK, but a competitor entered the market recently which means that impairment testing is required at 31 December 20X5 for KK.

Advice is therefore needed to determine the amount of any impairment and the carrying amount of KK's assets at 31 December 20X5 in the TC consolidated financial statements. Please show the allocation of any impairment losses to each type of asset.

Exhibit 2: New financing – prepared by Steve Gavinson

To support the reorganisation plan and to increase capacity, TC needs to raise new finance of £20 million on 1 January 20X6.

The TC board has decided that issuing ordinary shares is not appropriate at this time because it believes that the share price is significantly undervalued in financial markets, which have not fully recognised TC's growth potential following a reorganisation.

We have identified two alternatives:

Financing alternative 1 – Euro-denominated bank loan

Enter into a 5-year loan of €24 million on 1 January 20X6 at a variable annual rate of interest, which is currently 7% and which tracks the European Central Bank interest rate. Interest is payable annually in arrears. The principal is repayable after five years (that is, on 31 December 20Y0). There would be no issue costs payable by TC. We expect the exchange rate to be £1 = €1.2 on 1 January 20X6.

Financing alternative 2 – Redeemable 9% cumulative preference shares

Issue £20 million of 9% cumulative preference shares at par on 1 January 20X6. The shares will be redeemed at par after seven years (that is, on 31 December 20Y2). Dividends are payable half-yearly in equal amounts (ie, interim and final dividends would each be £900,000).

Exhibit 3: New supplier – prepared by Steve Gavinson

TC's existing factories across Europe provide good quality products and have proved reliable in delivering orders on time.

However, they are now operating close to capacity and have struggled to keep pace with increased demand in recent years.

hedging?   risk – pmt – quality – lead time – reputation

In addition, although our factories are performing well in terms of quality and service, it looks like there are a number of suppliers in Asia who could supply textile products for us more cheaply. However, some of the senior management team have raised concerns about using Asian suppliers, arguing that TC has no experience of operating outside Europe, and most of its revenue is achieved in the UK.

Exhibit 4: Memo from Kirsty Hall – tasks required

Please can you carry out the following tasks which have been requested by Steve Gavinson.

- With respect to the two underperforming business units (**Exhibit 1**): *VIU or disposal?*

  - evaluate, including calculations, the factors that should be considered in making a closure or disposal decision; and

  - determine and explain the appropriate financial reporting treatment in the financial statements for the year ending 31 December 20X5 for each of my two 'requests for financial reporting advice' notes in Exhibit 1.

    Please ignore the tax implications of the decision whether to sell Kidz Kitz or to allow it to continue trading beyond 31 December 20X5. These are being considered separately by our tax advisers.

- Determine the cost of finance in annual percentage terms for each of the two financing alternatives (**Exhibit 2**) and recommend the most appropriate alternative by comparing the risks and benefits. Also, so far as the information permits, explain the financial reporting treatment for each financing alternative.   *(-) affect on EPS??   (-) interest/divs   (+) longer   (-) liquidity   period.*

- Explain the nature of the key assurance procedures that you would perform with respect to the forecasts being made.

- Briefly discuss the issues TC should consider in order to decide whether or not to agree a deal with a new supplier in Asia.   *-) (+) expansion – close to capacity*

Please could you also draft a briefing note for me that sets out any ethical issues for SW and explains any actions that the firm should take.

(+) grow revenue

(-) var. rate but tracks... so predictable?   LD Hedge   (-) 5 yr pmt of cash   (-) currency risk

29 Western Wheels Ltd

Western Wheels Ltd (WW) makes high-quality, alloy wheels for motor vehicles, operating from a single factory located in northern England.

On 1 July 20X3, a large listed conglomerate, Integrated Metals plc (IM), purchased the entire ordinary share capital of WW. The relationship between the WW board and the main IM board has been difficult during the post-acquisition integration period. Particular sources of conflict have been the unexpectedly poor performance of WW since acquisition and the degree of control exercised by the main IM board.

You are an ICAEW Chartered Accountant, newly appointed as an assistant to the IM financial controller, Rachel Roberts. You have been given responsibility for monitoring and evaluating the performance of subsidiary companies, including WW. Rachel has provided you with background information on WW and the motor industry (**Exhibit 1**).

The management accounts of WW for the year ended 30 September 20X5 showed a loss before tax. The WW board prepared profit forecasts for the years ending 30 September 20X6 and 30 September 20X7 (**Exhibit 2**) and brief explanatory notes (**Exhibit 3**).

On receipt of the management accounts and forecasts, Rachel called you into her office for a briefing.

The briefing

Rachel opened the meeting. 'Thanks for coming along. The WW board forecasts a significant improvement in performance over the next two years. However, we just do not believe these forecast figures after the poor performance since acquisition and we are not happy with the explanations provided by the WW board. We need to analyse these management accounts and review the forecasts and the explanatory notes carefully. The board is thinking about asking a firm of independent accountants to provide an assurance report on the forecasts WW have prepared.

'The board is also concerned that, in hindsight, IM might have paid too high a price to acquire WW. I have summarised some of the key figures relating to the acquisition (**Exhibit 4**).

'Despite this, the board believes that WW can be an important part of IM's portfolio going forward. However, I believe that the WW board needs the right control framework and appropriate incentives. I have therefore made a preliminary analysis of the issues surrounding the degree of control exercised by the main board (**Exhibit 5**) and I have suggested a bonus scheme (**Exhibit 6**).

'I need to make a presentation to the IM board so that it can determine a future policy for WW. I would like you to help me prepare this, and will send you a list of tasks that I would like you to carry out for me (**Exhibit 7**).'

Requirement

Prepare the briefing notes requested by Rachel Roberts.

Assume it is now November 20X5.

Total: 40 marks

Exhibit 1: Background information – prepared by Rachel Roberts

The company

IM is a major international listed company operating globally in a number of manufacturing industries which involve the use of metals. It has many subsidiaries, each with a separate board. Each subsidiary is a separate division and the performance of the division is measured and monitored by IM management. There is little trade between group companies.

The IM group control framework is one of a high degree of centralisation where the key operating, investment and financing decisions are approved by the IM main board, even though they may be initiated by subsidiary company boards.

WW was set up twenty years ago by Texas Tyres Inc (TT), a large US company, which owned 100% of WW's share capital. By 20X3, WW no longer fitted into TT's strategic plan and the TT board therefore sold all of its WW shares to IM on 1 July 20X3.

While it was owned by the TT group, the WW board had autonomy over operations and could borrow independently using external sources. Control was exercised by the parent through the monitoring of profit before tax and return on capital employed, which were the key measures of performance.

WW operates a just-in-time manufacturing process, so minimal inventories are maintained.

The industry and market

Sales of alloy wheels are almost entirely to car manufacturers, with four new wheels required for each new car.

UK car production was 1.5 million vehicles in the year ended 30 September 20X4 and is expected to grow at around 2% per year over the next few years. Annual global car production is 66 million cars and is not expected to change over the next few years.

The quality and price of alloy wheels can vary significantly depending on the design and materials used, and also the size of the vehicle.

Exhibit 2: Management accounts – prepared by WW board

Statements of profit or loss: years to 30 September

	Actual 20X4	Actual 20X5	Forecast 20X6	Forecast 20X7
Units : (number of wheels sold)				
Home	352,000	315,000	346,500	381,100
Export	132,000	119,000	142,800	171,400
Total	484,000	434,000	489,300	552,500
	£'000	£'000	£'000	£'000
Sales:				
Home	35,200	31,500	38,115	45,732
Export	13,200	11,900	14,280	17,140
Total sales	48,400	43,400	52,395	62,872
Direct costs				
Materials	9,680	8,246	8,807	9,392
Factory payroll	14,520	13,020	14,679	16,575
Total direct costs	24,200	21,266	23,486	25,967
Contribution	24,200	22,134	28,909	36,905
Indirect costs				
Production overheads (including depreciation)	18,150	16,275	18,349	20,719
Other fixed costs	4,420	3,953	3,957	3,934
Development costs	900	1,500	0	0
Provisions	400	400	0	0
Total indirect costs	23,870	22,128	22,306	24,653
Operating profit	330	6	6,603	12,252
Interest on loan	140	140	140	140
Profit/(loss) before tax	190	(134)	6,463	12,112

Extracts – Statements of financial position

	Actual 20X4	Actual 20X5	Forecast 20X6	Forecast 20X7
	£'000	£'000	£'000	£'000
Equity	15,000	14,866	21,329	33,441
Loan	2,000	2,000	2,000	2,000

Exhibit 3: Brief explanatory notes to management accounts – prepared by the WW board

The WW board recognises that the performance for the year ended 30 September 20X5 was disappointing. Trading conditions were difficult in both the UK and overseas markets. Exchange rate movements did not help export sales.

In order to offset the decrease in sales, the WW board made cost reductions by stopping overtime for staff and not replacing staff who left the company.

WW continued to invest in the development of new products in 20X5 and, as a result, some design improvements will be implemented in early 20X6.

Faults were discovered in some types of wheel in August 20X4 and a provision of £400,000 was made in the financial statements for the year ended 30 September 20X4 for the expected costs that will arise from product recalls. This provision is likely to prove inadequate based on the latest estimates and a further provision of £400,000 was made during the year ended 30 September 20X5.

The WW board is optimistic that sales will improve and that the company will return to profit next year. A key strategy will be to improve the quality of the product design based on the development work and thereby increase sales volumes. We will also charge increased prices in the UK market, but not in export markets. Cost savings will be made in key areas to enhance profit.

Exhibit 4: Summary of figures relating to the purchase of WW – prepared by Rachel Roberts

	Forecast 20X4	Forecast 20X5	Forecast 20X6	Forecast 20X7
	£'000	£'000	£'000	£'000
Revenue	48,600	49,500	52,395	62,872
Operating profit	2,300	3,100	6,603	12,252
Profit before tax	2,160	2,960	6,463	12,112

The fair value of net assets acquired on 1 July 20X3 was £18.6 million, which included £550,000 for the WW brand name. IM has continued to use the WW brand post-acquisition.

IM paid £24 million to acquire 100% of WW's share capital.

Exhibit 5: Group control framework – prepared by Rachel Roberts

The WW board is responsible to the IM board for the performance of the company and it is required to prepare, report and explain its management accounts on a monthly basis.

A source of frustration for the WW board has been the rejection by the IM board of some key proposals on pricing and on the purchase and sale of assets.

The WW board is not allowed to borrow independently outside the IM group to finance its activities. Also, it is not allowed to raise new share capital. A £2 million loan from IM was made to WW on 1 October 20X3.

The IM board has expressed a willingness to make WW an exception in future to its normal policy of centralisation, in order to improve its divisional performance. My suggestion is that WW should have similar autonomy and measures of performance as was the case when WW was owned by TT (see **Exhibit 1**).

Exhibit 6: Bonus scheme for WW directors – prepared by Rachel Roberts

There are eight directors on the board of WW. They currently receive remuneration of a fixed annual basic salary, averaging £160,000 per annum. It has been recognised that this method of remuneration fails to give direct incentives to directors to improve the division's performance.

I am therefore suggesting a new remuneration structure for the WW directors. They would be asked to agree to a 15% reduction in basic salary with effect from 1 January 20X6. In return, they would each be awarded a cash bonus of £80,000 if they achieved their forecast operating profit (**Exhibit 2**) for the year ending 30 September 20X6; and a further £100,000 bonus each if they achieved their forecast operating profit for the year ending 30 September 20X7.

If the forecasts are not achieved, no bonus would be awarded.

If the forecasts are achieved, the bonuses for the years ending 30 September 20X6 and 30 September 20X7 would be paid on 31 December 20X6 and 31 December 20X7 respectively.

Exhibit 7: Briefing notes – prepared by Rachel Roberts

To help me with my presentation for the board, please prepare the following briefing notes.

- Evaluate the performance of WW for the year ended 30 September 20X5. Use the data and explanations provided (**Exhibits 2 and 3**) but, for this purpose, ignore the WW board forecasts. Indicate where further information is needed to make a more complete assessment of performance.

- Review and critically appraise the forecasts made by the WW board (**Exhibit 2**). In so doing, identify and evaluate any key underlying assumptions and discuss the adequacy of the supporting explanations (**Exhibit 3**), highlighting any key information omitted.

- Explain the implications for the asset values in the IM group financial statements for the year ended 30 September 20X6 of WW's actual trading performance compared to the forecast figures (**Exhibit 4**).

- Evaluate the benefit of asking a firm of independent accountants to review WW's forecasts, and assess the extent to which the accountants will be able to provide a report on the forecasts.

- With respect to the IM group control framework (**Exhibit 5**), explain whether the current approach is likely to have affected the performance of WW and comment on whether my suggested alternative approach is likely to improve WW's future performance.

- For the bonus scheme (**Exhibit 6**):

  - evaluate its likely impact on the motivation of the members of the WW board to improve performance; and

  - set out the impact on the financial statements of WW for the years ending 30 September 20X6 and 30 September 20X7 (assuming that the bonus is awarded).

Ignore tax issues. We will consider these later.

30   Stark plc

Stark plc is a listed company which operates a chain of retail stores throughout the UK, selling electrical products and appliances for domestic households.

You are recently qualified and working in the business advisory and assurance section of a firm of ICAEW Chartered Accountants, Karl & Kotter LLP (KK). Jim Mannister is the financial controller of Stark, which is a client of your firm. Stark is not audited by KK.

Jim called KK last week to arrange a meeting with your line manager, Jo Janus. You accompany Jo to the meeting. On arrival, Jim came straight to the point:

'What I am about to tell you is confidential. If we are to continue profit growth, we need to make an acquisition. Retail floorspace is currently a constraining factor, but we also need to widen the markets to which we appeal. I have provided some background details about Stark (**Exhibit 1**) as I believe neither of you have previously worked on a Stark assignment.

The Stark board has identified a target company, Halaga and Harbella Ltd (HH). This is a large unlisted company which retails electrical goods, related to home entertainment, through large out-of-town retail warehouses (**Exhibit 2**). We have had high-level discussions with the HH board and it has provided us with some limited information, from which we have made some working assumptions (**Exhibit 3**). HH has also provided draft financial statements and operating data (**Exhibit 4**). Negotiations are still at a preliminary stage, so we are a long way from agreeing a valuation, but things look promising so far.

We will request KK to carry out full due diligence when we are closer to a deal but, for the time being, I would like your firm to provide assurance by carrying out initial financial due diligence procedures on the draft financial statements that have been made available by HH. Also, before we can go further with the acquisition and then make a firm offer, the Stark board has asked me to produce some financial analysis to estimate a preliminary valuation of HH shares, as a basis on which to make a bid. I would like your help with this task.

The board is also keen to have a clear focus of the nature of our post-acquisition strategy for HH and how we can best integrate it into the existing Stark business model. One choice is to maintain Stark and HH as two independent operating units with two separate brands. The other choice is to rebrand all outlets in the new group under the Stark brand name, then operate as one unified business.

Two further issues related to the valuation of HH shares have arisen so far:

Brand valuation

We need some basis to value the HH brand. In part, we believe that this might affect the overall valuation of HH shares and also we need this value for separate recognition at fair value in the consolidated financial statement of the new Stark group should we eventually make the acquisition.

Pension fund deficit

The second of these issues relates to the measurement of the HH pension fund deficit. We consider this may affect the valuation of HH shares but the Stark and HH boards cannot agree on the basis for valuation of the deficit. To help us negotiate with the HH board, the Stark board would like KK, as ICAEW Chartered Accountants, to provide an independent valuation of the HH pension fund deficit. The HH board has agreed to give KK open access to any information required for this purpose. Please let me know if you would be willing to accept this engagement.'

'The board would like KK to help me, by preparing a report to address all the matters I have discussed. To help you, I am providing you with the following information:

Exhibit 1 – Background details – Stark
Exhibit 2 – Background details – HH
Exhibit 3 – Initial acquisition discussions and working assumptions
Exhibit 4 – HH financial statements and operating data
Exhibit 5 – HH brand valuation
Exhibit 6 – HH pension fund deficit
Exhibit 7 – External property valuer's report.'

After the meeting Jo Janus sent you an email requesting that you prepare each of the following sections of a report, so she can respond to Jim Mannister:

(1) In order to provide initial assurance, set out preliminary financial due diligence procedures on the draft financial statements and notes of HH for the year ended 30 September 20X2 (Exhibit 4) which: (1) explain any significant concerns you have with HH's financial reporting policies and estimates; and (2) review the financial statement items for reasonableness, so far as the information currently available permits. I am particularly concerned that, if earnings are to be used as a basis for valuing HH shares, they are measured in a way that is fit for purpose of an equity valuation. Do not worry about the brand value for this purpose.

(2) Estimate the value of the entire ordinary share capital of HH for the purpose of Stark making a bid. I would like you to make two alternative estimates using each of the following valuation methods: (1) discounted earnings based model; and (2) net assets based model. Use the working assumptions provided in Exhibit 3. Explain any key concerns you have with your valuation.

(3) Explain and evaluate the two choices available to Stark in respect of the post-acquisition integration of HH, being either to: (1) maintain Stark and HH as two independent operating units with two separate brands; or (2) rebrand HH outlets with the Stark brand and operate as one unified business.

(4) Explain the methods by which the fair value of the HH brand could be determined for the purpose of recognition of the brand asset in the Stark Group consolidated financial statements for the year ended 30 September 20X4 (**Exhibit 5**). Estimate the brand value for this purpose.

In addition to these sections of the report, please draft a letter responding to Jim's request for KK to accept an engagement to estimate the value of the HH pension deficit. The letter should explain the ethical issues which would be associated with accepting this engagement.

Requirement

Respond to Jo's instructions.

Assume the current date is October 20X2.

Total: 55 marks

Exhibit 1 – Background details: Stark

Stark was established 50 years ago as a retailer of large electrical appliances for kitchens, which were growing in popularity at that time. These are commonly known as 'white goods' and include, for example: cookers, dishwashers, fridges, freezers, washing machines and tumble driers.

Over the years Stark has expanded into other types of portable electrical products (sometimes known as 'brown goods') including for example: televisions, DVD players, personal computers, laptops and digital media players.

Stark owns a UK-wide chain of 72 upmarket electrical retail stores located in city centres and town centres. Due to the cost of city centre locations, retail floorspace is limited. The business model is therefore to sell a restricted product range, but only from the best quality global suppliers. Typically, Stark's prices would be two to three times the price of mid-market brands sold by other retailers and high profit margins are earned on each item sold. The company generates annual revenue of £360m. Stark has an excellent brand and the marketing position of the company was summarised by the Stark chairman who once said: 'we don't sell appliances; we sell image'.

The Stark finance director explained some issues:

'A particular concern has been with the white goods division, which is only breaking even overall. Floorspace is at a premium in our stores. Every store manager wants more floorspace in order to sell more goods. Our space problem is most acute in white goods, because the appliances are physically large and customers tend not to replace them frequently, particularly in a recession, so the inventory turnover is slow and getting slower. We are also competing against large out-of-town specialist stores which acquire much cheaper land and therefore have up to ten times the floorspace in one of their stores compared to a typical Stark store in a city centre.

It is not just floorspace. The upmarket image of Stark has prevented us from buying reasonable quality, low-cost brands from developing countries in East Asia. These products are just what customers of rival companies are now buying in high volumes because they are really good value. There is always a market for image but, for technologically advanced brown goods, products that are good quality today will become old technology next year. For example, the best quality televisions today will be outperformed by more up-to-date cheaper brands being produced in a couple of years.'

Exhibit 2 – Background details: HH

HH owns four large, out-of-town retail warehouse outlets, selling a wide range of electrical goods, based on home entertainment, including: televisions, DVD players, CD players, sound systems, home cinema and digital media players. HH sells goods at the lower end of the price range applying its 'low-cost, high-value' strategy.

The HH chief executive, Jed Bodine, founded the company fifteen years ago and sales have grown rapidly through discounting, with low prices appealing initially to low-income groups, but increasingly to mid-income groups in the recession. A key aspect of the business model is to display a significant range of inventories, using large warehouse outlets, in order to provide consumer choice.

Exhibit 3 – Initial acquisition discussions and working assumptions

Discussions with HH

In preliminary discussions, Jed Bodine has stated: 'HH is a growing business and it is important that any valuation, agreed upon for the acquisition, fully reflects the future potential growth in earnings of HH.' He pointed out that profit after tax grew significantly from 20X1 according to the draft financial statements for the year ended 30 September 20X2.

Jim Mannister agreed that earnings could be a possible basis for determining HH's share valuation, but is sceptical about the quality of HH's earnings and the apparent high growth in reported earnings claimed by Jed.

Working assumptions

The Stark board would like KK to use the following working assumptions in valuing the shares of HH:

- Given that negotiations may take some time, the acquisition will take place on 1 October 20X3 and the valuations should be determined at this date.

- When using a net assets based model use fair values, but exclude the brand value.

- Sales volumes for the year ending 30 September 20X3 will be 10% higher than for the year ended 30 September 20X2, but sales prices will be 5% lower.

- Sales volumes for the year ending 30 September 20X4 will be 10% higher than for the year ended 30 September 20X3, but sales prices will be 5% lower.

- Sales revenues and volumes for the year ending 30 September 20X5 and thereafter will be the same as for the year ending 30 September 20X4.

- After 30 September 20X4, annual fixed costs, selling price per unit and variable cost per unit will remain constant.

- The cost of equity to be used for discounting can be assumed to be 10% per annum.

- Operating cash flows occur at the end of each year.

- There will be no change in working capital requirements as a consequence of the acquisition.

- Future corporate tax rates will remain at 25% for all relevant years.

- Make, and state, any other reasonable assumptions.

Exhibit 4 – HH financial statements and operating data

HH draft income statement for the year ended 30 September 20X2

	Notes	20X2 Draft £'000	20X1 £'000
Revenue	1	37,250	35,600
Cost of sales	2	(19,800)	(18,000)
Gross profit		17,450	17,600
Operating expenses			
Administrative and other operating expenses	3	(6,000)	(6,000)
Depreciation	4	(3,000)	(4,000)
Impairment charge	5	–	(1,000)
Restructuring provision	6	–	(1,500)
Write-back of unutilised provision	6	1,150	–
		9,600	5,100
Finance costs		(600)	(600)
Profit before tax		9,000	4,500
Tax		(2,250)	(1,125)
Profit for the year		6,750	3,375

HH draft statement of financial position at 30 September 20X2

	Notes	20X2 Draft £'000
Assets		
Non-current assets		
Property, plant and equipment	7	39,000
Current assets		10,000
Total assets		49,000
Equity and liabilities		
Issued capital (£1 shares)		1,000
Retained earnings		11,230
Equity		12,230
Non-current liabilities		
Loans		12,000
Retirement benefit obligation		20,750
Current liabilities		
Tax payable		2,250
Trade creditors		1,770
Total equity and liabilities		49,000

Notes

1 Due to competitive conditions HH reduced all its selling prices on 1 October 20X1 by 5% in order to expand sales volumes.

2 Cost of sales for HH consists entirely of variable costs. The cost of purchasing each item is expected to remain constant for some years due to competitive market conditions.

3 Administrative and other operating expenses comprise entirely of fixed costs.

4 HH reviewed the useful lives of its non-current assets at 1 October 20X1 (see valuer's report in Exhibit 7). As a result of this review, it extended the remaining lives of property substantially. Had it not changed the asset lives, the total depreciation charge for the year ended 30 September 20X2 would have been £4m.

5 The impairment charge in the year ended 30 September 20X1 related to a decline of the value in use of a poorly performing outlet.

6 The provision in the year ended 30 September 20X1 related to an intended restructuring of the business that had been announced on 13 September 20X1. HH claimed that, due to union pressure, the size of the intended reconstruction was scaled down in March 20X2 and therefore some of the provision was no longer required, with the unutilised provision being written back in the year ended 30 September 20X2.

7 Property, plant and equipment includes the four retail warehouse outlets which are owned by HH.

All non-current assets are stated at historical cost less depreciation, as follows:

Cost	Warehouse outlets £'000	Fixtures and fittings £'000	Total £'000
At 1 October 20X1	42,000	20,000	62,000
Additions	–	5,000	5,000
At 30 September 20X2	42,000	25,000	67,000
Accumulated depreciation			
At 1 October 20X1	17,000	8,000	25,000
Depreciation charge for the year	2,000	1,000	3,000
At 30 September 20X2	19,000	9,000	28,000
Carrying amount			
At 30 September 20X2	23,000	16,000	39,000

The fair value of the owned properties at 30 September 20X2 is £34.5m and this amount has been unchanged for some years.

All land is held under operating leases.

Exhibit 5 – HH brand valuation

The HH company brand has been supported by national advertising and is well recognised throughout the UK. Consumer surveys show that the brand is trusted and the 'low price, high-value' slogan is one which is generally understood. Consumers also reported that they identify the brand with good service and honesty in being able to return unsatisfactory goods to HH after sale. All goods are sold under the manufacturer's brand name. No products carry HH's own brand, but the HH company brand attracts customers.

The HH board has claimed, based on market research that, compared to stores whose brand is unknown or little known, sales volumes are significantly higher in an HH outlet due to the HH brand name. Specifically, it is estimated that the HH brand accounts for 5% of its sales volume. Customers would not however be willing to pay any more for goods sold through HH outlets compared to rival companies, as they expect low prices from HH.

HH has spent significant amounts in recent years on advertising, which has been specifically targeted at brand support and promotion. It is estimated that for a competitor to establish a similar brand from a zero base would require many years' advertising expenditure, at about £200,000 per year, with a present value of £4.5m.

A large US electrical retailer, Dice Inc, offered HH £2m in 20X0 to acquire the global rights to the HH brand outside the UK. This offer was rejected by the HH board.

Exhibit 6 – HH pension deficit

HH operates a defined benefit pension fund for its directors and senior managers. It has been agreed that this would continue after an acquisition.

The boards of Stark and of HH have attempted to agree on a valuation of the pension fund deficit for the purposes of the acquisition. However, there are a number of key differences in estimates and assumptions that significantly affect their estimated amounts for the pension deficit. No valuation of the pension fund deficit has been carried out by actuaries for over two years.

One of these differences between the two boards' views is that the HH board believes the annual discount rate used to determine the present value of the pension obligations should be 7%, while the Stark board believes it should be 3%. The draft financial statements have been prepared on the basis of a discount rate of 5% as a temporary compromise, but without agreement or commitment to this figure. This has resulted in a preliminary estimate of £20.75m for the pension deficit. However, neither board is happy with this measurement, as they both believe that the pension valuation will be significant in agreeing a valuation for HH shares if an acquisition takes place.

Exhibit 7 – Extracts from external property valuer's report – prepared by Poon and Ponsonby, chartered surveyors

We have reviewed the value and the probable useful lives of the properties held by HH. These comprise four retail warehouse outlets.

The extension of the remaining useful lives of the warehouses from 14 years to 21 years is appropriate for the main structure of the buildings. However, when the warehouses were acquired, they comprised separate elements such as air conditioning, roofing and heating which were included in the value of the property, rather than as separate fixture and fittings. These separate elements would not have a remaining useful life of 21 years.

Land is excluded from this review as it is held under operating leases.

Poon and Ponsonby

31   Looster Lagoona plc

'We have two problems: liquidity and solvency. If we don't sort them out soon our next problem will be how to wind up the company.' Carl Zheng, the finance director of Looster Lagoona plc (LL), was summarising the company's current situation for his fellow directors at a board meeting. The meeting was eventually concluded by deciding that LL should seek independent external help from its accountants and business advisers, Sen and Sealy LLP (SS).

You are a senior working for SS and you have been asked to accompany the engagement manager, Gaynor Grimes, to a meeting with Carl Zheng. LL is not audited by SS.

Meeting with the finance director

LL is an AIM listed company which manufactures high quality furniture. Carl has been concerned for some time about a decline in LL's sales which he attributes to the market becoming more competitive. Although hoping for an upturn in market conditions, this has not materialised and operating cash flows have worsened, resulting in poor liquidity.

Carl commenced the meeting by summarising the current position: 'The company is facing a major financing crisis. LL has suffered poor operating results in the economic downturn. Despite drastically cutting back on new investment in plant and machinery, our overdraft has increased substantially and while the board has a plan for recovery from 20X3, this will not be implemented unless we can restructure our financing and thereby survive the short term.

When we prepared our management accounts for the nine months ended 30 September 20X2, we were in breach of loan covenants on our overdraft and our loan, both of which are with Brewster Bank plc (Brewster). A new manager, Rob Emerald, from the bank's recoveries department, has been assigned by Brewster to deal with our account. He explained that, as a result of the breach in the covenants, all borrowings are immediately repayable and that the bank is unwilling to continue with either the overdraft or the loan on the current terms. As a consequence, LL may need to enter into administration ⊛ if we cannot agree suitable new terms with Brewster, or refinance all our borrowing with an alternative   *or* lender. Winding up the company would be a tragedy for all our stakeholders.

Rob Emerald has suggested that Brewster may consider a refinancing package for both the current loan and the overdraft, if it can be convinced about the strength of our recovery and future cash flows. I have provided a letter from Rob Emerald which sets out an extract from the conditions suggested by Brewster for replacement financing (**Exhibit 1**). Frankly, the board considers the suggested annual interest rate of 10% to be punitive. Our existing overdraft and loan are both at an annual interest rate of 5%. I have also set out some thoughts on corporate governance following Brewster's demands for a review (**Exhibit 2**).

The board has investigated alternative sources of refinancing and we have found two further refinancing packages. I have outlined these in the supporting notes to this meeting (**Exhibit 3**). I have also provided you with some background information about LL and supporting financial information and forecasts (**Exhibit 4**).

What I would like from SS is a report that explains the current liquidity and solvency position of LL and a clear and reasoned recommendation regarding the best method of refinancing for LL. I am also concerned about how each of the refinancing arrangements would impact on our financial statements. I have set out what I require in more detail in the supporting notes to this meeting in the summary terms of our engagement (**Exhibit 5**).'

Summary of supporting notes to the meeting

LL has provided Sen and Sealy with the following supporting notes to the meeting:

Exhibit 1 – A letter from Rob Emerald of Brewster Bank, setting out the conditions for replacement financing and suggestions for improvements in LL's governance arrangements.

Exhibit 2 – Summary of LL's current governance arrangements.

Exhibit 3 – Thor: Refinancing packages:

      Package A: fixed term loan and issuing of options

      Package B: convertible loan

Exhibit 4 – LL company background and supporting financial information for LL.

Exhibit 5 – Summary of the terms of engagement with SS.

Engagement manager's instructions

Following the meeting, Gaynor called you into her office. 'I am concerned about the future viability of LL, so the three alternative refinancing arrangements available need to be considered urgently. I would therefore like you to prepare a draft response to each of Carl's requests in his summary of the terms of engagement with SS (Exhibit 5).'

Requirement

Respond to the instructions from the engagement manager.

Assume the current date is October 20X2.

Total: 45 marks

Exhibit 1 – Extract from letter from Rob Emerald, Brewster Bank to the board of LL

Brewster Bank
Threadeagle St
London W1

Brewster Bank has reclassified its financing arrangements with LL to high risk following the breach of the covenant in our loan agreement, based on the company's management accounts for the nine months ended 30 September 20X2.

It is the bank's view that responsibility for this situation rests with the LL board. Notwithstanding these concerns, Brewster Bank is willing to consider a new loan to LL on the following minimum key terms.

(1) A new loan arrangement for a term of six years from 1 January 20X3 at a fixed annual rate of interest of 10%. *more time to repay*

(2) The maximum amount of the loan would be the lower of: *liquidity / cash or £1m only / but must pay £2m.*

- £20m; and

2m? (£8m)

- 200% of net assets as recognised and measured in LL's statement of financial position in accordance with IFRS, at 31 December 20X2 (including the existing loan and overdraft).

(3) The new loan must be used in full by LL to repay the existing loan and overdraft with Brewster Bank.

(4) The LL board must take responsibility for the company's liquidity problem. Going forward, Brewster therefore requires that a review of corporate governance should take place with sufficient changes to assure the bank that LL has sufficient capability to deliver a strategy for recovery. My suggestions are:

likely to have strict loan covenants ↓ Breach?

- Remove the employee representative from board committees.
- Appoint two additional independent non-executive directors.
- Separate the chairman and chief executive roles.

The above terms should not be interpreted as an offer of a loan, but as minimum conditions for consideration by Brewster Bank of a potential loan application by LL.

kd = 10% Rob Emerald

Exhibit 2 – Summary of LL's current corporate governance arrangements

The ordinary share capital of LL and the board of directors comprise:

Investor or director	Role	Shareholding (000's of £1 ordinary shares)
Larry Lagoona	Chief executive and chairman	1,750
Carl Zheng	Finance director	150
Hazel Harvey	Production director	100
Victoria Venture Capital (VVC)	–	2,000
Hank Hogan	Non-executive director (representing VVC)	–
Employees	–	1,000
Jeff Manning	Non-executive director (representing employees)	–
Total		5,000

ICAEW

LL has always maintained a small board of five directors to be able to reach quick agreement and engage in rapid decision making.

All directors sit on the audit committee and risk committee except the employee representative. All directors sit on the remuneration and nominations committee.

↳ *not very independent*

Exhibit 3 – Thor: refinancing packages

Thor refinancing package A – Fixed term loan and issuing of options – prepared by LL treasury department

A financing house, Thor, has offered a refinancing package consisting of two elements as follows:

- A four-year loan from 1 January 20X3. The terms are a £20m, fixed-interest loan at 7% per annum, with interest payable annually in arrears on 31 December. The principal is repayable on 31 December 20X6; and

- The issue of options by LL to Thor on 1 January 20X3. These will allow Thor to acquire 4m newly issued ordinary shares in LL for £5 per share at any time up to 31 December 20X6.   ↳ *4 × 5 = £20m repay loan but not in out control*

The share price at 1 January 20X3 is expected to be £4.50 per share and is not expected to change significantly throughout 20X3.

Under the terms of this refinancing package, LL would not be allowed to pay any dividends before 20X7.

One of the treasury staff working for LL has estimated the fair value at 1 January 20X3 of an option to acquire one LL share to be £1.

Issue costs for this package can be assumed to be minimal. ← *ignore on recognition.*

Thor refinancing package B – Convertible loan – prepared by LL treasury department

Thor has also offered LL the following as an alternative choice to package A:

4m shares

LL would issue £20m of 7% convertible loan stock to Thor at par on 1 January 20X3. Thor would have the right to convert each £100 of convertible loan stock into 20 ordinary shares in LL at any time before 31 December 20X6. Alternatively, Thor could choose to redeem the loan stock at par on that date. Issue costs payable to professional advisers would amount to £500,000. The prevailing market interest rate for similar bonds of equivalent risk, but without conversion rights, is 10% per annum.

— *compound fin instrument.*

Under this agreement no dividends would be paid by LL before 20X7. *implicit*   *split acc/ng*

Exhibit 4 – LL company background and supporting financial information – prepared by Carl Zheng

£1m so can pay now but ↓ liquidity

LL is an AIM listed company which manufactures high quality furniture for use in private households. LL has a 31 December accounting year end.

LL was established over forty years ago by Charles Lagoona, who is the father of Larry Lagoona, the current chief executive. Charles had established a good reputation as a builder of quality furniture, and the business expanded greatly in the last ten years since his son Larry took over.

• EPS / DEPS? Amortised cost ∴ proceeds less trans cost.

Both = 4 yrs → D defencing solvency ⟹ enough cash to repay then?

(−) ↓ immediate liquidity 7%.

• Amount at beginning & end rate is different. ∴ capital cost.

A Redeemable ∴ IRR

Time	CF	DF @ 10%	PV	DF @ 15%	PV
T₀ (20 − 4)	16m				
T₁ – 4 Int	1.4				
T4 repmt	20m				
		2.1		(0.56)	

$$k_d = 10\% + \frac{2.1}{2.1 - -0.56}(15\% - 10\%) = 13.9\%$$

Forecast summary statement of financial position at 31 December 20X2

	Notes	£'000
Non-current assets		
Property, plant and equipment	1	20,000
Current assets		
Inventories		3,000
Trade receivables		3,000
Cash		1,000
Total assets		27,000
Capital and reserves		
Share capital (Ordinary £1 shares)		5,000
Reserves		1,000
Equity		6,000
Non-current liabilities		
5% bank loan		10,000
Current liabilities		
Overdraft		10,000
Other current liabilities		1,000
Total equity and liabilities		27,000

Forecast summary statements of comprehensive income – 20X3 to 20X6

The company does not expect to experience any growth over the period 1 January 20X3 to 31 December 20X6 and therefore the annual statements of comprehensive income for each of the years 20X3 to 20X6 are forecast to be identical as follows:

	Notes	£'000
Revenue		11,000
Operating costs	1	(7,750)
Operating profit		3,250
Finance costs	2	(1,000)
Profit before tax		2,250
Tax	3	–
Profit for the year		2,250

Notes

1   Depreciation amounts to £1m per annum and is included within operating costs. The cost model was used in 20X1 and previous years. The fair value of property, plant and equipment is £30m. The company expects to purchase £1.25m of new plant and equipment each year in order to maintain operations at their current level.   *CAPEX*   *adopt 1st dep^n*

2   The forecast does not take account of any refinancing of the loan and is therefore based on the existing annual interest rate of 5% on the bank loan and overdraft.

3   For tax purposes the company has substantial brought forward trading losses and capital losses. It does not therefore expect any tax liability over the period 20X3–20X6.

Could revalue for Brewer Loan.

Exhibit 5 – Terms of engagement with SS – prepared by Carl Zheng

(1) An assessment of the current and future liquidity and solvency of LL, ignoring any possible refinancing.

(2) A separate evaluation of each of the three alternative methods of refinancing ie the Brewster's offer (Exhibit 1) and the two refinancing packages being offered by Thor (Exhibit 3) under the following headings:

- Impact on liquidity and solvency

- Cost of financing (including calculations of annual percentage rates as far as the information permits)

- Impact on LL's financial statements for each of the financial years ending 31 December 20X3, 20X4, 20X5 and 20X6, with supporting calculations

(3) An assessment of the impact on corporate governance arising from: *– separation of responsibilities*

- the improvements suggested by Rob Emerald (**Exhibit 1**).
- each of the two refinancing packages being offered by Thor. (**Exhibit 3**).
  LR Dilution of SH?

(4) A comparison of the three alternative refinancing methods (ie Brewster and the two Thor refinancing packages), with a reasoned recommendation as to which one LL should select.

32 Funnel Cruises plc

Funnel Cruises plc (FC) is a listed company which operates cruise ships globally. The cruise line industry involves the operation of passenger ships for holiday voyages from 2 days up to longer cruises of over 30 days.

You are a recently qualified ICAEW Chartered Accountant working in the business advisory and assurance department of a large, international firm of ICAEW Chartered Accountants, Reez LLP (Reez). FC is a client, but not an audit client, of Reez.

Gary Gregory is the acting treasurer of FC. The previous treasurer retired in February 20X4, having reached normal retirement age. Gary called Reez last week to arrange a meeting with your manager, Helen Long. You accompany Helen to the meeting.

The meeting

Gary opened the meeting. 'The FC board believes that the company is generally progressing well in its long-term plans to become one of the leading operators in the global cruise line industry. However, the management accounts for the year ended 30 June 20X4 have just been finalised and there has been a fall in operating profit compared with the previous year. We will be carrying out an internal analysis, but we would also like some external, independent scrutiny by Reez of FC's performance.

'I have provided some background details for you about the cruise line industry and FC's operations (**Exhibits 1 and 2**).

I have also provided you with financial and operating information for FC (**Exhibit 3**).

In addition, there are some further issues where the FC board requires the help of Reez. I will provide an overview of these issues now, but I will also send a 'terms of engagement' document following the meeting with a summary of what will be required of Reez.

Foreign currency risk management

FC generates revenue in many currencies and it also incurs costs in different currencies. The board believes that, since the retirement of the previous treasurer, it has not had an adequate understanding of FC's foreign currency risks.

The board is concerned about the cash impact of foreign exchange risk, recognising that most customers pay FC, on average, four months before their cruise takes place.

The board would also like to understand the foreign currency issues relating to interdivisional trading, including settlement procedures for outstanding balances between divisions.

A further issue relates to foreign currency risks arising from payments for new ships that are currently being constructed for FC. These are long-term projects involving significant expenditure in euro.

I have provided some brief thoughts of my own on these issues (**Exhibit 4**), but the FC board has also requested the advice of Reez.

Potential acquisition

FC is considering making a bid for the entire ordinary share capital of Coastal Hotels Inc (Coastal). The board is aware that FC is very dependent on the cruise market and is therefore exposed to industry specific risks, particularly oil price volatility and overcapacity. The board believes that some related diversification is appropriate, while remaining within the wider leisure industry. Coastal fits into this model as it has hotels in a number of the US ports that our cruise ships visit. I have provided you with some initial, limited information (**Exhibit 5**).

A particular issue is that Coastal is making losses, so I am not sure whether the normal methods of valuation using earnings or cash flow would be appropriate. It would be easy just to use the net asset value, but the board would also like to explore other methods of determining an appropriate valuation for Coastal and it would welcome the opinion of Reez.

If we are not relying on earnings to determine the valuation, I am not sure whether detailed due diligence is necessary. If we do perform due diligence, the board is split about whether we should ask Reez to do this work or whether we should perform due diligence using our own staff, who are the industry experts, as the board is interested in more than just financial due diligence.

If FC eventually acquires Coastal's shares for a consideration of less than the fair value of its net assets, please explain how this difference would be dealt with in the FC group financial statements, particularly as Coastal is a US company so the transaction would be in US$.

Data analytics – website dashboard

FC has a website for customers providing details of cruises and the facility to book and pay for cruises and other activities. FC installed software to capture data about the website usage, but it has not yet made good use of that data for marketing purposes.

The FC IT director has provided a dashboard of some of the data captured and analysed (**Exhibit 6**) but he requires guidance to interpret this data and how it may be used in marketing.

Manager's instructions

Following the meeting, Helen called you into her office. 'The FC board would like Reez to prepare a report addressing the issues explained by Gary in our meeting. Gary has now provided more detail of what is required in a 'terms of engagement' document (**Exhibit 7**). Please draft a response to this document.'

Requirement

Respond to the instructions from Helen, your manager, based on the 'terms of engagement' document (Exhibit 7).

Assume the current date is July 20X4.

Total: 60 marks

Exhibit 1 – Background details, the global cruise line industry – prepared by Gary Gregory

The cruise line industry is dominated by multinational companies. The industry is defined as including ocean and sea cruises, but excluding river and lake cruises.

Industry data

In the year ended 30 June 20X4, the global cruise line industry generated revenues of £19.2 billion.

The cruise line industry has grown in recent years despite the economic downturn. Global passenger numbers and sales revenue each increased by 3.5% in the year ended 30 June 20X4.

The global fleet of all cruise line operators has 250 ships, with a total passenger capacity per night at sea of 410,000.

Competition

There is severe competition between cruise line operators with passenger capacity growing through the introduction of new, larger ships.

The largest of the new ships are over 225,000 tonnes, each with a capacity of about 5,400 passengers. By increasing capacity per ship, cruise lines are able to reduce cost per passenger, and encourage increased spending on-board by offering a greater range of amenities and activities.

The high capital cost of entering the market is a significant barrier to entry for new competitors.

Revenue generation

Passenger tickets make up about 75% of total industry revenues. Customers pay for tickets, on average, four months before departure. The other 25% of revenues are from other 'paid for' on-board activities (eg drinks, shopping, spa and beauty treatments) and on-shore excursions. Meals are included in the passenger ticket price, but other 'paid for' activities have become an important source of additional revenue in recent years for most operators.

Exhibit 2 – Background details, FC's operations – prepared by Gary Gregory

Introduction

FC is incorporated in the UK, but it has a dual listing on the London Stock Exchange and the New York Stock Exchange. Shareholders are mainly international institutions. FC reports under IFRS and has a 30 June accounting year end.

Organisational structure

FC is organised into three geographical divisions: UK, US and France. Each division is autonomous and owns and operates a number of ships.

Branding

The company offers mid-market cruises under the single FC brand name.

The fleet of ships

FC has a fleet of 24 ships of different sizes, ranging from 60,000 tonnes (with a passenger capacity of 1,000) up to 130,000 tonnes (with a passenger capacity of 3,600). All ships are owned by FC. There are no leases.

New ships

Two identical new ships are in the process of being built for FC and are scheduled for delivery from an Italian dockyard: *The Spirit of the Sea* in January 20X5; and *The Ocean Odyssey* in March 20X6. Each ship will be 130,000 tonnes, carry 3,600 passengers and each will cost €540m. The contracts are fixed price in euro and overall it will take 3 years to build each ship. Progress payments are made by FC while each ship is being built, and a final payment of €270m is to be made on delivery of each ship.

The treasury department

FC uses a centralised treasury department to co-ordinate the activities of the three divisions. The £ is used as the base currency and is also the functional currency of FC for financial reporting purposes. All divisions inform the central treasury department of their transactions with each other. Central treasury then informs each division of the outstanding amounts payable or receivable to settle the balances arising from interdivisional transactions.

Exhibit 3 – Financial and operating information – prepared by FC management accountant

Management accounts – Statement of profit or loss for years ended 30 June

	20X4	20X3
	£m	£m
Revenue		
Passenger tickets	2,925	3,040
'Paid for' on-board activities and excursions	920	909
Total revenue	3,845	3,949
Operating costs		
Fuel	425	378
Staff costs	435	431
Food	240	241
'Paid for' on-board activities and excursions	250	222
Depreciation	381	380
Other ship operating costs (Note 1)	1,239	1,398
Selling and administration	430	429
Operating profit	445	470
Gain on fuel derivatives	25	–
Gain on foreign currency derivatives	45	–
Earnings before interest and taxes	515	470

Note 1

'Other ship operating costs' are largely fixed and include: port costs, maintenance, repairs, consumables, freight and logistics.

Operating data for years ended 30 June

	20X4	20X3
Number of passengers in year	2,460,000	2,390,000
Occupancy (% of capacity utilised)	90%	92%
Total passenger capacity of fleet per night (at 30 June)	62,000	59,000
Number of staff	22,500	22,500
Number of ships in fleet at 30 June	24	23
Carrying amount of fleet at 30 June (£m)	5,190	4,940
Fair value of fleet at 30 June (£m)	7,000	6,500
Fuel consumption (000's tonnes)	839	849

Exhibit 4 – Foreign currency risks – prepared by Gary Gregory

Operating cash flows

The central treasury department manages foreign currency risks with third parties for the company as a whole.

FC receives cash inflows from customers in a variety of currencies and makes payments for costs in many currencies. In the past, FC has only occasionally hedged its exposure to fluctuations in foreign currency exchange rates on operating cash flows. I would like to recommend to the board that FC should start to use foreign currency derivative financial instruments (futures and options) to hedge currency risks on operating cash flows in a more systematic way.

Interdivisional balances

FC's ships travel around the world and each of the three FC divisions frequently performs maintenance and refuelling of the ships belonging to the other divisions. These services are paid for in local currencies. For example, if the US division pays for costs in US$ on behalf of the UK division then this amount will be owed in US$ by the UK division to the US division.

Similarly, customers in one country, for example the UK, may wish to book a cruise on a US ship. In this case, the UK division would take payment in £ sterling for the booking from the customer, but would then owe this amount in £ sterling, as an interdivisional balance, to the US division which operates the cruise. This results in significant outstanding interdivisional balances in multiple currencies.

The FC board wishes to introduce multilateral netting off of interdivisional balances, but the previous treasurer was dealing with this, so we would appreciate the guidance of Reez. The interdivisional balances at 30 June 20X4 are:

| | Payables division | | |
	UK	France	US
Receivables division			
UK (£)	–	£2.4m	–
France (euro)	–	–	€1.8m
US (US$)	US$6.4m	US$3.6m	–

The treasury department has determined that net settlements will be made in £ sterling and has set the following exchange rates for interdivisional settlements at 30 June 20X4:

	France	US
£1 =	€1.2	US$1.6

New shipbuilding currency risks

Our shipbuilding contracts are typically denominated in euro, as most ships are built in Italy. FC's decisions regarding whether, and how, to hedge foreign currency commitments for new shipbuilding are made on a case-by-case basis, taking into consideration the amount and duration of the exposure, market volatility, currency exchange rate correlation, economic trends, the overall expected net cash flows by currency and other offsetting risks.

In July 20X3, the previous FC treasurer entered into foreign currency, zero-cost collars with FC's bank to hedge the final payment for building *The Ocean Odyssey*. These collars mature in March 20X6 at: a ceiling rate of £0.85 to €1, amounting to £229.5m; and a floor rate of £0.77 to €1, amounting to £207.9m. If the spot rate is between these two rates on the date of maturity, then FC would neither owe any amounts, nor receive any payments under these collars.

I do not really understand the implications of these commitments for risk management. Please explain how the use of these collars affects our foreign currency risks.

Exhibit 5 – Potential acquisition of Coastal Hotels Inc – prepared by Gary Gregory

Coastal owns 10 hotels on the US coast. They have not performed well. The financial statements of Coastal show losses and the hotel carrying amounts have suffered an impairment charge in two of the past four years.

	US$m
Outline data for Coastal is as follows:	
Carrying amount of net assets at 31 December 20X3	32
Fair value of net assets at 31 December 20X3	30
Forecast loss after tax for year ending 31 December 20X4	4
Loss after tax for year ended 31 December 20X3	2

Coastal generated revenue of US$20m in the year ended 31 December 20X3 and forecasts revenue of US$19m for the year ending 31 December 20X4.

Notes

1   The Coastal accounting year end is 31 December.

2   An acquisition date of 30 September 20X4 seems most likely if the deal goes ahead.

3   An acquisition price of US$25m for Coastal's entire ordinary share capital has been suggested by the Coastal board, but this amount has not been agreed.

4   Coastal reports in accordance with IFRS.

5   Assume an exchange rate of £1 = US$1.6.

Exhibit 6 – Dashboard data

The FC website can be used by potential customers to obtain information about ships, facilities, cruises, on-board activities and excursions. The website can also be used to send emails, book cruises and activities and make payment. If customers prefer not to use the website to make bookings, they can also be made through travel agents and other intermediaries.

A new computer programme was installed last year to capture data from the FC website and analyse information for management about the number of hits, visits, unique visits, page views and traffic sources. Timings are also recorded so data patterns can be discerned. This produces large volumes of granular data which can be analysed in a variety of ways to produce management information. The dashboard below is just one configuration of the data.

Data dashboard – website analytics

Year ended 30 June 20X4

Data category	Outcome
Number of visits	32,869,754
Number of unique visits	12,965,982
Number of page views	97,878,296
Hits	1,157,974,936
Average duration of a visit	14.3 minutes
Most popular referral site	Trip advisor
Most popular source of hits – by country:	
UK	41%
US	28%
Other - Europe	22%
Other	9%
Most popular pages (by hits):	
Cruises	34%
Ships	33%
Facilities	15%
On-board activities and excursions	11%
Booking and payment	7%
Emails received from website	578,397

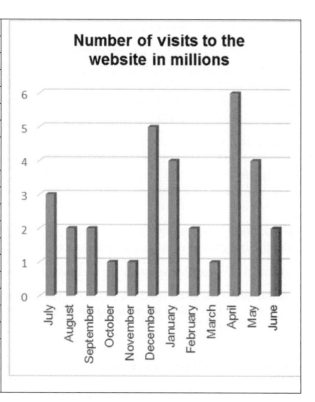

Advertising campaigns were run in April and December in the UK.

Exhibit 7 – Terms of engagement – prepared by Gary Gregory

The FC board requests that Reez prepares a report comprising the following:

(1) Using Exhibit 3 and the other information provided, analyse and explain the performance of FC for the year ended 30 June 20X4.

(2) With respect to FC's foreign currency transactions (Exhibit 4):

- Evaluate whether derivative financial instruments would be the most appropriate method for the centralised treasury department to manage FC's foreign currency risks in respect of its operating cash flows.

- Calculate the £ sterling settlements of interdivisional currency balances at 30 June 20X4 using multilateral netting off procedures. Explain how these procedures may be of benefit to FC.

- Explain how the use of zero cost collars can mitigate foreign currency risks with respect to payments under contracts for building new ships.

(3) So far as the information permits, with respect to FC's potential acquisition of Coastal (Exhibit 5):

- Identify and evaluate suitable methods to determine an acquisition price for Coastal's entire ordinary share capital given that the company is making losses.

- Explain, with calculations, how the difference between the consideration and the fair value of Coastal's net assets would be recognised and measured in the FC group financial statements for the year ending 30 June 20X5. For this purpose assume an acquisition price of US$25m. State any assumptions.

- Explain the benefits of carrying out due diligence for Coastal. Assess whether it would be preferable if this were to be completed by FC staff, or an independent assurance provider, such as Reez.

(4) Using the website dashboard data (Exhibit 6), analyse the results and explain how they may be used effectively in FC's marketing strategy. Identify further information that could usefully be extracted from the data captured.

33 Landex plc

Landex plc is a large-scale manufacturer of high-quality watches. The company's manufacturing facility is based in the UK, but it exports throughout the world.

You are Stella Savoy, an ICAEW Chartered Accountant who has just joined Landex. You have been asked to attend a meeting with the head of procurement, Kieran Black.

The meeting

Kieran opened the meeting. 'Thanks for coming to see me, Stella. I realise that you are new to Landex, so I have provided some background notes about the company (**Exhibit 1**).

The problem is that the directors are not happy. You would think they would be, given the increases in sales that have been achieved in recent years, but they are not. They are concerned that the recent growth achieved is not sustainable due to issues with our supply chain.

The board believes, in particular, that we need to review the procurement arrangements for watch casings. The casings provide the outer shell to hold the watch mechanism and so are critical to our final product. The casings are currently supplied by a local company, Gootle Ltd. However, Gootle no longer has the capacity to supply all our needs efficiently and the situation will worsen unless it invests in new equipment and a new factory.

Prior to making such an investment, the Gootle board is seeking assurances from the Landex board that Gootle will continue to be the sole supplier of watch casings for Landex over the next few years.

Opinion was divided on this issue at a recent Landex board meeting. As a result, three directors have produced briefing papers, each proposing different strategies for Landex's future procurement policy for watch casings over the next four years. I have provided you with these briefing papers (**Exhibit 2**) so that you can evaluate each of these three strategies. To help you, I have provided some forecasts of demand and some working assumptions (**Exhibit 3**).

There are some further issues I would like you to consider:

If, as suggested by the production director, we were to set up our own manufacturing facility in Moldovia (Exhibit 2, Proposal 3), we would need to decide how to finance this investment and I have identified two alternatives (**Exhibit 4**). I would like you to advise us on the more appropriate form of finance and to set out the financial reporting treatment for both alternatives.

Gootle was set up 10 years ago when Landex outsourced its production of watch casings to Gootle. Many of the Landex staff were made redundant as a result of the outsourcing, but transferred their employment to Gootle. They received lower redundancy payments as a consequence of obtaining alternative employment. The Landex chairman, at that time, promised that Landex would always use Gootle as its sole supplier of watch casings. I would like you to set out the ethical position for Landex if we were now to cease using Gootle as a supplier.

Also, the finance director of Landex, Catherine Jurys, has declared a conflict of interest, in that her brother is on the board of one of the suppliers she is proposing, Rotblat (Exhibit 2, Proposal 2). The board has expressed concern about any ethical issues that may arise from this relationship and whether any disclosures would be required in the financial statements. I would like you to draft some notes for the board addressing these issues. However, I advise you to be very careful with anything you may wish to say on this matter, as the finance director is very keen that her proposal should be implemented.

Finally, the board has recently become concerned about cyber security in Landex's supply chain following a cyber incident which affected accounting systems files. I have provided details and would like your advice on how the board should respond (**Exhibit 5**).

Thank you again for coming along to see me. I will provide you with notes of our meeting that set out more precisely what I require you to do (**Exhibit 6**).'

Requirement

Respond to the instructions (Exhibit 6) from Kieran Black, the head of procurement.

Assume the current date is July 20X4.

Total: 55 marks

Exhibit 1 – Landex business background – prepared by Kieran Black

Landex is a listed company generating revenues of over £300m per annum with sales in over 80 countries. The company has a single manufacturing site in the UK and most of its suppliers are also UK companies.

Landex manufactures high quality watches which retail from £1,000 upwards. The brand has widespread global recognition and is a symbol of quality and style. The watches have a traditional mechanism (rather than the quartz movement found in most watches) and are made by skilled employees, largely being assembled by hand.

The watch casings are the most significant bought-in component and are made from high quality glass, along with steel, silver or gold.

Demand, in volume terms, has increased by over 10% per annum in recent years. This has generated significant profit, but the increase in output has brought with it problems of maintaining quality. There have also been difficulties ensuring that the external procurement of components and raw materials is timely, efficient, flexible and within the production capacity of suppliers.

Landex has a 31 December accounting year end.

Exhibit 2 – Directors' briefing papers: three proposed procurement strategies

Proposal 1: Retain Gootle as the sole supplier of watch casings – prepared by operations director, Nancy Ritz

Gootle has supplied us with watch casings for many years and it has been reliable, provided generally good quality products and at a fair price. They also supply on a just-in-time basis so we can hold minimal inventories of watch casings.

Admittedly, Gootle has struggled to keep pace with the rate of expansion achieved by Landex in recent years, but we need to help them solve this issue, not just walk away at the first sign of a problem.

In my view, Landex should build a partnership supply relationship with Gootle, underpinned by a four-year supply contract and monitored by a service level agreement. This will give them the confidence to invest in new equipment and a new factory to expand their capacity and meet our needs in the medium term.

In initial negotiations, the Gootle board has stated that it can supply the watch casings at an average price of £100 each throughout the next four years.

Proposal 2: Have multiple global suppliers of watch casings – prepared by finance director, Catherine Jurys

The problem with Landex is that it is an international company on the demand side, but a very local company on the supply side. We have been too loyal to Gootle as our sole supplier of watch casings. We need to open up the supply contract for watch casings to global competition and have multiple suppliers. These suppliers can then compete on price, quality and service.

Initial investigations have revealed three potential suppliers: Mumbai Casings (India); Rotblat (China); and SH Watches (Vietnam). We can use all of these suppliers to meet our needs.

Contracts would be denominated in local currencies and transport costs would also be incurred in local currencies. Using expected exchange rates at 31 December 20X5, the watch casings could be supplied, on average, for the equivalent of £90 per casing, plus transport costs of £3 each.

Contracts would be renewable annually, so suppliers could be changed, prices renegotiated and competition reinforced on a regular basis. It is expected that, due to competition, the prices in terms of local currencies will not change over the period 20X5 to 20X8, although this is by no means certain.

Proposal 3: Set up Landex's own manufacturing facility in Moldovia – prepared by production director, Sue Harben

If we set up our own manufacturing facility solely for watch casings, we can exercise more control over production volumes, quality and costs. By setting up in a developing economy, like Moldovia, we can gain significant financial benefits from lower costs. Also, we will convert variable costs into fixed costs, which will be a major benefit if demand continues to grow.

The currency of Moldovia is the Moldovian dollar (M$).

I estimate that, on 1 January 20X5, we would incur initial set-up costs of M$40m to build the factory. Variable costs per watch casing are expected to be M$40 and annual fixed costs are estimated to be M$25m. We can exit after four years, if we need to, and sell the factory for M$20m, net of all disengagement costs.

Exhibit 3 – Demand forecasts and working assumptions – prepared by Kieran Black

Demand forecast

It is expected that global sales volumes for Landex watches over the next four years will be as follows:

	Number of watches
20X5	200,000
20X6	220,000
20X7	235,000
20X8	245,000

Each watch requires one casing.

Working assumptions

The following working assumptions should be applied for all three proposals for the procurement of watch casings (Exhibit 2).

- All three proposals would commence on 1 January 20X5 and run for an expected period of four years.

- Calculations are to be made over the four-year planning horizon (ie up to the end of 20X8).

- Landex evaluates projects using an annual discount rate of 10% for present value calculations.

- At 1 January 20X5, the exchange rate with Moldovia is M$2 = £1. However, the M$ will appreciate by 5% per annum against the £ thereafter.

- The basket of currencies used for Proposal 2 (the currencies of India, China and Vietnam) will depreciate at 2% per annum against the £ from 1 January 20X6.

- Operating cash flows will arise at year ends.

- Landex's functional currency is £ sterling.

Do not worry about tax for now. We can deal with this later.

Exhibit 4 – Financing the Moldovian factory – prepared by Landex's treasury department

There are two alternatives for financing the initial cost of M$40m for setting up a Moldovian factory (Exhibit 2, Proposal 3):

Alternative A – issue a zero coupon, M$40m bond at par in Moldovia, on 1 January 20X5, redeemable at a 17% premium on 31 December 20X8.

Alternative B – issue a £20m, 5% bond at par, in the UK, on 1 January 20X5. The financial institution handling the placing would charge 2% of the par value of the bond as a fee, which is payable when the bond is issued. The bond is to be redeemed at par on 31 December 20X8. Nominal interest is to be paid annually in arrears on 31 December.

Exhibit 5 – Cyber security incident and future actions

In June 20X4, an internal review of cyber security by the Landex IT department evaluated the company's technology, including hardware and software. It concluded that there was good resilience to direct cyber attacks on Landex's systems, but this review had not extended to suppliers' IT systems.

On 3 October 20X4, the Landex IT department produced an urgent report for the board notifying them that a malware infection had been discovered in the accounting system purchases and payments files. After an extensive investigation it was discovered that the source of the infection had been files received from a trusted supplier of watch movement mechanisms, Coggs Ltd.

Coggs is a small company with limited resources for managing cyber risks. Coggs IT system is partially integrated with that of Landex to improve the efficiency of ordering and this had been successful, until now.

A review of cyber risks in the supply chain is now taking place and the Landex IT department is seeking advice on the factors that it should consider. It is concerned about supply chain cyber security risk, but it does not want to damage critical business relationships.

Landex has a total of 508 suppliers. Many of these are small companies and some make sales of less than £10,000 a year to Landex. About 260 of the suppliers have some degree of integration with Landex's accounting IT systems.

Exhibit 6 – Extracts from notes of the meeting between Kieran Black and Stella Savoy – prepared by Kieran Black

Please prepare a report to the board addressing the following issues:

(1) Evaluate and compare the three procurement proposals put forward by the directors in their briefing papers (Exhibit 2). Include supporting calculations up to the end of 20X8, and also explain the wider operational and strategic implications of the three proposals. Use the working assumptions and demand forecasts provided (Exhibit 3).

  Also explain, without further calculations, the benefits and risks of each proposal if they operate for longer than four years.

(2) Assume that Landex decides to set up a manufacturing facility in Moldovia. With regard to the two alternatives for financing the Moldovian factory (Exhibit 4):

  • provide reasoned advice as to which of the two bonds should be issued. Include in your analysis supporting calculations of the bonds' annual effective rates of interest to Landex based on £ sterling cash flows.

  • set out the financial reporting treatment of both bonds in the financial statements of Landex for each year that they would be outstanding. Provide supporting calculations.

(3) In respect of the proposed procurement strategies explain:

  • the ethical implications for Landex of ceasing to use Gootle as a supplier.

  • the ethical implications, for Landex and its finance director, arising from her brother's position on the Rotblat board.

(4) Set out any corporate governance and financial reporting issues that may arise for Landex if Rotblat were to become one of its suppliers.

(5) Explain the issues that the Landex board should consider with respect to the cyber security in its supply chain for all suppliers (Exhibit 5). Make recommendations regarding any actions it should take in this respect.

34 Firebrand Forklift Trucks Ltd

Firebrand Forklift Trucks Ltd (FFT) is a manufacturer of diesel-powered forklift trucks with a factory located in Wales. It was established five years ago and exports globally.

Recent years have not been good for FFT. When the company was established, it borrowed to expand, but revenue has decreased since 20X2. Over the last year, FFT has struggled to meet debt interest payments and a long-term bank loan of £100m from Kittminster Bank becomes repayable in December 20X4. There is also an overdraft with Kittminster Bank. FFT cannot obtain the necessary funding to redeem this loan or repay the overdraft.

[handwritten: cash issues — loan — o/draft]

The chairman of FFT, Murray Moore, asked to meet with Rose Ready, who is a partner in Davies & Hyland LLP (DH), a firm of ICAEW Chartered Accountants. You work for DH as a senior in the advisory department.

The meeting

Murray opened the meeting. 'Rose, we are in a state of real crisis. FFT needs your firm's help urgently.

Despite taking all reasonable measures, including factoring of receivables, we are unable to obtain the funding to redeem the loan or repay the overdraft. As a result, Kittminster Bank is considering whether or not to put FFT into administration. Meanwhile, Kittminster Bank has given the FFT board the opportunity to put together a recovery plan in the form of a financial reconstruction and I would like your firm's help with this plan.

Given that FFT is a new client for DH, I have provided you with some information about the forklift truck industry and the market background (**Exhibit 1**). I have also provided the FFT company background (**Exhibit 2**), including some financial and operating data (**Exhibit 3**).

The FFT board has drafted a proposed financial reconstruction scheme (**Exhibit 4**). We would welcome DH's evaluation of this scheme, including whether it is likely to be acceptable to all stakeholders.

If we are allowed by Kittminster Bank to continue to trade, one new proposal to boost revenue is to offer customers the opportunity to lease our forklift trucks, rather than buying them outright. I need DH to evaluate this proposal (**Exhibit 5**) as I want to show it to the bank as a positive move forward, if it permits us to continue trading.

As if we did not have enough problems, last week we received an email from a journalist accusing us, in effect, of unethical trading (**Exhibit 6**). We need your expertise and independent support in this matter, so I would be grateful if you could advise us how we should reply. I also need DH to support our response and to argue that FFT has acted ethically, as we always inform our customers, before and after the sale, about the safe use of our vehicles.

[handwritten: not independent!]

I have attached terms of reference for an engagement between FFT and DH, where I set out more precisely what I require from your firm (**Exhibit 7**).'

Instructions

After the meeting, Rose asks to see you. She outlines what occurred during the meeting with Murray and gives you the following instructions:

'I would like you to provide a draft response to the requests from Murray, the FFT chairman, (Exhibit 7) for my consideration.

In addition, I am concerned about the implications for our firm of giving advice and support to FFT on its response to the journalist (Exhibit 6). Please provide a briefing note for me explaining any ethical issues arising for our firm from giving advice and support to FFT in this matter.'

Requirement

Respond to the instructions from the engagement partner, Rose Ready.

Assume it is now November 20X4.

Total: 60 marks

Exhibit 1 – Forklift truck industry and market background – prepared by Murray Moore

Forklift trucks are powered industrial vehicles used for lifting and moving materials over short distances. They are essential vehicles in warehouses and distribution centres for the movement of goods.

Forklift trucks differ according to how they are powered. The most popular type of power unit is electric, driven by rechargeable batteries. Larger forklift trucks are normally powered by diesel engines. Diesel engine trucks should not be used in an enclosed space because of the health risk from harmful emissions. Many countries have laws against the indoor use of diesel-powered forklift trucks, but there remain a number of countries where it is not prohibited by law.

Forklift trucks also vary significantly in size, which is a key factor in terms of load-bearing ability and price.

The industry is dominated by a number of large international companies. In 20X3, the top 20 global manufacturers generated revenues of about £19,000m from the sale of approximately 950,000 forklift trucks. Annual revenue growth has been around 2% for these companies.

More generally in the industry, the cost of a new forklift truck can vary from £9,000 to around £90,000, depending mainly on the means by which it is powered and the load capacity of the truck. When buying a forklift truck, customers need to consider not just the initial cost, but also the ongoing costs of usage.

Competition in the forklift truck industry is intense and is influenced by a range of factors including brand loyalty, customer service, price, availability, performance, quality, features and the cost of ownership over the life of the forklift truck.

Most major international manufacturers of forklift trucks offer the choice to customers of purchasing or leasing. Leases typically range from short-term hires of a few days to long-term leases of up to six years.

Exhibit 2 – FFT company background – prepared by Murray Moore

In the global forklift truck industry, FFT is a large company, but it is outside the top 20 companies. It was established five years ago as a spin-off from a large Japanese motor manufacturer, Jitsumi. FFT purchases all of its diesel engines from Jitsumi under a long-term contract, which has an exclusivity clause preventing FFT purchasing engines from other manufacturers. FFT is tied into this contract for a further five years and the FFT board believes that it is paying significantly more than the market rate for its diesel engines.

FFT has one factory, which is located in south Wales near the port of Milford Haven, from where it exports its forklift trucks and into which it imports Jitsumi engines and some other components.

FFT currently produces only diesel-powered forklift trucks. These are designed for use in large, outdoor distribution centres and storage facilities.

FFT trucks have proved popular and, as a result, FFT has had a problem in maintaining sufficient production capacity to meet demand. This has partly arisen from a lack of cash to expand its production facilities further after the initial investment five years ago. However, there is also a general feeling by the FFT board that production is not as efficient as it should be. It believes that output is below what could be achieved, even with the existing production facilities. As a consequence, there has been a growing backlog of unfulfilled orders, resulting in a long lead time for customer deliveries.

Exhibit 3 – FFT financial and operating data – provided by Murray Moore

Statements of profit or loss for the years ending 31 December

	Forecast 20X4 £'000	Actual 20X3 £'000	Actual 20X2 £'000
Revenue	667,000	694,300	703,500
Cost of sales	(480,000)	(499,900)	(492,400)
Gross profit	187,000	194,400	211,100
Distribution and administration costs	(195,000)	(199,500)	(201,800)
Operating profit/(loss)	(8,000)	(5,100)	9,300
Finance costs	(5,000)	(5,000)	(5,000)
Profit/(loss) before tax	(13,000)	(10,100)	4,300
Income tax expense	–	–	(860)
Profit/(loss) for the year	(13,000)	(10,100)	3,440

Forecast statement of financial position at 31 December 20X4:

	£'000
Non-current assets	
Property, plant and equipment	132,700
Current assets	
Inventories	23,300
Trade receivables	24,600
Total assets	180,600
Equity	
£1 ordinary shares	40,000
Retained earnings (deficit)	(7,300)
Current liabilities	
Bank loan 5% – Kittminster	100,000
Bank overdraft – Kittminster	35,300
Trade payables	12,600
Total equity and liabilities	180,600

Operating data

	Forecast 20X4	Actual 20X3	Actual 20X2
Operating cash flows (£'000)	2,100	14,600	27,800
Number of trucks sold	39,235	38,570	37,030
Backlog (ie number of trucks ordered by customers, but not produced at each year end)	16,350	12,855	9,260

The forecasts for the year ending 31 December 20X4 are reliable as they comprise actual data from the management accounts for the 10 months ended 31 October 20X4, plus the final two months of forecast figures.

Exhibit 4 – Proposed financial reconstruction scheme – prepared by Murray Moore

The terms of the proposed financial reconstruction are:

- FFT to issue to existing ordinary shareholders: 10m, additional new £1 shares, for cash of £10m.

- Kittminster Bank to accept a new arrangement: a new loan of £120m, at 8% per annum, redeemable on 31 December 20X9 at par, in exchange for cancelling its existing loan and overdraft. No cash would be paid or received on this exchange.

- FFT to make a payment of £2m to suppliers in partial settlement of trade payables, in order to secure the existing supply chain for the future. Of this total, it is proposed that £1.9m should be paid to Jitsumi. Payments would be made from operating cash flows.

The cash raised from the new share capital would all be invested in plant and machinery which will enable more efficient production and a gradual reduction in the backlog of orders. As a consequence, it is estimated, as a working assumption, that FFT will be able to generate operating profits of £14m in the year ending 31 December 20X5 and in each year thereafter for the foreseeable future.

If the financial reconstruction scheme is not accepted and FFT is placed into administration by Kittminster Bank, the most likely outcome is that FFT will be liquidated.

The proceeds generated from the sale of the assets in a liquidation at 31 December 20X4 are estimated to be:

	£'000
Property, plant and equipment	83,300
Inventories	13,300
Trade receivables	19,500

Other factors:

- Liquidation costs would be about £3.2m.

- Kittminster Bank holds a fixed charge, in respect of the loan, over all property, plant and equipment. In the loan agreement, there is also a floating charge over all FFT assets.

- All the overdraft is due to Kittminster Bank in respect of which it holds a floating charge over all FFT assets.

- Of the trade payables at 31 December 20X4, £9m is due to Jitsumi. The Jitsumi board has become aware of the financial problems that FFT is experiencing and is refusing to supply further diesel engines unless outstanding balances are paid immediately. FFT holds only a small number of engines as they are supplied on a just-in-time basis.

FFT has a cost of equity of 10% per annum. The tax rate is 20%.

Exhibit 5 – Lease or buy choice for customers – prepared by Murray Moore

FFT does not currently offer customers the choice to lease its forklift trucks. However, it is being proposed that, in order to boost revenue from one of our most popular types of forklift truck, the FZ101, we should introduce for customers the alternative of leasing from FFT.

We propose to offer the FZ101 to customers under a three-year lease agreement. The lease payment would be £1,200 per quarter, payable quarterly in arrears. At the end of the lease, after three years, FFT would sell the used FZ101 for about £4,000. The annual discount rate for this type of project is 8.24%.

The list price of a new FZ101 is £16,200 and the variable cost of manufacture is £12,300.

Under the lease agreement, FFT would not be responsible for repairs and maintenance.

Exhibit 6 – Email to the FFT board – from the journalist, Barry Bankhurst

The following email has been received from a journalist working for 'The Record', a major national newspaper:

To: FFT Board
From: Barry Bankhurst, Journalist with 'The Record'
Date: 1 November 20X4
Subject: Health and Safety concerns with FFT's exported forklift trucks.

We have been carrying out a piece of investigative journalism on the health and safety of exports by UK manufacturers.

It has come to our notice that some FFT diesel-powered forklift trucks exported to developing nations are being used inside warehouses by a number of employers. As a result, we believe that the emissions from the diesel engines have caused health problems for some of the employees driving them.

Moreover, we have discovered that FFT's sales documentation has not given clear warnings in the relevant local languages about the indoor use of diesel-powered forklift trucks.

We intend to publish an article in 'The Record' next week disclosing these discoveries. Before we do so, the editorial board has asked me to give you the right to respond and to justify FFT's actions. Your response may also be published in the article.

As part of this newspaper's contribution to the public interest, we are also requesting that the FFT board makes a public undertaking that the company will, with immediate effect, cease selling diesel-powered forklift trucks to those companies that are carrying out this practice of indoor use.

Barry Bankhurst
Journalist
The Record

Exhibit 7 – Terms of reference – prepared by Murray Moore

The FFT board would like DH to prepare a report which:

(1)   explains the decline in FFT's profit over the years ended 31 December 20X2, 31 December 20X3 and 31 December 20X4. Recommend actions which may improve profitability in future.

(2)   with respect to the financial reconstruction scheme (Exhibit 4):

- evaluates the effects of the proposed scheme and compares these with the effects of liquidation, setting out the benefits and risks for the various stakeholders and providing supporting calculations.

- shows and explains the financial reporting implications for the financial statements for the year ending 31 December 20X4 if, at that date, negotiations are still ongoing between FFT and Kittminster Bank regarding a restructuring of the loan.

(3)   with respect to the proposal to boost revenue (Exhibit 5):

- evaluates, with supporting calculations, the benefits and risks to FFT of leasing, compared with selling, the FZ101 forklift truck to customers.

- explains how a lease for an FZ101 forklift truck would be treated in the FFT financial statements.

(4)   advises the FFT board how it should respond to the email from the journalist. Please indicate any future actions that FFT should take with regard to this matter, now that the issue has been brought to its attention.

35   Washing Solutions Ltd

'I just don't understand what has gone wrong.' Richard Avebury, the managing director of Washing Solutions Ltd (WS), was opening a meeting with Xenon, Young and Zhang LLP (XYZ), a firm of ICAEW Chartered Accountants.

WS is a private company which manufactures washing machines used for cleaning clothes and other textiles. It has two divisions: the Industrial Division and the Household Division.

You are a senior working for XYZ, which acts as business advisers to WS. The XYZ engagement manager, Hayley Hughes, attended the meeting with Richard.

The meeting

Richard continued the meeting after his opening remarks: 'We appointed a new management accountant last year and he introduced a cost allocation system that has been a disaster. I had to dismiss him last month. The problem is that I do not trust the budget or the management accounts and unfortunately the finance director has been ill for some time, so I have little experienced internal financial expertise to call on.

'I have therefore sent you some background information about the company (Exhibit 1) but, in brief, WS manufactures two ranges of washing machine: large industrial machines and smaller machines for domestic households.

On 1 October 20X3, WS implemented a strategy of quality improvement for the industrial washing machines. This required additional labour hours and some overhead costs, but we thought these additional costs would be worthwhile as the changes would be appreciated by customers, who would then be willing to pay more for the machines.

However, since we made the quality improvement changes, we have won only a few tenders, when we would normally have won three to four times as many. It has been a terrible year for the Industrial Division. All we did was try to recover, in the tender price, the additional costs we incurred from quality improvements. I have sent you more information so you can see the details of our performance in tendering (Exhibit 2).

I have also sent you some data prepared by the management accountant who has now left the company (Exhibit 3A) and an analysis of actual overhead costs (Exhibit 3B) prepared by the production director. I would like XYZ to examine what has happened with our overhead cost allocations and their impact on pricing and on inventory valuation for external financial reporting purposes.

Unexpectedly, I recently received an email from a rival firm, Hexam, which also makes industrial washing machines. Their chief executive said that he had heard about the problems WS has been experiencing with its Industrial Division and enquired whether we would be interested in selling the division to Hexam, at a reasonable price.

We would not have been interested in selling the Industrial Division a few months ago but, given the problems we are now having, it might not be a bad idea to sell it. I am just wondering why Hexam is so interested in buying the division, just as it seems to be underperforming. I would like XYZ to evaluate whether selling the division would be the right thing to do. I have provided some more details on Hexam's offer (**Exhibit 4**).

I have set out more precisely what I require from XYZ in the terms of engagement document (**Exhibit 5**).'

Your instructions

Hayley updated you with what had happened at the meeting and provided you with the supporting documentation from Richard. She then outlined the following: 'I would like you to draft briefing notes for me giving a response to the instructions in the 'terms of engagement' from WS (Exhibit 5). Please be clear and provide as much relevant information as you can, as I will not have time to come back to you with any questions prior to my next meeting with Richard.'

Requirement

Respond to the instructions from Hayley, the engagement manager.

Assume it is now November 20X4.

Total: 40 marks

Exhibit 1 – Company background – prepared by Richard Avebury

WS is a private company that produces washing machines for cleaning clothes and other textiles. It operates from a single factory in the south of England. The company has two divisions: the Industrial Division and the Household Division. Each division has its own product range, although some manufacturing processes are common to both divisions and there is some shared production machinery.

The Industrial Division makes a range of large, industrial washing machines, for use in the public sector (typically in hospitals, schools, local authority premises, prisons and military establishments). Sales of industrial washing machines are achieved by winning government tenders. Normally, each tender is for between 10 and 40 machines. Tenders are not solely awarded on the basis of the lowest bid, but price is a key factor and there is a control procedure by government staff to make sure that manufacturers' profits on any contract are not deemed to be excessive, when assessed on a full cost plus basis.

The Household Division makes a range of washing machines for use in private households. Customers tend to be large retailers and prices are set by market forces in competition with rival companies. The WS machines are mid-market. They retail to consumers at an average price of £550, but typically, they are sold to retailers at an average price of £400. Prices may, however, fluctuate according to competitive conditions at different times of the year.

The manufacturing processes of both divisions are highly mechanised. The majority of manufacturing costs relate to the depreciation, maintenance and operation of the production machinery and the purchase of materials.

WS has an accounting year end of 30 September.

Exhibit 2 – Tendering by the Industrial Division – provided by Richard Avebury

The Industrial Division tenders only for UK government contracts. It is an approved supplier for the government and, as a consequence, reasonable profits have been made over time on most of these contracts. Many years ago, private sector tenders were made (eg to hotels, cruise lines and restaurants), but WS was less successful at winning tenders to supply industrial washing machines to private sector companies, so these were not continued.

The government uses a 'framework agreement' for the procurement of industrial washing machines. This is where the government knows that public sector bodies are likely to need a particular product, but is unsure about the exact type they will need, or when they will be needed. In this case, the government sets up a group of approved suppliers that it can use for a tender process when necessary.

The approved suppliers are invited to tender, following which the tenders are evaluated and then the contract is awarded.

This framework agreement process has restricted competition for WS and thereby enabled it to win, in most years, about 30% of the contracts for which it has tendered. The number of approved suppliers in the framework agreement for industrial washing machines is currently four, including WS. However, a new supplier is periodically introduced by the government in order to replace an existing supplier which is leaving the approved list. *}risk for WS.*

Hexam, a rival firm, has recently become one of the government's approved suppliers for industrial washing machines, replacing one of the other existing approved suppliers. *— Hexam.*

Tendering data for WS – Industrial Division washing machines

Years ended 30 September:

	20X3	20X4
Number of tenders made	900	800
Number of successful tenders	270 *30%*	80 *10%*
Number of washing machines tendered for	25,200	20,000
Number of washing machines sold under successful tenders	*32%* 8,100	1,760 *8·8%*
Value of tenders made (£)	30,240,000	28,000,000
Value of successful tenders (£)	9,720,000	2,288,000

Exhibit 3A – Budgeted and actual data – prepared by WS management accountant

Years ended 30 September:	20X3		20X4	
	Industrial	Household	Industrial	Household
Budgeted profit per unit				
	£	£	£	£
Average selling price per unit: (Note 1)	1,200	400	1,300	400
Average cost per unit:				
Materials (Note 2)	(468)	(124)	(460)	(124)
Direct labour costs (at £8 per hour) (Note 2)	(32)	(16)	(40)	(16)
Overhead allocation (at £100 per labour hour) (Note 3)	(400)	(200)	(500)	(200)
Budgeted profit per unit	300	60	300	60

Notes

1   The actual selling price per unit was equal to the budgeted selling price per unit. *→ no change in price.*

2   The actual direct labour cost per unit and actual materials cost per unit were equal to their budgeted costs per unit. *}not change in variable costs?*

3   The budgeted overhead allocation rates were based on budgeted overhead costs and budgeted labour hours.

	20X3		20X4	
	Industrial	Household	Industrial	Household
Actual data				
Units produced and sold	8,100	12,000	1,760	12,000
Budget data				
Labour hours	32,000	24,000	*5hrs* 40,000	24,000
Budgeted units produced and sold	8,000	12,000	8,000	12,000

per unit   *budget. 2 labour hrs per unit*

Total overheads for the years ended 30 September were as follows:

	20X3	20X4
	£	£
Actual overheads (£'000)	5,650	4,850
Budgeted overheads (£'000)	5,600	6,400

Commentary by management accountant

The additional quality improvement changes, implemented on 1 October 20X3, were estimated to require one extra labour hour per industrial machine. WS factored this into the budget, along with the associated overhead allocation, to determine the tender prices for the year ended 30 September 20X4. However, although the government claims to believe in quality improvement, it is clearly not willing to pay for it in terms of higher prices. We clearly got our budgeting badly wrong.

[handwritten margin note: 1 extra labour hr per industrial machine]

Exhibit 3B – Analysis of actual overhead costs – prepared by WS production director

In October 20X4, a review of actual overhead costs incurred found them to be a mixture of fixed costs and variable costs. For both the years ended 30 September 20X3 and 30 September 20X4, the actual variable overhead incurred is estimated at £16 per labour hour plus £1,000 per production run set-up, with all other overheads incurred being fixed costs.

Actual production run set-ups were:

	20X3		20X4	
	Industrial	Household	Industrial	Household
Number of production run set-ups	500	1,000	100	1,000

Exhibit 4 – Potential acquisition by Hexam – prepared by Richard Avebury

Hexam Ltd is a private company which manufactures a range of industrial cleaning equipment, including industrial washing machines. It does not make household washing machines.

Hexam has grown rapidly in recent years and is seeking to expand further through organic growth and acquisitions. I understand that it has the objective of obtaining an AIM listing in 20X8.

Last month, Hexam became one of the approved suppliers for government contracts for the procurement of washing machines. It also sells industrial washing machines in the private sector to hotels, cruise lines and restaurants.

The current share capital of Hexam is held: 30% by the founding Hexam family; and 70% by private equity firms.

Hexam does not have sufficient cash resources to acquire the Industrial Division of WS, but it has offered to transfer some of its shares to WS as full consideration for the trade and assets of the Industrial Division. The Hexam shares would be newly issued and, after the deal, WS would hold 20% of the total ordinary share capital of Hexam.

Exhibit 5 – Terms of engagement – prepared by Richard Avebury

The WS board would like XYZ to prepare a report which addresses the following:

(1) Analyse and explain, using the data in Exhibit 2, the decline in the Industrial Division's tendering success during the year ended 30 September 20X4, compared with the year ended 30 September 20X3.

(2) Using Exhibit 3A and 3B, so far as the information permits, explain with supporting calculations why the actual profit differs from the budgeted profit for each of the two divisions, and for the company as a whole, for the year ended 30 September 20X4.

(3) Analyse and explain:

- the effect that the overhead cost allocations had on pricing in the Industrial Division in the year ended 30 September 20X4.

- the problems which arise in using the overhead cost allocations for valuing inventories for financial reporting purposes in the WS financial statements.

(4) With regard to the offer from Hexam to acquire the Industrial Division explain:

- the strategic, operating and financial factors that the WS board needs to consider before deciding whether to sell the Industrial Division to Hexam.

- the risks arising, and the due diligence procedures that should be carried out by WS on Hexam, in respect of using shares as the consideration. I do not need all the normal due diligence procedures, only those relating to the extra risks arising from a consideration comprising shares, rather than cash.

36 Commex Cables plc

Commex Cables plc (CC) manufactures and maintains cabling equipment for the mining industry. Its only factory is based in the UK and all its sales are currently to customers in Europe.

You are a junior manager working for Myron & Merton LLP (MM), a firm of ICAEW Chartered Accountants. John Fimmel, the chief executive of CC, asked Helga Hughes, a partner in MM, to attend a meeting with him to discuss a potential geographical expansion strategy. CC is a client of MM, but not an audit client.

The meeting

John opened the meeting. 'I have provided you with some background information about the company (**Exhibit 1**).

CC wishes to expand the geographical scope of its sales into the Australia and South East Asia region, where there is significant mining activity. Australia has been identified as our favoured location for supplying this regional market. An initial feasibility study has identified two alternative strategies.

Strategy 1 is to set up an Australian subsidiary, Australian Mining Cables Inc (AMC), which would manufacture cabling equipment at a new factory in Australia for distribution to customers in Australia and South East Asia.

Strategy 2 is to build a distribution centre in Australia which would hold inventories of CC's products, manufactured in the UK factory, for distribution to customers in Australia and South East Asia. This would be a division, but not a separate subsidiary.

I have provided you with more details on each strategy (**Exhibit 2**). The board has not yet taken a final decision but, at the moment, Strategy 1 is our preferred alternative.

Under Strategy 2, we could finance the distribution centre from existing cash resources, but for Strategy 1, there are not enough funds available to finance the setting up of a new factory.

We would therefore need to raise additional finance if we opted for Strategy 1. The board has decided that there would be only a small amount of new equity finance available for Strategy 1, so most of the initial investment would be debt financed.

The CC treasurer has identified two alternative methods of debt finance for Strategy 1 and has provided more detail on these in a separate document (**Exhibit 3**). Unfortunately, the treasurer is ill and there are a few matters which I need to understand. I therefore require help from MM. The lenders will also require an assurance report before agreeing to a loan.

The CC treasury team has provided summary forecasts of operating profit for both strategies and some working assumptions (**Exhibit 4**). However, no risk assessment has yet been carried out. There are a number of risks to be considered, including the sensitivity of the project to exchange rate fluctuations. I would like to understand these exchange risks.

We tried to keep secret our entry into the Australian market, but a large Australian mining company, BTZ Inc, has become aware of our intention to enter the market because an employee, who was assigned to the feasibility study for this project, now works for BTZ and has informed its board of our plans. An email has been received from the BTZ procurement director making CC an offer of collaboration in Australia (**Exhibit 5**).

I have set out, in a terms of engagement memorandum, more precisely what the CC board requires of MM (**Exhibit 6**).'

Instructions

Helga outlines what occurred during her meeting with John and gives you the following instructions:

'I would like you to provide a draft response to the requests from John (Exhibit 6), the chief executive of CC, for my consideration.

I would also like you to address two ethical issues. I am concerned about the ethics of the offer of collaboration from BTZ to CC (Exhibit 5) and I am worried about a further ethical issue.

During my meeting with John, he had to leave his office for a few minutes. I took the opportunity to admire the artwork in his office, but while doing so I noticed a letter from the BTZ finance director on

shouldn't be reading the letter

Ethics!

BTZ headed notepaper. It stated that shares in BTZ, with a market value of £354,000, had been transferred to John. I did not have time to read the letter in full, but I am concerned about the ethical implications of this discovery.

Please provide a briefing note explaining any ethical issues for John, CC and MM, arising from: (1) the proposed collaboration between CC and BTZ (Exhibit 5); and (2) the letter to John from the BTZ finance director.

Also, set out the actions that should be taken by MM and me in response to both of these matters.'

Requirement

Respond to the instructions from the MM engagement partner, Helga, by drafting the required response to John and providing a briefing note on the ethical issues.

Assume it is now July 20X5.

Total: 60 marks

Exhibit 1 – Company background – prepared by John Fimmel

CC commenced trading over 20 years ago and grew rapidly, obtaining a stock market listing six years ago (in 20W9).

The company manufactures, supplies, installs and maintains cables and associated cabling equipment for the mining industry. The cables include high-technology products which are used to ensure the safe and efficient transfer of electrical power in mines throughout Europe.

Some products are fairly standard and can be supplied from inventory, without modification, to many different customers. Other types of product must be manufactured to order to meet the particular needs of a specific customer. This may take a few days for basic items but, for some high technology products, the lead time is up to five weeks. Sometimes the customer has planned the delivery many months in advance. Alternatively, it may be unplanned, such as when a broken cable has to be replaced urgently in order to recommence mining activity.

The only CC production facility is located in the UK and it is currently operating at around 80% of productive capacity. CC's products are too heavy to be transported economically by air, so mostly need to travel by sea where possible, and then by road or rail.

CC has a network of depots throughout Europe which provide both routine maintenance and emergency repairs for customers.

The company has long-standing relationships with major global mining companies, but it only operates in Europe.

Trading conditions in Europe were difficult in the year ended 31 December 20X4, as mining companies have been reluctant to invest significantly, given economic and political uncertainties and volatility in the prices of many mined commodities.

IFRS 8 disclosures of revenue and operating profit for the year ended 31 December 20X4 were as follows:

	Revenue	Operating profit
	£'000	£'000
UK	8,400	1,600
Eurozone	14,900	2,200
Other European countries	12,700	800
Total	36,000	4,600

The presentation currency of the group financial statements is £ sterling. Group revenue and profit for the year ended 31 December 20X4 were reduced by the decline in the value of the euro and other European currencies relative to the £ during the year.

Exhibit 2 – Alternative strategies for expansion – prepared by John Fimmel

In 20X4, the CC board decided that, in order to continue revenue growth, the company would need to expand outside Europe.

Australia, which has a significant mining industry, was identified as our most favoured location for expansion. A base in Australia would supply, not only customers located in Australia itself, but also those in the South East Asia region. An initial feasibility study identified two alternative strategies.

Under either strategy, construction work and other preparation would commence on 1 January 20X6, and would then take 12 months to complete. Trading in Australia and South East Asia would therefore commence on 1 January 20X7.

[handwritten: ↓ depreciation. construction → capitalise interest⊗]

Strategy 1

Under this strategy, a subsidiary, AMC, would be incorporated in Australia where the currency is the Australian dollar (A$). A new factory would be built in Australia for an estimated initial cost, including related plant and machinery, of A$63 million. This would be financed partly by an issue of share capital, but mainly by debt (Exhibit 3).

*[handwritten: * @ group level → translation risk.]*

Products would be manufactured and distributed from the factory to customers across Australia and South East Asia, over distances of up to 8,000 kilometres. *[handwritten: ↳How?]*

Many of the products would be similar to those manufactured in the UK, but there would also be variations to accommodate the particular needs of the Australian and South East Asian mining industries. The capacity of the Australian factory would be about one-third that of the UK factory. (Skilled staff, supply chains and production facilities would need to be developed.) *[handwritten: ↳ takes a while to find]*

Components and raw materials for the new factory would be sourced from Australian suppliers. Staff would be recruited locally and would include a group of engineers responsible for repairs and maintenance for customers. *[handwritten: → understanding * cultural impact. ↳ in A$]*

Strategy 2

Under this strategy, a distribution centre would be built in Australia, at a cost of A$4 million, which could be financed from CC's operating cash flows. Products would be manufactured in the UK, then transported to the distribution centre. From there, they would be distributed to customers in Australia and parts of South East Asia, up to a distance of 5,500 kilometres. *[handwritten: smaller distance; transportation costs; capacity?]*

A separate subsidiary would not be set up for Strategy 2. Instead, the Australian operation would be a division, managed and administered largely from the UK head office. *[handwritten: * translation risk]*

A group of engineers based in Australia (comprising about half the number required for Strategy 1) would be responsible for repairs and maintenance of the cabling equipment for customers.

Exhibit 3 – Finance methods for Strategy 1 – prepared by the CC treasurer

The CC board estimated that the financing needed for Strategy 1 would be A$63 million. Our initial working assumption is that the exchange rate will be £1 = A$1.8.

The board decided that there would be a low level of equity finance for Strategy 1, amounting to A$9 million. As a result, the remaining A$54 million would need to be debt financed. I have identified two alternative methods of debt finance:

Finance Method A

On 1 January 20X6, the Australian subsidiary, AMC, would raise, from an Australian bank, a 15-year loan of A$54 million, at an annual fixed interest rate of 5%. CC, as the parent company, would provide guarantees to the Australian bank for the repayment of the loan in the event that AMC were to default.

Finance Method B

On 1 January 20X6, CC would raise, from a UK bank, a £30 million, 10-year loan, at an annual fixed interest rate of 4.8%. CC would then immediately make a loan to AMC of A$54 million. This would be a 15-year loan, at an annual fixed interest rate of 5%.

Exhibit 4 – Summary forecasts of operating profit and working assumptions – prepared by the CC treasury department

A feasibility study was carried out by CC staff who travelled to Australia to undertake market research, explore operations and logistics and estimate costs.

Using this information, forecasts were prepared based on working assumptions, which are set out below.

Strategy 1

The feasibility study established that it would not take long for the reputation of AMC's new factory to become known in the industry in Australia. As a result, AMC would spend 20X7 penetrating the market, but sales for the year ending 31 December 20X8 would reach their steady state level for the future.

Summary forecasts of operating profit for AMC are as follows for the years ending 31 December:

	20X7 A$'000	20X8 and onwards A$'000
Revenue	18,000	27,000
Manufacturing costs:		
Variable production costs	(4,050)	(6,075)
Fixed production costs	(9,450)	(9,450)
Gross profit	4,500	11,475
Administrative and distribution costs	(4,600)	(4,600)
Operating (loss)/profit	(100)	6,875

[handwritten note in left margin: "tax benefit?"]

Strategy 2

Under this strategy it is expected that revenues will be lower than for Strategy 1 and will be constant from the year ending 31 December 20X7 onwards.

Summary forecasts of operating profit for the Australian division are as follows for the years ending 31 December:

	20X7 and each year thereafter £'000	Exchange rate	20X7 and each year thereafter A$'000
Revenue	N/A		9,000
Manufacturing costs:			
Variable production costs	(750)	1.8	(1,350)
Fixed production costs	(1,275)	1.8	(2,295)
Gross profit			5,355
Administrative and distribution costs	(2,500)	1.8	(4,500)
Operating profit			855

Working assumptions

The following working assumptions were used in determining the forecasts:

- For both strategies, construction of buildings and other preparation work will commence on 1 January 20X6 and all initial cash outlays will be made on that date.

- For both strategies, trading will commence on 1 January 20X7.

- The risk-adjusted annual weighted average cost of capital for both strategies is 8%.

- The exchange rate will be constant at £1 = A$1.8.

- For Strategy 1 all costs incurred, and all revenues earned, are in A$.

- For Strategy 2 all operating costs are incurred in £ sterling and all revenues are earned in A$.

- Operating profit equals operating cash flows.

- Operating cash flows will arise at year ends.

- Ignore tax for now, as it will be dealt with later.

[handwritten note in left margin: "unrealistic"]

Exhibit 5 – Offer of collaboration – email from BTZ

To: The CC board
From: Jeff Lilley: BTZ procurement director
Date: 10 July 20X5
Subject: Offer of collaboration

[handwritten: ® negotiate automatic terms]

It has come to the attention of the BTZ board that CC is considering opening a new factory in Australia, operated through a newly-formed subsidiary, called AMC.

As you will be aware, BTZ is a major global mining company. Our European operation already purchases cabling equipment from CC. Australia is, however, our main market and we are keen to do business with AMC.

We are constantly looking for new suppliers and cabling is a core product that we purchase on a regular basis. We would be interested in discussing whether AMC can become the preferred supplier of cables for our Australian and South East Asian operations.

However, the BTZ board would like a deeper involvement with AMC, rather than just a supplier-customer relationship. BTZ's collaboration offer is this:

> BTZ is willing to subscribe for a 20% equity holding in AMC at the nominal value of A$1 per share. In return, the BTZ board guarantees that it will make significant purchases of cabling from AMC, amounting to no less than A$5 million per year, on normal commercial terms.

As part of the proposal, the BTZ board would require a shareholder agreement specifying that:

- A minimum of 15% of AMC's operating profit is paid annually as a dividend; and
- A member of the BTZ board sits on the AMC board as a non-executive director.

I will probably take this role as the non-executive director myself. We can discuss director remuneration later.

The BTZ board requires all elements of its collaboration offer to be considered together as a package. To be clear, BTZ is unlikely to use AMC (or CC in Europe) as a supplier if our offer is refused. *[handwritten: } threat.]*

Please let us know your decision by 31 July 20X5 or we will have to assume that our collaboration offer has been refused. *[handwritten: very aggressive.]*

Jeff Lilley
Procurement Director – BTZ

Exhibit 6 – Terms of engagement memorandum – prepared by John Fimmel

The CC board would like MM to prepare responses to the requests below.

(1) For the two alternative strategies:

- determine the net present value (NPV) in £ sterling at 1 January 20X6.

- evaluate and explain the risks of exchange rate fluctuations. In so doing, provide illustrative calculations of the sensitivity of the NPV to future exchange rate movements. (Assume, for the purpose of assessing sensitivity, that the exchange rate at 1 January 20X6 will be £1 = A$1.8, but that a one-off change in the exchange rate occurs on 1 January 20X7, which would generate a zero NPV).

- compare and evaluate the key supply chain management and distribution issues.

For the analysis above, ignore the financing arrangements and the offer from BTZ.

(2) Compare the two proposed debt finance methods for Strategy 1 (Exhibit 3) and give a reasoned recommendation. Include an explanation of why the interest rate differs between the two finance methods.

(3) Explain the issues that MM would need to address in providing assurance to lenders for the debt finance methods for Strategy 1 (Exhibit 3).

I do not require a detailed list of assurance procedures, but I do need to understand the key risks to each of the lenders and how an assurance report would provide comfort for these.

(4) Identify and explain the key financial reporting issues affecting the CC consolidated financial statements arising from each of the two potential strategies (Exhibit 2).

37 Paige plc

You are Nat Ahmed, a member of staff at a firm of business advisers, Dancer Beeston Peters (DBP). One of DBP's partners, Josie Welch, advises Paige plc. Paige is an AIM-listed company which was established many years ago. It has several subsidiaries in the UK, most of which produce processed, packaged foods such as cereals, tinned foods and snack foods for the major UK supermarkets. Although sales are principally to UK customers, Paige has a growing amount of sales in the rest of Europe.

Strategic decision in respect of Slimsvelte Products Ltd

In 20W9, Paige purchased a majority holding (80% of the ordinary share capital) in Slimsvelte Products Ltd (SP). SP's original founder, Claudia Svelte, who holds the remaining 20% of the ordinary share capital, continued as chief executive of SP. The three other SP board members were appointed by Paige; they are also main board directors of Paige.

SP produces and sells a range of milkshake products which are designed to be used as meal replacements to help consumers to lose weight. Details about the market for weight-loss products are provided (**Exhibit 1**), together with background information on SP (**Exhibit 2**).

Paige has approached DBP for assistance in determining its future strategy in relation to SP.

Meeting with Paige's Chief Executive

Paige's chief executive, Charles Digby, called a meeting with Josie. Charles started the meeting:

'When we bought SP it was performing very well. However, since the acquisition, SP's performance has declined significantly. There are two principal reasons: firstly, the effects of the global recession and secondly, trends in the weight-loss market have altered. Growth in the meal replacement market has slowed and weight-loss products have become more diverse.

Two mutually-exclusive strategies have emerged in Paige's board discussions about the future of the investment in SP.

> **Strategy A** is to retain the investment in SP and to use SP as a vehicle to build up Paige's presence in the weight-loss market (**Exhibit 3**).

> **Strategy B** is to dispose of SP as quickly as possible and to use the funds released to build up the core business of food processing (**Exhibit 4**).

Strategy A, which has my support, is based upon an expectation that the weight-loss market will grow exponentially over the next few years. SP is Paige's only subsidiary operating in this important market, but its current narrow product range inhibits growth. We should be able to use the SP brand to introduce an exciting new range of products; we have had various ideas about this range, but would appreciate some advice from DBP.

Strategy B is favoured by Paige's finance director, Asha Kennedy. She thinks that Paige will maximise its future profitability by focussing on its food production business, and that Paige's 80% shareholding in SP should therefore be sold.

Key financial information for Paige (**Exhibit 5**) and summary financial statements and other information for SP (**Exhibit 6**) are provided.

What we need from DBP is an unbiased opinion. Please prepare a report before the next board meeting which presents a reasoned discussion of the two strategies.'

The partner's instructions

Upon her return to DBP, Josie provides you with a summary of her meeting with Charles Digby, and gives you various documents (see Exhibits). She then sends you the following instructions in an email:

To: Nat Ahmed
From: Josie Welch
Date: 20 July 20X5
Subject: Paige assignment

Nat

This email is to summarise what I require from you. I will be responsible for writing the report to the Paige board, but I need your assistance. Please prepare a working paper which comprises the following.

(1) An assessment of SP's market environment and an evaluation of the key risks currently facing SP. For this purpose, ignore the proposed strategies.

(2) An evaluation of Strategy A (Exhibit 3). You should explain the benefits and risks associated with each proposal identifying which, if any, of the four proposals are acceptable.

(3) An evaluation of Strategy B (Exhibit 4). You should:

- explain the benefits and risks associated with this strategy; and

- evaluate the acceptability of the £18 million offer that has been received from the private equity fund for Paige's 80% shareholding in SP. Determine and explain SP's cost of equity and price earnings (P/E) ratio implied by the private equity fund's offer. Determine and evaluate relevant alternative valuations and briefly note any additional information that you would require to refine your valuation.

(4) A preliminary reasoned recommendation as to which strategy Paige should adopt.

Requirement

Prepare the working paper requested by Josie Welch, the assignment partner.

Assume it is now July 20X5.

Total: 40 marks

Exhibit 1 – The weight-loss product market – prepared by Claudia Svelte in May 20X5

The World Health Organisation characterises obesity as a global problem, which is projected to become much more serious over the next few years. Since 1980, worldwide obesity levels have doubled, which some authorities attribute to an increased consumption of processed foods. It is estimated that, within the next 15 years, 2.2 billion people in the world will be overweight or obese. Currently, the highest concentration of overweight and obese people is in the USA. Other developed countries are fast approaching similar percentages, and some developing economies are experiencing similar trends.

The market for products that aim to help consumers to lose weight is also growing fast. The global weight-loss market is currently estimated to be worth nearly US$600 billion, of which over 40% is attributable to the USA and one-third to Europe.

The market for weight-loss products can be segmented as follows:

- **Diet food products**: ready meals, meal replacement products (such as the milkshake range produced by SP), artificial sweeteners

- **Weight management services**: consultation services, alternative therapies, diet clubs and support groups, diet food home delivery services, health clubs and gyms

- **Weight management drugs and supplements**: prescription drugs, over-the-counter drugs and herbal supplements

There are strong competitors in all segments of the market. Large international food processing companies are major producers of diet food products. Some smaller companies operate in particular market niches, for example in the herbal supplements business.

A significant part of the market comprises people who have been, often repeatedly, unsuccessful in dieting. For most dieters the ideal solution would come in the form of a pill. Although the pharmaceutical industry has produced diet pills, these have generally had unwanted side effects and have not been effective in the long term.

Handwritten margin notes:
Ethics?
CSR?
AIM-listed

Global
Weight
loss market
= US$600bn

40% = 240bn USA
⅓ = 200bn Europe

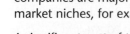

Exhibit 2 – Background information on SP – prepared by Asha Kennedy, finance director of Paige

[handwritten: Goodwill?]

SP was founded 11 years ago (in 20W4) by Claudia Svelte, who initially owned 100% of its share capital. Claudia had previously worked with Charles Digby, chief executive of Paige. Charles provided Claudia with a lot of advice, and in 20W7 he recommended that Paige lend SP funds to expand the business.

By 20W9, SP had become very successful, generating an annual revenue of £75 million and a profit after tax of £5.6 million. The Paige board decided to purchase 80% of SP's ordinary share capital, from Claudia, for £48 million on 1 April 20W9. Since 20W9, new entrants to the meal replacement market have had an adverse effect on SP's sales and profitability.

The global market for meal replacement products is expected to grow, especially in relatively new markets, such as parts of Asia. However, barriers to entry are low, and therefore it will remain a challenge to maintain and grow market share. *[handwritten: lots of competitors ⊗]*

Exhibit 3 – Strategy A – prepared by Charles Digby, chief executive of Paige

Strategy A is to use the SP brand to build up reputation and sales in the weight-loss market.

SP has a significant market share in the UK market for meal replacement products, although it is less well known in the rest of Europe and has virtually no sales in the USA.

Proposals over the three to five years from 1 April 20X6 include:

(1)   phasing out the meal replacement products gradually, in order to develop a range of low-calorie ready meals and promote them using SP's and Paige's existing sales channels;

(2)   establishing a range of web-based, paid-for, advisory services producing tailored dietary advice for individuals;

(3)   investing in existing chains of gyms and health facilities; and

(4)   establishing new markets in developing countries.

SP can undertake as many of the above proposals as it wishes.

[handwritten: re combos?]

Exhibit 4 – Strategy B – prepared by Asha Kennedy

Strategy B is to sell Paige's investment in SP and use the funds generated to invest in Paige's core business.

I believe that the investment in SP has been an expensive mistake, and that Paige should realise its residual value as quickly as possible in order to invest the funds in our core business of food production.

Paige has been approached by a private equity fund which is interested in making a bid for its 80% shareholding in SP. A figure of £18 million was offered in informal discussions as the acquisition price for Paige's 80% shareholding.

[handwritten: minority SH]

The private equity fund has indicated to the Paige board that it would only be willing to offer £2 million for Claudia's 20% shareholding in SP. The Paige board believes that, at this valuation, Claudia would prefer to retain her shareholding and her active involvement in SP. However, Claudia has not yet been informed of Paige's possible disposal of its investment in SP.

If Paige adopts Strategy B, the disposal of Paige's investment in SP is expected to take place on 1 April 20X6.

Exhibit 5 – Key financial information for Paige – prepared by Asha Kennedy

[handwritten: OPM X5 12.2% X4 12%]

	Year ended 31 March	
	20X5	20X4
Revenue	£503.0 million	£494.6 million
Operating profit	£61.3 million	£59.3 million
Return on capital employed (ROCE)	15.3%	15.5%
Food processing industry average ROCE	20.4%	20.3%

[handwritten: it's not utilising its capital effectively.]

ICAEW

Exhibit 6 – Summary financial statements for (SP) and other information – prepared by Asha Kennedy

Statements of profit or loss for the years to 31 March

	20X6 Forecast £m	20X5 Actual £m	20X4 Actual £m
Revenue	58.1 *↑?*	48.3	55.8
Operating profit	5.3	4.7	5.1
Net profit after tax	2.8	2.3	2.6

Statements of financial position at 31 March

where is cash coming from? *↑ buy new assets*

	20X6 Forecast £m	20X5 Actual £m	20X4 Actual £m
Non-current assets	65.1	60.1	60.8
Current assets	42.7	38.4	40.2
	107.8	98.5	101.0
Equity	28.8 *(Issue new shares)*	27.0	24.7
Non-current liabilities	40.5 *(no change)*	40.5	40.5
Current liabilities	38.5	31.0	35.8
	107.8	98.5	101.0

Other information

Revenue for the year ended 31 March 20X5 includes £4.3 million in respect of a contract with Purseproud Supermarkets (Purseproud) which is due to be renegotiated in early 20X6. There are rumours that Purseproud is unhappy with SP's products and is actively soliciting bids from other suppliers. This is one of SP's largest contracts.

↳ unlikely to renew? Why has revenue increased?

SP pays tax on profits at 20%.

SP paid a dividend of £500,000 in the year ended 31 March 20X4. No dividend was paid in the year ended 31 March 20X5. It is the directors' intention, if Paige retains its investment in SP, to pay a regular and larger dividend in the future. The dividend for the year ending 31 March 20X6 is forecast to be £1 million, growing subsequently at 8% per annum.   *g=8% DVM?*

→ distributable reserves? cash?

Property, plant and equipment is measured at cost less depreciation. The finance director estimates that the value in use of non-current assets at 31 March 20X6 will be £68.3 million and their fair value less costs to sell will be £60.2 million. SP's non-current liabilities consist entirely of a loan from Paige which is redeemable at par on 31 March 20X7. Annual interest is charged on the loan at 5% and is allowable for tax.   *intercompany loan P→S ↳ £2,025k*

VIU=68.3
FV = 60.2 less sell
CV = 65.1
no impairment needed.

Generally, the weighted average cost of capital (WACC) for a listed company in the food processing industry, with similar gearing to SP, is around 7.5% per annum.   *SP not listed*

SP's listed competitors typically offer a more diverse range of products and services and therefore there is no precise comparator company. However, an established listed company, Wensley Slimming plc, offers some similar products and its price earnings ratio is currently 9.4. Wensley Slimming is forecast to have stable profits into the foreseeable future. Paige's own price earnings ratio is currently 9.9.

38   Riller plc

Riller plc is a UK-based building company which constructs residential properties (ie houses and apartments). It is listed on the London Stock Exchange.

In common with many other companies that build residential properties, Riller performed poorly from 20W8 until 20X2, because of downward pressure on property prices and on sales volumes during the recession. However, Riller has now returned to profit, following an upturn in property prices since 20X2 (three years ago).

The chief executive of Riller, Gary Griffiths, asked to meet with Laura Lewis, who is a partner in Hayes & Scott LLP (HS), a firm of ICAEW Chartered Accountants. You work for HS as a senior in the advisory department. Riller is a client of HS, but not an audit client.

The meeting

Gary opened the meeting. 'Riller has been increasingly profitable over the past two years. Factors that have helped us return to profit include a reorganisation in 20X2 and also, more recently, the general improvement in the residential property market. In order to continue this growth in profit, however, the board has decided that the company needs to make a strategic acquisition.

I have prepared some information about the UK residential property building industry and market background, including an extract from the annual report of Mega plc, one of the UK market leaders (**Exhibit 1**). I have also provided some background information on Riller (**Exhibit 2**). The finance director, Julie Morton, who is an ICAEW Chartered Accountant, has provided some financial and operating data (**Exhibit 3**).

The Riller board has identified a possible target company, Minnen plc, and I have drafted confidential briefing notes relating to its acquisition (**Exhibit 4**). We would welcome HS's evaluation of this potential acquisition.

Financing the acquisition is a key factor. There are two alternative forms of consideration for purchasing Minnen:

(a)   Make an offer of a share-for-share exchange; or
(b)   Issue bonds to finance a cash acquisition.

Julie has provided some information about the financing of the acquisition (**Exhibit 5**).

In addition, if we decide to acquire Minnen, we will need HS to carry out due diligence procedures.

I appreciate that information is limited at the moment, but I have provided terms of reference for an engagement between Riller and HS where I set out more precisely what is required from your firm (**Exhibit 6**).'

Engagement partner's briefing

Laura asks to see you after the meeting. She outlines what occurred during the meeting with Gary and gives you the following instructions:

'I would like you to provide for me a draft response to the requests made by Gary, the Riller chief executive (**Exhibit 6**).

In addition, after the meeting, I received a phone call from Julie Morton (**Exhibit 7**) about an ethical concern. I would like you to prepare notes setting out the ethical issues arising for all relevant parties. Your notes should include the actions that HS and Julie should now take.'

Requirement

Respond to the briefing from the engagement partner, Laura, by drafting the required reply to Gary (**Exhibit 6**) and preparing notes on the ethical issues (**Exhibit 7**).

Assume that it is now November 20X5.

Total: 60 marks

Exhibit 1 – UK residential property building industry and market background – prepared by Gary Griffiths

The residential property market comprises two sectors: the new-build sector and the secondary market sector. The new-build sector is concerned with the construction and sale by building companies of new houses and apartments. The secondary market sector is concerned with the sale by individuals of their homes in private transactions with individual purchasers. Individuals buying a house or apartment normally obtain a loan to finance the purchase.

The prices of residential properties can fluctuate widely. In particular, there can be periods of rapid increases, sometimes as high as 20% in one year in some regions of the UK. However, prices can also fall, as occurred in the recession from around 20W8 to 20X2. Many residential property building companies failed in this period and most suffered losses.

As property prices started to increase after 20X2, most residential property building companies that survived the recession showed significant increases in profits. Residential property price increases have occurred throughout the UK. However, while the increases have been significant in London and the surrounding areas (where property prices have always been significantly higher than the rest of the UK), there have been smaller price increases in other regions.

The factors influencing residential property prices are varied but include: the level of personal incomes, loan interest rates, availability of credit to house buyers, consumer confidence, employment levels and available supply of properties.

Extract from industry magazine: House Builders Herald – 27 October 20X5

The UK's largest residential property building companies will see profits increase significantly in 20X5. Research shows that the UK's 10 largest companies in the industry own enough land to build around half a million homes. In total, they made pre-tax profits of more than £2,000 million in 20X4 – a 35% increase on 20X3.

Jeff Knight of the House Builders Association, whose members account for 75% of new residential properties built in the UK, said: 'Profits in the industry fell very steeply in 20W8 and the following few years, with most companies making losses and many companies failing. Those companies surviving the crisis have reorganised, with profits now returning to pre-recession levels.'

Extract from Mega plc's annual report for the year ended 30 September 20X5

Mega continues to be one of the UK's leading residential property building companies.

During the current financial year, Mega's total sales volumes grew by 24% to 3,785 residential properties. In the same period, the average selling price of our properties increased by 15%.

The substantial increase in the number of properties sold, combined with property price inflation in excess of build cost inflation, improved our gross margin from 20.7% to 22.8%.

Exhibit 2 – Riller company background – prepared by Gary Griffiths

Riller was established over 50 years ago. It grew by developing a good reputation for building residential properties and obtained a listing on the London Stock Exchange 14 years ago (in 20W1). The properties built by Riller are positioned above mid-market in terms of size and quality. It has focused its building activity in large towns and cities in the north of England.

The company has survived by adopting a prudent policy of acquiring a significant landbank (land on which houses can be built in future) and, unlike many companies that failed in the recession, its financial gearing is relatively low.

In common with many companies in the industry, Riller's profit has increased significantly in the past two years as a result of rising property prices and increased sales volumes. Industry profit growth is expected to continue for three more years at about 10% per annum, before stabilising to zero growth.

In the UK residential property building industry, Riller is in the top 25 largest companies, but it is outside the top 10 companies which dominate the industry.

Riller has a large central depot from which it operates in the north of England. It does not have a depot in the south of England, as it seldom has building projects in that area.

Riller's houses and apartments have proved popular because of its good reputation for quality building, and also as a result of careful selection of the location of the land it acquires.

Riller purchases land a long time before it needs to build on the land and it therefore has a substantial landbank in inventories. A key reason for the recent increase in profit has been that land was acquired at low cost during the recession. Increases in the value of land over the past three years have made recent land purchases significantly more expensive than was previously the case.

Inventories are the company's major asset and comprise primarily the landbank, but also building materials, work-in-progress on partially completed houses and unsold completed houses.

Revenue is recognised on legal completion of the sale of each house.

Riller's share capital is owned 27% by Financial First (a private equity company) and the remaining shares by a number of financial institutions.

Riller does not currently have any subsidiaries.   — first time for acqn.

Exhibit 3 – Riller financial and operating data – prepared by Julie Morton

Riller: Summary statements of profit or loss for the years ended 30 September

	20X5	20X4
	£'000	£'000
Revenue	285,300	232,500
Cost of sales	(218,900)	(189,400)
Gross profit	66,400	43,100
Distribution and administration costs	(28,500)	(21,200)
Operating profit	37,900	21,900
Net finance costs	(10,200)	(9,300)
Profit before tax	27,700	12,600
Income tax expense	(6,100)	(2,700)
Profit for the year	21,600	9,900

Riller: Summary statement of financial position at 30 September 20X5

	£'000
Non-current assets	
Property, plant and equipment	3,700
Current assets	
Inventories	566,300
Trade and other receivables	4,700
Cash	29,600
Total assets	604,300
Equity	
£1 ordinary shares	32,000
Share premium	108,500
Retained earnings	66,300
Non-current liabilities	
Loans	260,000
Current liabilities	
Trade and other payables	137,500
Total equity and liabilities	604,300

X5

gearing = 55.6%

Exhibit 4 – Potential acquisition of Minnen plc – confidential briefing notes prepared by Gary Griffiths

Negotiations

Preliminary negotiations have taken place with the Minnen board about the possibility of Riller acquiring 100% of the ordinary share capital of Minnen on 30 September 20X6.

The Minnen board believes that an appropriate bid price would be £4 per share and it would be willing to recommend that the shareholders accept an offer from Riller at this price. This would give a total proposed consideration of £80 million. *(land?)*

Minnen company background

profits ↑

Minnen is an AIM-listed company which builds residential properties mainly in the south of England, including London. Minnen has its main depot in the south east of England. *new market*

Minnen is not in the top 25 largest UK housebuilding companies, but it has an excellent reputation for quality. *smaller* *└ in line with Riller's CSF.*

The directors of Minnen own 20% of its ordinary shares, with financial institutions holding the remaining shares.

Minnen: Extracts from statements of profit or loss for years ended 30 September

	20X5	20X4
	£'000	£'000
Revenue	133,400	130,800
Gross profit	16,100	15,500
Operating profit	8,100	7,750
Profit before tax	7,000	6,700
Profit for the year	5,600	5,300

not big jumps but because prices are higher in South anyway.

Minnen: Summary statement of financial position at 30 September 20X5

	£'000
Non-current assets	
Property, plant and equipment	2,200
Current assets	
Inventories	184,800
Trade and other receivables	2,300
Cash	1,300
Total assets	190,600
Equity	
£1 ordinary shares	20,000
Retained earnings	22,000
Non-current liabilities	
Loan (redeemable in 20Y0)	87,000
Current liabilities	61,600
Total equity and liabilities	190,600

Notes

1 Inventories are measured at the lower of cost and net realisable value.
2 The fair value of Minnen's net assets, excluding internally-generated intangibles, is £58 million.

Comparison of operating data – Riller and Minnen

	Riller		Minnen
	20X5	20X4	20X5
Number of houses sold in year ended 30 September	765	820	242
Number of 'plots' of land held in landbank at 30 September	5,550	4,600	1,600

Synergies from the acquisition

The commercial and operating synergies, after tax, for the enlarged group which could arise from the acquisition, are:

- overhead efficiency savings of £200,000 per annum;

- material and subcontractor procurement gains from scale economies amounting to £100,000 per annum; and

- other cost savings amounting to £50,000 per annum.

Working assumptions

- The acquisition would take place on 30 September 20X6.

- In the absence of an acquisition, Minnen's profit after tax will increase by 10% per annum over the three years from 30 September 20X5, before stabilising to zero growth thereafter.

- An annual discount rate of 10% is to be used to evaluate the acquisition.

- Operating cash flows arise at the end of the year to which they relate.

- One 'plot' of land is used to build one residential property.

Share prices

Current quoted share prices on the London Stock Exchange are:

Riller   £7.20
Minnen   £3.20

These prices have remained around the same level since 30 September 20X5.

Post-acquisition integration

It has not yet been decided whether Riller would retain the Minnen brand name after acquisition or rebrand all its operations under the Riller brand.

Financial reporting concerns of the Riller board

The Riller board has a number of concerns about the impact of an acquisition of Minnen on the Riller group financial statements.

The Riller board's specific concerns about the acquisition are:

- the impact of the acquisition on the group statement of financial position, including the treatment of the Minnen brand name.

- the financial reporting implications of each of the two methods of financing the acquisition (Exhibit 5).

Exhibit 5 – Financing the acquisition of Minnen plc – prepared by Julie Morton

As a working assumption, the bid value for Minnen is unlikely to be affected by the method of financing the acquisition.

The acquisition can be implemented by two alternative methods of financing: a share-for-share exchange; or cash raised from the issue of a 10-year bond.

The amount under either method would be equal to the full amount of the consideration paid for 100% of the share capital of Minnen.

(a)   Share-for-share exchange

Acquire 100% of the ordinary shares of Minnen through a share-for-share exchange using newly-issued Riller ordinary shares.

The Riller board has specific concerns about the impact of the share-for-share exchange on Riller's share price and about any other implications for its existing shareholders.

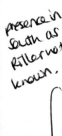

FV of bonds.

(b) 10-year bonds

Issue 10-year bonds at a fixed annual rate of interest of 5%. The funds raised will be used to make a cash acquisition of 100% of the ordinary shares of Minnen.

The Riller board is confident that market interest rates and expectations will remain stable until 30 September 20X6. However, the Riller board has specific concerns about how subsequent changes in market interest rates will affect the fair value of the bonds and about the implications of this for Riller. *Concern*

Exhibit 6 – Terms of reference – prepared by Gary Griffiths

The Riller board would like HS to prepare a report addressing the issues set out below.

(1) With respect to the potential acquisition of Minnen:

- analyse and compare the performance and position of Minnen and Riller; *P/L B/S*

- explain the factors that should be considered in deciding whether it would be beneficial to acquire Minnen;

- determine and justify a price per share that should be offered for the acquisition of Minnen, taking into account the proposal of £4 per share by the Minnen board. Use a variety of models; and

- explain the financial reporting implications for the consolidated financial statements of Riller, addressing the specific concerns raised by the Riller board (Exhibit 4).

(2) With respect to the two alternative methods of financing the acquisition (Exhibit 5):

- evaluate the factors that should be considered in deciding which method of financing should be used. Address the specific concerns of the Riller board (Exhibit 5), but do not restrict yourself to these; and

- provide a reasoned recommendation regarding the method of finance that should be used.

(3) Identify and explain the key risks to Riller relating to the acquisition of Minnen which will need to be assessed during the due diligence process. Set out the due diligence procedures that HS could undertake to address these risks. I do not need a long list of the standard due diligence procedures, just those relevant to the key risks.

Exhibit 7 – Note of telephone conversation with Julie Morton – prepared by Laura Lewis

The finance director of Riller, Julie Morton, called me confidentially today to raise an ethical concern.

Julie said that some of the Minnen directors have informally indicated that they might be prepared to recommend a lower bid price to Minnen shareholders. This would depend on Riller guaranteeing that they would retain their positions as directors after the acquisition, with their remuneration packages remaining at their current levels.

shareholder's interests at heart -

"bribe".

Julie explained that Gary is keen to minimise the cost of the acquisition and would therefore like to consider this suggestion, but she has concerns and would like some advice from HS.

39 Kinn plc

Kinn plc is a listed engineering company operating through three divisions: Mechanical, Electrical and Civil.

Kinn has performed poorly in recent years and, following a review of the business, it intends to restructure. The board is therefore seeking advice from Giplin and Linthwatt LLP (GL), a firm of ICAEW Chartered Accountants. You are a senior working in the business advisory department of GL.

Aisha Ashton, a partner in GL, has received an email from the Kinn finance director, Roger Reed, which she has forwarded to you.

To: Aisha Ashton
From: Roger Reed
Date: 3 November 20X5
Subject: Sale of Electrical Division

Dear Aisha,

The Kinn board needs GL's help.

As you have not previously worked on an engagement for Kinn, I have provided some background notes about the company (**Exhibit 1**).

Some segments of our business have not been performing well. In particular, we entered the electrical engineering market a few years ago, opening an Electrical Division in a newly-built factory in Germany, but it has not been a success. Following a review, we decided to sell the Electrical Division and withdraw from the electrical engineering market completely. I have provided you with some details (**Exhibit 2**).

The sale of the Electrical Division will generate net cash proceeds of £25 million for Kinn and we therefore have the short-term problem of how we invest this money to earn a pre-determined rate of interest. I have set out some details (**Exhibit 3**).

The board is still deciding how to use the net cash proceeds in the longer term and it would value GL's advice on this matter. I have set out the alternatives that we would like you to consider (**Exhibit 4**).

The Kinn board would like GL to prepare a report addressing the issues explained above. I have provided more details of what is required in a 'terms of engagement' document (**Exhibit 5**).

Partner's instructions

Aisha calls you into her office. 'I would like you to draft the report requested in Roger's 'terms of engagement' document (Exhibit 5).'

Requirement

Respond to the instructions from Aisha.

Assume it is now November 20X5.

Total: 40 marks

Exhibit 1 – Company background notes – prepared by Roger Reed

Products and divisions

Kinn plc is an engineering company. It has three divisions: Mechanical, Electrical and Civil. The divisions are autonomous, but they are not separate subsidiaries.

Division	Products	Location
Mechanical	Industrial machinery	UK
Electrical	Generators	Germany
Civil	Roads, railways, bridges	Italy

The Electrical Division was set up six years ago to diversify into electrical engineering products, but it has struggled to compete, despite significant investment. The decision to set up this division is now regarded by Kinn's management as a mistake.

The Mechanical Division and the Civil Division have performed reasonably well, but both of the divisional heads believe that these two divisions have suffered from under-investment, with most of the company's available funds being provided to the Electrical Division, in an attempt to help it to become established.

Performance

The performance of Kinn has been below expectations. This has been largely due to the Electrical Division. At first, it was believed that the poor performance of the Electrical Division was temporary and attributable to the division being in the start-up phase. However, while achieving profit, it has continued to perform below expectations.

Pressure from shareholders about poor share price performance resulted in the recent appointment of a new chief executive to implement a different approach. Following the review of the business, the Kinn board now has the aim of developing a strategy to increase the share price.

Based on currently available data, the forecast performance for the year ending 31 December 20X5 is:

	Mechanical £'000	Electrical £'000	Civil £'000	Total £'000
Revenue	16,600	4,500	22,900	44,000
Operating profit	4,250	620	4,600	9,470 ⟩ ∫ interest
Profit before tax	3,100	110	3,300	6,510
Net assets at carrying amount	34,000	26,400	46,400	106,800 ⟩ ∫ liabilities
Total assets at carrying amount	57,000	36,600	72,400	166,000

Head office costs are allocated between the divisions using a range of metrics and these allocated costs are included in the above data. *↳ how? may re-allocation would've helped E's performance?*

Exhibit 2 – Sale of Electrical Division – provided by Roger Reed

The Kinn board decided a few months ago that the Electrical Division should be sold. It has been successful in finding a buyer, a German engineering company, Reingold GmbH.

The details of the sale negotiations are being finalised, but a cash price has been agreed with Reingold. The date of sale is expected to be 31 March 20X6. On this date, Kinn will receive net cash proceeds of £25 million from the sale of the assets of its Electrical Division, after settlement of its liabilities.

The board has two main concerns:

(1) The impact on the future financial performance of Kinn for the year ending 31 December 20X6 arising from the disposal of the Electrical Division, including the effect on key ratios. *① Discontinued operations*

(2) The financial reporting implications arising from the sale agreement for the Electrical Division in the financial statements for the year ending 31 December 20X5. *→ non-current assets 'held for sale'.*

Working assumption

If there is no investment or restructuring, the performance of all three divisions in the year ending 31 December 20X6 will be the same as that forecast for the year ending 31 December 20X5.

Exhibit 3 – Short-term deposit of net cash proceeds of £25 million – prepared by Roger Reed *9m?*

The £25 million net cash proceeds from the sale of the Electrical Division is expected to be received on 31 March 20X6. At that date, the funds will be placed on short-term, fixed-interest deposit with Kinn's bank for three months until 30 June 20X6, when there will be a long-term use for these funds (**Exhibit 4**).

The board has expressed concern that short-term deposit interest rates might fall in the three months to 31 March 20X6, so it wants to lock into interest rates at 31 December 20X5. *HEDGING*

The board is considering using LIFFE 3-month sterling interest rate futures (contract size £500,000) to remove interest rate risk between 31 December 20X5 and 31 March 20X6.

The board expects at 31 December 20X5 that:

- the short-term, fixed-interest deposit rate will be 3.75% per annum; and
- the March 20X6, 3-month sterling interest rate futures contract will be trading at 96.00. *4%→ interest rate*

Exhibit 4 – Long-term use of net cash proceeds of £25 million – prepared by Roger Reed

There is disagreement on the board as to how the net cash proceeds from the sale of the Electrical Division should be used for long-term investment on 30 June 20X6.

Two alternatives were suggested. The board is keen to understand the likely impact on the risk of the company and on its share price for each of these alternatives.

① ②

Alternative 1

Purchase new production equipment for the Mechanical Division in order to improve its productivity and quality.

It is estimated that the new investment will generate a 9% annual return indefinitely.

The cost of new production equipment on 30 June 20X6 for the Mechanical Division would be £45 million. To finance this amount, Kinn would use the net cash proceeds of £25 million from the sale of the Electrical Division and also borrow a further £20 million, repayable after six years (on 30 June 20Y2.)

Kinn's current credit rating is BBB. Its bank has indicated that it would be willing to provide the £20 million debt finance at either a fixed rate of 6% per annum or a floating rate of 12-month LIBOR + 3%. The 12-month LIBOR is currently 3.75%.

[handwritten: Interest rate swap]

The board is unsure which of these types of debt it should use.

Alternative 2

Use the whole of the £25 million net cash proceeds from the sale of the Electrical Division to reduce some of the existing borrowing. *[handwritten: gearing levels?]*

Exhibit 5 – Terms of engagement – prepared by Roger Reed

The Kinn board would like GL to prepare a report in which you:

(1) (a) (1) Analyse the forecast financial performance of Kinn for the year ending 31 December 20X5.

   (2) Calculate and explain the impact on the company's future performance for the year ending 31 December 20X6 arising from the sale of the Electrical Division. Apply the working assumption in Exhibit 2.

   (b) Set out and explain the financial reporting implications arising from the sale agreement for the Electrical Division in the financial statements for the year ending 31 December 20X5.

   Ignore tax and deferred tax for now.

(2) Explain how the proposed interest rate futures could manage interest rate risk arising from the short-term deposit of the £25 million (Exhibit 3).

   Illustrate your explanation with calculations showing how the contract will work if interest rates fall by 1% (to 2.75%) between 1 January 20X6 and 31 March 20X6.

   State any assumptions.

(3) Explain the likely effects on the risk of the company, and on Kinn's share price, of each alternative long-term use of the net cash proceeds (Exhibit 4). Set out any assumptions you make.

   Advise whether Kinn should use the fixed or variable rate loan, from its bank, if the board were to decide on Alternative 1.

40 Kiera Healy Ltd

Kiera Healy Company Ltd (KHC) is a manufacturer of luxury toiletries with a good-quality brand name, Kiera Healy©. The brand name is reinforced by a distinctive floral design on all its packaging.

You are Jo Morris, a senior working for Peters, Hurst and Moore LLP (PHM), a firm of ICAEW Chartered Accountants. KHC is a new client, but not an audit client, of PHM.

When you opened your emails this morning you found the following communication from Jessica Patel, a manager at PHM.

To: Jo Morris
From: Jessica Patel
Date: 19 July 20X6
Subject: KHC – new engagement

PHM has a new engagement to provide advice to KHC and I am the engagement manager. I would like you to work on this assignment with me.

I met recently with Kiera Healy, the founder and chief executive of KHC, and the other two members of the KHC board: the finance director, Jeff Nunn; and the treasurer, Rachel Ridd. I have provided you with background notes (**Exhibit 1**).

At the meeting, Kiera explained her ambitions for international expansion to the US over the next few years, but she also has some concerns about the risks that this expansion might generate.

Kiera gave me a summary of her international expansion strategy (**Exhibit 2**). Rachel provided a document which raised some issues about managing the exchange rate risk from foreign currency operating cash flows over the initial six months of US trading (**Exhibit 3**). Jeff has been asked to consider the longer-term risks of the US operations, assuming that a warehouse is established there. Also, the board is concerned about the financial reporting issues arising from expansion to the US. Jeff has provided some details about these issues (**Exhibit 4**).

Kiera also asked me to meet with Paula Simmons, KHC's marketing manager. Paula has some ideas about how the Kiera Healy© brand and distinctive floral design can be used more effectively to develop the business in the UK. She would like our evaluation of this strategy. Paula has provided notes on these issues (**Exhibit 5**).

A potential ethical matter has also arisen, which I would like you to address (**Exhibit 6**).

<u>Instructions</u>

"KHC needs PHM's help and has raised a number of issues which they specifically refer to as 'requests for advice'. I would like you to address these 'requests for advice' (see exhibits) on the following matters:

(1)   The two strategic and operating matters raised by Kiera Healy in respect of KHC's international expansion (Exhibit 2).

(2)   Managing foreign currency exchange rate risk from foreign currency operating cash flows, as set out by the treasurer, Rachel Ridd (Exhibit 3).

(3)   Jeff Nunn's concerns (Exhibit 4) about whether to invest in, and how to raise finance for, a warehouse distribution centre in the US and the financial reporting issues arising from KHC's US expansion and its financing.

(4)   Branding and agreed-upon procedures, as outlined by Paula Simmons, the marketing manager (Exhibit 5).

In addition, please set out the potential ethical implications of the matter identified by Jeff and Rachel (Exhibit 6). Also, explain the actions that should be taken by PHM and by Jeff and Rachel in response to this matter."

Requirement

Respond to the instructions from the engagement manager, Jessica Patel.

Assume it is now July 20X6.

Total: 60 marks

Exhibit 1: Company background notes – prepared by Jessica Patel

Origins

KHC was founded almost 20 years ago by Kiera Healy. The company grew rapidly as the Kiera Healy[©] brand became increasingly well-known and by 20W1 (15 years ago) KHC products were being sold throughout the UK.

Products and manufacturing

KHC has a wide product range which includes: shampoos, conditioners, soap, shower gels and body lotions.

The toiletries are made at a factory in the UK. Good-quality materials are used, but most costs are fixed.

Distribution and marketing

KHC does not own any retail outlets. It sells and distributes to department stores and to chains of upmarket toiletry shops. The larger retailers normally only buy KHC products if they can obtain significant volume discounts. KHC aims to achieve a margin of 40% on its sales to retailers, but the discounts demanded by larger retailers mean that this has not always been achieved.

Retailers sell the KHC products at a premium price, with a mark-up which is often in excess of 50%. As an example, a 250ml container of shower gel sells at a retail price of about £12.

The budgeted pricing and costing for one container of 250ml shower gel is:

	£
Variable production cost	0.50
Packaging	1.00
Allocated fixed production cost	3.30
Full production cost	4.80
Margin for KHC	3.20
Price to retailer	8.00
Retailer mark-up	4.00
Typical retail price to consumer	12.00

Kiera has tried to negotiate higher prices with retailers, but this has normally been met with refusal and even the threat to cease purchasing KHC products.

Frequently, large stores will negotiate lower prices with KHC and thereby reduce KHC's margins. For example, for the 250ml shower gel, the price to a large retailer is normally less than £8.

Financing

Kiera owns the entire ordinary share capital of KHC. The company originally raised a loan to finance the factory purchase, but this loan has been repaid and now the company is almost entirely financed by equity. KHC has reinvested operating cash flows to grow the business.

Kiera wishes to maintain overall control of the company. She told me that she is reluctant to have other shareholders involved, as this could potentially create conflict if they wanted changes to the product or the business model.

Kiera is aware that KHC has been cautious and has grown slowly. However, the KHC board now wants to expand internationally and finance is therefore required. Kiera cannot afford to invest any more equity finance in KHC.

Extracts from the financial statements for the year ended 30 June 20X6

	£'000
Revenue	16,400
Gross profit	6,200
Operating profit	650
Net cash flow from operations	1,380
Property, plant and equipment	2,420
Net assets	5,800

Working capital at 30 June 20X6

	£'000
Inventories	3,100
Receivables	2,200
Cash	680
Current liabilities	2,600

Exhibit 2: Summary of international expansion strategy and operations – prepared by Kiera Healy

Further expansion of our toiletry sales in the UK market has become difficult as most retailers wishing to sell our products already do so. Also, the UK market is very competitive and it is becoming increasingly difficult to negotiate price increases with retailers. There is significant pressure on industry margins in the UK.

While the Kiera Healy© brand is well known in the UK, this is not the case elsewhere. As a result, we have not yet exported our products.

However, in early 20X6, KHC performed some test marketing in the US on a small scale by selling a range of toiletries to a few retailers in New York and Boston. We tried two different pricing strategies. In New York we attempted to penetrate the market by entering with a low price, which was around full cost. In Boston, we positioned the products as a premium brand and priced them at about 25% more than UK prices. To our surprise, the sales volumes in Boston were far greater than those in New York.

Although this was only small-scale market testing, we have been sufficiently encouraged to make the decision to enter the US market from 1 January 20X7.

We do not intend to manufacture in the US. For the initial six months trading to 30 June 20X7, KHC will supply each US retailer directly from the existing UK factory. From 1 July 20X7, however, the KHC board is considering two alternative ways of distributing to US retail customers:

- continue to supply each individual US retailer directly from the existing UK factory; or

- set up a warehouse distribution centre in the US to hold inventory and distribute throughout the US the products manufactured in the UK factory.

We do not intend to set up a separate US subsidiary, but there will be a US division which will be part of KHC and controlled from the UK.

Also, KHC needs to get its pricing strategy right. At the moment the Kiera Healy© brand is not well known in the US, so few people are aware that there is a price difference between Boston and New York. As we grow, we will need an agreed and consistent pricing strategy for the US.

Request for advice

I would like PHM to:

(1) evaluate, without calculations, the strategic and operating issues that arise from each of the following alternatives from 1 July 20X7: (a) continue supplying individual US retailers directly from the existing UK factory; and (b) set up a warehouse distribution centre in the US. Provide a reasoned recommendation.

(2) explain possible strategies for determining appropriate selling prices in the US market. Provide a reasoned recommendation.

Exhibit 3: Managing exchange rate risk from foreign currency operating cash flows prepared by Rachel Ridd

The board has asked me to consider foreign currency risks relevant to KHC's first six months of US operations. I have set out specific illustrative information below.

US operating cash flows – information to illustrate exchange rate risk

KHC will commence operations in the US on 1 January 20X7. KHC wishes to hedge its foreign currency exposure on operating cash flows from that date until 30 June 20X7.

On 31 March 20X7, KHC will make a payment in sterling of £435,000 for the set-up and initial manufacturing costs incurred from 1 January 20X7. Other cash flows to 30 June 20X7 will be in $.

The following are KHC's operating cash flow forecasts for its US activities (assuming that it does not set up a warehouse distribution centre in the US during the first six months of operations):

Cash outflows on 31 March 20X7	£(435,000)
Cash inflows on 31 March 20X7	$640,000
Cash outflows on 30 June 20X7	$(720,000)
Cash inflows on 30 June 20X7	$400,000

Forecast exchange rates at 1 January 20X7 (London forward foreign exchange market)

Spot ($/£)	1.5240 – 1.5275
3-months forward	0.72 – 0.67 cents premium
6-months forward	1.28 – 1.22 cents premium

Annual interest rates: (for 3-month or 6-month transactions)

	Borrowing	Lending
Sterling (£)	6.5%	4.5%
US Dollars ($)	5.0%	3.0%

Request for advice

I would like PHM to:

(1) explain the currency risks arising from the US operating cash flows for the six months to 30 June 20X7 and evaluate, without calculations, how those risks can be mitigated.

(2) prepare calculations and explanations, using the illustrative information above, showing the net sterling receipts and payments for KHC for both its 3-month and 6-month transactions if it hedges using:

- the London forward foreign exchange market; and
- the money market.

Exhibit 4: The risks of setting up a US warehouse distribution centre and financial reporting issues – prepared by Jeff Nunn

I have the following areas of concern about risks if the board decides to set up a warehouse distribution centre in the US:

- Operating returns and risks
- Raising finance

I am also concerned about the financial reporting implications of the US expansion and its financing.

Operating returns and risks

If the board decides to invest in a warehouse distribution centre in the US, it is expected that the purchase would take place on 1 July 20X7 and would cost $3 million.

While the KHC board hopes for growth, two alternative outcomes have been identified if a warehouse distribution centre is opened in the US:

- KHC products will have a niche position in the US market, in which case zero growth is expected and the net cash inflows in $ will be $400,000 in the year to 30 June 20X8. In addition, cash outflows, incurred in £, will be £100,000 in the same period. These $ and £ cash flows will be the same amount each year thereafter indefinitely.

- KHC products will have a wider market in the US, in which case the net cash inflows in $ will be $350,000 in the year to 30 June 20X8. In addition, cash outflows, incurred in £, will be £100,000 in the same period. These $ and £ cash flows would grow at 4% per annum thereafter indefinitely.

I have made the following working assumptions:

- Operating cash flows will occur at year ends.

- The weighted average cost of capital is 10% per annum.

- The probability of KHC products having a niche market is 40% and the probability of KHC products having a wider market is 60%.

- The exchange rate at 1 July 20X7 will be £1 = $1.5.

- Thereafter the $ will appreciate against the £ by 1% per annum indefinitely.

- The evaluation is to be in £ sterling.

Raising finance

I have no previous experience of raising finance for international ventures, but I am keen to use the best method of financing in order to reduce risks.

It has been made clear that there is no equity funding available. The additional funding requirement for a US warehouse would amount to the equivalent of $3 million.

Financial reporting issues

I would like advice about the key financial reporting issues which would arise from KHC's US expansion strategy and its financing. The impact on the financial statements is a matter of concern to the board.

Request for advice

I would like PHM to:

(1) recommend, with supporting calculations and explanations, whether KHC should invest in a warehouse distribution centre in the US. Use the information provided, including the working assumptions.

(2) advise on the best method of finance for the US warehouse distribution centre in order to mitigate risks.

(3) set out the key financial reporting issues which would arise from KHC's US expansion strategy, assuming that KHC invests in a warehouse distribution centre. Include the financial reporting treatment of your recommended method of finance.

Exhibit 5: Developing the Kiera Healy® brand – prepared by Paula Simmons

The history of the Kiera Healy© brand in the UK

The Kiera Healy© brand has been supported by national advertising and is well recognised throughout the UK. Consumer surveys show that the Kiera Healy© brand is fashionable and is regarded as a luxury brand, particularly by women in the UK aged 25 to 40.

The KHC board is satisfied, based on market research, that compared with similar toiletry products whose brand is unknown or little known, sales volumes are significantly higher for KHC products as a result of its brand name.

Specifically, when comparing a Kiera Healy© product with an equivalently priced unbranded product, it is estimated that the unbranded product would generate 60% less sales volume than the Kiera Healy© product.

KHC has spent significant amounts in recent years on advertising and brand development. It is estimated that a competitor wishing to establish a similar brand from a zero base would require ongoing advertising expenditure of about £450,000 per year, with a present value of £3.5 million.

In 20X4, a large international fashion house, Buckingham plc, offered to purchase the Kiera Healy© brand in order to use it for its clothing and handbag ranges. It offered KHC £2.5 million to purchase the Kiera Healy© brand, on the basis that it would grant KHC an exclusive and permanent right to continue to use, without charge, the Kiera Healy© brand name for toiletries in the UK. This offer was rejected by the KHC board.

Developing the brand

The KHC board believes that the Kiera Healy© brand is the most important asset owned by the company. It also considers that KHC is not taking full advantage of the increasing popularity of the brand.

I recently presented a new branding strategy to the KHC board. This comprises two alternative proposals, being either: (a) to license the brand; or (b) to sell the brand (see below). The board has requested that PHM review and evaluate these proposals.

The basis of the new strategy is to leverage the brand and the distinctive floral design that goes with it. KHC owns the legal property rights to the brand and the floral design.

My proposals

My first proposal is to license the brand. This idea came from a recent approach to KHC by a manufacturer of handbags, Mooton plc. Mooton would like to rebrand its 'Attitude' range of handbags with the Kiera Healy© brand name and distinctive floral design in order to increase its sales volumes.

The potential arrangement is that a four-year licensing agreement would be agreed, whereby Mooton would pay a licensing fee of £5 per Kiera Healy© branded handbag sold. The 'Attitude' handbags currently sell at an average price of £150 each and it is not proposed to change this price. Sales of the 'Attitude' range are currently 13,500 handbags per year and this is expected to increase to 30,000 handbags if they are rebranded as Kiera Healy©.

The marketing team believes that the Kiera Healy© brand and design could also be licensed to companies in different industries selling other products such as clothing, accessories and mobile phone cases.

I have concerns about how KHC would monitor licensee partners in order to ensure their compliance with the terms of any licensing agreement. I understand that PHM could perform agreed-upon procedures to assist us in this respect.

My second proposal, as an alternative to licensing, is to sell the Kiera Healy© brand to another company, but retain an exclusive and permanent right to continue to use, without charge, the Kiera Healy© brand for toiletries globally.

Request for advice

I would like PHM to:

(1)   explain the factors that KHC should consider in deciding whether to:

- license the Kiera Healy© brand to Mooton and to companies in other industries. Evaluate the factors to consider in agreeing a licensing fee with Mooton; or

- sell the Kiera Healy© brand to another company, but retain an exclusive and permanent right to continue to use, without charge, the Kiera Healy© brand for toiletries globally. Please estimate the minimum price that would be acceptable to KHC.

(2)   explain the benefits to KHC of PHM carrying out an agreed-upon procedures assignment to monitor licensee partners such as Mooton. Briefly explain the procedures that would be performed by PHM during such an assignment.

Exhibit 6: Potential ethical matter – prepared by Jessica Patel

At the end of my meeting with the KHC board, Kiera had to leave to attend another meeting and I was able to chat informally to Rachel and Jeff.

Jeff and Rachel told me, in confidence, that in April 20X4 they had both become unhappy with one of KHC's suppliers, Juno Ltd. They both believed that Juno products had declined in quality. However, when they informally suggested to Kiera that KHC should change to an alternative supplier, she refused, but gave no reasons.

In May 20X5, Juno notified KHC that it intended to increase its prices by 10%. Jeff and Rachel again spoke to Kiera suggesting a change of suppliers, but formally this time at a board meeting. Kiera refused to have the matter discussed and she approved the 10% price increase.

Last month, Kiera's personal assistant told Jeff, in confidence, that Kiera's nephew is the sales manager for Juno.

Jeff and Rachel, who are both ICAEW Chartered Accountants, thought that I should know about the situation, but they were unsure what action to take.

41 Quinter plc

Assume it is now July 20X6.

"When I took on the role of chairman I did not expect to find such poor information systems and inadequate management controls. Governance at all levels is questionable." Mike Fisher, the new chairman of Quinter plc, was opening a meeting with Rush & Woodrow LLP (RW), a firm of ICAEW Chartered Accountants.

Quinter sells imported electrical goods to individual customers and to electrical stores. All sales are made online. Quinter is planning to list on the AIM market within the next four year (ie before 20Y0.)

You are a senior working for RW, which acts as business advisers to Quinter. RW does not audit Quinter. The RW engagement manager, Tara Thierens, attended the meeting with Mike Fisher.

The meeting

Mike continued the meeting after his opening remarks: "I realise that you are new to Quinter, so I have provided some notes to explain the company background (**Exhibit 1**) and its governance and reporting (**Exhibit 2**).

"Following the recent acquisition of Quinter's entire ordinary share capital by a private equity firm, First Money Kapital (FMK), I was appointed as chairman three months ago to help plan Quinter's AIM listing before 20Y0. It has become clear to me that there are a lot of issues to resolve. The board has authorised me to take advice from RW.

"I have provided some financial and operating data, prepared by Quinter's finance director (**Exhibit 3**). I would like you to analyse quarterly performance and identify any areas of operational weakness.

"I do not consider that the data is sufficient to enable the board to manage and operate the business effectively. My concerns about data management, on which I would like RW's advice, relate to: firstly, sales and customer data; and secondly, inventory data. I have set out my views on these matters (**Exhibit 4**).

"Another issue is that Quinter has no policy on sustainability. This will become more of an issue in the period prior to the AIM listing and the company's corporate responsibility is already being questioned by stakeholders. I think we can use the annual report to publicise our sustainability policy as part of integrated reporting. I have provided some notes (**Exhibit 5**).

"I appreciate that information is limited at present, but I have provided terms of reference for an engagement, where I set out more precisely what is required from RW (**Exhibit 6**)."

Instructions

After the meeting, Tara asks to see you. She outlines what occurred during her meeting with Mike and gives you the following instructions:

"I would like you to provide, for my consideration, a draft response to the terms of reference (Exhibit 6) from Mike Fisher, the Quinter chairman."

Requirement

Respond to the instructions from the RW engagement manager, Tara.

Total: 40 marks

Exhibit 1: Company background – prepared by Mike Fisher

Products

Quinter sells two types of electrical products: items for the home (for example: fridges, cookers, irons, kettles, computer equipment); and items for the garden (for example: lawnmowers and electrical garden tools).

The products carry manufacturers' brand names, but these tend not to be well-known. Quinter describes them as the 'brands of the future'.

Suppliers

• cost differentiation

The Quinter business model is to import basic-quality, low-cost electrical goods from developing countries. The goods are safe and function adequately, but the technical features are approximately four to five years behind the market-leading brands. *old technology*

Quinter obtains volume discounts from suppliers by placing large orders. Each order has a separate contract. Every contract has a clause which specifies that there should be no more than three faulty items per 100 items purchased. Suppliers can be replaced if they do not meet Quinter's price and quality requirements. *→ a lot of suppliers available*

3/100 faulty

Inventories

Quinter holds significant amounts of inventories. The reasons given by the procurement staff when questioned about this are:

- lead times from suppliers can be long and uncertain
- demand can be variable
- there are many different product lines

Sales and customers

All customers order online. There are two types of customers:

- individual customers
- stores selling electrical goods

The prices that stores pay are 10% lower than the prices paid by individual customers, but stores are required to make an order with a minimum value of £1,000. Stores use a separate website from individual customers. There are many stores on Quinter's customer database and these tend to be small businesses with limited resources.

To place an order, individual customers are asked to provide details about themselves (name, address, gender, age, occupation, interests, family information). This information is held on a database along with the history of transactions with Quinter. Little use appears to be made of this database by Quinter staff. One comment by a staff member was that "there is too much detailed data to be useful to us. In the past five years over one million customers have bought products from us."

Big data social media information usage

Both stores and individual customers have the right to return goods to Quinter, for whatever reason, within 14 days of purchase. If the goods are faulty, they can be returned to Quinter within one year of purchase.

Exhibit 2: Governance and reporting – prepared by Mike Fisher

Governance

The board consists of four executive directors who have each held these posts for over 10 years. Before I was appointed, the chief executive also acted as chairman.

division of responsibilities

At board level, all major functions are carried out by the main board (ie there are no subcommittees of the board, such as an audit committee, nominations committee or remuneration committee).

↳ problem for AIM listing ⇒ no required but best practice

There is no internal audit department.

All Quinter's ordinary shares are held by the private equity firm, FMK. → *abuse of power?*

The remuneration of directors has increased by an average of 10% per annum over the past five years. *no check?* Over the same period, profits have not grown.

Reporting

The board receives quarterly, summary management accounts and operating data to monitor the performance of the business. These are similar, in terms of the level of detail, to that provided in Exhibit 3.

Exhibit 3: Financial and operating data – prepared by Quinter's finance director

Quarterly summary management accounts of Quinter for the year ended 30 June 20X6

	3 months to 30 September 20X5 £'000	3 months to 31 December 20X5 £'000	3 months to 31 March 20X6 £'000	3 months to 30 June 20X6 £'000	TOTAL £'000
Revenue by customer type:					
Individual customers	4,805	3,914	4,766	6,975	20,460
Stores	1,395	1,136	1,384	2,025	5,940
Revenue by product type:					
Home products	4,200	4,550	4,900	5,250	18,900
Garden products	2,000	500	1,250	3,750	7,500
Cost of sales by product type:					
Home products	2,940	3,185	3,430	3,675	13,230
Garden products	1,200	300	750	2,250	4,500

Operating data for Quinter for the year ended 30 June 20X6

	3 months to 30 September 20X5	3 months to 31 December 20X5	3 months to 31 March 20X6	3 months to 30 June 20X6	TOTAL
Number of items sold:					
Home products	120,000	130,000	140,000	150,000	540,000
Garden products	50,000	10,000	25,000	75,000	160,000
Number of items returned by all customers	8,500	7,000	8,250	11,250	35,000
Number of different types of product sold	480	380	420	560	–

Exhibit 4: Data management – prepared by Mike Fisher

In my view, while Quinter captures data, it does not analyse and disseminate data as efficiently and effectively as it should in order to manage and control the business.

Sales and customer data

Data being captured needs more detailed analysis for effective board-level decision making. (Exhibit 3 represents the level of detail available to the board.)

For example, we do not know enough about our customers to market to the needs of each sub-group. Also, we do not know how much profit each individual product is making and therefore whether it is worth selling.

Inventory data   → *demand + preferences*

We are holding too much inventory. I understand that we need to hold enough to meet customer needs quickly, but with better information we could lower overall inventory levels and therefore lower inventory holding costs.

I am also concerned that we may not be valuing inventories correctly for financial reporting purposes, particularly as there is a large amount of inventories purchased in a variety of foreign currencies.

Exhibit 5: Sustainability and integrated reporting – prepared by Mike Fisher

I would like Quinter to introduce a new policy called "return and recycle".

This policy goes beyond what is required by environmental regulations. It involves customers informing us that they intend to dispose of one of our products which they purchased in the past. We will offer to organise collection of the product and then either recycle it, or dispose of it in an environmentally friendly way. This would be at no cost to customers, if they purchase an equivalent new item from Quinter at the same time.

I don't think many customers will take advantage of this. However, I believe that this policy will give us a public profile as an environmentally-friendly company that promotes sustainability, something that we can publicise in our annual report.

Exhibit 6: Terms of reference – prepared by Mike Fisher

I would like RW to draft a report which:

(1) analyses the financial and operating data provided (Exhibit 3). This should explain quarterly performance and identify any areas of operational weakness.

(2) identifies and justifies the additional data that should be made available at board level which would aid its decision making for:

- sales and customer management; and
- inventory management.

(3) explains the financial reporting issues for the valuation of Quinter's inventories and recommends the information required to ensure that the company's inventories are valued appropriately in its financial statements.

(4) identifies and explains improvements in corporate governance that would assist Quinter's management control and performance management.

(5) evaluates whether the sustainability policy suggested (Exhibit 5) would:

- make a positive contribution to the public profile of Quinter; and
- generate additional useful management data.

42 Wooster Ltd

Assume it is now November 2016.

Wooster Ltd is a luxury sports car manufacturer, based in the UK.

You are Lisa Ling, and you work as a senior for Gieves & Wood LLP (GW), a firm of ICAEW Chartered Accountants which operates internationally. Wooster is a client of GW, but not an audit client.

You received the following email from Alex Khan, a GW manager.

To: Lisa Ling
From: Alex Khan
Date: 8 November 2016

Subject: Wooster – new engagement

GW has accepted a new engagement to advise the Wooster board.

I realise that you have not worked on this client before so I have provided background information for you (**Exhibit 1**).

I have also provided you with a briefing document (**Exhibit 2**) from Eric Edwards, Wooster's chief executive, setting out both the key decisions that the board needs to take about engine procurement and the nature of the advice required from GW.

The board's decisions need to be taken by 30 November 2016.

Last week, I received a confidential memorandum (**Exhibit 3**) from Harry Harris, Wooster's non-executive chairman, requesting GW's advice on share options and possible senior staff redundancies.

Instructions

Using the available information, I would like you to do the following:

(1) Draft a response to the request for advice set out in the briefing document from Eric Edwards (Exhibit 2).

(2) Prepare notes which respond to the request for advice from Harry Harris in the confidential memorandum (Exhibit 3).

(3) Set out any ethical implications for Wooster and for GW arising from the matters noted by Harry Harris (Exhibit 3). Explain the actions that GW should take.

Requirement

Respond to the instructions from Alex Khan.

Total: 62 marks

Exhibit 1: Background information – prepared by Alex Khan

Company history

Wooster is a private company, founded in 1920. It is a small company in the context of the car manufacturing industry, making luxury sports cars for a niche market.

Wooster has relied largely on the traditional engineering skills of its workforce. While there has been some automation of production processes, this is still not on the scale of most large competitors.

Following the onset of the recession in 2008, sales began to fall. Profits also declined and in 2013 the company made an operating loss.

At that time, the board and senior managers attempted to negotiate a management buy-out of Wooster, but they could not raise sufficient finance.

New ownership

On 1 January 2014, a private equity company, StockFin, acquired 90% of the ordinary share capital of Wooster for £432 million.

Prior to the acquisition, the Wooster board comprised the chief executive and four other executive directors. There were no non-executive directors. Immediately after the acquisition, StockFin removed the chief executive, and replaced him with Eric Edwards. The other four executive directors retained their positions. In addition, six new non-executive directors were appointed, including the chairman, Harry Harris, all of whom are employees of StockFin.

As part of the acquisition deal, all of the Wooster executive directors and some senior managers acquired the remaining 10% of the ordinary shares for £21 million. In addition, on 1 January 2014, they were granted share options, which vest on 31 December 2017.

StockFin plans to improve Wooster's operating efficiency and performance. Wooster will obtain an AIM listing in 2020, which StockFin will use as an exit route to sell its investment.

Wooster has not paid a dividend since 2008.

Production and capacity

Wooster manufactures all of its own car engines at its engine factory which is located in the UK. These engines are then transported to Wooster's car assembly plant where Wooster builds its sports cars. The engine factory is only five kilometres from the car assembly plant.

Over the two-year period 2014 and 2015, £20 million was invested to increase automation of the car assembly plant. Wooster financed this through bank borrowing. The increased automation resulted in a number of unskilled workers being made redundant.

The company sold 3,600 cars in 2015 and expects to sell the same number in 2016.

The engine factory is currently working at full capacity. However, following the recent investment in new equipment, the car assembly plant could potentially produce a total of 5,200 cars per year.

The company employs 1,200 people: 300 in the engine factory and 900 in the car assembly plant.

Sales

Approximately 70% of Wooster's sports cars are made according to the specific requirements of a customer order. The customer can specify the model, colour, size of engine and optional extras at the time of ordering.

As Wooster's engine factory is operating at full capacity, customers may need to wait up to six months from the time of ordering to the time of delivery. The length and variability of this lead time has resulted in the loss of some customers.

The remaining 30% of Wooster's sports cars are made to a standard specification in the most popular models, colours and engine sizes. These cars are delivered to independent car retailers (dealerships) and are available in inventory for immediate sale to customers.

Wooster sells its cars through dealerships mainly located in the US, the UK and the Eurozone.

Sales and production occur evenly over the year. In 2015, the geographical distribution of total sales revenue was:

	%
US	25
UK	40
Eurozone countries	30
Other regions	5

Financial and operating data

[handwritten: 80   85   90   91]

Extracts from the financial statements for the years to 31 December:

	2013	2014	2015	2016 (estimated)
	£'000	£'000	£'000	£'000
Revenue	240,000	270,600	309,600	313,200
Gross profit	60,000	85,800	104,400	104,400
Operating (loss)/profit	(20,000)	800	14,400	13,400
(Loss)/profit before tax	(23,000)	(2,700)	10,400	9,400
(Loss)/profit after tax	(18,400)	(2,160)	8,320	7,520
Property, plant and equipment	80,000	88,000	96,000	95,000
Net current assets	30,000	29,840	40,160	48,680
Non-current liabilities	60,000	70,000	80,000	80,000
Equity	50,000	47,840	56,160	63,680

[handwritten annotations: costs increase too?; fixed cost ↑?; 20%]

Operating data for the years to 31 December are as follows:

	2013	2014	2015	2016 (estimated)
Number of cars produced and sold	3,000	3,300	3,600	3,600
Number of employees	1,500	1,350	1,200	1,200

[handwritten annotations: price to increase?; materials ↑↑↑?]

Exhibit 2: Engine procurement briefing document – prepared by Eric Edwards

The Wooster board would like GW's advice on the future procurement of engines.

The current engine factory

Wooster currently manufactures its own engines in a separate engine factory. There has been a lack of investment in the automation of engine production and design over many years. Since the acquisition by StockFin, almost all the new investment has been in the car assembly plant.

Wooster's car engines are less efficient, less reliable and have higher emissions than equivalent engines made by rival, multinational car manufacturers using automated processes. In addition, the manufacture of engines using labour-intensive, traditional, engineering skills has become increasingly expensive.

[handwritten: – redundancies; – competitive advantage; quality & reputation.]

As a consequence, the board has decided to improve the current type of engine as soon as possible with a more modern design. The new engine design needs to be a substantial improvement on the existing version in terms of cost, efficiency, reliability and emissions.

It is not possible to achieve this improvement with the current plant and equipment in the engine factory. The Wooster board is therefore considering two alternative proposals:

- Outsource the manufacture of engines; or
- Automate and upgrade the engine factory

Proposal 1 – Outsource the manufacture of engines

On 31 December 2016, the existing engine factory would close. Future engine manufacture would be outsourced. Redundancies would occur in January 2017.

Negotiations are well developed with a rival company, Jadd Motors plc (JM), for the sale of the engine factory assets. JM accepts that the sale is conditional on the Wooster board selecting Proposal 1, but it requires a decision by 30 November 2016.

The disposal would occur in March 2017, raising net proceeds of £29 million, after deducting factory closure costs of £2.5 million, including redundancies. The contract would include all engine factory assets (ie. land, buildings and all equipment).

[handwritten: disposal group]

The engine factory assets are expected to have a total carrying amount of £22 million in Wooster's financial statements at 31 December 2016, after charging depreciation of £600,000 for the year. The fair value of these assets is expected to remain at £28 million until 31 December 2016.

Two multinational car manufacturers (Gratz, a German company; and Shensu, a Japanese company) have each expressed an interest in becoming the exclusive supplier in future for all Wooster's engines.

Both potential suppliers produce a wide range of luxury cars and have their own highly-automated engine production facilities.

Preliminary contract negotiations have taken place with both of these potential suppliers.

- German supplier – Gratz

  A German car company, Gratz, has offered a three-year supply contract from 1 January 2017. The contract would specify a minimum of 3,500 engines per year and a maximum of 4,200 engines per year. Engines would be delivered weekly. *10,000*

  The average price payable by Wooster, per engine, would be: €14,000 in the year to 31 December 2017; increasing to €15,400 in the year to 31 December 2018; and €16,800 in the year to 31 December 2019. *11,000* *12,000* .

- Japanese supplier – Shensu

  A Japanese car company, Shensu, has offered a two-year contract from 1 January 2017 to supply engines to Wooster at an average fixed price of yen (¥) 1,540,000 per engine. *↳ £11,000*

  The contract would specify a minimum of 3,800 engines per year. The maximum quantity is 5,500 engines per year. Engines would be delivered monthly.

Working assumptions (applicable to both suppliers)

- The euro exchange rate will be £1 = €1.4

- The yen exchange rate will be £1 = ¥140

- The discount rate is 6% per annum

- Operating cash flows occur at year ends

- The engines will be installed into cars as soon as possible after delivery, as there is very limited storage space at the car assembly plant

- Wooster's average total contribution per car, excluding the engine cost, will be £45,000

- Forecast demand for Wooster cars for the years ending 31 December is:

Year	Number of cars
2017	3,800
2018	4,100
2019	4,400

  There is uncertainty about demand in 2020 and beyond, but Wooster's management estimates that it will be at least 4,400 cars per year.

- Both supplier contracts can potentially be renewed.

Proposal 2 – Automate and upgrade Wooster's engine factory

A major capital investment would be required to automate and upgrade Wooster's existing engine factory, in order to produce a new type of car engine.

The new production line and all capital equipment would be purchased from a US supplier of industrial equipment, Silvez, for the equivalent of £40 million. During the upgrade, the engine factory would need to close temporarily, and engine production would therefore cease for three months from 1 January 2017. It would not be possible to purchase appropriate engines from another company during this period.

The required investment would be financed by issuing a 4%, 10-year, £40 million sterling-denominated bond.

It is estimated that the newly-equipped factory would be able to produce engines at an average variable cost of £6,000 per engine over the entire useful life of the new factory equipment. The useful life of the new plant and machinery is uncertain and current estimates are between 7 and 10 years. The equipment is highly-specialised and would have an insignificant net realisable value immediately after installation and thereafter. *↳ no residual value.*

The production capacity of the upgraded factory would be 8,000 engines per year.

Assurance for Proposal 1

If the board selects Proposal 1, the contract would include a service level agreement with the outsourcing supplier (Gratz or Shensu), setting out the performance criteria to be satisfied. The specific terms of the service level agreement would relate to the quality of the engines, the service provided and the environmental impact, including sustainability.

Wooster would need to renew the outsourcing contract and renegotiate the price when the initial contract period ends.

The board believes that assurance procedures should be carried out, by a combination of GW and Wooster staff, to monitor the selected key performance indicators (KPIs) in the service level agreement.

The board has not yet decided all of the KPIs in the service level agreement but, as a minimum, it would wish to develop KPIs for environmental impact and sustainability.

Request for advice

I would like GW to do the following:

(1) In respect of Proposal 1, compare and evaluate the Gratz and Shensu supply contracts under each of the following headings:

- Financial appraisal, with supporting calculations
- Supply chain risks, foreign exchange risks and risk management

Provide a reasoned recommendation for the preferred supplier, assuming that the Wooster board decides to select Proposal 1.

(2) Set out, and justify two KPIs that could form part of the environmental impact and sustainability conditions in a service level agreement for Proposal 1.

In addition, set out and explain the assurance procedures that should be performed to provide evidence of the extent to which these two KPIs are being achieved.

(3) Describe and evaluate, with calculations, the potential benefits and risks of Proposal 2 in comparison with Proposal 1 (using your preferred supplier for Proposal 1). Provide a reasoned recommendation.

(4) Explain, for each proposal, the key financial reporting issues and the appropriate treatment in the Wooster financial statements, for each of the financial years affected. In respect of Proposal 1, explain the issues for both potential supplier contracts.

Exhibit 3: Confidential - Share options and redundancies – prepared by Harry Harris

StockFin is not happy with the performance of its investment in Wooster and has asked me to make changes.

4 + 46 = 50.

My immediate concern is the number of share options held by Wooster's executive directors (who each hold a significant number of options) and 46 other members of the Wooster senior management. The options will vest on 31 December 2017, provided that the option holder is still employed by Wooster at that date. Each option gives the holder the right to subscribe for one share in Wooster, on 31 December 2017, at a zero exercise price. *→4yrs* *↳ vesting condition*

If all of these options were to be exercised, the shareholding of Wooster's executive directors and the senior managers would increase from 10% to around 20% of the company's total ordinary share capital. This would result in a major dilution of StockFin's shareholding in Wooster. Frankly, it was a mistake to issue so many share options.

I intend to prevent this dilution of StockFin's shareholding by making a significant number of the option holders redundant or dismissing them. As a result, their options will never vest as they will not still be employed at the vesting date. *↳ illegal & unethical.*

I will give the executive directors and senior managers two reasons for the redundancies. Firstly, the number of unskilled employees was reduced in 2014 and again in 2015, but no managers were made redundant. There are now fewer people to manage, so we need fewer managers. Secondly, the financial performance of Wooster has just not been good enough. StockFin normally requires a 20% annual return on its investment. *↳ not a valid reason.*

I want to be clear about this. It's not that the company's performance has got worse since the acquisition in 2014. What I am saying is that StockFin has invested significantly and, with competent management, performance should have improved a lot more than it actually has.

I am not suggesting that we make all the option holders redundant, as that would be unreasonable. However, I believe that we should make enough of them redundant to prevent about 60% of the options vesting.

Redundancy payments and compensation for dismissal will amount to about £1.7 million. In addition, we estimate that legal costs will be a further £150,000. However, this is better than a dilution of share ownership on the scale currently expected.

The redundancies will be announced in December 2016 and take place in early January 2017.

Request for advice

I would like GW to prepare an analysis of the financial and operating data (Exhibit 1) with supporting explanations. This should enable the board to understand the performance of Wooster, and the Wooster management team, in the period since the acquisition by StockFin.

I would also like you to write an additional short statement summarising performance. I intend to show this to the Wooster managers to justify our proposal to make redundancies on the grounds of poor performance. I hope that GW will agree that performance has been poor.

↳ intimidation?

43 Phantom West Airlines Plc

Assume it is now November 2016.

Phantom West Airlines plc (PWA) is a UK-based scheduled airline specialising in long-haul flights from London. It has both business customers and leisure customers. PWA is listed on the London Stock Exchange.

The chief executive of PWA, Kevin Gunn, asked to meet with Helen Hemson, who is a partner in Bowers & Bruno LLP (BB), a firm of ICAEW Chartered Accountants. You work for BB as a senior in the advisory department. PWA is a client of BB, but not an audit client.

The meeting

Kevin opened the meeting. "The PWA board has been considering two issues that have arisen for the business. The board cannot reach agreement, so we have decided to ask for independent advice from BB.

"As you have not previously worked on an engagement for PWA, I have provided some background notes about the airline industry and the company (**Exhibit 1**).

"The first issue relates to the possibility of PWA operating a new route from London to India. If the company decides to do this, new aircraft will need to be acquired and these will require financing. I have provided you with briefing notes (**Exhibit 2**) which include details of what the PWA board requires from BB.

"The second issue relates to PWA's total fuel costs for all routes, which are not only a high proportion of total costs, but also volatile. The finance director left the company in September 2016 and we are still looking for a permanent replacement. One of the finance team, Zara Zhou, is acting as the temporary finance director. She lacks experience and would appreciate some advice from BB. She has provided draft annual report extracts (**Exhibit 3**) and notes on some matters relating to fuel costs (**Exhibit 4**), including what the PWA board requires from BB."

↳ figures may be wrong.

Engagement partner's instructions

Helen asks to see you after her meeting with Kevin. She outlines the details of the meeting and gives you the following instructions:

"I would like you to prepare a draft response to the requests for advice from Kevin Gunn (Exhibit 2) and from Zara Zhou (Exhibit 4)."

Requirement

Respond to the instructions from Helen, the engagement partner.

Total: 38 marks

Exhibit 1: Industry and company background – prepared by Kevin Gunn

Industry background

The scheduled passenger airline industry operates to a published timetable. It includes airlines which operate flights on both short-haul and intercontinental, long-haul routes. Seats are arranged by class which may include, in increasing order of price: economy class, premium economy, business class and first class.

The scheduled sector also includes low-cost airlines which operate flights almost exclusively on short-haul routes, with economy-class seats only.

Airline profits have been affected by volatile oil prices, as fuel costs comprise a high proportion of total costs. Over many years, oil prices increased, reaching around US$140 per barrel prior to the recession in 2008. By late 2014, oil prices had dropped to about US$105 per barrel, before falling steeply over the following 18 months to around US$45 per barrel. These low fuel costs contributed significantly to an increase in airline company profits. *expected profits ↑*

PWA – company background *↳2016*

PWA was established in 1984, when it acquired its initial fleet of aircraft, along with the rights to routes and landing slots at London Heathrow Airport. PWA's fleet has since expanded, as it has both purchased and leased additional aircraft.

PWA has always operated in the long-haul, intercontinental market with routes from London to America, Asia and Africa. By operating long-haul flights, it has avoided competition from low-cost airlines. It provides a good-quality service to all passengers enabling it to charge a small price premium over many other airlines operating similar routes.

The PWA strategy has been to have a mixture of premium economy and business class seats, which has reinforced the quality brand image. It has avoided the price extremes of economy class and first class. *no eco or first*

Business class passengers mainly comprise two distinct groups: firstly, passengers travelling on business where the fare is normally paid by employers; and secondly, high-income individuals travelling for leisure. Premium economy passengers are mostly middle-income individuals travelling for leisure.

PWA has a 30 September accounting year end.

Exhibit 2: Proposal to operate a new route to India – prepared by Kevin Gunn

Introduction

A new route with landing slots has become available between London and New Delhi, India. This route would start on 1 October 2017.

Operating data

The new route would require the acquisition of two new identical aircraft which are capable of flying directly between London and New Delhi without stopping. PWA proposes to operate the route with one flight per day from London to New Delhi; and one flight per day from New Delhi to London. Each aircraft is only capable of operating one flight per day.

The proposed prices of seats for a one-way flight are:

Premium economy	£600
Business class	£1,250

max cap : 1 flight per day to and from 2 aircrafts

Market forecasts

Preliminary market research has indicated that the number of passengers per one-way flight, based on the proposed prices, is forecast as follows:

Day	Premium economy passengers	Business class passengers
Monday	150	120
Tuesday	150	60
Wednesday	150	60
Thursday	150	60
Friday	200	120
Saturday	200	60
Sunday	200	120

The market research undertaken indicates that there will not be much seasonal variation in demand, hence the above table represents a typical week. Flights are expected to operate 360 days of the year.

For premium economy passengers: if demand exceeds the number of premium economy seats available, then some passengers will be assigned to a business class seat, for no extra charge, if these are available. It is assumed that passengers will not wait a full day to travel if they cannot get a seat with PWA and will instead fly with other airlines.

For business class passengers: if demand exceeds the number of business class seats available, then passengers who cannot book business class seats with PWA are likely to fly with other airlines.

PWA is confident that the forecast level of demand will remain consistent for the next few years. However, if long-term demand for the new route to India is lower than anticipated, then one or both aircraft could be taken out of service (grounded) from 30 September 2020. It is estimated that the fair value of each aircraft will be £25 million at 30 September 2020.

Configuring the aircraft seating

The two possible configurations for one aircraft are:

- Configuration 1 – 80 business class seats and 180 premium economy seats.
- Configuration 2 – 60 business class seats and 225 premium economy seats.

Once the seats are installed, it would be expensive to change them, as it would require the aircraft being taken out of service for a number of weeks.

The seat configuration will be the same in each of the two aircraft.

Financing the aircraft

The purchase cost, per aircraft, is expected to be £40 million, payable on 1 October 2017. PWA would borrow to finance the aircraft purchase. Each aircraft would have an expected useful life of 10 years, after which time it is forecast that it could be sold for £15 million.

As an alternative to purchasing, PWA can lease the aircraft for 10 years. Annual lease rentals for each aircraft would be £5 million and would be payable annually commencing 1 October 2017. The lease contract would contain a break clause which would permit PWA to cancel the lease on 30 September 2022 in return for a penalty payment per aircraft of £14 million on that date.

There is no need for the two aircraft to be financed in the same way.

Request for advice from BB

(1) Calculate the revenue per week, for one aircraft, expected to be generated by each of the two proposed seat configurations. Provide a reasoned recommendation as to which seat configuration would be preferable, taking account of all relevant factors.

(2) Compare the two methods of financing the new aircraft, providing supporting calculations and explanations. Provide a reasoned recommendation. State any further information that would be needed before making a final decision.

(3) For each of the two finance methods, set out the financial reporting consequences of grounding one or both aircraft from 30 September 2020. For this purpose, assume that there will be no further use for the aircraft after 1 October 2020. If the aircraft had been purchased, they would therefore be sold, at fair value, as soon as possible after this date.

Notes

1   Ignore all taxes and deferred tax.
2   As a working assumption, use an annual discount rate of 7%.

Exhibit 3: PWA draft annual report extracts for the year ended 30 September 2016

PWA: Summary draft statement of comprehensive income for the year ended 30 September 2016

	£m
Revenue	2,815
Fuel costs	(942)
Other operating costs	(1,273)
Operating profit	600
Finance costs	(36)
Profit before tax	564
Tax	(73)
Profit for the year	491
Other comprehensive income	
Fair value changes in cash flow hedges transferred to fuel costs	56
Fair value changes in cash flow hedges in the year (fuel commodities)	(85)
Total comprehensive income	462

Risk management note – extract from draft annual report

PWA has entered into arrangements to mitigate the risk of volatility in fuel prices. These are primarily through forward contracts, on a rolling basis, applicable to the forthcoming 18 months of anticipated fuel purchases.

At 30 September 2016, these forward contracts covered approximately 90% of PWA's estimated future fuel requirements for the nine months to 30 June 2017; and approximately 60% of its estimated future fuel requirements for the following nine months to 31 March 2018.   *9m contracts*

Extracts from accounting policies note

All of the fuel forward contracts are matched against highly probable forecast commodity cash flows relating to anticipated fuel purchases.

PWA's fuel forward contracts are treated as cash flow hedges of forecast fuel purchases for risks arising from the commodity price of fuel. The contracts are recorded at fair value in the statement of financial position and are re-measured to fair value at the end of each accounting period, through equity, to the extent they are effective. Gains and losses on the forward contracts are recognised in profit or loss in the same period in which the hedged item affects profit or loss.

Exhibit 4: Managing fuel costs – prepared by Zara Zhou

Fuel is a major cost for PWA. It is highly correlated to the global price of oil, which has been very volatile in recent years.

The risk of oil price changes is a constant concern as, if PWA is exposed to higher fuel costs than our rivals, we lose competitiveness.

Until he left the company in September 2016, the finance director had been using forward contracts to hedge oil price increases. However, in 2015, and in the first half of 2016, oil prices did not increase; they fell. As a result, PWA was, in effect, locked into higher costs than the market rates for fuel, and losses were incurred on these forward contracts.

I do not fully understand the impact of the finance director's fuel price forward hedges on the company's reported profit (Exhibit 3).

Since taking on the role of acting finance director, I have not used forward contracts or any other type of hedging for fuel costs.

Concerns about hedging fuel costs

I am worried about using forward contracts in case oil prices fall next year and we are, in effect, locked into higher current prices again. I have heard that fuel commodity futures might be a better alternative than forward contracts.

I am also unsure about whether 18 months is the appropriate period over which we should be hedging and whether to hedge all our anticipated future fuel purchases or just a proportion of them.

I realise that I am exposing the company to the risk of fuel price changes by delaying my decision.

Request for advice

(1) Explain how fuel price changes and forward contracts on fuel prices have impacted PWA's profit and other comprehensive income in the year ended 30 September 2016. I need to know why the movements have been recognised in the financial statements in the manner shown in Exhibit 3, not just a general explanation of what has occurred.

(2) With respect to the hedging of fuel prices:

- Explain whether PWA should hedge, or accept the risk of fuel price volatility.

- If hedging is to take place, provide reasoned advice to PWA on the most appropriate hedging strategies. This should include addressing the concerns that I have set out above.

Answer Bank

1 Hobart plc

		Marks
		Up to
(a)	Introduction to memorandum	3
(b)	Valuation of Tasman assets	15
(c)	Discussion around valuation of assets	10
(d)	Risks relating to acquisition	8
(e)	Assurance over asset values	12
(f)	Draft memo: discussion of SID concerns	9
(g)	Draft memo: comments on corporate governance	12
Total marks		69
Maximum marks		55

Memorandum

To: Helen Dunn (assignment partner)
From: A. Senior
Date: 1 December 20X6
Subject: Acquisition of Tasman

(a) **Introduction**

The valuation of Tasman needs to be considered from the perspective of both an individual stand-alone company and also as a future integrated element of the Hobart group.

The key questions of valuation are therefore:

- What is Tasman worth to Hobart? (ie up to how much should Hobart be willing to pay?)

- For what amount will the administrator be willing to sell Hobart? The company needs to be sold or saved, and cannot remain in administration indefinitely as the Enterprise Act 2002 puts a one-year time limit on administration. In reality, the administrator would wish to act much more quickly than this. Thus, the administrator's alternatives to Hobart's offer are (1) the potential offers that may be received from other potential acquirers and (2) the break-up and sale of the company's assets.

In terms of what is being acquired, then the alternatives for Hobart are to:

- acquire the share capital of Tasman (although this is unlikely, as it would also involve acquiring the liabilities).

- acquire the business assets of Tasman, leaving the liabilities with the insolvent company.

- acquire individual assets of Tasman on a selective, piecemeal basis (eg some of the sites if the company is to be broken up).

The administrator will attempt to save the company as a going concern as the first priority but must act in the best interests of the creditors. Thus, whether Hobart will be able to exercise any of the above options will depend on the amount and form of the bids that may be made by other potential acquirers within the timescale set by the administrator.

The position of Rex is twofold, (1) as a major creditor; and (2) as a supplier who may have an interest in continuing Tasman as a going concern as it is a customer.

(b) **Valuation of assets**

While it has been stated by the FD that the firm carrying out the administration of Tasman requires a price of more than the fair value of the business assets, this value at least sets a base line figure. If there are no other bids, then the alternative to the overall business asset value would be the break-up of the business, which the administrator would be reluctant to do. The Enterprise Act requires that the administrator should attempt to save the business as a going concern.

In valuing the assets, a distinction needs to be made between the following values:

- Historic costs (which may form the basis of some of the financial statement values).

- Historic replacement costs – assets that have been revalued in the past but revaluations are not up to date.

- Current replacement costs.

- Net realisable values – ie what the liquidator can sell assets for on a break-up basis. (The financial statements may need to be restated on a break-up basis if the company ceases to be a going concern).

- Value in use – this will be considered collectively for all assets.

In the first instance, the asset valuation will examine the assets on a break-up basis as this would set a floor price for the administrator.

The valuation of the business assets is uncertain given the information available, however, the following may be a first estimate:

Item	Suggested value	Comment
Goodwill	Nil	As the company is loss making and its future as a going concern is in severe doubt, it is difficult to see why there should be any value attributable to goodwill. It needs to be ascertained why goodwill is not fully impaired, rather than only partially at 31 December 20X6.
		It may be that part of the brand value is subsumed in goodwill to the extent that it relates to the acquisition of Darwin, but this is very questionable.
Property, plant and equipment	£21.5m (probable maximum)	The fair value of the property (asserted to be £15m) should be capable of being ascertained with reasonable accuracy using a property valuer, and in accordance with IFRS 13 *Fair Value Measurement*. The replacement cost and the realisable value should be reasonably similar in an actively traded sector of the property market.
		The remaining PPE should be identified and itemised. It may be specialised equipment (eg used to electronically tune Rex cars) in which case the replacement cost may be substantially higher than the realisable value. On the other hand, an active market may exist in the motor trade for general assets used in the industry in which case the replacement cost may approximate to the realisable value.
		It needs to be ascertained whether any of the assets are capitalised under finance leases. In this case the net realisable value of the rights to use the assets under the lease may be much lower than the declared fair values of the assets themselves. (The administrator should have contacted all the leasing companies upon appointment, and should be able to provide a list of assets that are owned by such third parties.)
		Overall, a close examination of values on an asset-by-asset basis is required before a firm offer is to be made. The fair values suggested have been used in this estimate noting that they may turn out to be optimistic in a break-up situation.
		Selling costs have been deducted in arriving at an initial and approximate net realisable value.

Item	Suggested value	Comment
Inventories	£7m (maximum)	The retail values are an inappropriate basis on which to value inventories on acquisition of the company as these are selling prices to individual customers.
		More accurate figures are needed of the trade values of the cars ie the buying prices to dealers (there is an active market in second hand cars so this should not be a major problem).
		Meanwhile, the cost of acquiring the vehicles can be used as a rough measure of the net realisable value on break-up (ie their 'trade' value). Given that vehicles age and thus depreciate while being held in inventories the actual worth is likely to be lower than their cost. This is particularly the case as there are currently around eight months' sales of vehicles held in inventory.
		The consignment inventories would however be claimed by Rex and could not be held by the administrator for sale. These are valued at £4m and must therefore be deducted from the £11m carrying value.
		It may also be that the values of used cars traded-in against new Rex cars are at an artificially inflated cost as excessive trade-in values may have been awarded to give an incentive to buy a new Rex car.
Receivables	£500,000 (maximum)	Assumes full recovery of receivables.
		The actual receivables at the date of acquisition will need to be determined.
		Receivables may include deposits in respect of consignment inventories.
		It is possible that the administrator could be left with the responsibility for receivables collection if the business assets are acquired.
Off balance sheet assets		
Brand	Probably near zero	An offer was made to acquire the brand in 20X4 for £2m. As this was seriously considered, the offer may have approximated to the market value at that time.
		There must, however, be severe doubts regarding whether the brand is now worth anything despite the fact that Tasman has a good reputation for service. Specifically, the company's reputation may have been damaged by selling Rex cars and entering administration. Also, the fact that Tasman is loss-making, means that the brand has no current value in use. It would only acquire value by being purchased by another company. Care also needs to be taken over whether the offer was only for the brand alone or also with associated customer lists and any other rights and trade marks.
		The value of £2m therefore now seems optimistic. In the absence of any other data a nil value is initially adopted but it is noted that this may be understated and further information is needed.
Total	£29m	

Notes on the asset-based valuation

The asset valuation is the amount that the administrator is likely to obtain by a sale of the assets before deducting liabilities.

Noting the need for more information, the price that the administrator would (optimistically) desire for the business assets is thus around £29m, without any assumption of liabilities by Hobart or another purchaser.

The following points may also be noted:

- The Transfer of Undertakings (Protection of Employment) Regulations 2006 would mean that Hobart would assume obligations with respect to employees. This applies even though the business assets are being acquired rather than the shares of Tasman. These obligations may also extend to some sub-contractors. The obligations would not however extend to directors' service contracts unless the shares were being acquired.

- There may be other off-balance sheet contractual rights which would have value but which have not been included.

- There may be further rights or charges over the assets (in addition to those against property) held by third parties, which may either reduce their value or prevent individual sale (eg overdrafts).

- The costs to the administrator of liquidating assets individually on a piecemeal break-up may be greater than the costs of a sale of all assets to Hobart. There may thus be a 'discount' for a sale of business assets in their entirety to Hobart.

- If Hobart cannot gain access to all the assets this would clearly reduce the price. However, it would also impact on the ability of Hobart to operate Tasman as a going concern following acquisition.

- The valuation above is at the reporting date of 31 December 20X6. There needs to be a re-evaluation at the date of acquisition, as assets will have changed by that time.

(c) **Value of business assets to Hobart**

(1) **Introduction**

The value to Hobart of the business assets of Tasman may be greater than their break-up value and therefore, if there are other bidders, it may be necessary to bid above the break-up asset value in order to acquire Tasman.

Specifically, the going concern value of the business may be greater than the value of the business assets. This is because the discounted present value of the assets in use may be greater than their net realisable value. It is recognised that in their current use the company is generating losses and the NPV generated would be unlikely to exceed asset values. However, the value to Hobart is determined not by the current use, but by the future use of the assets with Tasman being part of the larger Hobart Group.

(2) **Value of Tasman with the Rex contract**

A key factor is the ability to disengage from the Rex contract. It would appear that under the Rex contract there will be growing losses over the next three years as sales are expected to decrease by around 10% per year.

Thus, for the next three years operating losses with the Rex contract are estimated as:

	20X7	20X8	20X9
	£'000	£'000	£'000
Sales	20,700	18,630	16,767
Cost of sales	18,000	16,200	14,580
Gross profit	2,700	2,430	2,187
Administrative expenses	2,800	2,800	2,800
Operating loss	(100)	(370)	(613)

The above table takes the assumptions of Exhibit 3 that all of 'cost of sales' is variable and administration and distribution costs are all fixed.

The Enterprise Act 2002 permits the administrator to continue to trade for a while if he cannot sell the company as a going concern immediately. The purpose of this rule is to give time to enable a sale on a going concern basis in the near future. However, where the company is making losses there is greater urgency for the administrator to find a purchaser as soon as possible in order to prevent further losses accruing to the creditors.

While it may be that under the ownership of Hobart the reduction in sales may be moderated, it seems reasonable that the proposed strategy for Tasman should include discontinuing trading with Rex. This does not therefore form part of the valuations.

Note: It is likely that the contract with Rex would have contained a clause that would cause the contract to cease on the appointment of an administrator. Any further dealings between Rex and the administrator or a new owner would therefore probably need to be agreed under new contract terms.

(3) **Value of Tasman business assets – Intended strategy**

The key point is that the contract is between Rex plc and Tasman Ltd. Acquisition of the business assets of Tasman does not therefore transfer obligations to Hobart under the Rex contract. As such, the exclusivity clause in the contract would probably not apply and Hobart would be free to seek a new manufacturer for which Tasman could act as a franchisee.

Despite this, care must be taken to ensure that Rex does not have the ability to exercise any other rights over the assets (eg as a result of the franchise contract or the loan agreement) that would make disengagement difficult, even though only the business assets are being acquired.

While the establishment of a new franchise may be far from certain, Hobart already has contracts with other car dealers and may be able to extend these to Tasman. Noting this uncertainty, if the assumption of a 100% increase with a new manufacturer is correct, then the value of the business assets could be obtained from discounting the future cash flows as follows:

	20X7 £'000
Sales	46,000
Cost of sales	(40,000)
Gross profit	6,000
Administrative expenses (2,800 – 400)	(2,400)
Operating profit	3,600
Add	
Depreciation (16,200 – 14,000)	2,200
Operating cash flow	5,800
Less	
Tax paid 23% (excl WDAs)	(1,334)
CAPEX	(500)
	3,966

The above table again takes the assumptions of Exhibit 3 that all of 'cost of sales' is variable and administration costs are all fixed.

Present value at 10% in perpetuity of the annual cash flow is:

£3.966m/0.1 = **£39.66m**

However, to this needs to be added the present value of the 20% WDAs on existing assets using a 23% tax rate which is:

£7m(0.2)(0.23)/(0.1 + 0.2) = **£1.07m** (approx)

Note: This calculation is similar to the geometric progression used in the dividend growth model but with a negative growth rate of 20% which applies to the pool WDAs.

The total value is thus **£40.73m**.

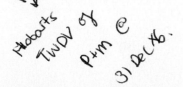

This value is greater than the break-up value of the assets, indicating that Hobart is adding some value to the break-up valuation. This is however dependent on the fact that it may be able to turn the company from a loss making entity into profit making by doubling revenue.

It should be noted however that the break-up value above was somewhat optimistic and further information is likely to produce a reduced figure. Similarly, the present values are of course rough estimates and they are likely to be sensitive to changes in cash flows and interest rates.

Other assumptions and qualifications on the present value calculations are as follows:

- Year end cash flows are assumed.

- The depreciation charge is high compared to the new CAPEX and cannot be sustained at this amount for more than a few years given the current carrying amount of the assets and the annual CAPEX. A more detailed capital budget and projections are needed.

- The increase of 100% in sales in 20X7 seems speculative and is dependent on a new franchise being established almost immediately.

- Conversely, the assumption of zero growth after 20X7 seems pessimistic.

- The new annual CAPEX of £500,000 to sustain the business seems low compared to the current level of depreciation.

- The perpetuity assumption seems unreasonable and more realistically a finite horizon should be determined to discount cash flows, along with a residual value of the business at that time.

(d) **Key risks**

The key overall risk is that of overpaying for the acquisition of Tasman in that it may not deliver the strategic and financial benefits expected.

This risk is, however, moderated in the circumstances where Hobart only pays the asset value, as there is then an exit route if Tasman does not succeed operationally. That is, if the benefits of operating Tasman do not fully materialise then the assets could probably be sold off to recover most of the outlay.

Despite this exit strategy, there are a number of risks:

- The strategy appears to depend fundamentally on disengaging from Rex and thus any rights, obligations and penalties under the existing franchise contract with Rex will need to be fully understood.

- There may be obligations to Tasman employees which will incur costs (eg redundancy pay).

- The business asset valuation based on present values of cash flows is sensitive to the 100% increase in sales and the interest rate used.

- The valuation overall of the sites may contain significant loss making sites and some profitable sites. It may be possible to 'cherry pick' the good sites and close the others but there are likely to be significant closure costs.

- Trading post year-end may reduce asset values but also alter the commercial viability of Tasman. The longer the deal takes to finalise then the greater these risks may be.

- The amount of unsold inventories is very high and may indicate more severe problems in making sales than indicated. Alternatively, it might imply there are minimum obligations under the Rex contract to acquire vehicles.

(e) **Assurance**

(1) **Context of assurance**

The 20X6 financial statements have not yet been audited. If they are still not audited by the time the acquisition needs to be agreed then financial assurance will be essential and will need to be more detailed than if an audit had taken place.

The nature of the assurance review will be determined by contractual agreement with Hobart. This in turn will determine the level of detailed investigation required but key factors would be:

- whether an assurance opinion is required;
- the timescale available to do the work; and
- access to information made available by the administrator.

The key issues are likely to be:

- risk; and
- valuation.

(2) **Financial assurance**

The key pieces of information relate to asset value and future projections.

If the shares are to be acquired, then greater emphasis needs to be placed on risk from assumed liabilities and obligations than if only the business assets are acquired.

Assurance relating to **asset values** includes:

Item	Assurance work
Goodwill	Enquire why full impairment is not being proposed in the financial statements.
	Assumed full write down in valuation so overstatement risk does not apply.
Non-current assets	Verify basis on which fair values have been determined. This needs to be in accordance with IFRS 13.
	Verify title to assets (eg not leased).
	Consider whether Rex owns any of the assets or has any rights or legal charges over them in respect of the loan.
Inventories	Review age analysis of inventories. Investigate nature, causes and value of slow moving items.
	Check vehicles to registration documents/invoices.
	Check valuations against trade guides.
	Establish the items of consignment inventories from Tasman records and documentation from Rex.
Receivables	Review age analysis of receivables.
	Check for normal recovery of older items.
	Use of debt factors in past?
Brand	Assess the terms and conditions of the offer of £2m for the brand in 20X4, eg does it include other rights and benefits.
	Have there been any other offers for the brand?
	Has the administrator made any attempt to sell the brand name separately, and if so at what value?
	If possible, roughly estimate the incremental cash flows that arise due to the brand name.

Financial assurance relating to projections and statement of profit or loss:

- Has revenue been enhanced by registering unsold cars or 'channel stuffing' Rex cars into trade sales? Examine year-end cut-off.

- Examine assumptions on which projections are made (eg 10% reduction in revenue if Rex contract maintained).

- Perform analytical procedures on financial statements to ascertain consistency. Separate analysis of new and used cars may be appropriate to assess each section of the business.

- Review basis of assumptions for doubling revenue after take-over by Hobart.

- Challenge assumption of whether revenue can be doubled.

- Review transactions post year end up to the date of possible transfer to ensure that ownership and condition of assets is maintained.

(3) **Commercial assurance**

Commercial assurance will be important as even though the business assets would be acquired there are likely to be rights, obligations and liabilities that will impact on asset value or in future operating of the assets.

Specific issues include the following:

- Legal review of the terms of the Rex contract including any purchase commitments to Rex (or others) that will need to be fulfilled. Check covenants, preferential interest rates or repayment terms and charges held over assets.

- Review obligations and constraints under any lease agreements.

- Ascertain any litigation, contingencies or contractual obligations or penalties (eg from correspondence with Tasman's solicitors).

- Consider tax issues outstanding (on-going correspondence, or disputes, with tax authorities, tax written down value of assets).

- Review market conditions and competitors (eg have total sales of Rex cars fallen nationally and have they fallen to the same extent as for Tasman?).

- Are Rex cars being discounted by other Rex dealers or does this reflect a particular weakness in Tasman's ability to make sales?

- Assess viability of each of the sites separately.

- Assess the credibility that a new franchise may be awarded with a different car manufacturer. For example, correspondence with car manufacturers relating to existing Hobart franchise relationships and whether offers of additional franchises have been indicated as feasible.

Draft memorandum

To: Chairman, Hobart plc
From: A. Senior
Date: 1 December 20X6
Subject: Concerns of the Senior Independent Director about the Tasman acquisition

We have submitted a report to James Lafon, your Finance Director, about aspects of the Tasman acquisition and a possible range of valuations for this company. This report was based on the assumptions that Hobart would be able to finance an acquisition at the proposed price and that the acquisition would not affect the company's cost of capital.

Your Senior Independent Director has challenged these assumptions and you may have some concerns about the implicatons for corporate governance of a possible rift between the executive directors on the board and some of the non-executives.

Financing the acquisition

We have not discussed the methods of financing an acquisition with your Finance Director. In our view the valuation of the business without its liabilities could be in the range £29m – £41m. The current market value of Hobart's equity is about £200m and loans have a value that we assume to be in the region of their nominal amount, £115m.

We would consider that subject to credit assessments by would-be finance providers, the company should be able to finance an acquisition entirely with new debt, should it wish to do so. Gearing would remain below 50%, which should be considered an acceptable level by lenders. Debt finance would probably need to be in the form of bank loans although a small bond issue in the domestic bond market might be feasible, depending on market conditions.

The board of Hobart may wish to consider financing an acquisition instead by means of a new equity issue, or a combination of new equity and new debt. Since Tasman is in administration, any new share issue would have to be for cash. If the offer price is in the region of £40m, which is about 20% of the current market value of Hobart's equity, we might be looking at a rights issue of between 1 in 5 and 1 in 6, or a large placement of new shares. Investor attitude to the proposed acquisition would therefore be very important.

Your Finance Director will no doubt provide the board with more information on the planned financing method, but your Senior Independent Director is justified in raising the issue as a matter for discussion.

Cost of capital and share value

The Senior Independent Director appears most concerned about the potential risk in the acquisition strategy and the effect that it could have on shareholder value.

In our report to the Finance Director we assume that an appropriate cost of capital for the acquisition would be 10%, but this assumption may not be correct. The cost of capital is affected by shareholder expectations about future returns and attitudes to risk.

In the short run, an acquisition of Tasman could have negative implications for dividends. In 20X5 dividend payments amounted to £9.6m, or 78% of profit after tax in the year. Shareholders may well expect a high dividend payout ratio to continue in the future. An acquisition of Tasman may not affect dividend payments, but this will depend on the profitability of the acquired company in the year or two immediately following the takeover, as well as the method of financing used for the acquisition, debt or equity.

Shareholders may also be concerned about the potential risk in the acquisition.

(1) In principle the cost of equity should rise if the company increases its gearing by borrowing more, and should fall if it raises new capital with a share issue.

(2) In principle there should be no additional business risk in the acquisition, since Tasman is in the same business as Hobart.

(3) On the other hand shareholders may have some concerns about acquiring a company that is in administration and question its future viability.

Hobart's shares are currently valued at about £200m. Earnings in 20X5 were £12.3m, giving a P/E ratio of 16.3. This is high, and indicative of shareholder expectations of rapid earnings growth (or recovery) in the future. It is appropriate to consider whether the acquisition of Tasman would affect future investor expectations, the P/E ratio and the share price.

Without further information it is not possible to provide a full response to the concerns of the Senior Independent Director. We would recommend that the Finance Director should prepare information for the board meeting about shareholder value and the risk that the acquisition could possibly destroy rather than create value.

Corporate governance

As you have correctly seen, the concerns of the Senior Independent Director do raise some issues about corporate governance, which it is your responsibility as chairman to address.

As a matter of good governance the board should have clear strategic objectives. In one way or another, the board should also establish its risk appetite, to provide a framework for risks that the board would consider acceptable and those that are unacceptable.

There seems to be some disagreement between the Senior Independent Director and the Finance Director about the risk in an acquisition of Tasman, and whether an acquisition is within or outside acceptable risk limits. This is a matter for the Hobart board to address specifically. If necessary, the board should agree and specify its policy on strategic risk more clearly.

A function of non-executive directors is to provide balance and independent perspective to the board of directors. It should be a matter of concern if the executive directors and a large proportion of non-executive directors have strong and continuing disagreements about strategy and strategic direction. As chairman and leader of the board, it is your responsibility to create a constructive relationship between board members, and in particular between executives and non-executives. It is essential for the future effectiveness of the board that any disagreements should be short-term and on specific issues, rather than long-term disagreements on strategy and risk.

It is important to emphasise that problems with governance are your responsibility and you should consider ways of dealing with them. We would, however, offer two suggestions.

(1) At the next board meeting, the discussions about an acquisition of Tasman should include a review of board strategy. You should try to establish whether there is agreement amongst board members that:

   • the board has a clearly-defined business strategy (for example for growth through organic development and acquisition, or through market development or market penetration, and so on); and

   • the board has reviewed and agreed its risk appetite.

   If there is general agreement on these issues, the discussion can move forward to whether the proposed acquisition is consistent with board policy or not. Even if the acquisition is not entirely consistent with board strategy and attitude to risk, the 'deviation' may be fairly small and acceptable.

   Focus on these issues, together with discussion of the business merits and method of financing an acquisition, may be sufficient to resolve problems at board level on this matter.

(2) In the longer term, if disagreements between executives and non-executives persist, the effectiveness of the board will be compromised. A formal annual review of board effectiveness, carried out perhaps by external consultants, might help to identify problems with the current board structure and membership, and any perceived ineffective decision-making at board or committee level.

2 Knowhow plc

		Marks Up to
(a)	Ratios and comments	
	Workings	6
	Ratio calculation	6
	Explanation	6
(b)	Discussion of issues	7
(c)	Accounting implications of share option scheme	8
(d)	Advantages and disadvantages for present directors	7
(e)	Corporate responsibility implications	5
(f)	Suitability of Flyzone as a strategic acquisition (low cost vs differentiation strategy)	11
(g)	Benefits of commercial due diligence	8
Total marks		64
Maximum marks		55

WORKINGS

Projected financial statements under each scenario

(1) **Projected statements of profit or loss and other comprehensive income for the year ended 31 December 20X9**

| | Knowhow Group | | |
| | No investment | 80% subsidiary | 40% associate |
	£m	£m	£m
Revenue	285.0	371.0	285.0
All expenses including tax expense	(146.0)	(194.0)	(146.0)
Non-controlling interest (£38m × 20%)		(7.6)	
Group share of associate's profits (£38m × 40%)			15.2
Profit attributable to equity holders	139.0	169.4	154.2

(2) **Projected statements of financial position as at 31 December 20X9**

| | Knowhow Group | | |
| | No investment | 80% subsidiary | 40% associate |
	£m	£m	£m
Non-current assets (W5)	1,578.0	2,582.0	1,578.0
Associate (W9)			242.2
Current assets	23.0	34.0	23.0
	1,601.0	2,616.0	1,843.2
Share capital (£1 shares, fully paid) (W3)	800.0	880.0	826.7
Share premium (W3)	200.0	800.0	400.3
Retained earnings (W7; W10)	349.0	379.4	364.2
Non-controlling interest (W6)		77.6	
	1,349.0	2,137.0	1,591.2
Non-current liabilities	240.0	460.0	240.0
Current liabilities	12.0	19.0	12.0
	1,601.0	2,616.0	1,843.2

(3) Shares issued

	£m
Subsidiary	
Million shares issued = 200m × 80% × 1/2 =	80.0
Value = 80m × £8.50 =	680.0
Of which share premium (680.0 – 80.0)	600.0
Associate	
Million shares issued = 200m × 40% × 1/3 =	26.7
Value = 26.7m × £8.50 =	227.0
Of which share premium (227.0 – 26.7)	200.3

(4) Goodwill purchased (subsidiary scenario)

	£m
Consideration transferred	680.0
Equity acquired = £350m × 80% =	280.0
Goodwill	400.0
Alternative calculation	
Cost of combination	680.0
Non-controlling interest at the acquisition date	
(20% × £350,000)	70.0
	750.0
Less total fair value of net assets acquired	(350.0)
Goodwill	400.0

(5) Non-current assets (subsidiary scenario)

	£m
Knowhow	1,578
Flyzone	604
Goodwill on acquisition (W4)	400
	2,582

(6) Non-controlling interest

Non-controlling interest = 388 × 20% = 77.6

(7) Retained earnings (subsidiary scenario)

	£m
Knowhow	349.0
Flyzone – post acquisition (38.0 × 80%)	30.4
	379.4

(8) Associate goodwill

	£m
Consideration transferred (W3)	227.0
Equity acquired = £350m × 40% =	140.0
Goodwill	87.0

(9) Investment in associate

	£m
Cost	227.0
Group share of post-acquisition profit (£38m × 40%)	15.2
	242.2
Or	
Share of associate net assets £388m × 40% =	155.2
Goodwill (W8)	87.0
	242.2

(10) Retained earnings (associate scenario)

	£m
Knowhow	349.0
Flyzone – post acquisition (£38m × 40%)	15.2
	364.2

(a) Ratios and interpretation

	No investment	80% subsidiary	40% associate
Earnings per share	$\dfrac{139.0}{800.0}$	$\dfrac{169.4}{880.0}$	$\dfrac{154.2}{826.7}$
	= 17.4 pence	= 19.3 pence	= 18.7 pence
Gearing	$\dfrac{240.0}{1,349.0+240.0}$	$\dfrac{460.0}{2,137.0+460.0}$	$\dfrac{240.0}{1,591.2+240.0}$
	= 15%	= 18%	= 13%
Non-current asset turnover	$\dfrac{285.0}{1,578.0}$	$\dfrac{371.0}{2,582.0}$	$\dfrac{285.0}{1,578.0}$
	= £0.18/£	= £0.14/£	= £0.18/£

Acquiring control of Flyzone Ltd will give the highest earnings per share. That is not surprising in itself because the group is permitted to record 80% of the subsidiary's profit and only a relatively small number of additional shares are being issued in order to make the acquisition because of the substantial premium on each share issued. Both of the offers to acquire an interest in Flyzone Ltd result in a higher earnings per share than not making an investment. The directors will not be discouraged from making an investment due to the impact on earnings per share.

The increase in earnings per share will however, have a negative impact on the price/earnings ratio unless the stock market agrees with the commercial logic behind the acquisition and the share price increases by more than 19.3/17.4 = 1.1 times the current share price (in the case of acquiring the subsidiary) in order to compensate. This may be part of the reason why the directors are concerned about the earnings per share figure and is therefore worth bearing in mind.

The acquisition will lead to the highest gearing ratio for Knowhow Group and, consequently, the highest perceived risk. This occurs because Flyzone is more highly geared than the existing group. As the investments will be financed through an equity issue and not debt, buying a 40% stake will increase group equity, so investing in an associate will improve the gearing ratio, making it an attractive option in relation to the impact on this ratio. Admittedly, none of the prospective gearing ratios is particularly high, although the group operates in an industry that can be quite volatile. It may be that the acquisition of the subsidiary still results in the gearing ratio being within acceptable limits to the directors.

Acquiring the subsidiary will lead to the lowest overall non-current asset turnover. The group will not earn a great deal of revenue per £1 invested in non-current assets in any case, but it will appear particularly unproductive if it buys a controlling interest in Flyzone Ltd. Both of the scenarios associated with investing in the company will reduce reported non-current asset turnover. This may again be unacceptable to the directors or the negative impact on this ratio may be within the acceptable limits to the directors.

It will be important for the directors to consider the overall impacts of these options on the ratios. For example, the 40% investment may be attractive in spite of the negative impact on the non-current asset turnover due to the positive impact on the other two ratios.

(b) Issues regarding Knowhow's shareholders

The shareholders may be concerned that these forecast figures do not give a convincing business case for investing in Flyzone Ltd.

Investing in an 80% stake will enhance earnings per share by a relatively small amount and will both increase gearing and reduce non-current asset turnover. The shareholders might be concerned that this is hardly a satisfactory outcome for an investment that will cost £680m.

The biggest reason for investing in Flyzone Ltd is to secure expertise and experience that might be difficult to obtain in any other way. The Knowhow Group will acquire the services of a management team that has the ability to help the group to grow in two directions that appear to be potentially lucrative. Acquiring control of the company will provide access to a bank of knowledge amassed by a host of staff working at all levels in dealing with low-cost airlines and transatlantic operations. However the issue of differing corporate responsibility philosophies needs to be addressed (see further discussion below).

There are also potential synergies to be had from acquiring a controlling interest in another airport. The group may be able to offer a better range of locations to existing or potential new customers.

Acquiring a 40% stake in Flyzone Ltd will enhance earnings per share, but by even less than the increase available from acquiring control of the company. It will, however, improve gearing but will lead to some deterioration in non-current asset turnover.

The case to be made to the shareholders is slightly more difficult in this case because the group does not really have the synergies associated with the acquisition of another airport and the degree to which it can draw upon the knowledge of Flyzone Ltd's staff will be more limited. The best that Knowhow plc can really hope for is that the terms of the contract for management and consultancy services will be met. The fact that the group has influence over Flyzone Ltd rather than control means that it has less opportunity to examine the books and records of the company or to explore areas that were not covered by the contract and were regarded as commercially sensitive.

Depending on how the approach was made, it may be possible to avoid making an announcement concerning the option to do nothing, however, it is likely that some commentary would be appropriate. Given the identified potential benefits of the investment the directors should address how they can achieve the benefits without the acquisition and in particular the significant future benefits that will result from having an international hub. A suitable defence may well be that the potential acquisition was not appropriately priced and the directors will continue to look for other opportunities.

(c) **Share options**

The share options will fall within the scope of IFRS 2 *Share-based Payment*. Knowhow plc is granting options to buy shares as an incentive to the directors in return for their consultancy advice and, presumably, as an inducement to them to advise the company to the best of their ability in order to maximise the value of the option. It would, by implication, not be appropriate to account for the issue of the options in accordance with IFRS 3 *Business Combinations*. The decision as to the correct treatment would be more difficult if the proposed new shareholders owned shares in Flyzone and had to sell these shares as part of the transaction.

It does not really matter which of the two methods of investing in Flyzone Ltd is taken because the payment is essentially for the purchase of a service by Knowhow plc. Thus, it would not matter whether Flyzone Ltd was a subsidiary or an associate. The directors of Flyzone Ltd would not be members of the parent company's board of directors.

This is an equity-settled transaction. Knowhow plc should recognise the fair value of the options as an expense over the vesting period and there should be a corresponding increase in the company's equity. This is effectively the issue of a capital instrument in return for consultancy advice.

These increases should be recognised over the course of the vesting period of the options. Presumably, this would be during the three year period from the date of joining the board. There could, however, be a case for recognising the cost over a shorter period if the directors were required to provide their advice as consultants over a shorter period than the three years. The terms of the contract should be studied to ensure that it is clear what conditions have to be met by the directors and over what period.

Ideally, the contract should be valued at the fair value of the consultancy advice that is to be received. In practice, it is unlikely to be possible to attach a meaningful valuation to this service. The directors providing this service are specialists in a very narrow field and so there is unlikely to be an observable market rate for this advice. Furthermore, they are unlikely to be expected to work for a specific number of hours. Instead, they will be asked to advise Knowhow plc as and when appropriate.

In the event that the fair value of the service cannot be measured reliably, the company should attempt to reach a fair value of the options themselves, as at the date the options are granted (effectively, as at the start of the three year period). This may well prove difficult to measure reliably because there are unlikely to be any observable market prices for similar instruments. The terms of the options granted for this type of payment are normally different from options that are traded freely on the open market.

It may be possible to estimate the value of the options by referring to the models in the finance literature, such as the Black-Scholes model. That is generally regarded as a reasonable measurement basis but assumes that the option will not be exercised until the end of its life. This latter assumption is quite relevant in this case because the directors have the option to buy shares on a specific date three years hence.

(d) Advantages and disadvantages to departing directors

The purchase of the 80% stake will give the outgoing directors quoted shares in Knowhow as consideration, with a market value of £680m (at current share prices). That is shared between only five individuals, so each is likely to be extremely wealthy.

The shares are quoted, which means that the directors will be able to liquidate their investment at almost any time. The shares in Flyzone are not quoted and therefore the sale allows the directors, who are approaching retirement, a convenient exit route which they would not have had before. It is unlikely that they will be privy to any sensitive information about Knowhow plc or the rest of the group that would make them insiders and so prevent them from selling their shares.

They will own 80/880 = 9.1% of a quoted company. They will have to be careful not to overload the market by selling too quickly, otherwise the market price could slump dramatically, so they may have to hold their investment for some time. This is not ideal because their portfolios will not be properly diversified and so they will bear a significant risk of loss until they are able to sell the shares.

Selling half of their stake in the company will yield quoted shares worth £227.0m (again at current share prices). That is still a sizeable amount of cash and the directors will still be wealthy. They will also retain 40% of a successful company that is an associate of a much larger group. That investment will have the capacity to increase in value, particularly if its association with the Knowhow Group leads to expansion or synergy. Retaining half of the company could turn out to be a wise decision if Flyzone Ltd subsequently flourishes as an associate of the Knowhow Group.

The most immediate disadvantage of this scenario is that the directors will receive less value per share. The fact that Knowhow plc is not acquiring control means that they are offering only one share for three Flyzone Ltd shares instead of one for two as before. The directors will need to consider whether the reduction in value on sale is compensated by the increased participation in potential future share price increase or enhanced dividends.

The second problem is that their remaining holding in Flyzone Ltd will not be particularly easy to sell if they ever wish to liquidate this investment. This could be a problem because the company's entire board is going to be replaced. While this leaves a layer of senior managers in place as before, the new directors will not necessarily be of the same calibre as the outgoing ones. Even the senior managers who are promoted from within are untried at this level.

It is unlikely that the directors of Knowhow plc will be influenced by the fact that the outgoing directors will own 40% of Flyzone Ltd. The only significant threat that this creates is that the former directors will act together with the owners of the remaining 20% of the shares in order to take back control. That might not be a problem in the longer term because Knowhow plc is trying to buy specialist knowledge rather than the assets and business of Flyzone Ltd itself. The ability to take back control by acting together with the other shareholders is an advantage to the present directors of Flyzone.

If the outgoing board members trust the three replacement directors who will be promoted from within then they should be reassured by the fact that these managers will have seats on the board. That will encourage them to remain with the company for the foreseeable future and should protect the value of their remaining investment in the company. The directors would, in any case, retain the right to appoint one further board member and that would give them some influence over the running of the company.

(e) Corporate responsibility issues

The difference in corporate responsibility stances has strategic implications as well as reflecting a difference in ethical philosophy. It affects board relationships, the need for post-acquisition integration and consideration of stakeholder interests such as customers and employees.

In analysing these issues, Knowhow's board needs to consider a number of risks. These include the legal risks of acting contrary to employment or environmental laws, and suffering costs and fines as a result. There is also a reporting risk, that Knowhow's corporate responsibility report will no longer be fair if Flyzone's policies do not change or are applied to other airports in the group. The board must consider a reputation risk, that a poor reputation will impact upon the actions of stakeholders that deal with the Knowhow group. It may be debatable how much Knowhow's responsibility stance on environmental matters and treatment of staff affects whether passengers use its airports. The greatest damage however may result from a loss of reputation for a good service, and ultimately passengers and airlines switching to other airports.

Therefore if the merger goes ahead, the board needs to decide whether the staffing and environmental policies of Knowhow, Flyzone or both need to be amended. This may affect the roles of, and autonomy given to, the new directors. The board needs to consider other organisational changes, whether for example an exchange of management at lower levels will help promote a common philosophy. It must also weigh up different passenger expectations in quality and low cost markets against the training costs and higher salaries required to improve passenger experience at Flyzone's airport.

(f)   **Basis of acquisition**

Generic strategies

Differentiation strategy v Low cost

In general terms, Knowhow has been pursuing a differentiation strategy; trying to differentiate its airports from potential competitors in terms of the quality of service and experience they provide to passengers who travel through them. By contrast, it appears that Flyzone is pursuing a low-cost strategy.

This difference can be seen not only from the fact that Flyzone has been able to attract low cost airlines to its airport while Knowhow has found it difficult to do so, but also from the differences in human resources management between the two groups. Knowhow pays its staff higher rates than staff in equivalent roles at other airports, but in return expects them to provide a high standard of service to customers. On the other hand, Flyzone pays a significant proportion of its staff the minimum wage only.

This difference in the generic strategies of the two companies also helps to explain why consumer ratings for Flyzone's airport are rated considerably below those for all of Knowhow's airports in respect of the comfort and ease of passenger experience offered.

In this respect, it may seem unsuitable for a company competing on the basis of quality and differentiation to acquire a company which competes on the basis of low cost.

HR and cultural issues

Equally, the differences in the way Knowhow and Flyzone are managed could also create problems in the cultural fit between the two companies. If Knowhow does acquire Flyzone, then Knowhow will need to consider how the organisational cultures of the different companies can be integrated, or whether they will remain, in effect, separate companies. Equally, Knowhow will need to consider the impact of the acquisition on the remuneration and reward systems of both companies. In particular, Flyzone's low cost business model means that its staff are likely to be earning less than Knowhow staff doing the same grade of job. If Flyzone's staff become aware of this wage differential this could potentially cause resentment and unrest among the staff, which in turn could potentially reduce the benefit to Knowhow from making the acquisition (for example, if staff go on strike).

Market opportunities

However, as we have already noted, acquiring Flyzone and the services of their management team, could be crucial in helping Knowhow capture a share of the transatlantic market as well as attracting low-cost airlines to fly from its airports. In this respect, the fact that Flyzone's strengths help to address areas of weakness within Knowhow suggest that the acquisition might be suitable.

As the Chief Executive has identified, low-cost airlines have grown in recent years, yet Knowhow has so far been unable to attract any of this new business. However, if the low-cost airline market is going to continue growing, then getting a foothold into this market could be strategically important for Knowhow – particularly in relation to the potential opportunities for growth it offers.

A similar argument also applies in relation to transatlantic flights. Flyzone's management have skills and experience in dealing with this market, and Knowhow could use this to help it attract transatlantic flights.

However, it is not clear how much spare capacity Knowhow's airports have to cater for additional flights. For example, if it wishes to attract additional long-haul flights alongside its existing short-haul flights, it will need sufficient take off and landing slots to accommodate the increased number of flights coming through its airports. Equally, if it wishes to accommodate low-cost airlines alongside its existing airlines, this will also increase the number of flights to and from its airports.

Knowhow's own generic strategy

Although growth of low-cost airlines appears to have reduced Knowhow's share of the market, its management need to be careful how they position their strategy for the group's airports. Perhaps the most important question is to evaluate how suitable and acceptable it will be to accommodate low-cost airlines alongside its existing airlines.

Knowhow's business currently appears to be managed with a view to satisfying passengers' requirements (for example, for high quality restaurants and shops at the airports). However, a key part of the low cost model is likely to be satisfying the airlines' requirements, for their costs associated with flights to and from an airport to be as low as possible.

In this respect, Knowhow has two different types of customer which it is serving: passengers, and airlines. Crucially, Knowhow will need to evaluate how far it can accommodate the requirements of both of these groups, or whether there is a danger it will end up being 'stuck in the middle.'

(g) **Benefits of commercial due diligence**

In order for Knowhow's directors to decide what course of action to take in relation to the potential acquisition, they need to have relevant and reliable information about Flyzone.

Knowhow's directors are justifiably concerned about the impact which investing in Flyzone could have on the company's share price, and the directors need to be satisfied that if they do invest in Flyzone they only do so at a reasonable price.

This could be a particular issue here because it seems that Knowhow might actually be more interested in acquiring the expertise and experience of Flyzone's directors, rather than acquiring an additional airport. If Knowhow acquires an 80% interest in Knowhow, based on the current projected figures, this will mean it pays £400m of goodwill on acquisition.

Potentially, however, the directors need to consider this goodwill figure not only in relation to Flyzone's airport but also in relation to the potential additional business which Knowhow might be able to generate in future; for example, if it is able to break into the transatlantic market.

Equally, though, the fact that Flyzone's directors have experience of the transatlantic and low-cost markets, and Knowhow doesn't, emphasises the importance of due diligence in relation to any potential investment in Flyzone. The difference in the perspectives and experience of the two sets of directors increases the degree of information asymmetry between them.

In this case, this asymmetry relates not only to Flyzone's own future earnings, but also potentially to the future earnings which Knowhow could generate through accommodating low-cost airlines and transatlantic business.

Consequently, it is not only important for Knowhow to undertake financial due diligence to confirm the accuracy of any figures and projections on which a bid is based, but also to undertake a broader commercial due diligence looking into the risks and opportunities linked to the investment.

In particular, commercial due diligence can complement financial due diligence by considering Flyzone's target markets and the external economic environment. In this case, issues such as the rate of growth which can be sustained in the low-cost airline market, could be crucial in understanding the benefits which Knowhow could gain from investing in Flyzone. For example, what are the expectations for growth in this market? In this respect, it will be important that the people carrying out the due diligence have a good understanding of the sectors of the market in which Flyzone operates.

An independent appraisal of Flyzone's management could also be valuable to Knowhow. Although Knowhow has identified three of Flyzone's senior managers to sit on the company's board after the acquisition, commercial due diligence should include an appraisal of the company's management and its resources after the acquisition. For example, how much of the company's success to date has been due to the five directors who are now retiring; and do their successors appear to have sufficient capabilities to sustain it?

Finally, given the concerns about the cultural 'fit' – or lack of it – between Knowhow and Flyzone, commercial due diligence should also indicate potential integration issues which could arise following an acquisition. Again, problems in integrating the two companies could reduce the benefits arising from an acquisition; and Knowhow's directors should consider this point when considering their courses of action.

3 Fowler Ltd

Marking guide

		Marks Up to
(a)	Costing system	
	Current vs ABC	10
	Breakdown between costs and activities	7
(b)	Profitability	
	Gross profit margins	7
	Operating and finance costs	7
	Dividends	4
(c)	Analytical procedures	6
(d)	Ethics	6
(e)	Operations management issues – eg cost, quality, volume, reliability	12
	Creating two separate operations	7
Total marks		66
Maximum marks		55

Briefing note

Client: Fowler Limited

Subject: Costing and pricing policies and comments on the trading results for the 9 months to 30 June 20X8

To: Janet Hales (Audit Manager)

From: Robert O'Hara (Audit Senior)

(a) Costing systems adopted by Fowler Limited

Background

After the takeover of Fowler Ltd by King plc profitability declined as sales volumes reduced. This reflects the fact that 60% – 90% of manufacturing costs of Fowler's products consist of overheads.

Therefore it is clear that in such an environment overhead absorption methods must be accurate and applied correctly in order for management to understand past results, the current position and where to direct the business in the future.

The 20X7 audit highlighted specific areas of concern in respect of overhead absorption. Our management letter recommended a review of costings of all products.

Current system adopted

At present a historically developed absorption method is used based on direct labour, direct machine hours and material cost.

This it is felt does not adequately reflect the automation levels used in production. This is specifically the case in the higher margin plastic mouldings sector.

Proposed system

Oliver Bradford is proposing to extend the areas over which costs are apportioned from 3 to 7.

This has necessitated breaking down overhead costs into far more specific areas.

These are:

	1	Direct labour support
	2	Machine operation
	3	Set up hours
	4	Production ordering activity
	5	Materials handling
	6	Product number administration
	7	General administration and marketing

Proposed results

This reclassification of costs has produced some interesting cost comparisons.

In particular the A7 and C4 components, used recently in the MOD tender have been re-costed under the proposed new system and this was followed by a re-costing of one of the plastic moulding products, P8.

Degree of difficulty	Original cost £	New cost £	Change %	Original tender price £	New tender price £
Complex A7	82.71	66.72	(19.3)	107.52	86.74
Simple C4	19.07	52.78	176.8	24.80	68.61
Complex P8	66.65	86.32	29.5	86.65	112.22

These re-costings demonstrate the subjective nature of absorbing overheads into cost production.

Under this new system the A7 tender price would have been considerably lower and as Fowler's original tender price was some 20% above the price that won the contract then it would appear likely the price that actually won was about £89.60. Therefore under the new system of costing the high volume A7 contract would have been won at Fowler's tender price of £86.74.

However the C4 tender price would have been almost three times higher under the proposed costing system and this price would almost certainly prove to be too expensive to the MOD and that contract would have been lost. However to the extent that the revised costings are a more realistic reflection of the incremental costs incurred, then the winning of the contract might have actually been at a loss with the price set below costs. In these circumstances it might have been preferable not to have won the contract.

No real conclusions can be drawn from these results. It would appear that out of the 60 MOD contracts that were tendered for some might have been lost, such as the A7 contract, due to the high costing and related tender price. However out of the eight contracts that were won, some such as the C4, might not have been won due to the high costing and tender price.

The P8 is an example of the new market (of plastic mouldings) that Fowler has entered. These have a more complex manufacturing process but if the P8 is representative of this type of product it would appear to have been significantly under-costed and therefore under-priced. This may mean that this new market is in fact a loss making market as the price of the P8 under the current system of absorption cost plus 30% (£86.65) only just covers the costs allocated to the product under the activity based costing system (£86.32).

Product types

Fowler appears to have three main product types – simple, complex and to customer specification (the new plastic mouldings). An example of each of these types of product have been costed under the current and proposed systems with the following conclusion:

Simple product – under-costed under current system

Complex product – over-costed under current system

Customer specification – under-costed under current system

It has to be questioned as to whether these classifications are correct and whether each of these products is representative of the product type. It would normally be expected under an activity based costing system that the more complex products would be under costed rather than has been indicated here.

General issues with proposed system

The data that is available to assess the new costing system is very limited as initially only two products were considered and then an additional product from the new range.

The purpose of activity based costing is to recognise the complexities involved in overhead apportionment. However if we consider the A7 and the C4 then the supposedly complex A7 has had its percentage of overheads to total cost reduced under the new system from 87.5% to 84.5% whereas the C4 which is classified as a simple product under the new system has overheads as a percentage of total cost of 85.6% compared to 60% under the current system.

This may be an indication of the fact that under the new system the low volume products such as the C4 incur higher percentage overheads than the high volume products. **✓✓**

Comparison of traditional products to new areas

Fowler Ltd has recently concentrated on the seemingly higher margin, injection plastic moulded products. These are produced in a highly automated fashion. Therefore the new costing system may apply more appropriately to these products regardless of levels of complexity. Taking the P8 as an example the current system shows a much lower amount of overheads compared to the proposed activity based costing system which may indicate that the current system is not capable of dealing with this level of automation.

More work is needed to establish which products are best suited to use the proposed new system. Contract volume for example must be a key factor in deciding on overhead rates.

Conclusion

A full revision of cost cards should be undertaken and monthly reconciliations of cost of sales to actual expenditure incurred should be made before recommending the adoption of these new standard costings.

(b) Discussion of trading profitability

Summary of performance

The first nine months of the year to 30 June 20X8 have seen a significant fall in profitability compared to the budget. This is particularly caused by the gross profit margin falling from 30% per the budget to just 22% in actual terms.

Gross profit margins

The gross profit margin overall is only 22% compared with the budgeted figure of 30%. This is entirely due to the increase in production overheads as a percentage of sales of 46% compared to a budget figure of 38%.

This could be a mixture of two factors. A large proportion of production overheads may be fixed and therefore as sales revenue is 6.5% down on the budgeted level this will affect the gross margin. However the other factor is that production overheads have increased in absolute terms from the budget indicating that the new plastic mouldings production has had a significant effect on the production overheads.

In terms of product performance rubber and leather seals are 25% down on budgeted sales and water pump seals are 7% down. However, as regards profit margins, both have shown a full 10 percentage point fall.

These results may be due to reduced sales prices or sales volumes. Equally the problems that are being considered with the costing and pricing system may be part of the reason for the reduced margins for these products. If products are under-costed then they will be underpriced and margins will be reduced.

The figures for plastic mouldings show that more units have been sold than budgeted for and indicate that the gross profit margin has been largely maintained at the budgeted level. However the work considered earlier on costings has raised concerns that due to the vagaries of the current costing system that these plastic mouldings are costed and sold at too low a price therefore this healthy profit margin may not in fact be the case. The plastic mouldings contracts will increase overheads due to the nature of their production but the selling prices may not be covering these increased costs.

In addition since the loss of the high volume MOD work, smaller job runs and batches have been produced, costing more per unit to produce and eroding the margins of traditional areas even further.

Marketing, selling, general and administrative costs

In total marketing, selling, general and administrative costs have increased in absolute terms above the budget by £200,000 and in terms of percentage of sales revenue by 1%. However Oliver Bradford has admitted that the allocation of these costs to product groups is not easy and further work is needed in this area. Therefore the budgeted and actual allocation of these costs to each product may not bear much significance. However they have increased in total.

One possibility is that the commitment of senior management to 'Total Quality' has been reflected in higher costs to administer the production facility. Quality checks and inspection visits have been increased both in terms of attention to detail and frequency. The costs of achieving this kind of quality however should be viewed as an investment especially if a BS 5750 standard could be obtained.

However there is seemingly no budget for TQM investment and therefore it cannot be necessarily stated that this has been the cause of the increase in general expenses. As TQM is a significant revenue investment Fowler would be well advised to set up a budget for TQM in order to help control such costs.

Interest payable

Interest charges are lower than budgeted but due to the reduced level of profit interest cover has reduced to 7 times from 12 times in the budget.

Other factors

The dividend payment of £2,000,000 is much higher than profit after taxation leading to retained losses for the year. However as Fowler is a wholly owned subsidiary of King then this dividend may have been imposed by King and will not affect the consolidated figures of King as it is an intra group item.

However the requirement to make a cash payment for this dividend, assuming that it has not yet been paid, does ask questions about the liquidity of Fowler. As the dividend is so much higher than reported profit unless that profit includes a lot of non-cash items such as depreciation then it may be difficult to find the cash necessary for the dividend payment.

We have little information on the production capacity for Fowler but given that market share and sales volumes are falling then there may well be some idle capacity which will serve to make fixed overheads more significant.

(c) **Analytical procedures**

- Obtain split of production overheads between fixed and variable overheads.

- Investigate changes in fixed overheads, and ascertain from cost records whether changes are consistent with factors driving the changes (for example increase in rent).

- Ascertain from production records and pricing lists the extent to which changes in sales are due to changes in prices or changes in volume.

- Ascertain from invoices and cost and sales volume records the reasons for changes in variable production overheads. Assess whether changes are consistent with factors driving the changes, for example smaller jobs runs and batches or changes in product mix.

- Ascertain the reasons for changes in selling, general and administrative costs by examining records of marketing initiatives, payrolls, invoices and other cost documentation, and confirm changes are consistent with supporting evidence.

- Review the assumptions on which budgets were prepared, and assess whether budgeted figures were realistic given the information known at the time the budgets were prepared.

- Seek explanations from management for changes in figures that cannot be verified independently, and consider the need for additional audit procedures on these areas.

It can be clearly seen that profitability for the nine months to 30 June 20X8 is considerably below the budgeted level. However the precise reasons for this cannot be determined without further analysis. There needs to be further testing of costings of products to determine whether contracts are being lost due to over costing and profits being sacrificed due to under costing.

(d) **Ethical issues**

    (1) **Reduce staff head count while avoiding redundancy payouts**

        This proposal shows a clear lack of integrity. Staff are not being dealt with fairly and are not being told the truth about their redundancy.

    (2) **Limit bonuses**

        This proposal also raises issues of integrity, that again there is a failure to deal fairly with staff. Objectivity is also a problem. Managers who are responsible for operating an appraisal system should assess staff with a lack of bias, giving credit and reward where due. Depressing staff grades so that profitability figures look better demonstrates a clear bias in decision-making.

    (3) **Reduce training costs**

        Again integrity may be an issue, if promises made to staff about the training they will receive are being broken. Professional competence and due care is also a significant issue, managers being responsible not only for their own training and performance, but those of their staff. A reduction in training may be particularly significant if it compromises the quality of production, since quality is a significant issue with Fowler.

    (4) **Terminate Fowler's apprenticeship scheme**

        Again integrity is an issue, if promises made to apprentices are not being kept. If apprentices were aware that their positions could be terminated without notice, the managers may still be guilty of acting with a lack of integrity towards them. Fowler may also be criticised for showing a lack of corporate responsibility, and this may be significant if either Fowler or King have tried to promote themselves as good corporate citizens.

(e) **Operations management issues**

Two of the main advantages which effective operations management can generate for a company are:

- It can reduce the costs of producing products and services.
- It can increase customer satisfaction through good quality and service.

Both of these will be attractive to King within the context of their TQM approach aimed at making high quality, low cost products which are delivered on time to customers.

The available management accounts extracts do not provide any information about the level of capital Fowler employs, but as a general principle we should expect effective operations management to reduce the amount of capital employed to provide the type or quantity of products required. In this regard, effective operations management could also reduce the need for additional investment – something which may be a consideration in King's plans.

Outputs

It is important that operational objectives and targets are based around customers' requirements; so if customers require a low-priced product, then performance objectives need to focus on achieving a low cost of output. This would seem likely to be the case, particularly for Fowler's simpler seals. (However, it is still important to confirm this is the case based on any discussions which Fowler's marketing and sales departments have had with customers.)

It appears that price is still an important factor for Fowler's more complex seals. The prices Fowler tendered to the Ministry of Defence are likely to have been a crucial reason why it secured so few contracts. In this respect, it appears that allowing prices to remain high, and using quality as its basis for competing with other suppliers is unlikely to be successful for Fowler.

Instead, Fowler would be better advised to focus primarily on achieving low costs, while still maintaining acceptable levels of quality. As the seals are viewed as 'commodity' products, then the most appropriate generic strategy would be one which aimed at becoming the lowest cost producer.

Plastic mouldings

By contrast, it appears that Fowler's new plastic mouldings business targets a market in which quality and customer service are more important than price. Consequently, Fowler's processes and performance objectives for this new market should focus on quality, because this appears to be the basis for its competitive advantage (over the low-cost competitors).

However, as the analysis of Fowler's costing system has indicated, the plastic moulding products currently appear to be under-priced. So, although it seems that quality and customer service have been critical in establishing Fowler's competitive advantage over its low-cost competitors, the position might be distorted by the under-costings which have occurred during the pricing process.

Delivery – Fowler's proximity to its customers also appears to contribute to its competitive advantage in the plastic mouldings market. This suggests that the 'delivery' elements of operations management (speed of delivery; reliability of delivery) are also important to the success of the product. So, in this case, the responsiveness of Fowler's supply chain is perhaps more important than its efficiency, whereas for commodity products efficiency is likely to be more important.

Volume and variety

The plastic mouldings are produced to individual customer specification, suggesting that there will be a high degree of variety in the manufacturing process. This means the process needs to be flexible and capable of adapting to individual customer needs, but this flexibility is also likely to make the work more complex and to increase unit costs as a result.

By contrast, the manufacturing process for the seals (especially the simple seals) is likely to be a higher volume, lower variety process. This would reinforce the point that unit costs for the seals should be low.

Individual customer specifications

The fact that the plastic mouldings are produced in response to individual customer specifications also has important implications for Fowler's manufacturing strategy. Whereas some simple seals can be made in advance and stored in inventory (if they are standard products used by a variety of customers) the individual mouldings will be produced directly in response to individual orders. This suggests that a Just-in-Time production strategy will be necessary for the moulding products.

More generally, we could suggest that this difference in manufacturing strategy reflects a difference in the underlying supply chain strategy for the mouldings compared to the seals. The aim of the mouldings' supply chain will be to respond quickly to demand, whereas the aim of the seals' supply chain (especially for the simple seals) will be to supply demand at the lowest cost.

Separate operations

The different characteristics of the complex mouldings versus the simpler seals might initially seem to justify King's logic of creating two distinction operations processes.

However, this ignores the fact that Fowler only started to manufacture the mouldings as a way of utilising spare capacity in its manufacturing process.

While sales of the plastic mouldings appear to be growing, it is not clear whether the mouldings business has yet reached a scale which justifies running them as a standalone operation. For example, is demand for the plastic mouldings sufficiently high for the new operation to be profitable in its own right?

However, perhaps more importantly, if the underlying aim of the 'seals' manufacturing process is to produce at as low cost as possible, then utilisation rates will be crucial. The higher the utilisation rate of the manufacturing process, the lower the unit costs of the seal are likely to be; for example, because fixed costs and overheads are spread over a larger number of units.

In this respect, moving the plastic mouldings to a separate operation could be counter-productive if it ends up leaving spare capacity in the rubber seals operations.

More generally, if King is suggesting two different operations in two different sites this would also seem to create inefficiencies due to two lots of fixed costs and overheads being incurred.

The impact of these inefficiencies will also depend on the extent to which the two operations (seals and plastic mouldings) share common inputs or common production processes. If they share components or processes then separating them is likely to mean that Fowler will lose some economies of scale which it currently benefits from. For example, if the same raw materials are used for making the seals and the plastic mouldings, then from a supply chain management perspective it might be more appropriate to have a single inventory of material inputs, but then two production lines making the different types of output.

However, we will need further information about the detail of King's proposal; in particular, whether they envisage splitting the operations into two parts as being a way of relocating the low cost, simple process away from Western Europe into a lower cost economy.

This kind of change could lead to reductions in labour and production overheads, although if Fowler continues to supply to customers in the UK and Western Europe its distribution and shipping costs will increase. A vital consideration will be the extent to which any savings made through the relocation exceed the additional costs generated by having two separate production centres.

The increased distance between the relocated operations and its existing customer base could also mean that Fowler will be slower to respond to customer demand; although it could compensate for this by holding a stock of key, standard products and fulfilling customer orders from stock. By contrast, the plastic mouldings business – which produces for individual customer specifications – will need to remain close to its market in the UK and Western Europe.

Cost and quality

When considering any cost reduction strategies, it is vital to think about the extent to which cost reduction can be sustained before the business starts to suffer in other ways. If any cuts Fowler makes reduce the quality of its products or the service customers receive, then it is unlikely the customers will view the cost reduction programme favourably. Regardless of how they are marketed, there is a danger that cost reduction programmes will be viewed by outsiders as not only reducing expenditure but also reducing quality and service as well.

Ultimately, Fowler needs to evaluate any potential cost reduction programmes according to the extent that they can add value to the company; for example, the extent to which the proposals will enable Fowler to compete more effectively.

It is also important to remember that cost reduction programmes are ultimately implemented to improve profitability. However, increases in Fowler's revenues could also improve profitability, so if devoting more resources to the plastic mouldings business enables the business to grow profitably, then this could be an appropriate strategic option as much as one focusing solely on reducing costs.

4 Archen plc

Marking guide

	Up to
Financial review	7
Due diligence:	
Analytical procedures	11
Assurance procedures	8
Risk management processes	7
Risks facing Merry	6
Non-financial measures	8
Strategic management accounting	4
Total marks	51
Maximum marks	45

To: Engagement Partner
From: Senior
Date: 31 March 20X9
Re: Archen

Performance evaluation of Merry Ltd

	Merry 20X8 Draft unaudited £'000	Merry 20X7 £'000	
Revenue	360,000	400,000	
Cost of sales	(240,000)	(250,000)	
Depreciation	(40,000)	(40,000)	Depreciation for 20X7 has been reduced to the new steady state depreciation figure in order to compare like with like.
Administration costs	(30,000)	(32,000)	
Impairment	–	(5,000)	Impairment has been charged in 20X7 but may have been cumulative from earlier periods. More information is needed.
Provision		(14,000)	Of the original provision of £28m it now looks as if only £14m is needed as the other £14m has been reversed. The charge for the provision is thus what would have been known with hindsight (assuming that the reversal is valid).
Operating profit	50,000	59,000	As a measure of operating performance the company has performed rather worse in 20X8 than in 20X7.
Financing income/(costs)	(18,000)	(12,000)	
Profit before tax	32,000	47,000	

More information is needed but on the basis of the revised figures Merry has performed rather worse in 20X8 than in 20X7 once reasonable adjustments are made to the accounting estimates. Merry's chairman's claim of doubling profits is clearly inappropriate.

Due diligence – Analytical procedures and assurance work

	Merry 20X8 Draft unaudited £'000	Merry 20X7 £'000	Analytical procedures comment
Revenue	360,000	400,000	The decline in revenue of 10% appears to reflect a decline in sales volume of 10% as the selling prices have remained constant. It may also however reflect a change in the sales mix.
			The key risk regarding the acquisition is that the decline in sales will be a continuing trend into 20X9 and thus any valuation based on the underlying cash flows should have a negative, rather than a positive, growth rate.
Cost of sales	(240,000)	(250,000)	Cost of sales has fallen by only 4% while sales volumes have decreased by 10%. Given, however, that cost of sales includes substantial fixed costs then the percentage reduction in cost of sales is likely to be lower than the percentage reduction in sales volumes.
			In this case the expected level of cost of sales for a 10% decrease in volumes sold assuming there had been no change in costs per unit would have been:

X7 $£250m \times 40\%$ = £100m
$£250m \times 60\% \times 90\%$ = £135m — revenue ↓10%
variable = £235m

The actual cost of sales figure is £5m higher than the predicted £235m. The apparent increase in costs per unit is thus 2.1% (£240m/£235m).

This increase is modest but it is greater than the zero increase in selling prices.

As a consequence, the gross profit margin has decreased from £150m (37.5%) to £120m (33.3%). Of this £30m reduction £5m (ie one-sixth) was due to cost increases and £25m (ie five-sixths) to sales volume changes. The source of the cost increases needs further investigation.

	Merry 20X8 Draft unaudited £'000	Merry 20X7 £'000	Analytical procedures comment
Depreciation	(40,000)	(50,000)	The change in the accounting estimate is substantial representing a 25% increase in asset lives. Given that IAS 16 requires regular reviews of asset lives, it is a concern that they have needed to be extended to such an extent all in one year.
Administration costs	(30,000)	(32,000)	This is probably not a material aspect of performance.
Impairment	–	(5,000)	The impairment in 20X7 appears to have depressed profits and hence increased the apparent growth rate. There is a risk that further impairment write-offs may be required.

ICAEW

	Merry 20X8 Draft unaudited £'000	Merry 20X7 £'000	Analytical procedures comment
Provision		(28,000)	The setting up and subsequent reversal of the provision in 20X7 and 20X8 respectively, has decreased the 20X7 profit and increased the 20X8 profit. This initial over provisioning has increased the apparent growth rate in profit. The measurement of the original provision and the necessity of the reversal need to be reviewed as the risk is that there has been intentional profit smoothing using the provisions.
Write back of unutilised provision	14,000		
Financing costs	(18,000)	(12,000)	There has been a substantial increase in finance costs. This should be reviewed against the amount of loans outstanding and interest rates charged. The risk is that increased finance costs and increased loans add to the financial risk of the company and may suggest liquidity problems. Covenants may also be at greater risk of being breached.
Profit before tax	46,000	23,000	
Tax	(10,580)	(5,290)	The effective tax rate is maintained at 23% which is in line with the actual rate of corporation tax. This assumes that any temporary timing differences reconcile, and either there are no permanent differences or the permanent differences net to £nil.
Profit after tax	35,420	17,710	

General comments

Although reported profit has doubled, revenue has actually decreased by 10%. This is cause for concern as a substantial increase in profit appears to have been generated from lower revenue and without any change in selling prices. The key risk is that the manipulation of accounting policies and estimates may have created increased profit rather than an improvement in the underlying commercial conditions.

Increases in profit generated by changes in accounting conventions should not be reflected in any real growth figure in a valuation model and would therefore not be reflected in an enhanced valuation of Merry as suggested by the Merry MD.

A further concern is the reliance that can be placed on the 20X8 financial statements without a statutory audit. In particular while financial due diligence may provide some assurance, typically it will not involve the detailed level of testing that would be carried out in a statutory audit. While due diligence procedures could be extended to cover further audit procedures this may have the same effect of delaying the transaction as waiting for the statutory audit.

Tax will also need to be investigated, as the 23% effective tax rate may indicate that tax is currently an estimate and has not been calculated in detail.

Assurance work

Audit area	Assurance work
Revenue	Substantiate the assertion that there have been no price increases: *price* { • Review sales invoices in 20X8 and 20X7. • Review price lists. • Review price documentation (eg catalogues). • Investigate reasons for the decline in sales. • Is there a new competitor? • Other market conditions. • The impact of the legal case. • Is the decrease spread throughout the year or is it concentrated into one or two quarters (eg are quarterly sales improving at the year end or declining into the next financial year)? *Is the decline evenly spread? or concentrated?* ↓ *particular products.* • Is the decrease limited to only certain types of product? If so, review these inventories held at year end for impairment.
Cost of sales — *Costs absorbed*	Review prices paid for raw materials for price increases. Review other variable costs for price increases (eg power, wage rates etc). Enquire of management why there were no increases in selling prices despite increases in costs. Review invoices for any increases in fixed overheads. Review methods of inventory valuation and inventory count documentation. Review allocation method of fixed overheads, particularly between inventories and cost of sales.
Depreciation *＊Enquire with mgmt (judgements + assumptions)*	Review evidence for extension of asset lives: • Average age of assets currently being used • Profits/losses on disposal Enquire of management the procedures for reviewing asset lives on a regular basis. Consider residual values. Review any expert evidence supporting reassessment of asset lives (eg surveyors/valuers, engineers).
Administration costs	Break down administration costs into each sub-account and review reasons for the differences.
Impairment	Consider impairment review in 20X8 of same assets as were impaired in 20X7 to investigate whether further impairment write-downs may be required. Enquire of management the reasons for 20X7 impairment and review calculations.
Provision and write back of unutilised provision	Investigate scale and nature of complaints regarding 'poor workmanship' (eg legal correspondence and documentation). Review provision calculation in 20X7 compared with 20X8 and enquire of management the reasons for the changes.
Financing costs	Verify interest rates and amounts outstanding to reconcile increase in finance charges. Review covenants for potential violation (eg interest cover and gearing).

Audit area	Assurance work
Tax	Tax assurance work to verify validity of corporation tax computation. CT Grup .
	Verify validity of deferred tax computation.
	Verify the existence of any outstanding tax liabilities.
	Enquire of management regarding any ongoing tax enquiries.

Risk review

✓ Objective setting

Because of its increased product and geographical diversification, the Archen group's strategic objectives will need to change. Archen's board must reconsider the group's objectives, since the risks it bears and the steps it takes to manage these risks, will be derived from its objectives.

✓ Risk appetite

Archen's directors will need to re-consider the group's risk appetite. This may be difficult as it is not easy to make an overall assessment of how much diversification has reduced overall risk. Some of the risks the group faces may be negatively correlated, for example exchange risks. On the other hand there is certainly some positive correlation between the demand conditions faced by the two companies, an economic slowdown being likely to hit both the home and office furnishings businesses.

✓ Risk culture

The board of Archen should ensure that there is a common risk culture across the group. This includes attitudes taken by, and examples set by, senior management, risk documentation, training and the emphasis placed on risk management in performance appraisal. Archen's board may be concerned with the attitudes of Merry's senior management as reflected in the inappropriate claims about profits and the possible manipulation of accounting policies. The recent claims against Merry for poor workmanship may also highlight failings in the operational culture with inadequate performance not being identified and corrected.

✓ Risk consolidation

Clearly Archen's directors will have to obtain evidence that Merry has systems in place for identifying and assessing risk. The process of profiling and consolidating risks will be very significant, since this will involve comparison of the risks Archen is bearing with those of Merry. As a result the relative importance of some of Archen's risks may change.

✓ Risk response

The re-assessment of the importance of Archen's risks may result in changes in the ways in which risks are managed and the priorities for action. The combination of Archen and Merry may result in benchmarking best practice, with one company adopting the other's practices in areas such as inventory management, health and safety and human resources.

✓ Risk reporting

Archen's management will need to review Merry's system of risk reporting to ensure that it is adequate for the group's needs. In particular it will need to assess whether significant risks are reported frequently enough and by the right level of management. It will also need to ensure that deficiencies in Merry's systems, identified for example by internal audit, are addressed. Archen's directors will also need to ensure that sufficient information is provided on Merry's activities for external reporting purposes.

✓ Risk monitoring

Given that Merry will be a material part of the Archen group, Archen's board will need to consider its activities as part of its review of risk that is required under the UK Corporate Governance Code. Archen's directors will probably require Merry's board to fulfil governance requirements – that is risk management being considered at every board meeting and a wider review of risks being carried out annually. The results of Merry's board's review would be fed through to Archen's board for its assessment.

Identification of key risks

✓ Currency risks

Merry appears to be more exposed to exchange risks than Archen. Archen may only have to be concerned with £/€ movements, whereas Merry's trade may be influenced by the £'s performance against a variety of currencies.

✓ Economic risks

Both Archen and Merry will be exposed to economic risks but in different ways. Archen will be vulnerable to a downturn in office building caused by recession, also offices currently operating increasing their replacement cycle. Merry will be vulnerable to pressures on the consumer market, leading to reduced demand for luxury goods. Merry however may also be vulnerable to local producers with lower production and distribution costs in some of the locations to which it exports.

✓ Transportation risks

Although Archen is vulnerable to damage of goods in transit, Merry's risk appears much greater given the greater transport miles and also the vulnerable nature of many of Merry's products.

✓ Financial and liquidity risks

The interest charge in Merry's accounts appears to suggest a need for a significant amount of loan finance, possibly to bridge gaps between goods being shipped and payment being received. Archen's board needs to consider the implications of a significant interest commitment and hence an increase in financial risk.

✓ Supplier risks

Merry's suppliers are likely to differ from Archen, and Archen's directors may find that Merry's supply chain is much more or much less integrated than Archen's. Archen's board will need to consider whether the risks Merry is bearing in relation to its suppliers are acceptable, particularly in terms of speed of delivery and quality. If the directors wish to rationalise the group's supply network, by using some of Archen's suppliers to supply Merry as well, the implications of making changes will require consideration.

✓ Customer risks

Archen's board needs to consider carefully the profile and features of Merry's customer base. A particular concern will be if Merry's customers have a much longer settlement period and a worse bad debt record. Credit controls may be more difficult to operate on Merry's customer base.

Potential benefits of using non-financial performance measures

✓ Competitive advantage

If the Board and, in turn, Archen's managers concentrate on financial performance measures there is a danger they will ignore other important variables which cannot be stated in monetary terms.

For example, Merry's success and its reputation appears to be based on the high quality of its furnishings. Therefore, quality appears to be an important part of Merry's competitive advantage, but it can't be stated in financial terms.

✓ Critical success factors and key performance indicators

In this respect, it would be useful for Archen and Merry to determine the key aspects of performance to measure based on the companies' critical success factors. Again, the importance of quality suggests that Archen needs to monitor aspects of performance relating to quality. In this respect, it would be useful for Archen to include some key performance indicators in the Board pack relating to this; for example, customer satisfaction levels.

Equally, we have identified supplier risks as being one of the main risks facing Merry, and supplier performance in relation to the reliability of delivery and the quality of inputs could have an important impact on the quality of the products Merry supplies to its customers, and its ability to deliver them on a timely basis. Therefore it could be important to monitor non-financial aspects of supplier performance (such as % of deliveries received on time) as well as financial aspects, such as the cost of products supplied.

Leading and lagging indicators

Traditional, financial performance measures tend to be lagging indicators, connected with past performance and past events. However, as such, they will not necessarily help Archen's directors or managers to understand future challenges the company will face.

By contrast non-financial performance measures can often act as leading indicators, and can highlight potential future performance issues. For example, if there were declining customer satisfaction levels with the quality of Merry's furnishings, in time this could damage the company's reputation and most likely its revenue and profits as well. However, if the initial indicators were identified quickly, appropriate action could be taken to address the issues which had caused the fall in product quality.

Links to objectives and strategy

The performance measures a company selects should allow it to measure the effectiveness of its operations and processes in meeting its objectives and contributing to its overall strategy.

Although we don't know what Archen's overall strategy is, the desire to open up new markets and to enhance its geographical presence suggests that at least an element of its strategy is linked to market growth and expansion. To some degree, performance in this respect could be measured through financial performance indicators (for example, revenue from different geographical regions), but non-financial indicators could also be useful (for example, market share in these different regions).

Short-termism

More generally, a potential danger of focusing on financial performance measures is that they could lead to short-termism. In particular, if the directors focus too much on achieving annual profit targets, this could come at the expense of longer-term investment and business sustainability. There is no indication that Archen or Merry are currently doing this, but using a balanced set of performance measures should help Archen manage performance for both the short and longer terms.

Equally, the notion of sustainability and the creation of value in the longer-term could also be linked to the development of integrated reporting. If, in time, Archen is going to report on its strategy, performance and prospects in the context of its commercial, social and environmental activities, then it follows that the directors should also monitor its performance across these different areas.

This is not to suggest that traditional financial performance measures will no longer be important for Archen. However, when selecting performance measures the company should try to balance traditional financial measures with non-financial ones.

Strategic management accounting

If Archen does place increased importance on non-financial performance measures in its reporting packs, then the use of strategic management accounting is likely to be consistent with this.

Unlike traditional management accounting which looks primarily at internally generated financial information, strategic management accounting also includes external factors and non-financial information. For example, strategic management accounting information might include information about competitors and market growth in different markets, alongside information about Archen and Merry's own performance.

Market share – In our assessment of the risks facing Merry we identified that it will be vulnerable both to pressures on the consumer market leading to reduced demand for luxury goods, and also vulnerable to local producers competing with it. In this context, it would be useful to assess Merry's performance not only in terms of its own revenues or profitability, but also in relation to the wider market performance; for example, by looking at changes in Merry's market share.

Equally, external information could help when analysing the group's own performance. We have already noted that Archen and Merry will be exposed to different economic risks, but it will also be important to assess what impact those risks could be having on the companies' performance. For example, if the companies' rates of sales growth slow down, it would be useful to know how far this might be caused by a general economic slow-down, or the actions of specific competitors.

Moreover, given that Archen will face different economic risks to Merry then it could be useful to understand the context in which the two companies are operating when analysing their performance. For example, if the market conditions in which Merry operates are more favourable than those in which Archen is operating, then the directors would be justified in expecting Merry's performance to reflect this.

The external focus needed for strategic management accounting, coupled with having an understanding of the market environments in which the companies operate, their competitors and their customers, will also be important for Archen's directors as they evaluate any future strategies for the group.

5 Pickering Packaging Ltd

Marking guide

		Marks
		Up to
(a)	Options for realising investment	12
(b)	Valuation of interest in PPL	12
(c)	Change of ownership	5
(d)	Share options:	
	Management issues	5
	Financial accounting/Assurance issues	6
(e)	Sustainability (environmental; social; economic; business sustainability)	10
Total marks		50
Maximum marks		42

Bob Graham
Pickering Packaging Ltd

Bright & Spencer
8 Holly Mews
Harrogate
Yorkshire
HA15 6QX

July 20X9

Dear Bob

I am writing concerning your wish to realise your investment in Pickering Packaging Limited (PPL) and to implement a share option scheme.

I understand your aims in proposing a realisation to be:

- to allow for personal reinvestment in alternative companies or industries.
- to allow PPL to continue to grow, potentially by acquisitive growth.
- to allow you perhaps to retain control of PPL after the proposed transaction.

I understand your aims in proposing a share option scheme to be:

- to incentivise key staff.
- to offset any adverse perception from your proposed realisation of your investment.

If any of my understanding of your aims is incorrect, please let me know at your earliest convenience.

I have dealt with these items in turn on the attached appendices, being:

Appendix

A   Options for realisation of part of your investment
B   Valuation of your interest in PPL
C   Problems associated with a change of ownership
D   Issues connected with offering share options to staff
E   Importance of sustainability issues to the company

I hope this is helpful. No doubt you will be in touch soon to discuss the possibilities available and other issues raised. I look forward to helping further.

Kind regards.

Yours sincerely

Max Spencer

Appendix A – Options for realisation of part of your investment

There are numerous ways in which you could sell part of your shareholding in PPL. I outline the possibilities of:

Option 1   Flotation of PPL with subsequent open market sale of shares to the general public

Option 2   Sale of shares to a private investor or institution prior to flotation/instead of flotation

Option 3   Sale of the business to a competitor or customer

Option 4   Sale of your shares to some of your fellow directors or employees

Option 5   Maintaining your existing shareholding but obtaining a cash withdrawal from the company

Option 1: Flotation

Should the company be floated, you would obtain a better price per share for your investment, since your shares would be more easily marketable than is currently the case as a private limited company. There are several advantages from PPL's viewpoint:

(+)
- Increased access to third party capital

- Increased marketability of shares

- An increased public profile for the company resulting in greater shareholder confidence

- The possibility of using a share-for-share exchange if in the future PPL wishes to expand by acquiring other companies

(-)
Disadvantages of flotation include the costs of obtaining a flotation and the management time involved. Regulation by the London Stock Exchange will mean increased reporting requirements, such as the need for interim financial statements. The UK Corporate Governance Code also requires a number of procedures to be introduced which limit the power of senior management (such as the appointment of non-executive directors and audit committees). These may not fit easily into the corporate culture of PPL.

You should also bear in mind that your wish to retain control of the company is likely to depress the price you could obtain for your shares, since any prospective shareholders would be buying into a non-controlling (minority) interest in the company. Since the non-controlling shareholders (minority interest) have little protection should you subsequently disagree with them over business decisions, they are likely to be prudent in valuing shares. Some investors are historically unwilling to invest in companies which have a dominant shareholder. The discount arising as a result of your dominant shareholding would be unlikely to be very large, however, as most listed company shareholders (other than large institutional shareholders) have virtually no ability to influence business decisions.

(+) Any shares which you retained would be quoted either on the London Stock Exchange or the Alternative Investment Market. This option would make any later disposals/realisations easier which may be of importance when, say, you retire.

Option 2: Sales of shares to third party

Flotation would increase the market value of your shares, since the shares are more easily realisable into cash. As discussed the costs of flotation are high and you will ultimately bear 85% of those costs.

It may be possible therefore to sell some of your shares to a private or institutional investor, using the valuation in Appendix B.

The valuation given in Appendix B includes a discount for non marketability of the shares. As noted earlier, a flotation increases the marketability and price of shares and so would be likely to raise more funds for you.

If you were willing to sell a shareholding of at least 50% of the voting shares, this would be likely to attract a control premium, increasing the proceeds you could obtain on realisation of your investment.

Once again, however, it is unlikely that a third party would be willing to pay a high sum for your shares while you retain a controlling interest.

Option 3: Sale of business to competitor or customer

The market you operate in is competitive, with more than twenty competitors headed by listed companies. I am aware that some companies are very similar to PPL and others may be interested in diversifying their business risk. They could do this by acquiring shares in your company in return for shares in themselves. Although it would be impossible to achieve your aim of retaining control of PPL by doing this (since the acquiring company would certainly require a controlling interest) this option may be a desirable method of increasing the liquidity and marketability of your investment while avoiding the costs associated with flotation.

Also, some of your customers may be interested in vertical integration and this may make them a potential acquirer. There are a lot of potential investors to allow you to choose the most beneficial offer.

Option 4: Sale of shares to fellow directors

It appears likely that some of your fellow directors would be interested in purchasing shares from you. As you have worked together for some time, you would be likely to obtain a fair price while still having investors who would be willing to accept your desire for a controlling interest in the short term.

This option would be unlikely to generate the most cash for you however, and it relies upon your fellow directors having the cash available to purchase your shares. It could easily be used as a means of satisfying your desire to reward your staff and fellow directors for their loyalty.

Option 5: Cash withdrawal

This could be achieved in one of three ways.

Bonus payment

As a controlling interest, you may elect to pay yourself a very large salary. Although not technically requiring the consent of the other shareholders, this may be seen as a breach of fiduciary duty and in an extreme circumstance could precipitate an action under the Companies Act for unfair prejudice against the non-controlling (minority) shareholders. It may not therefore be desirable.

Should you nevertheless decide on this method, PPL would obtain a corporation tax deduction for the payment, but you would be taxed on your earnings.

Dividend payment

A fair alternative to allow you to realise cash would be payment of a large dividend. This will have no impact on the corporation tax position of the company, but you would be taxed on this source of income.

Share buy-back

Finally, the company could buy back some of the shares you wish to sell. This is governed by the Companies Act, with the over-riding aim that the permanent capital of the company must be maintained. If the company were to buy back all of your shares then the premium on the repayment would need to be covered by distributable reserves and it would be necessary to transfer £85,000 to a non-distributable capital redemption reserve to cover the reduction in the share capital of the company. It would be necessary to ensure:

- that the Articles of Association of the company provided for the repurchase of capital in this method.

- that the off-market purchase of shares was approved by Special Resolution at a general meeting of the company. Your 85% shareholding would allow you to achieve the 75% vote required to pass a Special Resolution.

A share buy-back may be treated as either a capital distribution or an income distribution depending on whether it fulfilled the necessary tax conditions. A capital distribution would have the advantage of being taxed at a lower rate than an income distribution. If the company is interested in the idea of the share buy-back, one of my colleagues in the tax planning department will be happy to discuss the tax implications of the buy back with you.

These methods all have the following drawbacks:

- They will severely limit the company's ability to replace its assets and effectively manage working capital.

- They will probably remove the possibility of the company growing by acquisitive growth, since acquisitions of other companies are normally at least partially financed by cash.

- They rely upon the company having the necessary liquid resources, although the company is currently cash rich, holding cash balances of £17.6m following the sale of land.

In essence, realisation of your investment by these means is undesirable and should be discounted.

Appendix B – Valuation of your interest in PPL

Establishing a fair value of your holding in the company is extremely difficult since certain factors make PPL difficult to compare to other companies, specifically the following:

- PPL is a private limited company the share price for which would be lower than that of a similar public company (such as the shares listed under 'paper and packaging' in the FT) due to greater difficulty in transferring shares. A way around this might be to value a similar public company and apply an agreed discount of, say, 30% – 50%.

- Your desire to retain control means that the value of individual shares you intend to sell will be low since a purchaser would be buying a non-controlling (minority) interest. To cater for this any price established for a private company should be discounted by, say, 20% – 30%.

- An investor purchasing into PPL would be unlikely to participate in dividend policy, so the value they should ascribe to the company may rationally be based upon past dividend growth, using a method such as Gordon's dividend growth model.

- The earnings of the company in 20X8/X9 are significantly increased by the exceptional gains on the sale of property. Although this would be included in the EPS measure of the other similar companies it is unlikely that these companies will have included items of such a sale this year, so it is best to exclude the exceptional item when undertaking any comparative analysis.

Earnings based valuation

The current year sustainable earnings of PPL are the latest operating profit of £4.305m, less tax at 23%, ie £3.3m. Interest received has not been included as part of sustainable earnings as there is no guarantee that it will be received in perpetuity. The cash generating the interest may for example eventually be used for further expenditure on non-current assets. Applying the sector P/E of 9.625 gives

	£m
Value of an equivalent listed company = £3.3m × 9.625	31.8
Less discount on a private company (say 30%)	(9.5)
Value of controlling interest in a private company	22.3
Less discount for non-controlling holding (say 25%)	(5.6)
Total business value	16.7
Value of your proportion (85%)	14.2

Dividend growth model valuation

Dividend growth has been reasonably stable over the last six years, and we could calculate the growth rate using

$$(1 + g)^5 = (1,000/820) = 1.2195$$

which gives

$$(1 + g) = 1.040$$

so

$$g = 0.040 \text{ or } 4.0\% \text{ pa}$$

Based on the market information available, the required return for the business can be calculated using the capital asset pricing model as

$$k_e = r_f + \beta(r_m - r_f) = 5 + 0.67 (8 - 5) = 7.01\%, \text{ say } 7\%$$

And putting these into the dividend valuation model gives a business value of

$$P_0 = \frac{d_1}{r_e - g} = 1 \times 1.04/(0.07 - 0.04) = £34.7m$$

	£m
Value of an equivalent listed company	34.7
Less discount on a private company (say 30%)	(10.4)
Value of controlling interest in a private company	24.3
Less discount for non-controlling holding (say 25%)	(6.1)
Total business value	18.2
Value of your proportion (85%)	15.5

Free cash flows valuation

	20X9/Y0 £m	20Y0/Y1 £m	20Y1/Y2 £m	20Y2/Y3 £m	20Y3/Y4 £m
Sales	46.0	50.6	55.6	61.2	67.3
Gross profit	16.5	18.2	20.0	22.0	24.2
Operating costs excluding depreciation	(9.0)	(9.2)	(9.5)	(9.8)	(10.1)
Depreciation	(2.0)	(2.0)	(2.0)	(2.6)	(2.6)
Operating profit	5.5	7.0	8.5	9.6	11.5
Interest	0.6	0.6	0.6	0.6	0.6
Profit before tax	6.1	7.6	9.1	10.2	12.1
Tax at 23%	(1.4)	(1.7)	(2.1)	(2.3)	(2.8)
Add back depreciation	2.0	2.0	2.0	2.6	2.6
Capital expenditure				(6.0)	
Working capital	(0.5)	(0.5)	(0.6)	(0.6)	(0.7)
Free cash flow	6.2	7.4	8.4	3.9	11.2
Discount factor	0.935	0.873	0.816	0.763	0.713
Present value	5.8	6.5	6.9	3.0	8.0
	29.7				

	£m
Value of an equivalent listed company	29.7
Less discount on a private company (say 30%)	(8.9)
Value of controlling interest in a private company	20.8
Less discount for non-controlling holding (say 25%)	(5.2)
Total business value	15.6
Value of your proportion (85%)	13.3

The valuation is rather lower than the valuation suggested by the other two methods. However that is connected with the timeframe of the forecast, and extending it beyond 20Y4 is likely to give a higher valuation.

Conclusion

These different valuation bases have produced similar though different results, indicating that a value somewhere in the range of £13.3m – £15.5m should be achievable. This is clearly rather a broad range but leaves plenty of scope for negotiation. The value you may ultimately realise will be very dependent on market conditions and the market appetite for new issues at the date of any flotation.

With personal wealth of this magnitude, we strongly advise that you begin to plan for both capital gains tax and inheritance tax at your earliest opportunity. Our colleagues in the tax planning department will be pleased to assist you.

Appendix C – Problems associated with a change of ownership

If a controlling interest is sold to a competitor or another business, then the changes made to Pickering Packaging are likely to be more extensive than if you retain a controlling interest. Even if you keep a non-controlling (minority) interest, the power you have to influence matters may be limited, and the success of change of ownership will depend on the attitudes and actions of the new owners.

Problems may include:

- Lack of integration plans. Plans need to include changed reporting relationships, information and resource requirements and redefined strategic objectives.

- Inflexibility of integration plans. After the takeover the new owners need to be willing to adapt their initial plans.

- Poor man management. Even if managers are highly motivated under the current arrangements, they may not remain so if there is a lack of communication of goals and future prospects.

- Cultural differences may also result in a lack of communication, and these will be enhanced if the acquirer's management team show a lack of respect for what PPL has previously achieved.

Appendix D – Issues connected with offering share options to staff

Management issues

Attempting to ensure the continuing commitment of management by issuing share options has the following advantages:

- It links management reward into the success of the new ownership arrangements. Management will have a clear incentive to overcome problems and make the new arrangements work.

- Making the rewards share options rather than one-off or annual bonuses incentivises managers to consider the longer-term success of the business.

It may also have the following problems:

- Setting exercise prices at the right level may be problematic. If the prices are perceived as too high or their achievement is perceived as not being under the control of managers, they may have a very limited incentive effect.

- If managers are determined to leave, then issuing share options will not compel them to stay. A more effective means would be to persuade them to sign service contracts tying them to the company for a certain time (share options in the acquirer could be one of the terms in an enhanced service contract).

- You should also consider that potential acquirers may want to have the ability to make some changes to the management team, and may perceive share options as limiting their freedom to do so.

Financial accounting implications   SHARE OPTIONS.

Share options represent a share-based element of a remuneration package and their treatment is governed by IFRS 2 *Share-based Payment*.

For share options, IFRS 2 requires an entity to reflect as an increase in equity and a corresponding remuneration expense the fair value of the equity instruments granted as measured at the grant date. Fair value should be based on the market price of such instruments, if available. Few companies, however, have options regularly traded on their shares, and other companies must use a generally accepted valuation technique such as the Black-Scholes formula for options.

If the business undergoes a flotation and a stock market quotation is available for the shares then establishing an option value using the Black-Scholes formula is not problematic and we would be happy to provide assistance in this area. If, however, you choose to realise your investment by a route other than a flotation then this calculation becomes more problematic as establishing a fair value for the shares will be difficult, let alone the options. Once again, however, this is an area where we believe we can be of great assistance.

If the options are issued with what is called 'vesting conditions', such as the options are only received if the individual is still employed or if earnings growth exceeds a certain level, then the impact of these conditions needs to be reflected. Though they will not affect the fair value of any option, they may affect the number of options that will be exercised and hence the number of shares that may ultimately be issued. At each year end until any options are exercised, what you will need to reflect as part of equity within the accounts is your best estimate of the fair value of any options that will become exercisable. The movement in this estimate from one year to the next needs to be reflected in profit or loss for the relevant period.

Assurance issues

The assurance issues that will be relevant in this area relate to the above two factors, ie:

- the fair value of any options issued; and

- the estimate of the number of options that will be exercisable based on the vesting conditions and the conditions at the reporting date.

With respect to the fair value we will need to check the following:

- The share price – straightforward for a listed company
- The exercise price – specified in any option
- Time to expiry – specified in any option
- Volatility of the underlying share – reasonably straightforward for listed shares
- Interest rates – always known
- Dividend yields – which have been fairly stable for PPL

If the business is listed, the only figure that may be a little difficult to establish is volatility since ideally we want future volatility to expiry but we will need to base this on historical volatility.

With respect to the vesting conditions we need to check:

- what the conditions are and how many options may be exercised under any given circumstances.
- the likelihood of those conditions being satisfied given current circumstances.

Appendix E – Importance of sustainability issues to the company

Environmental concern – The concept of sustainability is often used in the context of environmental sustainability; for example, reducing greenhouse gas emissions, reducing waste or increased recycling. The newspaper articles highlight that these aspects of environmental sustainability are very important in the packaging industry.

Customer and consumer requirements – Importantly, however, this environmental concern isn't confined to the packaging and carton companies themselves, but environmental issues are becoming increasingly important to customers and consumers. As such, they could have financial implications for Pickering. If customers – particularly large B2B customers – want the packaging they use for their food products to be environmentally friendly, and Pickering's packaging doesn't meet their requirements in this respect, it is possible that the customers might switch suppliers – for example, to either Cradley or Coral who appear to be paying considerable attention to these issues.

In this respect, environmental sustainability could be more closely linked to the interests of your fellow shareholders than they might think.

Competitive disadvantage – The newspaper articles also highlight that Cradley and Coral have been developing new types of environmentally-friendly packaging. We are not sure whether Pickering has been taking any similar steps, but if not, this could lead to it being at a competitive disadvantage to its competitors.

On the one hand, it will increasingly not be able to offer customers the environmentally-friendly packaging they want; and on the other, Pickering is in danger of being seen as less innovative than its competitors.

Pickering has correctly identified a need to maintain its competitive advantage by employing the latest technology; but it needs to complement this by also offering innovative products and ones that meet customer requirements.

In this respect, the cost implications of different products could also affect Pickering's competitive advantage. It appears that, not only are the new products developed by Cradley and Coral environmentally friendly, they also allow the companies to make savings on their material costs. Here again, the links between sustainability and financial benefit might be closer than at first thought, and adopting an environmentally friendly approach would seem to create a 'win-win' situation for the business.

Sustainability and strategy – However, while environmental issues are an important aspect of sustainability, they are by no means the only aspect. Although the newspaper articles you have collected seem to focus primarily on environmental performance (for example, in relation to recycling or carbon emissions), you should look at sustainability in a wider context; including also social and economic dimensions.

Social dimension – You have already identified that you now have some very highly motivated managers in the business, and it is important to retain them. In more general terms, being seen as an attractive employer could help Pickering to recruit and retain high quality staff; and offering good quality working conditions, training and opportunities should help to maintain employee motivation. These social dimensions, in turn, should benefit the performance of the company.

Economic dimension – We have already alluded to the economic dimension of sustainability with reference to Pickering's competitive position and innovation, but more generally issues such as effective corporate governance, risk management and customer relationship management are all likely to be important to the continuing success of the business.

Business sustainability – The economic dimension of sustainability should also encourage a focus on the long-term viability and success of the business. Clearly, Pickering has been successful in recent years – with increasing sales, profits and productivity – but the notion of sustainability should challenge you and the other shareholders to consider how the business' success can be maintained into the future. In particular, is the group adopting strategies that can deliver it long-term competitive advantage?

Importantly, once your fellow shareholders start considering this idea of business sustainability they may also look at a more balanced range of performance indicators, rather than concentrating on short-term financial performance indicators only. Doing so should also encourage them to think about the risks and opportunities which could shape the longer-term prospects and performance of the business.

Perhaps more importantly though, the idea of sustainability should encourage the current shareholders and any future owners of the business to think about the longer-term consequences of any decisions they make, to ensure that those decisions have the best chance possible of creating value over time.

6   Zaltan plc

Marking guide

	Marks
	Up to
Business risks arising from the acquisition	8
Due diligence	5
Debt factoring – FR treatment	8
Debt factoring – advice	4
Loan notes FR – Proposal 1	8
Bank loan FR – Proposal 2	4
Recommendation – which debt instrument to choose	9
Retained earnings as a source of finance for the acqusition	4
Importance of HR in the acquisition process	7
Cyber security issues and actions to be taken	10
Total marks	67
Maximum marks	60

To: Hugo Hughes, Finance Director
From: Treasury Accountant
Subject: Draft briefing notes for board meeting
Date: 21 July 20X3

CORE COMPETENCIES

(a)   **Business risks of acquisition**

(1)   <u>Strategic risks</u>

This is a strategy of horizontal integration in acquiring a company with common elements in supply and manufacturing activities where management have experience in similar, but not identical, processes. The expansion is therefore in a related core area of the current business in copper piping manufacture and the risks of failing to understand the processes and supply chain arrangements are therefore likely to be low as there is some sharing of core competences.

The markets of Cupro are however significantly different to those of Zaltan, with little, or no, common customer base. Within the Ansoff matrix this could be regarded as market development.

The risk is that the customers of Cupro may not continue to be loyal under the new ownership of Zaltan (eg if there are valued business relationships with individual directors of Cupro). Continuance of these relationships is not guaranteed.

This is particularly the case with the three large contracts which may not be renewed. The Cupro sales are heavily dependent on these three contracts and so this is a key risk, although this is mitigated to some extent by the remaining contract terms of between two and four years. However, many supply contracts include change of ownership clauses that allow the third party to exit the contract or renegotiate its terms.

(2) Operational risks

There are risks that the post-acquisition integration of the two companies may not deliver the synergies and operational efficiency that was planned into the acquisition price.

In general, the merging (to the extent envisaged) of the manufacturing processes may give rise to unforeseen problems (eg in terms of compatibility of process, employee resistance, skills gaps). There may also be parallel problems in merging information systems and support processes (eg accounting, HRM, IT, internal controls, supply chain management, deliveries, marketing).

If the level of operating, marketing and financial synergies envisaged in the offer price does not materialise in the integration and post-integration period then there is a significant risk that Zaltan may overpay for Cupro.

Other operating risks may include:

- the sales of surplus assets may be uncertain in terms of the prices that may be obtained and the identification of assets that are no longer required due to duplication or strategic refocus.

- hidden contractual or other legal obligations.

- hidden financial liabilities (eg tax).

- while the specific method of financing is not to be considered, any debt financed acquisition will add to financial gearing of the new group and thus increase financial risk.

- management skills and available time may not be as appropriate for the new group as for Zaltan.

- asset security issues for providers of finance with a change of use or disposal of assets.

(3) Pricing the acquisition

Perhaps the key risk is making the acquisition at a price appropriate to the benefits that will be received from Cupro as part of the new group. Even if the acquisition is operationally and strategically a success then it is still possible to overpay.

Two key features in this respect are therefore that:

- the acquisition is based on full information currently available (see due diligence below) although there is still the risk that events may not turn out as expected. In particular, Cupro is still loss-making, has experienced industrial unrest and has just introduced new production and IT systems.

- the risk is related not just to the amount of the consideration for the acquisition but the form of the consideration.

(4) Due diligence – Managing the risks

Cupro will have more information about its business than Zaltan when setting a deal price. Due diligence helps to narrow this information gap to enable a more informed decision by Zaltan on the performance, position and risks of Cupro when offering an acquisition price. Specifically, due diligence may:

- identify legal title, intangible and legal rights to assets.
- confirm the accuracy and assumptions of financial data and projections.
- provide a commercial review of Cupro's business.
- identify and quantify areas of commercial and financial risk.
- give assurance to providers of finance (either the bank loan or loan notes).

- enable a more precise bid price to be ascertained by Zaltan.
- identify possible areas of synergy.
- identify key personnel to tie-in post acquisition.

Areas of due diligence will include:

Financial due diligence – giving assurance on the financial position, financial risk and projections (eg the assumptions on which a return to profit by Cupro following some years of losses will need to be established).

Commercial due diligence – giving assurance on markets and external economic environment (eg the potential for renewal of Cupro's three key contracts will need to be evidenced).

Technical due diligence – giving assurance on new technologies particularly as Cupro's new manufacturing technology is in its infancy.

IT due diligence – giving assurance on the nature, reliability and risks of IT systems and IT skills (the new IT system will need to be reviewed for reliability but also its compatibility with Zaltan's system).

Legal due diligence – giving assurance on legal rights and obligations including the acquisition contract. Employment law issues may also be important given the recent redundancies by Cupro.

HRM due diligence – giving assurance on the skills and HRM contracts particularly given the redundancies and resistance to new technology.

Tax due diligence – any tax liabilities and their impact on the new group will need to be reviewed (eg whether there are tax losses that correspond with the accounting losses and whether these will be available for relief in the context of the new group). Tax structuring of acquisition and finance.

[margin note: types of DUE DILIGENCE]

(b) **Debt factoring arrangement**

(1) **Financial reporting treatment**

The nature of debt factoring is addressed by IAS 39 *Financial Instruments: Recognition and Measurement* although the standard does not give specific detailed guidance on the treatment of debt factoring. The key question is whether factored receivables should be derecognised as a financial asset.

Derecognition (ie ceasing to recognise the factored debts) is appropriate only where the criteria for derecognition of a financial asset according to IAS 39 have been satisfied. Specifically, derecognition should only take place where the seller (Zaltan plc) has transferred substantially all the asset's risks and rewards of the receivables. (Note that if a transfer occurs and the seller neither transfers nor retains substantially all the risks and rewards the asset will only be derecognised if control has been lost.)

This is a question of judgement as to whether substantially all the risks and rewards have been transferred. In respect of the £7.2m (90% × £8m) that would be immediately received from the factor then it would appear that there is a strong case that this should be derecognised given that it is non-recourse finance. However, interest has to be paid until cash is received from receivables, which gives some slow-moving risk and it is a question of judgement as to whether this is 'substantial' in the context of the specific circumstances.

Zaltan is ultimately to receive a net total of at least £7,436,000 (see working below) thus the question arises as to when risk passes with respect to the remaining £236,000 and thus when derecognition should occur with respect to this amount. This is again likely to be a question of judgement as to what is a 'substantial' risk but it would not exceed three months before derecognition when the factor assumes unconditional responsibility.

The £12m of receivables which have not been factored will continue to be recognised.

The £7.2m received would be shown under 'cash and cash equivalents' in the statement of financial position.

WORKING

Receivables factored without recourse:

	£
Gross receivables sold to debt factor	8,000,000
Less credit protection fee (3% × £8m)	(240,000)
*Interest (£7.2m × 1.5% × 3 months)	(324,000)
	7,436,000

*This assumes the worst case that none of the receivables pay within three months.

Best case is that £7.2m is repayable after two months in which case interest payable would be £216,000.

(2) **Debt factoring advice**

This method of finance seems inappropriate as it is not incremental finance as the cash would have been received within a few months and better management of receivables could have achieved the same end. It is also very expensive over a three month period if only £7,436,000 of £8m is received. This is over 7% in three months which annualises to 31%. Unless there is a strong suspicion of high bad debts this seems inappropriate in terms of costs and timing.

There may be some savings in reduced administration but these seem unlikely to be large given that we need to maintain our sales ledger function for receivables which have not been factored. There may also be an adverse reputational effect if it becomes known that debts have been factored as it may imply poor liquidity.

(c) **Debt financing arrangements**

(1) **Proposal 1 – loan notes**

The implicit interest rate needs to be determined. Thus for a £100 loan note, where i is the implicit rate:

$$100 = 4/(1 + i) + 4/(1 + i)^2 + 4/(1 + i)^3 + 4/(1 + i)^4 + 128/(1 + i)^4$$

Solving for i by iteration or linear interpolation gives 10% approx

Year ending 30 June	Opening £'000	Interest 10% £'000	Paid £'000	Closing £'000
20X4 (6 months)	20,000	*976	–	20,976
20X5	20,976	2,098	800	22,274
20X6	22,274	2,227	800	23,701
20X7	23,701	2,370	800	25,271
20X8 (6 months)	25,271	1,233	800	25,704**

*6 months = $1.1^{1/2}$ = 4.88%
** rounding error 25,704k – (20,000k × 1.28) = £104k see note below)

Note:

- Only the first two years are required.

- Strictly the interest in the above table should be calculated with half year rests, as the £800,000 payments are made half way through each accounting period rather than at the end of the period.

Thus, in the financial statements for the year ended 30 June 20X4 interest charged should be £976,000 and there is a financial liability of £20.976m.

In the financial statements for the year ended 30 June 20X5 interest charged should be £2,098,000 and there is a financial liability of £22.274m.

(2) **Bank loan – Proposal 2**

It is not possible to determine accurately the interest to be charged to profit in respect of the bank loan as it carries a variable rate. The financial liability in the statement of financial position will however be known with certainty as £20m.

If the rate remains at 9% then in the financial statements for the year ended 30 June 20X4 interest charged should be £900,000 and there is a financial liability of £20m.

Note: The APR with six monthly rests is 9.2025% (because $1.045^2 = 1.092025$).

In the financial statements for the year ended 30 June 20X5 interest charged should be £1,800,000 and there will be a financial liability of £20m.

(3) **Recommendation on financing**

- **Difference in interest rates – loan notes and bank loan**

  In terms of costs, the bank loan is currently cheaper at 9% than the loan notes which have an effective rate of interest of 10%. This however is not a reasonable comparison as 9% reflects the current rate whereas 10% reflects the average expectation of future interest rates over the period of the loan to 31 December 20X7.

  This is likely to reflect the yield curve which normally is upward sloping whereby a risk premium is required by investors in the form of a higher yield for bonds of longer maturity. This may not however be the case if interest rates are expected to fall, in which case there may be an inverted yield curve with a lower yield on longer maturity bonds.

  The issue costs of the loan notes are likely to be higher than the bank loan and this will raise the effective interest rate further. Issue costs need to be quantified and included in the financing decision.

- **Financial risks**

  There are a number of risk factors to be considered:

  Refinancing risk

  Both the debt instruments are medium term but they are financing a long-term investment. The loan stock has a four year term while the bank loan has a six year term. A key risk is therefore whether at the end of these periods adequate replacement finance will be available, or whether Zaltan will have generated sufficient cash flows for the loan not to require replacement.

  Given that the bank loan is not repayable until 20X9 there is a lower repayment risk than the loan notes. This has a liquidity advantage from delaying refinancing or repayment by two years.

  Interest rate risk

  The bank loan is subject to interest rate risk as if LIBOR increases then the company will be required to pay more interest and it is tied into the loan agreement for six years. If this risk became unacceptable then a pay-fixed receive-variable swap arrangement could be entered into, but this would depend on a counterparty being available and agreement being reached on suitable terms.

  With the loan notes, after they are issued the interest rate and the cash interest payments are fixed so there is no interest rate risk. However, up until the time of issue, unexpected changes in interest rates may alter the terms of the agreement.

  Fair value risk

  The fair value of the debt varies inversely with interest rates. Thus, if interest rates fall in the economy, the fair value of the obligation to repay would increase. If the loans are held to maturity then this may not be a major factor but it may hinder any possible swap arrangement if interest rates change and would alter the terms of any refinancing deal.

  Gearing

  Both types of debt instrument will increase financial gearing and will therefore increase the financial risk of the business. This is as a consequence of increasing the volatility of equity returns but also it increases bankruptcy risks if interest or capital repayments cannot be met.

  Cash flow and liquidity

  In terms of cash interest payments, the loan notes provide a cash flow advantage as they are at only 4% nominal, compared to 9%. However, overall any liquidity advantage from the deferral of interest payments is far outweighed by the requirement on the loan notes for capital repayment plus the redemption premium in four years' time. This is a major liquidity risk compared to the bank loan.

Covenant risk

Typically there are more covenants on bank loans than publicly issued debt. To the extent that this is true of these arrangements, the bank loan may reduce financial flexibility in restricting the ability of Zaltan to raise additional finance elsewhere within the loan period. Private debt does however normally have less onerous public reporting requirements.

Availability risk

The relationship bank has indicated that the bank loan should be available, but the investment bank is only an intermediary and it may be that the loan note issue will not be taken up. The investment bank may underwrite the issue to ensure take up but this may add significant additional cost and therefore increase the implicit interest rate.

- **Advice**

  If debt markets are efficient then the two debt instruments should be more or less equivalent in terms of interest rates, risks and other terms. However, for our purposes the bank loan may be preferable on the grounds that there is more time to arrange refinancing, perhaps by an equity issue – particularly as the investment is long term.

  There is also an issue of diversity of funding sources – there may be an argument for taking public funding when it is available and leaving bank funding for a later date when quick access might be more advantageous.

  In addition however there is a lower cost of financing and more certainty over availability and lower costs of issue.

  Nevertheless, the interest rate on both instruments is very high, and therefore due consideration needs to be given to whether the financial risks and costs, in addition to the business risks, make the acquisition a viable proposition.

(d) (1) **Response to Chairman**

The notion that the £19m of retained earnings can be used to finance the acquisition is misconceived. The existence of retained earnings in the statement of financial position means that profits have been retained in the past, which are represented by net assets. However, it does not mean that cash or other liquid assets are available for financing an acquisition.

Indeed, it can be seen from the statement of financial position that there is no cash available as Zaltan has an overdraft.

(2) **Importance of HR in the acquisition process**

The Chairman's concern about the 'people' aspect of the deal appears justified, because a number of the key issues involved in an acquisition relate directly to human resource issues. Although in this case some people-related issues may have a higher profile due to the on-going disputes at Cupro, human resources are nonetheless important in relation to any acquisitions.

Although historically HR may not have been considered a strategic part of acquisition decisions, companies have increasingly realised the importance of people issues in acquisitions. One of the main reasons for this is that 'people' issues – poor cultural fit, poor communication – can often be the reason why acquisitions do not prove to be as successful as had been hoped.

The following issues could all be important when trying to integrate Cupro with Zaltan if the acquisition goes ahead.

- **Communicating to staff in both companies**, and addressing any concerns they may have about the acquisition. Staff (particularly at Cupro in this case) might be expected to resist the acquisition and the change and uncertainty associated with it. One of the main reasons why staff resist change generally is because they have not been told why the change is happening or what impact it is likely to have on them.

Equally, employee resistance is one of the single most difficult issues to deal with during the course of mergers and acquisitions, and HR is perhaps the department best-placed within an organsiation to deal with the causes of resistance.

- **Dealing with any redundancies** which may be necessary. The issue of redundancies is likely to be particularly sensitive at Cupro, given the redundancies which have already been suffered following the introduction of the new, capital intensive production methods. However, it is perhaps inevitable that there will be further redundancies after the acquisition. When companies merge, there are some departments or functions which can easily be consolidated (for example, accounting departments or marketing departments) and therefore staffing synergies can often be one of the first benefits to be achieved from an acquisition.

  Nonetheless, given the on-going employment disputes at Cupro, Zaltan will have to give careful consideration to how it handles any future redundancies.

- **Integrating the organisational cultures** of the two companies. At this point, we do not know much about the culture within Cupro. However, if Zaltan's organisational culture is different to the prevailing culture at Cupro, then Cupro's staff could feel uncomfortable with the culture of the new group post-acquisition. Depending on the strength of this clash of cultures between the two companies, it is possible that some members of staff may choose to leave.

- **Retaining key members of staff** and key managers. Although we have noted that acquisitions often cause staff redundancies, it is also important that key members of staff are retained in an organisation which has been acquired. In this case, it could be particularly important for Zaltan to retain key staff working on Cupro's long-term contracts with house-building companies.

- **Aligning the remuneration and reward systems** of the two companies. For example, if there are differences between the salaries Cupro's staff received compared to the salaries received by Zaltan's staff for similar jobs, and the employees become aware of these differences, this could lead to further discontent and unrest among the staff.

- **Deciding on HR policies and practice** in the new company. For example, if Cupro and Zaltan currently have different policies in relation to holidays or reward systems it seems likely that these will have to be integrated if the acquisition goes ahead. Again, however, it will be necessary to gauge the level of resistance to any proposed changes before they are implemented.

  Another issue to consider is the structure of the entity post-acquisition. For example, will Cupro be retained as a separate division, or will Cupro's existing staff simply be integrated into Zaltan's existing organisation structure, according to their job roles.

(e) **Cyber security concerns**

Incident at Cupro – issues for Zaltan to consider

The recent cyber incident that affected Cupro's contract management system has illustrated the potential for vulnerability to attack, whether maliciously or otherwise. Before any merging of the IT systems of the two companies (assuming that the acquisition goes ahead) the board of Zaltan will need to review the IT consultancy report to ensure that:

- the source of the virus at Cupro has been confirmed, and the circumstances of the incident fully understood.

- there has been a full investigation into Cupro's systems and there is no continued contamination from the exposure to the virus that could infect any merged system in the future.

- a similar incident could not occur with Zaltan's systems, or the merged systems following acquisition.

Actions to take

To protect the systems in the future, the following actions are recommended for the board of Zaltan.

ACTIONS TO TAKE

Undertake a review of Zaltan's systems

As a first step in avoiding similar occurrences in the future, a review of Zaltan's systems would be worthwhile, because there is an admission that cyber security is something that has been left to the IT department to manage.

Have a basic strategy in place

IT environments can be complex, and it is often the case that non-IT staff struggle to understand the importance or significance of security controls. Employees need to be formally trained in the importance of adhering to published company IT policies on acceptable use of IT (such as a ban on accessing non work-related websites) and the importance of access controls (with the use of strong passwords, firewalls and controlled access to only the relevant systems for each user). Staff should be made aware of the risks to the business that can be posed by ignoring these policies, or bypassing controls, and disciplinary procedures clearly communicated. IT systems should be regularly monitored for unusual activity, and the use of anti-virus software, scanning of all removable media and the application of regular vendor-supplied software updates should all be compulsory to ensure that applications remain supported.

Recognise that cyber security is not just the concern of the IT department

As well as being a technical risk, the neglect of cyber security represents a business risk that can affect the entire organisation, and so needs the involvement of a wider range of employees than just those in the IT department. Internal controls over the confidentiality, integrity and availability of data are important, but the focus needs to widen to include external risks to security posed by criminals, hackers, weaknesses in the supply chain, the prevalence of mobile devices and the increased use of cloud storage. All of these factors represent threats to the traditional approaches to the security of company data systems, and are particularly relevant to a company such as Zaltan that is considering an acquisition which will include the merging of data systems.

Identify the key sources of risk

The incident at Cupro highlights the risks posed to the infrastructure if cyber security is not taken seriously. In this case, it was apparently the actions of an employee that led to the breach, but external sources of cyber risks exist and could include customers, suppliers, business partners and service providers. External parties (such as customers and suppliers) with IT systems which are integrated with those of Cupro and Zaltan represent an area of significant risk. These parties should be expected to have strong security over their own systems, so that the risks to Cupro and Zaltan are minimised. Zaltan may insist in the future that suppliers obtain a satisfactory independent auditor's report (ISAE 3402) on their data security before entering into any contracts.

Focus on the most important information assets

Cupro's contract management system was affected by the breach, and this caused significant disruption. Zaltan needs to identify its key assets – those where breaches would have the most significant impact upon business operations – and focus its cyber security efforts here.

Implement a framework for risk management

Cyber security management should be an ongoing process at Zaltan. This is likely to require establishing appropriate processes and procedures that are regularly tested, revisited and updated as technology develops, and that will need communicating across the whole organisation after any acquisition takes place. ISO 27001 could provide a benchmark for the standard that is required, and should help to improve and maintain defences against cyber attacks, from whatever source, in the future.

7 Hottentot Hotels Ltd

		Marks Up to
(a)	Analysis and comparison of performance of divisions. Calculate and comment on the performance measures and suggest alternative measures. An assessment of whether Leisure Division is viable.	12
(b)	Explanation of importance of non-financial performance indicators (linked to CSFs and KPIs). Discussion of suitable multi-dimensional performance measurement system. Suggestions for suitable CSFs and KPIs.	12
(c)	Evaluation of new proposal: (1) Give advice on new proposal; and (2) Explain financial reporting implications of lease.	10
(d)	In respect of the fraud: (1) Recommendations on internal control weakness (2) Explain how to act concerning ethical issues arising.	6 5
(e)	Evaluation of impact of Big Data analytics on room pricing and customer relationship management.	12
Total marks		57
Maximum marks		55

(a) Divisional performance measurement

HH's performance measures:

	Business	Leisure
Room utilisation	75%	50%
Revenue per hotel (£'000s)	£4,050	£900
Return on assets (see working)	35.6%	Negative (9.7)
	£14.36m/(£32m – £640k + £9m)	£–1.24m/(£12m – £240k + £1m)

Tutorial note:

Net current assets are treated as non-divisional assets above but any reasonable split between the divisions is also acceptable.

WORKING

	Notes	Business £'000	Leisure £'000
Profit			
Original profit		15,000	(1,000)
Depreciation based on carrying amounts			
(£32m/50)	1	(640)	
(£12m/50)	1		(240)
Revised profit		14,360	(1,240)

Each of these measures can be criticised as not reflecting the underlying performance of the division. Thus, comparisons between these divisional performance measures are at best tenuous.

✓ **Room utilisation** is an important measure in the hotels industry but it is reflected already in the revenue measure used by HH as increased utilisation is likely to lead to increased revenue. Moreover, if taken as a metric on its own, utilisation may lead to excessive discounting which may actually reduce revenue and total contribution.

Revenue is an important measure of performance in considering year on year growth for each hotel and each division. However, revenue per hotel is not a reasonable means of comparing the two divisions as the size and value of hotels in the Business Division is much greater than that of the Leisure Division and therefore one would expect greater revenue generation potential from higher value assets. Moreover, while revenue is an important measure, on its own it is insufficient as it does not consider costs.

Return on assets appears, in concept, to be a reasonable measure of performance as it attempts to measure profit in relation to the value of the assets generating those earnings. In the case of HH however there are a number of weaknesses in relying on the return on assets figure as a measure for comparing the performance of the two divisions:

- The asset value used is the carrying amount. This is the cost less accumulated depreciation given the company's accounting policy of using the cost model. This means that the hotels of the Business Division, which were acquired some time ago, are significantly depreciated and are likely to have gone up in value substantially as the fair value of £4m per hotel is significantly greater than their carrying amount of £1m. In contrast, the Leisure Division hotels were acquired more recently and thus the carrying amount per hotel is £750,000 which is much closer to their fair value of £1m. As a consequence, the denominator in the return on assets calculation for the Business Division hotels is understated and thus the return on assets is overstated.

- The profit figure in the return on assets calculation includes depreciation. However, as the carrying amount is significantly less than the fair value, the depreciation charge is not a fair reflection of the consumption of the asset in commercial terms.

- The profit figures used in the return on assets calculation are after deducting head office costs. This is an arbitrary allocation between the divisions based on their relative revenues generated, as there is unlikely to be a cause and effect relationship between revenue generated and head office fixed costs incurred. A better assessment of return would be contribution by deducting only divisional specific fixed costs which are more likely to be avoidable if hotels were to be closed.

- The profit figures only relate to operating profit and do not consider finance costs and taxation in order to determine a net return.

Alternative measures of return on assets could be used to compare the performance of the two divisions based on fair values of assets and depreciation, also based on fair values and ignoring arbitrary allocations of head office costs.

Even here, however, direct comparisons should be treated with caution as the leisure hotels are, in many cases, newly established and therefore may take some time to reach steady state profits and establish a regular customer base.

	Notes	Business £'000	Leisure £'000
Profit			
Adjusted profit (see above)		14,360	(1,240)
Additional depreciation based on fair values	1	(1,920)	(80)
Revised operating profit/(loss)		12,440	(1,320)
Add back head office costs	3	50,400	5,600
Contribution to head office		62,840	4,280
Asset values			
PPE	2	128,000	16,000
Other assets		9,000	1,000
Total assets at FV		137,000	17,000
Return			
Operating profit/total assets %		9.1%	Negative (7.8%)
Contribution/total assets %		45.9%	25.2%

Notes

1 Depreciation

Depreciation is based on fair values. Depreciation in the financial statements should recognise the remaining useful life of 50 years and depreciate the carrying amount over this period as a change in an accounting estimate per IAS 8. *NOT cost*

For the Business Division, the annual depreciation charge per the financial statements would be £640,000 (£32m/50). The depreciation charge based on fair values would be £2.56m (£128m/50). This is an increase of £1.92m.

For the Leisure Division, the annual depreciation charge per the financial statements would be £240,000 (£12m/50). The depreciation charge based on fair values would be £320,000 (£16m/50). This is an increase of £80,000.

2 PPE

Business £4m × 32 = £128m

Leisure £1m × 16 = £16m

3 Fixed cost analysis

	Business £'000	Leisure £'000	Total £'000
Revenue	155,520	17,280	172,800
Total fixed costs	98,400	13,600	112,000
Head office costs			
(£112m × 50%) × 155,520/172,800	(50,400)		
(£112m × 50%) × 17,280/172,800		(5,600)	
Divisional fixed costs (residual)	48,000	8,000	
Divisional FC per hotel			
£48m/32	1,500		
£8m/16		500	

Summary

Based on the adjusted profit figures, the Leisure Division makes an increased operating loss. However, a key factor in the assessment of the divisional performance is the head office costs which are jointly incurred by both divisions, but appear to be allocated on an arbitrary basis. Head office provides key services on which both divisions depend so these costs are important in assessing the performance of the company as a whole, but they are difficult to trace to individual divisions.

In the extreme, if all the head office costs are fixed (which is unlikely) then the closure of the Leisure Division would cause the £5.6m of head office costs to be reallocated back to the Business Division which would significantly reduce its profit. Thus, if the Leisure Division is closed and assets sold at fair value to repay debt then the company profitability would be:

	£'000
Revised profit (from above)	12,440
Reallocation of Leisure HO costs to Business Div	(5,600)
Operating profit	6,840
Finance charge	
(£30m – £16m) × 8%	(1,120)
Revised profit before tax	5,720

This would be a substantial reduction in overall company profit arising from closure.

There would probably be some cost savings at head office arising from the closure of the Leisure Division but these may not be substantial, thus it is very likely that HH would be worse off from closing the Leisure Division.

(b)   **Non-financial performance information**

HH's performance reports need to provide relevant information which can be used for strategic decision-making and controlling the business.

Although HH already measures room utilisation, which is a non-financial measure, in general the three performance metrics currently used give little insight into the root causes of the hotels' performance. Moreover, they are lagging indicators (rather than leading indicators) and so give little insight about where HH's performance is heading in the future.

Objectives and critical success factors – As far as possible, the metrics used to measure HH's performance should be linked to its strategy and critical success factors. Given that we have identified that four aspects of the business will define its success, these four areas should also be the focus of its performance measures: financial performance; customer; staff and business processes. Currently, despite collecting information about customer satisfaction through the satisfaction survey, HH does not appear to have any performance indicators which monitor customer satisfaction levels nor business process efficiency. However, these would appear to be factors which will have a significant impact on its overall performance.

In effect, the performance of HH's staff and business processes will help determine customer satisfaction; and in turn, customer satisfaction levels in conjunction with the costs incurred to run the hotels have a significant impact on financial performance.

As such, improving the hotel's performance in relation to customer satisfaction (and therefore potentially repeat business or customer recommendations) should also lead to improvements in financial performance.

Importantly, however, improvements to business processes or customer satisfaction will ultimately only be beneficial to HH if they translate into improved financial results. Therefore any new performance measurement system introduced at HH needs to reflect this linkage between non-financial and financial results.

Balanced Scorecard – If HH introduced a balanced scorecard approach to performance measurement, this would encourage it to focus on non-financial aspects of performance as well as financial ones, but it would encourage HH to focus on the linkage between the different factors which drive performance.

The four aspects which define HH's success would appear to fit quite neatly with the four perspectives of the scorecard: financial; customer; innovating and learning/staff; and internal business processes.

Therefore, HH's financial performance metrics could still be used under a balanced scorecard approach, but they would be supported by other measures looking at the other three key aspects of the business.

Introducing a new performance measurement system

Any new performance measurement system should be planned carefully. At the moment, we do not know for certain which aspects of non-financial performance are critical to the success of the company.

Clearly, measures of capacity usage are important, even though these are retrospective in nature. Measures of 'capacity fill' for each hotel and the company as a whole should relate to the percentage of rooms occupied, and percentage of available business conference facilities sold.

It would seem probable that customer satisfaction is also a critical issue, although there are various aspects of performance that contribute to satisfaction. A KPI that could be used initially would be an average satisfaction score, obtained from the questionnaires completed by customers when they leave a hotel. (A target score could be set, and then actual performance compared to that target.)

The questionnaire system should also seek to discover reasons for customer satisfaction or dissatisfaction. By analysing the feedback in questionnaires, it may be possible to identify other factors which are important to customers, and therefore which could be key to maintaining – or improving – the company's performance,

For example, if it becomes apparent that the quality of service received from hotel staff is a key factor in customer satisfaction, the company should consider its policy for service quality, for example by trying to retain experienced staff (and reduce labour turnover) or improving skills through training. CSFs and KPIs may then relate to staff turnover rates or training days/hours per employee.

Finally, in the hotels and catering business, there are third party measures of quality and service standards, such as star ratings for hotels. The reputation of a hotel chain is related to the star ratings of its hotels, and star rating ought to be a KPI for the company's hotels over the long term.

(c) **Evaluation of the new proposal**

(1) **Proposal evaluation**

	Notes	£'000
Revenue	1	7,776
Variable costs	2	(2,333)
Fixed costs		(2,000)
Lease rentals*		(1,500)
Contribution to HO costs		1,943
Revenue per hotel		1,555
Contribution per hotel		388

* Treating the lease as an operating lease (see section (c) (2) below)

The figure of contribution divided by total assets would make little sense as, if the lease is an operating lease, it is not recognised and thus assets would be minimal. For management accounting performance measurement comparison, the lease could be deemed as capitalised, thereby deducting interest and depreciation as costs in order to assess return on assets on a comparable basis to divisions with owned assets.

Notes

1 **Revenue**

360 × £120 × 5 × 40 × 90%

2 **Variable cost**

30% × £7,776,000

Evaluation

There are two elements to the new proposal: (1) the acquisition by lease of five new hotels and (2) the divestment of 16 existing hotels. It appears that these are treated as a joint proposal although separation of the elements may be considered as independent decisions as the divestment proceeds are not being used to finance the acquisition of the new hotels.

The new proposal has been evaluated using an operating lease treatment. The treatment of the lease in the financial statements should not affect the commercial decision to accept the project. However, the operating lease treatment more closely reflects cash flows so this treatment is used below.

The new project generates a positive contribution (ie before head office costs) of £388,000 per hotel. This compares to £267,500 per hotel (£4,280,000/16) for the Leisure Division after fair value adjustments. Despite this difference, if rents rise with annual reviews (eg there are front end incentives in the lease contracts) then the two groupings may be similar. Indeed, the Leisure Division may become more successful.

Overall, the new project is smaller than the Leisure Division that it may be replacing, with 5 hotels valued at £10m (but not recognised in the financial statements) compared to 16 hotels valued at £16m.

Also, the Leisure Division data uses actual amounts, whereas the new proposal uses expected data and thus is subject to more uncertainty.

The data is short term whereas the future performance is key. In this respect, with projected utilisation at 90%, there is little scope for improvement in volume terms from the new proposal but with the Leisure Division there is significant scope to increase utilisation and performance.

Leaving aside comparisons and judging the new proposal on its own merits, a key factor is whether the new proposal will cause incremental costs to arise at head office. If, for instance, it causes the same head office costs as already allocated to Leisure (£5.6m) then the project is clearly not viable. Even if it creates the same head office costs per hotel to be generated as the Leisure Division, then the proposal is not viable. A detailed scrutiny of the incremental head office costs caused by the proposal compared to Leisure could therefore determine the viability of this proposal.

Treating the divestment of the Leisure Division as an independent decision, a possibility would be, if finance were required, to enter into a sale and leaseback of its operations rather than enter into the uncertainty of the new proposal. This would generate finance and enhance liquidity given the pressure from the bank.

(2) Financial reporting implications of new proposal

The treatment of the lease appears to be in doubt regarding whether substantially all the risks and rewards of ownership have been transferred to create a finance lease. One indicator is the residual value compared to the present value of the minimum lease payments, but the surveyor was unable to provide a reliable estimate. Another indicator is the proportion of the useful life. The lease term is 30 years compared to a useful life of the asset of 40 years. This period is probably marginal in terms of the transfer of risks and rewards. Other terms of the lease agreement would also need to be considered. These include whether there is a break clause in the lease which would allow early exit and point towards an operating lease; or whether the lease rentals may be increased substantially under the annual reviews which may point towards a finance lease.

Overall, in terms of the property element this appears to be an operating lease although more information would be needed to be more certain.

A further consideration is that the land element will be an operating lease. If the buildings are also an operating lease no problem arises as they are treated the same. If the buildings are ultimately deemed to be a finance lease, then they will need to be separated out from the land and treated differently.

The lease contract also includes fixtures and fittings. Given the lease contract is for 30 years these are likely to be a finance lease (unless there is a short term break clause in the lease contract). They will therefore need to be separated from the property. (Given the lack of data, the above calculations do not do this at this stage.)

The disposal of the Leisure Division is only currently being contemplated so would not constitute a held for sale asset at the current period end.

(d) Fraud

(1) Internal controls

The fraud committed related to controls over cash at the point of sale. This is a particular risk in the hotel industry as there are no goods to be exchanged which can be monitored in relation to sales.

This particular fraud included collusion between the manager who authorised a discount, and hence had control over the accounting record, and his wife who took the cash and hence had control of the asset. By understating both the asset and the record of revenue, the fraud was successfully carried out by circumventing normal segregation of duties controls.

Internal control systems do not normally attempt to control for collusion but instead rely on the integrity of segregation of duties. In this case however where there is a husband and wife it may be unwise to depend too heavily on segregation of duties. Possible actions could be:

- Separate system of recording and reporting of cash transactions
- Segregation of duties to be rotated periodically
- Internal audit to review cash transactions
- Segregation of duties to avoid close personal relationships
- Analytical procedures on cash transactions to identify high incidence in particular hotels
- Analytical procedures on high incidence of discounts or association with cash transactions

Overall, cash transactions are likely to be small compared to credit/debit card transactions, particularly amongst business customers. The scope for this type of fraud is likely to be limited and therefore the costs of new procedures should recognise that benefits may be limited.

(2) **Ethics**

The ethical issues surround the right or duty to disclose the fraud. These are ethical issues for the company and for Christine as an individual, as she is an ICAEW Chartered Accountant.

A key issue is whether the fraud would be deemed to be money laundering. If it is, it would fall under the Money Laundering Act which imposes additional duties of disclosure to the National Crime Agency (NCA). On the facts available, it would seem however that this is a straightforward fraud that does not fall within money laundering legislation, although legal advice may need to be taken if there is doubt.

If the company is advised that it is money laundering, then it should be disclosed to the NCA without informing the manager and his wife.

If it is not money laundering, then the 'victims' of the crime are the shareholders and, as a consequence, the directors have a duty to act in their interests. The size of the fraud is likely to be small, so the amount is not material. Disclosure to shareholders is likely to also involve public disclosure which may not be beneficial to the reputation of the company and to the shareholders. There would therefore not appear to be a duty to disclose publicly, although there is clearly the right to disclose.

A further more general ethical issue also arises in that a crime has been committed and if not disclosed then the perpetrators will go unpunished. This raises ethical issues of equity and justice.

The internal control deficiency is however important and, as a material issue, it should be disclosed to those charged with governance and to the external auditors.

Christine should consider obtaining advice from the ICAEW ethics helpline.

(e) **Potential impact of Big Data analytics**

Yield management and pricing

Managing the balance between price and occupancy rates is crucial in the hotel industry to try to ensure that each room attracts its optimal prices. Room rates need to take account of general fluctuations in demand throughout the year, as well as other more specific factors (for example, local events or competitor promotions) which can influence the number, and type, of guests checking in.

Although it seems that Hottentot's managers are applying already some of this logic, the discounting process appears to place significant emphasis on the managers' intuition and discretion.

By contrast, a crucial element of analytical approaches (whether based on Big Data or not) is that they are driven by data, rather than intuition.

Big Data analytics should enable demand to be forecast more accurately, by virtue of the range of factors which will be incorporated in the prediction. For example, analytics software could incorporate past data, recent trends, and local events (eg business conferences), as well as booking levels at competitor hotels and traffic patterns on their online booking sites in order to forecast demand, and in turn determine the optimum room rates.

In this respect, online shopping data could be very important. If the number of potential customers looking for hotel rooms for a specific date and in a specific geographical location is significantly higher than for similar dates in that location, this suggests there is a specific event taking place which is increasing demand for rooms on that date. As such, there is likely to be less price sensitivity on the 'peak' day, meaning that rates can be raised.

An important consideration in this respect is the level of demand at rival hotels and the prices they are charging. It is not clear whether the managers currently take account of these factors when setting their prices, but external data like this will be very important when setting prices. Potential customers are likely to compare Hottentot's prices with those offered by rival hotels, so we need to ensure that our prices remain competitive.

Nonetheless, making use of Big Data analytics could facilitate a new approach to pricing that could substantially alter Hottentot's existing pricing model. The current model appears largely based around a standard price approach (although managers have a degree of discretion to 'flex' prices against the standard). However, the new approach could enable rates to be automatically varied, based on continually changing demand forecasts. For example, based on the data in Figure 1 (Weekly forecast report) it seems surprising that the average room price for the business division on Friday is still at £150, given the relatively low forecast occupancy rate (78%).

If room rates are updated automatically, this could also have significant implications for Hottentot's management information. The weekly forecasts which are currently produced would have little value for decision-making purposes, and it would seem more useful for price and occupancy data to be monitored on a real time basis. Similarly, it would be useful for managers to drill down below the summary level to look at data for individual hotels.

Operational management

Being able to forecast demand more accurately not only affects room yield, but it should also help with operational management in the hotel. For example, if managers can predict occupancy levels with greater certainty, this will also help them plan how many staff they need on different shifts. Similarly, if analytical tools mean that managers are better able to assess the proportion of guests who will want to use other facilities (for example, restaurants) this will assist the planning of staff requirements in those facilities.

Customer relationship management

Customer feedback

Currently, the only customer feedback which Hottentot appears to be monitoring is that provided in the physical surveys which customers complete at the end of their stay. However, as the marketing director suggests, it is likely that customers are commenting about Hottentot's hotels on social media sites (such as Facebook or Twitter) as well as rating them on review sites (such as TripAdvisor). Using analytics to gather insights from unstructured data on social media sites is a commonly mentioned example of Big Data analytics, and arguably may provide more reliable and informative results than those Hottentot gets from its exisitng customer surveys if customers complete them hastily on departure.

If there are recurring themes in social media customer reviews (for example, about the layout, décor or comfort of the rooms; or the quality of customer service) these could highlight specific areas for improvement, or help us gain a better understanding of customer requirements. Alternatively, the review could also highlight areas where existing high standards need to be maintained.

More generally, the aspects of their stay which people comment on most frequently could also provide some useful insight into what is most important to them. People are less likely to comment on something which they do not feel is important, than something which is important to them and which could affect whether or not they stay at a Hottentot hotel again in future.

Customer segmentation

Although Hottentot recognises the benefit of keeping a database of customers to assess their buying habits, the database appears to be used primarily for tailoring discounts to individuals. However, there is no indication that this information is used for target marketing or customer relationship management.

In this respect, Hottentot could use data analytics to identify different groups among its customers (for example, distinguishing between business customers who typically stay only for one night and those who stay for longer periods), and then develop targeted marketing strategies, and/or promotional offers, tailored for different groups. Not only should such an approach increase the effectiveness of Hottentot's marketing promotions, it could also help to increase customer loyalty and retention among customers.

Similarly, being able to build up profiles of customers, and distinguishing between different types of customer, may help to ensure that we manage our customer relationships effectively. For example, a business person who spends very little on extra services could be someone who travels frequently for work and so could become a repeat customer if our hotels meet their needs. As such, that person could have a higher lifetime value, and be more valuable to the company, than a second customer who spends a lot of money in the restaurant and the bar during their stay because they know it is a one-off opportunity for them.

However, while segmentation and customer profiling like this results from data analytics, much – if not all – of the data being analysed could be held in Hottentot's database. As such, it doesn't necessarily constitute Big Data.

8 Zappo plc

Marking guide

		Marks Up to
(a)	Current situation in the industry	8
(b)	Acquisition of GameStar	6
(c)	Launch of LeagueStar	6
(d)	Valuation	
	Dividend valuation model	6
	Criticism of model and due diligence	4
	Alternative valuations	4
(e)	Comparison of financing methods and amount of finance required	10
(f)	Operational management issues:	
	Brand management	9
	Footfall and management information system	7
	Effect of change: culture, IT systems etc	6
Total marks		66
Maximum marks		60

From: Tish Hope
To: Ab Potts
Re: Notes concerning Zappo
Date: May 20X5

(a) **Strategic issues: current situation in the industry**

Conditions in the market appear to be difficult for all electronic games retailers.

(1) Retail stores are under threat from online buying of games. Although there may be practical difficulties at the moment with downloading large games from the Internet, these problems will probably be overcome at some time in the near future. This will enable producers of computer games to sell them directly to consumers, instead of through retail stores.

Online games products have minimal marginal production costs, and it seems probable that producers of computer games will be able to make a larger profit margin from direct sales to consumers than by selling through the retail stores of intermediaries.

Smartphone and tablet users can often download free games and pay very small amounts to enhance them. It appears that providers of games software can make high profits from the very large numbers of users that they attract. It may be difficult to predict whether this change in consumer habits (downloading games on to tablets or smartphones) will be a serious threat in future to the market for larger games.

(2) Town shopping centres may be in decline as more consumers switch to buying online. Shops depend for their sales on footfall, and if fewer people are visiting shopping centres to buy goods, it seems inevitable that sales in all retail stores, game stores included, may decline.

(3) Retail space remains expensive and is a fixed cost. Most labour costs are also likely to be fixed. Although I have not had time to investigate the figures, I expect that all game stores – including Zappo's – have high operating gearing. This means that its profits are vulnerable to even fairly small reductions in sales turnover. Even small shifts in market demand could have a dramatic impact on the profits of game stores.

Zappo has already experienced some decline in its business, which means that profits will be lower. The board and management need to respond to the threat that this creates. 'Doing nothing' does not seem to be a viable strategic option.

In order to improve its prospects for the future, Zappo needs to achieve either or both of the following:

- Higher sales turnover
- Lower costs

It is with these objectives in mind that the GameStar and LeagueStar proposals should be considered.

(b) Acquisition of GameStar

The purchase of GameStar will add to sales turnover, but this will not necessarily improve turnover at the existing Zappo stores.

Advantages

(+) Enhanced image

The acquisition may help to address the major image problem that Zappo currently faces. The Zappo brand name has a downmarket image, which I take to mean a fairly negative image, among consumers. The acquisition would provide a relatively easy method of transforming the Zappo brand – by replacing it with the GameStar brand. It is not clear, however, whether this would improve – or even have a negative effect on – sales in existing Zappo stores.

I have more comments on brand management later in this memo.

(+) Diversification

The acquisition allows Zappo to diversify geographically, and presumably buy some profitable retail sites. The costs arising from addressing duplication of stores in the same location, and the need to close stores, will largely be avoided.

On the other hand, geographical proximity of stores could be more desirable. It would mean closing one of the two stores that are located close to each other, and incurring redundancy costs and possibly costs of cancelling a lease agreement for the retail space. On the other hand there would be savings in operating costs and (hopefully) little or no adverse effect on sales turnover.

(+) Rationalisation

The acquisition also provides Zappo with what appears to be a cheaper head office to run. This will reduce its fixed cost base and generate additional funding, provided that it can dispose of Olde Towers.

Disadvantages

(–) Commitment to advertising spend

The financial advantages may be mitigated by the need to continue and perhaps even increase advertising expenditure, to attempt to keep the GameStar brand fashionable.

Long-term image problems

Because of the volatile nature of fashion in this sector, there may come a point where even substantial advertising expenditure has little positive impact. The biggest threat to GameStar, as suggested earlier, may be the growth in competition from online sales of games.

Computer game stores in general may become 'unfashionable'.

Property portfolio

The acquisition does not address (in fact it increases) the risk to the group of declining footfall across high street stores in general. This may not have been a problem for GameStar shops so far, but it may be so in future.

Summary: acquisition of Gamestar

The acquisition of GameStar would give Zappo a greater market share in what may well be a declining market.

I would question whether this is a valid basis for a long-term strategy.

The Zappo board would need to have clear objectives for the sustainability of the company over the longer term.

(c) **Launch of LeagueStar**

Advantages

(+) Diversification and footfall

LeagueStar provides a facility to customers that could generate a regular income stream to Zappo. This may result in a regular cash flow over the year.

By increasing the numbers of people visiting stores, there may be an increase in the sale of games products. Customers who visit a store to play in a league match or competition may also decide to buy a game. Each time they visit the store, they may then return a game for a refund, but take out another game.

(+) Promotion campaign

The launch of LeagueStar means that Zappo can undertake a promotions campaign that can be used to enhance awareness of its stores generally, as well as promoting LeagueStar.

(+) Development of supply chain

The development of LeagueStar may allow Zappo to develop closer relations with suppliers. This may result in various advantages, including price and inventory co-ordination to avoid problems and bottlenecks caused by short-term surges in demand such as promotions. Linked computer systems could save on paperwork and warehouse expense.

Disadvantages

(−) Uncertainty of market

The expectation that the system will have a useful life of ten years is probably over-optimistic. Technological advances are continuing at a fast rate, and this means that the system will almost certainly become obsolete and superseded some time before that. Also the facility offered may become less attractive to customers over time. Rival systems may be developed that enable customers to participate in national leagues at home.

(−) Security issues

Installation of the system in Zappo stores may make access to the rest of Zappo's systems easier to obtain. Enhanced security measures including firewalls may be required.

Required return

Ignoring taxation, the required return on an investment of £35m over ten years, at a cost of capital of 12%, would be about £6.2m. If the life of the assets is only five years, say, the required annual return would be about £9.7m.

If LeagueStar is introduced into the acquired GameStar stores as well as the existing Zappo stores, the investment cost may be higher than £35m.

I recommend that Zappo should review the financial projections for the LeagueStar investment, and re-assess whether there is a strong financial argument in favour.

Financing issues

If Zappo decides to go ahead with the acquisition of GameStar and investment in LeagueStar, it may have difficulty in raising the required finance. Financing is discussed later.

(d) **Valuation of GameStar**

One method of obtaining a valuation for GameStar is to use the dividend growth model.

The growth rate in after-tax profits and dividends in 20X4 was (1,701−1,590)/1,590 = 7%.

The projected growth rate in 20X5 is (1,888/1,701)/1,701 = 11%.

However it is only May and the projection for 20X5 could be optimistic.

DVM

The dividend growth model assumes the same rate of annual growth in dividends in perpetuity. An annual growth rate of 11% in perpetuity would seem much too high to be realistic, even allowing for future inflation.

If we assume that an annual growth rate of 7% will continue in perpetuity, a dividend growth model valuation of GameStar would be:

$d_0(1+g)/(k_e - g) = (1,888 \times 1.07)/(0.12 - 0.07) = £40,400,000$ (approximately).

However there are major flaws in this valuation.

Limitations of DVM

It assumes annual growth in dividends of 7% in perpetuity, which may not be realistic, as it is extremely difficult to sustain such a high rate of growth over the long term. The growth rate may be much lower. Perhaps more significantly, the business may have a limited life, for reasons already explained.

It assumes that a cost of capital of 12% should be applied, but this may not be appropriate. If a higher cost of capital is used, the valuation would be lower.

It assumes that the business will continue in its current form for the foreseeable future, but the business may have a limited remaining life, for reasons already explained.

It assumes that the estimated profit of £1.888m in 20X5 will be achieved. This assertion may be unrealistic. If a growth rate of 7% is applied to the 20X4 profits and dividends, the valuation would be 11% lower.

It assumes that dividends are a fair reflection of the strength of the company which may not be the case.

Due diligence work

The validity of the dividend valuation model depends mainly on two factors, k_e and g.

√ Growth rate is critical here. Expected growth in 20X5 is much higher than actual growth in 20X4, and we need to ensure that this is not a one-off figure.

√ The forecast results for 20X5 should be tested thoroughly. In the absence of any audit procedures having been done on them, the reasons for the increase in growth from previous year must be understood and validated.

√ Commercial due diligence work should then be carried out to test the growth assumption for future periods, to enable us to assess whether the GameStar growth will be continued. We should look at likely changes in the locations where GameStar has shops, also plans for future advertising.

Of course, the merger of GameStar and Zappo will render these projections somewhat obsolete, but they are however necessary in valuing GameStar on a stand-alone basis.

√ We should also consider any differences in risk profile between the two businesses which might make k_e different.

Alternative valuation method and alternative assumptions

A more appropriate valuation method would be to calculate a present value for estimated future annual free cash flows of GameStar for a limited payback period. The figures are not available to make such an estimate at the moment.

Alternative assumptions about the valuation should also be considered. For example, if it is assumed that the free cash flow of GameStar in 20X5 will be equal to the profit and dividend figure, but this will not increase any further due to deteriorating market conditions, and if we also assume that a discounted payback period of, say, ten years should be applied, the valuation of GameStar would fall to:

£1.888m × Annuity factor at 12% for ten years

= £1.888m × 5.650 = £10.667m

There are wide variations in possible estimates of value, and in view of the uncertainty about the future of the retail games stores business, the board of Zappo should be cautious, even if this means that the owners of GameStar reject Zappo's offer price for the business.

(e) **Financing of investments**

Zappo proposes to finance its investments by mean of a share issue, with any shortfall made up by bank finance.

After the purchase of GameStar, Zappo would seek to sell its head office premises for about £70m, and purchase the head office of GameStar for £22m. There would be tax implications in the sale of Olde Towers for a capital gain, but this would enable Zappo to pay back bank loans up to £48m less the tax.

The 60% owner of Zappo has agreed to subscribe £24m in new equity in a rights issue. As a 60% owner, this would suggest that the rights issue would seek to raise £40m in total, less costs (= £24m/60%). However, non-controlling shareholders may be unwilling to subscribe an additional £16m. The estimate is that they will subscribe at least £8m, but this view may be optimistic. We do not know whether other investors would buy the rights that minority shareholders do not wish to take up, but this may be doubtful.

Even if the company could raise £32m in new equity (= £24m + £8m), this would be insufficient for the purchase of GameStar and investment in LeagueStar.

The following figures are based on tentative assumptions.

70m
(22m)
48m
32m

- Zappo may acquire GameStar for about £40m.
- Zappo invests in LeagueStar and the cost is £35m in total.
- A new issue of shares would raise £32m.

80m   2m?

This would leave a funding gap of £43m, to be made up from bank loans at 6% interest (so interest would be about £2.58m in the first year, but this will attract tax relief).

The ability of Zappo to repay most of the borrowing quickly would depend on its ability to sell Olde Towers at the projected price of £70m within a reasonable time.

Zappo has no debt capital at the moment, but banks may have reservations about lending such a large amount of money – and they would almost certainly want security for the lending – presumably this would be provided by Olde Towers.

Uncertain future financing

There appears to be uncertainty over the funding that is available to Zappo. While the majority shareholder appears willing and able to invest the money required for now, he may not be so in future if the business requires further funding in the future.

The low level of existing gearing means financial risk at the moment may be low.

Conclusion about financing

The proposed methods of financing seem feasible but it depends on negotiating a suitable price for GameStar and a successful new share issue. However, the effect of borrowing on profits and of the new share issue on earnings per share and the share price should also be considered.

Sources of funding appear uncertain, with doubt over whether the non-controlling shareholders will subscribe to the rights issue, and doubt over the sales proceeds of Olde Towers (or indeed whether it can easily be sold at all).

The current lack of debt does give Zappo scope to introduce debt funding. However, the need to pay interest will further increase its committed fixed costs, and a fixed rate loan may prove expensive if interest rates are falling, although this may be reflected in the long term interest rate.

(f) **Operational issues**

You asked for my views on various operational issues facing Zappo after an acquisition of GameStar.

(1) **Brand management**

The board of directors considers the Zappo brand image to be poor. We do not know why this should be the case. It may be that Zappo stores are less well-kept and less well-presented than other retail games stores.

The board does not appear to think that the brand image can be restored, because it plans to re-name all its stores as GameStar stores after the acquisition of GameStar.

An issue for the Zappo board and management to consider is: Why is the Zappo brand name poorly regarded?

The reasons presumably lie with poor brand management by Zappo. We do not know what image the company wishes to project, but it is not succeeding.

A 'downmarket' image is not necessarily a bad thing, when 'downmarket' means low price and cheap. Several retail chains have been highly successful with a low-price strategy for customers, because customers believe they are getting value for money when they buy.

Zappo may have a low-price image but may not be charging low prices for its games. If this is the case, customers will not enjoy a shopping experience in Zappo stores.

The Zappo board believes that switching to the GameStar brand will resolve the branding issue. The risk, however, is that poor brand management could damage the GameStar brand name too.

Branding strategy: recommendations

There are two brand names to consider: GameStar and LeagueStar.

For each of these, the first requirement is to establish a brand identity or brand image that will appeal to the target market for the company's outlets and LeagueStar initiative. The brand image of GameStar and LeagueStar need to be consistent with each other. The brand also needs to create an image of a service or a product that customers want to buy: key features may be price and technological up-to-dateness etc. (Games users are likely to be deterred by yesterday's technology.) Customers need to know what the brand stands for, and must be able to recognise the brand name or logo.

The company, in creating a brand image, must be able to deliver the service or product that the brand is 'promising' to customers. In other words, the product must match up to the image that the brand seeks to create.

Creating a brand image that appeals to customers and differentiates the company's business will not be easy, given the poor reputation of the Zappo brand. The launch of the LeagueStar product could be a vital ingredient in the brand management policy, as a new idea with an appeal to potential customers in the target market.

The company should take measures to protect the LeagueStar name, through legal protection (trademark protection), to prevent rival businesses using the same name for a similar product.

As part of the Zappo's long-term strategy for the LeagueStar brand, it should seek an arrangement with the software provider(s), so that the provider is involved in any initiative to expand LeagueStar – if it proves successful – for internet/smartphone/tablet users.

The company also needs to consider its advertising strategy to promote the brand to create customer awareness and recognition. New brand initiatives are unlikely to succeed without substantial advertising, and perhaps also sales promotion initiatives such as early user price discounts.

(2) **Information about footfall**

Footfall is considered the most important factor in the industry, but Zappo management do not appear to have much quantitative information about it. The only information I am aware of also seems insufficient and so unreliable.

Fran Simmons obtained information about footfall and turnover from just two stores.

- The figures for sales turnover in the seven-day period were presumably reliable, but I do not know whether the two sets of figures are for the same seven-day period.

- The two stores may not be representative of the company's stores as a whole.

- The seven-day period selected will not be a 'typical' week. In retailing, there are peaks in retail sales at particular times of the year – especially approaching Christmas time. Other weeks will be much more quiet.

- I do not know how the figures for footfall were obtained, and the method (and reliability) of counting would need to be checked. For example, there may be inaccuracies in measuring by means of reviewing closed circuit TV cameras on the store entrances.

The figures from the two stores show significant variations in the ratio of sales turnover to footfall. In one store the ratio is turnover of £7.16 per visitor (£13,250/1,850). At the other store it was £10.50 (£12,600/1,200), but the footfall was lower. There are no figures for gross profit.

Information about footfall: conclusion

If footfall is such an important measure, it is surprising that Zappo does not have a more formal and reliable system for measuring footfall at its stores. The current information is incomplete and unreliable, raising questions about the quality of both the management accounting system and also management (for not insisting on having this information about footfall).

(3) **Merging operations of the two companies**

Fran Simmons appears to under-estimate the difficulties that will arise with an acquisition of GameStar.

Different cultures and management attitudes

Part of GameStar's appeal may be a different philosophy reflected in a different approach to customers and different style of management. If the GameStar brand is to be adopted, then arguably the staff currently working for Zappo should have to adapt to a new way of working – in stores as well as at head office.

Zappo's management may face considerable resistance to changes in Zappo's 'old' stores and head office. Fran Simmons claims that Zappo staff will quickly adapt because staff turnover is high. However, staff turnover could rise to an even faster rate if staff are dissatisfied and demotivated.

Fran's comments also raise questions about management attitudes to employees. There is likely to be poor morale throughout the company when management do not value employees. Poor morale leads on to poor performance. In a service industry such as retailing, this could have a significant impact on customers, footfall and sales.

If GameStar staff are required to adapt to Zappo's methods, there could be resistance to the change in corporate culture among GameStar staff.

Processes and IT systems

Fran Simmons intends to adopt the IT systems currently used by GameStar. Switching Zappo records and processing systems on to the GameStar systems could be extremely difficult.

- Existing files held by Zappo would have to be converted into a format for use on the GameStar system.

- Zappo staff would need training in the new systems and procedures.

- There will be resistance to using new systems among staff who are familiar and comfortable with their current system.

Cutting head office costs

After the acquisition, the two head offices will be merged into one. There will probably be scope for 'synergy' in the form of costs saved by making staff redundant.

Zappo management need to be prepared for the adverse effect on morale of redundancies among head office staff.

Merging the company systems and change management: conclusion

I would suggest that Fran Simmons is wrong in the view that changes after the acquisition of GameStar will be easy to implement. My recommendation would be that Zappo should give thought to the process of introducing change, and it may be appropriate to appoint a senior manager (and possibly an external consultant) as a 'change agent' with responsibility for the change process.

9   Safetex plc

Marks

Up to

(a)	Evaluation of proposed expansion strategies	15
(b)	Shareholder/corporate governance comments	6
(c)	Estimating forecast basic EPS and diluted EPS	12
(d)	Valuation of CAL	12
(e)	Discussion of financing issues	10
(f)	Discussion of HRM issues	5
(g)	Due diligence and assurance issues	10
Total marks		70
Maximum marks		60

(a)   **Comparison of the expansion strategies**

Strategy 1

The two strategies both build on the existing core competencies of Safetex as they are in the same industry. Strategy 1, however, is closer to the existing strategy as the product is more or less identical to the company's existing products. The strategy involves entry into a slightly different sector of the same market.

Using the terminology of the Ansoff growth (product/market) matrix, Strategy 1 can be described as market development – with the same product being sold in a different market sector, distinguished by pricing policy.

The advantages of this approach are as follows:

- It uses existing resources and thus increases their utilisation (it 'makes the assets sweat').

- The operational side of the business is identical to the existing business; so there is near complete overlap with existing core competencies in operational activities.

- It exploits a new market, when the core market is shrinking.

- The project appears to generate a positive net present value (see Working 1 below).

- It can be financed from existing cash resources (but only just). The investment would require £3m which is the projected cash balance of Safetex at the year end.

- The investment can be paid for from existing financial resources, and the growth strategy builds on the existing competencies of the company. Strategy 1 may therefore be considered a relatively low-risk strategy for growth; although much depends on the market potential for lower-priced alarms.

Limitations of the market development strategy include the following:

- Loss of sales of higher-priced alarms to customers who opt instead to buy cheaper products. Higher-priced alarms have a higher margin than sales in the new division would have.

- Reputational risk of being seen to have gone downmarket and thus losing sales to competitors. Safetex currently has a good reputation and offers a three-year guarantee on all products. It will have to decide whether it can afford to offer the same guarantee on its cheaper products.

- The investment and reorganisation costs are likely to be largely sunk costs if the venture fails.

- While the project generates a positive net present value, the cash inflows in the early years are low. Payback will be slow, especially if market conditions change for the worse. Therefore there could be significant pressure on liquidity. (Although sufficient cash is available for the investment without borrowing, the cash resources of Safetex would be fully used as a consequence.)

- Much of the risk assessment for this strategy will depend on the level of assurance given from market research. Safetex needs some assurance that the potential market for cheaper alarms is sufficiently large.

- In addition, revenue from annual maintenance contracts will continue to be important. Safetex needs to consider the pricing of maintenance contracts for the cheaper alarms. Demand for alarms may be adversely affected by relatively high annual maintenance and inspection costs.

Strategy 2

Within the Ansoff matrix, expansion Strategy 2 can be described as related diversification in that both the product and market have changed but in neither case is the change substantial.

Diversification is generally considered a greater strategic risk than either market development (Strategy 1) or product development. However the risk in the strategy would be reduced because growth would be achieved by means of takeover rather than organically.

The advantages of this approach are as follows:

- It accesses a new market where Safetex currently has no presence (the commercial market).
- The margins are greater in the commercial market than the household market.
- There is no loss of sales to existing customers.

Limitations of this strategy include the following:

- There is no current market knowledge in Safetex, although maintaining the existing management team of CAL would provide this knowledge. Even so, there is some risk in relying on the staff of an acquired company for development of the business.

- The product is a little different from the existing product so there is some departure from existing core competencies.

    - The products would be sourced from Hogsmood, the existing parent company of CAL. There are risks in reliance on a single supplier for a core product, and Safetex would need to consider urgently ways in which its supply chain could be protected from disruption.

- The level of synergies is questionable given the different products and different market.

    - There will be HR problems with a takeover. These are considered later.

    - There are significant initial costs required to make the acquisition in order to engage in this strategy. If the strategy fails there will therefore be significant sunk costs. Strategy 2 is therefore a high-risk strategy, as failure could threaten the financial stability and going concern status of the Safetex group.

In order to engage in this strategy it is necessary to make an acquisition which has major risks in addition to the strategy of diversification that it is making possible:

- The acquisition price needs to be determined. There is a risk that all the value of the business will be built into the acquisition price leaving no upside in the transaction.

- There may be a difficulty in obtaining accurate information despite due diligence.

The Safetex board believes that it does not have the financial or non-financial resources to undertake both strategies. It is understandable that management might not be able to undertake two different strategies at the same time, and an important limitation of non-financial resources would undoubtedly be management time.

However it is interesting to note that the board does not believe that it has the financial resources for both strategies, even though Strategy 1 would cost only £3m. This suggests that the board believes that Strategy 2 would stretch its financial resources close to their limit. If this is the case, the consequences of failure with Strategy 2 could be considerable.

Alternative growth strategies

Using the Ansoff growth matrix, Strategy 1 may be described as market development and Strategy 2 as concentric diversification.

The board may have considered other growth options. It appears that market penetration is not a viable option. The existing market for Safetex products is saturated, and possibilities for growth will be very limited.

The board should perhaps also consider the impact of technological change on its existing market. Although the current market is saturated, the development of more efficient alarm systems may provide opportunities for selling new products to existing customers. This would be a strategy of product development.

Before selecting its preferred strategy, the board may wish to consider whether there are significant technological improvements in the pipeline for alarm products to 'high end' customers.

Conclusion

Strategy 1 appears to involve much lower risk than Strategy 2, but the board should obtain assurance from market research about the potential size of the new market. The strategy has a positive NPV of £418,000 (see workings below), but the potential value to the company is limited, and the strategy may therefore deliver only limited added business value.

Strategy 2 is higher risk and requires a larger investment. The return would depend on the purchase price negotiated for CAL. If successful, the strategy offers much greater potential for growth, and may provide an opportunity for Safetex to progress from AIM to the main London stock market.

Overall it is difficult to make a quantitative comparison of the two options as the acquisition price for Strategy 2 has not yet been determined. On the basis of the information provided, Strategy 1 generates a positive NPV but this is dependent on the reliability of the working assumptions. The NPV is not large, so it is sensitive to changes in the cash flow assumptions. This is particularly the case as the major cash inflows are only expected to occur after three years, and growth in sales and profits in the first few years is assumed to be very high – doubling in both the second and third years.

More information is needed to assess the reliability of the data for both strategies.

WORKING 1 – NPV of Strategy 1

Year ending 31 Dec	Revenue £'000	Profit margin (5%) £'000	PV workings at 10%	PV £'000
20X9	3,000	150	150/1.1	136
20Y0	6,000	300	$300/1.1^2$	248
20Y1 onwards	12,000	600	$(600/.1)/1.1^2$	4,959
				5,343
			Opportunity costs*	(1,925)
			Outlay	(3,000)
				418

*It is assumed that the lost cash flow before tax from the reduction in sales of higher-priced alarms would be equal to the gross profit percentage on sales in the current year (= 6,000/24,000 = 25%).

Lost contribution margin each year	= £1m × 25%	= £250,000
Lost contribution net of tax at 23%	= (£250,000 × 0.77)	= £192,500
PV of lost sales	= 192,500/0.1	= £1.925m

(b) Implications for John Rawlings and corporate governance

John Rawlings

John Rawlings, as chairman of Safetex, would presumably agree to the acquisition of CAL on the terms that have been suggested.

The consequence of a takeover of CAL would be a significant reduction in the proportion of the company that he owns. A part of the acquisition price for CAL would be paid in new Safetex shares. It should also be assumed (although it is by no means certain) that the convertible bonds would all be converted eventually into new equity.

ICAEW

If the bond is converted this will create 3.75m new shares (25m × 15/100).

Also, following a share for share exchange on acquisition there would be 2m new shares. The shareholdings would then be:

Handwritten note (top right): Implied SP: £100/15 shares = £6.67

	Shares	
Original shareholders		
John Rawlings	4.50m	38%
Others	1.50m	13%
Issued to Hogsmood (share for share)	2.00m	17%
Convertible holders	3.75m	32%
	11.75m	

John Rawlings will still have the largest single shareholding but, to the extent that the other shareholdings are concentrated, these groups may have significant influence over Safetex.

The conversion rate for the convertible bonds (15 shares for every £100 of bonds) implies a share price of at least £6.67, compared with the current share price of £6. For the share price to rise by over 10% within three years, positive benefits from the CAL acquisition would need to be recognised by investors.

Other governance issues

If CAL is acquired under the arrangement suggested, there would initially be 8m shares in issue, of which only 1.5m – less than 20% – would be held by the general investing 'public'. Hogsmood might decide to sell some shares in the market, but given the limited liquidity of the AIM market this is unlikely to be its intention in agreeing to accept Safetex shares.

The response of the minority shareholders to the acquisition of CAL could have implications for the share price. They will be unable to prevent the acquisition, given the dominant shareholding of John Rawlings, but they may not give the strategy their support.

A separate issue is that since Safetex does not have any experience in the commercial market for alarms, it may be necessary to appoint at least one CAL executive director to the board of Safetex after the acquisition. Safetex is an AIM company and so is not required to comply with the UK Corporate Governance Code; however, if it has ambitions to go on to the main stock market, it will need to create a board of directors in time that complies with the Code requirements. The addition of additional executive directors to the board could make the board too large, and may also prompt the board to consider additional appointments of independent non-executive directors.

(c) **Determining EPS**

(1) **Strategy 1 – EPS year ending 31 December 20X9**

It is assumed that with Strategy 1, earnings from the existing business would be the same as in the current year plus the after tax profit from the new business, minus the opportunity cost of lost sales after tax, and minus a charge for depreciation of the new non-current assets purchased.

We know only that investment and reorganisation costs would be £3m. We do not know how much of this is investment, and we do not know the depreciation policy of Safetex.

As a rough estimate, it is assumed that investment costs will be £2m and the average depreciation rate will be 10% on cost, allowing for tax benefits. However, this figure will have to be re-assessed when more reliable information is available.

	£
Earnings from existing business	2,310,000
Earnings from cheaper alarms in 20X9	150,000
Loss of earnings (opportunity costs)	(192,500)
Additional depreciation	(200,000)
Total earnings	2,067,500

EPS = £2,067,500/6m shares = 34.46p

(2) **Strategy 2 – EPS year ending 31 December 20X9**

	Notes	Safetex £'000	Commercial Alarms £'000	Consolidated £'000
Revenue	1	24,000	12,480	
Cost of sales	2	(18,000)	(7,800)	
Gross profit		6,000	4,680	
Operating expenses	3	(1,500)	(3,000)	
Profit from operations		4,500	1,680	
Additional marketing	4		(300)	
Additional depreciation	5		(60)	
Finance costs	6	(1,500)	(1,612)	
Profit before tax		3,000	(292)	
Tax 23%	7	(690)	67	
Profit for the year		2,310	(225)	**2,085**

Notes

1 **Revenue**

$12,000 \times 1.04 = 12,480$

2 **Cost of sales**

Price paid after acquisition = 1/0.80 (*) = 1.25 of current costs. It is assumed that this will apply to the full cost of sales of CAL.

Cost in 20X9: $6,000 \times 1.25 \times 1.04 = 7,800$

* Adjustment of transfer price to fair value

3 **Depreciation adjustment**

Depreciation will increase following the adoption of fair values on acquisition according to IFRS 3. Assumed this to be pro rata to historical cost and fair values of PPE, thus depreciation is:

£1m × 40m/20m = £2m

This is an increase of £1m; therefore operating expenses are now £3m. (This assumes no adjustment for savings in centrally provided services.)

4 **Marketing**

£300,000: assumption given in the question

5 **Additional depreciation**

£1,200,000 × 5% = £60,000

This is a rough estimate of the depreciation of CAL on initial costs of £1.2m based on the existing ratio of depreciation to carrying amount of £1m/£20m.

6 **Finance costs – Convertible instrument**

This is a compound financial instrument which needs to be split between debt and equity components. The debt value is:

Cash interest is £25m × 4% = £1m

		£
PV of Interest payable 31/12/X9	$£1m/1.07 =$	934,579
PV of Interest payable 31/12/Y0	$£1m/1.07^2 =$	873,439
PV of Interest payable 31/12/Y1	$£1m/1.07^3 =$	816,298
PV of Principal payable 31/12/Y1	$£25m/1.07^3 =$	20,407,445
PV of liability component		23,031,761
PV of equity component (residual)		1,968,239
FV of bond		25,000,000

Finance charges are as follows:

Year ended 31 Dec	Opening bal £	Interest @ 7% £	Cash paid £	Closing bal £
20X9	23,031,761	1,612,223	1,000,000	23,643,984
20Y0	23,643,984	1,655,079	1,000,000	24,299,063
20Y1	24,299,063	1,700,934	1,000,000	25,000,000*

*Rounding = £3

7 **EPS and diluted EPS**

An effective tax rate of 23% is assumed.

Basic EPS

There are currently 6m shares in issue by Safetex.

If a share for share exchange plus cash takes place, then an extra 2m Safetex shares will be in issue, raising the total to 8m. These are assumed to be issued at the beginning of 20X9 so they will count in full.

Thus, basic EPS is: £2,085,000/8m = 26.06p

The acquisition therefore has a lower EPS than Strategy 1 in the first year.

Diluted EPS

[£2,085,000 + (£1,612,223 (1 − 0.23))]/(8m + 3.75m*) = **28.31p**

The convertibles are therefore **not dilutive**.

* (£25m/£100) × 15 = 3.75m

(d) **Valuing CAL**

(1) **Context of valuation**

The context of the valuation is to make an initial bid for CAL. The estimates therefore are made on the conservative side as the opening valuation is likely to be pushed upwards during the negotiation process. Nevertheless, the figures are drawn up to be justifiable both in terms of the methodology and the estimates used.

(2) **Adjusted earnings based valuation**

Revenue of CAL is £12m in 20X8 but growing at 4% pa.

The fair value of cost of sales when the company is not part of the group is £6m/0.8 = £7.5m. As these are all assumed to be variable costs, the growth rate will be 4% in accordance with volume.

Applying the valuation model for growth in perpetuity:

The present value of the gross profit income stream is:

(£12m − £7.5m)1.04/(0.10 − 0.04) = £78m

The present value of fixed cash costs then needs to be deducted from this figure.

	£'000
Fixed operating costs	2,000
Less depreciation (not a cash cost)	(1,000)
Additional Capex pa	1,200
Additional marketing costs	300
Fixed operating cost cash flows	2,500

PV of fixed operating cash flows = £2.5m/0.1 = £25m

MV of debt is   = £25m

The PV of the tax payments presents more of a challenge as revenues and variable costs are inflating at 4%, finance costs are increasing, but other costs are assumed constant. This has an uncertain effect on profit and thus on tax.

Also the tax rules are likely to change over time.

In addition, capital allowances will be based on the existing tax pool (which is unknown) plus Capex additions.

The calculation below is therefore prudent and based on a crude but simple assumption that tax will be at 23% of the cash flows calculated above. It is also assumed that it grows in line with sales volumes at 4%. This gives

	£'000
Gross profit	4,500
Fixed costs	(2,500)
Taxable	2,000
Tax at 23%	460

PV = (£460,000 × 1.04)/(0.10 – 0.04)

   = £7.97m, say £8.0m

Summary

	£'m
PV of gross annual profit in perpetuity	78
PV of fixed operating expenses	(25)
PV of annual tax payments	(8)
Enterprise value	45
PV of debt	(25)
Equity value	20

On the basis of the stated assumptions, an estimate of the equity value of CAL is £20m.

Tutorial note:

A range of reasonable assumptions could have been made to estimate a value. Alternative answers, which are justifiable, would therefore be acceptable.

(e) **Proposed financing arrangements for acquisition of CAL**

(1) **Assessment on the basis of information provided**

If a two-for-one share for share exchange takes place at a share value for Safetex of £6 each then this has a value of £12m. There is £3m cash in the Safetex statement of financial position.

Although there is £2.5m in the CAL statement of financial position, it is assumed that Hogsmood will withdraw this money, probably as a dividend, before the sale is completed.

This would leave a financing shortfall of £5.0m (£20.0m – £12m – £3m).

It is assumed that Safetex would be able to obtain this money in the form of a bank loan, although this would need to be checked. The interest on any additional borrowing would represent an additional charge.

Given that CAL would be expected to make a loss in 20X9 against an investment of £20m, then most of the value is dependent on delivering future growth. A bid of £20m may seem excessive unless there is a high degree of certainty about future growth estimates.

(2) The Safetex share price

Without a strategy for growth, the annual profits of Safetex are expected to remain static for the foreseeable future. The current share price is £6, and the expected EPS in 20X8 is 38.5p (2,310/6,000). The P/E ratio is therefore about 15.6 times (= £6/38.5p).

This is a very high ratio for a non-growth company whose shares are listed on AIM and it is difficult to see how such a high price is justified or sustainable.

The market for Safetex shares on AIM is probably illiquid, and the £6 may simply represent a transaction in the market that occurred some time ago.

My concern is that in arranging a deal for the purchase of CAL, Hogsmood will not agree to a valuation of £6. Similarly, investors in convertible bonds issued by Safetex should not accept a conversion rate of 15 shares per £100 of bonds, because the implied share price would be far too high.

I recommend that Safetex should obtain advice from its sponsoring bank about an appropriate valuation for the company's shares. If a £6 valuation is too high, the acquisition of CAL may be put into doubt.

For example, if a price of £20m is agreed for CAL and the fair value for the Safetex share price is just £4, an additional £9m of funding would be required (= £20m – £8m – £3m). A bank may not be prepared to lend this money. Convertible bond holders would want better conversion terms, perhaps better than 20 shares per £100 of bonds (in which case bonds would not be converted unless the share price exceeds £5).

In summary, the share price of Safetex is a critical assumption in the financing of the CAL acquisition, and I have strong doubts about the validity of this assumption.

(f) HR issues on acquisition of CAL

There are several HR issues to consider in the event that a takeover of CAL takes place.

(1) Location of head office

The two companies will remain as separate subsidiaries within the group, but they are likely to combine their head office operations. This may well be at the current head office of Safetex, and there is no obvious reason why an administration centre in Birmingham would be required.

Key staff may agree to be re-located to London, but it is quite possible that many will refuse to re-locate.

There will in any case be redundancies, which will damage morale among staff in the centre or centres affected.

(2) Selling the deal to CAL staff

CAL staff who remain with the group are likely to be hostile to the takeover, as they are unlikely to be aware of any reason for Hogsmood wanting to sell their company. The takeover will create uncertainty for them, and transfer them to a group whose culture is unfamiliar. There will be negative aspects for them in the change, and no obvious positive aspects.

(3) Remuneration schemes

The companies have different remuneration schemes. For a time after the acquisition of CAL it will probably be possible to retain the two different schemes for staff, depending on which company they 'come from'.

In the longer term, however, the board should expect greater integration of operations within the group, and the need for a single remuneration structure for all staff will increase.

(g) **Due diligence**

The following due diligence procedures are recommended prior to a takeover deal being completed.

	20X8 £'000	Reservations and due diligence work
Revenue	12,000	• Are any intra group sales at normal prices? • Test whether enhancement of revenue through group transactions or other means. • Are group transactions guaranteed to continue? • A question mark over whether Hogsmood will also sell systems through other channels and compete with Safetex in the market going forward.
Cost of sales	(6,000)	• Attest transfer price relative to fair values (eg by sales to third parties of same goods). • Consider prices of alternative suppliers.
Gross profit	6,000	
Operating expenses	(2,000)	• Ascertain the nature and value of services provided centrally by Hogsmood. • Does Safetex have the capacity to replicate these services at a similar or lower cost? • Working assumption of zero inflation needs to be reviewed.
Profit from operations	4,000	
Finance costs	(360)	• This represents only 1% interest rate. Not relevant to due diligence as will not continue. • Transfer pricing adjustment would apply for tax purposes. • Need to ensure no penalties etc in loan agreement with parent that would apply on acquisition. • Need time to put replacement finance in place.
Profit before tax	3,640	
Tax	(835)	• Need tax due diligence to ensure no outstanding tax issues (eg liabilities becoming due).
Profit for the year	2,805	
Net assets		
Property, plant and equipment	40,000	This is a key figure and independent valuations will be needed prior to any formal bid to assess the existence, condition, value and suitability of the property.
Current assets		
Inventories	6,000	Review sale or return contract to ensure that rights still exist to return the goods.
Trade receivables	4,000	Assumed full recovery but would need to assess recoverability through an ageing analysis. Responsibility of bad debts needs to be clarified.
Cash and cash equivalents	2,500	Assumes acquisition is not cash free. Need to clarify this and set out constraint on cash withdrawal prior to acquisition. Might also be intention to pay pre acquisition dividend.
Non-current liabilities		
Intra group balance owing to Hogsmood	(25,000)	To be refinanced. Need to be clear on conditions of loan and any covenants that will operate on repayment.
Current liabilities	(2,860)	Ascertain the nature of these liabilities and test for understatement. For example: • Possibility that the tax charge and deferred tax charge may be understated given that it is dependent on group relief. • Any provisions for warranties or other claims.

ICAEW

Other issues

Interest rate: real or money rate? Given that inflation is set aside, 10% should be the relevant real rate not the money rate.

Consider the appropriateness of the weighted average cost of capital as the relevant discount rate.

Rights of access to information and timing need to be clarified.

10 Coopers Coffee Company Ltd

Marking guide

		Marks Up to
(a)	Business strategy comments – strategies and risks associated with them	12
(b) (1)	Issues to consider in relation to customer relationship management	5
(2)	Evaluation of potential benefits of Big Data analytics	6
(c)	Calculation of additional revenue, and comments about initial franchise charge	12
(d)	Comments on controls	11
(e)	Comments on ethical issues	6
Total marks		52
Maximum marks		45

MEMORANDUM

To: Engagement partner
From: Senior
Date: X July 20X9
Subject: Coopers Coffee Company Ltd

(a) Strategy assessment

CCC has limited capital for achieving growth by opening outlets that it owns itself, but the CCC board has an objective of achieving rapid expansion. This presumably explains the main strategic reason for using franchises as a means of achieving growth.

Rapid growth inevitably creates problems for management control, but these problems are particularly severe with growth through franchising.

- Franchisees are of variable quality as entrepreneurs and managers of a business. Some will be better (and more successful) than others. With a requirement for rapid growth, CCC's assessment process of potential franchisees may not be effective in selecting capable managers and rejecting those most likely to fail.

- Some franchisees may over-commit themselves financially. Although the closure of a franchise would affect the franchisee financially rather than CCC, CCC's reputation would be damaged by outlet closures.

- There must be some control over the business from CCC head office, but it is more difficult to control the activities of franchisees than managers in company-owned outlets.

CCC is therefore faced with the problem that it must use franchising to grow quickly, but there are management and control risks with this strategy. Control is considered later in this memo.

Risks of owned and franchised outlets

There are business risks associated with both opening outlets owned by CCC and also making franchise agreements.

Owned outlets

handwritten: contribution / sales. ←

- These require large up-front investment by CCC. If outlets are opened with borrowed funds, the financial gearing of CCC will increase. Since 50% of costs of sales are variable costs, the contribution ratio is fairly high, which means that more self-owned outlets may add to the operational gearing of the company too. Higher financial gearing and higher operational gearing would mean higher overall risk.

- There would be significant exit costs for CCC if a new outlet fails.

- There is no up-front receipt, whereas franchisees pay £100,000 up front for their franchise.

- There is some risk of contribution from sales not covering fixed costs leading to losses.

- Owning premises may lead to excessive focus on admin/premises management rather than the business of running coffee bars.

Risks to CCC of franchising outlets   *handwritten: variable quality*

handwritten: risk of franchising

- There is limited control over the actions of franchisees who may damage the brand if the quality of service delivery is not up to CCC standards.

- Financial failure of franchisee may lead to non-payment of franchise fees (although up-front fee will already have been received).

- There may be some risk of understatement of the 10% franchise charge through understatement of sales. This is considered in more detail later.

- Risk that franchisees will not be available in sufficient numbers to meet the goal of 10% growth in the business plan. A strategy of growth through franchising depends on finding people who are prepared to operate a CCC franchise. The high initial fee may be a deterrent.

- Risk that franchises will not be renewed. Once franchisees are established with a local reputation they may not wish to reapply for the franchise in five years and may be a source of future competition for any new franchise. For franchisees, the risk that their franchise may not be renewed after five years may be a further deterrent, and reduce the potential for growth through opening new franchises.

- There are risks of operational and contractual disputes with franchisees.

- There will be increased monitoring costs as the number of franchises increases. These costs will depend on the perceived risk of the new franchisees.

Alternative strategies

CCC should look at what the main competitors are doing. The largest companies in the market may have reached saturation point with opening new outlets, and so are looking for new ways to expand. The biggest companies are able to expand internationally, but CCC does not have sufficient size yet to do this – although the potential for international growth may be investigated to establish whether opportunities in this area do exist.

Coffee shops are associated with town centres, transport hubs and motorway service stations. There may be opportunities for CCC in these locations. Other possible locations for coffee bars in other types of location may offer growth opportunities.

The major competitors are also limiting new franchises to companies with ten or more outlets. There may be two reasons for this. One would be to continue growing rapidly. Only one agreement needs to be negotiated to open ten outlets, instead of ten separate agreements. A second reason is that operators who are able to open at least ten outlets are more likely to be financially sound and also more competent at running businesses. Instead of dealing with ten individual franchisees, there would be just one corporate franchisee.

CCC may wish to consider arrangements for multiple outlets. An incentive may be to offer lower initial charges for any franchisee who is prepared to operate, say, at least three or four outlets.

(b) (1) **Customer relationship management (CRM)**

CCC appears to have a good brand name, but the board is concerned about its CRM policies.

Operating coffee shops is a service business, and the quality of service to customers is critical for success.

CCC's management are no doubt already aware of the importance of quality of service, the quality of the main product (coffee) and the attractiveness of the coffee bar environment.

However a problem for any company operating a chain of coffee bars is how to create and maintain customer loyalty for their own brand. CCC should be interested in how to persuade customers to buy their coffee at CCC's coffee shops, rather than at the coffee shops of rival companies.

One aspect of CRM policy must be to have a good understanding of customers and their motivation. CCC should conduct market research regularly, to obtain insight into:

* levels of customer satisfaction with CCC's products and service;
* the extent to which customers recommend CCC to other people; and
* customer loyalty – the extent to which they keep using CCC coffee bars, and how frequently.

Research should also gather data on the demographics of customers, to establish whether CCC appeals to some age groups (or social groups) more than others.

Research information can then be used to develop marketing activities to reinforce the good aspects of customer relationships and strengthen those which appear weak.

CCC should consider ways of strengthening customer loyalty. At least one leading chain of coffee bars has a members' club that offers additional benefits to members. A members' club arrangement would give CCC closer contact with customers, through emails and social networking, which should be used to attract customer interest without seeming a 'hard sell'.

Research can also be used to establish reasons why customers may be dissatisfied with CCC. Slow service, for example, may be a problem. If significant problems emerge from research, management can consider initiatives to deal with them.

(2) **Big Data analytics**

As noted in the previous section, one of the key aspects of customer relationship management is gaining a good understanding of customers and their behaviours.

Café 2 Go's analytics provide a means for gaining insights into how satisfied customers are with their coffee and the service they receive, without specifically carrying out separate research. Analysing customer responses can help Café 2 Go identify areas where performance may need to be improved (eg speed of service, or offering different products), which in turn should help to improve customer satisfaction and retention.

Although it is useful to have information about customer responses for individual periods, perhaps the greater use will come from monitoring trends, and trying to identify reasons for those trends. For example, although customer feedback about Café 2 Go has been less positive than Best Bean over the last year, the gap between the two has been closing since May. Therefore, Café 2 Go can assess what changes have prompted this improvement, and can then try to reinforce them in future, to maintain the improvements in customer sentiment.

Similarly, being able to analyse customer ratings for individual outlets could also be valuable, for trying to identify what the high-scoring outlets are doing better than the low-scoring ones, and in turn, whether there are any aspects of good practice which could be shared across all the outlets.

Although scores and customer comments are useful, the most valuable customer feedback will be that which provides some insight as to **why** customers feel the way they do (and therefore why they feel Café 2 Go is performing well/badly). The fact that a customer feels that a cappuccino at Café 2 Go is the 'best way to start the day' is nice to know, but it doesn't actually provide any insight as to why the customer feels this way. By contrast, the negative comment about the speed of service is potentially more useful – particularly if the comment be traced to a particular outlet and time of day so that the reasons for the slow service can be investigated.

In this respect, it is important to note that over 70% of Café 2 Go's customer sentiment in the last year has been 'neutral', and accordingly may provide little insight. As such, it could be necessary to consider whether the value obtained from the remaining 30% justifies the effort involved in analysing all the comments. Café 2 Go has a dedicated social media monitoring department, and so will incur the costs associated with running that department.

Similarly, it may also be necessary to consider how representative the feedback is of all Café 2 Go's customers. For example, what proportion of customers post comments on social media, and how does this proportion vary across different age groups?

(c) **Amount franchisees are prepared to pay**

I have been asked to provide an estimate of the amount of extra sales a coffee bar would need to earn in order to break even if it were to become a CCC franchise. To do this, I have been asked to use figures for Hoole Café.

I question the appropriateness of this approach. If Hoole Café becomes a CCC franchise, its sales prices are likely to change. Its costs are also likely to change, because it will have to buy its products through CCC instead of independently. Although CCC includes a profit mark-up for head office in the prices it charges its outlets, the strong central buying capability of CCC should mean that it can buy products at a lower cost than independent coffee bars.

(1) On the basis of Hoole's figures, the contribution per £1 of sales = (240,000 – 90,000)/240,000 = £0.625. There would be an additional franchise charge of 10% reducing the contribution/sales ratio from 62.5% to 52.5%.

(2) On the basis of the figures for a CCC-owned outlet, the contribution per £1 of sales would be (360,000 – 120,000)/360,000 = 66.7%. Deducting the 10% franchise charge would reduce this to 56.7%.

A franchisee has to pay the initial charge of £100,000 for a five-year franchise. Since the franchise may be terminated after five years, the franchisee would want to make a 10% return on this investment over five years. The required annual return to achieve this would be:

£26,380 (£100,000/Annuity factor at 10% for 5 yrs where AF10% 5 yrs = 3.7908.)

To break even, Hoole Café would need to make a profit of £10,000 per year. Contribution must therefore be sufficient to make this profit and cover fixed costs.

We do not know what Hoole's fixed costs will be if it becomes a franchise. CCC would provide marketing services, and some reduction in Hoole's fixed costs should be expected. The annual administration costs in a CCC-owned outlet are £10,000 for a 60-seat capacity outlet, but the fixed costs in the cost of sales are £120,000.

Hoole currently has £90,000 of fixed costs in its cost of sales, but administration costs (all fixed) of £50,000.

Without closer investigation of the cost figures, it is not possible to determine the annual fixed costs of Hoole if it were to become a CCC franchisee.

It will be assumed here that Hoole Café would be able to reduce its administrative costs from £50,000 to £30,000 (but this assumption needs to be investigated more closely).

	£
Profit needed to 'break even'	10,000
Fixed costs in cost of sales	90,000
Administration costs	30,000
Annual finance charge	26,380
Contribution required to 'break even'	156,380

If the contribution/sales ratio is 52.5%, Hoole Café would need annual sales of £297,867 (156,380/0.525) to be no worse off than operating independently. Say £300,000.

If the contribution/sales ratio is 56.7%, Hoole Café would need annual sales of £275,802 (156,380/0.567) to 'break even'. Say £275,000.

Current annual sales are £240,000. This means that additional sales of between £35,000 (14.6%) and £60,000 (25%) would be needed as a minimum to justify becoming a CCC franchisee.

An average 60-seat CCC coffee bar earns revenue of £360,000, or £6,000 per seat. Hoole Café has seating for just 50 people. If it achieves sales of £6,000 per seat, annual revenue would be £300,000 – at the top end of what the café would need to justify becoming a CCC franchisee.

Conclusion

The financial attractiveness of becoming a CCC franchisee for operators such as Hoole Café may be marginal. It is even possible that there is no financial benefit in becoming a franchisee, although the figures here are based on questionable assumptions.

The figures therefore suggest that an initial fee of £100,000 may be too high for an operator as small as Hoole Café. If CCC plans to continue with its strategy of rapid expansion using franchising, the following adjustments to initial fees may need to be considered:

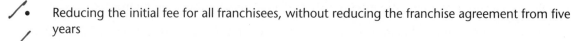

- Reducing the initial fee for all franchisees, without reducing the franchise agreement from five years

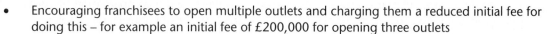

- Having stepped initial fees, with higher initial fees for outlets with bigger capacity and lower fees for smaller outlets

- Encouraging franchisees to open multiple outlets and charging them a reduced initial fee for doing this – for example an initial fee of £200,000 for opening three outlets

(d) Management control

CCC must be able to exert sufficient control over its business. This will require regular, reliable reporting to head office management about the performance of each outlet. Actual performance of outlets should be compared with budget targets, and also with each other. Outlets in similar areas and of similar size might be expected to achieve similar performance; and differences may be attributable to the quality of management (although the proximity of rival coffee bars would also have to be taken into consideration).

Poor-performing outlets should be investigated, to establish the reasons and initiate improvements.

Jack Johnson has particular concerns about under-stated revenues by franchises.

Understatement of cash receipts by individual employees

The key risk is that cash sales are significant and can be under-recorded at the point of sale by an individual employee, who may then misappropriate the cash.

Internal controls should be put in place to reduce this risk. These may include the following:

- Segregation of duties between the staff serving the coffee (or other goods) and the member of staff taking the cash. This would prevent the same member of staff having access to the cash receipt and serving goods to the customer.

- Secure point of sale recording of cash received. There should be an electronic till in all outlets which records the amount of the sales, the type of goods sold and the member of staff making the sale. This prevents misappropriation after initial recording in the till.

- The store manager will observe individual staff and processes of initial recording of transactions (possibly using CCTV). It is in the interests of the franchisee as well as CCC that staff should not misappropriate cash.

- Anonymous 'ghost customer' visits by CCC representatives.

- Performance comparisons between outlets and from day to day, as part of the reporting system referred to above.

Understatement of revenues by franchisees

Misappropriation of cash sales at the franchisee level can often be detected by management controls examining the relationship between purchases and related revenues. In the case of CCC however, the cost of materials is only 15% of variable costs, so comparisons between outlets of variable costs to sales ratios may not be an efficient or reliable method of identifying under-stated revenues.

It may therefore be difficult to exercise control over sales from amounts purchased using management accounting controls.

The franchise agreement needs to contain terms which allow CCC regular and random access to the accounting records and operations of franchisees.

Key control procedures should then include the following:

- Regular reconciliations of till control totals with amounts banked.

- Banking of all cash receipts intact (ie without any payments being made in cash from cash receipts) and implementing imprest type cash system with appropriate controls to cover cash payments.

- Bank reconciliations reviewed as regularly as is feasible. Bank reconciliations should be included as requirements in all new franchise agreements.

- Reconciliation of revenues reported to CCC, with franchisees' financial statements.

  As stated above, there should be regular management reporting by franchises to CCC. Where performance figures seem disappointing or unusual, CCC staff should inspect the management accounting records of the franchisee.

- The regular reviews of management reports from all outlets should compare monthly sales over time and between outlets for evidence of understatement (eg unusual fall in sales; movement in gross profit margins).

(e) **Ethical issues**

In general the FRC Ethical Standard Part B Section 5 does permit other work to be carried out for audit clients, but the ethical issue is one of self-review threat. Appropriate safeguards need to be established, although there may be instances where there are no appropriate safeguards and thus other work would be inappropriate.

(1) **Understatement of cash receipts by individual employees**

The key risk in this instance is that the controls recommended may need to be the subject of reliance in the audit which is a separate engagement. In reviewing our own work there is an element of self-review whereby it is difficult to be critical of systems which our firm has set up.

Safeguards

- Separate staff and partner on the audit engagement and the assurance engagement.

- Informing client that internal controls remain the responsibility of management.

- Limiting the engagement to advise on design, leaving implementation of internal controls as managerial responsibility.

(2) **Understatement of franchisees' income**

This instance looks at the internal controls of the franchisees which are not directly CCC's controls on which we are reporting. There is therefore a more limited ethical threat in this case. The audit would however concern itself with understatement of revenue so there is a limited self-review threat.

Safeguards would be as above.

(3) **Risk management**

Assessing risk is a key requirement of the audit. In this context the client is requiring an assessment of inherent risks. There is an ethical issue in that the client is asking us to identify and compare key risks for its franchised and non-franchised outlets. If the client implements risk management procedures based directly on our assurance assignment work it would be more difficult to be critical of these risk management systems.

Safeguards

- Clarify the context of the engagement, ie that we are not advising on risk management procedures but only identifying risks.

- Separate staff on the audit engagement and the assurance engagement.

- Inform client that internal controls remain the responsibility of management.

- Consider not accepting this work if the above safeguards may be deemed insufficient.

(4) **Franchise fees**

This is a reasonably objective piece of advisory work which does not impact directly on our audit opinion. There are therefore no additional material ethical implications.

11   Delta plc

		Marks
		Up to
(a)	Explanation of risks facing the company	8
(b)	Impact on profit and loss and reserves	
	Land	4
	Shares	5
(c)	Risk management strategies	
	Currency risk	10
	Interest rate risk	5
	Share price (market) risk	7
(d)	Accounting effects of hedging strategies	6
(e)	Acquisition of BC: financial analysis	9
	Acquisition of BC: strategic and risk analysis	6
Total marks		60
Maximum marks		55

Briefing notes

To: Jonathan Hubert
From: Group Financial Controller
Date: 31 December 20X7
Subject: Risks: accounting treatment and risk management strategies

(a) **Risks**

The board has identified two types of risk over the next twelve months. One is stock market risk, which is the risk that the market price of the shares in Lambda may fall. A fall in the share price has implications for the value of the investment and financial reporting. There are also cash flow risks, if the board has an intention (possibly) to sell the shares in the fairly near future. A fall in the share price would mean less cash income from the share sale.

Secondly, Delta is exposed to exchange rate risk (currency risk) on the French investment that it is committed to purchase. The risk results from changes in the spot rate during a given period. In this case, the risk originated with the contract to purchase the land in France. One aspect of currency risk is the resulting gain or loss reported in the financial statements. Another aspect of risk is the possibility that the cost of the purchase at the end of June 20X8 will be more than expected, due to a rise in the value of the euro against the British pound.

These briefing notes will consider the financial reporting implications of these risks.

In addition, I suggest that you should make the board aware of longer-term risks in these investments.

The board will be aware of its reasons for buying 10% of the equity in Lambda. If the reason was to make a return from a short-term investment, the only significant risk in the transaction is market risk. On the other hand, if the board intends to retain the investment over a longer period of time, short-term price movements are relatively unimportant. A much bigger risk would be the business risk in Lambda's operations, and the longer-term prospects for profit growth, dividend growth and, as a result, share price growth.

There is currency risk in the purchase of the land in France, but the risk does not end with the purchase of the land. Delta will expect to construct and develop a shopping centre, if planning permission is obtained, and this will involve substantial costs, presumably in euros. These costs will be incurred before the company begins to earn returns on the investment. The exposure to currency risk is therefore long term in nature.

If Delta intends to finance its investments with euro-denominated debt, there will also be interest rate risk. If the company borrows at a fixed rate, the risk is that interest rates may fall over the term of the borrowing. If the company borrows at a floating rate, there is a risk from rising interest rates. In either event, interest costs could be higher than they might have been.

As a final point on risk, market risk, currency risk and interest rate risk are all two-way risks, in the sense that actual outcomes may be better as well as worse than expected. Your immediate concern is with falling share prices and a fall in the value of sterling. The possibility that rates and prices could move in the other direction should not be overlooked.

(b) **Impact on profit or loss and reserves**

Purchase of land in euros

The payable relating to the land purchase is an amount fixed in foreign currency (since our functional currency is sterling) and this item therefore meets the definition of a monetary item per IAS 21.

1 October 20X7

As our functional currency is sterling, we will already have recorded the land and related payable at £66,205,679 translated using the current spot rate (€1.3594/£1).

31 December 20X7

The payable, being a monetary item, will be adjusted to a current sterling value of £69,050,176 based on the current spot (closing) rate (€1.3034/£1), and the corresponding loss of £2,844,497 will be recognised in profit or loss in 20X7.

30 June 20X8

The payable will be settled on this date and in order to do so we would have to purchase euros in the market at the spot rate, whatever this is at the time. If the rate is 1.2534, the payment will amount to £71,804,691. The consequent loss on settlement of £2,754,515 will be recognised in profit or loss in 20X8.

Purchase of shares in Lambda

The purchase of only a relatively small percentage of the shares in Lambda means it is most unlikely that the investment will be treated as a subsidiary or associate in our consolidated accounts. Under the rules in IAS 39 *Financial Instruments: Recognition and Measurement* there are two choices for treatment of the investment: financial assets (such as these) may be treated as either 'available-for-sale' or 'at fair value through profit or loss'.

We could have treated the shares as 'at fair value through profit or loss' in the following circumstances:

The shares were held for trading. This is only suitable when the financial asset is a derivative or part of a portfolio of instruments or principally bought for the purpose of selling in the near term. The last of these three indicators is a possibility, depending on our perception of 'near term'. As the purpose of the purchase was a part of our diversification strategy it seems likely that we have an intention to hold the shares for slightly longer than the 'near term'. You mentioned that you would prefer to keep them until 31 December next year at least.

They were designated at initial recognition as 'at fair value through profit or loss'. This seems very unlikely to be possible as there is no elimination of an accounting mismatch and it is not part of a group of financial assets evaluated on a fair value basis.

It therefore seems likely that under the provisions of IAS 39 the correct treatment would have been to show the shares as an available-for-sale asset which results in gains and losses being recognised in other comprehensive income. Thus there would be no impact on our profit or loss during 20X7 or 20X8 except for income relating to dividends where the right to receive payment has been established. If we did sell the shares on 31 December 20X8 then any gain or loss previously recognised in other comprehensive income would then be reclassified from equity to profit or loss as a reclassification adjustment.

The provisions of IFRS 9 *Financial Instruments* are different. All equity investments should be measured in the statement of financial position at fair value. Gains or losses should be reported in profit or loss, except that if the equity investment is not held for trading, the company can make an irrevocable election to measure it at 'fair value through other comprehensive income'(FVTOCI), in which case only dividend income is recognised in profit or loss. Gains or losses recognised in other comprehensive income are not reported in profit or loss on disposal.

If IFRS 9 is applied and the asset has been designated at FVTOCI, the unrealised gain of £20m at the year end will be reported in other comprehensive income, and profit or loss will not be affected. However any future losses on the investment will similarly not be reported in profit or loss.

(c) **Risk management strategies**

A distinction should be made between strategies for hedging short-term risks and those for hedging longer-term risks.

It should also be remembered that one risk management strategy is to do nothing. If the risk is considered fairly small, because of low impact or low probability of occurrence, an appropriate strategy may be to leave the exposure to risk un-hedged.

With the two investments, the risk is probably quite significant. A large fall in share prices is predicted and the euro is expected to increase substantially in value against sterling. The longer-term exposures to currency risk and interest rate risk may also be considered significant.

A strategy to hedge significant risks is likely to be preferred to a strategy of doing nothing.

Macrohedging

To respond to the board's concerns and to manage risk effectively, we need to take a portfolio view of risk management and hedging over all the group's business operations. This means grouping financial instruments or transactions with similar risks together and taking available opportunities to net assets and liabilities, and to net currency revenues and expenditures.

Exchange rate risk to 30 June 20X8

The immediate risk is that the sterling/euro spot exchange rate may fall from its current level of 1.3034 to 1.2534 by 30 June 20X8. If this happens the cost of buying the €90m to pay for the land will rise from £69.05m at the current spot rate to £71.80m at the expected spot rate at the end of June.

There are a number of ways in which we can hedge our risk relating to euro/sterling exchange rate movement and the payment of the €90m on 30 June 20X8.

(1) **Internal strategies**

Ideally we should be able to use some kind of internal hedging strategy to eliminate the foreign currency risk as efficiently as possible. Unfortunately commonly-used tactics such as invoicing in our currency, offsetting currency payments against receipts in the same currency, intercompany netting and leading and lagging are not available to us as we have no euro operations at present.

(2) **Matching assets and liabilities**

We should be able to negotiate with a bank to borrow euros to finance the payment. We would therefore borrow euros at the end of June and could use the currency to settle the liability. Once the supermarket was then built we would generate euro returns which could be used to pay off the euro loan.

This method has the advantage that it is less complex than the other methods although the bank is likely to charge us for setting up the future facility especially if we wish to fix the exchange rate now (the bank would in effect be hedging the risk position in their own books rather than us doing so).

Which one is the most appropriate?

This strategy has two major weaknesses. The first is that the term of the borrowing may have to be several years, and the bank is unlikely to agree to deferred interest payments. Delta will need to pay interest in euros that it is not earning from operations. The second problem is that having purchased the land, Delta will have to develop the shopping centre, which will take more time and involve additional costs in euros.

✓ Large and unquantified total borrowings in euros, without euro income to meet the interest payments and eventual capital repayment, would expose the company to ongoing currency risks.

(3) Money market hedge

To use a money market hedge for the short-term currency exposure we would buy euros now and invest them over a six-month term. This would then realise an amount which would accumulate to the €90m required after six months ie

$$€90m/(1 + 5.945\%)^{1/2} = €87,438,415$$

(where 5.945% = the annual € denominated interest rate for a six-month term – from now to end June)

We would either need to use surplus funds that we have to buy the euros (which seems unlikely given our short-term cash flow problems), or borrow money in order to finance the purchase. As a consequence we will incur interest at a market sterling rate (5.505% pa) if we borrow the money, or suffer a reduction in our interest income at our investment rate of return. A money market hedge has a similar effect to a forward contract, fixing the effective rate of exchange for a future transaction/payment.

• (4) Forward contract

We could buy the euros that we will need to make the payment using a forward contract. This would fix the exchange rate for the transaction. It would minimise our exposure to losses but would also mean that we would be unable to take advantage of any favourable movements in the exchange rate as the contract must be exercised irrespective of the spot rate at the time.

✓ As we expect a significant fall in the value of sterling against the euro over the next six months, we are not expecting a favourable movement in the rate (stronger sterling). As a hedge against the short-term risk a forward contract would seem the simplest and most effective hedge.

We can fix the forward rate at 1.3051, meaning that the cost of the €90m will be about £69.0m, rather than the £71.80m we would expect to pay if our prediction of the spot rate at the end of June is correct.

(5) Currency futures

Instead of arranging a forward contract to buy the euros, we could deal in sterling-euro futures. However this seems unnecessarily complicated, since we know the amount and timing of the payment we shall be making, and with futures there is an inconvenience of making margin payments to the futures exchange.

(6) Currency option

We could also buy an option to buy euros at a stated rate on payment of a premium which would then allow us to benefit from the option in the case of unfavourable exchange rate movements and to let the option lapse and use the market rates where there were favourable exchange rate movements.

Buying an option fixes a worst possible rate of exchange, while allowing the option holder to benefit if the spot price at expiry is more favourable than the option exercise price.

Since we are predicting an increase in the value of the euro over the next six months, an option would be unnecessarily expensive. It should only be considered a possible strategy if there is a reasonable chance that sterling will increase in value against the euro in the next six months. On the basis of our current expectations, this is highly unlikely.

matching asset and liabilities

Interest rate risk

If Delta has to borrow to finance the purchase of the land and the longer-term construction of the shopping centre, it will be exposed to interest rate risk. If it borrows in euros, it will be exposed to both interest rate risk and currency risk.

Interest rate risk is unavoidable. It is probably more obvious when borrowing at a variable rate of interest, because any rise or fall in the interest rate will result in higher or lower interest payments. There is also risk in borrowing at a fixed rate, because a fixed rate borrower loses the opportunity • to benefit from any fall in interest rates (as well as protecting himself against risk from higher rates).

With large loans, interest rate can be significant. For example a change in interest rates of 1% (100 basis points) on a loan of €90m implies a change of €900,000 in annual interest costs.

My recommendation, in the event that the company has to borrow to finance its French investment, would be to use interest rate swaps to manage the risk. Swaps can be used to shift between effective fixed rate and floating rate liabilities, in response to changing conditions in the debt markets.

A further possibility that may be considered, in the event that the board of Delta chooses to borrow long-term in euros, would be a currency swap between sterling and euros for the period of time between borrowing in euros and opening the shopping centre and earning revenues in euros. Interest obligations in euros could be swapped for obligations in sterling.

Share price risk

We bought 20m shares on 30 September 20X7 at £9 per share at a total cost of £180m. We are exposed to the risk of the share price going down, which may happen in 20X8 given market sentiment. On 31 December 20X7, the value of the shares has reached £10 per share creating a profit of £20m which we may wish to protect. We are not concerned by further appreciation in the shares as this is the outcome we are hoping for.

Whether we wish to protect ourselves against a fall in the share price depends on whether the board intends to hold the shares for a long time rather than sell them at a suitable opportunity, and whether the board is concerned about the implications of a falling share price on profit or loss (as discussed earlier in these notes).

As a protection against loss of market value in the short term, the company could use stock options, and buying put options on 20m Lambda shares. Put option contracts at an exercise price of £10 would give us a right to sell the shares at a price of £10 per share. We would do this if the market price of the shares is less than £10 at expiry date for the options. The current premium per share is £0.745 for put options on Lambda shares expiring on 31 December 20X8 at an exercise price of £10. So the cost of the premium will be £14.9m.

The intrinsic value of the option (ie the exercise price less the price per share of stock, times the number of shares specified in the option contract) is zero at acquisition. This is because the exercise price chosen is equal to the current market price. The cost of £14.9m reflects the time value of the option which depends on the time to expiry, the price of the stock and its volatility.

If the stock price falls below £10 the put option becomes in-the-money by the amount below the £10 strike price times the number of shares under option. For instance, if the price of Lambda stock fell to £9.50, the intrinsic value gain on the put option is £0.50 per share. If the stock price rises and stays above £10 for the term of the contract, the put option expires worthless to the buyer because it is out-of-the-money. We would lose the premium which is kept by the issuer of the option.

At a cost of £14.9m, we would be protecting ourselves against the effects of a fall in the share price, and the protection would amount to £10m for a fall of £0.50 in the price to £9.50 and £30m if the share price falls to £8.50.

So if the share price falls just £0.50 in the time to expiry of the options, the hedging strategy would produce a net loss of £4.9m. If the share price fell to £8.50, the hedging strategy would yield a net gain of £15.1m.

(d) **Accounting effects of the hedging strategies**

Exchange rate hedges: borrow euros at end of June 20X8

There would be minimal impact in our accounts prior to the loan being drawn down (any costs would be likely to be rolled up into the borrowings). On drawing down the loan it would be translated into sterling at the spot rate on the day (anticipated to be 1.2534 giving a value of £71,804,691) and then retranslated at each reporting date (being a monetary liability) with movements charged to profit or loss. The land is a non-monetary asset and would therefore be translated at the spot rate (as above) and retained in the accounts at this value.

Exchange rate hedges: money market hedge *(MMH)*

The money market hedge would give rise to similar accounting treatments compared to the matching points above but earlier as the loan will be taken out now in pounds and invested in euros. The euro foreign currency is a monetary item which will be translated at the spot exchange rate on 31 December 20X7 (being 1.3034 giving a value of £67,084,866 as per the payable that we have already recognised) and then retranslated at any subsequent reporting date or settlement. The exchange rate movement in this foreign currency asset will exactly offset the exchange rate movement on the payable and both the exchange gain and the exchange loss will be recognised in profit or loss giving no net profit effect at any point. Interest income on the euros and interest expense on the sterling loan will be accounted for in profit or loss in 20X8.

accounting treatment of MMH nil impact on profit

Exchange rate hedges: forward contract

The forward contract is a derivative. Derivatives are shown at their fair value with differences being recorded in profit or loss. The forward contract requires no initial investment and so no accounting is required on the purchase date of 31 December 20X7.

At the end of June the payable is adjusted to fair value of £71,804,691 based on the current spot rate (1.2534 €/£), and the corresponding loss of £2,754,515 is recognised in profit or loss.

The gain on the forward contract of £2,844,458 is the change in the fair value of the contract during the period, (£71,804,691 – £68,960,233) and is also recognised in profit or loss. The company settles the payable and the forward contract net.

Hedging of stock market risk

Without resorting to any of the hedge accounting rules within IAS 39 we would continue to hold the shares as available-for-sale assets (movements in fair value through other comprehensive income) and the derivative would be revalued each reporting period and the movements recorded in profit and loss.

IAS 39 allows special treatment when there is a relationship between a hedged item (in this case the shares) and a hedging instrument (the put option). In this case the relationship is that of a fair value hedge as we are trying to mitigate risks associated with the change in the value of the shares due to the movement in the share price.

However, in order to utilise the hedge accounting rules of IAS 39, it is not enough to state that there is a relationship between two items, we need to ensure that the qualifying criteria are met.

Conclusion on hedging stock market risk

Basing the scenario on the figures provided as you suggested, the conclusions are as follows:

If we choose not to hedge the position and the shares fall to £170m as expected we stand to lose £10m compared to our original purchase price. However, hedging these with a put option we can expect to make a net gain of £5.1m resulting from the gain on the security of £20m which occurred up to December 20X7 year end and the cost of the option of £14.9m.

(e) **Possible acquisition of Boolonga Construction**

A DCF evaluation can be applied to the possible acquisition of BC, using the assumptions given and a cost of capital of 12%.

It is assumed that the initial purchase price will be £40m, and that the acquisition should be evaluated in terms of its return in £ sterling rather than Australian dollars.

ICAEW

It is also assumed that since expected inflation in Australia is 3.5% and in the UK it is 2%, the Australian dollar will depreciate in value against sterling by a factor of (1.02/1.035) each year. This means that although BC earnings are expected to increase by 5% per annum, the growth rate in sterling dividends for Delta will be just 1.05 × 1.02/1.035 = 0.0348 or 3.48%, say 3.5%.

- A further assumption is that the acquisition will occur on 1 January 20X8. As a purchase would be expected to be completed within three months of now, this assumption would seem to be acceptable.

On the basis of 20X7 expectations, earnings of BC will be A$9m. Retained earnings will be (40%) A$3.6m, and dividends will be A$5.4m. If these were paid in dividends to Delta, the sterling value of the dividends would be (A$5.4m/1.50) £3.6m.

At a cost of capital of 12%, and assuming annual growth in dividends of 3.5% in perpetuity, the value of BC equity for Delta would be:

$$\frac{£3.6\,m \times 1.035}{(0.12 - 0.035)} = £43.835m \ (= A\$65.753m \text{ at the current exchange rate}).$$

Since the cost of the shares would be A$60m or £40m, the NPV of the expected acquisition would be + £3.835m.

In financial terms, on the basis of the assumptions used, the acquisition of BC would appear to be a worthwhile investment.

Strategic implications

Delta has decided on a strategy of growth through diversification, but its focus has been on Britain and, more recently, France. Although BC is in the construction industry, its location in Australia means that for Delta the acquisition would represent significant further diversification. It is most unlikely that there will be any synergy benefits from the acquisition and BC will operate in an entirely different (geographical) part of the construction industry.

A concern for the board of Delta is that by bringing completely different businesses within the same group, the group will in effect be a conglomerate, without any clear logical reason for its existence. This could make it the target for acquisition and break-up at some time in the future.

Risk implications

There would be substantial risks with an acquisition of BC.

Given the distance between Australia and Britain, there will be problems of management control. Senior management in the UK will presumably want to monitor and control the Australian business, but this will be very difficult at an operational level. In the short term, it may be necessary to appoint a senior British executive in Delta to a senior management position in BC, with a seat on the BC board. Even so, close control over the operations of BC will be difficult.

With any acquisition there are problems with merging two different cultures within the same group. It seems probable that, in the short term at least, BC will retain its own culture and management style, making it difficult to integrate the company closely into the Delta group.

The owners of BC plan to retire. We do not know about succession planning within BC, and whether there are senior executives within BC who have been 'groomed' to take over the running of the company. Unless successors to the senior management positions have been identified, there may also be problems with the transition of BC to new leadership at a local level (as well as at the Britain-Australia international level).

The board of Delta will no doubt assess the risk implications of an acquisition of BC, but the acquisition would possibly add about £3m to Delta's value. In the context of Delta's overall value, this is a relatively small amount. The costs of the acquisition, in terms of management time and effort as well as the financial cost, should be weighed against the potential financial benefits.

12 Rafford plc

Marking guide

		Marks Up to
(a)	Financial performance of Rafford	
	Comments	5
	Calculations	5
(b)	Valuation of Rafford	
	Comments	8
	Calculations	6
(c)	Valuation of Otnes	
	Comments	5
	Calculations	5
(d)	Accounting treatment and explanation of pension amounts	
	Comments	7
	Calculations	4
Total marks		45
Maximum marks		40

Notes on Rafford plc and Otnes plc

Prepared for: Tilliam Well
Prepared by: XXXX
Date: XX/XX/XXXX

Four issues have been raised:

- Financial performance of Rafford
- Valuation of Rafford
- Comparison with Otnes
- Accounting treatment of pension schemes

In dealing with the analysis of Rafford's performance (and that of Otnes) it is important to take account of the operating segments into which the two companies are organised.

(a) Financial performance of Rafford

op profit (M + absolute)

Rafford's profit from operations, a key performance measure, has increased by 75% ((63/36) – 1), when its revenue has increased by 66% ((1,410/851) – 1), implying an increase in net margin. In 20X7 the net margin was 4.5% (63/1,410) and in 20X6 it was 4.2% (36/851).

But both years are affected by profits on sales and leasebacks less restructuring costs and 20X7 by a change to the terms of its final salary pension scheme which cannot be repeated in the future. Stripping these net credits out of operating profit results in the following:

	20X7 £m	20X6 £m
Profit from operations	63	36
Less: sale and leaseback profits	(4)	(4)
pension scheme curtailment gain	(15)	–
Add restructuring costs	2	2
Adjusted profit from operations	46	34
Revenue	1,410	851
Adjusted net margin	3.3%	4.0%

* exceptional items were distorting the margins

ICAEW

So on this basis Rafford's performance was worse this year (20X7) than last year.

But Rafford has made substantial acquisitions in both years, so to obtain a clearer insight into like-for-like performance:

- adjustments should be made to the 20X6 results to include the effect of the 20X6 acquisitions for the full year.

- adjustments should be made to the 20X7 results to exclude the effect of the 20X7 acquisitions.

[handwritten margin note: adjusting to compare like for like.]

The results will then reflect only those businesses which were owned by Rafford for the whole of the two-year period.

This analysis is best made for the two operating segments separately

	Construction 20X7 £m	House building 20X7 £m	Construction 20X6 £m	House building 20X6 £m
Revenue				
Per financial statements	1,069	340	626	224
Less re 20X7 acquisition	(66)	–		
Add re 20X6 acquisition			249	29
Adjusted revenue (A)	1,003	340	875	253
Profit from operations				
Per financial statements	17	39	11	31
Less re 20X7 acquisition	(3)			
Add re 20X6 acquisition			3	3
Adjusted profit from operations (B)	14	39	14	34
Adjusted net margin (B/A)	1.4%	11.5%	1.6%	13.4%

[handwritten margin note: actually → has done badly in X7.]

Analysis on this annualised basis confirms that Rafford has done less well in 20X7 than in 20X6, even in its very low margin construction business.

This raises the question as to why Rafford is making acquisitions in both years in the low-margin construction business.

(b) **Valuation of Rafford**

It is not usual to value a business by reference to its revenue. Earnings or dividends are a more normal basis of valuation.

Tutorial note:

A valuation based on a multiple of EBITDA or free cash flow might be preferable, but information to make valuations on these bases is not available.

The realistic market price of a share can be derived from a valuation of estimated future dividends. The value of a share will be the present value of all future expected dividends on the shares, discounted at the shareholders' cost of capital.

Alternatively, but using the same logic, the value of a share can be said to be the present value of all earnings available for distribution to the shareholders (potential dividends or increases in the share price).

On these bases Rafford is valued:

- On a price/earnings ratio calculated as:

    - Earnings (profit for the year)   £44m
    - Weighted average shares in issue   305m
    - Earnings per share 14.4p (44/305)
    - P/E ratio of 3.7 (53/14.4)

- On a dividend yield of 5.7% (3p as a percentage of 53p)

Both of these show a weaker valuation than for Otnes plc (see next).

There are a number of factors which contribute to this low valuation, many of which may be seen as different aspects of the business being in a period of rapid change. Visibility of forward earnings prospects is usually quite poor when businesses are changing rapidly; this leads to lowered valuations.

- Rafford has increased its share capital very substantially over the last two years. The end-20X7 capital is £210m (£19m share capital and £191m share premium). The statement of changes in equity shows that capital has been increased by share issues totalling £191m (144 + 47) over the two years.

- Rafford is growing very quickly by acquisition. The goodwill acquired in the 20X6 and 20X7 business combinations can be calculated as:

	Consideration	Net assets acquired	Goodwill
	£m	£m	£m
20X6 acquisitions	101	44	57
20X7 acquisitions	111	59	52
			109

These are the amounts carried in the 20X6 and 20X7 statements of financial position, which imply that Rafford has only been making acquisitions in the last two years.

Visibility of forward earnings prospects is usually quite poor when substantial acquisitions are being made. Management may be confident about future prospects, but investors often are not.

- Rafford is making acquisitions in both years in the very low margin construction business. Businesses usually try to improve margins by acquisitions, not reduce them.

- The substantial increase in the carrying amount of land held for development is putting increasing pressure on Rafford's current asset/liability position:

		20X7	20X6
		£m	£m
Current assets	A	1,024	490
Less land held for development		(548)	(209)
	B	476	281
Less developments in progress		(157)	(75)
	C	319	206
Current liabilities	D	711	353
A:D		1.44:1	1.39:1
B:D		0.67:1	0.80:1
C:D		0.45:1	0.58:1

- Profitability is poor. The low net margins in the two segments have already been referred to. The 20X7 return on capital employed is also poor (particularly when the one-off net credits have been stripped out) and shows a sharp fall compared to the previous year:

	20X7	20X6
	£m	£m
Return = adjusted profit from operations (as above)	46	34
Borrowings: non-current	88	2
current	50	4
Cash and cash equivalents	(40)	(22)
Net debt/(cash)	98	(16)
Equity	307	120
Capital employed	405	104
Return on capital employed	11.4%	32.7%

[handwritten margin note: ROCE calculation]

The 20X7 acquisition took place late in the year (the revenue included of £66m is roughly a quarter of the total attributable to it for the year (£66m + £175m)). If this acquisition had been made at the start of the year, the profit from operations would have been £10m higher; the return on capital employed on this basis would be 13.8% ((46 + 10) as % of 405), still less than half that of 20X6. Investors would be right to be concerned about such a deterioration in profitability over a single year.

- Gearing is not a reason for the low valuation. Rafford had net cash at the end of 20X6 and net debt as a percentage of equity was only 32% (98 as a percentage of 307) at the end of 20X7.

Asset based valuation, Rafford:

Net assets per statement of financial position: £307m

An asset-based valuation method is often used for companies whose value can be accurately reflected by the value of the assets held, for example, property development companies. For many companies, there are sources of value which are not reflected in the statement of financial position (for example, brands, staff expertise) and so this method undervalues the business. It is sometimes used, therefore, to obtain a minimum valuation. In Rafford's case, its current market value (380m × 53p = £201.4m) is way below its net asset value.

It would be useful to have information about the market values of its assets and liabilities, and it may be appropriate to make an estimate of future losses, given the current problems and uncertainty in the property market.

request MV for A + L.

However, on the strength of the information provided, it would appear that the share price may reflect an underestimate of Rafford's value, for the reasons outlined above.

Other useful information:

- Market value of assets

- Existence and value of intangibles

- More detailed analysis of profits between ordinary recurring items and exceptional one-off items, which may have distorted the profits in individual years

- Details of costs or income that may be avoided or lost if a significant stake in the company is acquired, such as directors' remuneration

- More detailed/reliable growth forecasts

- Detailed risk analysis

- Cash flow details, to obtain a more fundamental cash-based valuation

Summary

Rafford operates in two business segments, house building and construction. House building provided a net margin (after adjustments) of 11.5% in 20X7, down from 13.4% in the previous year. Construction achieved a wafer-thin margin of 1.4%, marginally down on the previous year.

Rafford has expanded very quickly by acquisition in the last two years, which are centred on the low margin construction business.

With poor forward visibility and low profitability, the market is putting a low value on this company.

(c) **Valuation of Otnes**

The more usual bases show that Otnes is valued as follows:

- On a price/earnings ratio calculated as:
    - Earnings 20X7: £28m
    - Shares in issue 150m
    - Earnings per share 18.7p (28/150)
    - P/E ratio of 8.0 (149/18.7)

- On a dividend yield of 2.2% (3.3p as a percentage of 149p)

Both measures together indicate that the market appears to value Otnes more highly than Rafford.

There are a number of reasons:

- There have been no share issues for Otnes during either year, so its business is not changing so rapidly.

- There is no specific mention about acquisitions or the absence of them, but the fact that the carrying amount of goodwill is the same at both year ends indicates that there have been none in 20X7 at least.

- Profit from operations has increased by 20% ((36/30) – 1), when its revenue has increased by 42% ((142/100) – 1), implying a decrease in net margin. In 20X7 the net margin is 25.4% (36/142) and in 20X6 30.0% (30/100). The margins achieved by Otnes are very much higher than those of Rafford, suggesting a less risky as well as relatively more profitable business.

Because one of Otnes's segments is property development it will aim to make gains on its investment properties. So it is safe to leave the investment property gains on disposal and increases in fair value in as part of the recurring annual profit.

- The relative profitability of the two operating segments can be calculated as:

	Property and land 20X7 £m	Construction 20X7 £m	Property and land 20X6 £m	Construction 20X6 £m
Revenue (A)	81	61	43	57
Profit from operations (B)	35	6	29	6
Net margin ((B) as % of (A))	43.2%	9.8%	67.4%	10.5%

The development business is clearly very profitable. The construction business is less so, but it is much more profitable than the construction operations of Rafford.

- Otnes' return on capital employed can be calculated as:

	20X7 £m	20X6 £m
Profit from operations	36	30
Borrowings: non-current	28	20
current	3	4
Cash and cash equivalents	(15)	(3)
Net debt	16	21
Equity	139	116
Capital employed	155	137
Return on capital employed	23.2%	21.9%

The return has improved slightly.

- Gearing is not a problem, being 11.5% (16 / 139) at the end of 20X7 and 18.1% (21 / 116) at the end of 20X6.

- The carrying amount of land held for development is not putting much pressure on Otnes's current asset/liability position:

		20X7 £m	20X6 £m
Current assets	A	127	110
Less land held for development		(50)	(38)
	B	77	72
Less developments in progress		(45)	(50)
	C	32	22
Current liabilities	D	59	54
A:D		2.15:1	2.04:1
B:D		1.31:1	1.33:1
C:D		0.54:1	0.41:1

- There are substantial amounts of property in the course of construction held within property, plant and equipment (PPE). Perhaps in the future this property will be classified as investment property. If this is the case, there could well be substantial investment property gains to be recognised in the coming years.

Asset-based valuation of Otnes

Net assets per statement of financial position: £139m

For the reasons discussed above, the net asset value is likely to be a significant underestimate of the market value of the company.

Summary

Otnes operates in two business segments, property and land, and construction. Property and land provides very attractive margins, while construction achieves lower margins.

Otnes is concentrating on organic growth, since there have been no acquisitions in the last two years.

With good forward visibility and high profitability, the market is putting a high value on this company.

(d) **Accounting treatment of pension schemes**

The liability for retirement benefits is the difference between the actuarial measurement of the obligation to employees and the assets in the retirement scheme to meet that obligation.

Both amounts are rather volatile, for various reasons.

- The values of pension fund assets change as a result of changes in the market prices of the investments that the pension fund holds. Often these are shares and bonds (corporate bonds and government bonds), whose values can move by relatively large amounts within a financial period.

- The obligation changes as a result of increases in life expectancy; salary increases (on which the pension is based) being different from those previously expected; and employee turnover (and therefore length of pensionable service) being different from that previously expected.

- The present value of the obligation is arrived at by discounting the estimated future liability. Under current accounting standards the discount rate used should be based on the yields offered by high quality corporate bonds (normally AA-rated). If market interest rates move then the discount rate used by companies to value their future liabilities will also move: a fall in the discount rate would result in an increase in the present value of a fixed future cash amount. There is some balance built into the system however: economic factors which cause interest rates to fall often also cause the value of assets that the pension fund invests in (such as equities and bonds) to rise – so the net liability (or asset) may well change by less than would otherwise be expected.

- The actuary's expectations of interest on plan assets and on the liability may not match with the actual interest. This is referred to as the 're-measurement (actuarial) difference'. Gains on re-measurement in one period may be reversed by losses in the immediately following period as the actuary's estimates are updated.

- The question of affordability of final salary pension schemes is one that has been widely discussed recently, and it is true that there has to be some doubt over whether the amounts disclosed by companies in general today are an accurate estimate of the true value of future payments.

IAS 19 *Employee Benefits* (revised 2011) stipulates that re-measurement losses **must** be recognised in other comprehensive income in the period in which they arise. This eliminates volatility from the statement of profit or loss section of the statement of profit or loss and other comprehensive income, but does not eliminate it altogether.

It will be necessary to adjust Otnes's financial statements onto the same basis as Rafford's to conform with IAS 19, by recognising all gains in the year they arise, but in the 'other comprehensive income' section of the statement of profit or loss and other comprehensive income.

Adjustments to Otnes results:

	20X7 £m	20X6 £m
Profit from operations		
Per financial statements	36	30
Remove gains recognised in year	(7)	(5)
Adjusted profit from operations	29	25
Profit for the year per financial statements	28	24
Remove gains recognised in year as above	(7)	(5)
	21	19
Other comprehensive income per financial statements	–	–
Gains recognised in the year	7	5
Other comprehensive income for the year	7	5
Total comprehensive income for the year	28	24

13 Connor Construction plc

		Marks Up to
(a)	Financial reporting profit on Muldovian contract	8
(b)	NPV	7
(c)	Financial and operating risks	6
(d)	CSR issues relating to proposed contract	9
(e)	Advice on project viability	5
(f)	Steve Verdy tax	7
Total marks		42
Maximum marks		40

(a) **Profit**

PROFIT CALCULATION	20X2	20X3	20X4	20X5	Total
Exchange rates – constant	$	$	$	$	
Revenue	22,000,000	22,000,000	22,000,000	22,000,000	
Cash operating costs (in $)	11,000,000	11,000,000	11,000,000	11,000,000	
Cash operating costs initially incurred in £ (expressed in $ @ $2:£1)	4,000,000	4,000,000	4,000,000	4,00,0000	
Depreciation	3,000,000	3,000,000	3,000,000	3,000,000	
Operating profit	4,000,000	4,000,000	4,000,000	4,000,000	
Tax 30%	1,200,000	1,200,000	1,200,000	1,200,000	
Profit after tax	2,800,000	2,800,000	2,800,000	2,800,000	
	£	£	£	£	£
Convert to £s constant XR	1,400,000	1,400,000	1,400,000	1,400,000	5,600,000

Recognition of revenue and profit

Revenue and profit should be recognised by reference to the stage of completion (assuming no major problems arise over the period of the contracting). The timing of the cash flow does not determine the timing of profit or revenue recognition.

The stage of completion is currently determined according to IAS 11 *Construction Contracts*. In general the standard permits the timing of revenue recognition to be according to: contract costs incurred; surveys of work performed; or completion of physical proportion. In this case, the completion of physical proportion would be inappropriate as each section of the road is not equivalent and the contract recognises that some sections of road will be priced more highly than others. The overall price reflects the increased difficulty of the final 5 kilometres and this is also reflected in the timing of costs incurred. Revenue is therefore recognised equally in each of the four years of the contract which is in line with costs incurred.

Exchange rates

With constant exchange rates there is no issue of exchange rate movements as £1=$2 is used throughout.

(b) **NPVs**

NET PRESENT VALUE

	20X1 $	20X2 $	20X3 $	20X4 $	20X5 $	Total $
Outlay	-12,000,000					
Receipts		18,000,000	18,000,000	18,000,000	34,000,000	
Cash operating costs incurred in $		-11,000,000	-11,000,000	-11,000,000	-11,000,000	
Tax		-1,200,000	-1,200,000	-1,200,000	-1,200,000	
Net cash flow in $	-12,000,000	5,800,000	5,800,000	5,800,000	21,800,000	

(1) **Constant XR**

	20X1 £	20X2 £	20X3 £	20X4 £	20X5 £	£
Convert $ cash flows to £s at constant XR ($2:£1)	-6,000,000	2,900,000	2,900,000	2,900,000	10,900,000	
Less op cash costs incurred in £s		-2,000,000	-2,000,000	-2,000,000	-2,000,000	
Net cash flow £ (constant XR)	-6,000,000	900,000	900,000	900,000	8,900,000	
DF @ 10%	1	0.909091	0.826446	0.751315	0.683013	
NPV (constant XR)	-6,000,000	818,181.8	743,801.7	676,183.3	6,078,820	**2,316,987**

(2) **Depreciating XR**

	20X1	20X2	20X3	20X4	20X5	
Exchange rate (year end cash flows)		0.45	0.405	0.3645	0.32805	
Convert to £s	-6,000,000	2,610,000	2,349,000	2,114,100	7,151,490	
Less op cash costs in £s		-2,000,000	-2,000,000	-2,000,000	-2,000,000	
Net cash flow	-6,000,000	610,000	349,000	114,100	5,151,490	
DF @10%	1	0.909091	0.826446	0.751315	0.683013	
NPV (depreciating XR)	-6,000,000	554,545.5	288,429.8	85,725.02	3,518,537	-1,552,763
Expected NPV						**£382,112**

ALTERNATIVE PRESENTATION

	20X1	20X2	20X3	20X4	20X5	
Expected net cash flow (0.5 × net CF constant XR) + (0.5 × net CF depreciating XR)	-6,000,000	755,000	624,500	507,050	7,025,745	
DF @ 10%	1	0.909091	0.826446	0.751315	0.683013	
NPV	-6,000,000	686,363.6	516,115.7	380,954.2	4,798,678	
Expected NPV						**£382,112**

(c) **Financial and operating risks**

Financial risks

With constant exchange rates the project generates a positive NPV of £2,316,987. However if exchange rates depreciate by 10% per year then a negative NPV of £1,552,763 is expected. There is therefore a 50% probability of the project generating a significant negative NPV which is a major risk.

In addition it has been assumed that a 10% discount rate applies. However this is for UK projects of equivalent operational risk and would therefore not build in the additional risk of foreign currency fluctuations. A higher discount rate may therefore be appropriate for foreign projects to compensate for this risk which would lower NPVs.

Non-payment risk may be substantial. The government of Muldovia is dependent on the World Bank. The project financing is dependent on meeting any conditions in the agreement with the World Bank (eg quality, employment, environmental) and if these conditions are not satisfied then there may not be enough cash to pay CC. Even with the World Bank's help there is a possibility that the Muldovian government may choose to default.

In the early years there is significant liquidity risk. The net cash surplus is only £900,000 in each of the first three years of the project. This is not even sufficient to cover the initial outlay of £6m which is only recovered in the final year with the large terminal payment (ie the payback period is 4 years).

While estimates have been made of exchange rate variations, these may vary more substantially than expected. A key risk is that the Republicans are elected and the depreciation of the currency is greater than 10%, particularly in the early years of the contract. However, even if the Democratic Party is elected there may still be some currency depreciation against the £.

A further risk is that there will be inflation in Muldovia which may increase costs. This is particularly true if the Democratic Party is elected and there is a looser monetary policy with lower interest rates. At the moment, the assumption is that costs are constant over the period (or that 10% is a real interest rate). If inflation is significant this would increase costs, but not revenues as it is a fixed price contract.

Operating risks

The project is of significant size so the risk is likely to be material.

A key operating risk is if delays occur (eg due to unforeseen problems with the terrain). This is a particular risk in this case, as a large proportion of the payment is received towards the end of the contract. As a consequence, if the project is delayed, and therefore this payment is delayed, then the present value of the terminal payment would fall substantially.

In addition, problems in completion may cause cost overruns. With the contract being fixed price any cost overrun would reduce profit by an equivalent amount.

Risk mitigation

Financial risks

A key financial risk to mitigate is the exchange rate risk. This can be hedged in a number of ways in order to avoid a 50% probability of a negative NPV.

One method would be to borrow in $ to finance the outlay, in order to hedge finance costs in $ against net cash receipts to be generated in $. A money market hedge could however go further than this. This is achieved by borrowing an amount which, with interest on this loan, will be equivalent to the net cash receivable in $. This is then converted to £s and then invested. When the net cash amounts are received in $, they are then used to repay the $ loan with accrued interest.

Alternatively, the currency risk could be hedged by a forward contract to sell $. This locks in the $ amount of the net $ receipts to the forward exchange rates. This may however be costly given the long period of the contract and the expected volatility in the exchange rate.

Similarly, an option contract with the right to sell $ would achieve a similar result but would be even more costly given the volatility expected. It would however not bind CC into the exchange rate if the $ strengthened.

In terms of non payment risk then financial due diligence needs to be carried out on the Muldovian government (eg credit rating on sovereign debt) and on the terms of the contract, including the role and conditions of the World Bank.

The possibility of insurance could be investigated regarding default on the Muldovian Government debt to CC.

Operating risks

It is important to carry out operational due diligence on the terrain and feasibility of the project. This needs to be completed in some detail in order to consider the possibility of unforeseen delays or obstacles that may cause problems.

Also, consideration could be given to negotiating the terms of the contract as a condition of acceptance. This may include contingency payments for unforeseen operational problems that are not the fault of CC.

(d) **Corporate social responsibility issues**

Corporate social responsibility (CSR) is a business's responsibility to be accountable to all its stakeholders (including investors, employees, communities and suppliers) and to society as a whole. *] Defⁿ CSR*

＊ Behaving in a socially responsible manner demands that Connor manages the economic, social and environmental impacts of its activities to **maximise the benefits** and **minimise the negative side effects**. Equally, CSR means that Connor should take account of **social costs** and **benefits** when it is fulfilling its economic duties, and therefore these social considerations should be taken into account, alongside financial considerations, when Connor decides whether or not to accept the contract.

CSR issues arising from the construction project

Minimising environmental impact – Connor's policy is to ensure that the environmental impact resulting from the construction process in its projects is minimised.

In this project, environmental campaigners have highlighted that the proposed route for the road cuts through the habitat of several rare plant species, and also threatens a site of archaeological interest. There appears to be a high profile campaign against the construction of the road, and so Connor could suffer some negative publicity attached to this if it carries out the work.

There will, almost inevitably, be some negative environment impact from building a road. However, the issue here appears to arise mainly from the route the government has chosen from the road, rather than Connor's construction practices. If the government has a democratic mandate, then this would strengthen the case for Connor to act in accordance with its wishes. As such, we could argue Connor is carrying out its work in a socially responsible manner, if the techniques it uses in the construction of the highway are designed to minimise their impact on the environment. However, this is unlikely to reverse any public opinion about the negative environmental impact of the project.

Another potential environmental issue to consider is the impact that building the highway could have on vehicle emissions in the longer term. The new highway will help to link two important industrial towns in Muldovia. It is not clear how many vehicles currently drive between the two towns, and what route they use. However, if a large number of vehicles make the journey and the new road will make the journey shorter and more fuel efficient, construction of the highway could lead to an overall reduction in vehicle emissions, which could benefit the environment in the longer term.

Economic benefits of project – From an economic perspective, it appears that there will be considerable benefits to Muldovia as a whole from the construction of the road. Therefore, Connor could argue that building the road is socially responsible on the grounds of the benefits it brings to society as a whole.

Labour standards and health and safety – In general terms, Connor's policy of using local contractors and suppliers helps provide economic benefits to the communities in which it works. However, in this case, if contractors are taking on inexperienced staff this could create problems for Connor. If there is an accident on one of the sites, there could be significant adverse publicity for Connor – even if the accident was caused by one of the sub-contractors, and if the sub-contractor was operating within the local health and safety regulations.

If Connor does accept the contract, it would be advisable to require all the sub-contractors to operate to Connor's own health and safety regulations – even if these are more stringent that the legal minimum in Muldovia. Equally, Connor should obtain assurance that any sub-contractors it uses are employing suitably skilled and experienced staff.

Local communities – Assuming the highway is built along the route which is currently being proposed, then its construction will lead to several villages being destroyed.

Although this problem is ultimately caused by the route of the highway, rather than any decisions taken by Connor, it could be difficult to reconcile the destruction of the villages with Connor's latest CSR report which claims it brings benefits to the communities in which it works. It seems unlikely that destroying the villages can bring any benefits to them, especially as the government is only intending to offer a very low level of compensation to the people whose homes are being destroyed.

As well as CSR issues, the ethical principle of integrity could be at stake here, if Connor is perceived to be acting in a way – or to be associated with a project – which is inconsistent with the claims of its CSR report.

It is possible that Connor could try to persuade the government to change some of the detail in the route of the highway, or increase the compensation they pay the villagers, but since a decision needs to be made on the contract very soon, it seems unlikely there will be time for any such discussions before we have to decide whether or not to accept the contract.

Shareholder wealth – Despite the environmentalists' concerns, it appears that the government is going to go ahead and build the road, regardless of whether Connor is the lead contractor or whether a competitor accepts the contract.

Connor has to consider its economic obligations to its investors as well as the environmental interests. Connor is a listed company, and so it has a duty to its owners to maximise their wealth. As such, if the contract is strongly profitable and operationally viable, those considerations would be valid arguments in favour of accepting the project.

However, if the financial benefits of the project are only marginal, then the negative social and environmental impact could equally be valid arguments which support a decision not to accept it and may enhance reputation and therefore long term profitability.

(e) **Viability**

Overall, while the contract generates a positive expected NPV at a 10% discount rate, there are serious risks involved in acceptance which may not be fully reflected in using the same 10% rate applying to UK projects.

Given the NPV is small then it is likely to be sensitive to an increase in the discount rate (also the main cash inflow is at the end of the contract which increases the sensitivity of the NPV to changes in the discount rate).

Some consideration of the appropriateness of the 10% discount rate should therefore be carried out. However on the face of it, 10% seems understated for the level of risk and therefore despite the apparent positive NPV this project would seem to be of undue risk to be accepted.

As a sensitivity estimate, a recalculation of the NPV at 12% shows a negative NPV of £2,150 and it is therefore (given the likely risk premium required in Muldovia compared to the UK) probable that this project should be rejected.

The potential corporate social responsibility issues linked to the environmental impact of the highway and the destruction of villages during its construction would also support the argument to reject the project. If there were more time available to work with the government to look at possible ways to minimise the impact of the highway, then it might be possible to resolve some of the CSR issues. However, the fact that a decision needs to be made very soon, suggests the necessary time is not available, and therefore we should not accept the project.

(f) **Tax implications for Steve Verdy**

Steve is UK resident and in principle this means that he will be taxed on worldwide income in the UK and receive credit relief for income tax suffered on overseas earnings.

Leaving in January 20X2 for 15 months

In this case, Steve will not be resident for 20X2/X3 if he meets the full-time work overseas test throughout the tax year. This would mean working at least 35 hours a week overseas, with no significant breaks of more than 30 days, and should have less than the permitted 30 workdays in the UK during this period. The total days spent in the UK in the tax year must also be less than 91 days.

If he also meets these requirements (with the various limits pro-rated) for the parts of 20X1/X2 and 20X3/X4 when he is working overseas, split year treatment will apply. This will mean that he is treated as non-UK resident from the date on which he starts working in Muldovia in January 20X2, and will become UK resident on the day after his last day of work overseas.

On the assumption that he does meet the requirements to be treated as non-resident, any non-UK source income relating to the period in which he is not UK resident (including all of his remuneration relating to his overseas work) would not be subject to income tax, and the tax liability on UK source investment income (excluding UK property income) will be limited to the tax deducted at source.

Chargeable gains realised while he is not UK resident are not immediately taxable, but as he will be non-resident for a period of less than five years any gains realised while he is non-UK resident on assets which he holds when he ceases to be UK resident will be taxed in the year of his return.

Leaving in July 20X2 for 15 months

In this case, Steve will not meet the requirements for the full time work overseas test for an entire tax year. There is therefore no tax year in which he is automatically treated as non-UK resident.

Instead, he will meet the requirements of the automatic UK residency tests for both 20X2/X3 and 20X3/X4, as he will be working full time in the UK for part of each year, and in each case it will be part of a period of UK work which lasts for at least 365 days (although in both cases only part of the period falls within the relevant tax year). He will therefore be regarded as UK resident.

The split year rules cannot apply here as he is not non-resident for an entire tax year.

Under this scenario, Steve remains subject to UK income tax and capital gains tax on all of his income and gains for the whole of his period of absence.

If income is taxed both in the UK and abroad, double tax relief is available in one of two ways:

(1) A bilateral agreement between the UK and the country of destination will set out how income from employment is taxed and the reliefs available.

(2) If no double tax treaty exists, the UK authorities will mitigate the double tax charge by giving a deduction from the UK tax bill equal to the lower of:

- UK tax on overseas income; and
- overseas tax actually paid.

Any rental income he receives in the UK will be taxed to UK income tax. He will however continue to be eligible for his UK personal allowance.

14 Optica Scientific Instruments Ltd

Marking guide

		Marks
		Up to
(a)	Financial data	
	Westland profit calculation	6
	Eastland profit calculation	6
(b)	Valuation methods	6
	Other strategic issues	9
(c)	Practical issues surrounding expansion	6
(d)	Risks and hedging	8
(e)	Assurance issues	4
Total marks		45
Maximum marks		40

(Extracts of a) report to the board of Optica Scientific Instruments Ltd

Proposed overseas expansion
July 20X8
Grapeseed, Miley & Co, ICAEW Chartered Accountants

(a) **Financial investment appraisal**

Assessment based on Optica's criterion

The following criterion has been used to assess the two proposed expansion opportunities.

Maximise after tax sterling income to Optica over the next three years

Calculations have been prepared for the Westland operation and the Eastland operation and are attached to this report as Appendix 1.

Cumulatively over the next three years the Westland operation is forecast to generate a profit after tax of £2,297,000 while the Eastland operation is forecasting a profit after tax of £4,867,000.

Based on the above criterion, the Eastland operation will be preferred as it will maximise after tax income to Optica over the next three years.

(b) **Appropriateness of criterion used**

The after-tax income criterion used to assess the expansion opportunities may not be the most appropriate for Optica for the following reasons:

- After-tax income is a financial reporting based measure and may not reflect the cash flows of the operation.

- After-tax income does not consider the incremental, relevant cash flows of the operation or any savings made.

- After-tax income does not weight the results according to the level of risk involved.

- No allowance is made for the cost of financing the expansion, hence though the given criterion shows that the Eastland opportunity is preferable it does not determine whether it is worthwhile.

- This approach only considers the first three years of operation which may not be representative of future after tax results due to the inclusion of start-up costs and initial tax incentives.

 The approach takes no account of the skilled labour/training needs and the learning effect reducing costs over time, etc.

- The approach makes no consideration of opportunity costs, ie by investing in Eastland, is there a cost of not being close to the North America market place?

Alternative method of assessment

Net Present Value of relevant cash flows

An NPV analysis is widely considered the best method of evaluating an investment opportunity, especially when there is capital rationing (ie insufficient funds to pursue all options), as it evaluates the project by consideration of:

- all relevant cash flows over the entire life of the project rather than just a short term.

- a "risk-adjusted required rate of return" based on the source of finance used and the business risks involved.

Other strategic factors

Factors other than purely financial ones may be very significant in the investment decision. These factors may impact not only upon the decision of which subsidiary to choose, but also whether either of the subsidiaries is the best strategic decision for Optica.

Choosing between subsidiaries

The following factors may also be important.

(1) Availability of labour

Exhibit 1 identifies the need for substantial training. The costs of training a new workforce in either location are likely to be high, particularly if there is a lack of similar operations locally.

(2) Supply issues

The number of suppliers who can supply Optica with the quality of components it requires is likely to be limited. Optica may well have built up long-term relationships with these suppliers. Changing the country of manufacture will result in changes in the supply chain, probably pushing up costs. Alternatively if Optica wishes to limit the costs of supply by changing to suppliers that are near the subsidiary, it may find it difficult to choose suppliers who can guarantee delivery time and quality.

(3) Distribution issues

The Westland option may help with distribution in North America as the logistics of shipping from the UK would no longer be an issue. However Optica appears to be facing significant competition in North America, and Europe has been identified as a potential growth market. Possibly therefore the decision should depend on whether Optica wishes to focus most on expanding in America or Europe.

(4) Other opportunities

It is possible that neither the Eastland nor the Westland options offers the best way forward for Optica. Certainly other possibilities need to be considered.

(5) Subsidiary in another country

It is not clear whether Optica's board has considered options other than investing in Westland and Eastland. Investment in a third country may be better both on financial grounds and on the non-financial grounds described above.

(6) Different form of investment

Alternatively the board could consider a joint arrangement with a local manufacturer in Westland, Eastland or a third location. Possibly also some of the manufacturing currently undertaken in the UK could be outsourced overseas.

(7) Strategic alliance

Percy Toone has various other interests around the world. A strategic alliance with one or more of these may be a viable option, and may be preferable to seeking a new and unknown partner.

(8) Investment in marketing

Relocating the manufacturing base may not make much difference to the market penetration achieved by the AA Spectro, which is currently limited. A more urgent priority than relocating manufacture may be to refocus marketing efforts on the Spectro or on all the company's products.

(9) Investment in product development

A product as specialised as a Spectro may in time become obsolete. Optica needs to be mindful of what its competitors are doing to develop more advanced products. Investment in research and development may be a higher priority than investment in a subsidiary, either to develop the Spectro further or to develop other products (discussed below).

(10) Product diversification

The Spectro currently accounts for 48% of sales. Given the current limited penetration, it may be better to focus more effort on increasing sales of existing products or developing new products. Possibly a more diversified product range may yield higher profits.

(c) **Issues surrounding expansion**

General issues

Before considering Westland and Eastland separately, there are some common issues to consider:

- **Management structure** – Optica currently has a fairly simple structure, but this will be complicated by the investment in the overseas subsidiaries. The board will need to decide whether to recruit local management, or whether some senior management in Optica's home country will move abroad. It will also need to decide how much decision autonomy the subsidiary's management has. And how involved head office management will be in

- local v senior mgmt.
- Degree of autonomy
- targets
- performance monitoring

determining strategy. The extent of autonomy allowed will also affect how the subsidiary's activities are monitored, what performance targets are set, and how much stress is put upon achieving financial targets.

- **Information strategies** – Management structure and autonomy will also impact upon how information strategies need to change if Optica establishes a subsidiary. Optica will need to re-assess its strategic information needs if it expands into other countries. Investment in information technology will be a significant part of investment in any new subsidiary.

- **Repatriation of profits** – This could be achieved via dividends, but alternatives include royalties (for using Optica's technology) and management charges. It is important to establish a robust transfer pricing policy and have agreements in place in advance to avoid issues with the tax authorities.

- **Manufacturing quality** – By expanding production overseas it is harder to ensure that the quality of products manufactured meets Optica's specifications. To combat this threat, it is recommended that Optica's manufacturing director should be involved in establishing a quality management programme overseas.

- **Language barriers** – Optica will need a multi-lingual workforce, particularly at more senior and managerial levels.

- **Exchange rate exposure** – By trading internationally the group is exposed to exchange rate gains and losses on its transactions. In addition it will be exposed to translation risk on its overseas net assets and profits. I discuss both of these further below.

- **Company and other legislation** – There may be significant legislative requirements to be met in the countries being considered (eg health and safety, labour laws, age and other discrimination etc).

- **Governmental stability** – The economic and governmental situation should be researched to establish whether the environment will be conducive to running a profitable business.

- **Taxation** – The rates of taxation which will be charged on entities trading in these countries. The existence of double taxation treaties and their terms will be useful to consider.

Westland

The following issues need to be considered:

- The state of economic development of Westland

- The level of government assistance to foreign investors in Westland appears less favourable than in Eastland

Eastland

- There are significant financial and tax-based incentives for foreign investment in Eastland, including tax reliefs, grants, etc.

- Eastland has very high inflation (17% pa). Over three years this is a cumulative rate of 60%. From a financial reporting perspective it may become necessary for the financial statements to be maintained in a relatively stable currency such as sterling or euros.

- There is currently an available pool of cheap, but skilled labour in most eastern European countries. This should help lower Optica's costs and enable it to compete more effectively.

(d) **Foreign currency risk**

As noted above, expansion into overseas markets will increase Optica's exposure to foreign exchange risk. Given the potential volatility of exchange rates, this is a risk that should not be underestimated.

There are three forms of foreign exchange risk to consider:

(1) Transaction risk

Definition

Transaction risk is the risk that the local currency value of any foreign denominated transactions may vary as a result of exchange rate movements. For example, a cash flow of EAF 1,000,000 has a current sterling value of £2,857 but in Year 3 will have a value of only £2,000.

With costs denominated in either New Pesos or Eastland Forints but revenues being largely in other currencies, the subsidiaries will potentially be subject to significant transaction risk in relation to their revenues. This will clearly have a knock-on effect on their local currency profits.

revenues from over the world a diff. currencies

The primary factors influencing the level of transaction risk are:

- the scale of any foreign denominated transactions.

- the credit period offered on such transactions (the period over which exchange rates may vary).

- the volatility of the currencies involved.

Exposure

It is very difficult to comment on the scale of exposure here since we have no information regarding credit periods.

Methods of reducing risk

Transaction risk may be reduced by the following means:

- Denominating all transactions in local currency (New Pesos or Eastland Forints), although it is likely that this will be unacceptable to customers outside Westland or Eastland

- Selling at an agreed exchange rate (passing the exchange risk on to the customer) – again unlikely to be popular with customers

- Hedging with forward exchange contracts or other foreign currency derivatives (currency futures or options)

(2) Translation risk

Definition

Translation risk is the risk that the value of any foreign denominated net assets or profits may vary in terms of the reporting currency as a result of exchange rate fluctuations. When translated into sterling terms for incorporation into Optica's group accounts, net assets and profits will vary year-on-year even if only as a result of movements in exchange rates.

Though such movements have no direct cash flow impacts themselves they will impact on accounting ratios such as profit margins and gearing and, as such, impact on the ability of the business to raise finance.

Exposure

This depends on the extent to which the output from Westland and Eastland is exported to other countries. If the New Peso or Forint were to strengthen against the currencies of the export destination countries, then profits would be reduced.

On top of these risks which impact on the profits of the Westland and Eastland operations in local currency terms, we have the risk of a depreciation of the New Peso and/or the Eastland Forint against sterling, and a reduction in the sterling value of the profits made in those countries.

The translation exposure of the business is, therefore, quite complex, the overall result of which depends on the relative interactions between all currencies concerned.

matching and currency swap.

Methods of reducing risk

Translation risk can be minimised by minimising the scale of any foreign denominated assets, liabilities, income or expenses.

The scale of foreign net assets could be reduced by financing with a foreign currency loan bringing the net assets of the overseas subsidiary to zero. Alternatively a long-term currency swap could be used to switch the exposure on the sterling loan into the relevant foreign currency.

Reducing the scale of foreign denominated profits is clearly not optimal for the business.

(3) Economic risk

Definition

Economic risk is the risk that the value of a business's income may vary as a result of competition from overseas suppliers. Optica is currently experiencing this risk as it is finding it difficult to compete in overseas markets due to the strength of sterling.

Exposure

It is Optica's exposure to this risk that is driving the proposal of establishing an overseas subsidiary, though this risk cannot be analysed further without knowledge of the main business competitors.

Methods of reducing risk

Optica's proposal to manufacture overseas should help to alleviate this risk.

Assurance issues

The main assurance issues in relation to foreign currency will be confirming:

- historical rates used to initially record transactions in the subsidiary.

- closing rates used by the subsidiary for the evaluation of monetary assets and liabilities on its statement of financial position.

- closing rate used to translate the subsidiary statement of financial position into sterling for the group accounts.

- rate used (actual/average) for translating the subsidiary's profits or losses into sterling for the group accounts.

- any derivatives used for hedging purposes satisfy the requirements of IAS 39/IFRS 9 as hedging instruments where hedge accounting may be applied.

- fair values of such hedging instruments at the reporting date in accordance with ISA 540 *Auditing Accounting Estimates, Including Fair Value Accounting Estimates, and Related Disclosures*.

(e) Conclusions

In conclusion, the Eastland operation appears the most profitable based on the calculations in the Appendix. With a lower level of export sales they probably also minimise exchange risk, though the long-term volatility against sterling needs to be considered for completeness.

Further consideration should, however, be given to the cash flows forecast for each operation and included in a net present value analysis that reflects the inherent risks of such operations. This will allow a conclusion to be drawn on the impact of the expansion on shareholder wealth.

Appendix 1

Westland operation (W1)

	Year 1 £'000	Year 2 £'000	Year 3 £'000	Total £'000
Revenue	6,630	8,715	10,800	26,145
Direct costs	(3,465)	(4,985)	(6,860)	(15,310)
Indirect costs	(1,623)	(1,840)	(2,089)	(5,552)
Depreciation	(577)	(600)	(625)	(1,802)
Profit before tax				3,481
Tax charge at 34%				(1,184)
Profit after tax				2,297

Eastland operation (W2)

	Year 1 £'000	Year 2 £'000	Year 3 £'000	Total £'000
Revenue	7,680	11,400	15,120	34,200
Direct costs	(2,730)	(3,617)	(4,578)	(10,925)
Indirect costs	(5,450)	(5,251)	(5,222)	(15,923)
Depreciation	(660)	(544)	(462)	(1,666)
Profit before tax				5,686
Tax charge at 36%				(2,047)
Tax incentive (60% of tax charge*)				1,228
Profit after tax				4,867

* Assumes tax credits are given in loss making periods and are reduced by 60% in a similar way to tax charges.

WORKINGS

(1) Westland operation

Demand

	Market size	Market share	Units
Year 1	16,000	1.625%	260
Year 3	16,000	2.5%	400

1.625% × 16,000

Year 2

Average of Year 1 and Year 3 = $\dfrac{260 + 400}{2}$ = 330 units

Revenue

	Units	Selling price £	£
Year 1	260	25,500	6,630,000
Year 3	400	27,000	10,800,000

Year 2

Average of Year 1 and Year 3 = $\dfrac{6,630 + 10,800}{2}$ = £8,715 k

Direct costs

Year	Per unit N\$	Units	Total N\$	FX	Total £
1	173,225 × 1.00 = 173,225	260	45,038,500	13.0	3,464,500
2	173,225 × 1.09 = 188,815	330	62,308,950	12.5	4,984,716
3	173,225 × 1.09^2 = 205,809	400	82,323,600	12.0	6,860,300

inflation

General overheads

Year	N\$'000	FX	£
1	21,103 × 1.00 = 21,103	13.0	1,623,308
2	21,103 × 1.09 = 23,002	12.5	1,840,160
3	21,103 × 1.09^2 = 25,072	12.0	2,089,333

inflation

Depreciation

Item	Cost N$'000	UEL Years	Annual dep'n N$'000
Land	10,000	Infinite	0
Buildings	20,000	20	1,000
Equipment	52,000	8	6,500
Total			7,500

Year		Total N$'000	FX	Total £
1		7,500	13.0	576,923
2		7,500	12.5	600,000
3		7,500	12.0	625,000

(2) Eastland operation

Demand

	Market size	Market share	Units
Year 1	1,500	16%	240
Year 3	1,500	28%	420

Year 2

Average of Year 1 and Year 3 = $(240 + 420)/2 = 330$

Revenue

	Units	Selling price £	£
Year 1	240	32,000	7,680,000
Year 3	420	36,000	15,120,000

Year 2

Average of Year 1 and Year 3 = $\dfrac{7,680 + 15,120}{2} = £11,400k$

Direct costs

Year	Per unit EAF	Units	Total EAF m	FX	Total £
1	3,981,250 × 1.00 = 3,981,250	240	955.50	350	2,730,000
2	3,981,250 × 1.17 = 4,658,063	330	1,537.16	425	3,616,849
3	3,981,250 × 1.17 = 5,449,933	420	2,288.97	500	4,577,944

inflation

General overheads

Year	EAF m			FX	£
1	1,907.350 × 1.00 = 1,907.350			350	5,449,571
2	1,907.350 × 1.17 = 2,231.600			425	5,250,824
3	1,907.350 × 1.17^2 = 2,610.971			500	5,221,942

Depreciation (and amortisation of grant combined)

Item	Cost EAF m	UEL Years	Annual dep'n EAFm
Land	320	Infinite	0
Buildings	1,500 – 450 = 1,050	30	35
Equipment	1,960	10	196
Total			231

Year	Total EAF m		FX	Total £
1	231		350	660,000
2	231		425	543,529
3	231		500	462,000

15 Hyper-Thin Glass Ltd

Marking guide

		Marks
		Up to
(a)	EBITDA valuation	3
(b)	Discussion of EBITDA valuation	7
(c)	Alternative valuation	16
(d)	Valuation of a 25% holding	7
(e)	Comparison of the impact of the two proposals on the directors	16
(f)	Discussion of risk issues and factors that may make an AIM listing difficult to achieve	8
	Discussion of AIM listing and governance implications	4
(g)	Ethical issues	6
Total marks		67
Maximum marks		60

Draft report

To: HTG Ltd board
From: A. Senior
Date: XX.XX.XXXX
Subject: HTG Ltd – Departure of a director/shareholder

(a) EBITDA valuation

Using the formula provided, an unadjusted EBITDA based valuation figure would be

	£m
Operating profit	2.35
Add depreciation	1.50
EBITDA	3.85

Valuation: 5 × EBITDA	£19.25m

(b) Comments on EBITDA based valuation

EBITDA – Drawbacks.

Use of EBITDA

Earnings before Interest, Taxes, Depreciation and Amortisation (EBITDA) is a commonly used figure that attempts to bridge the profit-cash gap. It is a proxy for operating cash flows, although it is not the same. It takes operating profit and strips out depreciation, amortisation and (normally) any separately-disclosed items such as exceptional items.

Particular reservations in using EBITDA for an equity valuation include the following:

- EBITDA is not a cash flow measure and, while it excludes certain subjective accounting practices, it is still subject to accounting manipulation in a way that cash flows would not be. Examples would include revenue recognition practice and items that have some unusual aspects, but are not disclosed separately and, therefore, not added back.

- The presentation of items as exceptional may be subjective and therefore their inclusion or exclusion in the valuation formula needs to be clarified.

- EBITDA is not a sustainable figure as there is no charge for capital replacement such as depreciation in traditional profit measures or CAPEX (capital expenditure), as in free cash flow. This would seem to be a particularly important problem for HTG, where essential annual renewal and replacement of non-current assets seems to be necessary.

- The earnings figure is taken before interest. As such, it does not represent the flow of earnings to equity holders. Rather, it is more akin to valuing debt and equity jointly as from the EBITDA figure both the return to debt holders needs to be paid (ie interest) and the return to equity holders.

✓ • Taxes are excluded, which may be a significant cost.

✓ • The EBITDA figure is for the current year only. Any valuation based only on the current year ignores any future growth (in this case however zero growth has been specified as an assumption to be made) arising from changes in the business or in the environment.

✓ • The current estimate is a forecast and is unaudited. The actual figure may be different.

> **Tutorial note:**
>
> While there may be arbitrary transfer prices between the divisions this should not affect the overall profit of the company, as a distorted transfer price would mean overstatement of one division's profit and an equal understatement of the other division's profit.

Use of a multiple of 5

The multiple of 5 appears an arbitrary selection. It equates to a 20% return as a perpetuity discount rate.

The figure may have been adjusted to allow, in a crude manner, for the omission of tax and interest and for ignoring growth. However it is not clear whether, or how, this has been done.

The choice of an arbitrary EBITDA multiple leaves the negotiating process open to argument and disagreement, since there is no logical foundation on which to base the estimate of valuation.

(c) **Alternative valuation**

	£'000
Operating profit	2,350
Amortisation on unrecognised intangible (£2m/10)	(200)
Additional depreciation (Note 1)	(250)*
Revenue recognition adjustment (Note 2)	(184)
Directors' salaries (market adjustment)	(300)
	1,416
Finance costs	(200)
Profit before tax	1,216
Tax at 23%	(280)
	936

* Depreciation here is assumed to approximate to capital allowances

Using 8% as a discount rate to value earnings in perpetuity gives an earnings-based valuation of **£11.70m** (= £936,000/.08).

Notes

1 ✓ **Depreciation**

The fair value of the PPE in Division A is 20% greater than its carrying amount. As an approximation, the depreciation may be deemed to be 20% higher. An additional charge for depreciation in Division A is therefore £200,000.

The fair value of the PPE in Division B is 10% greater than its carrying amount. As an approximation, the depreciation may be deemed also to be 10% greater. Incremental depreciation is therefore £50,000 for Division B.

Total additional depreciation in order to provide a realistic charge for the consumption of the assets is £250,000.

2 **Revenue recognition**

Revenue recognised should only relate to goods where risks and rewards have passed. This would normally be when the goods are delivered and accepted by the customer. As a consequence, all of the revenue of £600,000 on the 600 items delivered should be recognised. These will be fully paid for by the year end so any deferred income account set up when the initial deposit was received in August would no longer be required in respect of the sold items.

In relation to the remaining 400 items, the cash of £120,000 paid in advance should be treated as a deferred income liability rather than as revenue.

The remaining revenue of £280,000 also appears to have been recognised for the 400 undelivered items. This entry should be reversed.

The costs of £240,000 (40% × £600,000) relating to the manufacture of the undelivered items should not be charged to cost of sales but should be recognised as inventories. However, this includes a profit element in the transfer price from Division A to Division B which should be eliminated. Thus, as half the costs are incurred internally, the inventory value should be ((£240,000/1.25) × 50% plus £240,000 × 50%) = approximately £216,000. The write down is therefore £24,000. The profit adjustment is therefore:

	£
Revenue (280 + 120)	400,000
Cost of sales	(240,000)
Inventory adjustment	24,000
	184,000

Note: There may also be a PURP adjustment for the remainder of Division B's inventory, if this has not already been adjusted.

(d) **Value of a 25% holding**

The value of the 25% shareholding is ultimately determined by how much someone is prepared to pay and how much Barry is prepared to accept.

Value to Barry

Currently Barry earns a return through being a director, but this is below market rates and hence could be regarded as a cost of involvement with HTG rather than a benefit.

There are no dividends paid.

As a result, the ultimate benefit from Barry's shareholding is to sell the shares when the company is listed. Prior to that date there is no right to sell and the benefit to the buyer is dependent on flotation.

The fact that Barry is being forced into a sale reduces the benefit to him as the forced sale price of a partial shareholding in a private company is likely to be significantly below the flotation price when there is additional liquidity for purchasers to make a subsequent sale.

Value to outside shareholders

The fact that Barry has been unable to find a third party to acquire his shares indicates that he has been unable to obtain his desired price.

The use of an earnings-based model would seem inappropriate for an external sale as the purchaser would be a minority shareholder and would therefore have no control. Moreover, there is nothing to suggest they would automatically be a director. There is also nothing to suggest any contractual protection or rights pertaining to minority shareholdings (eg through the Articles of Association or service contracts). No dividends are paid.

An external purchaser of Barry's shares would not have any short term benefits from share ownership. In the longer term, they would also be at risk of the directors' decision over the fact and timing of flotation. The price of Barry's shares would therefore be heavily discounted in any external sale.

The value is therefore likely to be significantly below £2.925m (ie 25% of the value of the entire equity of £11.70m).

(e) **Impact of Proposal 1 compared to Proposal 2**

Proposal 1 – Value to three remaining directors

If the other three directors were to acquire Barry's shares they would each have a one third share rather than the current one quarter. On flotation this would yield additional benefits but:

- prior to flotation there would be no incremental benefits accruing to the other directors as a result of acquiring Barry's shares.

- there would be an additional cost of £75,000 from paying Barry a market rate as a director (£300,000 between four is £75,000 which is then doubled to obtain a market rate).

- directors would have to borrow personally so their personal gearing would increase, making this a more risky investment.

- the directors would be less diversified personally by having more of their personal wealth in one company.

The change in ownership would also result in a change in control and governance of the company. Two directors acting in unison would now be enough to control both the board and the AGM and could therefore remove the third director.

One director could however now prevent a special resolution.

Overall the acquisition of Barry's shares for cash is not an attractive proposition unless they can be acquired cheaply and there is a short term, certain and profitable route to flotation where the increased shareholding can be realised to cash.

Proposal 2 – Value to three remaining directors

Proposal 2 would not require any personal cash from the directors but would involve a sacrifice of future income by the company and a loss of value on flotation.

Given that Barry's shares would be cancelled then the directors would, in common with Proposal 1, own one third of the equity. In this case however the company would be smaller.

The impact of the disposal of Division B needs to be assessed as this is, in effect, the purchase price paid for Barry's shares.

The fair value of the net assets of Division B is equivalent to the gross assets as no debt would be assumed by Barry.

	£
Book value PPE	1,750,000
Revaluation	175,000
Current assets	250,000
	2,175,000

This however only refers to tangible assets. Any claim by Barry for the intellectual property rights over intangible rights would also need to be considered. However this appears to relate to the glass itself rather than the double glazing units so it is assumed Barry would assume no rights in this respect.

In terms of assets therefore Barry would take £2.175m/£11.315m = 19.2%. (£6.84m + £1.925m + £0.55m + £2m = £11.315m).

This is below a pro rata share of 25% but, given the limitations on a minority shareholding, this would give Barry an effective exit route to realise his investment.

In viewing Division B as a going concern the value needs to take account of the artificially high transfer price that Division B is paying to Division A which is above market rates.

The adjusted earnings to shareholders for Division B would be

	£'000
Operating profit	750
Additional depreciation on PPE	(50)
Transfer price adjustment (Note 1)	120
Directors' salaries (market adjustment)	(75)
	745
Tax at 23%	(171)
	574

If these earnings are discounted at 8% then this gives a value for Division B of **£7.18m** (£574,000/0.08).

This would be 61% (£7.18m/£11.70m) of the whole company's earnings based market value. This is clearly excessive.

There may also be a case for arguing that, as Barry's new company is ungeared, the discount rate would be lower than 8% so the value would be even higher. On the other hand, given the relatively small size of Division B there is also an argument that the cost of equity should be higher.

Note 1: **Transfer price adjustment**

The cost of sales is 50% from Division A at a 25% mark-up. The market rate is only a 10% mark up.

Thus an adjusted figure is ((£1,000,000/1.25) × 1.1) + £1,000,000 = £1,880,000.

The adjustment is therefore £120,000 (£2,000,000 – £1,880,000).

Tutorial note:

An alternative way of looking at this issue is to take the earnings that would be left in Division A of £362,000 (£936,000 – £574,000).

If these were discounted at 8% then this would leave a residual value for the remaining shareholders of £4.53m (£362,000/0.08).

The value of the two holdings then reconciles back to the original value, but with Barry owning more value than the other three directors combined.

	£m
Division A	4.53
Division B (Barry)	7.17
Original value HTG	11.70

Note: In financial reporting terms HTG is effectively acquiring its own shares but using operating assets rather than cash. If an entity acquires its own shares ('treasury shares'), the amount paid should be deducted directly from equity and no gain or loss should be recognised on the transaction. The amount paid would be the fair value of the assets transferred.

(f) **Risk implications**

The shareholders and members of the board appear to expect that by obtaining a listing on AIM before the end of 20X9, many of their difficulties may be resolved. However, there is evidence from the limited amount of information available to suggest that obtaining an AIM listing may be much more difficult than they expect.

No dividends have been paid since the company was formed, which suggests that (unless debts have been repaid about which we have not been informed) all earnings are retained within the business. In 20X6, retained earnings were £1.655m. Total retained earnings to the end of 20X6 were £2.75m. This indicates that in the years 20X2 – 20X5 total retained earnings were just £1.095m. The large increase in 20X6 has no obvious reason or cause, and we do not know whether 20X6 was an exceptionally good year, or the first year of a large increase in the company's business. For the purpose of a listing, investors will want to see a track record of growth and success, and this does not yet appear to exist.

This point should be reinforced by the fact that the four directors have been paying themselves one half the market rate for their work, which means that in 20X6, if the directors had all been paid a market rate, pre-tax profits would have been £300,000 lower and earnings £231,000 lower. Depending on the tax rate in previous years, annual earnings would have been lower and so cumulative retained profits would have been much lower than shown in the company's financial statements for the end of 20X6.

In spite of the relatively large retained earnings in 20X6, the company had no cash at the end of the year and very little in working capital. Unless cash was used to repay debt, the indication is that a large proportion of the retained profits were used to invest in PPE. This may explain the large increase in earnings in 20X6 and may be the foundation for sustained growth in the future, but this is by no means clear.

As far as I am aware, the board of HTG have not discussed future business prospects with you. I am unable to comment, due to lack of information, on the nature of any technological or economic risks that may affect the company's business in the next few years.

HTG still owes £4,000,000. Before the company obtains a listing it might be necessary to repay this debt or exchange it for debt from another source, such as a bank. I do not have information about when this debt to Rowdean is repayable. Even so, the current large debt position of the company makes an AIM listing more difficult to achieve and the failure so far to make any repayment is a matter of some concern.

In summary, it may be appropriate to discuss with the board members of HTG their future intentions with regard to a listing, and the possible risks they may face in achieving that objective.

You also asked for brief comments on corporate governance issues with respect to an AIM listing. The UK Code of Corporate Governance applies only to companies with a main market listing, although there is an unofficial code for smaller quoted companies. Even so, a company obtaining a listing on AIM will be expected to make some changes in governance. Perhaps the change that the current directors should consider most carefully is the need to change the composition of the board. Other shareholders will not tolerate an arrangement in which four (or possibly three) major shareholders have positions on the board, without any other representatives on the board to protect the interests of the other (minority) shareholders.

It seems inevitable that it will not be possible for all three or four of the existing directors to remain on the board, and appointments of non-executive directors will be expected. This means that governance in the company will change, and the current shareholders will lose some representation on the board and have a somewhat smaller influence in shareholders' meetings/company meetings.

(g) **Ethical implications**

(1) **Acting for appropriate parties**

In acting for the company and the board as a whole, this would seem legitimate for Proposal 2 as this is a transaction to be undertaken by the company. However in advising the board, JJJ needs to be careful not to advise Barry also, as there is a potential conflict of interest in these circumstances between Barry and the company and the shareholders as a body.

In Proposal 1 it is more difficult to advise the board and the company as this is a transaction between individuals, not one to be undertaken by the company itself. As such, JJJ could act for one or more of the three remaining directors or act for Barry. If all parties agree however JJJ could act as an independent accountant giving an independent, but non binding, view on the valuation.

JJJ does not appear to act as auditors to HTG so there is no conflict affecting independence in this respect.

(2) **Request for information from Rowdean's auditors**

The major ethical issue in this case is one of client confidentiality. It would be inappropriate to disclose the circumstances of one client, HTG, to another client, Rowdean, as a means of justifying the impairment of its loan asset.

The approach by the audit senior on the Rowdean audit is ethically inappropriate. Any request for confirmation of an amount owing should be made to the client, not to the audit staff. The request should be treated on an arm's length basis and refused. Internal discipline procedures within JJJ should be considered for making the request.

16 Raul plc

Draft report

To: Finance Director
From: A. Senior
Date: XX December 20X3
Subject: Raul plc – Refinancing

(a) **Projected profit**

(1) **Lockington proposal**

This proposal would merely refinance the existing loan and overdraft with the new £20m loan at 15%. This gives for each of the years 20X4 to 20X7:

	£'000
Revenue	12,000
Operating costs	(8,000)
Operating profit	4,000
Finance costs	(3,000)
Profit before tax	1,000

Annual profit is reduced by the amount of the additional interest on borrowing.

The profit forecast (and the cash flow forecast below) assumes no change in the variable rate of interest throughout the period.

(2) **Walter Baffet financing package**

Loan

This is a straightforward loan of £10m at 10% with annual interest at £1m.

Option

The option is a derivative contract that can be settled by Raul delivering a fixed number of its own equity instruments in exchange for a fixed amount of cash.

The option is therefore recognised as an equity instrument at its fair value at the date of inception. The statement of profit or loss is not affected.

Subsequent changes in the fair value of the option are not reflected in the financial statements as they have no impact on the amount of the consideration paid.

If Walter ultimately subscribes for the shares then the amount of cash he pays to Raul would be added to equity at that time.

Sale and leaseback

This is a sale and operating leaseback as there is a significant value to the property after 10 years, which is only half way through its useful life.

The profit of £3m (ie the difference between the £8m fair value and the £5m carrying amount) is recognised immediately.

The excess proceeds over fair value of £2m is deferred and recognised over the lease period of ten years, ie £200,000 per annum.

The lease rentals paid of £1.3m are charged to profit or loss.

	Workings	20X4	20X5	20X6	20X7
		£'000	£'000	£'000	£'000
Existing profit before tax (per Q)		2,000	2,000	2,000	2,000
Add back depreciation on sale and leaseback of property	(W1)	250	250	250	250
Profit on sale and leaseback (FV – CA)		3,000			
Release of deferral (£2m/10 years)		200	200	200	200
Reduction in interest payments (£2m – £1m)		1,000	1,000	1,000	1,000
Rental payment		(1,300)	(1,300)	(1,300)	(1,300)
Revised profit before tax		5,150	2,150	2,150	2,150

(W1) **Add back depreciation**

The property is no longer depreciated as it is held under a sale and operating leaseback thus the £250,000 depreciation is added back.

(b) **Projected operating cash flows**

(1) **Lockington proposal**

	20X4	20X5	20X6	20X7
	£'000	£'000	£'000	£'000
Existing profit before tax	1,000	1,000	1,000	1,000
Add back depreciation	1,000	1,000	1,000	1,000
Cash flows	2,000	2,000	2,000	2,000
Opening cash	1,000	3,000	5,000	7,000
Closing cash	3,000	5,000	7,000	9,000

Notes

1 There may be other adjustments to profit in addition to depreciation (eg working capital adjustments). More information would be needed.

2 These cash flows assume that no new spending will be required on replacement non-current assets.

3 The refinancing would involve the £20m cash loan repaying the existing loan and overdraft. This has not been identified as a separate cash flow. The repayment of loan principal is repayable at the end of 20X9.

(2) **Walter Baffet financing package**

	20X4	20X5	20X6	20X7
	£'000	£'000	£'000	£'000
Revised profit before tax	5,150	2,150	2,150	2,150
Adjustments				
Profit on sale & leaseback	(3,000)			
Deferral	(200)	(200)	(200)	(200)
Remaining depreciation	750	750	750	750
Operating cash flows	2,700	2,700	2,700	2,700
Loan repayment				(10,000)
Opening cash	1,000	3,700	6,400	9,100
Closing cash	3,700	6,400	9,100	1,800

Notes

1   The initial refinancing arising from the new loan and the sale and leaseback, amounting to £20m cash, would be used to repay the existing loan and overdraft. These have not been identified as separate cash flows.

2   If the options were to be exercised this would lead to an additional cash inflow. The fact and timing of this receipt is however uncertain; therefore it has not been included.

3   For both financing methods surplus cash flows could be reinvested to generate some investment income or prepay part of the loan, if this is permissible under the contract.

(c) **Comparison of proposals**

A superficial comparison of the profits and cash flows of the two financing options would appear to indicate that Walter's package is superior to the new 15% bank loan from Lockington. However this comparison ignores a number of key factors including liquidity, risk and return.

(1) **Liquidity**

The time horizon is only four years and there are significant cash flow effects beyond this horizon. The package proposed by Walter means Raul loses use of the factory after 10 years and hence it needs to be refinanced or a new factory acquired. Under the bank's arrangement the factory is available for its entire useful life of 20 years and may have some residual value beyond that.

The period covered by the two financing arrangements differs, with the bank financing being for six years. The projected annual cash flows of £2m over six years would only generate £12m plus the existing £1m balance. This is not sufficient to repay the full £20m. On the basis of this forecast, we can therefore predict that at least some refinancing will be needed.

Walter's arrangement needs to be repaid in two tranches. The loan is repayable after four years. If the forecast operating cash flows prove accurate then there is sufficient cash to make the repayment. The sale and leaseback terminates in ten years, at which point a new factory needs to be acquired or leased.

(2) **Risk**

A key risk factor with the bank's package is the covenants. If any of these is breached, the bank will have the right to call in repayment of the loan immediately. As the company would be unable to do this, it would be forced into administration/liquidation. Given the bank's tough stance on the existing covenant breach, this is a significant possibility.

The forecast assumes that, except for the possible loss of one major customer, revenues will be maintained and will not fall further. This is a critical assumption and one that the directors of Raul should be advised to review or re-consider.

A further risk is the fact that the Lockington loan is at a variable interest rate (compared with Walter's loan, which is at a fixed rate). The key risk of the fixed rate is that, if interest rates move, the fair value of the loan changes inversely. With variable rates, the risk of interest changes is a cash flow risk since a rise in the LIBOR rate will result in additional interest payments.

Another key risk factor common to both arrangements is that 10% of revenues may be lost. This would result in a lost annual contribution of £800,000 [10% × (£12m – (50% × £8m))].

Whether or not Raul decides to borrow from the bank, its credit status or rating with the bank has declined considerably, which is why the bank would ask for interest at 15% compared with 10% before. This deterioration in credit rating could have long-term adverse implications for Raul's ability to borrow.

Consequences of loss of major customer

Lockington loan

	20X4	20X5	20X6	20X7
	£'000	£'000	£'000	£'000
Original cash flows	2,000	2,000	2,000	2,000
Loss of customer	(800)	(800)	(800)	(800)
Opening cash	1,000	2,200	3,400	4,600
Closing cash	2,200	3,400	4,600	5,800

Thus while cash flows are still positive they will now be significantly below what is necessary to repay the finance after six years.

The projected profit of £1m per year will drop to a profit of only £200,000, on revenue of £10.8m (90% of £12m).

Walter Baffet

	20X4	20X5	20X6	20X7
	£'000	£'000	£'000	£'000
Original cash flows	2,700	2,700	2,700	2,700
Loss of customer	(800)	(800)	(800)	(800)
Opening cash	1,000	2,900	4,800	6,700
Closing cash	2,900	4,800	6,700	8,600

Similarly, while cash flows are still positive they are now significantly below what is necessary to repay the loan finance after four years.

Steady state annual profits from 20X5 to 20X7 would fall from £2.15m to £1.35m.

If the customer's business is lost, the share price will fall and therefore the option held by Walter will be less valuable. This makes it less likely that Walter will exercise the option and although this reduces the dilution of shares it also removes a source of additional equity capital.

(3) **Return**

The cost of debt with the Lockington arrangement is 15% pa.

The bank loan from Walter is 10% pa.

The cost of the sale and leaseback arrangement is 12%.

The average cost of Walter's loan and lease arrangement is therefore 11% pa, which is significantly less than the 15% offered by the bank. However Walter also has the option.

The option held by Walter can affect future share values (as there will be more shares in issue subscribed at a discount) but has no immediate impact on profit or cash flows. The options could give rise to a significant 40% holding. This however assumes that the option would be to acquire shares already in issue rather than new shares. More likely, it would be new shares in which case the shareholding would be 29% (40/140), which is still substantial.

The fair value of these options would need to be measured using a model such as Black Scholes in order to assess the overall cost of Walter's package. However an examination of intrinsic values suggests some sensitivity.

The options are currently out-of-the-money, but with four years remaining to expiry and only being 50p lower than the current share price they are likely to have a significant time value and therefore fair value. If the shares increase at (say) 10% per annum for four years the shares would have a value of £6.59 (£4.50 × 1.1^4) by expiry. This would give the options an intrinsic value of £3.18m ((£6.59 – £5) × 2m) which would be a significant additional financing cost and may influence control of the company.

If the shares increase at (say) 15% per annum for four years, the shares would have a value of £7.87 (£4.50 × 1.15^4) by the time of expiry. This would give the options an intrinsic value of £5.74m ((£7.87 – £5) × 2m).

[Handwritten margin note: INTRINSIC VALUE EXAMINATION]

On the other hand, if share prices only increased by (say) 2.5% pa then the options would still be out of the money by the time of expiry and would be worthless.

(4) **Share value**. The analysis above assumes that the current share price is a fair market value for Raul shares. Some consideration may identify reasons why this may not be the case.

- It is generally assumed that share prices reflect the present value of future expected cash returns to the shareholders. The company is not intending to make any dividend payment in 20X3. Shareholders may also be aware that no dividend payments can be expected for the next few years either. The company has been through difficult times, and we are not aware of any reasons why the fortunes of the company should unexpectedly improve: our profit and cash flow forecasts assume constant annual revenues, or possibly a 10% fall in annual revenues, rather than an increase.

- When information about any refinancing arrangement is made known and shareholders are made aware that there are no prospects of dividend payments for five years or longer, there will almost certainly be a major correction to the share price.

(5) **An alternative: administration/liquidation**. The directors of Raul need to be satisfied that by accepting either of the financing arrangements, the company will be able to survive as a going concern for the foreseeable future. There may be a business plan for recovery and growth, but we are not aware of it.

There must be some doubts about the ability of the company to pay back any loan from the bank, or to survive successfully after repayment of the loan and the ending of the lease term with Walter Baffet.

Unfortunately, without further investigation, we do not know how much the net assets of Raul might sell for in a liquidation. There would be a high risk that the shareholders would receive nothing.

On this basis, the preference should be to try to keep the company 'alive', but only if the board is confident that the company will have the ability to survive the next few years.

(6) **Advice**

Given a decision to take one or the other of the two financing choices, Lockington or Walter Baffet, the preference may depend on the share options that Walter Baffet would receive.

The options potentially have a significant diluting effect on equity that can impact on control and they may be expensive in terms of the transfer of fair value that could occur.

On the positive side the company is very highly geared and the options would provide a much needed injection of equity, although at a discounted price – but only if the share price remains at a sufficiently high level to make exercise of the options worthwhile.

The key question therefore is whether the potential equity dilution is sufficient to compensate for the lower cost of debt compared to the bank loan, and for the lower risk of covenant breach in future with the threat of administration.

If there is confidence by the directors in their forecasts, and particularly that the major customer contract will be renewed, then the bank loan could be considered as the better choice in terms of maximising future share price. If these risks are considered too great, then Walter's package may be preferable where the option costs would only be significant if the company was trading successfully and share price was rising significantly.

My suggestion is that the board of Raul should consider the different risks with each financing option before making their choice, bearing in mind what information they will have to give to shareholders about refinancing, and the effect this may have on the share price – and the company's future business generally.

(d) **Assurance report**

(1) **Nature of the report**

Reporting on prospective financial information is covered by ISAE 3400 *The Examination of Prospective Financial Information*.

Prospective financial information means financial information based on assumptions about events that may occur in future and possible actions by an entity.

Prospective financial information can be of two types (or a combination of both):

A forecast: Prospective financial information based on assumptions as to future events which management expects to take place and the actions management expects to take (best-estimate assumptions).

A projection: Prospective financial information based on hypothetical assumptions about future events and management actions, or a mixture of best-estimate and hypothetical assumptions.

[margin handwritten note: Definition of PFI.]

A key issue in this respect for Raul is whether the key customer making up 10% of revenue will be retained. Another key issue is whether Walter's options will be exercised.

ISAE 3400 states that the assurance firm should agree the terms of the engagement with the directors, and should withdraw from the engagement if the assumptions made to put together the prospective financial information are unrealistic. It also lists the following factors which the auditor should consider:

[margin handwritten note: Factors to consider before accepting PFI engagement.]

- The intended use of the information (ie the new bank finance)

- Whether the information will be for general or limited distribution (primarily for Lockington and Walter)

- The nature of the assumptions, that is, whether they are best estimate or hypothetical assumptions

- The elements to be included in the information

- The period covered by the information

The auditor should have sufficient knowledge of the business to be able to evaluate the significant assumptions made. Our role as Raul's auditors would enable us to have this knowledge.

Procedures

When determining the nature, timing and extent of procedures, RR will need to consider the following:

- The likelihood of material misstatement

- The knowledge obtained during any previous engagements (annual audits by RR)

- Management's competence regarding the preparation of prospective financial information

- The extent to which prospective financial information is affected by the management's judgement

- The adequacy and reliability of the underlying data

We need to obtain sufficient appropriate evidence as to whether:

- management's best-estimate assumptions on which the prospective financial information is based are not unreasonable and, in the case of hypothetical assumptions, such assumptions are consistent with the purpose of the information.

- the prospective financial information is properly prepared on the basis of the assumptions.

- the prospective financial information is properly presented and all material assumptions are adequately disclosed, including a clear indication as to whether they are best-estimate assumptions or hypothetical assumptions.

- the prospective financial information is prepared on a consistent basis with historical financial statements, using appropriate accounting principles.

Specific procedures

The key issues which projections relate to are profits, capital expenditure and cash flows.

1) Profit forecasts

We need to verify projected income and expenditure figures to suitable evidence. While Raul's projections appear conservative by assuming zero growth, given the difficult industry conditions, some supporting evidence is needed (order books, long term contracts, customer satisfaction reports, market surveys).

2) Capital expenditure

This appears a key omission in the cash flow projections.

3) Cash forecasts

- We should review cash forecasts to ensure the timings involved are reasonable.

- The auditor should check the cash forecast for consistency with any profit forecasts (income/expenditure should be the same, just at different times).

Expressing an opinion

As prospective financial information is subjective information, it is impossible for an auditor to give the same level of assurance regarding it, as he would on historic financial information. In this instance limited assurance is given in the form of a negative opinion.

The ISAE suggests that the auditor express an opinion including:

- a statement of negative assurance as to whether the assumptions provide a reasonable basis for the prospective financial information.

- an opinion as to whether the prospective financial information is properly prepared on the basis of the assumptions and the relevant reporting framework.

- appropriate caveats as to the achievability of the forecasts.

If we believe that the presentation and disclosure of the prospective financial information is not adequate, we will need to express a qualified or adverse opinion (or withdraw from the engagement).

If we believe that one or more significant assumptions do not provide a reasonable basis for the prospective financial information, we will need to express an adverse opinion (or withdraw from the engagement).

(e) **Memo**

To: Helen Higgs
From: A. Senior
Date: XX December 20X3
Subject: Raul plc plans for financing and survival

This memo presents my views to you on the risks that seem apparent in the plans of Raul plc management for new financing and survival.

Raul business strategy

Raul is a manufacturer of central heating boilers for domestic use. The market is competitive and large producers with a strong brand name appear to be gaining market share by winning whatever growth there is in the market. A risk for Raul is that its strategic position in the market may be 'stuck in the middle'. It may have no obvious competitive advantage over rivals, although it has some reputation for quality, and we do not have any information about new product initiatives and innovations that might enable Raul to achieve market growth.

The company predicts stable sales revenues over the next few years, and no growth. However demand has fallen and the company has already lost some major customers.

As the company loses customers, there must be a risk that the sales decline will continue, with remaining customers possibly concerned about the ability of Raul to continue providing technical support and replacement parts for the products that it supplies.

Once a company's business goes into decline, the challenge of restoring sales and growth becomes much more difficult. This is a position that Raul appears to be in now. The company's management believes that the company can survive, but its strategy for survival does not contain any new business initiative that we are aware of.

Results for the 11 months to November 20X3

The results for the 11 months to 30 November 20X3 seem to reinforce this view. It is noticeable that the company's forecasts of operating profit for 20X4 – 20X7 appear to be identical to the budget for 20X3. The budgeted figures for the 11 months in 20X3 are exactly 11/12 of the forecast for future years.

A variance analysis of the results is as follows.

	£'000	£'000
Budgeted operating profit		3,667
Sales price variance (negligible)	0	
Sales volume (contribution) variance (W1)	480 (A)	
Materials cost variance 2,860 – (24% × 10,280)	393 (A)	
Labour cost variance (W2)	394 (A)	
Other operating costs variance (2,890 – 2,640)	250 (A)	
		1,517 (A)
Actual operating profit		2,150

Actual operating profit for the 11 months was £1,517,000 below budget expectation, which is 41% below budget. Unless December 20X3 is very different, the company may expect to achieve an operating profit sufficient to cover its finance costs for the year, but leave very little surplus as profit before tax.

WORKINGS

(1) **Sales volume variance**

Variable labour costs in the budget are (50% × 2,053)/11,000 = 9.33% of sales revenue. Material costs (assumed 100% variable) are (2,640/11,000) = 24% of sales revenue.

The contribution/sales ratio = (100 – 9.33 – 24) = 66.67% of sales revenue.

Check: Total budgeted variable costs = (50% × 2,053) + 2,640 = 3,666.5 = 50% of total costs.

Sales volume variance = (11,000 – 10,280) × 66.67% = 480 (A).

(2) **Labour cost variance**

	£'000
Expected labour cost	
Fixed: (50% × 2,053)	1,027
Variable: (9.33% × 10,280)	959
Total	1,986
Actual cost	2,380
Cost variance	394 (A)

Recovery in profits

The actual results for the 11 months to date in 20X3 must surely raise questions about the ability of the company's management to turn round the business and achieve the expected operating profit of £4,000,000 in 20X4.

Financing option: bank loan

The uncertainty about the company's future profitability raises questions about the risks with the bank loan. If Raul borrows from Lockington, the bank will apply strict covenants, and will monitor them throughout the term of the loan. These will include financial covenants. Breach of any covenant would give the bank the right to call in the loan and exercise any security that it has taken.

The bank is also likely to ask Raul to supply a budget to assist with monitoring the loan, and for regular performance reports. If Raul is unable to recover and achieve budget targets, the bank will be aware of the problem.

We do not know the nature of the relationship between Raul and the bank, but there is a strong possibility that if Raul fails to comply with the loan covenants or fails to meet loan payments on schedule, the bank will force the company into administration.

Financing option: Baffet financing package

The financing package under discussion with Walter Baffet is less 'risky', in the sense that the loan covenants would not be onerous, although he would become the owner of the factory and, if the company succeeds in returning to profitability, he may eventually acquire 2m shares or (2m/7m) nearly 30% of the company's equity.

When Mr Baffet is given updated information about the company's financial performance in 20X3, he may wish to re-assess prospects for 20X4 – 20X7, and either withdraw his financing offer or re-negotiate its terms.

Conclusion

We do not know what plans Raul management may have for turning round the business and increasing profitability. There is a risk that the company will lose another major customer, adding to the downturn in business. Management does not have, as far as we are aware, a clear strategy for survival.

I hope that these views are useful for you.

17 Geo Carbon Engineering plc

Marking guide

		Marks
		Up to
(a)	Structuring the joint venture, including advice on preferred structure	8
(b)	Financing the joint venture, with recommendation	10
(c)	Assurance services: initial and continuing	8
(d)	DCF analysis of the investment, with any supporting assumptions	14
(e)	Assessment of investment risks	10
Total marks		50
Maximum marks		40

(a) Joint arrangement structuring

Joint arrangements can take different forms. However there needs to be a contractual arrangement that establishes joint control in order for it to be considered as a joint arrangement (JA). IFRS 11 *Joint Arrangements* defines a joint arrangement as an 'arrangement of which two or more parties have joint control'. Joint control is defined as 'contractually agreed sharing of control of an arrangement, which exists only when decisions about the relevant activities require the unanimous consent of the parties sharing control'.

Definition ✱

IFRS 11 has a number of other definitions, which are important in this context:

(i) A **joint operation** is a joint arrangement whereby the parties that have joint control (the joint operators) have rights to the assets, and obligations for the liabilities, of that joint arrangement. A joint arrangement that is **not structured through a separate entity** is always a joint operation.

(ii) A **joint venture** is a joint arrangement whereby the parties that have **joint control** (the joint venturers) of the arrangement have **rights to the net assets** of the arrangement.

(iii) A **joint arrangement** that is structured through a **separate entity** may be either a joint operation or a joint venture. In order to ascertain the classification, the parties to the arrangement should assess the terms of the contractual arrangement together with any other facts or circumstances to assess whether they have:

- rights to the assets, and obligations for the liabilities, in relation to the arrangement (indicating a joint operation).

- rights to the net assets of the arrangement (indicating a joint venture).

The forms of JA identified in Exhibit 2 are:

Jointly controlled business (joint venture)

This involves the establishment of a separate entity under joint control. Each venturer then has an interest in the net assets of this entity rather than the individual assets of the JA. Rather than sharing the output of the JA operations, the venturers share the profits of the JA entity. While some arrangements structured through a separate entity may be joint operations, this structure indicates a **joint venture**.

Contractual arrangement with no separate entity

In this case there is no separate entity, partnership or financial structure. Each party uses its own assets and incurs its own costs jointly to create engineering equipment for the oil industry. The revenue is then shared according to the contractual arrangements. A joint arrangement that is **not structured through a separate entity** is always a **joint operation**.

Benefits and problems

If GCE and Moddo simply have joint operations, without a separate JA entity, then there are undivided assets with each entity retaining ownership of the assets it has contributed. This may create conflicts of interest over asset usage. This is in contrast with a jointly controlled entity, where it is this entity that owns the assets and incurs liabilities. The parties therefore each have a stake in this entity rather than the underlying assets which thus gives more control over JA priorities.

As a consequence for joint operations:

- the exit route is clearer and applies simply by withdrawing or selling the assets as they are under sole ownership of each party.

- each party manages its own contribution within a planned framework.

- the strategy is finite (with four years being the limit in this case).

In contrast if there is a joint venture there is a greater propensity towards joint governance and strategic decision making rather than a narrow contractual commitment. Presumably the intention would be to establish a joint venture in Muldovia, although an offshore company registration may be preferred.

Overall the planning horizon is relatively short term (four years) which may suggest that a joint operation is a more favourable option than the strategic commitment of a joint venture which may involve greater costs of disengagement. If, however, there are strong commercial incentives to renew the term of the joint arrangement beyond 4 years, or the minimum period can be extended then this may indicate a JA entity could be a more appropriate governance vehicle to manage a joint strategy.

(b) **Financing**

The implicit annual (pre-tax) interest rate on the UK loan is 8% as this is a plain vanilla loan.

The comparable cost of a loan in Muldovian dollars can be calculated in either of two ways, which produce slightly different results.

The M$ is expected to depreciate against the £. As the functional currency of GCE is the £, then there is a two stage process to determine the implicit interest rate on the Muldovian government loan.

(1) Convert M$ (capital and interest payments) to £ at depreciating exchange rates each year.
(2) Determine the implicit interest rate on £ amounts (ie the IRR).

In sterling terms the implicit interest rate is approximately **6.3%** (by linear interpolation or other approximation):

	01/01/X2	31/12/X2	31/12/X3	31/12/X4	31/12/X5
M$ (000's)	(30,000)	3,600	3,600	3,600	33,600
In £, at opening exchange rate	(15,000)	1,800	1,800	1,800	16,800
Adjustment to allow for 5% inflation on M$		0.95	$(0.95)^2$	$(0.95)^3$	$(0.95)^4$
Cash flow in £'000	(15,000)	1,710	1,625	1,543	13,684
Discount factor at 6.3%	1.000	0.941	0.885	0.833	0.783
PV (£'000s)	(15,000)	1,609	1,438	1,285	10,715

NPV = + 47 (close to 0)

Method 2

A slightly different interpretation of a 5% annual depreciation in the currency is as follows:

In sterling terms the implicit interest rate is approximately **6.7%** (by linear interpolation or other approximation):

	01/01/X2	31/12/X2	31/12/X3	31/12/X4	31/12/X5
M$ (000's)	(30,000)	3,600	3,600	3,600	33,600
Exchange rate: M$ = £1	2.000	2.100	2.205	2.315	2.431
Cash flow in £'000	(15,000)	1,714	1,633	1,555	13,821
Discount factor at 6.7%	1.000	0.937	0.878	0.823	0.772
PV (£'000s)	(15,000)	1,606	1,434	1,280	10,670

NPV = – 10 (close to 0)

The Muldovian Government loan is therefore cheaper at 6.7% than the UK bank loan at 8%. This is before allowing for taxation. Since the rate of taxation is 40% in Muldovia, the after-tax cost on the Muldovian loan should also be lower than on a loan in sterling.

Tutorial note:

As an alternative to linear interpolation, candidates could use the 8% rate of the sterling loan to discount the M$ loan cash flows to give a large negative NPV and thereby demonstrate that the implicit interest rate in the M$ loan is lower than the 8% of the UK loan.

Other factors to consider are as follows:

- As the Muldovian government loan is denominated in M$ there is currency matching between at least some of the sales to be made. However, to the extent that sales are to other South American countries then, unless these are correlated to the M$, there is no effective currency matching with the M$ loan on export sales from Muldovia.

- Some form of additional currency hedging may nevertheless be desirable even if the Muldovian government loan is used.

- There may be a risk of sequestration of assets by the Muldovian government if there is a return to a closed economy. In these circumstances a default on the loan may compensate some of these losses, which would not be possible under a UK loan.

- It needs to be established whether the M$ loan is to GCE itself or to the JA on behalf of GCE. If there is no separate entity, then the loan funds may be held in a separate JA bank account.

(c) **Assurance services**

Initial investigations

- Review JA agreement (in combination with legal advisers) for onerous, ambiguous or omitted clauses.

- Ensure that the purpose of the JA is clear and the respective rights of GCE and Moddo are established in the initial contractual arrangements.

Initial continued: *JA Agreement.*

- Ensure that the scope of the JA is clear so there is separation of the other operations of each company from those falling within the JA.

- Review tax status of JA entity (if applicable) or GCE operations including remittance of funds.

- Review governance procedures including shared management, control, rights over assets, key decision making processes to ensure that GCE management has an appropriate level of control over key decisions that may damage its interests.

- Establish that initial capital of £15m in cash and any amounts payable in-kind, has been contributed in accordance with the agreement.

- Establish the creditworthiness, going concern and reputation of Moddo based on local enquiries from stakeholders and a review of internal documentation as well as that in the public domain.

- Ensure the terms of the disengagement and residual rights in four years' time are clear in the initial agreement so there is a transparent and legitimate exit route.

- Where assets that are to be used in the joint arrangement are already held by Moddo or GCE, then they would normally be transferred nominally at fair value. This needs to be established.

- Clarify revenue sharing agreement with respect to existing sales under construction or orders contracted for but not yet commenced.

- Health and safety responsibility needs to be established and liability sharing agreed.

Continuing assurance

- Audit rights and access to information need to be established in the contract as this will affect the scope of the audit.

- Ensure that the operations of the JA are within the terms of the JA agreement (eg adequate unskilled labour is being provided by Moddo) ie no violations of the contracted agreement.

- Ensure that internal controls and accounting systems are being applied and are effective (eg that the revenue from sales to oil companies in South America relating to the JA is fully recorded and is separated from other sales that do not form part of the joint arrangement, such as existing customers within Muldovia or of other types of engineering equipment outside the oil industry).

- The accounting systems for a JA entity will need to be capable of recording accurately and completely the costs being incurred and the assets held by the entity. If the JA is set up as a jointly controlled operation then the costs will mainly be recorded in the individual accounts of each of the venturers (although there may be some joint costs met out of revenue). In this case the key audit issue for the JA is that operations and assets have been supplied in accordance with the contract rather than recording their costs. Risk areas for GCE may include overhead allocations as Moddo is supplying from a factory which has multiple uses.

- *OH allocation* If permitted within the terms of the contract, audit access to the accounting records of Moddo (not just PetroEng) would provide additional assurance. This may mean however that a reciprocal arrangement may need to be made available to the advisers for Moddo, by giving access to the GCE accounting systems. A compromise would be access to the divisional financial statements of PetroEng but not those of Moddo. This is less satisfactory as costs and revenues recorded within Moddo may be relevant to the JA (eg overheads or 'hidden' revenues).

- If a separate JA entity is established this may mean our firm is a component auditor in the context of ISA 600 and we will need to report to the principal GCE auditors. If so, there may be a question over our independence given the advisory work that we are doing.

- The dissolution of the agreement in four years creates additional assurance problems in terms of disengagement, return/sale of assets, intellectual property rights, rights to future customer access.

- The level of assurance needs to be determined (reasonable or limited).

- There may be a requirement for a separate audit for a JA entity.

(d) **DCF analysis**

Assumptions:

The initial investment of M$30,000,000 will be recovered as M$30,000,000 at the end of the fourth year.

Excluding the recovery of this M$30m (its sterling equivalent), annual cash flows in M$ will be sufficient to provide a constant cash return in sterling each year.

The annual cash returns (GCE after-tax share) in M$ must increase at a rate of 5% per year to provide a constant return in £.

Minimum annual cash flows required

GCE expects to receive back its initial investment of M$30m at the end of Year 4. The expected exchange rate then will be $2.00 \times (1.05)^4 = 2.4310$.

The expected sterling value of the returned investment will be 30,000,000/2.4310 = £12,340,600.

• This returned investment, plus the annual dividends from the Muldovian operations, are required to have a PV of at least £15,000,000 when discounted at 15%.

Let the annual sterling return from Muldovian operations be £R.

Year	Cash flow £	DCF factor at 15%	PV £
1 – 4	R per year	2.855	2.855R
4	12,340,600	0.572	7,058,823

Total PV of cash returns = 2.855R + 7,058,823

If the DCF return is exactly 15%:

£15,000,000 = £(2.855R + 7,058,823)

2.855R = 7,941,177

R = 2,781,498

To provide a constant annual cash flow from the investment, the annual after-tax return in sterling would need to be £2,781,498.

	After tax M$	Before tax M$
Minimum cash flows required, after tax and before tax		
Year 1: (£2,781,498 × 2 × 1.05: rounded)	5,841,150	9,735,250
Year 2 (× 1.05, rounded)	6,133,200	10,222,000
Year 3 (× 1.05, rounded)	6,439,850	10,733,000
Year 4 (× 1.05, rounded)	6,761,850	11,269,750
Year 4 recovery of investment	30,000,000	30,000,000

The after-tax returns on GCE's share of the investment would need to be in the region of M$5.8m to M$6.7m in each year, on an investment of M$30m. This is a very high and challenging return, and questions must be raised about whether returns of this scale will be achievable.

(e) **Investment risks**

There are several significant risks in this investment, most of them business risks.

The size of returns required to achieve the minimum 15% DCF return on investment is very large in relation to the amount of the investment. The average annual minimum cash returns for GCE from the operations would need to be about M$25m in the four years, which is an average of M$6.25m per year on an investment of M$30m. Although this size of return is not impossible, it will be difficult to achieve with the joint venture that is proposed.

The joint venture partner has no experience of exporting to other countries. It has been protected by a monopoly and it has no experience of competition and very little experience of operating in a private sector environment. Its annual operating profit is currently just M$2m, which means that the proposed new investment would increase its operating capacity enormously.

Its employees have no experience with modern technology; GCE would be required to provide all the skilled labour. But PetroEng would supply the unskilled labour with whom the skilled employees would have to achieve a good working relationship. Employees at PetroEng will have to change their attitude to working arrangements and efficiency, if the hoped-for returns are to be achieved.

The investment will be fairly large for GCE in terms of expected returns, but it has high risks attached, and there appear to be no options to invest gradually in stages or disinvest if the project is unsuccessful. This is an all-or-nothing investment in a foreign country, where management control by GCE may be restricted due to the joint venture arrangement.

If the joint venture is established as a separate joint venture entity, the board of the separate entity will control decisions about distribution of profits as dividends. In this arrangement, GCE could not therefore be certain that its share of the JV profits would be remitted in full.

There may also be some risk of political intervention by the government of Muldovia, for example to re-impose exchange controls on remittances out of the country, or restrict the convertibility of the M$ against other currencies. Any government measures that delay or defer the remittance of profits will affect the DCF return on investment.

The investment will also be exposed to currency risk. In particular there is a risk that the M$ will depreciate in value against sterling by more than 5% per year. If so, this may help the JV to export its products to other countries of South America, but it will also reduce the sterling value of the JV profits.

In summary, there are substantial business risks with this investment and some financial risks, but the anticipated return will need to be high. The finance director of GCE should be advised to confirm with the board of directors that this investment would be within the risk appetite and tolerance of the company.

18 Krown Jools plc

Marking guide

		Marks
		Up to
(a)	Valuation	11
(b)	Forecast EPS	12
(c)	Issues around method of financing the acquisition	9
(d)	Ethical issues	6
(e)	Strategic and operating risks	8
Total marks		46
Maximum marks		40

To:	Holly Harte – Engagement partner, Krown Jools
From:	A. Senior
Date:	XX.XX.XXXX
Subject:	Potential acquisition of Gubb

(a) Valuation

Free cash flow valuation

	£m
EBIT, year to 31/12/X2	4.80
Increase in directors' salaries	(0.50)
	4.30
Tax payments at 24%	1.03
Free cash flow	3.27

Depreciation should be added to free cash flow and essential capital expenditure deducted. Here it is assumed that depreciation equals essential capital expenditure.

The **maximum amount** that KJ should pay will reflect all the gains from synergies that will be obtained when Gubb becomes part of the group. This includes the temporary growth period, the sale of surplus assets and the terminal value. However the increase in directors' salaries seems inevitable, and since the adjustment will bring directors' salaries into line with market rates, it should be assumed that this annual effect on operating profits will be permanent.

Year		Free cash flow	Discount factor at	Present value
		£m	12%	£m
1	£3.27 + £2.1m sale of land	5.37	0.8929	4.79
2	£3.27 × 1.05	3.43	0.7972	2.73
3	£3.27 × 1.05^2	3.61	0.7118	2.57
4	£3.27 × 1.05^3	3.79	0.6355	2.41
				12.50

	£m
Total present value for forecast period (see above)	12.50
PV of free cash flows from Year 5 in perpetuity	
(3.79/0.12) × 0.6355	20.07
Total value of Gubb	32.57
Less value of debt	(9.00)
Value of Gubb equity	23.57
Shares in issue	10m
Value per share	**£2.36**

If the share-for-share exchange method of financing is used, given a share price of £3.95 for KJ shares, the exchange would be (3.95/2.36) = 1.67 shares in Gubb for every KJ share, or 5 Gubb shares for every 3 KJ shares.

KJ would therefore need to issue (10m × 3/5) = 6,000,000 shares

The above value per share attributes all synergistic gains to the Gubb shares to reflect the *maximum* KJ should pay.

Concerns

Free cash flow can be defined as follows:

Earnings before interest and taxation (EBIT)
Less tax on EBIT
Plus non-cash charges
Less capital expenditure (to replace ageing assets)
Less increase in net working capital *or* Plus: Decrease in net working capital
Plus value received from salvage of assets

The valuation of an enterprise, based on discounting future cash flows is similar to investment appraisal.

From a valuation perspective, the normalised cash flow and earnings figures are used together to estimate the free cash flows of a business. It is the free cash flow that is discounted to deduce an enterprise value for the business before deducting the value of debt to obtain an equity value.

The discount rate of 12% should be based on an ungeared beta for this level of business risk of Gubb.

The free cash flow method of determining the value of the equity is sufficiently flexible to allow for a period of temporary growth, followed by a perpetuity period of EBIT without growth. However, a concern is the sustainability of the cash flows in perpetuity, or indeed beyond a reasonable time horizon where markets may change.

In common with other valuation methods, it is dependent on the forecasts being reliable and the discount rate being appropriate and stable over time.

More detail on working capital cash flows, CAPEX outlays and taxes on capital expenditures would generate a better estimate.

The assumption that CAPEX equals historical cost depreciation appears unrealistic as it does not replace assets at their fair values and would lead to a shrinking business.

CAPEX → replacing assets @ their FV
So shouldn't equal historical dep^n

(b) **EPS**

(1) **Share for share exchange**

EPS for year ending 31 December 20X3:

	£
✓ Gubb earnings (£2.9m – £510,000) (W1)	2,390,000
✓ KJ earnings (£4.9m × 1.04)	5,096,000
Group profit after tax	7,486,000

Shares in issue

	£
KJ: current number in issue	20,000,000
New shares issued in share exchange to acquire Gubb (see above)	6,000,000
	26,000,000

EPS = £7.486m/26m
= **28.8p**

EPS in 20X2 = £4.9m/20m
= **24.5p**

WORKING 1

IFRS 3 requires net assets to be stated at fair value on acquisition, therefore the consolidated financial statements will require an additional depreciation charge.

Depreciation adjustment for 20X3 – Gubb head office

	£
Fair value depreciation (£10m/40)	250,000 ✓
Depreciation in Gubb financial statements (£6m/50)	120,000 ✓
Additional depreciation charge	130,000
Additional directors' salaries, less taxation: £500,000 × 76%	380,000
Downward adjustment to Gubb earnings in 20X3	510,000

(2) **EPS with debt financing**

Purchase price of Gubb = £23.57m

	£
Group profit after tax as stated above	7,486,000
Interest cost net of tax: (23.57m × 9% × (1 – 0.24))	1,612,188
Revised earnings	5,873,812

EPS = £5,873,812/20m
= **29.4p**

(3) **EPS with part share exchange and loan notes**

Acquisition financed by issuing 3m new shares in KJ and 10% loan notes for £23.57m/2 = £11.785m.

	£
Group profit after tax as stated above	7,486,000
Interest cost net of tax: (11.785m × 10% × (1 – 0.24))	895,660
Revised earnings	6,590,340

EPS = £6,590,340/23m
= **28.7p**

(4) **Impact of EPS on share price**

The EPS has increased from 20X2 under each of the three financing methods. However, this is not necessarily beneficial for the KJ share price, as it reflects the fact that Gubb, with poor growth prospects in the long term compared to KJ, has a higher EPS but lower P/E ratio. (Note that Gubb would not have a published EPS but it can be calculated in accordance with IAS 33 to assess the impact on the group). This means that **in the short run** EPS can be increased, as a smaller number of shares in KJ can be issued to acquire Gubb shares, as the price of each KJ share reflects future growth in its P/E ratio.

However, the stock market is likely to perceive that this increase in EPS is short term and does not represent a fundamental increase in shareholder wealth. The share price of the group is unlikely to increase as a consequence. This is also reflected in the 12% discount rate.

It should also be remembered that the valuation of Gubb shares was a **maximum price calculation**, based on the assumption that all the synergy benefits should accrue to the Gubb shareholders, and not to KJ shareholders.

(c) Method of financing

Superficially it would seem that borrowing to finance the acquisition would generate higher earnings and a higher EPS than the share-for-share exchange or partial share exchange and loan notes issue.

Comparison of share-for-share exchange with debt-financed share purchase

While interest is payable at 9% on debt and equity requires a 12% rate of return this fails to recognise that there is increased gearing with the debt-financed acquisition which would mean that there is likely to be an increase in financial risk and a higher required rate of return on equity. Strictly, the 12% rate of return relates to an ungeared beta as it reflects the return on total assets. Increased financial risk would increase the rate of return required on equity, based on a geared beta. A share-for-share exchange would conversely lower the level of gearing.

One advantage of debt is that it benefits from a tax shield, as interest payments are tax deductible. As such, in a world with tax deductible debt, this would mean that debt does have a tax advantage over equity finance.

Despite this, gearing would increase significantly with the debt financed option. The debt of the group would increase to £52.57m (£20m + £9m + £23.57m). Given the equity value of £79.0m (20m × £3.95) this would give a debt to equity gearing of 66.5% (£52.57m/£79.0m). This may reduce future debt capacity and reduce future financial flexibility to exploit new future opportunities through borrowing. In the credit crunch many firms have been de-gearing in order to reduce this risk notwithstanding the tax deductibility of interest on debt.

Issuing new shares through a share-for-share exchange is likely to change the balance of control amongst KJ shareholders. By issuing 6m new shares this is a 30% increase in the share capital of KJ. Perhaps more significantly, the Gubb family shareholders previously had a controlling holding in Gubb, but they are now minority shareholders in KJ. Although they have an exit route through selling as KJ is listed, the value may not reflect the control they had with Gubb. Moreover, their directors' remuneration may also be reduced or lost.

Consideration of partial share exchange and loan notes issue

This financing option has some advantages, because it is a mixture of the two financing options considered above.

- It is a way of using debt finance for the acquisition in the event that KJ is unable to raise the funding from a bank.

- EPS will be very similar to the situation with a 100% share-for-share exchange and members of the Gubb family will not acquire such a large equity interest in KJ, at least not for the first four years. defer

- Tax relief will be available on the debt capital, although the interest cost would be higher than with a bank loan.

Problems with this possible method of financing are that:

- the Gubb shareholders may not agree to it.

- if the Gubb shareholders do agree to accept convertible loan notes, these may influence the KJ share price in four years' time when the notes become convertible into KJ equity.

(d) **Ethics**

(1) **Share pricing**

If KJ shares are overpriced in the market at the time of a share-for-share exchange then the terms of the deal will be more favourable to KJ shareholders and less favourable to Gubb shareholders than would be the case if the shares were correctly priced.

However, unless the KJ board has deliberately attempted to manipulate the share price or conceal information **(Tutorial note:** *This would be a contravention of Listing Rules),* it is not responsible for market mispricing. It is incumbent on the management of Gubb to make their own judgement about the KJ share price and obtain the necessary information to do so (eg by doing their own due diligence). The ethical issue is one of transparency and there does not appear to be any obligation on the KJ board to express their view of overpricing. It is only incumbent on them to make the agreed information available to Gubb and their advisers.

(2) **Provision for reorganisation**

A provision needs to be made in the financial statements for the year ending 31 December 20X2 if the conditions of IAS 37 are met in that there is:

- a legal or constructive obligation at 31 December 20X2 as a result of a past event; and
- it is probable that an outflow of economic benefits will occur.

Thus, even if the reorganisation is delayed to 20X3, if there is an obligation created in 20X2 then a provision should be made in the financial statements for the year ending 31 December 20X2.

In ethical terms, however, if the management decision, and therefore the obligation, is to be delayed until 20X3 there is no constructive obligation and therefore no requirement to make a provision. As a result, no obvious ethical issue arises. For instance, this may be due to reassessing the timing of the reorganisation in light of the proposed acquisition which is a commercial decision.

Also, as the financial statements for the year ended 31 December 20X2 will not actually be published at the date of the acquisition, any provision, or an absence of a provision, would not impact on the share price at that date and would not therefore influence the terms of the share-for-share exchange.

(e) **Risks and due diligence**

(1) **Strategic risks**

The proposed acquisition would be a strategy of related diversification. The market of KJ is however significantly different from that of Gubb, as fashion jewellery has different customers from mid-market traditional jewellery. Within the Ansoff matrix this could be regarded as market development.

The industry is also different, as the composition of the jewellery differs and suppliers are therefore likely to differ, thus reducing the possibility of scale economies.

There are risks of failing to understand these elements of demand and supply in the new business where KJ management may not have the necessary core competences.

A period of doing little for a year after acquisition is one risk management response to these risks which KJ is intending to use. There is, nevertheless, the risk that KJ management will remain reliant on Gubb management for strategic knowledge and skills relating to the fashion jewellery market and industry.

The strategic fit between the two businesses is therefore less than perfect and there would be some change in strategic direction arising from any acquisition. On the other hand, there is some diversification away from mid-market traditional jewellery which may reduce risk.

A further strategic risk is that of reputational damage to KJ, as fashion jewellery is downmarket from mid-market traditional jewellery and this may affect customers' perceptions of the quality of KJ's products. This is particularly the case given that the quality of gold and diamonds is not easily observable by retail customers.

(2) **Operating risks**

There is a risk that the post-acquisition integration of the two companies may not deliver the predicted synergies and therefore offer little improvement in operational efficiency. The risk then arises that KJ may have overpaid for the acquisition, particularly if the price finally agreed is close to the maximum calculated above.

While the two businesses will remain operationally separate, merging the administration functions of the two companies may give rise to unforeseen problems where there are integration issues. These may include: differing corporate cultures, merging information systems and support processes (eg accounting, HRM, IT, internal controls, supply chain management, deliveries, marketing).

Other operating risks may include the following:

- Hidden contractual or other legal obligations, without indemnities.

- Hidden financial liabilities (eg tax) without indemnities.

- While the specific method of financing is not to be considered, any debt finance in future will add to financial gearing of the new group and thus increase financial risk.

- The Gubb business appears to depend on the Gubb family. Unless there is some form of contractual tie-in or conditional consideration for the acquisition then there may be loss of value as the family is likely to remain core to the fashion jewellery element of the business, at least in the short term.

- The ability to raise future debt might be limited as the group would have limited assets to secure it as the stores are held under operating leases: this may limit future financial flexibility.

- The sales of surplus assets may be uncertain in terms of the prices that may be obtained and the identification of assets that are no longer required due to duplication or strategic refocus.

19 Coriander plc

Marking guide

		Marks Up to
(a)	Assumptions about performance	10 ⎤
	Short-term performance and earnings per share	10 ⎦ 20
(b)	Accounting treatment of convertible bond	8 ·
(c)	Segmental analysis	6 ·
(d)	Valuation	10 ·
(e)	Raising the finance	4 ·
(f)	Conclusions	3 ·
Total marks		51
Maximum marks		45

MEMO

From: Paulina Constantine
To: Alex Davis
Date: [today's date]
Subject: Acquisition of Cortège NW Ltd

(a) (1) **Mark's assumptions**

Increasing sales by 25% in a single year would be an ambitious objective for any business. To do so while planning to cut costs is an even more difficult task, because generating the additional revenue will require increased spending on marketing, staff training and staff retention. There is a danger that this could lead to skimping on the quality of the food being purchased, which would have implications for business reputation and sales.

We can investigate Mark's assertions by exploring his reasoning.

Sales revenue assumptions

Does Mark plan to increase revenue by increasing the number of customers eating at CNW or will CNW change its pricing and aim to generate an increased spend per customer?

If he is planning to bring in more customers, (a) how will he attract them and (b) will CNW have sufficient capacity to service their requirements? There is no point in working with figures that would require 50 diners per sitting on a busy evening if CNW can only accommodate 40.

 His projections for revenue growth exceed those that are expected in 20X8 for the industry as a whole and also for Coriander. They also exceed historical revenue growth, which was 8% in 20X7 for Coriander and is expected to be about the same for CNW. On the other hand, if the company has not been run well in the past it might be argued that a major improvement in revenue can be achieved just by dealing with CNW's problems. We understand that a business similar to CNW but in other locations is capable of achieving annual revenues of £2.5m, which is 67% above the revenue of CNW in 20X7. The potential for strong sales growth may well exist.

If Mark plans to change the menu to appeal to a higher-spending clientele then he will have to demonstrate that there is sufficient demand in this market. Assuming that there are other restaurants in this price bracket in the local area of each of CNW's outlets then that should establish local demand, although it will also mean that there is already established competition.

The promotional budget of £50,000 will have to be analysed to establish exactly what is being purchased. While this sounds like a great deal of money, it amounts to slightly less than £1,000 per week, which might not go far in terms of a credible advertising presence. It would be reassuring to see what results Mark has had with similar spends in the work that he has done with Coriander. If there have been no comparable promotions then there is less reason to believe that this is possible.

Reducing the cost of sales and increasing gross profit margin

Reducing the cost of sales to 30% of sales revenue seems an impossible target. That is lower than Coriander can currently achieve in a sector of the industry in which it is highly experienced. It may be possible if Mark is planning to generate the increased sales by moving downmarket and massively increasing revenues by selling, say, fast food that is inexpensive but of low quality. Low cost of sales would also be possible in an upmarket restaurant where selling prices and indirect costs were high relative to cost of sales (ie ingredients). These projections can be checked by obtaining price lists or quotes from the suppliers whom Mark proposes to use.

 The argument that the previous general and local managers were incapable of keeping costs under control suggests that replacements might have some success in this area. It would be helpful to see some evidence of past performance just to demonstrate that poor cost control has been responsible for the disappointing performance. That would not prove that savings could be made, but it would give a slightly higher degree of confidence that savings were possible.

It is interesting that Mark has focused on cost of sales as the area where cost savings can be achieved. If he is correct about the inefficiency of the current management of CNW, it might be expected that there is potential to cut operating expenses, in spite of the higher planned marketing spend.

Finally, there is an assumption that working practices can be changed and that the unwanted staff and junior managers will leave of their own accord. It may not be possible to change working practices quite so easily, particularly if this would involve changes to terms in contracts of employment. It would be necessary to review the employment contracts to see how much flexibility there was. Certainly, however, it would not be possible simply to change the terms on which current employees were engaged, even if ownership of the business were to change.

ICAEW

Moreover, it would be somewhat unethical to simply 'make life uncomfortable' for existing managers in the hope that they will resign. There would also be a risk of legal actions by employees claiming constructive dismissal.

(2) **Impact on short-term performance and forecast of post-acquisition earnings**

The impact of the proposed acquisition on the short-term performance of Coriander is estimated by calculating the post-acquisition earnings of CNW and their contribution to the earnings of Coriander.

Under the post-acquisition assumptions that have been suggested, the statement of profit or loss for CNW post acquisition will be:

	Workings	20X8 £
Revenue	(W1)	1,887,500
Cost of sales	(W2)	566,250
Gross profit		1,321,250
Operating expenses	(W3)	750,000
Profit from operations		571,250
Finance costs	(W4)	280,000
Profit before tax		291,250
Tax	(W5)	58,250
Profit for the period		233,000

WORKINGS

(1) £1,887,500 = 1.25 × £1,510,000

(2) 0.3 × £1,887,500

(3) £700,000 + £50,000

(4) This assumes no change to finance costs. Actual finance costs will depend on how we finance the acquisition and how we then apportion finance costs over the group (see below).

(5) This assumes a constant effective tax rate of 20%, which is in line with our own effective tax rate: 20% × £291,250.

Basic earnings per share before acquisition

The basic EPS for Coriander for 20X8 before the acquisition of CNW is calculated as

Basic EPS = £4,151,280/3m shares = £1.384

CNW will make a contribution to Coriander's earnings of £233,000, before considering any change in finance costs. This is discussed below, after considering the accounting treatment of the convertible bond (as this will affect EPS post acquisition).

(b) **Accounting treatment of convertible bond**

For accounting purposes, the convertible bond is a compound financial instrument made up of a liability component and an equity component.

The liability component is calculated as the present value of the interest and capital payments discounted at the market interest rate of an equivalent bond with no conversion rights.

Year	Cash flow £	Discount factor (rounded)	£
1	70,000	0.909	63,630
2	70,000	0.826	57,820
3	1,070,000	0.751	803,570
Liability			925,020

The equity component represents the buyers' right to convert debt into equity at any time before maturity. In effect the holder has bought an equity call option from the issuer of the bond.

The value of equity is calculated as the difference between the total value of the bond and the liability component, ie:

Equity = Value of the bond − Liability = 1,000,000 − 925,020 = £74,980

This amount is not subsequently re-measured.

Interest payments

On the assumption that the bond will not be classified as at fair value through profit or loss, the £925,020 liability component will be shown at amortised cost. Assuming no issue costs, the amounts to be reported, using an effective interest rate of 10%, are as follows:

Year	Liability b/f £	Interest @ 10% £	Cash paid £	Liability c/f £
1	925,020	92,502	70,000	947,522
2	947,522	94,752	70,000	972,274
3	972,274	97,227	1,070,000	0 (rounded)

Accounting entries

The entries for 20X8 will be

	£	£
On issue:		
DEBIT Cash	1,000,000	
CREDIT Liability		925,020
CREDIT Equity		74,980
At the reporting date:		
DEBIT Interest expense	92,502	
CREDIT Cash		70,000
CREDIT Liability		22,502

Earnings per share post acquisition

This continues the analysis of earnings per share.

The revised forecast/statement of profit or loss for Coriander for the year ending 31 December 20X8 is

	£
Profit from operations	5,469,100
Finance costs (280,000 + 92,502)	372,502
Profit before tax	5,096,598
Tax (assuming a 20% effective rate)	1,019,320
Profit for the period	4,077,278

To calculate the impact on the basic earnings per share we need to calculate the consolidated earnings of CNW to be acquired and Coriander which is given below.

	£
Profit from operations (5,469,100 + 571,250)	6,040,350
Finance costs (372,502 + 280,000)	652,502
Profit before tax	5,387,848
Tax (20%)	1,077,570
Profit for the period	4,310,278

Basic EPS

The predicted basic earnings per share will be

BEPS = £4,310,278/3m shares = £1.437

The effect of the acquisition is to increase the Basic EPS of Coriander from £1.384 to £1.437.

Diluted EPS

To calculate the diluted earnings per share we need to consider the impact on both earnings and number of shares of the possible conversion of the convertible bond. On conversion, after tax earnings attributed to ordinary shareholders should be increased by the reduction in the interest charge payable to loan holders.

Profit for the period will increase if the shares are converted by the amount of interest on the convertible bond. Thus earnings will increase by £925,020 × 10% = £92,502. At the same time there will be an increase in the company's tax liability because the interest on the bond is no longer deducted from taxable profits. The net increase in the consolidated profits for the period will be

	£
Profit for the period (as above)	4,310,278
Post-tax effect of saved finance costs (92,502 × (100 – 20)%)	74,002
Profit for diluted EPS	4,384,280

On conversion the number of ordinary shares will increase by 125,000 shares, raising the number of ordinary shares after conversion to 3.125m ordinary shares.

The 20X8 diluted EPS is therefore

Diluted EPS = £4,384,280/3,125,000 shares = £1.403

The effect of funding the acquisition through the issue of a convertible bond is to increase earnings per share to £1.403, even if all the bonds are converted to shares.

(c) Segment analysis

As IFRS 8 applies to (debt or equity) listed entities we will need to consider the impacts of this transaction on our financial statements.

Under IFRS 8 we would need to consider whether we will keep discrete financial information about this business and, if so, whether this information will be reported to the chief operating decision maker (presumably Mark Jones) to assess performance and/or allocate resources. It is likely that this will happen as we do not currently have a significant amount of activity in the North West and due to the historical poor performance of CNW it may be prudent for him to review the activities on a regular basis, at least initially.

It is possible that the information will be aggregated with other parts of the business. The outcome here will hinge on whether the products (French food) are felt to be similar enough to the other activities of the business (Indian food in the main). The other criteria for aggregation seem likely to be met (similar production processes, customers, regulation and distribution methods).

Once we have identified if the segment is of management interest for IFRS 8 purposes and has not been aggregated, we will need to consider how much revenue, profits and assets the new acquisition represents of the whole. If the new business represents 10% of any of these indicators (profit making parts of the whole business in our case for identifying the profit level) then it will need to be disclosed as a separate segment. It is highly likely that as a minimum the revenue criteria will be met. We will also have to meet the 75% of total external revenue test (if insufficient segments are identified and for some reason the segment is not already disclosed – we will need to keep disclosing segments which may include this one, until 75% of external revenue has been analysed).

It is of course possible for us to voluntarily disclose the information concerning this business but this does not easily fit with our desire to minimise the information in the public domain.

(d) Valuation of CNW

Net asset basis for valuation

The net asset value method determines the value of equity as the difference between the market value of assets and the market value of liabilities. The assets of the company were estimated to have the following market values:

	Market value at 31 December 20X7
	£
Assets	
Owned premises	5,900,000
Fixtures and fittings	1,000,000
Current assets	100,000
TOTAL ASSETS	7,000,000

The market value of the premises has been provided by Cortège and may need independent confirmation.

The liabilities, as shown in the statement of financial position, are as follows:

Liabilities	Market value at 31 December 20X7 £
Loans	4,500,000
Current liabilities	500,000
TOTAL LIABILITIES	5,000,000

I have used the amounts in the statement of financial position and I am not able to verify the existence or not of covenants which could cause the loan to be repayable on take-over. This may cause liquidity problems and would need to be assessed during due diligence. It will also be necessary to assess the repayment schedule and whether loans will need to be refinanced. Finally, we need to ascertain the nature of current liabilities and explore the possibility that supplier terms and conditions may be improved.

Thus the net asset value of the company is approximately £2m based on these assumptions.

Price/Earnings multiple basis of valuation

Mark's forecast profits for CNW are £300,000 in 20X9 – so this figure can be used as a starting point for an optimistic valuation. The forecast figure of £233,000 for 20X8 (calculated previously in this memo) could also be used, but then we would have to adjust for predicted growth. The 20X9 value of £300,000 is perhaps likely to be a closer estimate of future maintainable earnings.

Current P/E ratio for Coriander is approximately 8, based on 20X7 amounts:

20X7 EPS = £3,744,640/3,000,000 = £1.248

Current P/E ratio: 10/1.248 = 8

Applying this to profits assumes that the CNW business will have the same long-term growth potential as Coriander as a whole.

A P/E multiple of 8 produces a valuation of £2.4m using earnings of £300,000, or £1.9m using earnings of £233,000.

(e) **Raising the finance**

Theta Bank has suggested that one half of the finance required could be raised by issuing £1,000,000 in convertible bonds. This would be a fairly small bond issue, and it would have to be questioned what the costs of the issue would be. Legal and other costs could be high relative to the amount of capital raised. We should also need to be confident that Theta Bank would be able to find investors who are willing to take on relatively small amounts of the convertible bond: demand for convertibles from investors can vary substantially over time. I suggest that Theta Bank is asked to confirm that the bonds could be issued, and at an acceptable cost.

The remaining £1,000,000 would have to be financed as equity. Coriander may well have sufficient cash to make the purchase. If it needed to raise the money by issuing new shares, an issue of about 100,000 shares would be required, given the current market price of £10 per share. This would be a small issue relative to the current issued share capital of 3m shares and it should be possible to issue these in a placing with institutional investors.

I also make an additional comment in the conclusion below about the total amount of financing required.

In conclusion, the only significant doubt about the proposal from Theta Bank is the feasibility of making a small issue of convertible bonds, but it should be possible to obtain confirmation from the bank about this.

(f) **Conclusion**

The impact of the acquisition on earnings of Coriander in the short-term is negligible. In the case where the acquisition is funded by issuing a convertible bond, then there will be a reduction in the diluted earnings per share, compared with the undiluted earnings per share after the acquisition.

The value of the restaurants is estimated using two alternative methods which both support a valuation in the region of £2m. However, forecast earnings, even for 20X8, are based on some rather optimistic assumptions.

- There is no evidence to suggest that Coriander will be able to reduce the cost of sales at each location to 30%, a level that is below that of the other Cortège locations, and below the level of Coriander, particularly given that the cost of sales is now in excess of the average for the industry.

- The growth expectations for CNW are higher than the current consensus expectations of financial analysts for Coriander, Cortège as a whole and for the industry.

- Despite the increased investment in advertising, it may not be possible to achieve the dramatic increase in sales assumed for the first year after acquisition, as the advertising campaign may need a longer time to become effective.

On the other hand, the break-even point for the CNW restaurants is roughly £0.75m. This is significantly lower than the more established Cortège restaurants or Coriander itself which may make it possible to achieve the planned level of profitability at a lower level of sales.

The capital committed by Coriander should be revised upwards from £2m, since it is highly likely that Coriander may be forced to make additional capital contributions to the business in order to maintain operations until they improve.

In conclusion, this could be a risky acquisition which makes economic sense only under optimistic assumptions about revenue growth and cost reductions.

20 Luminum plc

Marking guide

		Marks Up to
(a)	Working capital: operating cycle analysis	15
(b)	Benefits and risks of invoicing in euros	5
(c)	Working capital financing	5
(d)	German investment: analysis of financing	12
(e)	German investment: investment appraisal and risk analysis	10
(f)	Discussion of sustainability/CSR	12
Total marks		59
Maximum marks		55

To:	Karen Carter, CEO Luminum plc
From:	Accountant
Date:	XX January 20X5
Subject:	Business development projects

This memo sets out the information that you requested at our recent meeting. My workings related to the change in operating cycle are shown in the Appendices attached.

(a) **Exporting to France: change in operating cycle**

If Luminum goes ahead with its decision to export to France, the operating cycle will increase from 112 days to about 124 days. It is not possible to predict the exact increase in operating cycle due to uncertainty about the volume of export sales.

The reasons for the increase are as follows:

- There will be an increase in the average period for collection of payment from credit sales. This is because the average credit period will be 73 days (20% × 365) for customers in France compared with 58 days for UK credit customers.

- There will be slower inventory turnover periods, especially in finished goods. It is not clear why the turnover periods for raw materials and work in progress should be expected to increase, unless a change is expected in the sales mix as a result of selling to France. The increase in the finished goods turnover period from about 35 days to 41 days is presumably due to the longer period of time required to deliver the finished goods to customers in France.

(b) **Invoicing in euros**

Luminum proposes to invoice its French customers in euros.

The main benefit of invoicing in euros is competitive advantage. French customers are more likely to purchase goods priced in euros than goods priced in sterling, because they need not concern themselves with the administrative necessity of buying sterling to pay a UK supplier, and they do not have exposures to risks from adverse exchange rate movements.

The main disadvantage of invoicing customers in euros is that Luminum will be exposed to risks of adverse exchange rate movements and will need to consider whether measures to hedge these risks would be appropriate. If the euro falls in value against sterling, which is the current expectation, the sterling value of exports priced in euros will fall over time, unless the selling price in euros is increased.

Since the expected payment period from French customers will be 73 days, or more than two months, it may be appropriate to hedge the risk by selling euros forward in exchange for sterling in forward exchange contracts. I suggest that your treasury section calculate the potential benefits of fixing the exchange rate for credit sales to France, if the expectations of a weaker euro are well-based.

Another way of hedging the currency risk might be to raise borrowings in euros, instead of sterling (or swap sterling loans for euro loans) so that income in euros from sales to France is offset to some extent by interest payments on the euro loans. A switch from borrowing in sterling to borrowing in euros could be achieved by redeeming sterling loans and taking out new euro loans. Alternatively the same effect could be achieved by means of a euro-sterling interest rate swap.

(c) **Financing working capital**

Luminum currently finances its net current assets with medium-term loans. This may be described as a conservative approach to working capital financing. Net current assets fluctuate in amount, and with a policy of financing them with medium-term loans, the company is financing not only its 'permanent' net current assets, but also a large proportion of its temporary net current assets too. Short term financing, such as a bank overdraft, is only needed occasionally when net current assets exceed the amount of medium-term borrowing.

With this conservative policy, there will often be surplus cash. Interest earned from placing this surplus cash on temporary deposit (or investing it in other ways) is likely to be less than the interest cost of the borrowing. As a result, there will be a net cost to the company from having surplus cash through over-borrowing.

A more aggressive policy for financing net current assets would be to finance them entirely with short-term finance, such as a bank overdraft. Depending on the cash flow projections for the company, the cost of short-term borrowing on overdraft is likely to be lower than medium-term borrowing, because average borrowings over time should be lower (and the interest rate on an overdraft may also be lower than on a medium-term loan).

(d) **Financing the investment in Germany**

The investment in Germany would cost £6.25m initially, or €7.5m at the current exchange rate of €1.20/£1. The intention is to establish a separate subsidiary company, and to do this there must be some equity capital. Presumably the intention would be for the parent company to raise the capital and use the money raised to establish the subsidiary. As the details of the proposed arrangement are not available, I do not propose to comment further on the financial structuring of the subsidiary here, and shall focus on the group consolidated figures alone.

Current gearing level

If we define gearing as Long-term debt/(Equity + Long-term debt), the current gearing level is 9,350/(15,600 + 9,350) = 37.47%.

Sterling loan

If the investment is financed with a sterling medium-term loan, there must be a plan for re-financing if required at the end of the loan period.

A sterling loan to purchase euro-denominated assets for the subsidiary would expose the company to currency risk. There would be translation risk arising from translation of the euro assets into sterling for the purpose of consolidation. If the euro falls in value from its current rate of €1.20/£1, a loss on translation will arise.

In addition to this translation risk, there will inevitably be transaction risk arising from transactions between the subsidiary and the parent company, involving exchange of sterling for euros (or vice versa).

If the investment is financed with a sterling loan, a summary consolidated statement of financial position would be as follows, depending on whether the exchange rate is €1.20 or €1.30.

	Exchange rate €1.20/£1	Exchange rate €1.30/£1
Assets	£'000	£'000
UK	28,050	28,050
• Germany (€7.5m)	6,250	5,769
Total assets	34,300	33,819
Equity: initial	15,600	15,600
Loss on translation[1]	–	(481)
	15,600	15,119
UK borrowings	15,600	15,600
Euro borrowings	0	0
Current liabilities	3,100	3,100
Equity plus liabilities	34,300	33,819

— OCI ✓

[1]: [€7,500,000 at €1.30] – [€7,500,000 at €1.20] = £5,769,231 – £6,250,000 = £(480,769).

The gearing ratio would be:

- At exchange rate €1.20: 15,600/(15,600 + 15,600) = 50%
- At exchange rate €1.30: 15,600/(15,119 + 15,600) = 50.8%

Borrowing would increase the gearing ratio, although the gearing level may not be excessive, and a fall in the value of the euro against sterling would increase gearing slightly.

[handwritten left margin: Bond-too small!]

[handwritten right margin: High yield needed for bond.]

There is a suggestion that the debt finance might be raised by means of a bond issue. Given the fairly small amount of capital required, and the status of the company as AIM-listed, it is unlikely that investors would be willing to invest in a bond issue by the company. The bonds would not have a secondary market, and investors would demand a high yield to justify their purchase of the company's bonds.

Loan in euros

If the investment is financed with a medium-term loan in euros, there must be a plan for re-financing if required at the end of the loan period.

A loan in euros to purchase euro-denominated assets for the subsidiary would enable the company to avoid currency risk with the initial investment. There would not be any translation risk arising from translation of the initial euro assets into sterling for the purpose of consolidation, because any change in the sterling equivalent value of the assets would be matched by an equivalent change in the sterling value of the euro loan.

However, as commercial operations get under way in the German subsidiary, currency risk exposures will arise from business operations – for example as the subsidiary makes profits (or losses) in euros.

	Exchange rate €1.20/£1 £'000	Exchange rate €1.30/£1 £'000
Assets		
UK	28,050	28,050
Germany (€7.5m)	6,250	5,769
Total assets	34,300	33,819
Equity	15,600	15,600
UK borrowings	9,350	9,350
Euro borrowings	6,250	5,769
Current liabilities	3,100	3,100
Equity plus liabilities	34,300	33,819

The gearing ratio would be:

- At exchange rate €1.20: 15,600/15,600 + 15,600) = 50%
- At exchange rate €1.30: 15,119/(15,600 + 15,119) = 49.2%

Gearing would fall if the euro loses value (but would increase if the euro gains value against sterling).

Equity issue

To raise £6.25m in equity, the company may be advised to make a rights issue. Alternatively it may be advised to issue the new shares in a placing, with prior approval from the shareholders. This is an issue on which the company's investment banking advisers or sponsor would be able to make a recommendation.

An equity issue has the advantage that it provides an additional buffer against potential losses, and equity may be the preferable method of financing when the risk is very high. Dividend payments do not have to be made, whereas interest payments on loans must be. It is not clear, however, that risk is so high that debt finance should not be considered.

Like a sterling loan, an equity issue would not provide any hedge against an adverse exchange rate movement (a weaker euro).

	Exchange rate €1.20/£1 £'000	Exchange rate €1.30/£1 £'000
Assets		
UK	28,050	28,050
Germany (€7.5m)	6,250	5,769
Total assets	34,300	33,819
Equity: initial	21,850	21,850
Loss on translation	–	(481)
	21,850	21,369
UK borrowings	9,350	9,350
Current liabilities	3,100	3,100
Equity plus liabilities	34,300	33,819

The gearing ratio would be:

- At exchange rate €1.20: 9,350/(21,850 + 9,350) = 30.0%
- At exchange rate €1.30: 9,350/(21,369 + 9,350) = 30.4%

Because it provides protection against adverse exchange rate movements, the euro loan may be preferred. However the choice also depends on expectations of the future exchange rate movement and also the perceived level of risk in the German investment.

(e) **Project analysis: German investment**

It is surprising that the same cost of capital should be applied to the project, regardless of the currency of financing. However, this assumption is accepted here for the purpose of the analysis.

Annual depreciation:

Distribution centre: Cost €5,400,000. Annual depreciation (20 years) = €270,000.

Delivery trucks: Cost €2,100,000. Annual depreciation (5 years) = €420,000

Total annual depreciation = €690,000.

Estimated cash flows

Year	Profit before interest and tax	Tax	Depreciation	Estimated cash flow
	€'000	€'000	€'000	€'000
1	0.5	(0.1)	0.69	1.09
2	1.0	(0.2)	0.69	1.49
3	2.0	(0.4)	0.69	2.29
4	3.0	(0.6)	0.69	3.09
5	3.0	(0.6)	0.69	3.09
	Value of dist'n centre			
5	5.4			5.40
				16.45

DCF analysis

The project is evaluated in the table below. If it is financed by a loan in euros, it is sufficient to discount the euro cash flows and compare these with the initial cost of the loan. If it is financed by a sterling loan, we should evaluate sterling cash flows, and to do this we can assume that 100% of profits after German tax are remitted to the UK as dividends, and that any remaining cash flows would be remitted at the end of Year 5.

Loan in euros:

Year		Cash flow	Present value at 10%
		€'000	€'000
1	Profit before interest and tax	1.09	0.991
2		1.49	1.231
3		2.29	1.721
4		3.09	2.111
5		3.09	1.919
			7.973
5	Value of dist'n centre	5.40	3.353
			11.326
0	Initial investment		(7.500)
	NPV		3.826

Loan in sterling:

Amount remitted each year in Years 1 – 4 = Profit after tax

Balance remitted in Year 5.

Year	Cash flow in € €m	Exchange rate	Cash flow in £ £m	Present value at 10% £m
1	0.40	1.22	0.328	0.298
2	0.80	1.24	0.645	0.533
3	1.60	1.26	1.270	0.954
4	2.40	1.28	1.875	1.281
	5.20			3.066
5 (16.45 – 5.2)	11.25	1.30	8.654	5.373
				8.439
0				(6.250)
NPV				2.189

The project is expected to provide a positive NPV, ignoring risk and uncertainty in the cash flow estimates.

If the project is financed with a bank loan in euros, the project can be evaluated on the basis of the euro cash flows. This indicates a positive NPV of €3.826m, and the project should therefore add to the company's value. However the value in sterling will depend on when the cash flows from the project are remitted (if at all) to the UK.

If the project is financed with a sterling bank loan, we need to consider the NPV in terms of sterling cash flows. Since remittances to the UK will be restricted to a maximum of post-tax profits, the NPV is reduced by the delay in obtaining sterling returns and also the decline in the value of the euro against sterling over the period.

The cash flows from the project profits are insufficient to pay back the investment, and payback at the end of Year 5 is achieved from the terminal value of the distribution centre.

Even if all the project cash fows are retained in the German subsidiary and are not remitted to the UK until the end of Year 5, the €16.45m would have an expected sterling value of (/1.30) £12.654m at the end of Year 5, which has a present value of £7.857m discounted at 10%. This would still exceed the cost of the investment.

In purely financial terms, the project would appear to be a worthwhile undertaking, regardless of whether it is financed by a euro or a sterling loan.

(f) **Sustainability**

Sustainability and CSR compared

You are correct to make a distinction between sustainability and corporate social responsibility (CSR), although they are related issues.

The term 'sustainability' can have two meanings. It can refer to the ability of a business to operate commercially without putting at risk the ability of future generations to enjoy a prosperous life for themselves. In this respect, sustainability refers mainly to the ability of a business to operate without causing irreparable damage to the environment, through irreversible pollution and contamination, and through consumption of scarce and irreplaceable natural resources.

A second meaning of 'sustainability' considers the broader issue of how a business can develop and succeed commercially in the long term as well as the short term. Traditionally the success of a business has been judged by its profitability and its growth, measured perhaps in terms of the quantity and value of its net assets.

Traditionally, it is assumed that if a company is profitable and continues to grow, it will be successful.

The concept of 'business sustainability' challenges this traditional view to some extent. It takes the view that although a business must be profitable and should maintain or grow its net assets to survive in the long term, it should also have regard to sustainability of the natural environment in which it operates, its relations with its work force ('human capital') and the tacit support of the community in which it operates. Sustainability requires management of natural capital, human capital and social capital as well as financial and net asset growth.

Corporate social responsibility (CSR) is the concept that a company has a moral or ethical responsibility, as a 'citizen' of the society in which it operates, to act for the good of society as well as to make profits for shareholders. Companies should therefore take measures to protect the natural environment, because this belongs to all society. Similarly a company has an ethical obligation to consider the well-being of its work force and the interests of society more generally.

One aspect of sustainability is concerned with the commercial objective of long-term survival. CSR focuses more on ethical responsibilities. These two different views, however, are compatible. Companies can – and it may be argued should – concern themselves with both.

Sustainability, CSR and the detergents, soaps and hygiene products industry

The challenges of sustainability, and the CSR issues associated with them, vary significantly between different industries. For the oil and energy industries, for example, a major issue is the extraction and use of diminishing natural resources. For many manufacturing industries, key issues are emissions from production processes and pollution of land, air and water.

The detergents, soaps and hygiene products industry, like other manufacturing industries, must deal with the problem of emissions from production processes, and recycling waste. It seems inevitable that over time, regulations to restrict emissions and environmental damage will become more strict. Companies in the industry will have to become 'cleaner' in order to survive.

A problem, however, is the time scale over which production standards are improved. Companies that invest now in 'greener' production methods may put themselves at a cost disadvantage to rivals that continue to use old technology.

Our industry has additional challenges where sustainability and CSR policies can benefit companies commercially. Already leading global companies in the industry are taking initiatives in this area, particularly in developing countries.

A major aspect of social policy is hygiene and health. Producers of soap, detergent and other hygiene products should be at the forefront of initiatives to improve hygiene throughout societies in all parts of the world. The commercial benefit of selling more product and the social benefit of better hygiene and health standards are closely linked. Our industry will benefit from improving worldwide hygiene standards.

CSR policies include policies to help local communities. Major producers are already implementing policies to educate local communities in developing countries about hygiene and health care. This is another example of how sustainability and CSR policies are consistent with the aim of commercial profit.

Soaps and detergents are associated with the use of water and creation of polluted water. A sustainability challenge, with potential commercial benefits, is to develop products that use less water and possibly also allow water to be re-cycled and re-used.

In summary, sustainability and CSR issues are possibly much more significant in our industry than in many other industries. The company's concern about the matter is fully justified.

Appendices to the memo/workings

Sales to France

Expected sales: (€6.75m × 0.6) + (€8.5m × 0.4)	€7.45m
Average exchange rate in 20X5: (1.2 + 1.3)/2	1.25
Expected sales in £	£5.96m
Accounts receivable in £, sales to France: (20% × £5.96m)	£1.192m

Revised financial outcomes

	UK £'000	France £'000	Total £'000
Credit sales	20,934[1]	5,960	26,894
Receivables	3,339	1,192	4,531
Inventory			
Raw materials	1,906[2]	535[3]	2,441
WIP	811[2]	230[3]	1,041
Finished goods	1,338[2]	646[3]	1,984
Total current assets	7,394	2,603	9,997
Cost of goods sold	13,959	3,577[4]	17,536
Purchases	9,306	2,385[5]	11,691
Accounts payable	1,956	501[6]	2,457

Notes

1   90% × £23,260,000 = £20,934,000

2   Raw materials 47% × £4,055,000 = £1,906,000
WIP = 20% × £4,055,000 = £811,000
Finished goods = 33% × £4,055,000 = £1,338,000

3   Raw materials: £2,441,000 − £1,906,000 = £535,000
WIP: £1,041,000 − £811,000 = £230,000
Finished goods: £1,984,000 − £1,338,000 = £646,000

4   (13,959/23,260) × £5,960,000 = £3,577,000

5   (9,306/23,260) × £5,960,000 = £2,385,000

6   (1,956/9,306) × £2,385,000 = £501,000

Revised operating cycle

		Days
Inventory		
Raw materials	(2,441/11,691) × 365	76.2
WIP	(1,041/17,536) × 365	21.7
Finished goods	(1,984/17,536) × 365	41.3
		139.2
Receivables	(4,531/26,894) × 365	61.5
		200.7
Payables	(2,457/11,691) × 365	(76.7)
Revised operating cycle		124.0

The revised operating cycle is **124 days**

However this estimate is based on an expected value of sales in France in 20X5.

Current operating cycle

		Days
Inventory		
Raw materials	(1,906/9,306) × 365	74.7
WIP	(811/13,959) × 365	21.2
Finished goods	(1,338/13,959) × 365	35.0
		130.9
Receivables		58.2
		189.1
Payables		(76.7)
Current operating cycle		112.4

The current operating cycle is 112.4 days, say **112 days**.

21   Horora plc

To: Horora CEO
From: Financial adviser
Date: XX February 20X6
Subject: Proposed merger and proposed product development

This memo provides responses to your recent requests.

(a)   Estimate of post-merger values

The post-merger value of the company is estimated as £5,300m (market capitalisation) and the predicted EPS is 81.5p. The Appendix to this memo shows that these estimates are based on the assumption of total earnings equal to the combined 20X5 earnings of the two companies and a P/E ratio of 10, which is higher than the current P/E ratio for Horora shares.

↑ P/E ratio - stock is overpriced (ie gp compared to growth potential)

The estimated market capitalisation of the merged entity may ignore the market value of the patents, and may be based on an assumption that total earnings would be the sum of the earnings of the two separate companies in 20X5, and an increased P/E ratio of 10 would apply. Alternatively, the estimated market capitalisation includes an element for earnings growth in 20X6, or possibly includes the estimated £125m sale value of the Blaze patents.

This may appear consistent with the view that Horora's growth rating can be applied to the earnings of Blaze, but there is no evidence to support the estimate of a higher P/E ratio, which may therefore be optimistic.

(b) **Effect of merger on equity investors in each company**

If we assume that the forecast market capitalisation of £5,300m will apply post-merger, the value of the shares of the existing Horora shareholders would be £8.15 per share or (£8.15 × 450m) £3,667.5m in total. This is higher than the current market price of £7.00 per share.

Blaze stockholders will each receive one share (estimated value £8.15) for every two stock units they hold. The current market value of two stock units is 2 × $5.06 = $10.12 or £6.75 in equivalent sterling value. On the basis of the forecast figures, Blaze stockholders would therefore benefit financially from the merger.

The equity holders of both companies will therefore benefit from this proposed merger, but only if a P/E ratio of 10 can be applied to the group after the acquisition. A lower P/E ratio may apply and still provide benefit to both sets of equity holders.

For example if the current P/E ratio of Horora (9.1) applies to the merged entity, the estimated post-merger market capitalisation would be (9.1 × £530m) £4,823m. The share of the 'old' Horora shareholders would be (69%) £3,328m or £7.40 per share. This is still higher than the current share price of £7.00.

On this lower P/E ratio, Blaze stockholders would also benefit.

Both sets of equity investors benefit because a higher P/E ratio has been applied to the earnings of both companies, but particularly to the earnings of Blaze. The higher P/E ratio rather than higher earnings appears to explain the increase in total market capitalisation.

Much will therefore depend on the market's views of the merger and whether it believes that strong earnings growth will result from it.

(c) **Maximum offer price, assuming share for stock exchange**

The forecast market capitalisation of £5,300m and the sale of the patents for £125m would produce a total maximum value for the merged entity of £5,425m.

If shareholders in Horora gain nothing from the merger in terms of market capitalisation for their shares, the value of Blaze stock would be:

£5,425m – £3,150m (the current value of Horora shares) = £2,275m.

This gives a value of £5.69 or $8.54 for each stock unit.

This equates to approximately four Horora shares for every five Blaze stock units, as opposed to the current offer which proposes that one share in Horora be given for every two held in Blaze.

(d) **The proposed merger and Horora's financial objectives**

The current financial objectives are:

- to increase EPS by 5% per annum
- to keep the gearing ratio below 30%
- to maintain a P/E ratio above the industry average of 9.2

EPS

Earnings over the past four years, since 20X1, have increased by about 5% a year for Horora and by just 4.4% per year for Blaze.

If these rates of earnings growth were to continue after the merger, the objective would be achieved in the first year (Appendix 3).

However, earnings as a percentage of revenue have been falling in recent years for both companies, so sustained rates of earnings growth in the future may be difficult to achieve, unless the market is increasing in size. In addition, sustaining the growth rate beyond 20X6 so that it remains above 5% may be difficult.

Gearing

Appendix 2 shows the calculation of the estimated financial gearing for the merged entity. This is less than the objective level of 30%. The forecast increase in the market value of Horora shares would reduce the gearing ratio of Horora from 27.2%, which is currently below the maximum target, to an even lower level of 22.7%.

However the gearing level would increase if Horora makes a hostile bid for Blaze and offers a cash price for the stock, financed by debt capital.

Horora could not make a cash offer for Blaze stock without scrapping its financial objective for gearing.

P/E ratio

Horora's P/E ratio is currently 9.1 (£7 × 450m/£346m). The industry average is 9.2. Horora is therefore currently failing to achieve its financial objective for P/E ratio.

The ability of a merged company to achieve a P/E ratio in excess of the industry average will depend on investors' assessment of the merger and its future prospects for earnings growth.

The current estimate appears to be that the merged company's P/E ratio will be re-rated to 10.

(e) **Cost of borrowing and the proposed new product development**

It has been assessed that the financial viability of the new product development will depend to some extent on keeping the cost of borrowing below 6.5% for the next five years, even though the project will be financed by a variable rate loan.

Horora should be able to borrow at LIBOR plus 1%. The current six-month LIBOR rate is 5.25%; therefore borrowing at this rate for five years, with interest payable six monthly, would initially cost 6.25%. This is below the maximum tolerable level.

However LIBOR could rise at any time in the next five years. This is an interest rate risk for Horora. The risk could possibly be hedged in either of the following ways, although more information is required about current prices and rates.

(1) One possible method of fixing the effective rate of borrowing would be to arrange a five-year interest rate swap with notional principal of £150m and six-monthly coupon swaps.

Horora should arrange to pay the fixed rate in the swap, and receive the floating rate (usually LIBOR). The effective interest cost of this arrangement would be kept at 6.5% or below if the fixed rate payable in the swap is 5.5% or less.

For example if the fixed rate in the swap is 5.5%, Horora would pay 5.5% on notional principal of £150m, and would receive LIBOR on this amount in the swap. It would also pay LIBOR plus 1% on its loan, and the net effective cost would be 6.5%.

This would apply for the full five-year term of the swap.

(2) A second possible arrangement would be a zero cost collar, or something close to a zero cost collar. A collar consists of a pair of interest rate options – a cap and a floor. In the collar Horora would:

- buy a five-year cap, with option exercise dates at six-monthly intervals, giving Horora the right to borrow at the exercise rate for the cap for the next six month period. The exercise rate may be set at 6.5%.

- sell a five-year floor, with option exercise dates at six-monthly intervals, which would oblige Horora to lend at the exercise rate for the next six-month period. This may be set at 6.5%.

The cost of the cap would be offset to some extent (or possibly completely) by the revenue from selling the floor.

The effect of a collar with a cap and a floor both with a 6.5% exercise rate would be to fix the effective borrowing rate at 6.5%, with option exercise dates at six-monthly intervals, for the full term of the collar.

Appendix 1/Workings

Terms of offer: 1 new share in Horora for two stock units of Blaze.

Total number of new Horora shares issued: 400m/2 = 200m

Total number of shares after the merger = 450m + 200m = 650m

	Horora		Blaze	
Current EPS	346/450	76.9p	276/400 = $0.69 at $1.50	46p
Current P/E ratio	700/76.9	9.1	$5.06/$0.69	7.3
Current market capitalisation	450m × £7	£3,150m	400m × $5.06 = $2,024m at $1.50	£1,349m

The post-merger market capitalisation of the merged entity has been estimated at £5,300m, excluding the value of the patents. This £5,300m total is more than the combined current values of the two companies.

This indicates a post-merger share price of £5,300m/650m = £8.15.

The combined earnings of the two companies in 20X5 = £346m + $276m/$1.5/£1 = £530m. Post merger there will be 650m shares, so if there is no growth in earnings, EPS would be £530m/650m = 0.815 = 81.5p.

A share price of £8.15 and an estimated EPS of 81.5p indicates a P/E ratio of 10, which is higher than the current P/E ratio for Horora shares.

Number of shares in merged entity	Horora shareholders	Blaze stockholders	Total
Number	450m	200m	650m
Percentage of total	69%	31%	100%

Appendix 2

Assumed market capitalisation of equity post-merger = £5,300m

The current market value of debt is [£1,150m × (1.025)] + [$550m × 1.018 at $1.50/£1]

= £1,178.75m + £373.27m = £1,552.02m, say £1,552m

Therefore gearing ratio = 1,552/(1,552 + 5,300) = 22.7%.

This is below the maximum gearing ratio (of 30%) that has been set as a financial objective.

The gearing ratio would exceed 30% if the market capitalisation of the shares post-merger is less than (1,552 × 7/3) £3,621.3m.

Current gearing of Horora:

Value of equity = £7 × 450m = £3,150m

Value of debt: £1,178.75m

Gearing = 1,178.75/(1,178.75 + 3,150) = 27.2%

Appendix 3

Assumed earnings in 20X6 at average annual growth rates and assuming no change in the exchange rate = (£346m × 1.05) + [($276m/1.50) × 1.044] = £555.4m

EPS would be £555.4m/650m = £0.854

Horora EPS in 20X5 = £0.769 (see Appendix 1)

Growth in EPS = (854/769) − 1 = 0.11 or 11%.

22 Puller plc

		Marks Up to
(a)	Valuation	
	General considerations	3
	Net asset values	6
	Earnings valuation	15
	Cost of equity considerations	3
	Evaluation of approach and valuation	3
(b)	Financial reporting and other data	6
(c)	Risks of the acquisition	6
(d)	Impact on profit after tax	8
(e)	Evaluation of post-acquisition strategies	10
Total marks		60
Maximum marks		55

Note: Valuation is not an exact science. Some of the assumptions made in this answer are not therefore the only reasonable assumptions that could be made. Other alternative assumptions may be acceptable.

(a) Valuation for Rantz – initial bid

The context of the valuation is to make an initial bid for Rantz. The estimates therefore are made on the conservative side as the opening valuation is likely to be pushed upwards during the negotiation process. Nevertheless, the figures are drawn up to be justifiable both in terms of the methodology and the estimates used.

Other key general considerations are:

(1) Acquisition of entire equity or a majority holding

It is necessary to consider whether we are bidding to acquire all of the shares, or whether a majority holding is attainable and would be sufficient for our objectives. If we wish to acquire all of the shares then the relevant valuation is for the equity holding overall. We may however acquire only a majority of the ordinary shares. This may be either because this is our aim (perhaps in order to reduce the acquisition cost) or alternatively because some shareholders are unwilling to sell. In this case the valuation is unlikely to be pro rata to the overall valuation of the equity. This is because there is likely to be a significant control premium as we will control the financial and operating activities of the business in accordance with the group's objectives, even though the benefits may be shared with non controlling shareholders. In this context, the fact that the company does not pay a dividend may severely diminish the value of the non controlling holding.

(2) Key shareholdings

We need to know the expectations and intentions of the vendors individually. Jeff Rantz wants to retire, so he would presumably be a key shareholding to obtain. However, he only owns 45% of the shares, so it would be necessary to obtain an additional 6% in order to guarantee overall control. This may come most easily from a subgroup of managers and employees. It may be however that a 75% shareholding is required in order to be able to alter the Articles of Association. This would mean that the acquisition would need to include Charles Fang's shareholding. Conceivably, if Jeff Rantz was asking too high a price, then control could be obtained without his shares.

A base-line comparison – net asset values adjusted to fair value

Statement of financial position at 31 December 20X8

	£'000	£'000	Comments
ASSETS			
Hotels – owned		52,000	This is a key figure and independent valuations will be needed prior to any formal bid.
Hotels – finance leases		11,000	The basis of the fair value needs to be considered. How has it been calculated and what were the key judgements involved?
			Note that the fair value is lower than the outstanding lease obligation of £13m, so acquiring these hotels solely on an assets value basis may not be appropriate.
Fixtures and fittings		2,000	This is the carrying amount but the fair value will need to be assessed during the due diligence process.
Current assets		8,000	Much of this amount appears to be cash which, subject to normal audit verification, has few valuation difficulties. It is not however clear why the company wished to retain so much cash. Particularly while increasing borrowing. We need to make sure that the acquisition terms are not 'cash free', with the vendors stripping out cash balances prior to sale.
			The remaining current assets of £4m will need to be verified.
			Current assets in 20X7 presumably include the discontinued depot at £4m (which would not have been treated as a non-current asset under IFRS 5 as the contract was signed in December 20X7). Excluding this and excluding cash proceeds, the other current assets have increased from £1m to £4m.
LIABILITIES			
Loans	28,000		There may be covenants which could cause the loan to be repayable on take-over which may cause liquidity problems. This would need to be assessed during due diligence.
			It will also be necessary to assess the repayment schedule and whether loans will need to be refinanced.
Finance leases	13,000		This is the capital element of the finance lease obligation. Consideration would need to be given to the total lease obligations, their fair values and the repayment scheduling.
Provision	1,000		Need to review with legal advice.
			Also assess the need for other provisions and contingencies.
Current liabilities	1,600		Ascertain the nature of these liabilities.
			Can supplier terms and conditions be improved?
Total liabilities		(43,600)	
Net assets		29,400	

Thus the asset value of the company is approximately **£29.4m** based on these assumptions.

An earnings based valuation

An assessment of normalised earnings needs to take place and, as far as it is possible from the information provided, earnings need to be adjusted to cash flows.

	Workings	20X8 Draft £'000	20X9 £'000	20Y0 and thereafter £'000
Revenue	(W1)	45,900	57,703	63,473
Cost of sales	(W2)	(34,400)	(43,246)	(47,570)
Gross profit		11,500	14,457	15,903
Operating expenses	(W3)	(6,000)	(5,000)	(5,000)
Executive salaries reduction	(W3)	–	200	200
Marketing	(W3)	–	(500)	(500)
Operating lease discontinued	(W4)	–	–	(270)
Adjusted profit from operations		5,500	9,157	10,333
Add back depreciation	(W5)		4,000	4,000
EBITDA			13,157	14,333
Finance costs	(W6)	(4,000)	(4,000)	(4,000)
Adjusted profit before tax		1,500	9,157	10,333
Tax	(W7)	(420)	(2,106)	(2,377)
Adjusted profit after tax		1,080	7,051	7,956
CAPEX			(3,000)	(3,000)
Residual cash flow			4,051	4,956

Tutorial note:

The 20X8 column in the above table is included as a base year. As the acquisition is assumed to be on 1 January 20X9, then the 20X8 earnings do not form part of the valuation calculations.

WORKINGS

(1) **Revenue**

20X9	£45,900 × 80/70 × 1.1 = 57,703
20Y0	57,703 × 1.1 = 63,473

However the hotel under an operating lease should (prudently) be assumed to discontinue next year as the lease may be terminated. See (W4) below.

(2) **Cost of sales**

20X9	£34,400 × 80/70 × 1.1 = 43,246
20Y0	43,246 × 1.1 = 47,570

However the hotel under an operating lease should (prudently) be assumed to discontinue. See (W4) below.

(3) **Operating expenses**

The exceptional charge is a non-recurring item and is thus not part of sustainable earnings. Zero inflation is assumed. (See interest rate discussion below.)

The marketing costs are the incremental advertising costs.

The salaries of the directors have been adjusted to market rates resulting in a cost saving. This assumption may need to be varied if a preferential salary is for example given to Charles Fang if he remains in the business as a director and significant shareholder. Alternatively, the high salaries may have been paid in lieu of dividends.

(4) **Operating lease discontinued**

A two-star hotel is to be discontinued.

Revenue is £75 × 50 rooms × 80% × 360 days	=	£1.08 m
Approx gross profit margin*	=	25%
Profit forgone before tax	=	£270,000

* This is the approximate gross profit percentage, for the whole of the business, in the 20X8 statement of profit or loss. This is applied in accordance with the working assumptions suggested (**Exhibit 3** – 'additional notes') that cost of sales is variable. As there may be different margins achieved in the larger hotels compared to the smaller hotels, this assumption needs to be questioned during due diligence (see below).

Similarly, there is a working assumption provided that operating expenses are fixed. This should also be questioned during due diligence.

(5) **Depreciation**

Depreciation is not a cash flow and thus should not be discounted into the valuation.

There will be extra depreciation on new CAPEX, but as it is excluded from the analysis of cash flows, it has been ignored.

(6) **Finance costs**

It may be that as positive cash flows are generated even after CAPEX then debt may fall and thus finance costs may fall. A prudent assumption of maintaining finance costs at their 20X7 level has however been made.

(7) **Taxation**

The tax rate is 23% per Exhibit 3.

Valuation calculation

Using the 10% working assumption for the cost of equity, then the value of the equity is:

$$£4,051,000 / 1.1 + \frac{£4,956,000 / 0.1}{1.1}$$

= £48.74m = **£49m** approx

Cash flows are assumed to be in perpetuity. (Alternatively, any terminal value could be assumed equal to the remaining present value at that date.)

Qualifying assumptions

It may be that the £4m surplus cash could be added to the above valuation figure to obtain a fuller reflection of value (ie approx **£53m**) as this cash does not appear to generate operating cash flows. More detailed data of cash flow predictions would need to be made however to ascertain whether these were truly surplus cash balances (or the deal could be 'cash free' as already noted).

The four hotels held under finance leases only have a ten year average remaining life, whereas the above assumption is based on the fact that their leases will be renewed at the end of this period on similar terms. Assuming the worst case scenario that the leases will not be renewed and that these hotels will be discontinued, then the loss in present value is approximately as follows:

Revenue from the four two-star hotels:

£75 × 80% × 50 × 360 × 4 hotels	= £4.32m
Approx gross profit margin	= 25%
Profit before tax	= £1.08m

For simplicity, ignoring the other items as fixed costs, then the value of these in the terminal calculation of present value should have been:

£1.08m × 1.1^2 × AF10% 9 yrs × (1 – 0.23)/1.1
= £1.08m × 1.1^2 × 5.759 × (1 – 0.23)/1.1
= £5.268m

The amount at which the four hotels were actually included in perpetuity was:

= £1.08m × 1.1^2 × (1 – 0.23)/(0.1 × 1.1)
= £9.148m

The difference of (£3.880m) should be deducted from the £48.74m above giving approximately **£44.86m**

Note: It is assumed in these calculations that the lease rentals are included in cost of sales and hence form part of these calculations. This needs to be established.

Explanation of the general approach

The approach is to value the future cash flows to Puller as a result of the acquisition. While some of the estimations are conservative an alternative approach would be to estimate the worth of the company to the present owners in discounted present value terms, ie as an indication of their price to sell. There seems to be insufficient data to do this but as an opening bid it seems appropriate to commence significantly below £40m, as the current owners are unlikely to experience the same growth rate.

Crudely, if profit stays at its current level and a 10% discount rate is used:

	£'000
Profit after tax from continuing operations	1,080
Add depreciation	4,000
CAPEX (20X8 figure)	(2,000)
Cash flow	3,080

Valuation = £3.08m/0.1   = £30.8m

This valuation is little above the asset value but, even this may be unsustainable, as depreciation is double CAPEX and one hotel on an operating lease may need to be discontinued as above.

Interest rate

The valuation is of the equity of the company, not the entire value of the entity. As the residual returns to equity are measured, the interest rate is therefore a proxy for the risk adjusted cost of equity.

As inflation has not been applied to the cash flows then the 10% rate can be deemed to be a real rate. If general inflation is say 3%, then this may be equivalent to a money rate of around 13.3% (1.1×1.03).

The key question is whether the rate of 10% adequately compensates for risk. As a listed company, Puller may view risk in systematic terms and attempt to estimate an adjusted (ie geared) beta for Rantz.

The interest rate has also been deemed to be constant over time, whereas more realistically, the term structure of interest rates and changing risk profiles are likely to lead to changing discount rates.

Discount rates should strictly apply only to cash flows, but while adjustments have been made (eg to use EBITDA) then these are still not cash flows but adjusted profit figures that are only proxy cash flows.

Weaknesses in the approach

- The 10% growth assumption in price is unclear and needs to be ascertained in terms of market conditions.

- Increased utilisation is significant particularly given the price increases and therefore market research data will be needed to support this assumption.

- The impact of general inflation has been largely ignored on data (unless it is partially included in revenues in the 10% growth, but even this is only for two years). The most obvious explanation is that the 10% is a real rate of return (see above).

- There may be additional cost savings when the company is brought into the group. For example, there may be synergies from administration costs which may be common to both companies (eg only one head office may be needed).

Overall the difference between the £30.8m for the value to the existing owners and the £49m valuation to our company is dependent largely on the key assumption of increased prices and increased occupancy. The asset value of £29.4m would also set a floor price. Any initial offer much above £30m may therefore be imprudent until more data is obtained.

(b) **Data provided by Rantz**

- Rantz has incentives to provide data that may inflate the offer price. This may involve overstating profits/revenues and understating costs.

- Rantz also has incentives to classify expenditure as exceptional so it would not form part of the sustainable earnings calculations.

Issues from the financial statements

- It is not clear why Rantz has increased borrowing during 20X8 while at the same time it appears to be holding £4m of cash from the sale of the storage facility. An explanation is needed but also it needs to be clear whether the cash balance would be part of the acquisition. Undertakings will be needed in this respect or it may be paid out as a late distribution to existing shareholders.

- The treatment of the leasehold hotels needs to be verified. The land on which the leased hotels stand should be treated as an operating lease. This needs to be clearly established and the calculations adjusted for rentals which will terminate after ten years or be renegotiated.

- We are told there have been no new hotel purchases but there are additions in the non-current asset note. These are therefore presumably improvements or additions to existing assets. This needs to be verified as these costs could be normal maintenance and have been capitalised to inflate profit rather than expensed.

- If the assets are in disrepair then, even though collectively their fair value may exceed their carrying amount, impairments may be needed on individual assets.

- The provision needs to be examined both for understatement (the potential costs could turn out very high and we would take this obligation as the new shareholders) and for overstatement (the costs within the provision may include normal costs which are being reclassified as a provision to present them as exceptional and therefore being excluded from the valuation calculation).

- Review the data for reasonableness using industry norms for this type of hotel group to see if any unusual ratios or relationships are apparent.

Other issues

- We need to examine the Articles of Association to see if there are any constraints on the acquisition of a majority shareholding rather than needing to acquire the entire share capital. This may reduce the acquisition cost but is likely to leave a minority with rights. There are various combinations of shareholdings that we could acquire to obtain a majority – indeed, any two of the three shareholder groupings would be enough.

- The condition of the hotel real estate needs close inspection as the asset values are a key resource in the take-over. Maintenance is also a major cost.

- There is a lot of debt and the terms of the debt need close scrutiny. The loan agreements need to be examined by legal advisors to establish clearly any covenants and the repayment terms (eg a change of ownership clause might be triggered making debt repayable or debt terms may need to be renegotiated). Otherwise there may be unexpected liquidity pressures on the Puller group.

- Tax due diligence will be required to examine the status of the taxation computations, group tax implications, change of ownership, correspondence with tax authorities and any outstanding employee tax and VAT matters.

- Commercial due diligence will need to inspect the assumptions of growth having regard to local competitors.

- Similarly, existing occupancy rates will need to be verified as they are a key driver of profit.

- The lease agreements will need to be reviewed to ascertain any clauses over renewal, penalties for condition of assets, rent inflation clauses etc.

(c) **Risks with the acquisitions**

There is a significant element of risk in the acquisition as it has high operating gearing given the high fixed operating costs. This makes any profit highly dependent on occupancy rates as is typical for the industry. The future projections are highly sensitive to minimal changes in underlying assumptions. Sensitivity calculations should be carried out when better information is available, and before making a final offer.

The level of debt is also very high. Non-current loans and finance lease obligations total £41m at 31 December 20X8. This is 79% of total assets at their carrying amounts. It is 93% of the carrying amount of property, plant and equipment. In terms of fair values, however, the owned property is £52m compared to loans (excluding the finance leases) of £28m. This is only just over 50% and thus the property represents good security for the non-current loans.

Rantz is an unquoted company, therefore there are additional uncertainties regarding valuation as there is no existing observable market price. A key issue is that in valuing an unquoted company there is normally a discount for lack of liquidity compared to a listed company, but this is uncertain given that the valuation is in the context of an acquisition by a listed company.

The risks are limited by the fact that the going concern values are not considerably in excess of the fair values of the net assets. The strategy of selling off underperforming hotels is thus a possible exit route if the acquisition does not produce the required returns. This is, however, dependent on obtaining competent, professional and independent valuations of the assets prior to the bid being finalised.

The law suit needs legal due diligence as it may be far larger than indicated by the provision. Indemnities from the directors may be appropriate to reduce risk. More generally, legal due diligence is needed.

The disposal of the storage facility was completed in the year. Legal due diligence is needed in respect of any remaining obligations, indemnities or contingencies outstanding.

Other contracts and agreements with suppliers, finance providers, employees and directors (including exit clauses) need to be reviewed for any hidden costs. This might include terms that may be triggered by a take-over or any onerous contracts that have not been recognised in the financial statements in accordance with IAS 37.

(d) **Impact on group profit**

	20X9
	£'000
Revenue	57,703
Cost of sales	(43,246)
Gross profit	14,457
Operating expenses	(5,000)
Executive salaries reduction	200
Marketing	(500)
Additional depreciation (Note 1)	(500)
Operating profit	8,657
Finance costs	(4,000)
Profit before tax	4,657
Tax	(2,106)
Impact on group profit after tax	2,551

Notes

1 **Depreciation**

IFRS 3 requires that assets should be revalued to their fair value on acquisition, with fair value measured in accordance with IFRS 13. The fair values then form the basis for determining depreciation in the group accounts. As the fair value of the properties (£52m) is higher than their carrying amount in the individual financial statements of Rantz (£30m) there is likely to be an additional depreciation charge. While the total useful life is 50 years the remaining use life is lower. As the company was established over 30 years ago, if we assume that assets were acquired gradually over this period then perhaps assume that they have a remaining useful life on average of say 35 years. The extra depreciation will therefore be £22m/35 years, which is about £600,000.

However with regard to the properties held under finance leases the fair value is £1m less than the carrying amount (£12m – £11m). Using the average life of ten years this will lower depreciation by £100,000.

The net effect is to increase depreciation by £500,000.

(Note the above are very subjective calculations, credit would be given for sensible alternative approaches.)

2 Other potential effects

Impairments – the assets have been revalued thus there is a greater probability of impairment. This will include any goodwill attaching to each hotel as a CGU. The goodwill will be written down for impairment first before PPE.

Group accounting policies may be different from those of Rantz. When restated in accordance with group policies then adjustments may be needed to group profit.

If the acquisition is financed partly by debt then additional finance costs will be incurred in the group accounts. If, in the extreme, the acquisition was all financed by debt for say £30m at 10% then after tax there would be a charge of say £2.3m.

(e) Post-acquisition strategy

If Puller acquires Rantz, the acquisition will represent a horizontal integration, because both companies operate in the same (hotel) industry.

Nonetheless, there appear to be some important differences between Puller and Rantz's current positioning strategies, which need to be considered before deciding the extent to which the two chains should be integrated post-acquisition or whether they should be maintained as separate businesses.

Although Puller's hotels and Rantz's in-town hotels are both four-star hotels, they appear to have different target markets. Puller's main focus is on business travellers who value the contemporary style and facilities offered by its hotels, while Rantz appears to have targeted leisure customers who value the character of its hotels.

Puller has to decide whether to continue to operate the Rantz hotels as a separate brand post-acquisition, or whether to integrate them into its existing portfolio and rebrand them as Puller hotels.

An important factor in this decision is likely to be the purpose of the acquisition. Puller is having to acquire smaller chains of hotels because it cannot get the planning permission it needs to build new hotels itself and thereby grow organically. This suggests, however, that the main driver behind the acquisition of Rantz Ltd is the desire to acquire the additional capacity needed to facilitate growth, rather than to acquire the Rantz brand as such.

It is not clear what level of brand loyalty or customer loyalty existing customers have to the Rantz brand, and this is something which needs to be assessed before any decisions about post-acquisition strategy are finalised. However, since Rantz is a small privately-owned chain, its brand strength is likely to be considerably less than Puller's. There is no indication that Puller's offer to acquire the hotels will include any consideration for Rantz's brand or any associated trademarks or logos.

As noted under 'Risks' earlier, the need to increase occupancy rates will be a priority for Puller if it acquires the hotels. It is not clear how much of the difference between Rantz and Puller's in-town occupancy rates can be attributed to the lack of capital expenditure in Rantz's hotels, or how much could be attributed to the difference in target market, pricing and marketing strategies or differences in brand strength.

Whatever post-integration strategy Puller adopts, it seems clear that the Rantz hotels will require significant capital expenditure. However, if Rantz has become seen as a 'tired' brand, due to historic under-investment in its hotels, it may be beneficial for Puller to convert the in-town hotels to the Puller brand as part of the process of refurbishing and decorating them.

Converting the in-town hotels to the Puller brand might also permit economies of scale in relation to the additional advertising expenditure.

The counter argument, though, is that if there remains significant market demand from leisure travellers for in-town hotels which retain period charm, Puller should consider the Rantz hotels as a distinct brand rather than trying to integrate them into the Puller brand. In this respect, it would be useful to undertake some market research into demand and supply for different types of hotel in the towns where the hotels being acquired are located, before finalising a course of action.

As well as the in-town four-star hotels, Puller also has to decide what to do with the two-star out-of-town hotels. Apart from the difference in their geographic positioning, they also seem to have a different strategic position to the rest of the portfolio: with their average room rate per night being half that of Rantz's in-town hotels.

It seems unlikely that out-of-town, two-star hotels will be attractive for business travellers – Puller's current target market. Therefore, one option might be to try to re-sell them. However, given the relatively short life left on the operating leases it is debatable how attractive these would in their own right be to any potential buyer.

Alternatively, Puller could retain the two-star hotels in the group, but operate them as a separate business unit to the four-star hotels. As such, Puller would be able to apply different competitive and marketing strategies for the two-star hotels, compared to the four-star hotels; enabling each to retain distinct competitive positions.

In this respect, it is possible that Puller could convert the in-town hotels to the Puller brand, while leaving the out-of-town hotels as Rantz hotels. Puller could still improve the external and internal condition of the hotels, and provide additional advertising expenditure and marketing expertise needed to increase occupancy rates, without having to rebrand the hotels.

23 Quanta

Marking guide

	Marks
(a) Review of forecast for 20X6	10
(b) Comment on proposal for 'war chest' up to £50m	10
(c) Offer price for potential target company	10
(d) Reporting on risks from company pension scheme	5
(e) Assessment of inventory management	10
(f) Assessment of strategic option to sell more online	5
Total marks	50

(a) Review of forecast for 20X6

The forecast for 20X6 is for the company to increase its operating profit by 33% (from £50.6m to £67.5m) and profit after tax by 38%, although forecast growth in sales revenue is only 4.5%. The improvement in profit is attributable to the sales revenue growth but also a slight increase in the gross profit margin from 64.3% to 64.4% of sales and (more significantly) a reduction in the ratio of other costs to sales from 57.3% to 55.4%. The most significant item in other costs is selling costs, which are forecast to rise by less than 1% even though revenue is expected to grow by 4.5%.

The expected results for 20X5 are comparable with actual results in 20X4, in the sense that the gross profit margin in both years was similar (64.2% in 20X4 and 64.3% in 20X5) and so too was the ratio of other costs to sales (57.5% in 20X4 compared to 57.3% in 20X5). Revenue growth between 20X4 and 20X5 is 2.5%.

The forecast improvement in 20X6 profits is therefore attributable mainly to an increase in the rate of revenue growth and a reduction in the ratio of other costs (particularly selling costs) to sales revenue. Improvements may well be justifiable, especially if the forecast is for an upturn in the global economy and consumer spending. However these optimistic forecasts should be supported by information about the measures that the company expects to take to achieve these improvements. Without convincing explanations for the improvements, some questions may be asked about the reliability of the figures. If the operating profit to sales ratio in 20X6 is the same as in 20X5 (7.03%), the operating profit in 20X6 would be, assuming 4.5% growth in revenue, only £52.9m, which is £14.6m lower than the current forecast (and an improvement of only 4.5% on 20X5).

There is some information about exchange rates. The pound fell in value against the euro and strengthened in value against the South Korean won in 20X5 by 3%. Quanta appears to incur a fairly high proportion of its costs in South Korea and to sell a large proportion of its products into Europe. It might therefore be expected that the company's reported profitability was improved to a certain extent by the lower won and stronger euro (assuming that sales to Europe are priced largely in euros). There is insufficient data to assess the effect of currency movements on group profits. There is also no information about how the company expects exchange rate movements in 20X6 to affect profitability next year.

In conclusion, the forecast improvements in results in 20X6 may be wholly or partly justifiable, but without more information about the assumptions that were used to make the forecasts, it would be appropriate to have some scepticism about the reliability of the figures. The assumptions in the forecasts should be questioned more closely.

(b) **Proposal for war chest**

The current market capitalisation of Quanta's shares is £512m (160m shares at £3.20) and gearing measured by market values is low. (The book value of debt is expected to be £96.8m (73.5m + 23.3m) at the end of 20X5.) Investors or banks may therefore be willing to finance a war chest of £50m, provided that they believe the company will make a suitable return on the investments they make with the money.

If the company were to raise £50m by means of a syndicated loan, its expected gearing and interest cover would change. On the basis of the expected figures for 20X5, and ignoring any takeover of Lorgnetta, the expected debt: equity ratio for Quanta at the end of the year will be (using book values) 96.8:153.5 = 63%. The interest cover for the year is expected to be 8.7 times (50.6:5.8). These ratios are well within the covenant limits for the company's existing loans. Increasing the level of debt by £50m would increase the gearing ratio (using book values) to 95.6% (146.8:153.5). This is close to the maximum gearing ratio permitted by existing loan covenants. If the company unexpectedly began to make losses, the 100% gearing limit might be breached and the company would technically be in default.

Furthermore, unless some of the war chest is invested quickly to start earning profits, the payment of a dividend of £12m might also result in a breach of the gearing covenant.

The interest cover covenant does not appear to be a problem. Interest costs would rise by £2.5m if borrowing is at 5%, and (ignoring any interest income from placing unused cash on deposit) the interest cover ratio would remain well above 5 times.

From a financial perspective, the company would appear to have the capacity to take on extra debt of £50m, and the gearing covenant would seem to be too restrictive. The company may be able to re-negotiate the covenant with the lender, thereby removing the risk that the covenant might be breached.

From a strategic perspective, the merits of creating a 'war chest' for future acquisitions should be assessed in terms of strategic aims and objectives. Insufficient data is available to do this.

(c) **Offer price for Lorgnetta**

Lorgnetta was only marginally profitable in 20X5. Its profit after tax of €60,000 represented a net profit margin of just 0.09% of sales revenue. Return on capital employed, measured by book values, was 3.03% (1,820,000/(25m +35m)) and return on equity was 0.17% (60,000/35m).

Unless there is significant potential to turn round the company and improve its operating performance, it does not seem to be an attractive acquisition. In addition to its low profits, it also has just 105 outlets across Europe, indicating that it does not own a major chain of retail outlets.

The poor financial performance of Lorgnetta compares unfavourably to Quanta. In 20X5, Quanta is expected to make a profit after tax of £35.8m (net profit margin = 5% of sales), with return on equity of 23.3%(35.8/153.5).

The EPS of Quanta in 20X5 is expected to be 22.38 pence (35.8m/160m shares). On the basis of the current share price of £3.20, this gives a P/E ratio of 14.3.

Even allowing for expected sales growth for Lorgnetta in 20X6 of 4%, and for synergy benefits of €1m per year from an acquisition, it would be inappropriate to value Lorgnetta on a P/E ratio that is at all similar to that of Quanta. In addition, the estimates of sales growth of 4% for the next five years may be over-optimistic, as there is no apparent basis for expecting sales growth of this magnitude from a struggling company.

If the board decides that it would like to make an offer for the shares in Lorgnetta, an offer based on a P/E ratio valuation may be appropriate. A P/E ratio for valuation purpose should probably not exceed 50% of the P/E ratio of Quanta. This would suggest a P/E ratio for valuation of around 7.2 times. The taxation rate seems to be 20%, therefore the after-tax benefits from synergy would be €800,000. If, say, the value of one half of these benefits €400,000) is offered to shareholders in Lorgnetta, a maximum offer price might be, using a P/E ratio of 7.2 applied to 20X5 earnings and one half of the after-tax synergy benefits:

[€60,000 + €400,000] × 7.2 = €3,312,000.

For a company the size of Quanta, this would be a small acquisition. As indicated above, the strategic value of such an acquisition should be questioned. Although Quanta may be looking for vertical integration by acquiring a retail chain of opticians outlets, a larger target company might be more appropriate.

(d) **Company pension costs and liabilities**

If Quanta acquires Lorgnetta, it will take on the obligations of the company to the defined benefits scheme of that company. This will not create any new business risks for Quanta: the company will have an ongoing obligation to pay contributions into the pension fund, but unlike a defined contributions scheme, there is some uncertainty in the amount of contributions that may be required. As the scheme is currently in deficit, Quanta will need to consider how the deficit will be eliminated: this may require additional contributions into the fund over the next few years, and this will affect the group's reported profits.

There will be some financial risk from a defined benefits scheme, since the value of assets in the pension fund will be affected by market factors, such as share price movements and interest rate changes. Higher market interest rates, for example, will reduce the value of any bonds held by the fund, thereby increasing the deficit in the fund (or reducing any surplus).

As a result of a takeover of Lorgnetta, Quanta will be required (by IAS 19 *Employee Benefits*) to report on its net obligation to the defined pension scheme (as an asset or liability) and to report a cost of the scheme which may vary each year, depending on the contributions of the employer into the fund, changes in the fund asset values and changes in the present value of future obligations. The cost chargeable to profit or loss each year is therefore not predictable and may vary.

However given the small size of Lorgnetta relative to Quanta, it seems likely that the uncertainty and variability in profits that will arise as a result of the defined benefits scheme are likely to be small and not significant in terms of the group's reported profits. My initial conclusion is therefore that there is some financial risk and financial reporting risk from Lorgnetta's pension scheme, but the risk is unlikely to be significant.

(e) **Inventory management**

The concerns of the NED about inventory costs are understandable. Her attention is focused on the provision for writing off finished goods inventory, but there will also be a charge against profit for the actual amount of goods written off each year, which will presumably be an amount similar to the provision as at the beginning of the year.

The NED may be criticising inventory management generally. As an approximate guide, the average inventory turnover period in 20X5 is expected to be 108 days [(76.3/256.9) × 365], excluding the finished goods for which a writing-off provision has been made. Most of the inventory turnover period is attributable to the length of time that stocks of finished goods are held.

To assess whether the NED's criticisms of inventory management are justified, it would be useful to obtain comparisons of average turnover periods. Comparisons can be made with previous years, and it may also be possible to obtain information about inventory turnover from the financial statements of major competitors to Quanta.

The Marketing Director attributes the high level of provisioning (and possibly also the slow turnover of finished goods) to the fact that products are distributed to retailers on a sale or return basis. Until the retailer sells the items, they have not been sold and the inventory remains inventory of Quanta (application of the principles of revenue recognition as set out in IAS 18 *Revenue*). This means that large quantities of inventory are outside the physical control of Quanta, but still a part of Quanta's finished goods inventory.

The Marketing Director may also be correct in stating that since many glasses products are fashion items, large returns from retailers should be expected.

The argument can be simplified. The NED believes that costs are too high and inventory (especially finished goods inventory) is badly managed. The Marketing Director argues that these costs are an inevitable consequence of distributing products on a sale or return basis.

A recommended way forward to resolve this disagreement is to compare current levels of inventory turnover and inventory write-offs, to assess whether inventory management is not as efficient as in the past. At the same time, the marketing department should be asked to consider whether any measures might be taken to improve the system of distributing products to retailers. If total inventory levels can be reduced, it should be possible to reduce the amounts (and costs) of write-offs.

(f) **Online sales strategy**

Without more data, only an initial and brief assessment of an online sales strategy is possible. As a broad guiding principle, it seems reasonable to develop a strategy for online selling of goods. The volume of online sales, although still relatively small compared to in-store sales, is growing at a fast rate. Companies that are unable to offer an online sales option to customers are likely over time to find themselves at a serious competitive disadvantage.

However, if the general principle is accepted by Quanta that an online selling option is necessary, the strategy will require careful planning and efficient implementation. The overall strategy will need to include plans for web site design, marketing and advertising the online service, online payment arrangements, and arrangements for distributing goods to customers (globally), for selling prescription glasses online and for after-sales service and returns.

The company would also need to decide on a timetable for implementing the strategy, with a target date for 'going live'.

24 Galaxy Travel plc

		Marks
(a)	Financial assessment of company	15
(b)	Strategic drivers and KPIs	12
(c)	Critical analysis of investment appraisal	10
(d)	Framework for monitoring project management	8
(e)	Treasury operations and risk management	6
	Accounting for financial instruments	4
(f)	Advice on cyber security measures	5
Total marks		60

(a) Assessment of financial position and company's prospects

The statement of profit or loss for 20X5 shows revenue growth of 2.6%. There was a fall in the gross profit margin from 10.3% in 20X4 to 10.2% in 20X5, so that gross profit increased by just 1.2%. With a 1.5% increase in administrative expenses, operating profit in 20X5 was the same as in 20X4. These results show that increases in costs have offset modest revenue growth, and the company made little progress in 20X5. The company is expecting revenue to grow at 3% per year for the next five years, which is slightly faster than in 20X5, but we do not know the basis for these expectations.

Operating profit was much higher in the UK (3.9% of sales) than in other countries and operations in the Netherlands ran at a loss in 20X5. The difference in performance may be attributable mainly to the revenue earned from each customer – highest in the UK and lowest in the Netherlands.

20X5	£ revenue per customer
UK	927
Netherlands	528
Scandinavia	763
Other countries	781

It would be useful to compare profitability in each geographical segment with other companies in the same business sector. For example the operating profit in Scandinavia in 20X5 was £11.46 per customer, which seems a very low amount. Selling prices may be too low, or operating costs may be excessively high.

Prospects for the future do not seem to be attractive to investors. In 20X5, earnings per share were £0.70 and dividends per share were £0.60 but the share price is currently just £4.35. This gives a low P/E ratio of 6.2 times and a high dividend yield of 13.8%. These investor ratios might suggest that investors consider Galaxy to be a high-risk investment, perhaps with little or no earnings growth prospects.

Financial gearing is high. Total loans are £271m and the current market value of the company's shares is £174m (40m × £4.35). Of the total loans, £99m are repayable within 12 months. Presumably the company will expect to renew these at maturity, or negotiate new borrowing; however it should be a matter of some concern to the company that a large amount of liabilities will become due for payment in such a short time.

The statement of financial position shows a substantial amount of goodwill. Total tangible non-current assets were £354m and of these £168m (47.5%) represent aircraft or advance payments for aircraft. It may seem surprising that such a large proportion of the assets of a travel company should be aircraft.

It is difficult to assess the company's working capital position, without more details. The company had a large amount of cash (and receivables) at 30 September 20X5, but it also had current liabilities of nearly £600m. Total current liabilities exceeded total current assets, suggesting that the liquidity position of the company is not as strong as a cash balance of £301m might indicate. The company's dividend policy appears to be to pay out most earnings as dividends, and it is by no means certain that the company has sufficiently strong cash flows to afford this. We would recommend strongly that the company should review its cash flow position, and manage working capital so as to keep the need for cash within limits that the company can afford.

The board of Galaxy has expressed confidence in the strength of the company's position, but for the various reasons explained above, their optimism may be misplaced. The company is profitable, but margins are low, growth in revenue is slow, the Netherlands operation is running at a loss, and there may be liquidity problems, especially with up to £99m of loans maturing in the next year.

(b) Strategy drivers and Key Performance Indicators (KPIs)

KPIs should be quantifiable measures that can be used for setting strategic targets and monitoring actual performance by comparing actual with target.

It is assumed that the board has identified appropriate strategy drivers for the business, and the only requirement in this report is to suggest measures of performance that may be appropriate as KPIs.

Becoming an online business

If becoming an online business is a key strategic aim of the company, targets should be set and performance monitored in terms of growth in sales volume and also the proportion of total annual sales of the company. Recommendations for KPIs are:

- increase in the volume of online bookings, measured in terms of percentage annual revenue growth. This KPI will focus on volume growth. This KPI will focus on volume growth.
- increase in online sales as a percentage of total annual sales revenue. This KPI will measure the extent of the change to becoming an online business.

Selling tailored holidays

The board of directors presumably believes that the potential for future sales growth lies with tailored holidays rather than packaged holidays, possibly because tailored holidays provide a higher profit margin. Recommendations for KPIs are therefore:

- percentage annual growth in sales revenue from tailored holidays.
- average operating profit margin on tailored holidays.

Selling the Galaxy brand

Successful promotion of the Galaxy brand should result in growth in tailored holiday sales as well as growth in packaged holidays and other services. This strategy driver therefore overlaps with selling tailored holidays. The success of a brand is evident in sales revenue and profit; but the strength of the brand also depends on customer perceptions, which may change over time. Success in selling the Galaxy brand should also be measured to some extent in terms of customer feedback. Recommendations for KPIs are therefore:

- percentage annual growth in sales.
- operating profit margin.
- a suitable measure of customer response to the Galaxy name, such as brand awareness, as measured by an annual market research survey.

Exploiting technology and Big Data

There are at least two aspects to exploiting technology. One is to use technology to attract potential customers to buying holidays from the company. Another is to use technology to analyse customer data in order to target specific customer groups with tailored holidays.

Two suitable KPIs for attracting customers through technology might be:

- growth in the number of visits to the web site.
- target average time for visitors to remain on the web site (the length of stay).

It is more difficult to recommend a KPI for the use of Big Data to develop products or services that will attract customers. It may be appropriate to set a target for the number of new product or service offerings to customers each year that make use of the company's IT resources and databases. However, successful use of Big Data will depend on which aspects of data are used, and how it is applied to operations. In other words, the successful use of Big Data will have an effect on revenues, costs or profits – measures covered already by 'traditional' KPIs.

Geographical expansion

I assume that this strategy driver refers to geographical expansion of operations, since the company presumably already provides holidays to all parts of the world. Geographical expansion should be planned and targeted at particular countries or regions. However, suitable KPIs might be:

- growth in annual sales revenue in specific geographical areas.
- a measure for total sales growth in geographical areas where the company has established new operations within the previous three to five years. new businesses

Developing the company's people

This strategy driver is presumably concerned with attracting and retaining talented employees, and developing them into highly capable workers. Recommendations for KPIs are therefore:

- minimum retention rates (or maximum labour turnover rates) for employees, or strategically important employees.
- training provided to employees, measured as either average training days per employee or average expenditure on training per employee.

(c) **Analysis of investment appraisal**

The DCF analysis prepared by the management accountant indicates that the proposed investment would require an initial outlay of £50m and yield a positive NPV of £22.67m, suggesting that the investment will add value and should be undertaken.

However there are several aspects to the calculations that should be questioned. Several of these relate to estimates of cash flows.

Cash flows: revenue per customer

The estimated revenue per customer in the first year is £978 per customer (£220m/225,000 customers). This is more than the revenue per customer in the UK in 20X5 and much higher than the revenue per customer in the rest of Europe in 20X5. We do not know where this estimate came from, but the assumptions on which it is based should be questioned rigorously. For example, if the revenue per customer in the first year is just £781 (the same amount as for the rest of Europe in 20X5), and if we assume 225,000 customers, revenue in the first year will be about £175m rather than £220m, a difference of 20%.

Cash flows: profit margin per customer

Net operational cash flows in the first year of operations are estimated at £5.22m in sterling (£2.44m + £2.78m), giving a net operating profit margin of 2.37% on estimated revenue of £220m. The net operating profit margin for the company in 20X5 was 2.14% (53/2,472). If a profit margin of 2.14% is applied to the estimated revenue figure for year 1 of the investment, the net operational cash flows would be lower in that year by £506,000 (£220m × (2.37% – 2.14%)). This is almost 10% of the estimated cash flows for the year.

Cash flows: forecasts of exchange rates

The cash flows of the project will be in euros and US dollars, but the NPV is calculated in sterling, using exchange rates that are estimated using Purchasing Power Parity theory and estimates for inflation in the three currency areas in perpetuity. These exchange rate estimates are speculative, and actual rates are likely to be different. The application of these rates to the cash flows also assumes that the net cash flow after tax will be remitted to the UK in full on the last day of each year.

Cash flows: other issues

The positive NPV for the project depends to a large extent on the realisable value of the project or investment at the end of Year 5. Any such estimate can only be a 'best guess'. Here it is the present value of assumed future cash flows from Year 6 onwards in perpetuity. The actual value could be higher than this, or much lower – especially if the project is not as successful as expected.

It is assumed that sales revenue and operational cash flows will increase by 3% per year for five years. This is consistent with the company's expectations for annual revenue growth of 3% for all its business. Even so, this assumption should be reviewed, especially if there is a capacity limit to the number of customers that the new operation is capable of handling each year.

The estimated net operational cash flows are after tax, but we do not know what assumptions have been made in calculating tax payments. The assumptions should be questioned.

Timing of cash flows

The estimated cash flows appear to be based on the assumption that the project to implement the new operation will be completed on time, by June 20X7. A delay in the project completion date might have a major effect on the start date for the new operation. A delay in the start of operations would reduce the PV of total benefits, for example, by a factor of $1/(1 + r)$, where r is the cost of capital.

Discount rate

No information is available about why 9% has been used as the cost of capital or discount rate for the project. This should be questioned. A different (and higher) discount rate might be appropriate for the project.

Sensitivity analysis

For the reasons explained above, it is strongly recommended that sensitivity analysis should be applied to the estimated cash flows for this proposed project. This would provide information about the scale of risk in the project, and a decision about the investment could then be made on the basis of assessing both expected returns and risk.

(d) Monitoring project management

The committee responsible for monitoring the progress of a project should use the same criteria for assessing performance that the project manager himself/herself uses.

Aspects of the project (and the operation that the project will implement) that should be monitored are:

- Targets
- Timing
- Cost and keeping within budget
- Risks and risk management

Targets

The project should achieve the performance targets that have been set. Targets should relate to the procedures and systems for the new business that the project will establish. The project requirements may include, for example, establishing an IT system that fulfils specified operational requirements. There may also be a requirement to design, test and implement operating procedures that achieve certain performance standards. The project should achieve all (or most) of targets that are set.

A list of key targets should be drawn up when the project is initiated, and progress towards each of the targets should be monitored.

Timing

The project should be completed within the planned time. The overall project can be broken down into activities, each with estimated times for completion. A critical path chart (or something similar) can then be used to monitor progress in completing the various activities, and ensuring that the activities that are time-critical are given the most attention.

Delays in the project completion time can be identified in advance by reviewing actual progress on each activity and re-assessing the expected completion time. When critical activities are running late, a decision can be made whether to commit more resources (and cost) so that it can be completed more quickly.

Costs and budget

There should be a budget for the project, ideally broken down into time periods, and actual costs should be compared regularly with budgeted costs (and any revised forecast of costs).

Risks and risk management

The project manager and the review committee should also consider operational risks with the project work and with the operational system that it establishes. A system should be established for identifying and assessing risks, and taking measures in advance to manage the material risks. For the project itself, risks will relate to failure to achieve target, late completion and over-running on costs.

For the operation that the project will establish, there need to be suitable and effective internal controls. The monitoring committee may ask internal auditors or an external firm of accountants to review the effectiveness of the planned internal controls for the new operation.

(e) Treasury operations, financial risk and accounting for financial instruments

Percentage of exposures hedged

Hedging transactions for currency exchange rates and fuel prices are largely short-term in nature. Forward contracts or derivative instruments might have a settlement date several months ahead, or possibly just several weeks ahead. Because of the short-term nature of many instruments, the company hedges a higher proportion of its near-term exposures than its longer-term exposures. As at 6 December, Galaxy had hedged most of its exposures relating to Winter 20X5/20X6. We should expect the proportion of exposures that are hedged for Summer 20X6 will increase over the next few months, as Summer 20X6 approaches.

Galaxy's operations involve a large number of small transactions in a number of different currencies. The Treasury department's task is to measure, as accurately as possible, the company's net exposures to each currency, as well as its exposure to fuel purchases. Complete accuracy is impractical, as exposures change continually. Galaxy does not hedge 100% of any of its exposures, although in principle it could make hedging transactions for more than 100%. Hedging effectiveness, for practical reasons, will rarely be exactly 100%.

The Treasury department should be given some discretion in deciding not to hedge an exposure, when it considers that there is a probability that spot prices will move in the company's favour rather than adversely. In these cases, there should be a good prospect of benefiting by not hedging, in order to benefit from the favourable price movement (assuming that it does occur). For this reason, we might expect less than 100% of exposures to be hedged.

Forward contracts and currency futures

Most non-bank companies normally use forward contracts rather than currency futures to hedge exposures to currency risk. Forward contracts have the advantage of administrative convenience: it is agreed over the counter with a bank, and nothing further is required until settlement date when the currencies are exchanged.

Currency futures are administratively more complex, due to the system of regular margin payments to cover potential and actual losses on futures positions. Futures positions therefore have to be managed continually until the position is closed.

However futures have an advantage over forward contracts in the sense that a position can be closed at any time before settlement date. With a forward contract it is more difficult to re-arrange the settlement date.

A combination of forward contracts and futures may therefore be used in order to benefit from the advantages of each type of instrument.

Hedging fuel price exposures

In retrospect, a company purchasing fuel should not have hedged exposures to fuel price increases when prices were falling. By not hedging, the company would be able to buy at the available (lower) spot rate.

However, oil prices have now fallen and the relevant issue to consider is the likely direction of future changes in the spot price, not the fall in prices in the past. If it is thought likely that spot prices will rise in the near future, it would make sense to hedge. If prices are expected to fall further, or if the company thinks it likely that the oil price will remain stable for a while, a decision not to hedge would be appropriate.

Accounting for hedging instruments

The chairman's concern appears to be with profitability and the consequences of hedging currency risk. When a hedging instrument is settled in the same accounting period that it was originated, the effect on profit is reported during that period. With a forward contract used for hedging, the effective cash flow is the amount received or paid on settlement of the transaction. When currency futures are used for hedging, the effective cash flows are the amount received or paid in a spot transaction for the currency, offset by the gain or loss on closing the futures position. In both cases, hedging achieves its intended purpose, and this is reflected in the profit or loss for the period.

A different situation arises when a hedged position has not reached settlement date at the end of the financial period. The accounting standard that currently applies to accounting for financial instruments is IAS 39 *Financial Instruments: Recognition and Measurement*.

Financial instruments, including forward contracts and futures contracts, should be re-valued at fair value at the end of the period. This will create a gain or loss. To the extent that the financial instrument provides an effective hedge for an underlying transaction, the gain or loss is reported as other comprehensive income and transferred to an equity reserve. It is transferred from the reserve and into profit or loss when the hedged transaction is eventually settled. Only gains or losses on an ineffective part of a hedging transaction are taken to profit or loss at the end of the period.

In summary, the chairman's concerns are unnecessary. Where financial instruments are used to hedge exposures to financial risk, the impact on profit or loss will be reported in the period that the hedged transaction is settled. Most of the gains or losses arising from hedging will therefore be included in profit or loss in the same period as the hedged transaction.

(f) **Cyber security**

Actions to take to protect Galaxy's systems

The recent cyber attack that resulted in the loss of Galaxy customers' confidential data has illustrated the vulnerability of business to cyber attack, whether from malicious intent or weakness in company systems. A significant proportion (33%) of Galaxy's sales were online in the most recent financial year, and the company plans to invest heavily in its online operation as a key business driver. Galaxy also uses external companies for selling late holidays online. Its exposure to cyber threats therefore represents a key risk. In order to protect its developing systems, customers' transactions and business relationships in the future, the following actions are recommended.

Protection of damaged reputation

Galaxy's customer database was affected by the breach, but it appears that nobody has suffered any loss. However, it may still be subject to regulatory penalties for its failure to protect customer data, and it was a very damaging incident. Customer trust will have been damaged, so Galaxy needs to act quickly to show both customers and wider interests that it is committed to ensuring that such incidents do not recur.

Ensure confidence in systems

The incident highlights the risks posed to the infrastructure if cyber security measures are not strong enough. In this case, it was the actions of hackers exploiting a weak point in Galaxy's network, showing that risks can come from the systems of customers, suppliers or even business partners (as happened here) as well as from a company's own systems. As Galaxy seeks to develop its online business, external parties with IT systems which are integrated with those of Galaxy will represent an area of significant risk. These parties should be expected to have strong security over their own systems and it is recommended that ,where practical, Galaxy insists that partners with integrated IT systems obtain a satisfactory independent auditor's report (ISAE 3402) on their data security before entering into any contracts. It should conduct a full investigation into how the breach occurred and what the external company has done to rectify the problem. If Galaxy cannot satisfy itself that appropriate measures have been taken, it should consider terminating the relationship.

Identify the key systems

Galaxy needs to identify where breaches would have a significant impact upon business operations and focus cyber security efforts in those areas. IT systems should be regularly monitored for unusual activity, and the use of anti-virus software, firewalls, scanning of all removable media and the application of regular software updates should all be part of company policy. Appropriate processes and procedures need to be regularly tested, revisited and updated as the online business develops.

ISO 27001

In assessing its own systems, Galaxy may wish to apply standard ISO 27001, which describes best practice for an information security management system, and identifies key requirements for establishing an effective system against cyber threats. Complying with the standard would increase the confidence of customers and other parties in Galaxy's systems.

Staff competence

Galaxy has already identified the need for IT competence in its employees, and this will go a long way to helping improve cyber security. People are the weakest link in implementing effective security measures, so if staff can be made aware of the risks to the business that can be posed by ignoring company IT policies, or bypassing access controls, then systems will be safer.

25 Latchkey Ltd

		Marks
(a)	Assessment of restructuring arrangements, including brief comments on the company's market niche and possible governance arrangements	22
(b)	Assessment of the company's recovery plan, focusing mainly on the assumptions used in the plan	10
(c)	Comments on brand strategy	8
(d)	Comments on how to improve the company's performance	12
(e)	Suggestions how to deal with the option scheme	8
Total marks		60

(a) **Views on restructuring and Gammon's exit route**

Ignoring the recovery plan of the Latchkey board, a reconstruction arrangement might be agreed on the basis of what we know from the historical information about Latchkey.

The company performed badly in 20X4. UK property prices fell on average by 5%. If this price reduction applies to retirement properties, some of the 10.1% decrease in revenue in 20X4 is attributable to lower prices. However there was also a fall in 'real' sales of about 5%. We do not know the reasons for this.

There is also evidence of poor cost control. The cost of sales in 20X3 as a percentage of revenue was 74.8% (86.2/115.3). In 20X4 it went up to 78.6% (81.4/103.6). However, adjusting the figures for the 5% fall in property prices, a comparative figure for 20X3 is 78.7% (86.2/95% of 115.3). Building costs in 20X4 therefore seem comparable with those in 20X3. The poor cost control is evident in the increase in administrative costs and other operating expenses, in spite of a fall in the real volume of sales.

Even so, the main reasons for the deterioration in performance in 20X4 were the fall in sales prices and the fall in sales volume.

A reconstruction or refinancing scheme would need to be based on a reasonable expectation that volumes and prices will recover in future years.

Latchkey incurred interest costs of £10.5m in 20X4, which indicates that the interest rate on the loans of £120m was 8.75%. Gammon would hope to buy the loans from the company's banks for 70% of their face value, or £84m. Gammon would expect a high yield on lending to a restructured company, but in a restructuring, it should be able to agree to a re-negotiated interest rate on the loans. For example, a high-risk yield of 10% would be obtainable by Gammon even if the interest rate on the £120m were reduced to 7% (costing £8.4m per year for the company, but providing a 10% yield on Gammon's investment).

Lower interest charges for the company, combined with some improvement in operating performance, would be sufficient to return the company to profit. Other companies in the same business sector appear to be performing well, and (subject to closer investigation) it might be expected that the potential for improving profits does exist.

A restructuring of Latchkey will also depend on the agreement of its shareholders. Gammon would expect an equity stake, and may be prepared to provide additional finance for the company. On the other hand, the existing shareholders must be offered a deal that is sufficiently attractive to persuade them to accept it, rather than put the company into liquidation.

The size of Gammon's equity stake, and the amount of new financing that it provides, would be a matter for negotiation. A suggestion might be for Gammon to obtain a 25% share of the equity by investing £5m in 5m new £1 shares at par. If this is paid for in cash, the company will have what might be a much-needed increase in cash, for investing in working capital.

Retirement homes as a market niche

The distinguishing feature of the market for retirement homes is that they are purpose-built for retired and older people, and there is an identifiable group of potential customers. Barriers to entry into the market niche may be relatively low for companies in the building industry, although companies such as Latchkey have knowledge of the particular features of the market, its products and its customers. In addition, their land bank may consist of plots that are particularly well-suited to building retirement homes. Any company entering into the market might need to invest a large amount of money to acquire a suitable land bank of their own.

Corporate governance

An essential requirement for a successful restructuring deal must be the ability of Latchkey to improve its operational performance. Gammon will want to have some influence over Latchkey's management. The board of Latchkey may refuse to consider the appointment of a Chief Executive Officer appointed by Gammon. However at the very least, Gammon should insist on the appointment of at least one non-executive director to the board of Latchkey, to represent its interests and to monitor management and the business performance closely.

Conclusion regarding a restructuring arrangement

In conclusion, future prospects for Latchkey may be encouraging and Gammon should continue with detailed discussions about a restructuring deal.

Exit route for Gammon's investment

If Gammon purchases the loans from the banks, it can hold them until maturity, earning interest and receiving repayment of the loan capital at maturity. The interest receivable on the loans should provide a high yield. However, if the company is unable to meet its loan repayment obligations, Gammon would have the option of initiating insolvency proceedings, or possibly of negotiating a further refinancing scheme in which it swaps loans for equity, and so acquires control of the company.

If the company recovers successfully, Gammon may also choose to sell the loans to another specialist fund.

If Gammon acquires an equity interest in Latchkey, its exit route might be through an eventual IPO for the company, or by means of a trade sale to another construction company, or possibly a sale to a private investment organisation such as a private equity fund.

Exiting from the investment, having made a good return, should be possible, but only if the company is successful in improving its operational performance.

(b) **The recovery plan of the Latchkey board**

If the assumptions used by the board of Latchkey turn out correct, the company's operating profit in 20X5 will be as indicated in their recovery plan.

Forecast operating profit for the year to 31 December 20X5

	£m
Turnover: sale of homes (103.6 × 1.04 × 1.02)	109.9
Cost of sales (81.4 × 1.02 × 1.01)	(83.9)
Gross profit	26.0
Income from care home management (3.2 × 1.05)	3.4
	29.4
Administrative expenses (15.7 × 1.01)	(15.9)
Other operating expenses (3.2 × 1.01)	(3.2)
Operating profit	10.3

If the company's interest costs are reduced, as suggested previously, this would be sufficient to restore the company to profitability in 20X5.

However, the assumptions used in this plan should be reviewed critically, to establish how they have been obtained and how reliable they might be.

Recovery in property prices

Large property selling agents provide predictions of property price changes. A survey of forecasts, together with any official forecast produced by government, would provide a means of assessing the reliability of the assumption of an average 4% increase in prices in 20X5.

Recovery in sales volumes

We do not know why sales volumes fell in 20X4. It would be useful to look at the report and accounts that are available for other companies in the same market sector, to establish whether there was a decrease in sales in the market generally, or whether the decrease occurred for Latchkey only.

An increase in sales volume of 2%, after a fall of about 5% in the previous year, may not seem unreasonable. Forecasts of major property/real estate agents for 20X5 may provide a useful guide to market expectations.

Income from managing care homes

The company is forecasting a 5% increase in revenues, but this is not a significant amount. Presumably there are associated operating costs of care home management. This item in the recovery plan can therefore be ignored for the purpose of assessing the overall validity of the plan.

Increase in costs of 1%

Operating costs cover a wide range of items, and a more detailed breakdown of costs should be made to establish which items of cost are the most significant. Clearly they will include costs of building materials, employee costs, hire of equipment, property rental and so on. Estimates of wage inflation, increases in commodity prices, and the general rate of inflation are available from a variety of sources, and the validity of the assumptions in the Latchkey recovery plan can be assessed.

It would be appropriate to carry out some sensitivity analysis to establish how profitability might vary given variations in the assumptions that have been used.

(c) **Creating a strong brand**

The board of Latchkey have a strategic objective of creating a strong brand for the company's name. Without the benefit of detailed research, my view is that the company is not sufficiently well-established, having been in existence for only five years, to have a strong brand image among potential customers. A brand can only be developed over time.

In the market for retirement homes, the strength of a brand is likely to depend largely on product quality and a reputation for good customer service and ethical business practices (including concerns for health and safety). High product quality should also help to improve the resale value of retirement homes, adding further to the company's reputation. The company's board has identified key risks in the business. These include reputational risks linked to the quality of homes that are built and customer satisfaction, and also health and safety risks (which would have a consequence on the company's reputation in the event of a serious accident in a property under construction or in a completed home).

Brand image also depends on successful marketing, including advertising.

In my view, given the fact that Latchkey is a fairly new company and a relatively small competitor in its market, brand strategy is an issue for the longer term, and is not necessarily something that the company should be concerned about at the moment. The quality of built homes, customer service and health and safety issues are all important, but at the moment they are important for establishing a successful business rather than a strong brand image.

(d) **Improving operational performance**

As indicated earlier, the turnaround for Latchkey's business will depend largely on a recovery in property prices and in demand for retirement properties. Property prices are dependent on the market, and so are largely outside the company's control. Sales demand may also be influenced largely by market conditions; however there may well be scope for improvements in sales performance.

An important factor in constructing and selling residential properties is the length of the cycle between acquiring land for development and completing the sale of constructed properties. A long cycle means fewer sales than if the cycle is shorter. For example if the cycle for building and selling homes is one year, sales potential will be twice what it would be if the length of the cycle were two years.

The board of Latchkey has identified a problem with the building cycle, with delayed starting times for new building and late completion of construction projects. The problems with delays should be investigated, and an attempt should be made to remove or reduce delays in the construction process. Provided that there is sufficient demand for completed homes, any reduction in the building cycle time will result in higher sales volumes.

There may also be weaknesses in the performance of the sales department. Clearly there is some delay in selling completed homes. At the end of 20X4, inventory of finished housing was £63.4m, representing a turnover period of over 9 months (63.4/81.4 × 12). If there is sufficient demand for retirement homes, it is surprising that it takes over nine months on average to sell a completed home. Improving the building cycle time will not result in higher sales if the outcome is simply to add to inventories of unsold finished apartments.

Even though there may be weak demand in the market, it would be surprising if measures could not be taken to reduce the overall length of the cycle between acquiring land for development and selling completed properties. Latchkey appears to have an arrangement for the sale of some properties where it retains the right to some of the proceeds from re-selling. I would recommend further investigation into this selling arrangement, to establish whether it might offer opportunities for more sales. As a more general recommendation, the performance of the sales department should be monitored, and if the company does not yet have one, an incentive scheme to reward successful sales and marketing personnel might be considered.

There are probably also opportunities for cost savings. The increase in administrative and other operating costs in 20X4, in spite of a fall in sales volume, would suggest that expenditures may be out of control. Even a 1% reduction in total costs (cost of sales, administrative costs and other operating costs) would improve operating profit by about £1m. One aspect of spending to consider is the local responsibility of project managers for purchasing and hiring labour. Although it may be necessary to hire labour locally for building projects, there may well be opportunities for cost savings if purchasing is organised centrally for building materials and equipment hire.

My comments have so far focused on profitability. It is important to recognise also that Latchkey needs adequate funding for its operations. A shorter cycle between land purchase and selling completed homes should reduce working capital and improve cash flows. However the company needs sufficient finance for its working capital, including land sales and costs of constructing new buildings. It is critically important that the company should continue to acquire land for its land bank, and that it should be successful in obtaining planning permissions to build. In view of the small amount of cash held by Latchkey at the end of 20X4, my view is that new funding is required. Without further investigation, I cannot estimate how much would be sufficient.

(e) **The share option scheme**

A reconstruction scheme involving the issue of new shares in Latchkey will affect the rights of option holders under any existing share option scheme, and we would need to study the terms of the option scheme to establish what the altered entitlements of scheme holders might be, and what implications this would have for the company's profitability as well as Gammon's investment.

My recommendation would be to make a proposal to buy out the existing option holders from their scheme, with the promise that if the company's financial situation recovers, a new share option scheme will be considered at some time in the future.

The offer to buy out the existing options and cancel the scheme should be a fair one. It could be based on an estimate of how the value of the options might be expected to increase over the next three years, and the offer price could be a discounted value (present value) of the estimated future value of the options.

A tougher negotiating line would be to argue that the existing share option scheme should be cancelled as a condition of a refinancing agreement, on the grounds that the options will have no value unless the resonstruction goes ahead. In negotiations, a nominal value may then be offered to win agreement for cancelling the option scheme.

It should therefore be possible to estimate the likely effect of the new share option scheme on the company's annual profits, if Gammon is unable to scrap the scheme as part of the restructuring arrangement. If only a small number of senior executives are affected, the cost may not be large. If it seems too large, Gammon can refuse to participate in a restructuring deal, leaving Latchkey exposed to an uncertain future for its business.

26 Plumbrite plc

		Marks
(a)	Calculation of relevant performance statistics	
	Comparison of performance between UK and Taiwan, including reasons for potential differences in performance	20
(b)	Critical success factors for each country	6
(c)	Performance measures for evaluating staff training and development	6
(d)	Evaluation of the proposal to reduce the supplier base and to revise the contract terms	
	Issues involved in revising the contract terms	10
(e)	Evaluation of rebranding proposal	
	Assurance which could be provided in relation to the rebranding proposal	8
(f)	Financial reporting implications of rebranding programme	5
Total marks		55

(a) Performance comparison between UK and Taiwan

	UK	Taiwan	Taiwan vs UK
Gross profit (%)	30.0%	21.9%	−8.1%
Operating profit (%)	3.5%	4.4%	0.9%
Return on capital employed	12.3%	14.1%	1.8%

	UK	Taiwan	Taiwan – UK	% diff
Revenue per store (£m)	4.67	6.38	1.71	37%
Gross profit per store (£m)	1.40	1.40	–	–
Operating profit per store (£m)	0.16	0.28	0.12	75%
Employees per store	13.0	15.1	2.1	16%
Revenue per employee (£m)	0.36	0.42	0.06	17%
Training days per employee	14.0	10.0	−4.0	−29%
Cost of returns	1.96	5.61	3.65	186%
On time deliveries (%)	97.6	92.4	−5.2	−5%

	UK				Taiwan			
	RM	NC	SB		RM	NC	SB	
Sales revenue per sector (£m)	367.5	83.3	39.2		74.0	176.0	5.1	
Cost of sales (£m)	267.8	50.9	24.3		63.4	130.8	5.0	
GP (£m)	99.7	32.4	14.9		10.6	45.2	0.1	
GP (%)	27.1%	38.9%	38.0%	30.0%	14.3%	25.7%	2.0%	21.9%
Relative market share (*)	1.65	0.67	0.64		0.83	0.89	n/a	

* Plumbrite's Market share/Market share of largest competitor

Profitability and Revenues

Gross Profit margin in UK is 8 percentage points higher than for Taiwan. This is likely to be due to the higher cost of sales in terms of transport and distribution costs to the Taiwanese outlets where no distribution warehouses are located nearby. It could also be because the retail price for the products is lower in Taiwan than the UK, although we do not actually have any information about price differentials between the two countries. Nonetheless, the threat from the two locally based building suppliers suggests that competitive pricing is important in Taiwan.

Interestingly, despite having a lower gross margin, BM's operating profit percentage in Taiwan is about 1 percentage point higher than in UK. This is likely due to the lower operating costs in Taiwan compared to the UK. In particular, it seems likely that this is driven by lower staff costs and less investment in staff training in Taiwan. Again, however, in this respect it would be useful to have more information about the relative wage rates BM pays its staff in both countries.

The operating profits earned in both UK and Taiwan were higher than the BM division's overall operating profit of 3.1% for 20X3 (214/6,843; see Exhibit 1). Therefore, both countries are making a positive contribution to the overall profitability of the division.

BM has been operating in the UK significantly longer than it has been in Taiwan. As a result it is better established in the UK and has more outlets there. Nonetheless, BM's revenue per outlet in Taiwan is £1.7m (37%) higher than in UK. This may be due, in part, to differences in the size of the stores between the two countries (if Taiwan has larger stores). However, a more significant factor is likely to be the differences in the range of products sold in the two countries. BM sells a range of large, high value industrial products in Taiwan (to the New construction sector), whereas in UK it primarily sells smaller domestic repair and maintenance products.

However, despite the revenue per outlet being considerably higher in Taiwan, the gross profit per outlet is the same between the two countries. This again reflects the difference in the gross profit margins, with UK sales generating a higher gross profit margin than those in Taiwan.

Employees

BM employs more than twice as many employees in UK than in Taiwan, which is to be expected, considering that the number of outlets in UK is also much higher.

However, in terms of the number of employees per outlet, on average BM employs two people fewer per outlet in the UK than in Taiwan. This again could be because its outlets are larger in Taiwan than UK, although there may also be other factors which affect staff numbers per stores – for example, differences in the level of service which customers want, particularly in relation to different product ranges; or differences in the skills and experience of the employees in the respective countries.

On average, BM's staff in Taiwan received four days less training during the year than staff in the UK (29% less). If this leads to the staff in Taiwan being less efficient than their counterparts in the UK, this could be a reason why the outlets in Taiwan require more staff.

The greater investment in training in the UK may also help to explain the low employee turnover rate (1% in the year) – compared to 3.5% in Taiwan. Although 3.5% still seems a relatively low staff turnover rate, the very low rate in the UK may indicate that BM's staff are motivated and dedicated to their jobs. This could also help to explain the high customer satisfaction scores – because motivated and dedicated staff are likely to provide their customers with a high standard of service.

Nonetheless, the revenue per employee is marginally higher in Taiwan than the UK. This is likely to be driven by the lower number of overall employees operating in fewer and larger outlets, selling higher value products.

Product returns

The cost of product returns in Taiwan was almost three times as high as in the UK (£5.61m vs £1.96m).

Although these figures suggest that this is an area where performance improvements and cost savings could be made in Taiwan, the high level of returns there may result from the higher value products sold there.

Equally, to some extent they may be a result of the transportation distances required to ship products to Taiwan from BM's warehouses – in the UK and in USA. Products damaged in transit could be a cause of returns. Equally, returns could be caused by delays in delivery – if the delay means that a customer no longer wants a product they have ordered. Again, it could be useful to have more information about the levels of inventory held in each country, and between new construction (NC) and repairs and maintenance (RM) products. If a number of NC products are ordered on a JIT basis, but the majority of RM products are held 'just in case' this could also affect levels of returns between the two countries.

Nonetheless, its distribution and logistics networks appear to be the main area which BM needs to address. If Taiwan, and Asia more generally, are seen as a potential growth area, then BM should investigate the possibility of investment in more local distribution and warehousing facilities. It appears that the Board is already aware of the need to acquire additional logistics resources (see Strategic developments in Exhibit 1), but this performance comparison reiterates the potential strategic importance of such an acquisition.

However, in part, the low level of product returns in the UK is also likely to be a further reflection of the knowledgeable and well trained employees who are able to correctly advise customers on the products they need – reducing the scope for customers returning products because they were not what they wanted/needed. In this respect, as well as knowing the number of products returned it would also be useful to analyse the reasons why products are returned, so that BM can address the underlying causes.

On time deliveries

The relative performance information indicates that deliveries are much more time efficient in the UK, with 97.6% being delivered on time, compared to 92.4% in Taiwan.

The figures for on time deliveries suggest this is an area of risk for BM in Taiwan, as the NC customers, in particular, demand prompt and accurate delivery of goods. However, as well as comparing performance internally, it would also be useful for BM to compare its performance externally. In particular, it would be useful to know what proportion of orders the two national suppliers in Taiwan deliver on time.

The goods being delivered to the NC sector are high value products, and are likely to be required on large projects with tight deadlines to be met. Late or unreliable deliveries could be a serious competitive disadvantage for BM in this respect. Again, the fact that it has no local warehouses is likely to be a significant factor in its ability to deliver on time, which reinforces this as an issue which BM should look to address if it wants to develop its market position in Taiwan and/or other Asian countries.

Analysis by market sector

Revenue per market sector

There are significant differences in the revenues generated by the different market sectors in each country. In the UK, revenues are dominated by the repairs and maintenance market, which accounts for 75% of total revenue. In Taiwan, revenues are dominated by the new construction market, which accounts for 69% of total revenue.

The new construction market generates the highest gross profit margin (%) in both countries, though; and it is more than ten percentage points higher than the margin earned from repairs and maintenance sales. This is likely to be due to the repairs and maintenance products being smaller, low value items whose prices earn lower margins.

The gross profit margins BM earns in all three sectors are significantly higher in the UK than in Taiwan; for both the repairs and maintenance sector and the new construction sector, the UK margin is approximately 13 percentage points higher than Taiwan's. It seems likely that transport costs are again a major factor behind this difference, because materials have to be transported very long distances in order to be sold in Taiwan.

As we have already noted, though, we do not know anything about price differentials between the two countries, but this information would be useful when comparing gross profit margins.

Sustainable Building (SB) sector

The gross profit margin for the SB market in the UK is very strong (38%), and this suggests that the SB market provides an opportunity for BM to exploit in the future, as this sector is currently the smallest of the three in both countries.

Moreover, as the UK government has been actively promoting the development of more sustainable building projects this should provide an opportunity to increase revenues in this sector.

Currently, BM is the third largest competitor in the sustainable buildings market, with a 9% market share. (The market leader holds 14% of the market). If the government's support, coupled with the inherent growth potential in this market sector, leads to high growth rates in the sustainable business market as a whole, then this business unit should be viewed as a 'question mark' in BM's product portfolio. This suggests that BM should continue to invest in, and develop, this business area.

However, the margin for the sustainable building materials market in Taiwan is currently very low (2%). This may be because the SB products require specialist transportation or delivery methods (which incur additional costs) to get them to Taiwan. However, it may equally be because the sector is still very small, and therefore the margin may increase as volumes increase and BM can begin to benefit from economies of scale. Nonetheless, this is an area which BM should review closely.

New Construction (NC) sector

The UK government has also been promoting investment in large scale regeneration of derelict housing stock across the country. This regeneration should help to promote growth within the new construction market and, as such, should increase revenues and profits in the NC sector in the UK.

In Taiwan, revenues are already dominated by the new construction market, which is driven by the country's growing and developing economy and the building of large scale infrastructure. This growth should provide an on-going source of business development in Taiwan, and so it seems appropriate for BM to concentrate on this sector.

Again, in terms of BM's product portfolio, its NC business in Taiwan should be viewed as a 'question mark', and therefore BM should be looking for opportunities to develop this sector further. However, its ability to do so could depend on investing in efficient transport facilities to ensure that new construction customers receive their products on time. Timely delivery of materials is a critical success factor in this market sector.

With strong local competition in the new construction market, BM must focus upon improved customer service and price competitiveness in order to strengthen its position in the market. As the gross profit margin earned in the NC sector is currently higher than the average in BM in Taiwan there may be scope for BM to reduce its prices to NC customers in order to improve price competitiveness. However, in order to be effective, any such initiatives still need to be supported by efficiency in delivery and high levels of product quality.

Market position

One of Plumbrite's overall strategic objectives is to be the market leader in the regions of the world where it operates. To help it achieve this, BM should also strive to be the market leader in the markets and sectors where it operates.

Currently, the only sector where BM is the market leader is the RM sector in the UK. In Taiwan, BM holds second place in the RM sector, with a market share 4 percentage points behind the market leader (20% vs 24%). Therefore, it should consider how it can strengthen its market share, either through improved price competitiveness or through improved customer service and speed of delivery. Again, though, this is likely to require significant investment, and so should be considered alongside an assessment of the long term growth potential of the RM market sector in Taiwan. If it becomes clear that BM is unable to become the market leader, and the RM sector has only low growth, then the RM sector in Taiwan is effectively a 'dog' in terms of the BCG matrix classifications. As such, Plumbrite should 'hold' the division, rather than continuing to invest in it any further.

In the NC market sector, BM occupies the second position in both the UK and Taiwan. Its market position in the UK may change in the coming years as more growth occurs in the new construction industry which BM can then aim to exploit. In Taiwan, BM's market share is already quite close to that of the market leader (17% vs 19%) but again there appears to be scope for growth in this sector. BM needs to consider the possibility of future investment in improved transport networks and distribution facilities and range of products if it is to compete against strong local competitors and to gain its position as market leader – or perhaps even to retain its second place as market supplier in this sector as the market grows and potentially becomes more attractive to other competitors.

The SB sector appears to be a source of future development for BM and more research must be carried out on the predicted growth in this market sector in both countries. In order for BM to grow and increase its market share, though, investment is likely to be necessary – particularly in Taiwan. Nonetheless, the SB sector seems to be a new and developing area, and if BM can be one of the first companies to establish itself in this market sector it could gain significant advantages in both countries.

Customer satisfaction

BM has set a target rate of 96%. All three of BM's business units in the UK have achieved this target level, and overall BM's customer satisfaction rating in the UK (using a weighted average approach based on sales revenue) is 97.2%. By contrast, none of BM's business units in Taiwan have achieved the target level, and the overall customer satisfaction rating is 95.2%.

The Taiwanese figures provide cause for concern, and BM should investigate ways of improving customer satisfaction levels in Taiwan. In particular, improved levels of employee training could help. Employees in Taiwan currently receive less training than their counterparts in the UK, and it seems likely that this is reflected in the level of service they are able to provide their customers.

Although the sustainable building sector is currently a very small part of BM's business in Taiwan, it is likely to become increasingly important in the future as governments and companies are forced to consider more sustainable building methods and products. Therefore, staff training should include sustainability issues, to support the development of this area of the business.

(b) **CSFs for the UK retail outlets**

High levels of customer service – A critical success factor for BM's retail outlets in the UK is the delivery of high levels of customer service provided to all customers, across all of its market sectors. Although customer service is important to all customers, it is particularly valued by the small independent builders and tradesmen who are currently BM's main customers. Therefore, providing high levels of customer service is likely to be critical in sustaining BM's market position in the UK, where the market is dominated by sales to the repairs and maintenance sector.

This CSF highlights the need for BM to maintain its staff training and staff development, to ensure that employees' product knowledge and their commitment and loyalty to BM continues to deliver sustainable competitive advantage for the company.

Wide product range – A second critical success factor for BM in the UK could be offering the widest choice of products to its customers. Customers in the UK value the range of products offered by BM and this should be an area which BM focuses on in relation to maintaining sustainable competitive advantage. However, it is important that a wide range of products is supported with high levels of customer support and knowledgeable staff (as highlighted in the first CSF).

CSFs for the Taiwanese retail outlets

Speed of product delivery – A critical success factor for BM's retail outlets operating in Taiwan is the speed with which products are delivered to customers, ensuring that high quality products are delivered to the right place at the right time.

BM faces competition from two large nationally based building materials suppliers who sell competitively priced products. This means price is an important factor. However, by itself, price is not likely to be a critical success factor for BM against its main rivals, as customers want guaranteed on-time delivery, at the correct location. Therefore it is critical for BM to ensure that speed and accuracy of delivery is the primary focus, in particular to its NC market sector customers.

BM's NC customers not only expect prompt and accurate delivery, but also demand high quality products.

Quality products – Therefore, a second CSF should be the delivery of high quality products. BM should focus on ensuring that, where possible, it provides higher quality products than its rivals, because this could provide it with a means of differentiating itself from those rivals and thereby gaining a competitive advantage. It may also mean that customers will buy their products from BM even if its prices are slightly higher than those offered by the local competitors.

Nonetheless, BM must also be able to ensure it consistently delivers its products on time, to sustain the competitive advantage it gains through the quality of its products.

Once again, this highlights that investment in local warehousing and distribution facilities is an important consideration for BM if it wishes to develop and enhance its competitive position in the Taiwanese market.

(c) **Staff training and development**

Providing excellent customer service is the key critical success factor for the BM division. In turn, this also means that staff development and employee retention are very important to BM's business strategy and its long term success. A skilled and motivated workforce is more likely to deliver excellent customer service than a less skilled or less motivated one.

Therefore, the performance measures selected for evaluating the success of staff training and development activities need to consider employee satisfaction and engagement, as well as customer satisfaction.

Performance measures

Tutorial note:

Only three measures were required. More are provided here for tutorial purposes.

Customer satisfaction rating per outlet – The underlying purpose of BM's staff training and development activities should be to improve the level of service its staff provide to their customers. Therefore, the success of those activities can be measured through customer satisfaction scores.

BM's target is to achieve an overall customer satisfaction target rating of 96% across all outlets in every country. If BM measures customer satisfaction at each outlet this will help it to identify areas where it is not performing as well as intended, and therefore where additional training or other performance improvements may be required.

(BM could potentially even identify how customer satisfaction levels vary according to the staff members who have served the customers.)

Training – % of staff per country who have been trained – As a division, BM places considerable emphasis on staff training. However, it appears that the numbers of staff who have received training varies between different countries, and this may also reflect that staff training is given less emphasis in some countries than others. For example, less time and effort appears to be given to training in Taiwan than in the UK.

However, these differences in the level of training also appear to be reflected in the level of customer service provided in the different countries.

Monitoring the quality and quantity of training provided to front-line employees – as well as the proportion of staff who are completing the online training modules provided – will help to identify countries or regions where sufficient training is not being provided. Improving the training should, in turn, also help BM to achieve its customer service targets.

Employee satisfaction scores – BM carries out employee engagement surveys in all of its retail outlets, in order to measure levels of employee satisfaction.

Within these employee surveys, BM could ask staff specifically about the training they have received, and their roles (eg development; career development/progression etc). The feedback from these questions could provide BM with useful information about how the training could be improved, or ways in which the development activities available to staff could be improved.

Staff retention rates (%) per outlet – Staff retention as well as staff development is an important factor which contributes to BM's long term strategic success. There will be little benefit to BM from training and developing staff if they then leave the division or Plumbrite as a company.

However, measuring the level of staff retention can also indicate how satisfied employees are with BM as a place to work. If staff do not feel valued, adequately trained to perform their job effectively, or are not satisfied with BM as a place to work more generally, they are more likely to leave the company and therefore staff retention levels will fall.

(d) **Reducing the number of suppliers**

Better economies of scale – Increased margins

Over the last five years, the Plumbing and Heating (PH) division has increased its product range by 29%, but in doing so it has increased the number of suppliers it uses by 44% ((65,000 – 45,000)/45,000). Given that the percentage increase in the number of suppliers is greater than the increase in the product range, this suggests that the division is using more suppliers who supply fewer products. In turn, this is likely to increase the administration costs per product.

If the number of suppliers is reduced across the division, and across Plumbrite as a whole, this should reduce administration costs due to the economies of scale achieved by purchasing a greater number of products from each supplier. These economies of scale may also mean that Plumbrite can negotiate lower purchase prices as well, on account of the volume of products it is buying from a supplier.

Supply chain efficiency

Given that Plumbrite prides itself on having an efficient supply chain, then one of its primary goals in managing its supply chain should be to satisfy customer demand at the lowest cost.

This again suggests that reducing the number of suppliers, and benefitting from economies of scale in supply, would appear more consistent with the goals of an efficient supply chain.

Relieve pressure on logistics

Plumbrite's warehouses are struggling to cope with the increased product range in recent years. If the number of suppliers is reduced – and, with it, the number of different products supplied – this pressure will be relieved, and stepped fixed costs (for example, from having to move to bigger warehouses within the UK and the USA) could be avoided.

Many products will be generic

As many products in the Plumbing, Heating and Building materials markets are generic, it should be possible to ensure that suppliers are rationalised without any significant loss of consumer choice. General plumbing parts, such as taps and pipes, have little 'differentiating' quality, and if carefully selected, duplicate suppliers may be removed without compromising customer choice.

For products where there is a greater degree of customer choice (such as baths or showers), PH division may have less scope to reduce the number of suppliers without affecting the level of choice it offers its customers though.

Reduction of competitive edge on product range

The PH division appears to have differentiated itself by offering the widest and most diverse range of products, meaning that this product range is a source of competitive advantage. Cutting the number of suppliers would therefore represent a significant change to the current strategy, and so could make it more difficult for the division to deliver a clear marketing message to its consumers.

Difficult to establish the criteria for supply

Although we know the Logistics Director has proposed a 'standard set of criteria' for selecting suppliers, we do not know what these criteria are. The criteria may be too rigid – given the huge range of products sold by PH – and could lead to successful products (and good supplier relations) being damaged.

However, it is important that the criteria which PH uses for evaluating its suppliers are defined in advance and are applied fairly, given Plumbrite's corporate responsibility aim to adhere to the highest ethical standards with respect to supplier relationships.

For example, decisions should be made according to the price and quality of the products, demand for them, and the reliability of the suppliers in supplying them, rather than any financial incentives suppliers might be prepared to make in order to secure the continuation of their preferred supplier status.

Revising the terms of the contracts

Legality and penalty clauses

Given that Plumbrite offers its preferred suppliers long term (three year) contracts, we are assuming that it has formal, legally binding contracts with those suppliers. Therefore, any proposal to change these terms will either take time (if the contract is either followed in full, or a required period of notice is given) or lead to a breach of contract. This could in turn result in significant legal costs for Plumbrite.

It appears that Plumbrite's legal team have helped to draw up the existing contracts (or are at least aware of them), so the management team should discuss the implications of the proposed changes with a suitably qualified member of the legal team before finalising any changes.

Increased flexibility for Plumbrite

Currently suppliers have the benefit of a three year contract term and a minimum order guarantee.

Although this enables Plumbrite to develop long-term relationships with its suppliers, the commitment for minimum order guarantee appears more beneficial to the suppliers than to Plumbrite. For example, there is no suggestion that the suppliers are required to make any incentive payments to secure their preferred status with Plumbrite, and such a policy should be avoided, given Plumbrite's commitment to maintaining high ethical standards with its suppliers.

Nonetheless, the new terms would appear to redress the balance of power between Plumbrite and its suppliers, and will allow the company to make quicker decisions about discontinuing less profitable or slow-moving products.

(e) Evaluation

Positive net present value

Assuming the Marketing Director's figures are reliable, the rebranding exercise gives a positive net present value of £5.2m, which would suggest it is beneficial from a financial perspective.

In addition, although the physical shop fittings are refurbished every five years (which justifies the five year investment appraisal period) the benefits accruing through increased revenue and higher margins should extend beyond that. As such, the financial benefit of the programme may actually be greater than the NPV calculation suggests.

Capital cost and relevant cost

The Marketing Director's figures suggest that the capital cost of the rebranding programme in the UK has been estimated at £58m (580 shops × 80% × £125,000 each).

However, given Plumbrite's rolling refurbishment programme, approximately one fifth of these stores would have been refurbished in a year, regardless of the rebranding exercise. Therefore, it would be more relevant to reduce the cost of refurbishment for the costs which would already be committed under the normal five year refurbishment programme. As such, the 'relevant' capital cost to include in the investment appraisal would be nearer to £46m (580 shops × 80% × 80% × £125,000 each).

Brand identity and product ranges

The underlying logic of the Marketing Director's proposal appears to be that, because many of the goods Plumbrite sells are largely generic – bricks, timber, pipes etc – there is little benefit in retaining individual trading names, due to the operating inefficiencies which result from them advertising separately and the inherent difficulty they could face in creating customer loyalty. This may be one of the reasons why Plumbrite has already had to write down the goodwill on some of the businesses it has acquired.

As such, the rebranding exercise could enable all of the shops to benefit from being part of Plumbrite's main brands.

However, the reason why Plumbrite has retained the retail outlets it has acquired under their own trading names is because each has specific lines of business – such as the sale of complete bathrooms or kitchens. As such, the product ranges sold through these outlets are not the same as those sold through a general 'building materials' store which sells bricks and timber etc.

Therefore, while the Marketing Director's logic in reducing the number of different trade names being used appears valid, there is a danger that combining the different types of outlet into only two trade names means that Plumbrite will no longer be able to distinguish between outlets which offer a wide range of general products and those which focus on selling a narrower range of specific products. In effect, the Marketing Director is proposing a 'one size fits all' policy, which may not be appropriate in this context.

Assurance

The business case which the Marketing Director has prepared represents prospective financial information. Therefore any assurance work RH undertake should be governed by ISAE 3400 *The Examination of Prospective Financial Information.*

ISAE 3400 highlights that prospective information is based on assumptions about the future and is therefore highly subjective in nature and a considerable amount of judgement has to be exercised in its preparation.

This is clearly the case here; in particular, in relation to the impact that rebranding will have on Plumbrite's revenues.

Nonetheless, RH could still undertake assurance procedures to obtain evidence that the assumptions on which the business case are based are not unreasonable; for example, what evidence is there to support the claim that annual revenue will increase 5% following the rebranding.

RH could also undertake procedures to ensure that the business case is properly prepared on the basis of the assumptions.

ISAE 3400 identifies that capital expenditure is a key issue in projections, and so RH could undertake procedures to check the capital expenditure for reasonableness; both in terms of the expected cost per outlet, and also that the capital expenditure included in the business case only relates to refurbishments required by the rebranding (and not outlets which were due for a routine refurbishment anyway).

Limited assurance

However, as with any forecast, it is important that RH recognises that the assumptions may subsequently prove incorrect, even though they appeared reasonable. As such, RH cannot give Plumbrite the same level of assurance over the business case as it could over historical financial information.

RH could give limited assurance in the form of a negative opinion – saying that there is nothing to suggest that the business case is inappropriate.

(f) **Financial reporting consequences of rebranding**

When Plumbrite acquired the different chains of retail outlets, in accordance with IFRS 3 *Business Combinations* this will have given rise to two different types of intangible assets in its financial statements: trade names, and goodwill.

Trade names

While the chains have been trading under their own names, future economic benefits are attributable to the trade names. The trade names were also separable and therefore identifiable. Therefore Plumbrite has been able to carry the trade names as intangible assets in accordance with IAS 38 *Intangible Assets.*

However, following the rebranding it is unlikely that the trade names will continue to have any value.

As Plumbrite has been amortising the trade names, some may already be fully written off. However, any remaining unamortised amounts will have to be written off, and charged to profit or loss.

Goodwill

Goodwill in a business combination is defined by IFRS 3 as:

'An asset representing the future economic benefits arising from other assets acquired in a business combination that are not individually identified and separately recognised.'

Goodwill recognised in a business combination is an asset and is initially measured at cost. Cost is the excess of the cost of the combination over the acquirer's interest in the net fair value of the acquiree's identifiable assets, liabilities and contingent liabilities. These identifiable assets include the trade names of the acquired chains of retail outlets.

After initial recognition goodwill acquired in a business combination is measured at cost less any accumulated impairment losses. It is not amortised. Instead, it is tested for impairment at least annually, in accordance with IAS 36 *Impairment of Assets.*

While the rebranding will affect the trade names, which are no longer generating economic benefits, there is no reason for it to affect the goodwill arising on the acquisition of the business concerned. This is a historical figure representing the difference between the price paid and the fair value of the identifiable net assets (including trade names), and it would not necessarily change as a result of the rebranding.

However, in the case of those acquired businesses which have already been identified as underperforming, the goodwill arising on acquisition is probably impaired. Impairment tests should therefore be carried out in accordance with IAS 36, that is by allocating the goodwill to cash generating units and testing the cash generating units by comparing the carrying amount of the unit, including the goodwill, with the recoverable amount. If the carrying amount is greater, there is an impairment loss to be treated as per IAS 36.

Store refits and new signage

The cost of refitting the stores and rebranding the shop front signage (£58m according to the Marketing Director's estimates) should be capitalised as non-current assets, in line with IAS 16 *Property, Plant and Equipment.*

This cost should then be depreciated over five years, in line with Plumbrite's policy of refurbishing its outlets on a five year programme.

Disposal of old shop fittings and signage

However, in addition to capitalising the new shop fitting costs, Plumbrite will also have to write off the cost of its existing shop fittings and signage.

The extent to which these have already been depreciated will depend on when each outlet was last refurbished.

The undepreciated amount will need to be charged to profit or loss.

Marketing costs

Any expenditure relating to brand building or advertising should be expensed as incurred. Therefore the expected marketing costs of £1.75m which will accompany the rebranding will all be charged to profit or loss.

27 Liebitz & Luber plc

Marking guide

		Marks
(a)	Explanation of the financial risks and evaluation of how these risks may be managed	8
(b)	Explanation of the financial reporting treatment of the purchase of ammonia and for possible hedging arrangements	8
(c)	Briefing note on whether LL should insure against spillage risks or accept the risks; with supporting calculations	5
(d)	Explanation and justification of the level of assurance that RR could provide and the benefits to LL	7
(e)	Evaluation of the potential benefits to LL of adopting integrated reporting; with particular reference to reporting on social and manufactured capital	12
(f)	Evaluation of the potential impact that the new EIS could have on performance management at LL	5
Total marks		45

(a) **Risks**

The purchase of the ammonia exposes LL to two key and interrelated financial risks: (1) commodity price risk; and (2) foreign exchange risk of the US$ moving against the £. In the context of the specific transaction to purchase 2,000 tonnes of ammonia, if the price of ammonia rises, and/or the US$ strengthens against the £, before 22 December 20X4, then the cost, in sterling terms, will increase.

Unless any cost increase can be passed on to the customer, in the form of a higher selling price, then the sales contract on which the ammonia is to be used will be less profitable, or indeed, it may make a loss.

In addition there are health and safety risks from the transport and storage of ammonia as a dangerous substance. If there is an incident then this could have financial consequences (see below).

There are also compliance costs arising from regulations and laws governing the transport and storage of dangerous substances such as ammonia. Breach of these regulations could result in fines or other measures against the company and its directors.

Risk management

Commodity price risk

The commodity price risk for an individual purchase transaction could be mitigated most easily by a futures contract for delivery of ammonia in 5 months' time. This would lock-in the current price in US$ terms and prevent further commodity price movements. However, it would lock the price at the forward rate of $520 per tonne giving an overall price of $1,040,000. This would remove any upside benefit if the price of ammonia fell by 22 December. In addition, although this hedge arrangement may be successful against any US$ denominated commodity price movement, there is still a risk of exchange rate movement affecting the sterling cost of the ammonia.

The futures contract could be margin traded so physical delivery on the contract is not required. Thus the profit on the margin trade from an increase in the price of ammonia would offset the increase in costs on the underlying contract.

Currency risk

Any potential currency movement could be separately hedged (from the commodity price movement) by a number of methods:

- Money market cover. LL could exchange an amount of £s sterling immediately into US$ such that, with interest, it will accumulate to $1,040,000 by 22 December.

- Currency forward contract. This would operate similarly to above, but LL would wish to acquire US$1,040,000 at a predetermined exchange rate in 5 months.

- Currency option. Similarly LL could acquire an option to purchase US$ at a fixed rate in 5 months. This is thus a call option. This would be more expensive upfront than a forward contract because it is a one way bet.

However LL's approach to risk management for individual transactions should take a broader 'strategic' view of risk. Futures and forward contracts, when used for hedging, are intended to fix a price for transactions that will be settled at a future date, but in doing so, they prevent the company from taking advantage of any favourable movement in the spot price.

In this example the spot price is $500 per tonne. The futures price is $520, but has fallen from $530 in just a few days. The company may not wish to commit itself to a fixed price of $520 if the spot price seems more likely than not to stay below this level.

For large transactions, when the future movement in the spot price is difficult to predict, it may be worth considering the use of call options, although these obviously have a cost (the premium). Alternatively, the choice may be 'not to hedge', taking the view that the spot price will be lower than the forward price or futures price at settlement date.

LL's Treasury department should hedge transaction exposures within the framework of an overall policy towards the management of price risk for different commodities and exchange rates.

Other points should also be considered.

- Hedging needs to be considered collectively for all transactions (macro hedging) rather than for each contract. For instance, 15% of LL's revenues are generated in the US, but there is no factory in the US. As a result, US$ denominated costs may be a natural hedge against US$ denominated revenues. It would only be the net US$ exposure that would require hedging.

- Hedging policy may be to partially hedge transaction exposures and leave them partly unhedged. It might not be necessary to hedge the whole amount of future income/expenditure. If LL is willing to take some risk, only a proportion of the exposure would need to be hedged (eg in the example of the ammonia transaction, 50% or 1,000 tonnes). This would leave some upside potential.

- If the highly probable need for ammonia does not materialise (eg a cancelled sales contract) then, perversely, hedging could actually increase risk as there is now an exposed one-sided commitment from the hedge instrument (ie an unmatched hedge position). This might be mitigated if we need ammonia for other contracts, but timing is crucial given the costs and dangers of storage of ammonia.

(b) **Financial reporting**

The purchase of the ammonia would be treated as a normal purchase transaction at the time the ammonia is delivered to LL. Given that the purchase is in December it is also likely to be included in inventories at the 31 December 20X4 year end.

Hedging is about risk management. Hedge accounting is about offsetting profits and losses on hedging arrangements in a similar manner, in the same financial statement, in the same period. As a result, the accounting treatment is intended to reflect the underlying commercial reality of a hedge arrangement.

Hedge accounting is specifically allowable according to IAS 39 *Financial Instruments: Recognition and Measurement* subject to the following:

- The risks being hedged are clearly defined (ie in this case foreign currency risk and commodity price risk).

- The hedged item and the hedging instrument must be clearly identified.

- The values in the hedge arrangement must be measurable.

- The hedge is expected to be effective and it turns out to be effective within an 80% – 125% range.

- The hedge must be pre-designated and documented.

Hedge accounting is normally only permitted where derivatives are used as the hedging instrument (eg commodity futures for ammonia). The exception is that foreign currency may be hedged by non-derivatives (eg this may include a money market cover arrangement specified above).

Here the hedged item is a forecast highly probable transaction. This can only be accounted for as a cash flow hedge (unlike a firm commitment which could be treated either as a cash flow hedge or a fair value hedge for foreign currencies; per IAS 39 para 87).

As it is a non-financial item being hedged then it can only be designated as a hedged item:

- in respect of foreign currency risk only; or

- in its entirety for all risks (ie for foreign currency and the commodity price risk for ammonia) (per IAS 39 para 82).

The effect of the cash flow hedge accounting is as follows:

The hedged item is the forecast purchase of 2,000 tonnes of ammonia at the spot price on that date.

The hedge instrument is a combination of (for example):

- a 5-month commodity future for delivery of 2,000 tonnes of ammonia on 22 December 20X4; and

- a FOREX forward to buy US$1,040,000 and sell £s at an exchange rate of £1 = US$1.6.

Hedge effectiveness (prospective and retrospective) is assessed by comparing changes in the fair value of the hedging instruments with changes in the fair value of the hedged item.

As it is a cash flow hedge, changes in the fair value of the hedging instruments are recognised initially in other comprehensive income and accumulated in equity and then later reclassified from equity to profit or loss as a reclassification adjustment when the hedged item (ie the purchase of ammonia) affects profit or loss.

(c) **Health and safety risks – chemical spillages**

Quantitative evaluation

Expected insurable cost of a spillage:

[(0.07 × £100m) + (0.93 × £10m)] = £16.3m

Expected number of spillages per annum:

Occurrence of spillages per annum	0	1	2	3
Probability	90%	5%	3%	2%
Probability × Occurrences	0	0.05	0.06	0.06

Expected number of occurrences per year = 0.17

Expected cost of spillages:

£16.3m × 0.17 = **£2.771m**

Qualitative evaluation

The annual insurance premium at £4m is greater than the expected insurable cost of spillages of £2.771m per year. If the company is risk neutral then accepting the risk and not insuring is the preferred solution.

However, most investors are risk averse and would consider insurance even though the expected cost is higher.

Arguments favouring insurance

- Scale. The cost of a major spillage is significant at £150m being around twice the operating profit. This may significantly impact operations requiring divestment to finance the major spillage costs. Insurance would only cover the first £100m of such costs but the remaining £50m may be manageable within operating cash flows.

- There may be a much higher occurrence of spillages than expected.

- The proportion of major incidents may be higher than expected.

- If spillage costs are high then, in the absence of insurance, going concern may be in doubt creating further indirect costs arising from cumulative spillages.

- Insurance would enable LL to show that it is environmentally responsible in having financial backing to pay for environmental damage and personal injury, even if the company did not have sufficient resources itself.

- From a public interest perspective, insurance would finance a clean-up to protect third parties if the scale of the spillage was beyond the capability of the company if it was forced into liquidation.

Arguments against insurance

- Higher cost. The insurance premium has a higher expected cost than accepting spillages.

- Present value (liquidity). Insurance premiums are payable at the beginning of the period whereas spillage costs may be payable for some years after the spillages have occurred, resulting in a lower present value and less pressure on liquidity.

- Uninsurable costs. Some costs are uninsurable such as financial costs over £100m on a single spillage and indirect costs such as reputational damage. As a result, insurance only partially offsets the financial costs of some spillage.

- Insurance coverage may lead to greater claims by those affected by the spillage, knowing that the insurance companies have deep pockets.

Advice

Although the expected cost is higher from insurance than from accepting the risk, an insurance policy demonstrates corporate responsibility and gives a greater probability of business sustainability if a major catastrophe occurs. It is also in the public interest. Insurance is therefore recommended based on the terms suggested.

(d) **Assurance assignment**

Level of assurance

Provided that the directors' disclosure of LL's system of internal controls is sufficiently detailed, RR may be able to gather sufficient appropriate evidence to express a conclusion that certain internal controls have operated as designed.

However, judgement is needed in assessing the likelihood and potential impact of risk. In most circumstances, it is likely to be impossible for RR to determine, with any degree of certainty that all potentially significant risks that threaten the achievement of business objectives have, in fact, been identified and have been properly evaluated and managed.

As the risk identification and assessment process is highly judgemental, RR is unlikely to be able to obtain sufficient evidence to be able to express more than limited assurance, in the form of a negatively expressed conclusion, regarding the effectiveness of LL's processes used to determine risks.

Benefits

The benefits would depend on the scope of the engagement. ISAE 3410 identifies varied procedures depending on the nature and purposes of the assurance to be provided. In the case of the risk assurance assignment requested by LL, it is necessary to have clarity over the desired purpose of the assurance report distinguishing clearly between:

(a) Providing assurance on the **design** of risk management procedures and internal controls; and

(b) Providing assurance on the **operation** of risk management procedures and system of internal controls in accordance with their design.

The nature and scope of each of these engagements would be different and therefore the benefits derived by LL would also differ.

Investors will be concerned about risk assessment as the risk that the company enters into, has a direct impact on the risk of their investment. Stakeholders need assurance that the risk taken by the company is acceptable to them and that the returns that they receive are in accordance with that level of risk.

It is the duty of management to implement and monitor the effectiveness of risk management procedures to manage the risk for investors and other stakeholders. Risk management is therefore the responsibility of the LL board. As LL is a listed company, it needs to comply with the disclosure requirements of the FRC's UK Corporate Governance Code. Specifically, the UK Corporate Governance Code main principle: Risk Management and Internal Control states:

'The board is responsible for determining the nature and extent of the significant risks it is willing to take in achieving its strategic objectives. The board should maintain sound risk management and internal control systems.'

A risk assurance assignment would therefore carry out an independent examination by a professional accountant with relevant experience applying the highest standards to examine data, processes, or information and expressing an assurance conclusion which provides a strong signal of reliability and offers attestation to stakeholders.

Any assurance report that RR could provide would be in the context of the assertions about risk management made by the board in the LL annual report.

In identifying deficiencies in internal control and risk management procedures, this helps LL's management to enhance the quality of its internal systems and controls. The assurance conclusion and any related recommendations resulting from the work of RR, can be used by LL management to improve the quality of systems and controls, and the information derived from them.

(e) **Integrated reporting**

Integrated reporting (IR) aims to combine the different strands of reporting (financial, management commentary, governance and remuneration, and sustainability reporting) into a coherent whole that explains an organisation's ability to create and sustain value in the short, medium and long term. As such, integrated reporting also highlights the importance of long-term business sustainability for an organisation.

By encouraging entities to focus on their ability to create and sustain value over the longer term, IR should help them take decisions which are more sustainable and which ensure a more effective allocation of scarce resources.

Context of performance reporting – In an integrated report, LL will still report on its financial and operational performance, as it currently does, but it will also report on social and environmental aspects of its performance.

Given the potentially dangerous nature of the chemicals LL uses in its production processes, and the damaging consequences of a chemical spill, it is important that LL maintains an appropriate system of controls over its physical processes, and regularly reviews those controls, to minimise the risk of a spill or any other damaging impacts on the environment.

Bearing in mind the adage that 'What gets measured, gets done' then the increased focus on environmental performance which IR brings, should help to reinforce the attention given to environmental controls at LL.

Impacts on different categories of capital – More generally, IR requires an organisation to explain the outcomes of its performance in terms of six categories of capital: financial; manufactured; intellectual; human; social and relationship; and natural.

Using these six categories could provide LL with a more comprehensive framework for analysing its performance than its current approach, which appears to focus predominantly on financial performance.

However, the 'integrated' nature of the reporting also means that in its report LL should highlight the interrelatedness and dependencies between different factors which affect its ability to create value over time. For example, investing in new machinery or factory upgrades should help to improve the efficiency and safety of LL's production processes, and possibly to reduce pollution, but these benefits will come at the financial cost of acquiring the new machinery.

Future strategy and outlook – Another important contrast between IR and traditional performance reporting, is that IR has a greater focus on future strategy and outlook. The main focus of LL's current report is likely to be the performance in the past year; so, the report is backward-looking.

However, in an integrated report, LL's management would provide not only a summary of past performance but also a summary of how the company's strategy, governance and performance can lead to the creation of value in the future. As such, IR underlines the importance of planning and looking forward.

Integrated reporting and performance measures

Two of the key questions which an integrated report should address are: to what extent has a company achieved its strategic objectives; and, what are the outcomes of its performance in terms of the six capitals? Integrated reporting is based on the belief that in order to achieve sustainable long-term growth in a business and in business value, there must be accumulation of all six types of capital – although the significance of each type of capital may vary between different types of business.

In order to do this, it will need to establish key performance measures for each of these six capitals, and to set targets for each. These measures should relate to aspects of performance that are expected to have a significant impact over the long term in helping the company to achieve its strategic objectives.

Assuming that LL's current performance measures focus primarily on financial capital, then introducing IR will require LL to develop a range of new (non-financial) performance measures looking at its manufactured capital, human capital, intellectual capital, social capital, and its impact on natural capital. For example, performance measures linked to LL's health and safety standards could be relevant to social and natural capital.

Several directors have reservations of the value of reporting on some of these aspects of capital. They are correct to take the view that integrated reporting should focus on performance that affects long-term value, so the benefits of reporting on social capital and manufactured capital, for example, would need to be considered in the context of how these add to the long-term value of the business.

Although definitions vary, social capital refers to matters such as company reputation, brand reputation and relationships with stakeholders. Given the nature of LL's business, social capital may be of less concern than it is for manufacturers of consumer products. Even so, a reputation for fair dealing with suppliers and customers, and compliance with regulations, can affect the long-term status of the company in its industry. A problem however is to establish suitable key performance indicators (KPIs) that measure the company's relationships with stakeholders.

Manufactured capital refers to 'performance' in terms of machinery and equipment, and other manufactured items. For a manufacturing company, this can be a critical measure of performance. Successful manufacturers are those that not only increase the amount of their capital assets: they also have assets that are efficient and use up-to-date technology. So in addition to reporting on the growth in the amount or value of property, plant and equipment, LL should also consider measures such as output per machine hour (or a similar measure of productivity) and average age of key equipment (or a similar measure of up-to-dateness).

These measures should help LL and its shareholders to focus their attention on the long term as well as on the shorter term financial aspects of performance, because performance that affects the long term will contribute to growth in business value.

(f) **Impact of new executive information system (EIS)**

Benefits

Facilitates improved decision making – At the strategic level, LL's management should be looking at how well the company is performing in relation to its key performance indicators. By summarising key information, and providing managers with easy access to it, the EIS should help senior managers to be better informed when making strategic decisions.

However, the EIS should also allow management to drill-down to the more detailed operational records to help understand the reasons for any variances in performance, and to identify ways of improving performance.

Amount of information available – The new system should increase the amount of information that will be available to managers, and the speed with which it becomes available to them. In particular, the system will allow the managers to use more up-to-date (real-time) information than they are currently able to use. In turn, having more information available to them should increase the amount of analysis managers can perform in relation to any strategic decisions.

Consistency – Whereas summary data used to come from a range of different systems, it will now come from a single database, which should again improve the quality of data available to management. For example, there should no longer be any inconsistencies in the data being submitted by different factories. This means that LL's head office staff and management will now be able to focus more on analysing the data rather than having to spend time reconciling different figures or reports prepared by different factories.

Tactical information – The EIS will also give access to tactical information such as budgets, which will help managers control the business more effectively; most obviously by comparing actual financial performance against budget.

External information – Executive information systems typically include data and information from external sources as well as internal information. Given the impact that external factors (for example, exchange rate movements or commodity price movements) can have on LL's performance this information could be very useful to managers – both in terms of analysing current results or in planning for the future.

Management should also be able to make use of the external information in the EIS more generally when identifying risks and opportunities for the business. This could also be useful if LL does introduce integrated reporting, because one of the questions which its integrated report needs to cover is the risks and opportunities which could affect its ability to create value in the future.

Potential problems and issues

Information overload – Although allowing managers access to more information could be a benefit of the EIS, if the amount of information available is not controlled then information overload could become a problem. For example, managers could become obsessed with looking at detailed information rather than focusing on strategic issues and overall performance against key performance indicators.

Training – Because the EIS is a new system, in order to maximise the benefit which managers can get from using it, they will need to be trained in how to use it.

Extent of data captured – Although the new system will improve the speed with which information is available, and the consistency of that information across different factories, it is still not clear how much non-financial information it will collect or provide to management. For example, will the system collect data about the level of emissions or leaks from the factories' production processes?

If this data is not recorded anywhere in the factories, then despite having the new integrated system, management will still not be able to monitor performance in some of the key areas of LL's business.

28 Textiles with Care plc

Marking guide

		Marks
(a)	Evaluation of relevant factors to be considered in making the closure or disposal decision Identify and explain the appropriate accounting treatment	13
(b)	Determine the cost of finance for the two financing alternatives Recommend the most appropriate alternative; and explain the financial reporting treatment for each alternative	6
(c)	Explanation of assurance procedures relevant to forecast information	10
(d)	Discussion of relevant factors to consider before deciding whether or not to agree a deal with a new supplier in Asia	5
(e)	Set out ethical issues for SW and explain appropriate actions the firm should take	6
Total marks		40

(a) **Underperforming Business Units**

Chester factory

Closure decision

If the Chester factory were to stay open, it would generate an annual return of 2.5% pa (200/8,000). While the risk may be different to the KK business unit (see below) the after tax WACC in that case is 6% pa which is far above the 2.5% pa return generated by the Chester factory.

An alternative way of looking at the valuation issue would be to discount £200,000 at 6% in perpetuity. This gives £3.333m (£200,000/0.06) which is far below the £8m that it could be sold for immediately.

Although there are some closure costs associated with immediate closure (see below) these are small compared to the £8m cash that would be generated on disposal.

Some factors to consider are as follows:

- Although expected to earn only £200,000 per annum, efficiency improvements could increase this to a level where it would be better to retain it in the group. A basic calculation using the 6% figure (which may not be appropriate for this business unit) is £480,000 profit pa (6% × £8m). This would therefore require a very significant increase in profitability.

- The Chester factory may be interdependent with other TC divisions and the disposal of this business unit may lead to loss of profits elsewhere in the group. For example, retail units may depend on the Chester factory for their inventory and the transfer prices may be below market values.

Unless the above issues have a major impact, there is a clear rationale for disposing of the Chester factory.

Financial Reporting

Costs to be provided	£'000
1 Statutory redundancy costs	220
2 Discretionary redundancy costs	340
3 Retraining of staff who would be redeployed to other sites	–
4 Legal costs of solicitors handling redundancies	22
5 Impairment of assets to be sold off	–
6 Expected profit on sale of patent rights	–
7 Penalty to exit a contract with a supplier as a result of closure	88
8 Operating losses to be incurred between the date of the announcement and the date of closure	–
Total provision	**670**

Notes

1   Legal obligation. The legal obligation creates the requirement for a provision in accordance with IAS 37 *Provisions, Contingent Liabilities and Contingent Assets*.

2   Constructive obligation. The constructive obligation creates the requirement for a provision in accordance with IAS 37.

3   Retraining of staff who would be redeployed to other sites. No provision can be made as retraining costs are <u>associated with the ongoing activities</u> of the entity so cannot be included in a restructuring provision, IAS 37 para 81(a).

4   Legal costs of solicitors handling redundancies. These costs are necessarily entailed in the reconstruction and are directly attributable expenditure, IAS 37 para 80. As a result they are provided for.

5   Impairment of assets to be sold off. The write-down would be credited to the asset (IFRS 5 *Non-Current Assets Held for Sale and Discontinued Operations*), rather than being a provision.

6   Expected profit on sale of patents. Gains on expected disposal of assets are not taken into account in measuring a provision, IAS 37 paras 51 and 83.

7   Penalty to exit a contract with a supplier as a result of closure. The penalty to exit means that the contract can be considered as onerous following the closure. These costs are therefore recognised as a provision as they are directly attributable to the restructuring.

8   Operating losses to be incurred between the date of the announcement and the date of closure. Provisions for future operating losses are not permitted as a provision as they do not meet the definition of a liability, IAS 37 para 63 (as there is no present obligation arising from past events).

Even though the conditions for recognising some costs as a provision are satisfied, it seems unlikely that the Chester factory would constitute a discontinued operation per IFRS 5, based on the information available. While the closure will be announced before 31 December 20X5, there is no suggestion that the factory will be available for immediate sale or will be actively marketed by this date as required by IFRS 5 paras 7 and 8.

Kidz Kitz Ltd

WORKINGS (in £'000)

	20X6	20X7	20X8	20X9	NPV
Cash receipts from sales	5,200	6,400	6,600	6,300	
Cash paid to buy inventories	(3,680)	(3,760)	(3,840)	(3,580)	
Salary payments	(620)	(620)	(620)	(620)	
Overheads paid	(900)	(900)	(900)	(900)	
Restructuring	0	–	–	–	
Operating cash flows	0	1,120	1,240	1,200	
Interest payments on loan	–	–	–	–	
Cash flow before tax	0	1,120	1,240	1,200	
Tax payments @ 20%	0	224	248	240	
Cash flow after tax	0	896	992	960	
NPVs					
@ interest rate 7% (before tax flows) for impairment calculation	0.0	978.3	1,012.2	915.5	**2,906.0**
@ interest rate 6% (after tax flows) for closure decision	0.0	797.4	832.9	760.4	**2,390.7**

Closure decision

Discounting the after tax cash flows at the after-tax discount rate gives a positive net present value of £2.39m.

Keeping KK open and generating this NPV needs to be compared to the value generated by immediate disposal. If the trade and assets are sold as a single transaction this would generate £2.2m. This is lower than the NPV that could be achieved by keeping the store trading, which would suggest that the store be kept open.

Factors to consider other than the above numbers are as follows:

- Any taxes payable on the disposal. This would depend the assets' tax written down value.

- Other opportunities may present themselves over the next few years and keeping the business trading would maintain the real option to take advantage of these.

- Liquidity may be a factor in the group and the immediate generation of cash may provide much needed liquidity, particularly as KK only plans to break even in the coming year, so little cash would be generated from operations next year if it were to be kept open.

Overall, the advice would be to keep KK open, but the decision is not clear cut and could be reviewed on a periodic basis in case there is a change in any of the estimates.

Financial Reporting

The purpose of an impairment test is to ensure assets, and groups of inter-related assets (cash-generating units), are stated at no more than their recoverable amount, being the higher of: fair value less costs of disposal; and value in use (present value of net cash inflows relating to the asset). This is, in effect, the best return the entity could generate by either selling the asset or retaining it to generate cash flows in the business (See closure decision above).

IAS 36 *Impairment of Assets* requires an entity to discount at a rate that reflects the 'current market assessments of (a) the time value of money, and (b) the risks specific to the asset for which future cash flow estimates have not been adjusted'. It also requires the use of the before-tax interest rate (IAS 36, para 55) so, in this case, it is 7% rather than the 6% used previously for the closure decision. Similarly it requires tax and interest to be excluded from cash flows from the asset or cash generating unit (IAS 36, para 50). Any impairment losses would however generate a deferred tax adjustment.

Based on the above calculations the value in use is therefore £2,906,000.

Fair value is determined using the criteria in IFRS 13 *Fair Value Measurement*, and represents the market value of the assets at a point in time, normally the year end.

Recoverable amount

Higher of:

	£'000
Fair value less costs of disposal	2,200.0
Value in use	2,906.0

Therefore value in use of £2,906,000 is the recoverable amount.

As this exceeds the carrying amount of £2,760,000 there is no impairment.

(b) Financing

(1) Assessment of financing alternatives

Alternative 1 – Euro denominated bank loan

The current annual rate of interest on the loan is 7%, but this may vary, up or down, over the life of the loan. While in an efficient market it is not possible to predict with any accuracy how market interest rates will change over a five-year period, some indication in the short term is given by forward £/€ exchange rates. In the longer term, fixed rate bonds will give a broad indication of market expectations of future movements in short term interest rates.

Interest rate parity would suggest that if markets expect the £ to strengthen against the €, then sterling interest rates will be lower than € interest rates, or there would be inefficient arbitrage opportunities.

[handwritten margin note: If ℤ↑ then UK Interest rate (than foreign currency)]

A key risk is that the finance is being raised in euro so the sterling equivalent of the amount outstanding is subject to exchange rate risk. Thus, if the € were to strengthen against the £, then the amount repayable in sterling terms would increase. Over a five year period this movement could be substantial. Conversely, if the € weakens against the £ then TC would benefit on redemption.

Given that TC has activities in Europe, then if revenues in € exceed costs in € then this loan could be a natural hedge. If this is not the case, then £/€ exchange rate risk could be increased by this loan.

Compared to the WACC rate of 7% before tax this loan appears to be expensive at 7%. We would need to investigate why this is the case as the 7% WACC includes a cost of equity element.

[handwritten margin note: 7% WACC (cost debt + equity) ∴ high?]

In terms of liquidity, this would favour the preference shares as more cash is available for longer given the earlier redemption date with this loan.

In terms of credit risk, if TC defaults on the repayment of interest or capital then the bank could potentially wind up the company with a creditors' voluntary liquidation.

Interest charges are tax allowable hence the implicit interest rate on the loan after tax is:

$[(\text{AFi 5 yrs}) \times (\text{€ 24m} \times 7\%) \times (1 - T)] + (\text{€ 24m}/(1 + i)^5) = \text{€24m}$

By linear interpolation or iteration = **5.6%**

Alternative 2 – 9% preference shares

The annual cost of finance for the preference shares is:

$(1.045)^2 - 1 = 9.2\%$

The gross nominal rate of dividend is higher for the preference shares at 9% than the bonds at 5.6% but in addition the preference dividend needs to be paid half yearly so the annual rate is the compound half year rate at 9.2%.

Also, however, preference dividends are not relieved for tax whereas interest on the bond is tax allowable. The after tax cost of the bond is therefore lower.

While the cost of finance for the bond is lower than for the preference shares there are other factors to consider.

- The preference shares are redeemable after seven years rather than five years with the bond, so there is greater liquidity with the preference shares and more time for the reconstruction to take effect.

- If there is a default on the preference share dividend it is cumulative and therefore merely deferred. There are no rights for the preference shareholders to wind up the company.

- The preference shares are denominated in sterling so there is no currency risk.

Recommendation

The loan is the lower cost form of finance. The gap in the cost of finance between the two instruments is significant and is widened by the fact that the loan interest is tax relievable. As the currency risk can be largely offset by hedging, the loan therefore appears to be the preferred choice.

(2) **Financial reporting for financing alternatives**

As most of TC's costs and revenues arise in the UK, its functional currency is the £.

Alternative 1 – Euro-denominated bank loan

The loan would initially be recognised at £20 million.

However, the euro-denominated loan is a financial liability and therefore needs to be translated at each year end at the year-end exchange rate. Any exchange gains or losses are recognised in profit or loss.

Interest is variable in euro terms and so would change each year in accordance with the basis of the contract. In addition, however, even if the euro amount of interest did not change, then it would need to be translated at the actual rate when interest accrues. If exchange rates move evenly over the year and interest accrues evenly, then the average exchange rate for the year may be used as an approximation.

Alternative 2 – 9% preference shares

The preference shares are redeemable and therefore they have the characteristics in substance of a debt instrument, even though their legal form is equity.

As a result, the preference shares are treated as a liability and the preference dividends are treated as a finance cost.

(c) **Assurance**

Providing assurance in respect of forecasts is covered by ISAE 3400 *The Examination of Prospective Financial Information*.

Prospective financial information means financial information based on assumptions about events that may occur in the future and possible actions by an entity. This would relate to the forecasts of profits made by TC to support its application for finance.

In this respect, a forecast is defined as prospective financial information based on assumptions as to future events which management expects to take place and the actions management expects to take (best-estimate assumptions).

The following are areas where SW needs to perform procedures to obtain sufficient appropriate evidence:

- SW needs to satisfy itself that TC management's best-estimate assumptions on which the prospective financial information is based are not unreasonable and, in the case of hypothetical assumptions, that such assumptions are consistent with the purpose of the information (ie to raise new finance in the form of a loan or preference shares). This will require ascertaining that TC sales volumes are realistic for the prices being charged in the markets being accessed (eg similar ventures by other companies, existing market prices and revenues generated by retail outlets selling textiles and related products). As TC operates in the fashion industry this will require evidence on seasonal cycles and trends in the industry. To be able to do this SW will need clear evidence (eg market research) collected by TC to support the forecasts provided. Given that TC is made up of a number of business units then separate projections (similar to those provided for KK) and assumptions would be needed for each significant business unit. They can then be aggregated.

- The prospective financial information is properly prepared on the basis of the assumptions ie that the financial information produced (ie TC's revenues, costs, cash flows) is consistent with the assumptions in amount and timing. As TC is divisionalised, this will need to be done for each division or profit centre separately (such as KK and the Chester factory if they are retained) and then all the divisions should be aggregated.

- The prospective financial information is properly presented and all material assumptions are adequately disclosed, including a clear indication as to whether they are best-estimate assumptions or hypothetical assumptions (disclose assumptions for example about timing, the level of sales, the impact of advertising, costs, the number of new divisions opened each year). For example, the budget provided for the KK division would need to be reviewed for consistency if this division were to continue in operation.

- The prospective financial information is prepared on a consistent basis with historical financial statements, using appropriate accounting principles (for TC profit forecasts).

It is clear that, as prospective financial information is subjective information, it is impossible to give the same level of assurance regarding forecasts for TC as would be applicable to historic financial information for its historic performance. In particular it covers at least a five-year horizon for the loan and seven years for the preference shares.

In this instance, the procedures carried out should gather sufficient appropriate evidence consistent with providing limited assurance in the form of a negatively expressed opinion.

ISAE 3400 suggests that SW should express an opinion including:

- a statement of negatively expressed assurance as to whether the assumptions provide a reasonable basis for the prospective financial information.

- an opinion as to whether the prospective financial information is properly prepared on the basis of the assumptions and the relevant reporting framework.

- appropriate caveats as to the achievability of the forecasts (eg, where there is a new venture following the CEO's reorganisation there may be little internal precedent on which to substantiate assumptions).

(d) **Possible new supplier**

The textiles business units seem to be performing well, in contrast to some of TC's clothing business units. As such, it would appear sensible for TC to increase its supply capacity in order to meet the increasing demand.

Historically, TC appears to have manufactured all its products in its own factories. Therefore, before deciding which supplier to use or where they should be located, TC should consider whether it wants to change this policy of in-house manufacturing and start using external suppliers. The alternative would be either to expand some of its existing factories, or to build a new factory of its own.

Agreeing a deal with an external supplier is likely to provide TC with extra supply more quickly than if it expands its own production capacity, and will not involve any capital expenditure. Similarly, the costs of the additional supply will be variable costs. This could be significant if demand falls again in future, because it means TC would not be lumbered with the additional fixed costs associated with the greater factory space, nor left with excess capacity. *unless min. amounts negotiated.*

However, using its own factories provides TC with greater control over its supply chain than if it uses external suppliers – particularly in relation to the quality of its products. Product quality, and reliability of delivery, appear to be important factors in TC's current success, and TC needs to be confident that using external suppliers will not have an adverse effect on performance in these respects.

In addition, TC has no experience of managing external suppliers. This again could present control issues (in relation to managing the supplier's performance), but there could also be practical operational issues, for example in relation to how orders are communicated to the supplier.

Although price is also an important factor in the sourcing decision, TC should not select a supplier simply because they charge the lowest prices. Although such a decision might seem profitable in the short-term, it may prove not to be if quality issues subsequently affect sales and TC's brand reputation in the longer term. Similarly, if any social responsibility issues emerge at a supplier, this could also damage TC's reputation by association. As such, TC would be advised to carry out supplier assurance work before signing any deals with external suppliers, wherever they are located.

If TC does decide to start using external suppliers, it then has to decide whether an Asian supplier is preferable to a European one. It seems likely that the Asian suppliers will be cheaper than the European ones, but here again TC should also consider a range of non-price factors.

The geographical distance between TC and the suppliers means that there are likely to be longer lead times, and also could lead to greater uncertainty over delivery times. Dealing with suppliers in a foreign country could also produce regulatory, language and cultural problems. If TC pays for the goods in the supplier's local currency, it could also be exposed to exchange rate risk.

(e) **Ethics**

It is an ethical principle that, as ICAEW Chartered Accountants, we should maintain confidentiality. The ethical issue of concern is not therefore confidentiality as such, but the reasons why the CEO wishes to maintain confidentiality, including the possibility of making a personal gain. Additionally, external confidentiality to the public is different from internal confidentiality to other directors, which is essentially a question of corporate governance.

The timing of the announcement of the reconstruction is a matter for the TC board. If the CEO were buying or selling shares then there is a risk of illegal behaviour based on insider trading, but as it is part of a remuneration package this does not appear to be the case. Indeed, there is no evidence that the CEO can control the timing of the issuing of shares to him.

The ethical issue is, however, that the CEO is altering the timing of decisions which may affect TC shareholders and other stakeholders in order to make personal gains.

Similarly, issues arise with the CEO bringing forward the closure decision so profits of the current year are affected by the provision, rather than future years on which Steve's performance will be judged.

Again, companies are entitled to vary the timing of transactions to gain commercial advantage, but the ethical issue in this case is one of the conflict of interest of the CEO, where the delay is made for personal, rather than corporate, benefit.

The ethical principles arising are:

Ethical principle	Explanation
Integrity: Straightforward and honest in business and professional relationships.	Steve may be promoting his own interests above those of the company and other stakeholders.
Objectivity: Not allowing bias, conflict of interest or influence of others to override professional or business judgement.	There is a self-interest threat to Steve in the suggestion that there may be some personal gain from timing transactions in accordance with Steve's best interests. This can create conflict of personal interest with the fiduciary duty of directors.
	For SW, the question is whether the duty of confidentiality should be overridden by the requirement for transparency. In the first instance, those charged with governance could be made aware of the facts and our concerns. This may be the audit committee if there is one or the company chairman if not.
Legal issue or breach	Legal advice could be taken by SW to ascertain whether there is any breach of laws or regulations by the CEO.
	If this is the case, then there may be a duty or right to disclose the behaviour of the CEO if those charged with governance refuse to do so.

Actions

The SW engagement partner should discuss the issues with Steve including: his motivations; confidentiality; and governance. If there are grounds to suspect that Steve is promoting his self-interest beyond the corporate interest then the issues should be discussed with those charged with governance or with the chairman.

Based on legal advice if Steve's behaviour is deemed to be illegal then there may be a duty to disclose the relevant facts, which would override the principle of confidentiality.

29 Western Wheels Ltd

Marking guide

		Marks
(a)	Analysis of performance data for year ended 30 September 20X5 and evaluation of WW's performance	
	Identify additional information needed to make a more complete assessment of performance	10
(b)	Critical appraisal of the forecasts made by WW's board	
	Evaluation of the underlying assumptions and the adequacy of the supporting explanations	7
(c)	Explanation of the implication of post-acquisition trading on asset values in IM group financial statements	5
(d)	Evaluation of the benefits of asking a firm of independent accountants to review WW's forecasts	
	Assessment of the level of assurance the accountants could provide on the forecasts	7
(e)	Explanation of whether or not the IM group control framework is likely to have affected WW's performance	
	Evaluation of whether or not the alternative approach is likely to improve WW's future performance	6
(f)	Evaluation of the likely impact of the bonus schem on the motivation of WW's board members	
	Explanation of the appropriate financial reporting treatment of the bonus scheme	5
Total marks		40

Data analysis for (a) and (b)

Years to 30 September	20X4	20X5	20X6	20X7
Price home £	100	100	110	120
Price export £	100	100	100	100
Materials per unit £	20	19	18	17
Direct labour per unit £	30	30	30	30
Units sold				
Home	352,000	315,000	346,500	381,100
Export	132,000	119,000	142,800	171,400
Total	484,000	434,000	489,300	552,500
ROCE % [Y/E capital]	1.94	0.04	28.30	34.57
Contribution margin %	50.0	51.0	55.2	58.7
Operating profit margin %	0.68	0.014	12.60	19.49
Sales revenue growth				
Home %		(10.5)	21.0	20.0
Export %		(9.8)	20.0	20.0
Total %		(10.3)	20.7	20.0
Contribution growth %		(8.5)	30.6	27.7
Operating profit growth %		(98.2)	109,950	85.6
Sales volume growth:				
Home %		(10.5)	10.0	10.0
Export %		(9.8)	20.0	20.0
Total sales %		(10.3)	12.7	12.9
% of sales revenue from				
UK Market	72.7	72.6	72.7	72.7
Exports	27.3	27.4	27.3	27.3
% change Production overhead		(10.3)	12.7	12.9
% change Labour costs		(10.3)	12.7	12.9
Industry data:				
UK sales (no. of wheels)	6,000,000	6,120,000	6,242,400	6,367,248
Global sales				
(66m x 4 wheels)	264,000,000	264,000,000	264,000,000	264,000,000
Market share				
UK %	5.9	5.1	5.6	6.0
Global %	0.18	0.16	0.19	0.21

(a) **Performance of WW in year ended 30 September 20X5**

Revenues

Sales volumes declined by 10.3% in 20X5 compared to 20X4. This decrease was reflected broadly equally in both the UK market (down 10.5%) and the export market (down 9.8%).

The decrease in sales volumes occurred despite no change in sterling equivalent prices, which remained at £100 per wheel. Exchange rate movements may however have caused a price increase denominated in local currencies for export markets. This is suggested in the WW board report but no clear causal link is identified to specific geographical markets or specific currencies in the WW notes.

Given constant prices, sales revenues declined by the same % as sales volumes.

The decline in UK sales was against a background of a growing UK market for cars and therefore for car wheels. This meant that UK market share fell from 5.9% in 20X4 to only 5.1% in 20X5.

The commentary from the WW board provides a limited explanation of the fall and a degree of professional scepticism is appropriate to the explanation they offer. They point to 'difficult trading conditions' but the UK market was growing. If there were new entrants to compete against for market share, there was no indication of this in the WW board notes.

Costs

The WW board notes indicate that cost reductions were made, for example by reducing staff. Given the lower output achieved, one would expect total costs to be lower. Indications of cost cutting and efficiencies may be given by looking at costs per unit. This shows no change in direct labour costs per unit despite WW management's assertion.

There has been a reduction in material costs per unit from £20 to £19 which has had a favourable effect in constraining the reduction in profit. However, it may have affected the quality of the output resulting in the fall in sales volumes. More information would be needed in respect of customer complaints to substantiate this view.

The production overhead has fallen by 10.3% which has had a favourable effect on profit. However, one would expect most of the production overhead to be fixed costs, yet it has moved in line with payroll costs. This requires investigation as to whether the production overhead is being recovered on a labour cost or labour hour basis, or whether this is the actual total cost.

There has been a significant increase in development costs. It is not clear whether this is an increased cash spend that has not qualified for capitalisation in accordance with IAS 38 *Intangible Assets* or whether this includes an impairment of capitalised costs or amortisation of capitalised costs. The WW board notes point to design improvements from development activity, but more information is needed regarding the significance of these changes and the likely impact on sales.

Other fixed costs have decreased, but may require further consideration in assessing the division's performance as these may not be under the control of the WW board.

Omitted costs should be considered. For example, given the loss making situation, it is slightly surprising that there are no impairments. More information is required that impairments have been appropriately considered.

Consideration also needs to be given as to whether all relevant provisions have been made, particularly as losses are being incurred.

Profit

The consequent effect of revenue and cost movements has been to reduce operating profit from £330,000 to near break-even level at only £6,000. After interest is deducted there is a loss before tax in 20X5 of £134,000.

Given that costs are not split between the UK market and Export markets it is not possible to identify profits for each revenue stream. Given the arbitrary allocations that would be required this would probably not be a useful exercise. Nevertheless, there is a clear pattern of poor performance in both the years ended 30 September 20X4 and 20X5, with a decline in performance in the latter year.

ROCE

There has been no movement in capital employed other than the retained earnings but the overall ROCE has fallen significantly as a result of the reduction in operating profit.

(b) **Appraisal of forecasts**

If the forecasts are to be believed, they represent a major turnaround in the fortunes of the WW business in 20X6 and 20X7 compared to the figures for 20X5 reviewed above. A degree of professional scepticism might be appropriate to these forecasts given the lack of explanation of clear causal factors in the WW board explanatory notes which should have explained the underlying reasons for the expected improvement.

Revenues

The prices charged in the UK are forecast to increase by 10% in 20X6 and 9.1% in 20X7. Prices in export markets are constant. Unless the product mix has changed (eg a new large contract) this seems a significant price increase for what was described as a 'difficult market' for 20X5 in the WW board notes.

Notwithstanding the price increases, sales volumes in the UK are forecast to increase by 10% in each of 20X6 and 20X7. This is against a background of UK market volume growth of only 2% per annum. This would see WW more than recover its 20X4 UK market share of 5.9% by 20X7 when it would reach 6.0%, despite a price rise of 20% over the 2 year period to 30 September 20X7.

The WW market report provides little explanation for this sales volume increase other than pointing to design improvements arising from development activities. This would require substantiation by market research or specific evidence of large new contracts agreed with motor manufacturers arising from the improvements.

There are no development costs expensed in 20X6 or 20X7. This may be because they are being capitalised in accordance with IAS 38 *Intangible Assets*, following the success of the development project but this requires attestation.

Export markets also show volume growth of 20% in both 20X6 and 20X7 but in this case there is no price increase. These are very challenging targets but at least they are not forecast to be achieved alongside price increases, as with the UK market.

It should be noted that WW is moving from uniform pricing in 20X5 to price discrimination in 20X6 between UK prices and export prices. There is no indication as to why this policy has been introduced and care needs to be exercised that there is no leakage between domestic and export markets. This may not be feasible under the contractual terms agreed with customers and any best price assurances given.

Overall, sales revenues are forecast to increase substantially, largely due to UK sales which continue to dominate overall sales at around 73% of total revenue. There is a distinct lack of evidence to support this optimism.

Costs

Material costs per unit are forecast to continue to fall by £1 per annum over the period 20X4 to 20X7. Significant doubt should exist about whether this can be achieved without impacting on quality and therefore sales volumes. The fact that there has been a fault in the wheels requiring a recall and a provision underlines the question marks over quality.

The production overhead is forecast to increase by over 12% in each of 20X6 and 20X7. This is less than the 20% sales volume growth, but this is to be expected given that fixed costs are likely to form a large element of production overhead. Indeed, it may be surprising that production overhead is forecast to rise so much, given the likely fixed cost content. Moreover, production overhead is forecast to continue to move in line with direct payroll costs, which is surprising given the fixed and variable cost elements expected for these two cost headings. The underlying assumptions require investigation.

It is surprising that no provisions are required for either 20X6 or 20X7. While the recall issue causing the original provision may have been resolved by 20X6 it would be unusual for no provisions to be required. Consideration should also be given as to whether there should be any impairments in respect of the recall.

Profit

Overall significant increases are forecast in both absolute terms and percentage terms for contribution, operating profit and profit before tax. The assumptions and causal factors on which these forecasts are based are inadequately explained in the covering notes and significant scepticism should exist as to whether they can be achieved.

The forecasts appear to rely on assumptions based on the simultaneous achievement of potentially conflicting factors, including significant increases in sales volume being achieved with large price increases (despite reductions in raw material costs per unit and lower selling costs per unit).

Without further explanation and evidence the forecasts lack credibility.

(c) **Financial reporting implications of asset values post-acquisition**

IM acquired WW for £24 million, when the fair value of WW's net assets was £18.6 million, indicating a payment for goodwill of £5.4 million. This amount will have been capitalised as an intangible asset in the Group statement of financial position.

As the WW brand has continued to be used after the acquisition, the fair value of the brand acquired (£550,000) should have been capitalised separately in the Group statement of financial position. It is not clear whether the brand is being amortised, but even if it is, WW's recent performance suggests the carrying value should also be reviewed for impairment.

The shortfall in WW's actual performance post-acquisition, compared to the figures forecast at the time of acquisition, indicates that an impairment review of the asset value of goodwill will also be required, to ensure that its carrying value reflects its value in use, in accordance with IAS 36 *Impairment of Assets*.

WW's actual profit before tax in 20X4 (£190k) was 91% below the forecast figure (£2,160k); and WW's performance declined further in 20X5, leading to a pre-tax loss of £134k compared to a forecast profit of £2,960k.

IAS 36 requires that the value in use calculated for the Group financial statements should be based on the future cash flows IM expects to derive from WW, with those cash flow projections being based on reasonable and supportable assumptions. Although we are currently looking at profit figures rather than cash flows, it seems inevitable that the profit shortfall will have had a significant negative impact on WW's cash flows. Moreover, given the apparent lack of credibility in WW's forecasts, IM would be advised to produce its own forecasts as the basis of the impairment review, to ensure that the figures used are reasonable and supportable.

IAS 36 requires that any impairment loss required as a result of the review should be recognised as a loss in Group profit or loss for the year. However, the standard also specifically requires that goodwill must be subject to an annual impairment review. Therefore, by 30 September 20X6 the initial goodwill figure of £5.4 million may have already been substantially impaired, thereby also reducing the potential charge to profit or loss in 20X6.

(d) **External assurance reports**

In order for IM to make rational decisions about WW, it needs to have credible and reliable information about WW's performance. However, there are concerns that the forecasts prepared by WW are neither credible nor reliable. If a firm of accountants carried out a review of the forecast, they would be able to provide independent assurance about the level of confidence IM can have in the forecast.

If the accountants accept an assurance engagement to review the forecasts, the guidelines for such an engagement are provided by ISAE 3400 *The Examination of Prospective Financial Information*.

The forecast prepared by WW's management should be based on certain specified assumptions. In part, these may be based on historical information about the company, but they will also be based on future expectations about WW's competitive environment.

In an assurance engagement, the accountants will need to satisfy themselves about the reliability of any historical information that has been used as a basis for the forecasts. They will also need to consider the reasonableness of the assumptions used to prepare the forecast, and then check that the forecast has been accurately prepared on the basis of those assumptions. The aim of their engagement will be to obtain sufficient evidence to decide whether or not this is the case; and provided they are able to obtain this evidence then they will be able to issue a report at the end of their engagement.

In this scenario, a key part of the accountants' work is likely to involve establishing whether the factors which give rise to the expected improvement in performance appear reasonable or not.

However, a major problem with any financial forecast is that, even if there are valid and verifiable reasons for the assumptions that have been made, predicting the future is a subjective exercise. Similarly, the assumptions in a forecast are, by their nature, speculative, so actual performance will differ from the forecast.

As such, the accountants will not be in a position to express an opinion on whether the results in the forecast will be achieved. Instead, they will only be able to provide limited assurance.

If the accountants believe that the assumptions provide a reasonable basis for the forecast, and that the forecast has been properly prepared, they will issue a statement of negative assurance – that there is nothing to suggest the forecast is inappropriate. This will be accompanied by a caveat that, nonetheless, the results in the forecast may still not be achieved.

If the accountants believe the assumptions do not provide a reasonable basis for the forecast, they will issue an adverse opinion.

In this case, however, it appears that Rachel has already identified that the forecasts are not credible, and has her own (qualified) staff available to review WW's performance. As such, it is not clear what additional benefit IM would gain from asking the independent accountants to carry out an independent review of the forecast.

If anything, as the engagement is for the benefit of IM's management, a consultancy engagement might be more appropriate. In this type of engagement, the accountancy firm would assess the degree of reliability in the forecast, and perhaps provide an alternative forecast based on different assumptions. Again though, this may be something which IM could do internally, rather than needing to use an external firm.

(e) **IM group control framework**

The IM board operates a highly centralised system for controlling its subsidiaries with limited devolvement of decision making to subsidiary board level.

Each subsidiary is, therefore, responsible to the main board for its performance, despite having limitations on its control over that performance.

The internal governance arrangement is therefore one of centralised control on a divisionalised basis, with WW being one such division.

In terms of financial autonomy, the WW board is not able to borrow from external institutions. The only source of funding is from IM which imposes an annual interest charge of 7% over which WW appears to have no control. Similarly, the IM board retains control over investment decisions, so WW could not be regarded as an investment centre.

In terms of other operating decisions, the WW board appears to have limited control over pricing and the purchase and sale of assets. There are therefore questions over whether WW could even be regarded as a profit centre.

If WW is to be monitored on the basis of ROCE then it seems reasonable that the WW board has some discretion over the capital base and the ability to borrow to buy assets to form part of the capital employed. But no group, however devolved, is likely to give up parent company board control over capital/borrowing decisions entirely.

The suggested alternative control framework gives more autonomy to WW management to take local decisions, while maintaining accountability to the parent company board for overall performance.

This would restore the situation to a similar governance structure that existed when WW was part of the TT group. This would enable localised decision making and probably more rapid decision making.

In this context, the main IM board would need to set clear objectives and monitor achievement of these objectives, but the WW board would control the means by which these are to be achieved.

By enabling local decision making by the WW board, it would be more feasible to incentivise managers to improve performance as their actions can now impact on performance (see below).

(f) Bonus scheme

(1) Impact on motivation

This scheme is directly linked to the performance of WW rather than the group and hence it is more within the control of the WW board.

The major disadvantage is that it is an accounting-based measure rather than a market-based measure and may therefore give rise to incentives for creative accounting by the directors in order to achieve their bonus.

The major advantage is that it has a truth-inducing element in that if the directors have made forecasts that they know not to be credible (see above) the scheme would be unattractive as they would lose 15% of salary (£24,000 per year on average) and not meet the conditions to be awarded the bonus. On the other hand, if they believe in the forecasts, they would be in favour of the scheme as they would gain £80,000 each in 20X6 and £100,000 each in 20X7, while only losing £24,000 each in basic salary.

(2) Financial reporting impact

This is a short term bonus payment in accordance with IAS 19 *Employee Benefits*. It would be recognised on an accruals basis as it would be known at the year end whether the forecasts had been met.

In the year ending 30 September 20X6, the following amount would be recognised if the forecasts had been achieved:

	£'000	£'000
DR Payroll expenses	640	
CR Liability (£80,000 × 8)		640

In the year ending 30 September 20X7, the following amount would be recognised if the forecasts had been achieved:

	£'000	£'000
DR Payroll expenses	800	
CR Liability (£100,000 × 8)		800

The liabilities would be cleared when payment was made on 31 December each year.

30 Stark plc

Marking guide

		Marks
		Up to
(a)	Financial due diligence and initial assurance on HH	13
(b)	Valuation of HH equity	18
(c)	Post-acquisition integration	11
(d)	Brand valuation	11
(e)	Ethical issues	7
Total marks		60
Maximum marks		55

(a) Financial due diligence on the financial statements of HH

A key concern is the reliance that can be placed on the draft 20X2 financial statements to form the basis for a valuation without a statutory audit. In particular while financial due diligence may provide limited assurance, typically it will not involve the detailed level of testing that would be carried out in a statutory audit. While due diligence procedures could be extended to cover further audit procedures, this would inevitably cause a delay in completing the acquisition. It would probably be advisable (if possible) that the directors wait for the statutory audit to be completed.

The analysis below shows a line by line review of the financial statements explaining significant concerns with reporting policies and estimates:

	30 Sept 20X2 Draft £'000	30 Sept 20X1 £'000	Comments
Revenue	37,250	35,600	The increase in revenue reflects a 10% increase in sales volume and a 5% reduction in sales prices. However if this change were precise then revenue would be (£35.6m × 1.1 × 0.95) £37.202m.
			This is close so as not to present a major risk of overstatement of revenue and may be explained by a small change in the sales mix.
			Due diligence procedures will need to verify price and volume changes, including the timing of the price change.
Cost of sales	(19,800)	(18,000)	Cost of sales has increased by 10% in line with the sales volume increase hence some assurance is given that the figure is not misstated as cost per unit has not changed, although this could be affected by the mix of sales.
			Additional assurance can be given by due diligence procedures to verify the volume change.
Gross profit	17,450	17,600	The gross profit has fallen despite the contribution from the 10% volume increase. This is because cost of sales has increased by 10% (£1.8m) and sales prices have fallen by 5%.
			The key risk regarding the acquisition is that the decline in gross profit will be a continuing trend into 20X3 due to the reduction in sales prices. As a result, any valuation based on the underlying operating cash flows could have a negative, rather than a positive, growth rate after

	30 Sept 20X2 Draft £'000	30 Sept 20X1 £'000	Comments
			cost of sales is considered.
Depreciation	(3,000)	(4,000)	The change in the accounting estimate is substantial representing a 50% increase in life of the property. Given that IAS 16 requires regular reviews of asset lives, it is a concern that they have needed to be extended to such an extent all in one year. However of additional concern is that the properties have been treated as a composite asset rather than as separate assets being separately depreciated over each asset life in accordance with IAS 16. No detail is provided but the depreciation charge would increase if some of the property is to be reclassified as fixtures and fittings with a short useful life.
			The prospective treatment of a change in an accounting estimate would be correct in accordance with IAS 8 although there is doubt whether such an adjustment should be made based on the valuer's report.
Administration costs	(6,000)	(6,000)	This is a significant, but stable, figure as it appears to be a fixed cost.
Impairment	–	(1,000)	The impairment in 20X1 appears to have depressed profits in 20X1 and hence increased the apparent profit for 20X2. The reasons for the impairment need to be investigated during due diligence to ascertain whether further write offs may be necessary for other warehouses or the same warehouse in later years. The impairment may imply doubts over future profitability based on value in use.
Provision		(1,500)	The setting up in 20X1 and subsequent reversal of the provision in 20X2 is a material concern and professional scepticism needs to be applied to the judgement of the directors in this case.
Write back of unutilised provision	1,150		
			Causes and consequences both require consideration.
			The underlying causes of the provision relating to the restructuring need to be investigated to ensure that there was a constructive obligation at 30 September 20X1 and that the provision was made in compliance with IAS 37.
			In terms of consequences, the provision and reversal has decreased the 20X1 profit and increased the 20X2 profit. This initial over-provisioning has increased the apparent growth rate in profit. The measurement of the original provision and the necessity of the reversal need to be reviewed as the risk is that there has been intentional profit smoothing using the provisions to enhance apparent growth.

	30 Sept 20X2 Draft £'000	30 Sept 20X1 £'000	Comments
Financing costs	(600)	(600)	There has been no increase in finance costs. This needs to be verified by due diligence but represents low risk.
			Comparing the interest charge with the loan liability gives 600/12,000 as a 5% cost of finance which appears reasonable.
			The movement in the net pension obligation may be included but this is not obvious from the information provided.
Profit before tax	9,000	4,500	Despite the fall in gross profit, the profit before tax has increased very significantly by 100%.
			Finance costs and administrative and other operating expenses are unchanged. The reason for the increase in profit before tax is therefore due to accounting adjustments rather than improvements in underlying trading conditions and cash flows.
			These accounting adjustments require investigation and should not form the basis of a valuation measure as they are non recurring and unrelated to sustainable business activity.
			They may also be due to managerial manipulation which may bring into question the validity of other information.
Tax	(2,250)	(1,125)	The effective tax rate is maintained at 25%. If this is in line with the actual rate of corporation tax then this implies that any deferred tax adjustments reconcile the actual and effective tax rates with no adjustments for permanent differences.
			This assumption is questionable and requires further investigation.
Profit for year	6,750	3,375	

	20X2 £'000	Comments
Non-current assets		
Property, plant and equipment	39,000	The depreciation policy will impact on the value of the assets as recognised in the financial statements. (See depreciation note above).
		The valuer's report provides some evidence that no impairments are required.
		It should be noted that a degree of professional scepticism should be applied to the depreciation rate on fixtures and fittings as it appears very low.

	20X2	Comments
	£'000	
Current assets	10,000	A physical inventory count will be needed at the date of acquisition with attention to cut off. The acquisition date will be the key risk date in this respect rather than the year end. Impairment is a key issue as 'significant inventories' are held and obsolescence is a risk with technology based goods.

A physical inventory count will be needed at the date of acquisition with attention to cut off. The acquisition date will be the key risk date in this respect rather than the year end. Impairment is a key issue as 'significant inventories' are held and obsolescence is a risk with technology based goods.

If inventory turnover is rapid this would suggest there is no general problem but if isolated product lines are not moving then this could be a focus for concern.

Sales returns are also an issue with impairment.

Receivables are likely to be low for a retail business so are low risk.

Cash is low risk but it needs to be established whether it will be 'cash free' acquisition.

	20X2 £'000	
Total assets	49,000	
EQUITY and LIABILITIES		
Issued capital (£1 shares)	1,000	
Retained earnings	11,230	
Equity	12,230	
Non-current liabilities		
Loans	12,000	The carrying amount of the loan needs to be ascertained in accordance with IAS 39/IFRS 9. The detailed terms of the loan agreement will need to be reviewed, but there are no significant concerns based on the evidence presented.
Retirement benefit obligation	20,750	There is a key risk here of both over and understatement. (KK do not have the professional competence of an actuary to value the deficit hence this section only refers to the discount rate and the likely impact – see later section on pensions).

The lower the discount rate, the higher the PV of the obligation, and therefore the higher the liability.

According to IAS 19 the discount rate should be the yield on good quality corporate bonds (AA rated). This needs to be reviewed against market indicators, including interest rate spread, at the relevant date of acquisition.

It is not clear where the accounting entries relating to the pension appear in the income statement (possibly in administrative expenses). This needs to be ascertained, as if the interest rate is inappropriate then this will impact on the service cost, the interest cost and the actuarial difference. This may have a material effect on profit and valuation.

	20X2 £'000	
Tax liability	2,250	This is consistent with the tax charge but need to consider under or over provisions from last year and any tax payments made need to be considered.

The absence of a deferred tax balance requires investigation.

		20X2	Comments
		£'000	
Trade payables		1,770	A key risk is around the acquisition date cut off rather than the year end cut off date. However payables' days are 33 days (365 x 1,770/19,800) which appears reasonable.
Total equity and liabilities		49,000	

General comments

Income statement

Although profit after tax for the year has doubled, gross profit has decreased. This is a cause for concern as a substantial increase in profit after tax appears to have been generated from lower gross profit. The key risk is that the manipulation of accounting policies and estimates seems to have created the increased profit, rather than an improvement in the underlying commercial conditions.

Increases in profit generated by changes in accounting conventions should not be reflected in any real growth figure in a valuation model and would therefore not be reflected in an enhanced valuation of HH as suggested by Jed.

Statement of financial position

Unrecognised assets include the brand (which we have been instructed to ignore) but there may be other intangible assets and rights.

There may also be unrecognised contingent liabilities and provisions which would need to be reviewed for understatement.

Procedures and reliance

These financial due diligence procedures can only provide limited assurance. They do not form the evidence to rely on the financial statements as a basis for determining the value of HH shares for the acquisition. We have also raised a number of matters of concern which cast further doubts on the reasonableness of the draft financial statements, as presented, in being used for this purpose.

Limited reliance can therefore be placed on the draft financial statements, without a statutory audit. While financial due diligence may provide some assurance, typically it will not involve the detailed level of testing that would be carried out in a statutory audit.

Statutory financial statements are prepared in accordance with IFRS. They are not intended to be used directly, without adjustment, for the specific purpose of equity valuation. Even in the absence of the above concerns, they should not be regarded as fit for that purpose.

(b) **Valuation of HH equity**

An assessment of normalised earnings needs to take place and projected forward then discounted to a present value at the acquisition date of 1 October 20X3.

	Working	20X2 Draft	20X3 (Forecast)	20X4 and thereafter (Forecast)
		£'000	£'000	£'000
Revenue	(W1)	37,250	38,926	40,678
Cost of sales	(W2)	(19,800)	(21,780)	(23,958)
Gross profit		17,450	17,146	16,720
Admin and operating expenses	(W3)	(6,000)	(6,000)	(6,000)
Depreciation	(W4)	(4,000)	(4,000)	(4,000)
Adjusted profit from operations		7,450	7,146	6,720
Finance costs	(W5)	(600)	(600)	(600)
Profit before tax		6,850	6,546	6,120
Tax	(W6)	(1,712)	(1,636)	(1,530)
Adjusted profit for the period		5,138	4,910	4,590

WORKINGS

(1) Revenue

20X3: 37,250 × 0.95 × 1.1 = 38,926
20X4: 38,926 × 0.95 × 1.1 = 40,678

This allows for the 10% increase in sales volumes and the 5% decrease in selling price.

(2) Cost of sales

20X3: 19,800 × 1.1 = 21,780
20X4: 21,780 × 1.1 = 23,958

This allows for the 10% increase in sales volumes.

(3) Operating expenses

These are fixed costs.

(4) Depreciation

From the information provided, the fair value of owned properties is £34.5m compared to a carrying amount of £23m. As fair value is 50% greater than the carrying amount, the depreciation is 50% greater than the historic cost depreciation ie £3m (£2m × £34.5m/£23m).

Depreciation on fixtures and fittings is a further £1m.

Therefore total fair value depreciation is £4m (£3m + £1m).

(5) Finance costs

Finance costs are prudently assumed to be constant although operating cash flows may be used to repay debt over time and thereby reduce interest costs.

(6) Taxation

The same effective tax rate of 25% is used as per working assumptions. This is however a crude assumption as the current tax obligations would need to be separated from the deferred tax. This is relevant given that fair value depreciation is used which is likely to exceed capital allowances, but more information would be needed to make a quantitative adjustment.

Earnings valuation calculation

Using the 10% working assumption for cost of equity, then the value of the equity at 1 October 20X3 is based on the earnings for the year ended 30 September 20X14 discounted as a perpetuity:

£4.59m/0.1 = £45.9m

Net assets valuation

	20X2	Comments
	£'000	
Non-current assets		
Property, plant and equipment	50,500	Fair value at 30 September 20X2 as per information provided (£34.5m PPE + £16m F&F).
Current assets	10,000	As per financial statements provided.
Total assets	60,500	
Non-current liabilities		
Loans	(12,000)	The carrying amount of the loan is assumed to equal fair value. This may not be the case if the amortised cost method is being used.
Retirement benefit obligation	(20,750)	This may vary significantly with the discount rate change but is not investigated further in accordance with instructions.
Tax liability	(2,250)	Assumed.
Trade payables	(1,770)	Assumed.
Net assets	23,730	

This is the net assets valuation at 30 September 20X2 using fair values. However the acquisition is assumed to be at 1 October 20X3. Assuming there are no changes in the fair value of the PPE (or other movements through OCI) then the change in the value of the assets is given by the profit after tax for the year ending 30 September 20X3 which is £4.91m (per calculations above).

The estimate of the fair value of the net assets at 1 October 20X3 is therefore:

At 30 September 20X2	£23.73m
Profit for year to 30 September 20X3	£4.91m
At 30 September 20X3	**£28.64m**

Key concerns with the valuation

- The brand is a key asset which has been omitted from the net asset valuation.

- The pension fund entries require further investigation as they could affect both net assets and earnings.

- The working assumptions are fundamental to the valuation therefore, to the extent they are unrealistic, they may have a material impact. While they may all be questioned, key issues would be:

  - perpetuity assumption appears unrealistic – although the present value of a long term annuity may approximate to a perpetuity

  - constant prices and costs in perpetuity (but the cost of equity may be a real rate – see below)

  - cost of equity of 10% (eg is this a real or money rate?)

(c) **Post acquisition integration**

The acquisition is a form of horizontal integration by Stark, as HH operates in the same industry. There are however a number of key differences between Stark and HH that need to be considered before deciding on the extent to which the business should be integrated post acquisition or maintained as separate businesses. These differences include the following:

- Scale: Stark is far larger than HH both in revenue and number of outlets.

- Market positioning: Stark is at the very top end of the quality market, while HH is towards the bottom end.

- Location of stores: Stark has town centre locations, while HH has stores which are out of town.

- Size of stores: Stark stores are small, while HH stores are large with significant floorspace.

- Product range: Stark sells both brown and white goods, whereas HH only sells home entertainment related brown goods.

A key problem with full integration is that the two companies serve two different sectors of the market. The consumer perception and interpretation of the brands is therefore entirely different. The Stark brand signifies quality and image, whereas the HH brand suggests low price and value.

Merging the two elements of the business, post integration, under the one Stark brand would therefore seem to be a high risk strategy as the Stark brand would no longer represent quality but a wide range of product qualities and prices. This may damage Stark's policy of selling image and its reputation for high service and relationships with quality suppliers.

The counter argument is that while the existing Stark business may suffer from unification, the existing HH business may benefit from a higher quality image by using the Stark brand. Even this might be in doubt however if customers are shopping for low price and value rather than image.

The issue is also raised that if the businesses are separately operated then there may be limited synergies, other than using the additional floor space for Stark. The motivation for making the acquisition therefore needs to be questioned as the greater the extent to which the two businesses are kept separate post acquisition, the lower are the synergies achieved.

One solution may be to maintain the HH business model and outlets, but have a 'shop within a shop' as Stark, being a premium and separately branded, separately identified section within HH outlets, to attract two types of customer to the one location. This would enhance the store space for Stark goods which is a constraining factor. It could be that only white goods are sold in this way, in order to avoid brand confusion but then the two elements of the 'shop within a shop' would be disparate in both product nature and product positioning.

A further problem of the integration of a 'shop within a shop' idea is that if an HH outlet and a Stark outlet are geographically proximate, then the existing Stark store may lose business. However it may well be the best way to attain additional floorspace and perhaps some synergies, while maintaining the separate market positions and perceptions of each brand. These locations would need to be investigated.

(d) **Brand valuation**

It is necessary to provide a value for the Stark group consolidated SOFP as at 30 September 20X4 where the HH brand would need to be recognised as a separately identifiable asset at fair value, notwithstanding that it would not be recognised in the individual company financial statements of HH.

IFRS 13 para 9 defines fair value as 'the price that would be received to sell an asset or paid to transfer a liability in an orderly transaction between market participants at the measurement date'.

IFRS 13 requires the fair value to be determined on the basis of its 'highest and best use' from a market participant's perspective. This needs to consider what is physically possible, legally permissible and financially feasible.

The fair value is determined from the perspective of a market participant. The previous section on business integration is also relevant to financial reporting measurement. If Stark intends to acquire the HH brand but not use it (ie branding all outlets under the Stark brand) this does not however mean that the brand has no fair value, as the assumption is the highest and best use by a market participant (eg an alternative buyer of the brand such as Dice Inc).

If, however, Stark management intends to use the brand then it is entitled to assume that its current use is the highest and best use without searching for alternatives unless market or other factors suggest otherwise (IFRS 13 para 29).

The fair value is therefore in part dependent on the post-acquisition strategy adopted by Stark with respect to usage of the HH brand.

In order to quantify fair value IFRS 13 has a fair value hierarchy:

Level 1 inputs are quoted prices in an active market for identical assets. This is not normally feasible for a brand given its unique nature, so is probably currently inapplicable to Stark.

Level 2 inputs are other observable prices. This might include prices in markets which are not active, such as the Dice Inc quote, but this is weak as it excluded the UK which is the primary market for HH and the bid was rejected as inadequate, implying it was too low.

Level 3 inputs are unobservable inputs, including internal company data.

Based upon these three levels, IFRS 13 sets out three possible valuation bases which Stark may use to value the HH brand:

The market basis – This uses market price and other market transactions. Given the nature of a brand is unique this would be difficult to use (noting, as previously, the Dice offer is not appropriate but, had it been for the entire global rights, serious consideration could have been given to this method of valuation).

The income basis – This would consider the present value of the incremental income generated by the brand. No price premium is obtained by the HH brand, but additional sales volume is obtained. Based on the information provided for HH, this gives a value of:

Contribution (£16.72m* × 5%)	£0.836m
Advertising cost	(£0.200m)
Net contribution before tax	£0.636m
Tax 25%	(£0.159m)
Net contribution after tax	£0.477m

* Contribution for year ended 30 September 20X4 (see above workings)

PV = £0.477m/0.1 = £4.77m (using cost of equity of 10% as the discount rate)

The **cost basis** – this is the current replacement cost of the brand which is the PV of the advertising expenditure in the HH case which is £4.5m. The basis on which this value was determined would need to be considered, including allowance for risk and how the expenditure could replicate the brand in varying market conditions. Given annual advertising expenditure of £200,000 the implied discount rate to give a PV of £4.5m seems unreasonably low, hence some scepticism is appropriate regarding this estimate.

Based on the above three calculations the brand's current use is the highest and best use giving a value of £4.77m. This would not however be applicable if Stark was not going to retain the brand in the new group.

(e) **Ethical issues**

Stark Board
Stark plc
[Address]

Thank you for your request to engage KK in an assignment relating to the valuation of the HH pension fund deficit.

The request raises various professional ethical principles for KK if this engagement were to be accepted. These are as follows.

Professional competence and due care – We must question whether KK, as a firm, has the necessary skills and experience to undertake the work.

While the professional competence of accountants extends to financial reporting for pension funds, the expertise for estimating the underlying value and assumptions more properly extends into the profession of actuaries. This particularly applies to defined benefit funds such as that of HH where estimates and assumptions relating to investment returns, mortality, wage inflation, and future interest rates are beyond our expertise. This work should therefore be referred to a qualified actuary and we are unable to accept the engagement on this basis.

Independence and conflict of interests – We are acting for Stark in its negotiations for the potential acquisition of HH. This would present us with an issue of conflict of interest between the two parties. Assisting with a valuation of HH's pension fund deficit may give us privileged information about HH which could be perceived by a reasonable and informed third party as being used to benefit Stark in price negotiations for the acquisition. Again on this basis we could not accept the engagement as there are no adequate safeguards that we could put in place.

We would however be willing to act for you in the other matters you have requested in the potential acquisition of HH.

31 Looster Lagoona plc

Marking guide

		Marks
		Up to
(a)	Assessment of current and future liquidity and solvency	11
(b)	Evaluation of refinancing packages	22
(c)	Corporate governance	8
(d)	Comparison of packages, and recommendation	8
Total marks		49
Maximum marks		45

Draft report

To:	Finance director – Carl Zheng
From:	A. Senior
Date:	1 October 20X2
Subject:	Looster Lagoona plc – Refinancing

(a) An assessment of the current and future liquidity and solvency of LL

Future cash flow projections

Over the current planning horizon of four years (from 1 January 20X3 to 31 December 20X6) for which data is available the operating and investment cash flows are as follows (assuming finance continues to be available at 5%):

	20X3	20X4	20X5	20X6
	£'000	£'000	£'000	£'000
Existing profit before tax	2,250	2,250	2,250	2,250
Add back depreciation	1,000	1,000	1,000	1,000
Operating cash flows	3,250	3,250	3,250	3,250
Less CAPEX	1,250	1,250	1,250	1,250
Net cash flow	2,000	2,000	2,000	2,000
Opening cash	1,000	3,000	5,000	7,000
Closing cash	3,000	5,000	7,000	9,000

Notes

1 There may be other adjustments to profit in addition to depreciation to obtain operating cash flows (eg working capital adjustments). More information would be needed.

2 The increase in the cash balance may be used to reduce the overdraft and therefore reduce overdraft interest each year. If this assumption were to be made then cash flows would be as follows:

	20X3	20X4	20X5	20X6
	£'000	£'000	£'000	£'000
Operating profit	3,250	3,250	3,250	3,250
Finance cost @ 5% pa (W1)	(1,000)	(850)	(742)	(630)
Profit before tax	2,250	2,400	2,508	2,620
Add back depreciation	1,000	1,000	1,000	1,000
Operating cash flows	3,250	3,400	3,508	3,620
CAPEX	(1,250)	(1,250)	(1,250)	(1,250)
Net cash flow	2,000	2,150	2,258	2,370
Cash less overdraft	(9,000)	(7,000)	(4,850)	(2,592)
Closing overdraft	(7,000)	(4,850)	(2,592)	(222)

WORKING 1 – **Finance costs**

Finance costs relate to the loan plus overdraft

20X4 (5% × £10,000) + (5% × 7,000) = £850

20X5 (5% × £10,000) + (5% × 4,850) = £742

20X6 (5% × £10,000) + (5% × 2,592) = £630

These calculations prudently assume year end cash flows.

In terms of liquidity, on the basis of operating and investment cash flows LL is generating surplus cash which is sufficient to cover interest payments and increase net cash balance by £2m in 20X3 and more than £2m in each subsequent year due to the reduction of the overdraft and therefore the reduced overdraft interest.

By 20X6 the overdraft will therefore be almost completely repaid from operating cash flows net of investment cash flows (CAPEX).

The key issue in terms of solvency is however financing cash flows. While sufficient cash is being generated to meet interest payment obligations and new investment requirements (CAPEX), the breach of the covenant has generated the possibility of the need for an immediate capital repayment of £20m (£10m overdraft and £10m bank loan).

Operating cash flows are not sufficient to make these capital repayments immediately hence the solvency of the business is in question unless the debt can be refinanced.

The issue of solvency concerns the probability of being able to refinance the £20m of loan and overdraft given the bank's declaration that it is unwilling to continue under the present arrangements. Indeed, BB may be unwilling to refinance at all, given that the suggested terms 'should not be interpreted as an offer of a loan, but as minimum conditions for consideration by BB of a loan application by LL'.

As a consequence, failure to arrange refinancing quickly seems likely to place the company in an insolvent position. However given the alternative forms of finance being negotiated there seem reasonable prospects that a refinancing package can be obtained.

Even if refinancing is acquired, then it seems unlikely that it will be on such favourable terms as the current 5% under any of the suggested arrangements (the specific liquidity and solvency implications of the separate new financing packages are considered below). The implications of servicing a higher interest rate have consequences for current liquidity and future solvency as lower annual cash flows will be generated and the overdraft will take longer to repay. There is limited capacity however to service capital repayments. If for instance the interest rate on the new loan doubles this would increase interest payments and reduce profit by £1m per year. Therefore cash available to repay the £20m of capital would reduce from £2m per year to £1m.

refinancing reclassifies the ST loan into LT term (medium term solvency).

However, the transformation of the short term overdraft into a longer term loan under all the financing options provides greater medium term solvency as it precludes immediate demands for repayment by the finance provider (unless there is another covenant breach).

Conclusion

*need for reorg-recovery plan *.*

LL's continuing solvency is dependent on the ability to refinance the current £20m of overdraft and loan with Brewster. Insolvency seems almost inevitable if refinancing cannot be achieved.

With a high interest rate, interest on the new loans can be covered but, unless the directors' plan for recovery engenders growth, greater profitability and cash inflows, it is difficult to see how significant capital repayments can be serviced beyond the medium term.

(b) **Evaluation of refinancing packages**

(1) **Brewster Bank Refinancing Loan**

- **Liquidity and solvency**

    Assuming that the new Brewster loan arrangement goes ahead with the full £20m being available, then the above cash flow calculation can be revised as follows:

reinvest surplus cash to generate add'l income .

(if permissible by Brewer)

	20X3	20X4	20X5	20X6
	£'000	£'000	£'000	£'000
Operating profit	3,250	3,250	3,250	3,250
Finance costs (£20m @ 10%)	(2,000)	(2,000)	(2,000)	(2,000)
Profit before tax	1,250	1,250	1,250	1,250
Add back depreciation	1,000	1,000	1,000	1,000
Operating cash flows	2,250	2,250	2,250	2,250
CAPEX	(1,250)	(1,250)	(1,250)	(1,250)
Net cash flow	1,000	1,000	1,000	1,000
Opening cash	1,000	2,000	3,000	4,000
Closing cash	2,000	3,000	4,000	5,000

    Note: The above table does not consider the reduction in overdraft interest payments arising from the declining overdraft. This is because the short term overdraft is being refinanced into longer term debt which is entirely repayable in 20X8. However, surplus cash flows could be reinvested to generate some investment income or prepay part of the loan, if this is permissible under the contract.

ICAEW

Nevertheless, extrapolating the trend in the above table shows that the cash flow generated after CAPEX is only £1m per year. LL would therefore not be able to repay the £20m new Brewster loan on 31 December 20X8, from current cash inflows and would need to refinance again at this date. The directors' plan for recovery may improve cash flows but any additional cash investment required by the new plan would need to be recoverable within the six year term of the loan if it is to make a favourable difference.

Therefore, while a new loan of £20m with Brewster would address the immediate liquidity and solvency issue it would really only defer it to 20X8 when the new loan becomes repayable. A key reason for this, is the higher rate of interest which, at 10%, is a significant additional cash outflow each year.

The key risk is therefore insolvency risk when the new loans become repayable in six years. Also, if operating cash flows decline in future, the interest payments may not be serviced and insolvency may arise before 20X8 (ie the higher interest payments under the new loan mean that there is less headroom between operating cash flows and interest payments). New covenants such as interest cover may also mean that a decline in operating cash flows would cause a breach.

This leaves the issue of whether Brewster would be willing to extend the full £20 refinancing loan.

According to Rob Emerald, the maximum amount of the loan would be the lower of:

- £20m; and

- 200% of net assets as recognised and measured in accordance with IFRS, in LL's statement of financial position at 31 December 20X2 including existing loans.

Using the draft statement of financial position net assets at the expected carrying amount are valued under the cost model at £6m giving a maximum loan of £12m. This would not be enough to refinance the existing loan and overdraft in the absence of alternative or additional financing. Additional debt finance may be difficult to obtain or expensive as Brewster is likely to require a first charge over assets.

A possible solution is to revalue some, or all, of the assets to fair value as a change in accounting policy under IAS 8. This may be permissible under IAS 8, para 14, if it 'results in financial statements providing reliable and more relevant information'. Arguably the revaluation model would do this for LL compared with the cost model used previously.

Assuming a revaluation would be acceptable to Brewster, this would mean that if all PPE were to be revalued to £30m then net assets would increase to £16m and therefore, under the Brewster formula, all £20m would be available (ie £20m < 200% × £16m = £32m). *capped @ £20m.*

- **Cost of finance**

This is a straight vanilla loan so the nominal cost is the same as the effective rate at 10% per annum. Any transaction charges may increase the rate but these are likely to be small on this type of loan.

- **Impact on the financial statements**

As a straight vanilla loan this would again be straightforward as the interest would be the recognised expense and the initial capital amount of £20m would be a non-current liability until the year before repayment (ie 20X7) when it would be reclassified as a current liability.

This gives for each of the years 20X3 to 20X6:

	£'000
Revenue	11,000
Operating costs (W1)	(8,250)
Operating profit	2,750
Finance costs	(2,000)
Profit before tax	750
Tax	–
Profit for the year	750

WORKING 1

The 50% increase in the fair value of the PPE means depreciation increases by 50% from £1m to £1.5m. The operating cost increases from £7.75m to £8.25m. (Cash flows remain the same)

(2) **Thor: Package A – Fixed term loan with options**

- **Liquidity and solvency**

This package makes the full £20m available. It thus prevents the immediate solvency concerns by enabling the current Brewster loan and overdraft to be repaid in full.

The above cash flow forecast calculation can be revised as follows:

	20X3	20X4	20X5	20X6
	£'000	£'000	£'000	£'000
Operating profit	3,250	3,250	3,250	3,250
Finance costs (£20m @ 7%)	(1,400)	(1,400)	(1,400)	(1,400)
Profit before tax	1,850	1,850	1,850	1,850
Add back depreciation	1,000	1,000	1,000	1,000
Operating cash flows	2,850	2,850	2,850	2,850
CAPEX	(1,250)	(1,250)	(1,250)	(1,250)
Net cash flow	1,600	1,600	1,600	1,600
Opening cash	1,000	2,600	4,200	5,800
Closing cash	2,600	4,200	5,800	7,400

If the options were to be exercised this would lead to an additional cash inflow of £20m (4m × £5) which could be used to repay the £20m loan element of the Thor package at 31 December 20X6. The fact and timing of this receipt from option exercise are however uncertain (being dependent on LL's future share price movements) and therefore it has not been included. The options element of the package will never have to incur a cash outflow as they are part of equity.

As for the Thor loan element, surplus cash flows could be reinvested to generate some investment income or repay part of the loan, if this is permissible under the contract, but given the uncertainties this has not been included in the above cash flow forecast.

A key issue is that this is a four year repayment term (rather than six years with Brewster) and from the above cash flow forecast it is clear that refinancing of the £20m loan cannot be made unless the options are exercised by Thor in four years' time. Thus, the immediate solvency crisis is likely to be deferred four years rather than avoided unless the LL share price is greater than the exercise price of £5 at 31 December 20X6. If the share price is lower than £5, then the options will not be exercised and the loan will become repayable at that date when the above cash flow forecast suggests that there will be insufficient cash to repay the loan.

The directors' plan for recovery may improve cash flows, but any additional cash investment required by the new plan would need to make a quick recovery of the outlay within the four-year term of the loan if it is to make a favourable difference to the cash balance at 31 December 20X6 when the loan becomes repayable.

- **Cost of finance**

  The nominal cost of this loan is 7% which is lower than the 10% on the proposed new Brewster loan. However the cost of the Thor loan needs to be viewed as part of a package with the attached options. The required return on the options is not immediately observable given the information provided. However in order to make a rough comparison with the other methods of finance we can use the fair value at £1, as measured by the member of LL's treasury staff, and assume a repurchase of the options in order to strip out the options from the calculation. Thus, if some of the cash generated from the loan of £20m were to be used by LL to buy back the options at their fair value of £4m on the issue date of 1 January 20X3 the remaining proceeds would be £16m [£20m – (4m × £1)].

  A crude rate of return would therefore be the nominal interest payments on the £20m loan divided by the remaining cash available after repurchase of the options which would be:

  £1.4m/£16m = 8.75%

  This calculation is naïve however as this is a four-year loan, not a perpetuity. The implicit rate on the package could however be estimated by taking the initial repurchase as an outflow and determining the cost of the debt package on this basis as an effective implicit interest rate (ie the internal rate of return).

  Using linear interpolation or by trial and error the effective implicit interest rate is 13.84%. (**Tutorial note:** Any reasonable method of approximation is acceptable.)

  This is demonstrated as follows:

31 Dec	Cash outflow £	DF@ 13.84%	PV £
20X2	4,000,000	1	4,000,000
20X3	1,400,000	1/1.1384	1,229,796
20X4	1,400,000	$1/1.1384^2$	1,080,285
20X5	1,400,000	$1/1.1384^3$	948,950
20X6	21,400,000	$1/1.1384^4$	12,741,900
			20,000,000*

  *Rounding 931

  If repurchase of the options is not possible, then there are risks for (1) volatility in option values (2) corporate governance (see Section (c) below) and (3) dilution of shareholding and control. These risks may then be reflected in a higher required rate of return on the package.

  However taking the above calculation at face value then the cost of finance is 13.84% (which is somewhat higher than the Brewster loan).

  There is some uncertainty over the fair value of the options as by their nature they are not actively traded. This creates uncertainty over the cost of financing of this package of 13.84%. The methodology and data of the member of treasury staff needs to be investigated. The use of a model such as Black Scholes or Monte Carlo simulation could be used to estimate the value of the options.

- **Impact on the financial statements**

  Loan

  This is a straightforward loan of £20m at 7% with annual interest at £1.4m.

  The interest would be the recognised expense and the initial capital amount of £20m would be a non current liability until the year before repayment 20X5 when it would be reclassified as a current liability.

  Options

  The option is a derivative contract that can be settled by LL delivering a fixed number of its own equity instruments in exchange for a fixed amount of cash.

The option is therefore recognised as an equity instrument at its fair value of £4m at the date of inception. The income statement is not affected.

Subsequent changes in the fair value of the option are not reflected in the financial statements as they have no impact on the amount of the consideration paid.

If Thor ultimately subscribes for the shares then the amount of cash paid to LL of £20m would be added to equity at that time.

Overall this generates the following profit for each of the years 20X3 to 20X6:

	£'000
Revenue	11,000
Operating costs	(7,750)
Operating profit	3,250
Finance costs	(1,400)
Profit before tax	1,850
Tax	–
Profit for the year	1,850

Diluted EPS

The existence of options gives rise to the possibility of a diluted EPS disclosure. However as the options are out-of-the-money (ie the exercise price exceeds the average market price) then there is no dilution in 20X3.

If the average share price in any financial year up to 20X6 rises above £5 then the options become in the money and a diluted EPS should be disclosed by adding to the denominator in the basic EPS the implied number of 'free' shares to be issued.

(3) Thor: Package B – Convertible loan stock

- **Liquidity and solvency**

    This package also makes the full £20m available. It thus prevents the immediate solvency concerns by enabling the current Brewster loan and overdraft to be repaid in full.

    The interest rate, at 7%, is the same as Thor Package A, thus the cash flow forecast for Package B is the same as that set out above and is therefore not replicated here.

    By 31 December 20X6, if the LL share price is greater than £5, then Thor would probably have the incentive to convert the loan into equity shares. In so doing, the amount of equity capital will be increased by £20m and the loan will be cancelled.

    If however, by 31 December 20X6, LL's share price is less than £5, then Thor will have the incentive to demand repayment of the loan. The cash flow forecast suggests that there will be insufficient cash to repay the loan and the current solvency crisis will be revisited at the end of 20X6.

- **Cost of capital**

    The nominal cost of the loan is 7%, but the loan element needs to be viewed as part of a package with the equity conversion rights element. The required return on the equity element is not immediately observable given the information provided. However, as with Package A, in order to make a rough comparison with the other methods of finance we can use the equity value, as measured below, and assume a repurchase of these rights immediately after issue in order to strip out the equity element from the calculation.

    In the financial reporting calculation below (see Financial reporting section below) the equity element value has been estimated at £1,901,920 before issue costs.

    One method of determining the cost of capital of this package would be to take the weighted average of the cost of equity and the cost of debt. The cost of debt has been determined below at 10.776%. The cost of equity would need to be estimated using a suitable model. The relative weightings would be £1,901,920 and £18,098,080 for equity and debt respectively (see Financial reporting section below).

Alternatively, if some of the cash generated from the loan of £20m were to be used by LL to buy back the equity conversion rights at fair value on the issue date of 1 January 20X3 the remaining proceeds would be £18,098,080 ignoring issue costs.

A crude rate of return would therefore be the nominal interest payments on the £20m loan divided by the remaining cash available after repurchase of conversion rights which is:

£1.4m/£18.098m = 7.74%

As with the option package however, such a calculation is naïve as it assumes a perpetuity rate whereas this is a four-year loan. The implicit rate on the package could be estimated by taking the initial purchase cost of equity (£1,901,920) as an outflow and determining the cost of the debt package on this basis. This is the equivalent of the 10% rate determined below (ie the net inflow at 1 January 20X3 is £18,098,080 (being the £20m loan receipt less the £1,901,920 payment for equity). Using the table below (see 'Financial reporting') this gives a zero NPV.

If issue costs are built in, then the rate rises to 10.776% (see below).

- **Financial reporting**

  The convertible bond is a compound financial instrument in accordance with IAS 32 *Financial Instruments: Presentation*. IAS 32 paragraph 28 requires separation of the equity and liability components.

  The liability component should be measured first at the present value of the capital and interest payments. The discount rate used should be the prevailing market interest rate for an instrument with the same terms and conditions except for the ability to convert to shares. At the date of issue the value of the liability is therefore:

	Cash flow	DF	PV
	£	@ 10%	£
20X3	1,400,000	$1/1.1$	1,272,727
20X4	1,400,000	$1/1.1^2$	1,157,025
20X5	1,400,000	$1/1.1^3$	1,051,841
20X6	21,400,000	$1/1.1^4$	14,616,487
			£18,098,080

  The equity component is then the residual amount: being the difference between the liability and the value of the bond:

  £20m – £18,098,080 = £1,901,920

  IAS 32 para 38 requires that transaction costs directly attributable to a compound financial instrument should be allocated to the equity and liability components in proportion to the allocation of the proceeds. Thus:

  Liability component £500,000 × £18,098,080/£20m = £452,452
  Equity component £500,000 × £1,901,920/£20m   = £47,548
                                                  £500,000

  The liability component is therefore = 18,098,080 – 452,452
                                        = £17,645,628

  The equity component is therefore = 1,901,920 – 47,548
                                     = £1,854,372

  It is assumed that the bond is not treated as at FVTPL (it is clearly not held for trading so there is no reason why this should be the case).

  Due to the issue costs, the effective rate on the bond to determine the finance charge differs from the prevailing market rate of 10% used to determine the value of the liability element, as the issue costs reduce the liability and thereby increase the required rate.

  Using linear interpolation or by trial and error the effective annual interest rate is 10.776%. (**Tutorial note:** Any reasonable method of approximation is acceptable.)

Tutorial note: Proof of interest rate:

	b/f	Int @ 10.776%	Cash	c/f
	£m	£m	£m	£m
20X3	17,645,628	1,901,493	1,400,000	18,147,121
20X4	18,147,121	1,955,534	1,400,000	18,702,655
20X5	18,702,655	2,015,398	1,400,000	19,318,053
20X6	19,318,053	2,081,713	21,400,000	0

Rounding – 234

Diluted EPS

The issue of convertibles would have an effect on diluted EPS.

Thus for instance in the year to 31 December 20X3 the basic EPS is:

Profit for year	£2,250,000
Shares	5m
EPS	45p

The diluted EPS (given there is no tax) is:

	£
Profit for year	2,250,000
Add interest saving	1,901,493
	4,151,493
Shares	5m
Potential new shares	4m
Potential shares	9m
Diluted EPS	46.13p

For 20X3, as the diluted EPS is greater than the basic EPS the convertibles would therefore be antidilutive and not disclosed in accordance with IAS 33.

For each of the years 20X4 to 20X6 the interest saving added back in the diluted EPS calculation is even greater than the £1,901,493 figure for 20X3, so the diluted EPS will rise over time and become even more antidilutive. Diluted EPS will not therefore need to be disclosed in any of the years 20X3 to 20X6.

(c) Corporate governance

(1) Brewster offer

The current corporate governance structure regarding shareholdings is as follows:

	Shares (000's)	% shareholding
Larry Lagoona	1,750	35%
Carl Zheng	150	3%
Hazel Harvey	100	2%
Victoria Venture Capital (VVC)	2,000	40%
Employees	1,000	20%
Total	5,000	100%

Regarding the board of directors there are only three executive directors and two non executives who represent the interests of VVC and employees.

Corporate governance includes the set of processes, customs, policies, laws and institutions affecting the way in which an entity is directed, administered or controlled. Corporate governance serves the needs of shareholders, and other stakeholders, by directing and controlling management activities towards good business practices, objectivity and integrity in order to satisfy the objectives of the entity.

The role of the board in corporate governance requires a service/strategy role and a control role. The service/strategy role requires a level of expertise and experience by individual directors that enables appropriate strategies and operations to be pursued. The control role requires non executive directors to have an appropriate degree of independence from the executive directors and managers in order to monitor performance and risk on behalf of shareholders and other stakeholders.

what is corporate governance .

The suggestions by Rob Emerald are representative of the interests of one stakeholder group, Brewster Bank. They may not therefore be appropriate to the interests of all stakeholder groups. However, to the extent that it is necessary or desirable to take new loan finance from Brewster, rather than, for example, Thor as an alternative finance provider, then the future solvency of the company, and therefore the interests of all stakeholders, depend on meeting the demands of Brewster in order for them to extend new loan finance.

Regarding each of the demands of Brewster:

- **Removal of the employee representative from the remuneration committee and nominations committee**

  Employees are a legitimate stakeholder group on which the company's operations depend. Moreover 20% of the shareholding of LL is held by employees. The employee director, Jeff Manning, therefore represents employees in their role as staff and also in the role as shareholders.

  While Jeff could be removed from the remuneration committee and nominations committee, this may disenfranchise the employee stakeholder group and fail to represent legitimate interests of the employees.

- **Appointment of two additional Non Executive Directors (NEDs)**

  At the moment, the executive directors outnumber the NEDs. Best practice, according to the UK Corporate Governance Code, is that the number of NEDs should be at least equal to the number of executive directors. Two new appointments would redress this balance in favour of the NEDs in terms of simple numbers. However, it is questionable whether the existing NEDs can be regarded as independent since they each represent one stakeholder group.

  Moreover, the audit committee, according to the UK Corporate Governance Code, must include at least three members, as independent non-executive directors. At the moment LL has only one non executive director (as the employee director does not sit on the audit committee and risk committee) and, as noted above, it may be questioned whether the VVC NED is independent.

  It should be noted however that as LL has an AIM listing, rather than a full listing, it is not required to comply with the UK Corporate Governance Code, although there may be an expectation of compliance amongst stakeholders.

- **Separate chairman and chief executive roles**

  Where one individual has the dual roles of chairman and chief executive it may give that person a disproportionate amount of authority to run the company and dominate the board. The UK Corporate Governance Code regards the separation of these roles as best practice.

  In this case the situation is worsened by the fact that Larry also has a 35% shareholding which makes him influential, if not dominant, in shareholder meetings as well as board meetings.

  This demand by Brewster therefore seems reasonable in asking for a separate chairman to act as a counterweight to Larry. It is not however specified as to who might take this role (eg an existing director or a NED). The effectiveness of separation would therefore depend on the independence and skills of the new chairman.

(2) **Impact of Thor refinancing packages**

There do not appear to be any demands for board representation by Thor. However given the scale of their potential investment this is surprising and Thor may require representation on the board when agreeing the details of the financing package arrangements.

The key effect of the Thor packages is on the balance of power of shareholders in the event that the options are exercised in Package A or the shares are converted in Package B. In each case a further 4m new shares would be issued to Thor.

The balance of shareholding would then become:

	Shares (000's)	% shareholding
Larry Lagoona	1,750	19.4%
Carl Zheng	150	1.7%
Hazel Harvey	100	1.1%
Victoria Venture Capital (VVC)	2,000	22.2%
Employees	1,000	11.1%
Thor	4,000	44.5%
Total	9,000	100%

If the options are exercised in Package A or the shares are converted in Package B the above table demonstrates that Thor will become the largest single shareholder, although it would not have a controlling interest. As such, this becomes significant for the balance of control in LL's AGM.

A number of points are relevant:

- The above shareholdings would only apply from 31 December 20X6 and not from 20X3 when the packages are initiated.

- They would only apply if the share price exceeded £5 per share.

- The existing holdings of Larry and VVC are 35% and 40% respectively. Under the current arrangement they can therefore block any resolution that requires a 75% majority (eg a special resolution). Under the new arrangement the respective holdings are 19.4% and 22.2% and would not therefore be sufficient to block a vote requiring a 75% majority.

- If Thor exercises the options in Package A or the shares are converted in Package B it may not wish to hold onto these shares as a long term investment. Instead, it is likely to seek an exit route by selling the shares in the open market or directly to another shareholder. If one of the other major shareholders had enough cash to acquire these shares (eg VVC or Larry), then this could be sufficient to give them a controlling holding.

(d) **A comparison of the three alternative refinancing methods**

All three financing packages would provide £20m in cash immediately in order to repay the existing Brewster overdraft and loan and would therefore alleviate the immediate solvency crisis.

(1) **Brewster loan compared to Thor Packages**

The Brewster offer differs significantly from the other two packages in being straight debt, without any equity element.

The key differences between Brewster's new loan and the two Thor packages are as follows:

- There is a six year term with Brewster rather than four years, which would give the LL board's recovery plan more time to yield benefits and recover any initial investment.

- Uncertainty – Thor has made an offer, but Brewster has only suggested minimum terms on which an offer may be made. If LL tries to strike a deal with Brewster, negotiations may fail (eg if additional terms are added such as covenants which are unacceptable to LL; or Brewster is not convinced about the detail of the recovery plan).

- Uncertainty – foreclosure. If the terms of the new loan (eg a covenant) are breached, Brewster has shown it is willing to place the company into administration. Thor has some incentive to maintain the company as a going concern as it potentially has an equity stake with either the options in Package A or the conversion rights in Package B.

- The Brewster loan has a higher annual cash interest rate at 10% than either of the Thor packages which are only 7%. However for Brewster the 10% rate is also the effective rate, whereas the Thor packages have an equity element which in each case means the effective rate is greater than 10% (see calculations above but these comparisons are also discussed in more detail below).

- A key difference between the Brewster loan and the Thor packages is the equity element. While this must be considered from the inception of the agreement in determining the expected cost of finance, the ultimate consequence of the two packages is that the options or conversion rights will be taken up or they will not. The comparison of options and conversion rights is considered below, but relative to the Brewster loan the key differences of either package are that:

- corporate governance and control will be affected by the issue of a significant number of shares (increasing share capital from 5m shares to 9m shares).

- there is an opportunity in four years' time that the £20m debt in either package A or B can be cancelled or repaid if the share price is greater than £5, thereby providing a key increase in equity and boost to liquidity.

(2) **Thor Package A compared to Thor Package B**

The debt element of these two packages is identical being a straight vanilla four-year loan of £20m at 7% per annum.

The two packages are therefore distinguished by their equity elements.

In each case the LL share price would need to exceed £5 for there to be a possibility of exercising the options or the conversion rights. If the share price is in excess of £5 then Thor is likely to exercise its rights as follows:

Package A: Thor has the option to subscribe for 4m shares at £5 per share which would be a cash injection to LL of £20m and an increase in equity of £20m arising from the issue of 4m new shares. The loan element of the package of £20m would become due on the same date (or later if early exercise is taken). The proceeds from the option exercise of £20m could be used to repay the debt of the same amount.

Package B: Thor has the right to convert each holding of £100 convertible bonds into 20 ordinary shares. Therefore, as for Package A, the break even price is £5 per share (£100/20). There would be no cash impact to conversion, but the loan element of £20m would be cancelled and 4m new shares issued at a cost of £5 per share.

Comparing three possible alternatives of share price at the exercise date:

- **Share price is £5.** The net effect of the two packages is identical for the convertible and the option exercise at £5 as demonstrated above.

- **Share price is less than £5.** In this case, neither the options nor the conversion rights would be exercised and the transaction would be the same for both Thor packages ie the loan repayment of £20m would be required by Thor.

- **Share price is greater than £5.** If the share price is above £5 then, from the perspective of the company, there is no difference in the terms of the basic transactions, as the exercise/conversion terms would be the same. However the value sacrifice to LL in market value terms would be greater.

Comparing the two packages from the perspective of Thor, rather than LL, then it has been shown that they are identical if the share price is at or below £5. The calculations below show the impact of the packages on Thor at a price above £5 (this being £6 in the example but the same principle would apply at other prices in excess of £5).

Package A – LL share price £6

Before exercise

Intrinsic value (and fair value) of shares = (£6 – £5) × 4m = £4m

After exercise

Cash injected as new equity (£5 × 4m shares)	£20m
Cash repaid (by LL to repay debt instrument)	£20m
Value of shareholding (£6 × 4m shares)	£24m

Thus a financial asset (debt) with a nominal value of £20m has in effect been exchanged for equity of £24m.

Package B – LL share price £6

Value of shares after redemption (4m × £6)	£24m
Debt cancelled on conversion (fall in value of debt instrument)	£20m

Thus a financial asset (debt) with a nominal value of £20m has been exchanged for equity of £24m.

It can be seen therefore that the two Thor packages are more or less identical in their outcomes both from the perspective of Thor and LL.

This therefore raises the question as to why the cost of finance determined above differs in each case (13.84% for Package A; and 10.776% for Package B). The difference arises from the difference in the estimated fair values of the equity element. However, if the outcomes (ie payoffs to Thor) demonstrated above are near identical, then a degree of professional scepticism should be applied to the significant differences in fair values provided by LL's treasury staff. It could be that the model used to determine the fair value of the options at £1 each by treasury staff is inappropriate. Alternatively it could be that the prevailing market interest rate of 10% on loan stock without conversion rights is not directly comparable (eg because of corporate risk differences with respect to default). However in this case it should be noted that Brewster is offering the possibility of a straight loan at 10% which indicates it is likely to be an appropriate market rate.

Further analysis is needed to assess the fair values in order to make better comparisons. However the fair values are in effect accounting estimates and they are not amounts paid and should not be a factor in determining which package is preferable.

One further issue is that there is no certainty that Thor will take up the option if share price exceeds £5 by a small amount. The reason for this is that the price per LL share before conversion is based on having £20m debt on the balance sheet and 5m shares making up share capital. After conversion there would be 9m shares and no debt. There is therefore a significant difference in financial risk which may impact on the value of the shares. There may also be a tax effect on valuation of the gearing change in the long run if interest is tax allowable and dividends are not (recognising however that tax is not currently payable by LL).

(3) Recommendation

The required interest rate of 10% per annum from Brewster is high for corporate bond yields however it may reflect a high risk of LL's insolvency for the bank.

The other two packages have a lower nominal rate of 7% on their loans, but after considering the equity element have higher cost of capital than Brewster at 13.84% for Package A; and 10.776% for Package B. There is some uncertainty over the fair value which may have distorted these rates but, on face value, the required rates of return would suggest a recommendation for the Brewster Bank arrangement. Two further factors also suggest that Brewster Bank would be the favoured choice.

First, that the term of the Brewster loan is six years which gives more time before repayment for the board's recovery plan to work compared to four years for the other two packages.

Second, the number of shares to be issued for Package A or Package B is significant at 4m compared to the number of shares currently in issue of only 5m. For shareholders and director stakeholder groups there is therefore a significant risk that in saving the company as an entity from insolvency the value of their equity and their control exercised through their equity will be very much reduced.

It is possible that Brewster will not in the end extend the loan as Exhibit 1 makes clear that it is not an offer of a loan but 'minimum conditions for consideration of a loan application'. If the loan offer is not forthcoming, then the two Thor Packages are near identical and the recommendation would be one of indifference between the two (subject to any differences in detailed terms imposed by Thor in the individual contracts).

It may also be that Brewster will extend the loan but impose additional terms beyond the minimum ones specified in Exhibit 1 (eg strict covenants which will never realistically be satisfied).

However, if the minimum terms become actual terms, an offer is made by Brewster and there are no other refinancing offers in the market than those specified, then it is recommended that the Brewster offer be accepted.

32 Funnel Cruises plc (July 2014, amended)

		Marks
(a)	Analyse and explain the performance of Funnel Cruises for the year	19
(b)	Assess whether the use of derivatives is appropriate to manage foreign currency risks on operating cash flows	
	Calculate and explain the sterling settlements of interdivisional currency balances using multilaterial netting off procedures	
	Explain how the use of zero cost collars can mitigate foreign currency risks with respect to payments under contracts for building new ships	16
(c)	Identify and evaluate suitable approaches to determine an acquisition price for Coastal given that it is making operating losses	
	Explain, with calculations, how negative goodwill would be dealt with in the FC group financial statements	
	Explain the benefits of carrying out due diligence for Coastal and whether a professional assurance firm should carry out such procedures	14
(d)	Interpretation and analysis of dashboard data for marketing purposes	
	Identification of further information that can be extracted from the data	11
Total marks		60

(a) **Performance analysis**

To 30 June	20X4	20X3
Fuel cost per tonne (£s)	507	445
Profit on 'paid for' on-board activities (£m)	670	687
Loss on Passenger tickets (£m)	(225)	(217)
Total operating profit (£m)	445	470
Revenue per ship (£m)	160.2	171.7
Profit per ship (£m)	18.5	20.4
Revenue per passenger (£s)	1,563	1,652
Profit per passenger (£s)	180.9	196.7
Revenue per passenger per night (£s) (W1)	188.79	199.32
Revenue per staff member (£s)	170,889	175,511
Profit per staff member (£s)	19,778	20,889
Operating profit margin	11.6%	11.9%

WORKING 1

Passenger numbers analysis

	20X4	20X3	Increase
Number of passengers per night	55,800	54,280	2.8%
	(90% × 62,000)	(92% × 59,000)	
Passengers nights per year (365 days)	20,367,000	19,812,200	

Overall performance – adjusting the data

In comparing the data for the years to 30 June 20X4 and 30 June 20X3, it is necessary to distinguish underlying trading operations from other activities such as hedging using derivatives.

While relevant to current performance, gains on fuel and currency derivatives are unlikely to be repeated systematically and arise from random currency movements in an efficient market. They are therefore not part of underlying operating performance.

Thus while EBIT has increased in 20X4 from 20X3 the operating profit has fallen.

Two operating streams

Total revenue has declined by 2.6% in 20X4 compared to 20X3. There are however two separate operating streams.

The 'paid for activities on board' can be analysed as follows:

	20X4 £m	20X3 £m	% change
Revenue	920	909	1.2%
Costs	(250)	(222)	12.6%
Profit	670	687	(2.5)%
Operating margin	72.8%	75.6%	

Paid for activities on board have declined slightly in terms of profitability, but remain an extremely high margin activity.

Stripping out the 'paid for activities on board' from the total revenues and costs enables the residual core activity of running cruises through passenger tickets to be evaluated:

	20X4 £m	20X3 £m	% change
Revenue	2,925	3,040	(3.8)%
Costs	(3,150)	(3,257)	(3.3)%
Loss	(225)	(217)	3.7%

The core activity of running cruises would therefore appear to be making losses. Moreover, the losses have increased by 3.7% in 20X4 compared to 20X3.

However, such a clear distinction between the two operating streams is likely to be invalid as they are so highly interdependent. If the management accounting system had allocated more overheads to 'paid for activities on board' then the result could have been very different.

It therefore remains necessary for the core business of attracting passengers to cruises to succeed. This is fundamental to an appraisal of the performance of the business as a whole.

Revenue

The decline in passenger ticket revenues of 3.8% should be compared with the increase in passenger numbers in order to compare price and volume effects on revenue. Passenger numbers have actually risen by 2.9% which could imply that there has been a significant adverse price effect. This could be reflected in the fall in revenue per passenger from £1,652 to £1,563 (down 5.4%). The revenue per passenger night has also decreased by 5.3%.

Revenue per ship has fallen by 6.7% and revenue per employee by 2.6%.

In seeking causal factors to explain the fall in revenue, there are indications that price has been reduced in an attempt to increase passenger numbers. Marginal costs are low from taking an extra passenger so it is important to attract as many passengers as possible per cruise to improve utilisation which has fallen from 92% in 20X3 to 90% in 20X4. In addition to the ticket price for any incremental passengers, there is the opportunity to sell other paid for activities on board.

If there is overcapacity in the industry as more large ships are launched then there is increasing pressure on cruise operators to lower ticket prices to maximise utilisation.

One additional explanation is that price per passenger booking may have fallen due to the average length of a cruise being lower in 20X4 than it was in 20X3. In these circumstances the lower revenue per passenger would reflect lower prices for shorter cruises rather than discounting. Further information is needed to evaluate this proposition.

Operating profit and costs

Operating profit has decreased by 5.3% from £470m to £445m. This is significantly greater than the fall in revenue of 2.6%.

Many of the costs will be fixed. Staff numbers for example are constant.

Where the costs are variable the cost drivers are likely to be:

- the number of passenger bookings (up by 2.9%)
- the distance travelled on voyages (an indicator is that fuel consumption is down by 1.2%)
- the number of ships (increase from 23 to 24)
- the number of voyages or stop-overs at ports (no data available)

While the indicators are mixed regarding the level of activity, the key changes in costs are discussed below:

(1) **Fuel**

Fuel costs have increased by 12.4% despite the number of tonnes of fuel used falling by 1.2%. This is reflected by the increase in the price of fuel per tonne from £445 to £507, an increase of 13.9%.

However the absolute increase in fuel costs of £47m has been offset by derivatives hedging on fuel, resulting in gains of £25m and leaving a net increase of £22m.

(2) **Employee costs**

The number of employees is constant at 22,500 and payroll costs have increased by 0.9%. This does not therefore seem a major contributory factor in explaining the change in profit, despite the fact that payroll is a major cost.

(3) **Other ship operating costs**

These costs had a major favourable effect on operating profit as they decreased by 11.4% and they are one of the largest operating costs. Further investigation is needed; as if some costs continue on an upward trend then it seems unlikely that other ship operating costs can continue to decrease at the current rate to compensate. The significance of these costs is indicated in that, if they had stayed at their 20X3 level, then operating profits would have fallen by around one third to £286m.

(4) **Food**

Food costs have remained constant despite the increase in the number of passengers. This might be because lower quality food has been purchased, smaller portion sizes have been given or improved discounts have been obtained from suppliers.

(5) **Depreciation and ships**

It is slightly surprising that depreciation has not risen, as a new ship has been brought into use.

This might be because it was brought into use near the year end or it might be that older ships are now fully depreciated.

(b) **Foreign currency transactions**

(1) **Use of foreign currency derivatives**

FC is unusual in receiving cash at least 4-months in advance of providing the services it delivers. Also, some cash is likely to be received as a deposit to secure the booking when the contract is made. While there may be some FOREX movement between the contract date and the date of receipt of the residual cash, few costs will be incurred in this period as it will still be at least 4-months before the cruise commences. In the short term, therefore, for each sale there is limited transaction risk which would be common to normal international trading. In the case of FC, monies received can be converted on receipt to the currency in which costs will be incurred (subject to netting) using money markets as a means of hedging.

For longer time horizons, there is economic foreign currency risk exposure. **Economic risk** is the risk that exchange rate movements might reduce FC's international competitiveness. It is the risk that the present value of the future cash flows might be adversely affected by exchange rate movements. Derivatives are normally relatively short term instruments and are likely to be ineffective in mitigating such long term risks.

Exchange rate fluctuations of the euro, US dollar and other currencies against £ sterling will affect FC's reported financial results since the reporting currency for its consolidated financial statements is the £. Any strengthening of the £ against these foreign currencies has the financial statement effect of decreasing the £ values reported for cruise revenues and expenses. Any weakening of the £ has the opposite effect.

The use of derivative financial instruments can offset cash flow risks, but may not be the most suitable means to do so in the case of FC.

By utilising derivatives such as forwards and options and other financial instruments (such as foreign currency swaps, foreign currency debt obligations and foreign currency cash balances) exchange risk can be managed by locking into agreed exchange rates and avoiding future fluctuations. However, this is largely unnecessary for FC's revenues (as cash is received in advance) and therefore using derivatives is probably not desirable.

(2) **Interdivisional sterling settlements**

Multilateral netting off occurs when each of the three divisions of FC interact with the central treasury department to net off their transactions. The arrangement should be co-ordinated by the central treasury (or alternatively by FC's bankers). The process involves establishing a 'base' currency to record all intra-group transactions.

This procedure has the advantage for FC of reducing the number of transactions and thus transaction costs, including foreign exchange purchase costs and money transmission costs. There will also be less loss of interest through having money in transit. However, it requires strict control procedures from the central treasury. In addition, there may be some countries which FC deals with which have severe restrictions on, or even prohibition of, netting because it is seen as a means of tax avoidance. There may also be other legal and tax issues to consider.

In terms of the data provided, multilateral netting off would take place as follows.

Convert to £:

Receivables division	UK (£)	France (euro)	US (US$)	Total receipts £	Total payments £	Net receipt/ (payment) £
UK (£)		£2.4m		£2.4m	£(4.0)m	£(1.6)m
France (euro)			£1.5m	£1.5m	£(4.65)m	£(3.15)m
US (US$)	£4.0m	£2.25m		£6.25m	£(1.5)m	£4.75m

All transactions are handled in £. Therefore:

The UK division should pay £1.6m to the US division.

The France division should pay £3.15m to the US division.

(3) **New ship building**

Using a collar arrangement, FC has bought a foreign exchange rate cap and at the same time sold a foreign exchange rate floor, which locks the exchange rate between these two limits.

If the euro appreciates significantly against the £, then the risk, without hedging, would have been significant as the cost of the ship would increase materially in £ sterling terms. Conversely, if the £ appreciates against the euro then the cost of the ship in £ sterling would be reduced.

The collar would accept the risk of currency movements within the ceiling to floor range of £0.85 = €1 and £0.77 = €1. Outside these limits, the upside and downside potential of currency fluctuations is removed by the collar.

Given that the final payment for the ship is €270m then the maximum that can be paid is £229.5m at the ceiling rate of £0.85 to €1. The minimum that can be paid is £207.9m at the floor rate of £0.77 to €1.

The collars however only cover the final payment for one ship and end in 20X6. There remains foreign currency risk exposure for the final payment in respect of the second ship. The progress payments for both ships also remain unhedged.

(c) **Potential acquisition of Coastal**

(1) **Valuation methodology**

The normal models used to determine valuation based on future earnings or cash flows cannot be readily applied to a business making losses as, on the face of it, this would give a negative value.

The most obvious alternative would be to use the fair value of the assets as a means of valuation. This would give a fair value at 31 December 20X3 of $30m.

Confirming this value would be a key factor in due diligence (see below). Fluctuations in fair value between the date of valuation and the date of acquisition would also need to be considered.

However, both the earnings model and the net asset valuation need some further consideration.

Regarding the net assets model, the method of determining fair value needs consideration. The hotels are worth only what a potential purchaser is willing to pay. There is unlikely to be an active market and the potential sale price may be subject to significant variation according to market conditions and the needs of any potential purchaser. Further consideration is therefore required of the fair values.

In addition, there may be value attributable to unrecognised assets. This is likely to be limited given the loss making position and the nature of the hotel business, but there may be intangible assets that could demand a price. This might include the use of the brand name if Coastal is withdrawing from the market.

Regarding the earnings model, the straightforward acceptance of financial reporting losses as a measure of contribution to the business may be inappropriate.

A key question is: why is the Coastal business loss making? The following should be considered:

- While the current Coastal management is making losses, this may reflect the performance of the management, rather than the potential of the hotels. An alternative management may yield more potential and generate profit which would increase the value to FC. Most obviously, if FC used the hotels for their cruise passengers (where the hotel is located at a port used by FC) prior to, or after, cruises, this may generate a significant new source of income and therefore return Coastal to profit.

- Alternative explanations for the losses could be:

    - the current adverse phase of the economic cycle
    - lack of funds and other resources for investment by the current owners
    - start-up phase of development

- The measure of profit is likely to be imperfect and will include non cash items such as depreciation. Once these are backed out, then the free cash flows generated may be positive which could indicate a valuation greater than the fair value of the assets. Cash flow models may therefore be used where free cash flow is positive. Also, a rough initial estimate could be a multiple of EBITDA.

- It may be that Coastal is making operating profits, but loan interest creates a loss after tax. In this case, it may be that for operational purposes Coastal is profitable and a different financing structure under FC ownership may generate profits.

Overall, the price to sell is likely to be determined by negotiations which are constrained by:

- the maximum amount a purchaser is willing to pay (which may include an alternative use of the hotel buildings and alternative acquisitions); and

- the minimum amount that Coastal shareholders will accept for the sale.

(2) Financial reporting

Fair value is the price that would be received to sell an asset or paid to transfer a liability in an orderly transaction between independent and knowledgeable market participants at the measurement date.

The fair value of the Coastal assets will need to be determined in accordance with IFRS 13. The three levels of inputs used to measure fair value are as follows:

- Level 1 measurements are based on unadjusted quoted prices in active markets for identical assets or liabilities that we have the ability to access. Valuation of these items does not entail a significant amount of judgement.

- Level 2 measurements are based on quoted prices for similar assets or liabilities in active markets, quoted prices for identical or similar assets or liabilities in markets that are not active or market data other than quoted prices that are observable for the assets or liabilities.

- Level 3 measurements are based on unobservable data that are supported by little or no market activity and are significant to the fair value of the assets or liabilities.

The fair value on acquisition for Coastal will therefore probably use Level 3 measurements unless there are very similar hotels in similar locations.

If the acquisition price is below this value, then there is negative goodwill. IFRS 3 requires that FC should:

- reassess the identification and measurement of Coastal's identifiable assets, liabilities and contingent liabilities and the measurement of the cost of the business combination; and

- recognise immediately in profit or loss any excess (ie negative goodwill) remaining after that reassessment.

In the case of FC acquiring Coastal on 30 September 20X4 then the negative goodwill would be:

	US $m
Fair value of net assets at 31 December 20X3	30
Less forecast loss for period to 30 September 20X4 ($4m × 9/12)	(3)
Fair value of assets at 30 September 20X4	27
Consideration	(25)
Negative goodwill (Bargain purchase)	2

On consolidation, negative goodwill is measured at $2m/1.6   £1.25m

The £1.25m gain is recognised in profit or loss on the date of acquisition (30 September 20X4) (IFRS 3 para 34):

DEBIT   Negative goodwill   £1.25m
CREDIT Profit or loss   £1.25m

Note: It is assumed that there are no further fair value changes between 31 December 20X3 and 30 September 20X4 other than those relating to retained earnings.

(3) **Due diligence**

The acquisition would be material to FC and assurance over a number of aspects of the business can mitigate some risks of the acquisition, even though the purchase price is not primarily dependent on Coastal's future earnings.

Due diligence is a means of attesting that information, normally on behalf of a prospective bidder. It can take place at different stages in the negotiations, although the timing is likely to affect the nature of the due diligence process.

Due diligence will attempt to achieve the following objectives.

- Confirm the accuracy of the information and assumptions on which the bid is based.
- Provide the bidder with an independent assessment and review of the target business.
- Identify and quantify areas of commercial and financial risk.
- Give assurance to providers of finance.
- Place the bidder in a better position for determining the value of the target company.

There are several different forms of due diligence which generate different types of benefits. Some of these can be carried out by independent assurance providers (such as Reez), others require specialist skills, while others can be carried out by FC's own staff.

Financial due diligence

Financial due diligence is a review of the target company's financial position, financial risk and projections. The primary role in this case would be to attest the fair value of the hotels and make projections of future cash flows based on current commitments and contractual obligations. The benefit to FC would be to have a credible valuation based on the assets of Coastal. If this acquisition takes place, but the business then fails, this also provides the value to be attained by FC as an exit strategy.

The financial due diligence may support the bargain purchase review required by IFRS 3 (see above).

Property valuers will be needed for part of this process rather than Reez staff or FC staff.

Commercial due diligence

Commercial due diligence work complements that of financial due diligence by considering the target company's markets and external economic environment. Information may come from the target company and its business contacts. Alternatively, it may come from external information sources.

Such information is useful for advanced planning of an appropriate post-acquisition strategy.

Reez staff would provide some expertise and objectivity in carrying out this task but FC may also have competent staff in this respect but without any specialist experience in the hotel industry.

Operational due diligence

Operational due diligence considers the operational risks and possible improvements which can be made in a target company. In particular it will:

- validate vendor assumed operational improvements in projections.

- identify operational upsides that may increase the value of the deal to return Coastal to profit.

Again, Reez staff would provide some expertise and objectivity in carrying out this task but FC may also have competent staff in this respect, but probably without any specialist experience in the hotel industry.

Information technology due diligence

IT due diligence assesses the suitability and risks arising from IT factors in the target company. This may be a factor in improving the level of hotel bookings.

Specialist IT staff would be best placed to carry out this work.

Legal due diligence

Legal issues arising on an acquisition are likely to be relevant to the following:

- Valuation of the target company – eg hidden liabilities, uncertain rights, onerous contractual obligations

- The acquisition process – eg establishing the terms of the takeover (the investment agreement); contingent arrangements; financial restructuring; rights, duties and obligations of the various parties

- The new group – eg new articles of association, rights of finance providers, restructuring

Reliance will need to be placed on lawyers for this process rather than Reez staff or FC staff.

Human resources due diligence

Protecting and developing the rights and interests of human resources may be key to a successful acquisition. There may also be associated legal obligations.

Tax due diligence

Information will need to be provided to allow the potential purchaser to form an assessment of the tax risks and benefits associated with the company to be acquired. Purchasers will wish to assess the robustness of tax assets, and gain comfort about the position re potential liabilities (including a possible latent gain on disposal due to the low base cost). The nature of the acquisition may also be influenced by tax considerations (eg share purchase or trade and assets purchase), which in turn may be influenced by the value of the assets.

Reez tax staff would be well placed to carry out this work with respect to UK tax, but US tax specialists may also be required.

(d) **Dashboard data interpretation**

Visits and unique visits

The number of visits was 2.5 times higher than the number of unique visits indicating that potential customers are likely to make repeat visits to the site. This may be to obtain further information, demonstrating some interest, before making a booking. Targeting information towards potential customers making multiple visits using cookies may identify the most probable future customers for marketing. Further useful information may include identifying the number of visits made before a booking actually took place using the website. This may indicate the level of usage of the site before a booking is made and therefore usefulness.

The timing of visits is also important. The increased visits in April and December may be indicative of the effectiveness of the advertising campaigns. Similarly, the timing of visits when at their lowest may indicate when best to make discount offers to generate more interest.

Page views and most popular pages

The data shows that each visitor to the website looks at an average of almost 3 pages. Key further information would be to identify which pages are most popular. In developing a marketing strategy this may be indicative of what potential customers most value. For example, the 'excursions' page is one of the least popular and this may therefore be regarded as a low priority for customers in deciding whether to book an FC cruise.

Hits

A 'hit' refers to the number of files downloaded from a website, this could include photos, forms and other information. A detailed analysis of which files had the most hits would be further information as to which aspects of the cruise are of most interest to potential customers at the stage they are considering booking.

Average duration of a visit

The duration of the visit may indicate whether the interest of a potential customer is casual (a short visit) or serious (a longer visit). Targeting marketing towards those customers making longer visits could make best use of marketing resources.

Changes in the average duration of a visit from year to year may also reveal the continued attractiveness of the website as a whole.

Most popular referral site

Identifying the most popular referral sites would focus marketing attention on where to advertise (eg social media) and where to attempt to gain higher profile for FC (eg Google).

Most popular source of hits – by country

Identifying the geographical source of hits may most obviously identify where to focus advertising, but changes in the number of hits could also be indicative of shifts in popularity of a given market. If there have been movements in exchange rates this may also reflect whether this has had the effect of increasing or decreasing customers' interest. Changes in the number of hits may also be indicative of new geographical markets, particularly if further analysis of the 'Other - Europe' and 'Other' groupings can be carried out. This may indicate whether it is worth promoting marketing in these countries or increasing operations, for example by have some ships visit a port in that country to facilitate access.

Booking and payment

There were 5.27 unique visits for every actual passenger in 20X4. This indicates that over 80% of potential passengers, identified by a unique visit to the FC website, decided not to book a cruise with FC. Comparisons with other companies in the industry would need to be made to assess whether this is a reasonable success rate.

It may be difficult to link back how many actual customers used the website but a more conventional questionnaire of actual passengers during their holiday may provide some corroborative data.

The low level of bookings from the site is also indicated by the fact that only 7% of hits were on the booking and payment pages. Investigation of reasons for reluctance to use the site to book and pay may be useful in avoiding third party commissions eg to travel agents.

Email

The emails received via the website is a useful indicator of escalation of interest by potential customers from mere browsing, to an individual enquiry. This may be regarded as a stepping stone towards a booking. An analysis of these emails using software to detect key words may assess the nature of the emails and whether they ultimately resulted in a booking. This may give marketing information as to how best to respond to each type of email and where to place most focus and follow-up.

33 Landex plc (July 2014, amended)

Marking guide

		Marks
(a)	Evaluate and compare, with supporting calculations, the three investment proposals, and explain the wider operational and strategic implications	16
(b)	Provide reasoned advice on which of the two bonds would be preferable, and set out the financial reporting treatment for both bonds	11
(c)	Set out the ethical issues relating to: Ceasing to use Gootle as a supplier FD's brother and related party transactions	7
(d)	Set out any corporate governance and financial reporting issues that may arise for Landex if Rotblat were to become one of its suppliers	6
(e)	Set out the issues surrounding cyber security highlighted by the incident, the risks for the supply chain Recommend actions Landex should take in relation to improving cyber security across its supply chain	15
	Total marks	55

(a) **Proposal 1**

31 December	Price		Number of casings	Total	DF 10%	PV
	£			£		£
20X5	100		200,000	20,000,000	0.9090909	18,181,818
20X6	100		220,000	22,000,000	0.8264463	18,181,818
20X7	100		235,000	23,500,000	0.7513148	17,655,898
20X8	100		245,000	24,500,000	0.6830135	16,733,830

NPV £70,753,364

Proposal 2

31 December	Price	Exchange rate	Number of casings	Total	DF 10%	PV
	£			£		£
20X5	93	1	200,000	18,600,000	0.9090909	16,909,091
20X6	93	0.98	220,000	20,050,800	0.8264463	16,570,909
20X7	93	0.9604	235,000	20,989,542	0.7513148	15,769,754
20X8	93	0.941192	245,000	21,445,060	0.6830135	14,647,264

NPV £63,897,018

Proposal 3

Variable cost M$		40	40	40	40

31 December	20X4	20X5	20X6	20X7	20X8
Number of casings		200,000	220,000	235,000	245,000
Outlay	40,000,000				
Variable cost		8,000,000	8,800,000	9,400,000	9,800,000
Fixed costs		25,000,000	25,000,000	25,000,000	25,000,000
Proceeds on closure					(20,000,000)
Total M$	40,000,000	33,000,000	33,800,000	34,400,000	14,800,000
Exchange rate	2	1.904762	1.814059	1.727675	1.645405
Total £	20,000,000	17,325,000	18,632,250	19,911,150	8,994,746
DF 10%	1	0.9090909	0.8264463	0.7513148	0.6830135
PV	20,000,000	15,750,000	15,398,554	14,959,542	6,143,533

NPV £72,251,629

Procurement strategy – casings

Evaluation and comparison of the three proposals

Quantitative financial analysis

Comparing the figures in the above table, the choice with the lowest present value over the four-year horizon is Proposal 2 with multiple overseas suppliers. The next best is Proposal 1 which is Gootle and the highest present value is Proposal 3, which is in-house production in a new factory in Moldovia.

However the figures warrant some further analysis.

While no calculations have been performed beyond 20X8 as instructed, there is a clear trend that costs per item are decreasing with Proposal 2 due to the depreciation in the exchange rate in the basket of currencies. If this were to continue then this option would become even more attractive in narrow financial terms over time.

While Proposal 3 is the highest cost in PV terms over the four year period, it has the lowest variable cost per item of the three proposals. As a result, if demand continues to expand this is more likely to become the lowest cost option due to the high operating gearing.

The above analysis is however only a narrow financial analysis. As instructed, the operating and strategic implications of the three proposals also need to be considered.

Operating and strategic analysis

There are three choices:

(1) A single UK supplier (the existing supplier Gootle)
(2) Multiple suppliers (three internationally based suppliers)
(3) Bring production back in-house (with the Moldovian factory)

The current arrangement with Gootle can be described as one of strategic procurement. This is the development of a partnership between a company and a supplier of strategic value. The arrangement is usually long-term, single-source in nature and addresses not only the buying of parts, products, or services, but product design and supplier capacity.

This type of relationship can be beneficial for some organisations which may need to establish close links with companies in the supply chain to meet their own production needs or strategic objectives.

The following are some of the advantages to Landex from single sourcing with Gootle:

- Consistency (shape, size, quality, design) from a single supplier.

- Easier to monitor quality.

- Gootle is dependent on Landex, and is therefore more responsive to Landex's needs, if a large amount of its income is being earned from it.

- More scale economies can be earned by Gootle to reduce costs if Landex's entire supply is sourced with it. This can then be passed on to Landex in reduced prices.

- Communication, integration and synchronisation of the two companies' systems are easier (eg integrated IT systems).

- Collaboration is easier and more mutually beneficial in developing new products because all the benefits come to one supplier.

- Gootle has an existing and proven relationship with Landex and therefore there is less risk and greater awareness of its strategic capability.

However, there may also be some problems with Gootle as a single source supplier, some of which have already been experienced by Landex in recent years arsing from Gootle's inability to match Landex's rate of expansion:

- If there is an inability by Gootle to supply Landex in full then this may disrupt Landex's production. This means Landex may need to hold inventories in future.

- If there are variations in demand by Landex, a single supplier such as Gootle may not be able to satisfy these in the short term (which may be another reason for Landex to hold inventory).

- Gootle might exert upward pressure on prices if it knows Landex is tied into it for a number of years as the sole supplier and therefore has no alternative source of supply.

If Landex has multiple suppliers (as in Proposal 2) there are a number of benefits:

- Landex can drive down prices charged to it by encouraging competition between suppliers who know that Landex has a choice of alternative suppliers.

- Switching sources of supply is possible by dropping a supplier altogether if it is delivering a poor quality product or service, or at least reducing the number of purchases.

- Landex can benefit from innovation in future product development from many companies rather than just one.

However, if Landex has multiple suppliers there may be a number of problems:

- Each supplier has a smaller income from Landex than a single source supplier and so may lack commitment to development of watch case design.

- Multiple communications become more difficult and more expensive for Landex (eg more difficult to integrate multiple IT systems).

- Reduced scale economies.

- Suppliers are less likely to invest in bespoke equipment and produce a bespoke product for Landex as production volumes may be insufficient.

- All of the potential suppliers would be new and therefore this may create some initial uncertainty and front-end costs in establishing new relationships and communications systems.

Along with the issue of single and multiple suppliers, there is the simultaneous decision of UK or international suppliers. Having suppliers that are geographically remote creates a series of problems:

- The lead times and uncertainty of delivery time are greater if the geographical distances are greater such as from India, China and Vietnam. This is made worse if the watch casings vary in size or style.

- Cross border supply chains may produce regulatory, language, cultural, exchange rate and tax problems.

- Exchange rate risk exists – if the overseas currencies appreciate, then operating costs in £ terms will increase. Conversely, if the M$ fails to appreciate in the final year of the planning horizon then the disposal proceeds will be worth less in £ sterling terms.

Setting up in-house production in Moldovia (Proposal 3) has some benefits:

- Control is exercised over product quality and delivery, as the supply chain is internalised within the company.

- If demand increases, variable costs are low and profit will increase more rapidly than the other alternatives due to high operating gearing.

- Price negotiation and renegotiation are avoided, as prices are internal transfer prices.

- Landex can benefit from controlling innovation in future product development and it stands to gain the entire benefit from doing so, without sharing with external suppliers.

Setting up in-house production in Moldovia has some risks:

- There is high operating gearing from fixed costs so if planned expansion does not occur, then profit would be very sensitive to a shortfall in sales.

- Management may be distracted from the normal day-to-day operations by setting up a production site in Moldovia and this may have an adverse effect on sales.

- Landex may no longer have the core competences in watch casing production as it has not made them for 10 years, and even then only in the UK. As such, to invest in what is not a core activity or a core competence may be subject to high risks that need not be taken.

Advice

The current supplier, Gootle, has proved reliable and therefore reduces risk and gives assurance over quality. Landex may thus be best continuing with Gootle as sole supplier but, in negotiations on price and service, the possibility of multiple suppliers could be raised in order to obtain the best possible contract terms.

Any decision need not be permanent and any commitment to Gootle could be made conditional on service levels achieved over time and commitments on price.

Four-year horizon

Four years may be considered to be too short a planning horizon to recover the initial outlay for Proposal 3. A longer and more realistic planning horizon seems likely to favour this proposal strongly. The low variable cost per unit means that over a long time period increased output can benefit from higher contributions per unit for Proposal 3 compared with the two other proposals.

There are other factors to consider:

- The assumed annual exchange rate movements (5% appreciation of M$; and 2% depreciation of the basket of currencies) are unlikely to be sustained in the longer term with efficient currency markets unless there is a long term disparity in interest rates with £ sterling rates. The PV changes over the four year horizon are therefore unlikely to be sustained beyond four years.

- Contracts may be renegotiated after four years under Proposals 1 and 2 which may mean either more favourable or less favourable pricing. Such negotiations would not apply to Proposal 3.

(b) **Methods of financing initial investment in Moldovian factory**

Financial assessment

Alternative 1 – M$40m, zero coupon bond

The annual cost of debt is M$ terms is $[(117/100)^{1/4} - 1] = 4\%$ per annum

However, the functional currency of Landex is the £ and the M$ is forecast to appreciate against the £ over the 4-year term of the bond from its current level of M$2 = £1. As a result, the exchange rate on 31 December 20X8, when the bond is due to be redeemed, is expected to be £1= M$1.645405 (ie M$2/1.05^4).

As a consequence, in £ sterling terms, the bond generates £20m when issued and requires £28.4428m (ie M$40m × 1.17/1.645405) to redeem it.

The annual cost of debt to Landex in £ sterling terms is therefore $[(28.4428/20)^{1/4} - 1] = \textbf{9.203\%}$ per annum.

Alternative 2 – £20m, 5% bond

The coupon rate on the bond is 5% giving annual interest payments of £1m in arrears. However, the cost of debt needs to consider the 2% fee for the investment bank. Under this alternative, the effective rate of interest on the bond (i) is:

$$(£20m × 0.98) = £1m/(1 + i) + £1m/(1 + i)^2 + £1m/(1 + i)^3 + £21m/(1 + i)^4$$

Solving for i (by iteration, estimation or linear interpolation) the effective rate of interest on the bond is **5.57%** per annum.

Thus, in sterling terms the UK bond has a lower cost of debt by some margin.

Advice

Not only is the 5% sterling bond lower cost, but it is also lower risk. There is a risk with the zero coupon bond that the M$ may appreciate even more than the 5% pa expected.

Also the M$ bond adds to the operating foreign exchange risk rather than hedging it, as it adds even more costs in M$.

The clear advice is therefore to issue the 5% sterling bond.

Financial reporting

Alternative 1 – M$40m, zero coupon bond

This bond is a monetary item thus the liability, including accrued interest, is translated at the year end exchange rate each year in accordance with IAS 21. Any exchange rate movement is recognised in profit or loss.

The effective interest on the bond is recognised through profit or loss each year, even though it is not paid.

Year	Opening balance M$m	Interest 4% M$	Closing balance M$m	Exchange rate M$	Closing balance (SOFP) £m	Movement (profit/loss) £m
20X5	40	1.6	41.6	1.904762	21.84	1.840
20X6	41.6	1.664	43.264	1.814059	23.849	2.009
20X7	43.264	1.73056	44.99456	1.727675	26.043	2.194
20X8	44.99456	1.7997824	46.794342	1.645405	28.439	2.396

REDEMPTION
17%   46.8
ROUNDING   0.0056578

The movement goes to profit or loss comprising both the loan interest and the retranslation of the liability as a monetary item.

Alternative 2 – £20m, 5% bond

Year	Opening balance £m	Interest 5.57%	Cash paid £m	Closing balance £m
20X5	19.6	1.09172	1	19.69172
20X6	19.69172	1.096829	1	19.78855
20X7	19.78855	1.102222	1	19.89077
20X8	19.89077	1.107916	21	0

Rounding   -0.00131

The interest is charged to profit or loss in accordance with IAS 32.

The closing balance at the end of each year is shown as a liability in the statement of financial position.

(c) **Ethics**

Ceasing to use Gootle

An ethical principle in this case is one of honesty in assessing whether there was an intention by the chairman, 10 years ago, to honour his statement or to mislead to gain short term advantage of reduced redundancy costs.

A key factor is the passage of time and the capacity of the chairman to bind the board's actions 10 years later. On this basis, there does not seem any overwhelming ethical obligation to maintain Gootle as a supplier.

However, Landex could consider whether there is any ethical obligation to employees to make additional payments now.

Indeed, to maintain Gootle as a supplier, if they were not the best choice on commercial grounds would be an ethical breach by the Landex board towards its shareholders to whom the board owes their primary duty.

Use of Rotblat as a supplier

The ethical principle in this case is a conflict of interest by the finance director both in being influential in determining who obtains the contract and, if the contract is awarded to Rotblat, in obtaining more favourable terms than would be available on an arm's length basis to other suppliers.

The ethical safeguards would be transparency so the board is aware of the relationship (the FD seems to have done this in 'declaring an interest'). Also, the role of the FD in the decision as to who should be awarded the supply contract should be minimised. The fact that two other directors are putting forward alternative proposals appears to be some safeguard, showing that there is active debate within the board.

There may be a suggestion of an intimidation threat if non board members, such as myself, make arguments contrary to the proposals of the FD. This needs to be safeguarded against by openness and transparency and, if the FD is an ICAEW Chartered Accountant, he is bound by their ethical code.

(d) **Corporate governance and financial reporting**

Corporate governance

The board of directors is a key stakeholder and is fundamental to corporate governance. In this case a key member of the board, the finance director, has potential influence over two key decisions:

- Whether to have Rotblat as a supplier.

- If Rotblat becomes a supplier, the terms on which the contract is made and manner in which the service monitored.

A key corporate governance issue is that the finance director, as a key member of the board, can potentially influence these decisions in which she has a personal interest. There is therefore a risk that contracts may be undertaken or continued that are not in the best interests of the company.

One safeguard would be for the finance director to be excluded from decisions in respect of the supply contracts for watch casings. If this is not possible or reasonable then she should be excluded from voting on such matters.

Financial reporting

Consideration needs to be given as to whether a contract with Rotblat would be a related party transaction in accordance with IAS 24.

The finance director, Catherine Jurys, as a member of the board is part of key management personnel and is therefore a related party.

IAS 24, para 9, also deems close family members of key management personnel to be related parties if they may be expected to influence, or be influenced by, them in their dealings with the company. While a brother is not one of the examples given of close family members in IAS 24, the general test of influence applies.

It is a question of fact whether Catherine Jurys' brother is likely to influence her, or be influenced by her, in respect of the Rotblat supply contract. A safe underlying initial assumption, in the absence of evidence to the contrary, is that there is such an influence. The fact that Catherine is strongly supportive of the Rotblat proposition, rather than being neutral, is indicative of such influence.

If it is ultimately deemed that it is a related party contract, then the nature of the contract should be disclosed in accordance with IAS 24, para 19. In addition, the amount of the transactions, outstanding balances, commitments, guarantees and bad debts should be disclosed.

(e) **Cyber security**

The cyber incident and the existing response

The cyber incident in October with Coggs has illustrated Landex's vulnerability to cyber attacks from external sources in the supply chain.

As a first step in respect of that data incident the board needs to establish that:

- there has been full data cleansing and systems cleansing such that there is no continued contamination from the breach.

- a similar incident could not occur such that files from suppliers are in future tested for malware with a firewall, the same as from non-trusted external communications.

While the specific cause of the attack and its consequences can be addressed by the above measures the incident highlights the risk from other types of cyber attack and from other sources in the supply chain. This emphasises that the earlier report by the IT department was too limited in focusing only on internal direct risks. It also appears to be too limited in viewing cyber security as a technical risk, rather than a business risk where responsibility is throughout the organisation, not just in the sphere of the IT department.

Supply chain risks – issues to consider

The supply chain is just one set of external partners from which cyber risk could arise. Other external sources of cyber risks include: customers; business partners; IT service providers; and subcontractors. All these external relationships should be part of a wider review, but suppliers are the focus of the current report.

It may be unproductive and unrealistic to gain assurance over all suppliers and therefore a degree of prioritisation is required in any cyber security risk management strategy. It is important to target efforts on the greatest risk suppliers, which may not be the same as the highest value suppliers.

Those suppliers with IT systems which are integrated with Landex represent one of the greatest risks. Small companies which do not have a significant IT security budget may also be a significant risk.

It is also important to make cyber assurance part of an ongoing process, not a one-off exercise. This is likely to require establishing appropriate processes and procedures over the entire life cycle of a supply contract.

In the October cyber incident, the attack accessed the procurement system. This is a key risk as it can trigger payments. The payments system should therefore be a key focus in reviewing cyber risks in the supply chain.

Recommendations for action

For selected suppliers which have been identified as a significant cyber risk, it is important to consider the nature of any critical business relationships alongside IT security. This may require building a culture of a common approach to risk and a common risk vocabulary, rather than imposing conditions. This may involve sharing data security across the supply chain, including tier 2 and tier 3 suppliers (ie suppliers of suppliers). ISO 27000 series could provide a benchmark for required standards and for due diligence.

If co-operation is not forthcoming, the business consequences of losing the services of a supplier may need to be weighed against cyber risks.

Service level agreements with suppliers may need to include transparency and access conditions to suppliers' files and systems in order to obtain assurance as a condition of doing business. This will facilitate ongoing IT due diligence procedures throughout the life cycle of the supply contract. Service level agreements may also include penalty clauses for cyber breaches in order to provide incentives for suppliers to comply with conditions and install IT security systems.

34 Firebrand Forklift Trucks Ltd (November 2014)

	Marks
Prepare a report which:	
(a) Explains the decline in FFT's profit over the years ended 31 December 20X2, 20X3 and 20X4. Recommend actions which may improve profitability in future.	(13)
(b) With respect to the financial reconstruction scheme:	
Evaluates the effects of the scheme and compares these with the effects of liquidation, setting out the benefits and risks for various stakeholders and providing supporting calculations.	(17)
Shows and explains the financial reporting implications for the financial statements for the year ending 31 December 20X4 if, at that date, negotiations are still ongoing between FFT and the bank regarding restructuring of the loan.	(8)
(c) With respect to the proposal to boost revenue:	
Evaluates, with supporting calculations, the benefits and risks to FFT of leasing, compared with selling, the FZ101 forklift truck to customers.	(5)
Explains how a lease for an FZ101 forklift truck would be treated in the FFT financial statements.	(5)
(d) Advises the FFT board how it should respond to the email from the journalist. Please indicate any further actions that FFT should take with regard to this matter, now that the issue has been brought to its attention.	(6)
(e) Sets out any ethical issues for DH arising from giving advice to FFT in response to the journalist's communication.	(6)
Total marks	60

Handwritten annotation: } 12

(a) Decline in profit

	Forecast 20X4	Actual 20X3	Actual 20X2
% change sales revenue	(3.9%)	(1.3%)	
% change sales volumes	1.7%	4.2%	
% change gross profit	(3.8%)	(7.9%)	
Gross profit %	28.0%	28.0%	30.0%
Operating (loss)/profit %	(1.2%)	(0.7%)	1.3%
Price per truck £	17,000	18,001	18,998
% change in price	(5.6%)	(5.2%)	
Operating profit per truck £	(204)	(132)	251
Backlog (days)	152	122	91

Revenue

There has been a clear decline in sales revenues over the period 20X2 to 20X4 represented by decreases of 3.9% in 20X4 and 1.3% in 20X3.

Sales volumes and prices are two possible causes of why these decreases in sales revenues have occurred. However, sales volumes have actually increased by 1.7% in 20X4 and 4.2% in 20X3, so this was not the cause of the decrease in revenues.

The explanation therefore relates to decreases in average prices of 5.6% in 20X4 and 5.2% in 20X3, which outweigh the volume increases. In trying to identify underlying causal factors, it may be that there has been a uniform decrease in price in an attempt to sell more units. This explanation may lack plausibility, however, due to the backlog in demand, which means it would be difficult to satisfy a price induced demand increase as production is at capacity. Also, if this was the policy, then it appears unsuccessful with inelastic demand producing a fall in revenues.

An alternative explanation is a change in the product mix being sold, with a higher proportion of lower price trucks being purchased by customers in 20X4 compared to earlier years.

Profits

Despite the decrease in selling price, the gross profit % remained constant at 28% in 20X4 compared with 20X3. This may be indicative that the mix argument may have weight as, although prices were lower, the cost of sales was also commensurately lower. The gross profit margin was however lower in 20X4 and 20X3, compared to 20X2, when it was 30%.

In looking at absolute figures, rather than % margins, gross profit decreased by 3.8% in 20X4 and 7.9% in 20X3, thereby setting the conditions for an operating loss.

Indeed, while administrative expenses and distribution costs have been reduced in 20X3 and again in 20X4 this has not been sufficient to prevent an operating loss being made due to the lower gross profit.

Operating efficiency

A key factor in generating the loss has been an inability to satisfy customer demand as reflected in the backlog of unsatisfied orders. In terms of days sales, the backlog has grown from 91 days in 20X2; to 122 days in 20X3; and then to 152 days in 20X4 (16,350/39,235 x 365 days). At 20X4 prices this represents approximately £278m in lost sales which, at the average gross margin, would mean £77.8m in lost profit.

The raw backlog figures may also understate the severity of the problem, as there may be many customers who would wish to buy from FFT, but are unwilling to wait and therefore have not placed orders.

Improvements in operating efficiency may generate an ability to satisfy the backlog by increasing capacity and therefore increasing sales volumes, which could generate significant additional revenue and profit.

Recommendations for actions

Possible actions could be to:

- improve operating efficiency to generate greater output from the existing asset base. For example review operating management procedures, labour productivity and production scheduling.

- increase the scale of operation by investing in new assets to raise production capacity.

- increase prices until the backlog is removed or reduced through lower demand at higher prices.

- renegotiate the onerous contract with Jitsumi – as it has a significant amount to lose if FFT is forced into liquidation.

(b) **Financial reconstruction plan**

  (1) **Evaluation**

  Liquidation

  Funds generated on liquidation (legal rights)

	£'000
Property, plant and equipment	83,300
Inventories	13,300
Trade receivables	19,500
Total	**116,100**

With a liquidation, the funds would be distributed:

	£'000
Proceeds	116,100
Liquidator's fee	(3,200)
	112,900
Paid to holders of fixed charge: (PPE proceeds)	(83,300)
Remaining funds	29,600

The remainder of the fixed charge in respect of the loan becomes a floating charge ie £16.7m (£100m – £83.3m).

Floating charge:

	£'000
Loan	16,700
Overdraft	35,300
	52,000

Funds available: (£112.9m – £83.3m) £29.6m

The liquidator would pay 56.9p in the £ to creditors holding a floating charge.

Unsecured creditors and shareholders would receive nothing (but see tutorial note below).

Overall, the bank would recover £112.9m (£83.3m + £29.6m) of the £135.3m owing to it. This is an 83.4% recovery giving a write off to the bank of £22.4m.

Tutorial note:

Unsecured creditors would actually receive a small sum as the prescribed part.

Comparison of liquidation and financial reconstruction scheme

If the proposed financial reconstruction goes ahead on the suggested terms then stakeholders will be impacted in a variety of ways as follows:

Kittminster Bank

Under the proposed reconstruction scheme Kittminster Bank is being offered a medium term loan at 8% of £120m. This is greater than the £112.9m which would be received by the bank under statutory liquidation terms but there are a number of further factors to consider:

- Under liquidation, the bank has cash of £112.9m to reinvest elsewhere and is able to reassess the risk of the new investment.

- Under the financial reconstruction the £120m remains invested in FFT and therefore continues to be risk capital.

- The new 8% interest rate is a higher return for the bank than previously at 5% but the risks are likely to be different (or at least the perceived risks) so an assessment needs to be made of the adequacy of the 8% return for the risks now to be taken by the bank following the reconstruction.

- The shareholders would inject new equity capital under the reconstruction scheme which would lower gearing and lower the risk of the bank. This assumes that they are willing to invest again (see below).

- If the projected operating profit of £14m is achieved, there may be a reasonable return overall (but assurance over this figure will be needed) and there would be sufficient earnings to pay interest in future with a margin of safety as follows:

	£'000
Operating profit	14,000
Interest (£120m × 8%)	(9,600)
Profit before tax	4,400
Tax	(880)
Profit after tax	3,520

This gives an interest cover of 1.46.

An alternative way of considering the issue is to look at sensitivity, such that if operating profit falls by 31.4% there is only just enough profit to cover interest (interest cover of 1) and nothing is left over for shareholders.

Shareholders

On <u>liquidation</u>, the shareholders would not receive any distribution.

Under the reconstruction scheme they would be required to inject £10m of new capital and they are assumed to require a 10% return on this capital.

The original loss on existing share capital is a sunk cost so the current question for shareholders is whether the £10m injection is as good as a new stand-alone investment.

The forecast annual return is £3.52m which is 35.2%. An alternative way of examining the issue is that discounted in perpetuity at 10% the income stream would be worth £35.2m for a £10m investment.

However, a degree of professional scepticism needs to be applied to the projections as there appears to be no supporting evidence for these figures and FFT management have strong incentives for optimism to persuade shareholders to invest.

Trade suppliers

Suppliers have a lot to lose from liquidation and have no direct control over this decision.

Suppliers are unsecured creditors and would not receive any distribution on liquidation (other than a small amount in respect of the prescribed part) whereas they are intended to be paid £2m under the reconstruction scheme and, if FFT continues to operate, then in time they may receive full repayment. It is not clear from the terms of the arrangement whether operating cash flows would be sufficient to pay the suppliers. On liquidation, suppliers would also lose a future customer and the profits on this business.

For Jitsumi the long term contract with FFT would be void on liquidation and any excess profits being earned on this contract would be lost in future.

As a result, it may be unnecessarily generous to pay suppliers £2m in a reconstruction scheme and it may be an opportunity to renegotiate contracts and search for alternative suppliers.

If the suppliers attempted to force settlement through the courts they would not receive anything on liquidation, as the secured creditor (the bank) would stand ahead of them.

(2) **Financial reporting**

According to IAS 1 *Presentation of Financial Statements*, going concern means that an entity is normally viewed as continuing in operation for the foreseeable future. Financial statements are prepared on the going concern basis unless FFT management either intends to liquidate the entity or to cease trading or has no realistic alternative but to do so.

IAS 1 makes the following points:

- In assessing whether the entity is a going concern management must look at least twelve months into the future measured from the end of the reporting period (not from the date the financial statements are approved). Realistically the negotiations with Kittminster Bank should be completed by then.

- Uncertainties that may cast significant doubt on the entity's ability to continue should be disclosed. This would require disclosure of the situation when the financial statements are authorised for issue. Although the negotiations with Kittminster may not be completed by 31 December 20X4, they may well be completed when the financial statements are authorised for issue. Full disclosure of the agreement could then take place.

- If the going concern assumption is not followed (eg because the negotiations have been concluded and the liquidation decision has been decided upon, or it is apparent that this is the most probable outcome) that fact must be disclosed together with:

  — The basis on which financial statements have been prepared
  — The reasons why the entity is not considered to be a going concern

- IFRSs do not prescribe the basis to be used if the going concern assumption is no longer considered appropriate. A liquidation or break-up basis may be appropriate, using the values provided in Exhibit 4, but the terms of the insolvency arrangement may also dictate the form of preparation.

When making the judgement of whether the going concern basis is not appropriate, the following indications taken from ISA 570 *Going Concern*, may be significant:

— Financial indicators, in this case the default on Kittminster Bank
— Operating matters, competitive conditions leading to operating losses
— Other matters

In relation to going concern, IAS 10 *Events after the Reporting Period* states that, where operating results and the financial position have deteriorated after the reporting period, it may be necessary to reconsider whether the going concern assumption remains appropriate.

In addition, it may be appropriate to make a provision for the onerous contract with Jitsumi.

All bank borrowings will be shown as immediately repayable at year end – ie bank loan is a current liability.

(c) New financing package for customers

(1) Evaluation

If 8.24% is the annual interest rate, then the quarterly rate is $1.0824^{1/4} - 1 = 2\%$.

We therefore need to discount the quarterly income stream of 12 receipts of £1,200 over 3 years and residual of £4,000 after 3 years as follows:

$(AF12@2\% \times £1,200) + 4,000/(1.0824)^3$

$= £12,696 + £3,154$
$= £15,850$

On this basis the present value of the lease rental receipts is lower than the cash sale price. This would indicate that if this scheme came into operation FFT would be worse off if a customer substituted a leasing arrangement for a straight purchase at £16,200.

In addition, there is liquidity risk whereby, if running out of cash continues to be a problem then leasing will defer cash receipts compared with a straight sale and thereby add to liquidity problems.

In favour of the leasing arrangement it may be attractive to customers, particularly if they themselves have liquidity issues. It may therefore generate additional customer orders. However this is only of benefit if the production capacity is increased and the backlog of unfulfilled orders is reduced or removed, so the additional orders can be satisfied.

(2) Financial reporting

FFT would be recognised as a dealer lessor in accordance with IAS 17.

It would appear that, on balance, the lease arrangement for the FZ101 is an operating lease. The factors that indicate this are:

- The useful life appears to be significantly longer than the lease term (some lease contracts in the industry are for six years and if this also applies to the FZ101 then the lease term is only half of the useful life).

- The residual value of £4,000 after three years indicates that FFT as lessor retains material risks and rewards in the asset. (Using the interest rate provided as an approximation to the implicit interest rate then, using the above calculations, the present value of the residual at £3,154 is almost 20% of the fair value of the asset.)

As a consequence, the rentals are credited to the statement of profit or loss over the lease term on a straight line basis. Thus, for any one year, credit would be taken as revenue for £4,800 per machine.

In the statement of financial position of FFT the FZ101 would continue to be recognised as an asset, as risks and rewards have not transferred to the lessee.

No selling profit is recognised by FFT on entering into the operating lease because it is not the equivalent of a sale (IAS 17 para 55).

(d) **Advice to FFT**

The formal response should be minimal at this stage until the full facts of the situation are established.

There appear to be two issues:

(1) Is FFT providing clear instructions such that customers are aware that they should not use FFT trucks indoors as they have diesel engines which can cause harmful emissions?

(2) Has FFT any responsibility for customers who, having understood the instructions and are therefore aware of the emission issues, decide to use them in an inappropriate way?

FFT claims to make clear that its diesel engine forklift trucks should not be used indoors. It does this both prior to the sale and in the documentation accompanying the product when it is delivered.

FFT should look again at its documentation and procedures to ensure that a full understanding is conveyed. It may not necessarily be the duty of FFT to provide this information in every local language, so long as the information is communicated clearly. Legal advice should be obtained in this respect.

Regarding the use of the vehicles indoors, this may be illegal or legal depending on the countries in which they are being operated. It may be that FFT does not have responsibility or liability in this respect for the way in which the vehicle has been used. It cannot know or monitor every customer's usage, nor be responsible for the consequences of reckless actions so long as it has made the customer aware of the appropriate usage. Where it becomes aware of illegal behaviour it should consider its duty to disclose to the relevant authorities based on legal advice.

Overall, the incident raises questions of FFT's corporate responsibility which need to be addressed in order to protect reputation. In this respect, FFT needs to manage the underlying substance of the accusations and also the related capacity of the publicity to change perceptions of customers, potential customers and other stakeholders.

(e) **Ethical implications for DH**

It is important with any ethical issue that we first obtain the facts, rather than rely on information from the journalist or FFT.

Having established the facts we need to make a judgement whether FFT has acted legally, ethically and appropriately before providing any type of support in this matter. It is not appropriate to provide legal or technical support which is outside our firm's areas of expertise.

With regard to the instructions accompanying the vehicle, the ethical issue is one of transparency. This means that FFT needs to have made clear how the trucks can be used and conveyed an understanding of this irrespective of the language.

An additional ethical issue is honesty. The FFT board needs to ensure that FFT staff have not tried to claim that the trucks are suitable for indoor use in order to make a sale.

If an illegal act has been, or is being, committed, we need to ascertain our responsibility as to whether we have a duty to disclose this matter to the appropriate authorities in the relevant jurisdiction. We should take our own legal advice in this respect.

It may not be appropriate to support FFT in any legal dispute as this may give rise to an advocacy threat.

35 Washing Solutions Ltd (November 2014)

		Marks
(a)	Analyse and explain the decline in the Industral Division's tendering success during the year ended 30 September 20X4, compared with the year ended 30 September 20X3.	10
(b)	Explain, with supporting calculations, why the actual profit differs from the budgeted profit for each of the two divisions, and for the company as a whole, for the year ended 30 Septmber 20X4.	13
(c)	Analyse and explain:	
	The effect that the overhead cost allocations had on pricing in the Industrial Division in the year ended 30 September 20X4; and	4
	The problems which arise in using the overhead cost allocations for valuing inventories for financial reporting purposes in the WS financial statements.	4
(d)	With regard to the offer from Hexam to acquire the Industrial Division, explain:	
	The strategic, operating and financial factors that the WS board needs to consider before deciding whether to sell the Industrial Division to Hexam; and	4
	The risks arising, and the due diligence procedures that should be carried out by WS on Hexam, in respect of using the shares as consideration.	5
Total marks		40

(a) Tendering performance

Data analysis – Industrial Division tenders

	20X3	20X4	% change
Number of tenders made	900	800	(11.1%)
Success rate	30%	10%	(66.7%)
Number of washing machines sold under successful tenders	8,100	1,760	(78.3%)
Number of machines per tender	28	25	(10.7%)
Number of machines per successful tender	30	22	(26.7%)
Price per machine tendered	£1,200	£1,400	16.7%
Price per machine sold under tenders	£1,200	£1,300	8.3%

Tenders made

There has been an 11.1% fall in the number of tenders made in 20X4 compared to 20X3. It is not clear whether this is because there were fewer tenders available from government, or whether WS considered it was not worth making some tenders due to the poor success rate. More information is needed.

Tenders won

There has been a significant fall (66.7%) in the proportion of tenders won in 20X4 compared to 20X3. The most obvious apparent causal factor for the reduced tender success rate is the increase in the average price tendered, which has risen 16.7% from £1,200 to £1,400.

A word of caution is that we may not be comparing like with like in that the type of washing machine sold in 20X4 may be larger or better than those in 20X3.

However, we are informed that extra labour costs have been incurred with additional overhead allocated and that these have been built into the price for customers (see Section (c) below). It seems therefore that the most obvious explanation is that the additional price charged has meant the loss of more tenders, notwithstanding the quality improvements.

Machines sold

The fall in the number of tenders won has resulted in the most revealing statistic which is the fall in the number of washing machines sold of 78.3%.

The fall in machines sold is actually greater than the fall in tenders won, because when tenders have been won they have been smaller in 20X4 than 20X3 by 26.7%, falling from 30 to 22 machines sold per tender won.

Conclusion

Overall the key factor has been the fall in tenders won due to the increase in price. This severely questions the reasons for the extent of the increase in price. This issue is addressed below when looking at the costing systems.

(b) **Evaluation of performance**

Data analysis – actual data

		20X4	
	Industrial	Household	Total
	£'000	£'000	£'000
Sales	2,288.0	4,800.0	7,088.0
Materials	(809.6)	(1,488.0)	(2,297.6)
Labour	(70.4)	(192.0)	(262.4)
Variable overhead: set ups	(100.0)	(1,000.0)	(1,100.0)
Variable overhead: labour hours	(140.8)	(384.0)	(524.8)
Contribution	1,167.2	1,736.0	2,903.2
Fixed overhead			(3,225.2)
Loss			(322.0)

Reconciliation 20X4

	£
Variable overhead set ups	1,100,000
Variable overhead labour hours	524,800
Fixed overhead (residual)	3,225,200
Total overhead (per exhibit 3A)	4,850,000

Overview

Based on actual data, the performance for the household division has been constant, while the performance of the industrial division has declined significantly. The overall contribution of the Industrial Division has fallen by 74.9% from £4,651,600 to £1,167,200.

In the above table, fixed overhead costs are not allocated, but are treated as an actual company-wide cost. When these fixed costs are deducted, the company has made a small loss of £322,000 in 20X4.

Budgetary cost allocations

		20X4	
	Industrial	Household	Total
	£'000	£'000	£'000
Sales	2,288.0	4,800.0	7,088.0
Materials	(809.6)	(1,488.0)	(2,297.6)
Labour	(70.4)	(192.0)	(262.4)
Overhead allocated at £100 per budgeted labour hour	(4,000.0)	(2,400.0)	(6,400.0)
Budgeted profit	(2,592.0)	720.0	(1,872.0)
Over/(Under) recovery			* 1,550.0
Profit/(Loss)			(322.0)

*£6.4m – £4.85m

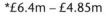

This table shows that the cost allocation system attributes fixed overheads to each division. This method generates a significant loss for the Industrial Division for 20X4 as the additional labour hours attribute not just additional labour cost but also the share of overhead which is allocated on a labour hours basis.

Additionally the high fixed cost budget has meant an over-recovery of fixed costs as actual overheads reflect the lower variable overhead cost which fell with the lower output in 20X4.

While the allocations distort divisional profit, the overall profit for the company is identical in both the above tables once adjustment is made for under/over recovery.

The distortion in divisional profit through arbitrary overhead allocations between the two divisions shows a large loss for the Industrial Division. This can be contrasted with the positive contribution for the Industrial Division in the earlier table.

Reconciliation of actual profit with original budgeted profit

20X4

	£
Original Budgeted profit	3,120,000
(£300 × 8,000) + (£60 × 12,000)	
Sales Volume Variance [(1,760 – 8,000) × (£1,300 – 460 – 40)]	(4,992,000) (A)
Overhead expenditure variance	
(£6.4m – £4.85m)	1,550,000 (F)
Actual loss (see table above)	(322,000)

(c) **Effect of cost allocations**

Effect on pricing

The key causal factor in reducing profit has been the fall in revenue from the Industrial Division. This in turn has arisen from pricing the product too highly in tenders. The high price seems to have stemmed from the effect of overhead cost allocations on the cost plus pricing policy.

The following analysis shows an apparent increase in full cost per unit of £100 for industrial machines (from £900 to £1,000).

Cost per unit:	20X3	20X4
	£	£
Materials	468	460
Labour (@ £8 per hour)	32	40
Overhead (@ £100 per labour hour)	400	500
Cost per unit	900	1,000

The selling price has also increased by £100 per unit (from £1,200 to £1,300), presumably in an attempt to cover the additional costs. In so doing, volumes sold and profit have fallen dramatically.

The error made was in assuming that costs had increased by £100 per unit when in fact the actual cost arising from the quality improvements only increased by one labour hour at £8; plus the variable overhead recovery element on labour hours of £16. This is a total of £24 additional costs incurred, rather than £100 which included arbitrary allocations of fixed costs. The fall in materials costs offered the opportunity to restrict the price increase further, although it is unclear whether this relates to the quality improvements.

The arbitrary allocation of fixed costs based on labour hours, when labour hours do not cause most of these costs, has led to an incorrect pricing decision.

If WS's present costing and pricing system continues, the government may no longer see WS as a cost efficient and effective supplier and remove it from the approved list.

Valuing inventory

Valuation of inventories is addressed by IAS 2. This standard requires production overhead to be included in inventory, based on the normal level of activity. This creates three problems for WS:

- Overheads appear to include all overheads for WS. Only production overheads are permitted by IAS 2 to be included in inventory values. The budgetary cost system therefore needs to identify administrative overheads separately.

- The 20X4 level is not the normal level of activity for WS for the Industrial Division, so some of the overhead will have to be written off in the period rather than carried forward into the next period as part of the value of inventories.

- For the Industrial Division, the total cost appears to exceed the sales value. As a result these inventories would need to be written down to net realisable value.

As a consequence, the information gathered by the WS budgetary system would need to be adjusted in the above ways in order to determine a figure for inventories in the published financial statements.

(d) **Offer from Hexam**

Factors to consider

Strategic factors

The industrial division has been part of the long term strategy of WS for some time. There would appear to be some synergies between the household machines and industrial machines on the production side, even if not on the marketing side.

One poor year of performance, based on a mispricing decision that can be reversed, should not deflect WS from its long term strategy which appears to have been successful prior to 20X4.

There therefore seems little imperative to alter the strategic direction either because of one bad year or because an offer is being considered by Hexam. There is however a strong need to review the changes to the costing systems and review the changes made to pricing and products.

Operating factors

There appear to be some joint processes between the industrial and household machines. The impact of removing the Industrial Division may therefore have a significant impact on the efficiency of the remaining Household Division production facility. Examples might be: under employed production lines; and specialist staff who work on both products who may be under employed.

Also at a practical level if there are shared assets between the two processes it is not clear whether these will be taken by Hexam (in which case WS may not have an operational factory or may need to buy new assets). Alternatively, if WS retains the assets, it is not clear what Hexam is buying.

Financial factors

The acceptance of any offer will depend on price. In this case, it is the value of the shares being offered in consideration. If this price is sufficiently high then this could compensate for the strategic and operational issues above and still make a deal acceptable to WS.

However, credibly, it may be doubtful if Hexam could gain sufficient additional value from operating the Industrial Division that such a price would be offered.

If the Industrial Division is sold, then there is a major financial issue for WS that in future it would need to cover all its fixed costs, which are a high proportion of total costs, just from the Household Division revenues.

Risks and due diligence

Hexam is an unlisted company hence there are significant risks around determining a value for Hexam shares.

There are further risks for determining the value of a minority holding of Hexam shares. This is particularly the case where the holding, as in this case, is less than 25%, so the majority shareholders can change the articles of association. A shareholder agreement could provide some protection, but this would depend on the terms of the agreement.

In determining a value for Hexam, due diligence could obtain evidence from market transactions as a best source. For example:

- Has a bundle of shares in Hexam been acquired recently (eg by one of the private equity firms)?

- Have credible offers been made for Hexam or a bundle of its shares?

- Have companies similar to Hexam (size; same industry) been traded recently?

- Have bundles of shares in companies similar to Hexam been traded recently?

In the absence of such market evidence then models could be used to determine a value for Hexam (eg earnings growth models; free cash flow). Discounts on pro rata values would need to be made to reflect a lack of liquidity and a lack of control.

A key factor affecting any liquidity discount would be the level of certainty surrounding the possible AIM listing in 20X8. If this occurs it would give a possible exit route for WS to sell Hexam shares. Given that most of the other shares are held by private equity there is some assurance that they also would wish to obtain an exit route through an AIM listing to realise their investment in the medium term.

Legal due diligence would be needed for any shareholder agreement. This could give rights to WS to protect their interest in the shares. For example, a right to a dividend or other distributions. Perhaps also the right for a seat on the Hexam board.

36 Commex Cables plc (July 2015)

Marking guide

		Marks
(a)	Apply working assumptions to perform calculations to determine NPV. Perform sensitivity calculations. Use judgement based on the sensitivity calculations to evaluate the extent of exchange rate risk. Identify the nature of different supply chains and structure answer to address each.	23
(b)	Structure answer around the key features of the two types of loan. Draw comparisons between the two types of loan under each of the headings, distinguishing key differences. Judgement to provide a reasoned recommendation which uses and follows on from the preceding analysis Assimilate information to provide an explanation of why the interest rate should differ between the two loans.	10
(c)	Use judgement to identify key risks to be addressed by an assurance report. Identify issues of providing assurance over forecast information (ISAE 3400). Address specific assurance issues with each loan.	10
(d)	Use judgement to identify and select key issues for each strategy. Identify and explain issues relating to consolidation and foreign currency as key issues.	9
(e)	Use ethical language and principles. Identify key ethical issues with respect to the letter to John from the BTZ finance director. Set out the actions to be taken by relevant parties.	8
Total marks		60

(a) Alternative strategies

NPV

Strategy 1

	1 Jan 20X6	31 Dec 20X6	31 Dec 20X7	31 Dec 20X8 & thereafter	Total PV
Initial outlay A$'000	(63,000)				
Operating CF A$'000			(100)	6,875	
DF	1		$1/1.08^2$	$1/(1.08^2/0.08)$	
PV A$'000	(63,000)		(86)	73,678	10,592
XR	1.8		1.8	1.8	
PV £'000	(35,000)		(48)	40,932	5,884

Strategy 2

	1 Jan 20X6	31 Dec 20X6	31 Dec 20X7 & thereafter	Total PV
Initial outlay A$'000	(4,000)			
Operating CF A$'000			855	
DF	1		$1/(1.08/0.08)$	
PV A$'000	(4,000)		9,896	5,896
XR	1.8		1.8	
PV £'000	(2,222)		5,498	3,276

Exchange rate fluctuations

Strategy 1

The initial outlay is at a known exchange rate and therefore is, in effect, fixed in £ sterling terms. All subsequent operating cash flows are in A$ for Strategy 1. This exchange mismatch could be reflected in a significant depreciation of the A$ against the £ sterling which would make cash inflows less valuable and therefore it would be more difficult to recover the initial outflow in NPV terms.

The sensitivity calculations (see below) show that a one-off exchange rate shift of 16.8% depreciation of the A$ against the £ would generate a zero NPV based on the data provided.

Other exchange rate considerations for Strategy 1 are that revenues are generated from South East Asian countries and the revenue generated from these countries is also subject to fluctuations of their currencies against A$, and ultimately against the £, thereby increasing the exchange risk.

Strategy 2

As for Strategy 1, the initial outlay is at a known exchange rate and therefore is, in effect, fixed in £ sterling terms. The key difference is that, in absolute terms at least, the outlay is much smaller for Strategy 2 at A$4m compared to Strategy 1 at A$63m. The risk of future cash flows not covering this outlay is therefore reduced in absolute terms.

However, our working assumption is that the operating cash outflows are all in £ sterling, whereas the revenues are generated in A$. There is therefore a currency mismatch as if the A$ depreciates against the £ then revenues in sterling terms fall while costs remain constant.

The sensitivity calculations (see below) show that a one-off exchange rate shift of only 6% depreciation of the A$ against the £ would generate a zero NPV based on the data provided. This makes Strategy 2 more sensitive than Strategy 1 to exchange rate movements based on the assumptions of the illustrative calculation.

Sensitivity calculations

Strategy 1

Initial outlay	=	A$63,000
PV inflows (at £1 = A$1.8)	=	A$73,592 (73,678 – 86)
Break even exchange rate	=	(73,592/63,000) × 1.8 = 2.1026
% sensitivity 2.1026/1.8	=	16.8% depreciation of A$ against £

Proof (not required)

	1 Jan 20X6	31 Dec 20X6	31 Dec 20X7	31 Dec 20X8 & thereafter	Total PV
Initial outlay A$'000	(63,000)				
Operating CF A$'000			(100)	6,875	
DF	1		$1/1.08^2$	$1/(1.08^2/0.08)$	
PV A$'000	(63,000)		(86)	73,678	10,592
XR	1.8		2.1026	2.1026	
PV £'000	(35,000)		(41)	35,041	0

Strategy 2

All costs are incurred in £ sterling and are therefore unaffected by exchange rate movements. (Note: some professional scepticism may be applied to this working assumption that all costs are incurred in £s. It seems implausible, as some costs must be incurred in A$. Nevertheless, for calculation purposes it is accepted as a working assumption.)

Only revenues are affected:

$$\text{PV revenues (at £1 = A\$1.8)} = \frac{\text{A\$9,000}}{1.08/0.08} = \text{A\$104,167}$$

NPV in A$ = A$5,896

Break even exchange rate = $(104,167/(104,167 - 5,896) \times 1.8 = 1.908$

% sensitivity $(1.908 - 1.8)/1.8 = 6\%$ depreciation of A$ against £

[handwritten annotations: "costs", "revenue", "DON'T UNDERSTAND THIS CALCULATION"]

Supply chain management and distribution

[handwritten annotation: "WHAT IS IT?"]

Supply chain management is the planning and management of all activities involved in sourcing and procurement, conversion, and all associated logistics and distribution activities. Supply chain activities therefore include: procurement, inventory management, production, warehousing, transportation, customer service, order management, logistics and distribution.

For CC and AMC different types of products and services can be identified which require different types of supply chain management. Specifically:

Goods (mining cables):

- Standard products (supplied from inventory)
- Made-to-order products

Servicing and maintenance:

- Routine maintenance and servicing
- Emergencies

All activities in the supply chain should be undertaken with the customers' needs in mind; and, to this end, all supply chains ultimately exist to ensure that a customer's needs are satisfied. The way that customers can be satisfied differs for each of the above choices. The relative merits of Strategy 1 and Strategy 2 therefore depend on the type of product or service being considered.

For CC and AMC, made-to-order products and emergency services require a response to a customer order or request. This is a supply chain 'pull' process as it is demand driven.

Key factors include:

- Being aware of customers' needs and keeping in communication. With made-to-order products, the holding of adequate raw materials and components to make the goods is essential as, if these need to be ordered from CC's or AMC's own suppliers, then this may lengthen the lead time significantly. Strategy 1 has a greater strategic presence in the geographical location of the customer (Australia and SE Asia) hence may have a comparative advantage in this respect.

- Flexible manufacturing systems are also key to being able to commence manufacture as soon as a bespoke order is received. The UK factory used in Strategy 2 is larger and more established and may therefore provide an advantage in terms of flexible manufacturing over the factory in Strategy 1.

- Transportation is perhaps the greatest difference between the two strategies. The maximum scope of Strategy 1 is 8,000 kilometres, with many customers being much closer within Australia. In contrast, in order to supply the Australian market under Strategy 2 the goods need to be transported across the world. As they are significant in size they need to be transported by ship which takes many weeks.

Similarly, to supply emergency maintenance there needs to be a significant local presence with associated expertise. This seems more likely with a factory that makes the goods located in Australia, particularly if some components are needed as part of the maintenance. The maintenance group is also larger with Strategy 1 than Strategy 2.

Overall therefore Strategy 1 is very much favoured for made-to-order goods unless the customer knows significantly in advance of delivery which products are needed and therefore the lead time becomes unimportant. Thus, for instance, if a cable breaks unexpectedly and needs to be replaced it would be difficult under Strategy 2 to make and supply the item within a reasonable timeframe as there is no local manufacturing facility.

For standard goods and routine maintenance the problems of supply chain management are different. For standard goods, the 'push' model is appropriate and the response to uncertainty in customer orders can be to hold inventories to reduce lead time and improve customer service. In the 'push' model, CC or AMC can produce goods according to schedules based on historical sales patterns. At first, as Australia is a new market, demand may be hard to predict but, once demand patterns have become established, Strategy 2 may be able to accommodate this type of demand by holding sufficient inventories in its distribution centre.

Strategy 1 can similarly hold inventories but, as it can fine tune inventory levels more quickly from local factory production, it has a more flexible system of supply and distribution and inventory management. Thus the levels of inventory and associated holding costs are likely to be lower.

For routine maintenance there appears little difference between the two strategies as appropriately skilled staff can be employed under either option with adequate human resource planning.

Overall, the essence of the decision for the most appropriate supply chain and distribution system is a balance between responsiveness and efficiency. Strategy 1 seems superior in being able to satisfy customer needs. While the initial cost of Strategy 1 is much greater than Strategy 2 it reduces transport costs for the delivery of finished goods to the customer. Raw materials and components are also supplied locally with Strategy 1 and so it is independent of deliveries of any inventories from Europe. Also, revenues are higher under Strategy 1, presumably because more types of products can be supplied to customers to meet local needs and supplies are more efficient with a much shorter lead time for many types of product.

Overall for the above reasons Strategy 1 seems the preferred choice.

(b) **Methods of finance**

The key differences in the methods of debt finance for Strategy 1 are:

- the currency in which the debt is denominated.
- whether the parent should raise the loan or AMC.
- differences of detail in the terms of the loan arrangements.

Currency

A key difference is that with Method A the loan is raised in A$ while with Method B it is raised in £ sterling.

The key currency risk is the risk to the group rather than the risk to the subsidiary, as ultimate ownership rests with the group.

Strategy 1 is generating operating profits in A$, therefore this presents a currency risk to the parent as it is based in the UK. The functional currency of the parent is likely to be the £ as all costs are incurred in £s, even though more revenues are earned in euro.

Borrowing in A$ therefore provides a hedge against A$ denominated net operating cash inflows. Also, however, assets are based in Australia and are therefore valued in A$. Having an A$ denominated liability would therefore also provide a hedge against exchange rate movements affecting asset values.

Thus borrowing in A$ (Method A) is a more effective method of hedging than borrowing in £ (Method B).

Parent or Subsidiary

Leaving aside the above currency argument, the parent as an established entity may be better placed to raise a loan (Method B) than the subsidiary, which lacks a track record or a significant asset base. It also has a forecast income stream that is deferred for at least one year (or two years with a year-end operating cash flows assumption). CC is also likely to have a longer term relationship with the bank. These factors would reduce the risk to the lender and might reduce the cost of borrowing.

The fact that CC is offering the bank guarantees under Method A would reduce the reputational risk difference as CC as parent is standing behind the subsidiary. However the terms of the guarantee would need to be considered (eg whether there are limits or restrictions on the guarantee).

Differences of detail

It is apparent that the parent can borrow at a lower interest rate than AMC. This is discussed further below.

Another difference is the term of the loan. Under Method A the term of the loan is 15 years, whereas under Method B it is only 10 years. This favours Method A as it improves liquidity in not having to refinance a major loan after 10 years, in a new venture.

Method B has another problem. CC is borrowing over 10 years but relending to AMC over 15 years. The terms of the two loans are not therefore matched and CC could be exposed to repaying a loan in 10 years without receiving the repayment of its loan from AMC for a further 5 years.

There may be other differences which would need to be verified. These may arise from different national laws, different tax allowances and reliefs and different covenants in the loan agreement.

Difference in interest rates

There may be many reasons for the difference in interest rates of 5% and 4.8%, some of which are included below:

- The loans are denominated in different currencies. Interest rate parity would suggest that currency markets would compensate for expected differences in foreign currency movements by adjusting interest rates to leave an investor indifferent when considering where to invest surplus cash (taking both interest rates and currency movements into consideration).

- The risk on the loans may be different due to the company which is undertaking the borrowing, the security being offered or different covenants in the loan agreements.

- The time periods of the loans are different and therefore the term structure of interest rates would suggest that liquidity preference risk for the lender would be higher on a longer term loan and therefore the rate of interest would be higher. A further factor to consider is expectations where the long term yield curve is a function of the market's expectations of future interest rates. Changes in the supply of debt may also influence interest rates.

Recommendation

More information is needed (on covenants, tax, forward currency rates) but based on the information available a preliminary recommendation is that Finance Method A is to be preferred, despite the slightly higher interest rate of 5% compared to 4.8%.

The key factors are that it provides better currency matching with Australian operations; the longer term of 15 years provides more long term liquidity; and the issue of mismatching terms of the loan for CC is avoided (although this latter issue can also be avoided by changing the internal refinancing arrangement rather than the selection of the external loan).

(c) **Assurance report**

Many of the assurance issues are common to both methods of finance. These common issues are therefore considered first, then issues specific to each financing proposal are addressed.

Two key risk issues for the bank are as follows:

[Handwritten margin note: major risks with loan for lender]

(1) Assurance over whether the business is viable and whether sufficient cash flows will be generated from operations in order to repay principal and interest over time (debt servicing ability).

(2) If the repayments cannot be made are there sufficient assets that can be realised on liquidation to repay the loan (security in the event of default).

Providing assurance in respect of forecasts is covered by ISAE 3400 *The Examination of Prospective Financial Information*.

Prospective financial information means financial information based on assumptions about events that may occur in the future and possible actions by an entity. This would relate to the forecasts of cash flow and profits made by AMC to support its application for finance.

In this respect, a forecast is defined as prospective financial information based on assumptions as to future events which management expects to take place and the actions management expects to take (best-estimate assumptions).

The following are areas where MM needs to obtain sufficient appropriate evidence:

[Handwritten margin note: GENERAL]

- MM needs to satisfy itself that CC management's best-estimate assumptions on which the prospective financial information is based are not unreasonable and, in the case of the hypothetical/working assumptions, that such assumptions are consistent with the purpose of the information (ie to raise new loan finance). This will require ascertaining that AMC sales volumes are realistic for the prices being charged in the markets being accessed (eg existing market prices and revenues generated by rivals selling cabling products in Australia and South East Asia). To be able to do this MM will need clear evidence (eg market research) collected by AMC staff (perhaps during the feasibility study) to support the forecasts provided.

- The prospective financial information is properly prepared on the basis of the assumptions ie that the financial information produced (ie AMC's revenues, costs, cash flows) is consistent with the assumptions in amount and timing.

- The prospective financial information is properly presented and all material assumptions are adequately disclosed, including a clear indication as to whether they are best-estimate assumptions or hypothetical/working assumptions.

- The prospective financial information would normally need to be prepared on a consistent basis with historical financial statements, using appropriate accounting principles. However this is not possible as AMC is new to the Australian and South East Asia market and hence there is no historical information to support the assumptions and forecasts. This is a key risk issue.

It is clear that as prospective financial information is subjective information, it is impossible to give the same level of assurance regarding forecasts for AMC, as would be applicable to historic financial information for its historic performance. In this instance, limited assurance, in the form of a negatively expressed opinion, is the best that could be achieved.

Finance Method A

Providing security for the loan in the form of available assets that can be sold on liquidation is a key issue. In this case however the asset base comprises not just the assets of AMC but also those of the parent, CC, which has guaranteed the loan.

A key issue would be the type of charge taken over the assets. If there is a fixed charge over the factory then this would need to be valued by an expert in property valuation. However, at the time the loan is taken out it may be that only the land is owned, and maybe not even that.

If there is a floating charge, then the assurance report would need to consider all assets falling under the floating charge.

Given the infancy of AMC at the time the loan is to be raised, then the parental guarantee is crucial. The assurance report needs to assess the validity of the terms of any agreement from the perspective of the bank and the ability for CC to fulfil these terms from its own asset base.

Another key concern is the high level of financial gearing resulting from the low proportion of equity, which means that the bank is subject to significant risk.

[Handwritten note: ↑gearing - bank = ↑ risk]

Finance Method B

Providing security for the loan in the form of available assets would in this case mean assessing the value of CC's assets that form the basis of any fixed or floating charge. It would also need to be considered what other charges are held over these assets by other lenders.

A particular issue is the going concern of CC and therefore its ability to fulfil any guarantees. A risk in this respect is that CC wishes to borrow from the bank over a 10-year term but has made a loan to AMC for the amount borrowed for a 15-year term. CC's ability to repay the loan to the bank in 10 years therefore needs to be assessed.

(d) **Financial reporting**

Strategy 1

Consolidated financial statements

AMC is a subsidiary of CC (either wholly owned or 80% owned depending on whether the offer from BTZ is accepted – see below).

For the preparation of financial statements, AMC needs to determine its functional currency which is likely to be the A$. At the year end, however, it is necessary for AMC to translate its results into the presentation currency of CC, which is the £, in order to be included in CC's consolidated financial statements.

Variations in the £/A$ exchange rate will impact upon the consolidated results so, for example, if the A$ depreciates against the £ then the value of A$ denominated revenues will fall when expressed in the presentation currency of the group (ie the £).

Intra group items will need to be adjusted on consolidation. There is little trading between group companies as AMC sources its raw materials and labour locally. However there may be group management charges.

Also, a key intra group item is financing under Financing Method B. Here there is an intra group loan from CC to AMC denominated in A$. This would cancel on consolidation with exchange gains and losses netting off.

Foreign currency transactions

AMC will enter into transactions denominated in a currency other than its own functional currency (the A$) eg from sales in SE Asia. It must translate these foreign currency items into its own functional currency according to IAS 21, in its individual company financial statements. Thus, for example, sales made in South East Asia and any receivables outstanding in respect of these, as monetary items, will need to be translated into A$ in the individual company accounts of AMC. These in turn will then be translated into £s as the group presentation currency, as noted above.

Construction costs

The first year following incorporation will be spent constructing the factory. These costs will be capitalised but also the interest on borrowing to build the factory will be capitalised with an offset for interest earned on unused funds.

Related parties

If BTZ acquires 20% of the share capital of AMC (see below) then potentially it could have significant influence and AMC would need to be treated as an associate of BTZ. If this is the case then transactions with BTZ would be treated as related party transactions, including any transaction with the directors.

Contingent liability

The guarantee for the bank loan under Finance Method A may need to be disclosed as a contingent liability.

Operating segment

AMC is largely independent of CC, which is a listed company. AMC would, in accordance with IFRS 8, therefore qualify to be treated as an operating segment in the group financial statements. Under IFRS 8, para 5, AMC would qualify as an operating segment from 20X6, even though no revenues are expected to be earned in that year. As an operating segment, there would be separate disclosure of AMC's operating results (revenue, expenses, segment profit), assets and liabilities, in the group financial statements.

Strategy 2 — Division. (functional currency = £)

Under this strategy, the division is part of CC for accounting purposes so its results, assets and liabilities are treated as those of the CC parent company.

The foreign currency translation issues relating to the division therefore relate to transactions and balances being translated into the functional currency of CC (most likely, but questionably, the £). The issue of presentation currency does not arise as there is no issue of consolidation.

Assuming that the CC functional currency is the £ then the Australian and South East Asian revenues are required to be recognised in £s at the spot exchange rate at the date on which the transaction took place. The date of the transaction is the date on which the transaction first satisfied the relevant recognition criteria. If there are a high volume of transactions in foreign currencies by the division, translating each transaction may be an onerous task, so an average rate may be used. *non-monetary asset.*

The new distribution centre represents a foreign currency asset which is a non-monetary asset. Non-monetary items will not require retranslation so those acquired on 1 January 20X6 will be translated at £1 = A$1.8 and would not be retranslated. Their value in the statement of financial position of CC would not therefore be affected by subsequent exchange rate fluctuations.

historic cost

Receivables represent another foreign currency asset but they are a monetary asset. These assets will need to be translated into £s as CC's functional currency at each reporting date.

Monetary assets would therefore be affected by subsequent exchange rate fluctuations and resulting exchange gains or losses impact on profit.

The division would also probably qualify as an operating segment in accordance with IFRS 8 (see above).

(e) **Ethical issues**

Proposed collaboration between CC and BTZ

BTZ became aware of CC's intentions in Australia due to one of our ex-employees on the feasibility study team joining them. This may be regarded as a breach of confidentiality but more information would be needed on employee obligations in the employment contract to form a firm conclusion. If the ex-employee is a member of a professional body such as ICAEW, then disciplinary procedures may be appropriate as a breach of confidentiality.

part of normal business

The email from the BTZ procurement director is making a commercial offer. The declared intention not to purchase goods from AMC unless BTZ is allowed to acquire a 20% shareholding may be regarded as part of normal business negotiation. It is directed towards the company rather than an individual so could not reasonably be considered to be an intimidation threat. *NV<MV*

An ethical risk is however that the offer to acquire shares at their nominal value is likely to be below market value and not at arm's length. The nominal value on incorporation is only A$9m so 20% would only be a consideration of A$1.8m (or £1 million). This is unlikely to be helpful in financing AMC.

conflicts of interests

While more facts are needed there are potential ethical risks arising from conflicts of interests between the personal interests of directors and those of their companies.

The procurement director has control over purchases including any from AMC. He is also suggesting that he should have a seat on the AMC board, and perhaps receive personal remuneration for this. The ethical risk is therefore that he will treat AMC favourably to the detriment of his company, BTZ, in return for inflated remuneration for his services to AMC as non-executive director.

The appropriate action would be transparency so the BTZ board is aware of all arrangements between AMC and the procurement director.

BTZ letter to John

The letter to CC's chief executive may suggest a further conflict of interest between the personal interests of a director and the company. In accepting the transfer, John may have received a personal benefit in the form of BTZ shares, although more information is needed.

The risk here is that John may <u>approve</u> the acquisition of a 20% shareholding in AMC by BTZ (even though it is likely to be a poor commercial transaction for CC) as he is receiving a personal benefit.

Unfortunately, the manner in which this information was acquired is itself ethically questionable on the grounds of integrity and confidentiality in looking at private information.

The most appropriate action would be to disclose to John the means by which the information was acquired but then require an explanation of the letter. <u>Informing</u> the <u>CC</u> chairman of the <u>facts</u> would be appropriate.

There is an additional ethical risk that the two conflicts of interest may be <u>illegal</u> particularly with reference to the Bribery Act. <u>Legal advice</u> should be acquired once the facts are established.

37 Paige plc (July 2015)

		Marks
(a)	Identifying that UK market is saturated and Paige does not have a presence in other markets Identify business, product life cycle and financial risks Evaluation of the risks	8
(b)	Identify relevant risks Identify relevant benefits Discussion – brand value may be lost if operations are transferred to a new range of products Use of appropriate analytical approach (eg Porter's Five Forces) Proposals 2 and 3: link need for new infrastructure investment with Paige's existing high gearing Discuss relative ROCE of SP and Paige Discuss problems of entering new markets Identify problems in entering new markets in developing countries. Reasoned conclusion as to the viability of each proposal	14
(c)	Identify relevant risks Identify relevant benefits Calculation of implied value of Ke and P/E Evaluation of relevant alternative valuations Identify additional information required and alternative approaches to valuation. Identify embedded point that sale of SP would mean transfer of obligations including the debt that falls due for repayment on 31 March 20X7	14
(d)	Make a recommendation based upon findings in (b) and (c)	4
Total marks		40

To: Josie Welch
From: Nat Ahmed

WORKING PAPER

(a) SP's market environment and key risks

Market environment

SP currently operates in a market where barriers to entry are low, and where competition has eroded its market share and profitability. Although the market for weight loss products is buoyant and likely to grow significantly, SP is not currently benefiting from the strong market. The strongest growth in the market for meal replacement products is projected to take place in relatively new overseas markets such as Asia, where SP does not have a presence.

SP's strength, such as it is, lies in the UK market which is likely to be saturated, and where competition will be keen. The company's sales and profitability have fallen, a decline which Paige attributes to the presence of new entrants in the market. While this may well be a relevant factor, other explanations are possible. For example, the company may not have been well-managed since its acquisition by Paige.

Key risks

The following risks can be identified.

Business risks:

- Barriers to entry to the market for meal replacement products are assessed by Paige as low. This means that there is a constant risk of new competitors who may be able to price their product more competitively, or advertise it more effectively, thus potentially eroding SP's market share.

Product life cycle risks:

- Charles Digby, Paige's CEO, attributes SP's loss of profitability to a slowing down of growth in the meal replacement market. There may be a risk that meal replacement products are nearing the end of their life cycle, and that they will be replaced by other products.

- There is no indication that SP is actively researching new products, and there is a risk that competitors may be making better progress in bringing new product variants to market.

Financial risks:

- The financial information provided indicates that SP is currently quite highly-geared. Taking gearing as debt/equity, the actual gearing ratio in 20X5 is 1.5 (40.5/27). No information is available about the company's cash resources or cash flow, but it may be that SP is subject to liquidity risk. If SP plans to extend its presence in markets outside the UK this will potentially expose it to a greater range of financial risks, such as exchange rate risks.

(b) **Strategy A: proposals for developing SP's activities in the weight loss market**

Although the market for weight loss products is likely to increase substantially over the next few years, the four proposals under Strategy A require careful evaluation as there are significant weaknesses associated with all of them. The proposals are not mutually exclusive and Paige's management would have to appraise the extent to which available investment should be apportioned between the proposals.

The first proposal is to gradually phase out the meal replacement products and to use existing sales channels to promote a range of low-calorie ready meals. A reduction in one type of product will be matched by the build-up of another, and it is even possible that the production facilities for the meal replacement products could be adapted for production of ready-meals. The second and third proposals (web-based advisory services and investment in gyms and health facilities) would both be completely new directions for SP.

The final proposal, of establishing an overseas growth strategy in developing countries, could be applied to any of the three proposed new ranges of products and services.

Strategy A involves retention of the investment in SP. Its retention would form part of a major strategic move for Paige, ie strengthening and building its position in the weight loss market.

Potential benefits

- Could help to diversify risks to Paige from its involvement in the food processing business.

- Could use Paige's existing experience and sales channels in the food industry to sell a new range of low-calorie meals.

- The potential market for the range of products and services suggested in Strategy A is obviously very large and is growing rapidly.

Potential risks

There are several risks involved in this strategy:

- The proposed strategy is diverse in nature and potentially involves entering markets in which Paige has little or no experience and no obvious core competences: web-based advisory services, gyms and health facilities and the market for diet products in developing countries.

- Paige has not, on the evidence of SP's performance figures, made an outstanding success of running SP's current product line as revenues have been falling. However, the company has produced a net profit of over 4% over that period, despite the falling revenues, suggesting that costs are under control. Strategy A would involve exiting the market for the current product range which is, at least to some extent, profitable.

- If the investment in SP is retained, it will presumably remain under the control of its directors who have apparently failed to make any significant return on the investment since its acquisition. Even if the investment was 'worth' £48 million upon initial acquisition (which is perhaps unlikely) its value has dropped significantly over a period of some six years.

- In the event that an effective diet pill is developed by the pharmaceutical industry, the market for conventional diet products could disappear overnight. This is considered to be an unlikely contingency, but the uncertainty does exist, and if possible the risk should be quantified.

- Barriers to entry to the market for diet products and services are low and there is a high risk of effective competition taking away market share.

Examining each of the four proposals in turn:

(1) Gradual phasing out of meal replacement products and promotion of a range of low-calorie ready meals

SP's success has been built upon the production and sale of meal replacement products. Any brand value that it has built up is entirely associated with this range of products. Paige is proposing to exploit the brand value by transferring its operations over a relatively short timescale to a different range of products. It may be that the old and new product ranges are sufficiently similar to allow for the transfer of brand value from one to the other but this is not guaranteed, and SP may lose value unnecessarily.

The proposed strategy is radical, and may not be necessary. It seems that demand still exists for meal replacement products and SP is an established supplier. Therefore, it might be preferable to retain this range of products, adding to it, rather than substituting it.

Porter's analysis of the competitive environment for businesses identifies five forces:

- Threat of new entrants
- Threat of substitute products or services
- Bargaining power of customers
- Bargaining power of suppliers
- Rivalry amongst existing competitors in the industry

Threat of new entrants: The market for low-calorie ready meals may well be poised for growth because of the anticipated increases in the numbers of people worldwide who are overweight or obese. However the products themselves are not likely to be technologically very complex and can easily be imitated. Any company that has existing sales channels through, eg supermarkets and other retailers, would be able, like Paige, to utilise these channels for distribution of meal replacement products. The threat of new entrants is high.

Threat of substitute products or services: There are many food producers in the market. Many of those producers are likely to be engaged in research and development into new products or variants on old products. If one producer succeeds in bringing a marginally-improved product to market, competitors can easily imitate the innovation. The threat of substitute products or services is high.

Bargaining power of customers: Demand for weight-loss products is high, but one product can easily be substituted for another by a customer. Customers are unlikely to develop strong attachments to one particular brand of low-calorie ready meals. Supermarkets are likely to carry several different product ranges which will be easily substitutable. From the customer's point of view there is no cost in substituting one product range for another. Therefore, it seems likely that customers collectively have a high level of bargaining power in the market for low-calorie ready meals.

Bargaining power of suppliers: This is likely to be very low. Suppliers of food products for low-calorie meals will probably be the same generic suppliers as are already used by Paige. Paige's position as a bulk buyer will mean that suppliers have little bargaining power.

Rivalry amongst existing competitors in the industry: Where barriers to entry are low, rivalry is likely to be at a high level. The market for weight-loss products is buoyant, with many existing suppliers. Although the expected rapid future growth of the market will allow for new entrants to the market in low-calorie meals to flourish, competition is likely to remain intense and existing market leaders will be unwilling to cede their leadership positions to new rivals.

(2) **A range of web-based paid-for advisory services**

There are already well-established players in this market, and SP would be entering it for the first time. The threat of new entrants to this market is probably lower than for reduced-calorie ready meals, because of the need for investment in infrastructure and specialist staff. Nevertheless, barriers are not insuperable, and if SP were to succeed in entering this market it would face the threat of new entrants. The threat of substitute products or services is also high.

Customers' position is potentially somewhat weaker. Although there are substitutes, if the advisory services are provided in exchange for a monthly, or annual, subscription customers' power to switch is constrained.

Rivalry with existing suppliers will be high. Existing providers of such services will be unwilling to lose market share. Because the service they are providing is, to some extent, personal, they may have been successful in building brand loyalty. SP's potential market would probably lie in new consumers who have not previously signed up for such a service.

Entry into this market would involve potentially significant investment. Assuming that SP's cash resources are limited any new investment would probably have to be supplied by Paige. SP is already highly-geared to a point where commercial lending arrangements might not be available or would be highly-priced. *↑ gearing*

(3) **Investment in existing gym and health facilities**

ROCE = $\dfrac{op\ profit}{Equity + loan}$

The proposal is to invest profits from other products and services into existing gyms and health facilities. This would require a great deal of further investigation. SP's current ROCE is just below 7% (based on 20X5 actual figures [£4.7 million/(£27.0 million + £40.5 million) × 100]. Therefore a threshold requirement is that any investment should be able to yield at least 7%. Paige's own ROCE is significantly higher at just over 15%. Therefore it would make sense to invest any surplus generated by SP into Paige's own operations (if marginal return on capital can match the current average return), and to invest in other activities like gyms only if there was a high probability of returns above 15%.

There is a significant risk involved in this proposal, in that Paige has no existing presence in the sector and, presumably, lacks knowledge, experience and core competences.

long payback .

A final point is that profits generated by SP are relatively insignificant. In 20X6 the company is forecast to generate a net profit after tax of £2.8 million. After deducting dividend, this would leave a maximum of £1.8 million in surplus retained profits. It would take many years to allow for significant investment in gym and health facilities businesses.

(4) **Establishing new markets in developing countries**

There is clearly significant potential for expansion of the market for weight loss products into developing countries, given the scale of the obesity problem across the world. However, Paige is not necessarily best placed to exploit these opportunities; it has only limited experience of expanding its markets into other countries. The group's sales are principally within the UK. It has a growing presence in other parts of Europe, but this experience of markets outside the UK would not necessarily be helpful in establishing markets in developing countries. This fourth proposal could be combined with any or all of the first three proposals.

The least risky combination is likely to be with the first proposal; Paige could explore the possibility of exporting low-calorie ready meals to developing countries without committing significant resources. It may be possible to find a partner business or businesses already well-established in the target markets. Proposals two and three, however, present much more significant challenges. The provision of web-based advisory services would have to be carefully tailored to suit cultural conditions in developing countries. Investments in gym and health facilities, as noted above, are risky, but would be even riskier in developing countries because of eg currency risk, and the challenge of operating successfully in distant locations.

Evaluation of the four proposals

The analysis of the various proposals outlined above suggests that some are higher risk than others. SP may well be able to take advantage of the forecast increase in volume in the market for weight loss products and services, but the company should be advised to be selective in its targeted growth areas. Investment in gyms and health facilities does not appear to be a viable or realistic option. Expansion into paid-for web-based advisory services carries significant risks, and should probably be rejected.

With a high level of competition and low barriers to new entrants, the SP business may not prove to be particularly profitable. There is a further problem in that Strategy A proposes an overseas growth strategy, specifically in developing countries. However, it appears that Paige has no experience in such markets and only limited experience in establishing markets outside the UK.

A final point is that a significant threat to the whole weight loss market exists in the form of a potentially effective pharmaceutical product. As noted in Exhibit 1, dieters would most welcome an effective pill. If such a product were to be developed, the market for other weight loss products and services would most likely disappear.

Although this outcome currently appears unlikely in the immediate future, it is a risk, and it should inform future strategy if Paige stays in the weight loss market.

This analysis should be firmed up by more detailed investigation of the existing and potential market for weight loss products and by detailed competitor analysis.

(c) **Strategy B: proposal to dispose of investment in SP**

Potential benefits:

- The investment could realise cash of at least £20 million which would be available for investment in Paige's core business. Paige can earn a ROCE of around 15%, which is substantially in excess of SP's ROCE (which can be estimated for 20X6 as [5.3/(28.8 + 40.5) × 100] = 7.6%).

Potential risks:

- Paige may have overpaid significantly for its investment in SP. Disposing of the business could have adverse reputational effects for Paige, at least in the short term.

- In adopting Strategy B Paige could be exiting a highly lucrative and rapidly growing market. Although barriers to entry to this market are low, it would require time and investment to re-enter and the disposal could prove to be an error.

SP's Cost of Equity and P/E ratio implied by the private equity fund's offer

Valuation of SP

A private equity fund has set an 'informal' valuation figure of £18 million for Paige's 80% holding in SP. This compares very unfavourably to the £48 million paid for the investment in 20W9. The offer of £2 million for Claudia Svelte's 20% share of the company is, apparently, insufficient to induce her to sell. If the private equity fund genuinely wishes to purchase her 20% of the company it will probably have to offer more. However, the two offers taken together do allow for an overall valuation of £20 million for the company which is based on a firm offer and which is therefore a useful benchmark for further work on valuation.

SP's implied cost of equity

SP's cost of equity can be estimated using the food processing industry WACC of 7.5%, with similar gearing to SP.

First, the cost of SP's debt can be calculated as follows:

Cost of debt at 31 March 20X6 (per £100 of debt) using 5% as the appropriate before tax yield and a 20% tax rate:

K_d = 5% (1 – 0.2) = 4%

Because WACC and Kd are known, Ke can be estimated as follows, based upon a valuation for the whole company of £20 million:

WACC (0.075) = [K_e × (20.0/(20.0 + 40.5)) + (0.04 × (40.5/(20.0 + 40.5)))]
0.075 = (K_e × 0.33058) + 0.026777
K_e = 0.146 (approximately)
 = 14.6%

This is a relatively high cost of equity, because it reflects the high business risk attached to the entity and also the equity is subject to high gearing.

SP's implied P/E ratio can be calculated as the reciprocal of K_e as follows, using the K_e estimated above:

1/0.146 = 6.85

Valuation: income-based models

Dividend valuation model

A dividend valuation model could be used to estimate SP's value. The constant growth model is likely to be suitable given the assumption provided. This is expressed as follows:

$$P_0 = \frac{D_0\left(1+g\right)}{\left(K_e - g\right)}$$

Where:

P_0 = Market value
D_0 = Dividend
g = Growth rate in earnings and dividends
K_e = Cost of equity

Although the dividend actually paid in 20X4 was £0.5 million it would be reasonable to use the intended annual future dividend of £1.0 million.

Using these values for a 31 March 20X6 valuation:

$$P_0 = \frac{\left(£1 \text{ million} \times 1.08\right)}{\left(0.146 - 0.08\right)}$$

= **£16.36** million

P/E ratio model

Using the implied P/E ratio of 6.85 and the 20X6 forecast earnings of £2.8 million produces a valuation of:

£2.8 million × 6.85 = **£19.18** million

Alternatively, the valuation can be estimated by using the P/E ratio of a suitable comparable company. However, neither Wensley Slimming nor Paige are directly comparable and therefore a valuation based on the P/E of either must be treated with caution.

There is further uncertainty regarding whether or not current levels of profitability can actually be maintained. If SP loses the contract with Purseproud Supermarkets revenue will be reduced by around £4.3 million per annum. It is not possible to estimate the effect that the loss of this revenue would have on profitability without further information about fixed and variable costs. Also, it is possible that the loss of the contract could have adverse reputational effects and other contracts may be lost.

For the reasons given above any valuation based on P/E ratios that takes projected earnings for 20X6 into account must be treated with professional scepticism.

Using Wensley Slimming's P/E gives a valuation of 9.4 × SP's forecast profit for 20X6 of £2.8 million: £26.3 million. A similar calculation using Paige's own P/E produces a valuation for the whole company of 9.9 × £2.8 million: £27.7 million. However, much depends upon the reliability of the 20X6 projected profit figure. The forecast statement of profit or loss suggests an increase in revenue of over 20%, and an increase in net profit of 21.7%. Increases of this magnitude, under the same management in a declining market, seem inherently implausible.

The same calculations as above based on reported 20X5 figures would give the following:

Using SP's P/E: 6.85 × £2.3 million = £15.76 million.

Using Wensley Slimming's P/E: 9.4 × £2.3 million = £21.6 million.

Using Paige's P/E: 9.9 × £2.3 million = £22.8 million.

These valuations are much closer to the offer price, and may be more realistic.

Asset-based model

Net asset value can provide some indication of company value, especially if assets and liabilities are stated at fair values.

The value in use of the non-current assets is estimated by the finance director to be £68.3 million at the proposed date of sale. This is (£68.3m – £65.1m) £3.2 million above the carrying amount. Assuming that the fair value of all other assets and liabilities at 31 March 20X6 approximates to the carrying amount, this gives a valuation for equity at that date of (£28.8m + £3.2m) £32 million. However, a degree of professional scepticism needs to be applied to this figure from the finance director as the dividend and earnings models give a much lower figure of future earnings to be generated from the assets.

More realistically in terms of the value of non-current assets is the fair value less costs to sell which is £60.2m which is lower than the carrying amounts. (No impairment is required as the recoverable amount is greater than the carrying amount if the finance director's estimates are to be believed.)

This is (£60.2m – £65.1m) £4.9 million below the carrying amount of the assets. Again assuming that the fair value of all other assets and liabilities at 31 March 20X6 approximates to the carrying amount, this gives a valuation for equity at that date of (£28.8 m – £4.9m) £23.9 million.

Summary of valuations:

Informal private equity fund valuation	£20 million
Dividend growth	£16.36 million
P/E basis – current earnings	£15.76 to £22.8 million
P/E basis – forecast earnings	£19.18 to £27.7 million
Asset basis	£23.9 million

The information provided by the finance director allows for the application of income-based and asset-based models of valuation. There are other, potentially more useful, approaches that could be taken that would focus upon cash flow and value-based models, but more information would be required. For the purposes of this initial report we can use a relatively limited number of approaches in order to establish a range of values, but Paige and/or ourselves should produce a more exhaustive range of valuations before any negotiations are undertaken.

Valuation: discussion

The private equity fund informal valuation of £20 million may represent a reasonable starting point for negotiation. It seems from the information available that a realistic valuation for Paige's holding in SP may be in the range of about £16 million to £27 million. However, the valuation methods outlined above would require further refinement. Using the P/E model on the basis of comparable companies is valid only where a suitable comparator company can be found and neither of the P/Es cited appear more than superficially comparable.

Use of the implied P/E ratio is likely to be more reliable. The dividend valuation model is based upon the directors' intention that a dividend of £1 million, growing at 8% pa, would be paid. Although the company would appear to have been capable of paying a dividend at that level (based on profit after tax) in both 20X5 and 20X4 it did not actually do so. Also, there is no indication from the information given of SP's cash position.

The asset-based model can constitute a realistic approach to company valuation. However, it would require a much more rigorous valuation of the component elements of assets and liabilities. The only adjustments made so far have been in respect of the finance director's estimate of the value in use of non-current assets. These valuations would require refinement in the form of an unbiased third-party valuation.

A further, very important, point is that if SP is sold to the private equity fund, the fund will take over responsibility for SP's liabilities, and the obligation to repay the debt to Paige on 31 March 20X7. This factor alone is likely to make the offer by the private equity fund worth considering. If the sale does not take place, the debt remains a substantial intra-group item.

Other approaches to valuation are possible, and arguably have greater validity. Information in the form of cash-flow forecasts for a three- to five-year period would provide the means for a valuation based on net present values.

Any valuation information that is provided in DBP's report must be accompanied by appropriate caveats and requests for further information.

(d) **Preliminary reasoned recommendation**

The preliminary recommendation is that Strategy B should be adopted. The key argument in its favour is that Paige is capable of earning 15% ROCE, which is far higher than the comparable figure for SP. Also, if the offer from the private equity fund is accepted, a significant amount of debt, between Paige and SP due for repayment in 20X7, can be removed from the Paige Group's liabilities. However, a great deal more analysis and information would be required in order to turn this from a tentative into a firm recommendation. Strategy A is muddled and contains too many proposals, none of which appear attractive on the basis of current analysis.

38 Riller plc (November 2015)

Marking guide

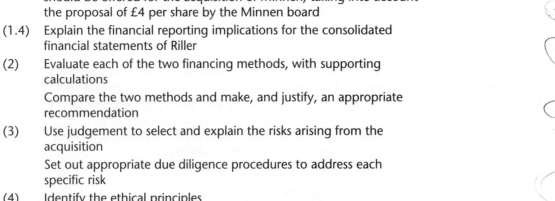

		Marks
(1.1)	Analyse and compare the performance of Riller and Minnen	10
(1.2)	Explain the factors which should be considered when deciding whether to acquire Minnen	8
(1.3)	Using a variety of models, determine and justify the price per share that should be offered for the acquisition of Minnen, taking into account the proposal of £4 per share by the Minnen board	11
(1.4)	Explain the financial reporting implications for the consolidated financial statements of Riller	6
(2)	Evaluate each of the two financing methods, with supporting calculations	
	Compare the two methods and make, and justify, an appropriate recommendation	9
(3)	Use judgement to select and explain the risks arising from the acquisition	
	Set out appropriate due diligence procedures to address each specific risk	9
(4)	Identify the ethical principles	
	Consider a range of actions and recommend the most appropriate	7
Total marks		60

Data summary table (amounts in £'000)

	Riller 20X5	Riller 20X4	Change %	Minnen 20X5
Revenue	285,300	232,500	22.7%	133,400
Cost of sales	218,900	189,400	15.6%	117,300
Gross profit	66,400	43,100	54.1%	16,100
Operating Profit	37,900	21,900	73.1%	8,100
Profit before tax	27,700	12,600	119.8%	7,000
Profit for the year	21,600	9,900	118.2%	5,600
Net asset value (book value)	206,800			42,000
Houses sold	765	820	(6.7)%	242
Cost per house sold (CoS/houses sold)	286.1	231.0	23.9%	484.7
Plots	5,550	4,600	20.7%	1,600
No. of shares ('000)	32,000	32,000		20,000
Price per house (£'000)	372.9	283.5	31.5%	551.2
Time to use plots (years)	7.3	5.6	30.4%	6.6
Gross margin	23.3%	18.5%		12.1%
Operating margin	13.3%	9.1%		6.1%
Interest cover	3.7	2.4		
Gearing (debt/equity)	125%			107%

1.1 Analysis of performance Riller

Revenue

Total revenue has increased by 22.7% in 20X5 compared to 20X4. The increase has been achieved despite a reduction in the number of houses sold of 6.7%.

The underlying cause of the increase in revenue appears to be the increase in the average price per house sold of 31.5%. This could reflect the buoyant housing market where Riller has benefitted from favourable trading conditions in the market, rather than any internal actions by Riller. Alternatively (or additionally), it could reflect a trend for Riller to build larger, and therefore higher priced, houses in 20X5 compared with 20X4, thereby generating a higher price but more costs. There is some evidence that this may be the case as the cost per house has increased by 23.9%.

The underlying cause of the decline in demand could be the increase in prices charged by Riller (ie a downward sloping demand curve) whereby the high prices have meant fewer sales at a greater margin.

The relationship between price (+31.5%) and volume (−6.7%) can be demonstrated as jointly impacting revenue (22.7%) as:

$1.315 \times 0.933 = 1.227$

Profit and costs

The gross margin has increased significantly from 18.5% to 23.3% which is likely to reflect the higher average price per house sold as the main causal factor.

These higher margins have generated a significant increase in absolute gross profit of 54.1%.

Despite an increase in distribution and administration costs of 34.4% operating profit has increased by 73.1%. Some investigation of the extent of the increase in distribution and administration costs may be appropriate as it might be expected that these costs are largely fixed and, in respect of any variable element, the volume of sales has fallen.

The profit after tax figure has increased significantly by 118.2% reflecting the operating gearing effect of fixed costs, which do not increase despite rising revenue.

Liquidity

The improved profitability has increased the interest cover significantly from 2.4 to 3.7, thereby reducing the risk of being unable to make interest payments.

Gearing appears high at 125% but the nature of the business means there is significant investment in assets (land and buildings) which can normally be sold without incurring significant losses against cost. Indeed, sales from the landbank could be made. In this respect the value of the inventory is almost double the value of the loan. If the loan became repayable, then sales of properties and some of the landbank would be able to realise enough to repay the loan. Given this is the case, the inventory generates debt capacity and provides good security for the loan.

Asset base

The landbank has 5,550 plots and 765 houses have been sold in the year. If sales were to continue at this level there would be sufficient houses in the landbank to service sales for 7.3 years. Riller has therefore secured a key resource.

Moreover, in 20X5 there has been a significant increase in the landbank of 20.7% thereby securing a resource for the future.

Comparison of the performance of Riller and Minnen

Riller is a larger company than Minnen producing 216% more residential properties. It therefore benefits from economies of scale.

Minnen however produces the higher value residential properties with an average price of £551,200, being 48% higher than Riller's average price in 2015 of £372,900. The higher price for Minnen might be attributable to its location in the south of England where property prices are generally higher.

Despite the higher price for Minnen it has a lower gross margin (12.1%) than Riller (23.3%). Minnen also has a lower operating margin (6.1%) than Riller (13.3%). Part of the cause of this is that Miller has a cost per house of £484,700 compared to £286,100 which is 69.4% higher. This may reflect the higher cost of land in the south.

 Overall Riller appears to have performed better than Minnen even after allowing for the larger scale. A key piece of data is that revenue is 114% higher for Riller in 20X5 but profit for the year is 286% higher.

1.2 Acquisition of Minnen

Factors to be considered

The acquisition is one of horizontal integration whereby a company in the same industry is acquired. This does not diversify risk but, as both companies are listed, the shareholders (or institutional shareholders at least) are able to diversify their portfolios and diversify unsystematic risk themselves without operational diversification by individual companies in their portfolios.

It may be that the risk of Minnen is different from that of Riller (eg due to different markets; cost structures; finance structures; and management's risk appetite). The acquisition of Minnen may therefore alter the risk of the group, up or down. This should be reflected in the discount rate used to assess the bid price.

By expanding in the same industry it enables the Riller board to <u>use existing core competences</u> to manage the newly acquired business. Moreover, as it is in the same industry, there are more likely to be <u>synergies</u> and therefore cost savings resulting from the acquisition which are estimated to amount to £350,000 per annum. However, this level of synergistic gains is very small in the context of the size of the two companies, but it may be explained by the fact they operate in different geographical regions so there is limited overlap of activities and operations.

In strategic terms the acquisition appears to be a good fit.

- It provides geographical <u>diversification</u> in the key market of the south of England. This could enable geographical diversity in the form of a new physical location in the south of England, but also reputation in the region. It may have been possible for Riller to enter the south of England market by organic growth, but an acquisition enables quicker market entry and circumvents some of the barriers to entry in this geographical market.

- There is also <u>diversity by market sector,</u> as Minnen appears to build houses that are more upmarket than those built by Riller. This is indicated by the fact that the average house price in 20X5 for Minnen is £551,200 compared to £372,900 for Riller. Part of the explanation, (perhaps a significant part) for this difference may be that land is more expensive in the south of England, but the scale of the difference implies that the property is also of greater size or quality.

Operational advantages are reflected in the sources of the <u>synergistic gains.</u> These reflect operational savings (eg where there are common functions that can be merged into one); <u>procurement</u> and subcontractor gains (eg where greater discounts can be obtained for larger quantities); and changes in rationalisation, in design and in specification, so greater economies of scale can be achieved.

There may also be <u>duplication of assets</u> (eg two head offices) where one could be sold giving a <u>one-off cash inflow.</u>

In financial terms, Riller would be assuming a significant amount of debt onto its statement of financial position amounting to £87m. The <u>gearing</u> of Minnen is high:

Book gearing at fair value (debt/equity)   =   £87m/£58m =   150%

Market value gearing (debt/equity)   =   £87m/£80m =   109%

The <u>timing</u> of the acquisition appears to be good as it coincides with a period when the housing <u>market is growing.</u> However, ultimately the viability of any acquisition is a question of price and any advantages may already be priced into the proposal made by the Minnen board.

There may also be problems with the acquisition:

There are problems of <u>integrating</u> the two companies, which may include <u>different cultures,</u> IT systems, governance and control systems. While there may be cost savings from integration there may also be additional costs from integration difficulties.

There may be <u>additional uncertainties</u> which <u>due diligence procedures may not identify</u> (see below). This may mean that risks become apparent after the acquisition has been made, that were not anticipated.

A further issue is that the directors of Minnen own 20% of its ordinary shares. If a share-for-share exchange takes place, then they will hold a much smaller proportion of the combined entity. Even if there were to be a debt-financed cash acquisition, the value of the directors' 20% shareholding may be worth more per share, than the price of individual shares sold on the market. This may be the case if the 20% holding gives the board significant influence. There may therefore be a reluctance by directors to sell at any given price, compared to other Minnen shareholders.

1.3 Price per share

The proposal from the Minnen board is for an acquisition at £4 per share. There are 20 million ordinary shares so this would give a consideration for the acquisition of £80 million.

There is a range of possible estimates. For each one, it should be remembered that the valuation date is 30 September 20X6 rather than 30 September 20X5 so the estimates need to be rolled forward.

Existing share price

The existing share price in trading individual shares is £3.20 per share which gives a market capitalisation of £64m. Based on the proposed offer price of £4, there is therefore a bid premium of £16m in order to gain control, compared with the current share price of £3.20 for smaller bundles of shares in daily trading. This is a 25% bid premium. It could be argued that this is part of the time difference between 30 September 20X6 and 30 September 20X5 (or at the current date of November 20X5), but 25% is a significant increase in one year, and so it is unlikely to account for the whole difference.

Net asset value

The net asset value (excluding intangibles) of Minnen at fair value is £58m. Thus, at the acquisition price of £80m, this would represent a payment of £22m for goodwill and other intangibles (eg the Minnen brand name).

Given that the tangible asset value mainly comprises land and buildings in this industry (in inventories), the fair value of £58m sets a reasonably low risk floor value of assets that could be realised if the acquisition needed to be reversed. The rising property market, for the short term at least, lowers this risk.

An asset value of £58m would give a share price of £2.90, which is lower than the current share price in market trading of £3.20 and below the proposed price of £4 per share.

If however the retained earnings of £5.6m for the year ending 30 September 20X6 is added to the net asset value of £58m (ie assuming no revaluation differences or other movements on reserves) then this would give a value per share of £3.18 ((£58m + £5.6m)/20m).

Note: The excess of the fair value of net assets (£58m) over the carrying amount (£42m) is £16m which is relatively modest on a landbank carrying amount of £184.8m (8.7%). This implies that Minnen has not benefitted significantly from property price increases following landbank purchases during the recession in the same way that Riller has.

P/E ratio

An alternative method is to use the P/E ratio. As both Riller and Minnen are listed and are in the same industry this may seem reasonable as a rough guide. If the P/E ratio of Riller were to be applied to Minnen then:

EPS of Riller	=	£21.6m/32m	=	67.5p
P/E ratio of Riller	=	£7.20/0.675	=	10.7
EPS of Minnen	=	£5.6m/20m	=	28p
Share price Minnen	=	28p × 10.7	=	£3.00

This is above the net asset value of £2.90 at 30 September 20X5, but below the current share price of £3.20, so it seems too low to be useable. The most probable explanation is different rates of anticipated growth compounded into share price for the two companies. More specifically it implies that the Minnen P/E ratio should be higher than that of Riller as there are greater growth expectations for Minnen by financial markets. (The P/E ratio of Minnen is £3.20/£0.28 = 11.4)

Earnings based valuation

Earnings for Minnen for years to 30 September

Year	Money cash flow £ million	Discount factor @10%	PV £ million
20X5	5.6	Not relevant	
20X6	6.16	Not relevant	
20X7	6.776	1/1.1	6.16
20X8	7.4536	$1/1.1^2$	6.16
20X9 and thereafter	7.4536	$(1/0.1)/1.1^2$	61.6

PV at 30 September 20X6	=	£73.92m		
Share price	=	£73.92m/20m	=	£3.70 per share

This value of £3.70 is above the net asset value of £2.90 at 30 September 20X5, and above the current share price of £3.20. However it is below the proposal of £4 from the Minnen board, so it seems to be within a reasonable range as a counter proposal.

Synergy gains

The above values for all valuation methods represent the value to Minnen shareholders for continuing the existing business. In addition, there are synergy gains which would make the acquisition more valuable in the Riller group than for Minnen as a stand-alone company.

The value of the synergy gains is £350,000/0.1 = £3.5m.

Thus as an example using the earnings based method the value to Riller of Minnen is:

Share price   =   (£73.92m + £3.5m)/20m   =   £3.87 per share

On this basis any price above £3.70 would mean that Minnen shareholders would capture some of the synergy gains in the value of the consideration.

Advice

In terms of negotiating an offer price, £4 per share is above what Minnen would be worth to Riller.

As a negotiating position £3.60 is suggested which would be below the earnings based measure and the initial offer from the Minnen board, but above the current share price by a bid premium of 40p.

1.4 Financial reporting issues

Statement of financial position

The acquisition would require that the net assets of Minnen would be revalued to fair value in accordance with IFRS 3 *Business Combinations*. This would mean they would be consolidated on a line by line basis at their fair value at 30 September 20X6. A particular feature is that the value of land in the landbank appears to have increased in line with increases in property prices. This would need to be revalued to fair value for consolidation purposes.

While the statement of financial position would be consolidated in full at that date, the statement of profit or loss of Minnen would not be consolidated until after the acquisition in the year ending 30 September 20X7. The return on capital employed and return on equity for the year ending 30 September 20X6 would therefore be distorted as the net assets would be recognised, but not the profit.

The consolidation of intangibles would also be an issue.

It is necessary to provide a value for the Riller group consolidated Statement of Financial Position for the year ended 30 September 20X6 where the Minnen brand would need to be recognised as a separately identifiable asset at fair value, notwithstanding that it would not be recognised in the individual company financial statements of Minnen.

IFRS 13 *Fair Value Measurement*, para 9, defines fair value as 'the price that would be received to sell an asset or paid to transfer a liability in an orderly transaction between market participants at the measurement date'.

IFRS 13 requires the fair value to be determined on the basis of its 'highest and best use' from a market participant's perspective. This needs to consider what is physically possible, legally permissible and financially feasible.

The fair value recognised is determined from the perspective of a market participant. The issue of business integration is relevant to financial reporting measurement. If Riller intends to acquire the Minnen brand, but not use it (ie branding all housing developments under the Riller brand) this does not mean that the brand has no fair value, as the assumption is the highest and best use by a market participant (eg an alternative buyer of the brand).

If however Riller management intends to continue to use the Minnen brand, then it is entitled to assume that its current use is the highest and best use without searching for alternatives unless market or other factors suggest otherwise (IFRS 13, para 29).

BRAND VALUE

The fair value is therefore, in part, dependent on the post-acquisition strategy adopted by Riller with respect to usage of the Minnen brand.

In order to quantify fair value IFRS 13 has a fair value hierarchy:

Level 1 inputs are quoted prices in an active market for identical assets. This is not normally reasonable for a brand given its unique nature, so is inapplicable to Riller.

Level 2 inputs are inputs other than quoted prices which are observable. This might include prices in markets which are not active.

Level 3 inputs are unobservable inputs, including internal company data.

Based upon these three levels, IFRS 13 sets out three possible valuation bases which Riller may use to value the Minnen brand:

(1) **The market basis** – This uses market price and other market transactions. Given the nature of a brand is unique this would be difficult to use.

(2) **The income basis** – This would consider the present value of the incremental income generated by the Minnen brand.

(3) **The cost basis** – This is the current replacement cost of the brand which could be the PV of the advertising expenditure.

Goodwill

Any excess of the consideration transferred over the fair value of the net assets acquired should be recognised in the group accounts as the asset, goodwill (the value of any non-controlling interest is zero in this case so goodwill is not affected by this).

As goodwill is a residual amount, any variation in the value of other assets at the date of acquisition (eg the brand value) will alter the amount attributable to goodwill.

After initial recognition, goodwill is stated in the group accounts at cost less any impairment charges.

Financing methods

The 10-year bonds would be recognised and measured at amortised cost in accordance with IAS 32 *Financial Instruments: Presentation* with the interest of 5% being recognised as a finance cost.

The share-for-share exchange would recognise, as the consideration, the fair value of the shares in Riller at the date of the exchange (30 September 20X6) in the transaction. As Riller is listed, the published price is to be used. This would normally be the bid price.

The fair value of the shares would therefore be the cost of the business combination and used in the calculation of goodwill. Consolidation in the normal manner would then take place in accordance with IFRS 3.

For the new shares issued the difference between their fair value and their nominal value would be credited to share premium account.

(2) **Financing methods**

Finance method 1 – Share-for-share exchange

Acquiring 100% of the ordinary shares of Minnen using a share-for-share exchange using newly issued Riller shares would have the effect of lowering financial risk for Riller as there would be no use of existing cash resources. In addition there would be a reduction in gearing as additional equity would be issued with no extra debt.

Ignoring consolidation adjustments (other than fair value adjustments) the gearing of the new Riller group, if consolidation had taken place on 30 September 20X5, would be:

Book gearing at FV (debt/equity) = (87m + £260)/(£58m + £206.8) = 131%

MV gearing (debt/equity) = (£87m+£260)/(£80m + £230.4) = 112%

Thus while book gearing is lower for the combined entity than for Minnen, the market gearing is approximately the same.

As both companies are quoted then there is greater assurance over share values than would be the case if one were a private company. The fact that Riller shares are quoted also makes them more liquid and perhaps more acceptable to Minnen shareholders who can sell them post acquisition. If they all try to sell them immediately, however, then this may force down the share price.

In terms of Riller's share price if the market regards the acquisition as value enhancing then it is likely that share price will rise. This however depends on the bid price. If Riller overpays for the acquisition it is likely that its share price will fall.

A further issue is that the directors of Minnen own 20% of its ordinary shares. If a share-for-share exchange takes place then they will hold a much smaller proportion of the combined entity. The value of the 20% shareholding may, collectively, be worth more than the price of individual shares sold on the market and thus there may be some reluctance by directors to sell.

Finance method 2 – 10-year bond

The issuing of a 10-year bond will increase the financial risk of the Riller group. Gearing will increase due to the increased debt.

This will make share price more volatile and will increase the beta by gearing it up.

In terms of the concerns of the directors, if market expectations of future corporate bond rates increases then the fair value of the Riller bonds will fall. This will increase the bond yield.

Advice

A share-for-share exchange appears to be the lower risk option as it means that: gearing is not increased; there is greater liquidity to make more landbank purchases, as debt capacity is maintained; and the need to refinance the debt in 10 years is removed as a share-for-share exchange is a permanent method of financing the acquisition. Given the business risks of the industry, in terms of house price volatility, then adding further financial risk into the package would seem undesirable.

This advice is given on the assumption that this form of consideration is acceptable to Minnen shareholders and that a higher bid price is not demanded compared to a cash acquisition.

(3) Key risks and due diligence

The acquisition would be material to Riller and due diligence over a number of aspects of the Minnen business can mitigate some risks of the acquisition.

Due diligence is a means of attesting information, normally on behalf of a prospective bidder. It can take place at different stages in the negotiations, although the timing is likely to affect the nature of the due diligence process.

[handwritten margin note: DD definition]

The key risks and the due diligence procedures to address each risk include the following:

Bid price and forecasts

Risk: The bid value, based on the forecasts provided, may be over optimistic, resulting in over payment for the acquisition.

Due diligence: Examine appropriateness of the forecasts and underlying assumptions. The assumption about 10% annual growth rate is significant in this context. Assurance, in the form of financial due diligence, could include examining the order book of forward purchases on houses off-plan, demand in the sector, demand in the region. Forecasts by similar companies, if available, would also act as a benchmark. Operational due diligence could assess the capacity of the company to achieve growth (eg resource audit including physical and human resources; peaks and toughs in forecast demand; historic issues of capacity constraints).

Valuation of assets (particularly the landbank)

Risk: There is a risk that the asset-based valuation is overstated, particularly with respect to the landbank. If the acquisition fails then the fair value of the assets represents a floor price for an exit value. An incorrect estimate of the landbank value may mean that this risk is not appropriately quantified.

Due diligence: The value of the landbank is a key asset. As inventory in the financial statement is stated at the lower of cost and NRV, the carrying amount is not a reflection of the fair value which has not therefore been subject to annual audit. Due diligence procedures can identify upside potential (high fair values compared to the estimated £58m fair value of assets) and downside risk (inadequate impairments and lower fair values than the estimates included in £58m fair value of assets). Due diligence procedures may involve the use of an expert in residential property and land valuation. Any recent sales from the landbank could be a test of the achieved price against attributed fair values.

Ownership and rights over assets and relevant legal obligations (particularly the landbank)

Risk: The landbank acquired may not have all the appropriate permissions and rights to build the planned residential properties. For example, there may be covenants limiting the size or specification of residential properties that can be built on a plot (eg houses may be permitted, but not apartments on some sites; there may be a minimum limit on the number of houses that must be built on a site).

Due diligence: Legal due diligence would be needed to establish the rights and restrictions on building land to ensure that it would be suitable for the intended purposes of the proposed new group. Legal obligations may also arise from land ownership which may cause unforeseen costs (eg ground rent; obligations to make-good any disruption to landscape from building work; obligations to maintain aspects of the site such as water and drainage; other hidden liabilities; and onerous contractual obligations).

Costs and uncertainty over integration

Risk: The costs and difficulty of integrating Minnen into a new Riller Group may be greater than expected. This may result in additional costs, a reduction in efficiency, less control and delay on delivering any synergies or other benefits.

Due diligence: An assessment of the compatibility of the two companies' operations, governance and information systems needs to be assessed through operational, human resources and IT due diligence. For example, an assessment of whether the two companies' information systems can be integrated or whether a new common system is needed, giving rise to additional costs. An operational assessment of commonalities in procurement and building methods also needs to be assessed using operational due diligence.

(4) **Ethics**

Ethics pertains to whether a particular behaviour is deemed acceptable in the context under consideration.

In making any ethical evaluation it is first necessary to establish the facts. In this case, the claims made by Julie Morton need to be established to assess their validity. This may be difficult if the indication has been oral and not written. The Minnen directors may deny the claims if anyone challenges them.

However assuming the claims are valid, a number of issues arise.

The issue of legality applies where an inducement may be given (ie continuing the role of director at the same remuneration in return for influencing shareholders toward a less favourable deal) which may come under the Bribery Act. It may also be fraud.

It should be noted however that no inducement has yet been given so no issue may yet have arisen. Legal advice should be taken.

A key ethical issue is **self-interest**. The Minnen directors may be attempting to act in their own interests rather than those of the shareholders to whom they owe a fiduciary duty. These interests are likely to be in conflict in the circumstances of the takeover recommendation.

In making a decision as to how to act, it may be helpful to apply the Institute of Business Ethics three tests:

- Transparency
- Effect
- Fairness

Transparency – Would the Minnen board mind people (existing shareholders, suppliers, customers, employees) knowing the terms of the agreement? In particular, the issue of transparency will apply to the Minnen shareholders.

Effect – Whom does the decision to provide inducements affect/hurt? Clearly this includes the Minnen shareholders who may be induced to give up their shares for an amount which is lower than could be obtained in a commercial arm's length transaction.

Fairness – Would the inducement be considered fair by those affected? The issue for the Minnen board is that they may be using their position and inside information in order to gain what many would consider to be an unfair personal gain at the expense of Minnen shareholders.

Honesty – A final issue is one of honesty. The inducements fail the honesty test on the basis of not basing advice to shareholders on an honest assessment of the value of the offer from Riller in the relevant commercial circumstances.

Response

An initial action would be to speak with the Riller board to ensure that no offers of directorships have been made to Minnen directors which may be considered an illegal inducement for them to recommend a low acquisition valuation to their shareholders.

If there is any doubt, then HS should not act for Riller and, if there are reasonable grounds to suspect that an inducement is to be given, HS should seek legal advice as to whether there is a duty to disclose this to the police.

If negotiations for the takeover are to be completed before the negotiation for continuing director contracts commences, then this may give some assurance that the former is not influenced by the latter.

39 Kinn plc (November 2015)

Marking guide

		Marks
(1.1)	Analyse the forecast financial performance of Kinn for the year ending 31 December 20X5.	
	Calculate and exlain the impact on the company's future performance for the year ending 31 December 20X6 arising from the sale of the Electrical Division (in line with the working assumption in Exhibit 2).	12
(1.2)	Set out and explain the financial reporting implications arising from the sale agreement for the Electrical Division in the financial statements for the year ending 31 December 20X5.	9
(2)	Explain to the board how the interest rate futures contract that it is proposing to use could manage the interest rate risk arising from the deposit of the £25 million	
	Set out calculations showing how the interest rate future provides an effective hedge.	10
(3)	Explain the likely effects on Kinn's risk profile and share price of the two alternative uses of the funds	
	For Alternative 1, provide advice on the two potential financing methods (fixed or variable rate loan).	9
Total marks		40

(1) Sale of the Electrical Division

1.1 Financial performance for the year ending 31 December 20X5

	Mech	Elect	Civil	Total	Mech & Civil ✳
Revenue	16,600	4,500	22,900	44,000	39,500
Operating profit	4,250	620	4,600	9,470	8,850
Profit before tax	3,100	110	3,300	6,510	6,400
Net assets at carrying amount	34,000	26,400	46,400	106,800	80,400
Total assets at carrying amount	57,000	36,600	72,400	166,000	129,400
Liabilities	23,000	10,200	26,000	59,200	49,000
Interest	1,150	510	1,300	2,960	2,450
ROCE	7.5%	1.7%	6.4%	5.7%	6.8%
ROE	9.1%	0.4%	7.1%	6.1%	8.0%
OP profit %	25.6%	13.8%	20.1%	21.5%	22.4%
PBT %	18.7%	2.4%	14.4%	14.8%	16.2%
Gearing (debt/net asset)	67.6%	38.6%	56.0%	55.4%	60.9%

[Handwritten annotations in left margin: "op.profit / total assets" → pointing to ROCE; "PBT / Net assets ie. equity" → pointing to ROE; "comparing the removal of E division with M+C"]

The table above sets out some key financial performance indicators based on the limited information available.

Liabilities have been taken as total assets less net assets (but may include non-interest bearing liabilities such as provisions and trade payables).

Interest has been taken as the difference between operating profit and profit before tax (but this may include other finance charges eg lease interest).

As indicated by the finance director, the Electrical Division appears to have underperformed the other two divisions on the measures of margin and return on capital. The return on equity for Electrical Division is only just positive at 0.4% and therefore appears to be making little contribution to shareholder return. This can be contrasted with the better ROE rates of 9.1% and 7.1% for the Mechanical and Civil Divisions respectively. However, it could be argued that even these rates are not high when considering the risks.

Even the funds placed on bank deposit at 3.75% are earning a better rate of return than the Electrical Division. In addition the bank deposit funds are virtually risk free.

The ROCE of the Electrical Division is only a little better than the ROE at 1.7%.

In terms of margins, the PBT% is only 2.4% for the Electrical Division which is extremely thin, especially when compared to those of the other two divisions at 18.7% and 14.4%.

Some notes of caution are however appropriate. These rates are based on accounting numbers which may be distorted by accounting policies or unusual items in the year. However if the projection is the same for next year then this seems less likely.

The end two columns of the table show the impact on the group of the removal of the Electrical Division. While the total column shows all three divisions, the right hand column shows the total of the other two remaining divisions.

It can be seen that while the removal of the Electrical Division has some impact on the group, it is only by one or two percentage points. The reason is that the Electrical Division is much smaller than the other two divisions and therefore has a relatively lower weighting. The removal of the poor performance of the Electrical Division therefore has some impact on the group, but it is not major.

The use of the £25m funds from the sale of the Electrical Division has not been considered in the assessment of the change in performance as this will depend on how these funds are to be used. This is considered further below but clearly there will be a favourable effect.

Performance so far has been taken to mean the impact on the overall profitability of Kinn from the sale of the Electrical Division. There will also be an impact on the risk profile of Kinn as a result of the disposal.

The direction of the impact will depend on whether the Electrical Division was a higher or lower business risk profile compared with the other two divisions. It might however be noted that the Electrical Division had lower gearing than the other two divisions and hence the group gearing has risen. (This of course ignores the surplus cash and how it will be used in the longer term which is considered below.)

Forecast performance for the year ending 31 December 20X6

If the disposal of the Electrical Division occurs on 31 March 20X6 then it will make a time apportioned contribution to the group of 3/12 of the full year amounts for item in the statement of profit or loss. The forecast for the year ending 31 December 20X6 will therefore be (in £'000):

	Mech	Civil	Mech & Civil	3/12 Electrical	Total
Revenue	16,600	22,900	39,500	1,125	40,625
Operating profit	4,250	4,600	8,850	155	9,005
Profit before tax	3,100	3,300	6,400	28	6,428
Interest	1,150	1,300	2,450	325	2,775

It can be seen that the impact of the Electrical Division in 20X6 is relatively insignificant in the context of the company as a whole for the year ending 31 December 20X6 in terms of operating performance.

The sale of the division may also impact upon profit in the period. The net assets have a carrying amount of £26.4m and the net sale price is £25 million. However if there is evidence of impairment in 20X5 then this would be recognised in the year ending 31 December 20X5. As a consequence, no loss on sale would be expected to be recognised in the year ending 31 December 20X6.

1.2 Financial reporting

The assets in the Electrical Division are being disposed of collectively under a single contract. They therefore appear to form a 'disposal group' under IFRS 5 *Non-current Assets Held for Sale and Discontinued Operations*. According to the standard a disposal group is defined as a group of assets to be disposed of, by sale or otherwise, together as a group in a single transaction.

The following criteria must be met:

- The division must be available for immediate sale in its present condition.

- The sale must be 'highly probable', that is:

    - being actively marketed at a reasonable price;
    - changes to the plan are unlikely;
    - management must be committed to the sale;
    - there must be an active programme to locate a buyer; and
    - the sale must be expected to be completed within one year from the date of classification.

Given the information about the planned sale, it seems clear that the disposal group meets the definition of 'held for sale' at or before 31 December 20X5. (The disposal group is available for immediate sale in its present condition and has been actively and successfully marketed at a reasonable price. The sale appears virtually certain and will be completed within one year.)

Immediately before the classification of a disposal group as held for sale, the carrying amounts of the assets need to be adjusted (IFRS 5).

On this basis, evidence of impairment should be assessed on each individual asset (or cash generating unit (CGU)) immediately prior to the held-for-sale date. After classification as held for sale, any test for impairment will be based on the disposal group as a whole.

There is evidence of impairment as the net sale price is £25m and the net assets have a carrying amount of £26.4m.

An adjustment that will need to be made prior to classification as held for sale is in respect of the depreciation charge up to the date the assets are classified as held for sale.

On re-classification as held for sale, IFRS 5 requires that a disposal group shall, at the date when reclassified as held for sale, measure the relevant assets at the lower of:

- Carrying amount
- Fair value less costs to sell

Any test for impairment will be based on the disposal group as a whole. As the expected proceeds from the sale of the disposal group to the German company is £25m and the carrying amount immediately before reclassification as held for sale is £26.4m or as the date it is classified as held for sale may be before the year end slightly less, (as £26.4m is the year end net asset value) there is an impairment charge of approximately £1.4m.

The impairment charges will be treated as reductions in the carrying amounts of individual assets (IAS 36 *Impairment of Assets*).

One qualification is that the non-monetary assets would normally be measured at the exchange rate at the date of purchase, and would not be normally be retranslated. However, where there is an impairment, non-monetary assets are retranslated at the exchange rate at the date of impairment. As a result, the sterling amount of the net asset value may change.

Consideration also needs to be given as to whether the sale is a discontinued operation under IFRS 5.

The Electrical Division is likely to be a component of the entity as a CGU. It is revenue generating, it is clearly distinguishable from the rest of the company and it is material. It appears to be a separate major line of the business as it makes a different types of engineering product from the rest of the company at a separate location.

IFRS 5 provides an analysis of the contribution of the discontinued element to the current year's profit ie the part that will not be included in future years' profits. Showing separate information about discontinued operations allows users of financial statements to make relevant future projections of cash flows, financial position and earnings-generating capacity.

(2) Interest rate futures contract

Interest rate futures contracts offer a means of hedging against the risk of adverse interest rate movements. If Kinn buys an interest rate futures contract, it contains the entitlement to receive interest; if it sells an interest rate futures contract, it sells the promise to make interest payments. Buying an interest rate futures contract, therefore, equates to lending, while selling an interest rate futures contract equates to borrowing.

An interest rate futures contract is effectively a binding, standardised forward rate agreement similar in effect but with conditions, amounts and terms which are standardised. As a result, they cannot always be matched precisely with a specific interest rate exposure, not least because a number of whole contracts must be bought or sold (based on the standard contract size) and because of the effects of 'basis risk'.

Interest rate futures contracts represent interest receivable or payable on notional lending or borrowing for a three-month period beginning on a standard future date eg the end of March, June, September or December for LIFFE contracts. The notional period of lending or borrowing starts when the contract expires eg at the end of March or the end of June.

Interest rate futures are priced at 100 minus the three-month interest rate contracted for.

In this particular situation, as a depositor (ie lender) Kinn can hedge against the possibility of interest rates falling by buying 50, March sterling interest rate futures contracts at 31 December 20X5 at the prevailing market price of 96.00 and selling futures on the date that the actual deposit (lending) begins ie the end of March. If interest rates do fall, Kinn will suffer a loss of interest income on the actual deposit but this will be offset by the gain on the futures contract, whose price will have risen in line with the fall in market interest rates.

To hedge the deposit, Kinn should buy 50 contracts at 31 December 20X5 and sell 50 contracts at the end of March. If the current deposit interest rate is 3.75%, then Kinn's target interest receipt will be £234,375 (£25m × 3.75% × 3/12).

If the deposit interest rate at the end of March is 2.75% (a fall of 1%), the three-month deposit with the bank from the end of March will only yield £171,875 (£25m × 2.75% × 3/12), which is a shortfall of £62,500.

However, assuming that the futures price has converged to equal the spot interest rate at the end of March (ie the futures price moves from 96.00 to 97.25) this will give Kinn a gain of 1.25%. The gain from selling 50 interest rate futures contracts at the higher price is £78,125 (£0.5m × 1.25% × 3/12 × 50), which more than compensates for the shortfall in interest on the actual deposit £62,500 (the excess compensation being due to the effects of 'basis risk').

(3) **Alternative uses of net proceeds**

Alternative 1 – Purchase new production equipment for the Mechanical Division

This strategy is simultaneously a new operating investment and a new financing arrangement.

The operating strategy is further investment in an existing line of the business and so may be lower business risk than an investment in a new line of business. However, the increased borrowing represents additional gearing and financial risk.

The sale of the Electrical Division involved repaying some liabilities amounting to £10.2m. However this project involves borrowing a further £20m thus the net effect is to increase borrowing significantly. This raises financial risk.

The new project earns a rate of return of 9%. This is in excess of the rate of return on either of the suggested debt instruments. However, the increase in gearing as a result of borrowing will mean the required return on equity will rise.

The hurdle rate for the project is therefore the risk adjusted marginal weighted average cost of capital (ie allowing for changes in financial risk and business risk) not the cost of debt. Share price will rise if the risk adjusted marginal cost of capital is lower than 9% and will fall if the risk adjusted marginal cost of capital is greater than 9%.

Risk adjusted should mean systematic risk, based on the project beta as the company is listed.

Fixed or variable rate loan

Turning to the type of debt, there is a choice between fixed and variable rates. The initial fixed rate is 6% to compared the initial variable rate of 6.75%. The fixed rate will however reflect the expectation that short term interest rates will fall over the period of the loan.

Variable rate loans give rise to cash flow risks as the coupon rate may vary over the life of the loan and the cash interest payments will therefore change.

Fixed rate loans give rise to fair value risk as the value of the loan will increase if market interest rates fall in order to adjust the yield to the market rate. Conversely, the value of the loan will decrease if market interest rates rise.

Advice

If the loan is to be held to maturity, then the fixed rate loan offers lower interest rate risk as the rate is certain over the period of the loan. Although the fair values may vary, this will have no significant impact if held to maturity and the cash interest payments will not change, even if market interest rates change.

Alternative 2 – Degearing

This is a lower risk and more conservative approach than Alternative 1.

After the Electrical Division has been sold and its liabilities paid off, the total liabilities of Kinn amount to £49m. Using the £25m net sale proceeds to repay debt would therefore more than halve the company's debt and reduce gearing substantially.

The impact would be to reduce the cost of equity as there is lower risk due to lower financial gearing. The impact on the weighted average cost of capital would be difficult to determine but in the absence of tax and in a perfect market it is likely to remain constant. Whether it will in fact do so would depend on the market's view of whether Kinn had been over geared.

The equity beta of the shares would be lower as the gearing is lower and may therefore generate a lower return at a lower risk.

If profitable investment opportunities were to present themselves in future then the debt capacity of Kinn would be greater if there is degearing now.

40   Kiera Healy Ltd

		Marks
(1.1)	Evaluate the strategic and operating issues that arise from KHC's expansion into the US. Provide a reasoned recommendation as to which of the alternative supply chain strategies is preferable for KHC.	
(1.2)	Explain possible pricing strategies for the US market, and analyse key market issues which will affect pricing. Provide a reasoned recommendation for KHC's pricing model.	11
(2)	Explain currency risks arising from multi-currency operating cash flows, and evaluate how those risks can be mitigated. Perform foreign currency risk management calculations using the data provided, and the methods suggested, to demonstrate effective hedging. Explain the implications of the calculations for foreign currency risk management.	13
(3)	Recommend, with supporting (expected value) calculations and explanations, whether KHC should invest in a warehouse distribution centre in the US. Advise on the best method of finance for the US warehouse distribution centre. Set out and explain the key financial reporting issues arising from KHC's expansion strategy in the US.	15
(4)	Explain the factors KHC should consider in deciding whether to license the brand or to sell it (on the basis described by Paula Simmons). Explain the benefits to KHC of PHM carrying out an agreed-upon procedures assignment to monitor licensee partners, and explain the key procedures that would be performed during such an assignment.	14
(5)	Identify the potential ethical implications of the matter identified by Jeff and Rachel, and explain the actions to be taken by the relevant parties in response to the matter.	7
Total marks		60

(1)   Strategic and operating issues

1.1   Distribution and warehousing

The decision to build a warehouse distribution centre in the US is partly an issue of cost and partly an issue of distribution strategy.

In terms of cost there is a greater fixed cost (both initially and annually) in having a warehouse distribution facility in the US, compared with supplying each retailer, directly from the UK.

A US warehouse distribution centre would need to be justified in terms of sales volumes as although fixed costs would be higher, the variable costs could be reduced by more efficient local distribution to the US and within the US. As an example an agreement with a US wholesaler might reduce distribution costs and widen access to US retailers.

At the moment, it seems clear that KHC's scale in the US is not sufficient to justify a warehouse distribution centre. Moreover, if a warehouse distribution centre was set up and the US operations subsequently failed, then there are likely to be more significant exit costs.

As KHC grows in the US, the arguments, based on costs, about whether to have a warehouse distribution centre may become more finely balanced. If export volumes rise significantly, then demand may exceed the warehouse capacity in the UK, and a US warehouse could become more cost effective than a new UK one if labour and property prices are lower. The impact on distribution strategy may then become the major factor.

Distribution is part of the downstream supply chain and the management of all supply activities through to delivery to customers is an important part of becoming successful in the US. Distribution is therefore part of demand chain management, reflecting the idea that the customers' requirements and downstream orders should drive activity of end-to-end business (e2e).

The distribution channel comprises a number of stakeholders including: manufacturer (KHC); wholesalers; retailers and consumers. The local holding of inventory in the US enables the distribution channel to be shortened in some cases, but there may still be significant delays in supplying from the UK (particularly if supplied by ship rather than by air) unless demand is stable or significant inventories are held at the US warehouse.

Supplying directly from the UK might result in more significant delays for consumers unless wholesalers and retailers are prepared to hold significant inventories and suffer the costs of doing so in order to make sales of KHC products.

Benefits of a US warehouse distribution centre

- The lead times and uncertainty of delivery times are greater if supplied from the UK as the geographical distances are larger. Inventory can be held 'locally' in the US with a warehouse distribution centre to meet surges in demand more quickly and with less uncertainty for customers than by supplying directly from production output in the UK.

- As a consequence, this strategy is driven by customer need, which is central to the end-to-end business model. The US presence means that KHC is closer to the customers and could perhaps better understand their needs.

- Presence in the US, rather than delivery directly from the UK, means more local employees with local knowledge can be used.

- Reputation with customers may improve if they know they are being supplied locally (ie their supply chain becomes within the US to a greater extent).

- Managing customer service from the UK becomes more difficult as US sales volumes grow and a distribution facility will, at some point, in the growth curve be a minimum response to satisfy the needs of the US market.

- A more substantial response to US sales growth would be to have a US production facility. However, having a distribution facility holding inventory is a much cheaper alternative than a second manufacturing site in the US which would increase fixed costs and would need an appropriate skills base without any history of production in the US.

- Having more costs in the US will mean more costs incurred in $ which would be a natural hedge against the $ revenues that will be earned as a partial protection against currency risks.

Risks

- Mere location within the US still leaves a large geographical distance between the warehouse distribution centre and much of the US population. A single distribution centre may therefore only be a partial solution to the need to improve customer service. A network of multiple distribution facilities may be warranted at a later date if and when sales grow more substantially.

- The fixed production facility increases fixed costs and therefore increases risk from operating gearing if US sales are volatile. Exit costs are also increase if the US venture fails.

- High risk of a stock out. May need higher inventory levels than would be the case for an equivalent level of UK sales, as there is only one warehouse and there is a risk that there may be inventories in the UK which cannot quickly be used to supply the US market.

Recommendation

Initially, for market entry, sales volumes are likely to be low and supplying from the UK directly to retailers located across the US is likely to be the most efficient means of distribution while there are few economies of scope. As sales grow a little, the use of wholesalers may facilitate wider distribution but there may be a sacrifice of some margin to achieve this, as there would be an extra step in the supply chain.

Over time, if conditions change and sales expand, a larger number of customers geographically dispersed across the US may be more efficiently supplied, with shorter lead times and therefore better customer service, from a US warehouse distribution centre. If sales expand further, then multiple US warehouse distribution centres serving different regions of the US may become appropriate.

1.2 Pricing strategy

It is important for the Kiera Healy© brand to gain a foothold in the US market in terms of recognition and reputation.

The pricing policies used in New York (price penetration) and Boston (price skimming) represent two extremes.

Price penetration can help to gain market share by setting a low price initially to enter the market and get the brand name known amongst as many consumers as possible. Price penetration may also help in obtaining economies of scale which could render KHC's US operations more viable as a long-term strategy.

Price penetration is a temporary policy, as prices need to be increased later to generate profit if sales are being made at full cost price as in New York. It may be difficult however, to increase the price once this lower price has been established.

The low initial prices may also damage the brand name, particularly for toiletries products where quality is not easily observable, and it may be difficult to establish a quality brand image later.

Price skimming is where the initial price is set high for new products launched into a market and a smaller market share is normally gained but at a greater margin. This policy was intended by KHC in Boston.

Typically a price skimming policy will involve a company charging high prices when a product is first launched; then spend heavily on advertising and sales promotion to win customers. The company may later lower its prices in order to attract more price-elastic segments of the market; however, these price reductions will be gradual.

For KHC, the Boston price model has been successful in generating a higher sales volume at a higher price.

One possible reason is that the price is a signal of the quality and image of the product and it has become successful in this area partly because of, rather than despite, the price. Another consideration however is that it was non-price factors that caused the difference in sales volumes (eg differences in culture between the two cities, differences in retailers selected or locations within the cities).

There are significant questions whether the price skimming model is either sustainable within Boston or extendable to other regions of the US.

Perhaps a more sustainable pricing model would be based on market research including what similar products are selling for in the US market and what the target market group is willing to pay. This group may differ from the females aged 25 to 40 applying in the UK market.

(2) **Managing exchange rate risk from foreign currency operating cash flow**

(a) **Currency risks of the US operating cash flows**

By entering the US market, KHC will suffer economic foreign currency risk. This refers to the effect of exchange rate movements on international competitiveness. For example, KHC uses raw materials which are priced in sterling as manufacturing is in the UK. However, it exports products to the US so revenues are in $. A depreciation of the dollar against sterling would erode the competitiveness of the company compared to local US producers.

Techniques for protecting against the risk of adverse foreign exchange movements include the following:

- KHC could invoice in £, thus transferring all risks to suppliers and customers. However, this seems implausible in the circumstances as KHC is small, perhaps dealing with large wholesalers and retailers in an advanced economy with a stable currency.

- KHC could enter into forward contracts, under which an agreed amount of $ will be bought or sold at an agreed rate at some fixed future date or, under a forward option contract, at some date in a fixed future period. Where there are many transactions it would be inappropriate to hedge each one but hedging the net cash flow exposure would be reasonable. However these are only short term measures. (See illustrative example below.)

- KHC could buy foreign currency options, under which the buyer acquires the right to buy (call options) or sell (put options) a certain amount of a currency at a fixed rate at some future date. If rates move out-of-the-money, the option is simply allowed to lapse.

- KHC could buy foreign currency futures on a financial futures exchange. Futures are effectively forward contracts, in standard sizes and with fixed maturity dates. Their prices move in response to exchange rate movements, and they are usually sold before maturity, the profit or loss on sale corresponding approximately to the exchange loss or profit on the currency transaction they were intended to hedge.

- KHC could enter into a money market hedge. One currency is borrowed and converted into another, which is then invested until the funds are required or funds are received to repay the original loan. The early conversion protects against adverse exchange rate movements, but at a cost equal to the difference between the cost of borrowing in one currency and the return available on investment in the other currency. (See illustrative example below.)

  Where there are many transactions it would be inappropriate to hedge each one but hedging the net cash flow exposure would be reasonable. However, these are still only short term measures and would not manage a risk of a drift of £/$ exchange rates over a longer period.

(b) **Forward exchange market**

The rates are:

	$/£
Spot	1.5240 – 1.5275
3 months' forward	1.5168 – 1.5208
6 months' forward	1.5112 – 1.5153

The net payment three months hence is £435,000 – ($640,000/1.5208) = **£14,169.**

The net payment six months hence is ($720,000 – $400,000)/1.5112 = **£211,752.**

The $ receipts can be used in part settlement of the dollar payments, so only the net payment is hedged.

Money market

Three-month transaction

$640,000 will be received three months hence, so $632,098 ($640,000/(1 + (0.05 × $\frac{3}{12}$)))

may be borrowed now and converted into sterling, the dollar loan to be repaid from the receipts.

The net sterling payment three months hence is:

£435,000 − {[$640,000/(1+(0.05 × 3/12)] / 1.5275 × [1 + (0.045 × 3/12)]} = **£16,532**

The equation for the $640,000 receipt in three months is to calculate the amount of dollars to borrow now (divide by the dollar borrowing rate) and then to find out how much that will give now in sterling (divide by the exchange rate). The final amount of sterling after three months is given by multiplying by the sterling lending rate.

Six-month transaction

$320,000 net ($720,000 − $400,000) must be paid six months hence. We can borrow sterling now and convert it into dollars, such that the fund in six months will equal $320,000. The sterling payment in six months' time will be the principal and the interest thereon. A similar logic applies as for the equation above except that the situation is one of making a final payment rather than a receipt.

The sterling payment six months hence is therefore:

[$320,000/((1 + (0.03 × 6/12))//1.5240 × (1 + (0.065 × 6/12))] = **£213,594**

An alternative approach

The intertemporal nature of the $ cash flows can be recognised as a $ **inflow** of $640,000 occuring after 3 months and a net $ **outflow** of $320,000 after 6 months.

Unless the $ cash inflows need to be converted to £s for use in the UK, some of the $640,000 inflows could be maintained in $ and be put on deposit in $ in the US for the three to six-month period, rather than converted to £s. The amount invested would be $317,618 (ie $320,000/(1 + (0.03 × 3/12)) such that it would accumulate to $320,000 after three months. This amount could then be used to settle the net $ outflow of $320,000 ($720,000 − $400,000) after six months. This would avoid the need for hedging the six-month $ net cash outflow by a forward or money market hedge.

(3) **The risks of setting up a US warehouse distribution centre and financial reporting issues**

(a) **Investment decision for warehouse**

If the $ appreciates against the £ at 1% pa then the $ cash flows, expressed in sterling, will grow by 1% per annum irrespective of any increase in underlying $ cash flows.

NPV

	£
Niche	
[($400k/1.5)/(0.1 - 0.01)] =	2,962,963
£100k/0.1	(1,000,000)
PV	1,962,963
Wider market	
[(350k/1.5)/(0.1 - 0.05*)] =	4,666,667
£100k/(0.1 – 0.04)	(1,666,667)
PV	3,000,000

5% reflects 1% exchange rate appreciation and 4% $ cash flow growth (more precisely should be 5.04% (1.04 × 1.01)).

The outlay in sterling will be $3m/1.5 = £2m

NPV = (0.4 × £1,962,963) + (0.6 × £3m) - £2m = **£585,185**

Recommendation

While there is an expected positive NPV, there is also a 40% probability of a negative NPV (ie if there is a niche market the PV is less than the outlay of £2m.) Even these figures are dependent on the accuracy of the underlying assumptions.

Nevertheless, based on these assumptions, for which the test marketing exercise has given some assurance, there is a significant positive NPV. Also the downside loss in terms of the negative NPV for a niche market outcome is relatively small.

A tentative recommendation is therefore to invest in the warehouse but any commitment should be delayed as long as possible to gain the maximum amount of information from market entry.

(b) Raising finance

The financing need of $3 million is substantial when measured against the company's net assets of £5.8 million. However brands are internally generated and represent a significant unrecognised asset.

Leasing

It should not be assumed that debt is the only alternative when equity finance is not available. Leasing may be a useful choice that would restrict the US financial commitment depending on the term of the lease. A short-term lease would reduce exit costs if the US venture failed. A long-term lease may be an alternative to borrowing, but it may, in commercial terms, amount to a similar commitment with similar characteristics. Local advice on the tax implications of a lease and debt may be needed.

As a compromise, a short-term lease may be a stepping stone for a few years between direct supply from the UK and a debt-purchased warehouse distribution centre.

The currency in which the debt is denominated

In financing operations overseas, there may be a currency (foreign exchange) risk for KHC arising from the method of financing used. For example, if KHC decides to acquire the distribution centre in the US, using a sterling denominated loan, the investment will provide returns in $, while the bank will want interest and capital paid in sterling. If the $ falls in value against sterling, the sterling value of the project's returns will also fall, but the financial commitment to the bank will remain unaffected.

To reduce this currency risk, KHC might finance it with funds borrowed in the same currency as the investment ie in dollars.

The advantages of borrowing in the same currency as an investment are that:

- assets and liabilities in the same currency can be matched, thus avoiding exchange losses on conversion in the Group's financial statements (see Section (c) below).

- revenues in $ can be used to repay borrowings in the same currency, thus reducing losses due to fluctuating exchange rates.

KHC therefore has three options when financing the US project by borrowing in:

- The same currency as the inflows from the project (ie in $). This can be done in the US or using KHC's UK bank.

- Raise finance in the UK, denominated in sterling, with a hedge in place.

- Raise finance in the UK denominated in sterling, but without hedging the currency risk. This exposes KHC to exchange rate risk that can substantially change the profitability of US operations.

The type of debt

A bank loan would be the obvious type of borrowing as this scale is far too small for a bond issue.

Fixed or floating rate

Fixed rate loans are where the coupon rate of interest paid on the loan is at a set level for the entire life of the loan. If the loan is held to maturity, this gives certainty over the cash flows of interest and principal that will need to be paid by KHC in terms of the local currency. If it is a $ denominated loan, the sterling equivalents will not be certain, but there is scope for currency matching as noted above.

The risk with fixed rate loans is that if market interest rates rise, then the fair value of the instrument will fall as yields increase (and vice versa).

Variable rate, or floating rate, loans are where the coupon rate varies according to market interest rates (eg LIBOR). Rates are reset periodically. For a $ loan, KHC would have the variation in cash interest paid according to US market interest rates and for a sterling loan according to UK market rates.

The term of any loan

Careful consideration needs to be given to the term or period of any loan.

A long term, fixed rate agreement would give certainty of cash flows for many years. A variable rate agreement would mean KHC would be subject to variations in short term interest rates over time.

In either case, the risk of refinancing a long term loan would be deferred for many years providing liquidity advantages during the period KHC is trying to become established in the US market.

A downside to a long term $ denominated loan would be that if the US venture failed, then KHC would be locked into making $ interest and capital repayments for many years with no corresponding $ revenues. Additional hedging arrangements would be needed if this became the case.

(c) Financial reporting issues

Foreign currency – assets and financing

Under this strategy, the division is part of KHC for accounting purposes so its results, assets and liabilities are treated as those of the KHC parent company.

The foreign currency translation issues relating to the division therefore relate to transactions and balances being translated into the functional currency of KHC (most likely the £). The issue of presentation currency does not arise as there is no issue of consolidation.

Assuming that the KHC functional currency is the £, then the US revenues are required to be recognised in £s at the spot exchange rate at the date on which the transaction took place. The date of the transaction is the date on which the transaction first satisfied the relevant recognition criteria.

If there is a high volume of transactions in foreign currencies by the division, translating each transaction may be an onerous task, so an average rate may be used.

The new warehouse distribution centre would represent PPE as a foreign currency asset which is a non-monetary asset. This would be depreciated over its useful life.

Non-monetary items such as the warehouse will not require retranslation so the warehouse distribution centre when acquired on 1 July 20X7 will be translated at the assumed spot rate on that date of £1 = $1.5 and would not be retranslated. Depreciation on this cost would therefore also be based on the same historic exchange rate. The value in the statement of financial position of KHC would not therefore be affected by subsequent exchange rate fluctuations.

Receivables arising from US sales represent another foreign currency asset but they are a monetary asset. These assets will need to be translated into £s as KHC's functional currency at each reporting date.

Monetary assets and liabilities would therefore be affected by subsequent exchange rate fluctuations and resulting exchange gains or losses impact on profit. Exchange gains/losses on monetary operating items (eg receivables) would be recognised in operating costs. Exchange gains/losses on monetary finance items (eg a $ loan) would be recognised in finance costs.

Hedging

The investment in the US and its financing cannot be designated as a net investment in a foreign operation in accordance with IAS 21 as this rule applies only to consolidated financial statements and KHC does not prepare these as the US operations are only a division, not a subsidiary.

Also, a foreign currency borrowing in US$ cannot be designated as a fair value hedge of the US assets purchased in $ (eg a warehouse) because these assets are non-monetary. As such, they are not subsequently remeasured under IAS 21 and therefore they do not contain any separately measurable foreign currency risk.

If a future sale of the warehouse is highly probable, then it could be designated as a cash flow hedge, but this seems unlikely as it has not yet been purchased.

Where the $ denominated revenues and costs are highly probable, as seems the case, and they are to be hedged with a forward or a money market hedge (hedge instruments) then, if other hedge accounting conditions are met, this may be treated as a cash flow hedge. That is:

- the portion of gain or loss on the hedging instrument that is determined to be an effective hedge should be recognised in other comprehensive income; and

- the ineffective portion should be recognised in profit or loss.

The gain or loss on the hedging instrument that has been recognised in other comprehensive income should be reclassified to profit or loss on receipt/payment of the related operating cash flow.

Leasing

If leasing is to be used to finance the warehouse this may be a finance lease or an operating lease.

Finance leases – where substantially all the risks and rewards of ownership of the leased asset are transferred to the lessee and the asset is a resource for which future economic benefits will flow. Both the asset acquired and the obligation to make lease payments are recognised in the statement of financial position and the effective 'interest' expense is recognised in profit or loss.

Operating leases – other leases where the transfer of risks and rewards does not take place. Lease payments are recognised in profit or loss and the lessee does not recognise the asset or obligation in the statement of financial position.

The land element of the warehouse would be an operating lease.

Buildings are normally operating leases largely because they have a significant residual value. Much would depend on the term of the lease and the conditions on completion of the minimum term but a warehouse may be a less substantial structure than a traditionally constructed building so it may be a finance lease.

(4) **'Kiera Healy©' brand issues**

Licensing the brand

A licence grants a third-party organisation (the licensee) the rights to exploit an asset belonging to the licensor.

Licences over brand rights are common. The licensee, Mooton, would pay an agreed amount (in this case £5 per bag), to KHC, as licensor, relating to the sales generated on licensed products, for the right to exploit the Kiera Healy© brand for its Attitude range of products in the specified geographical area of the UK.

The total annual payment from Mooton would be £150,000 per annum (30,000 × £5). In perpetuity (assuming that the four year contract was constantly renewed or replaced) discounted at the WACC this would give a value of £1.5 million.

This compares favourably with the £2.5 million offered by Buckingham for the brand rights to all its products (except cosmetics). There may be some annual monitoring costs to be incurred which will reduce the PV but these are not likely to be significant.

Licence agreements will vary considerably in the constraints placed on the licensee. Some will dictate branding, pricing and marketing issues. Others will leave these decisions to the licensee.

Licensing can be a method of financing rapid growth without having to make an initial investment, as KHC would need to do to exploit different product markets itself. Mooton will also bring core competences in handbag manufacture that KHC does not have and may find difficult to acquire.

There needs to be some incentive for the companies involved to purchase the licence but as Mooton has already approached KHC presumably it believes it will benefit from the licensing agreement.

From KHC's perspective, the financial risk is low as there is a low risk new revenue stream with no operating costs to be incurred other than setting up and monitoring the arrangement. There is however a potential reputational risk.

A key issue is whether Mooton will enhance, damage or have neutral effect on the Kiera Healy[©] brand.

The licensing arrangement may enhance recognition of the Kiera Healy[©] brand name and stimulate sales of toiletries. Alternatively, it may damage the brand name if Mooton's product or customer service is not of the same quality as KHC. Contractual protection against this could be built into the licensing agreement to protect against this risk. This might involve control over production quality, service quality and controls over the advertising image presented.

Also in order to manage risks:

- a break-date or exit route from the contract needs to be established in case the relationship fails within the contract period.

- controls measuring sales volumes are needed so Mooton does not exploit the contract and underpay on the licence royalties. A clear cut-off date needs to be established in the contract as triggering a royalty payment (eg date of production, date of sale to retailer, date of sale to consumer).

Selling the brand

The decision to sell the brand would depend fundamentally on the price that could be obtained. Three ways of determining the brand value are:

The market basis – this uses market price and other market transactions. Given the nature of a brand is unique this would be difficult to use (note, the offer of £2.5 million from Buckingham plc was not appropriate but, had it been for the entire global rights, serious consideration could have been given to this method of valuation, although as the offer was rejected the valuation itself seems too low).

The income basis – This would consider the present value of the incremental income generated by the brand. No price premium is obtained by the Kiera Healy[©] brand, but additional sales volume is obtained.

The cost basis – this is the current replacement cost of the brand which is the PV of the advertising expenditure of £3.5 million. The basis on which this value was determined would need to be considered, including allowance for risk and how the expenditure could replicate the brand in varying market conditions.

Aside from the valuation there are adverse strategic factors which are as follows:

- The ability for KHC to leverage the brand in future in order to expand is lost permanently

- While the brand sale involves a clause to "retain an exclusive and permanent right to continue to use, without charge, the 'Kiera Healy©' brand for toiletries globally" the use of the brand by other companies may damage the brand for KHC (eg if the other companies used it for downmarket products).

On the positive side, larger companies could leverage the brand more efficiently than KHC and Kiera may obtain a higher price in expectation of this. As a stand-alone company, KHC may take many years to be of sufficient size to exploit the brand as effectively.

Minimum price

The minimum price is likely to be higher than the £2.5 million as: this price was rejected; it only related to non-toiletry products; and the company has developed since the offer was made.

The £1.5 million for licensing to Mooton just for handbags seems indicative of the value of the brand if it can be spun out to other types of product.

Cost basis of £3.5 million has no element of added value above cost so a minimum of around £4 million to £5 million may seem appropriate.

Ignoring tax this would give a P/E ratio of around 6.2 to about 7.7.

PHM engagement

Agreed-upon procedures

In an agreed-upon procedures (AUP) engagement, PHM would provide a report of factual findings from the procedures and tests performed, which need to be agreed with both KHC and Mooton. The procedures and tests required should be sufficiently detailed so as to be clear and unambiguous, and discussed and agreed in advance with both KHC and Mooton, so that the factual findings are useful and appropriate to the licensing contract.

When performing an AUP engagement on historical financial information, PHM, as practitioners, are required, as a minimum, to comply with International Standards on Related Services (ISRS) 4400 *Engagement to Perform Agreed-upon Procedures on Financial Information*.

Our report for an AUP will not express a conclusion and, therefore, it is not an assurance engagement. It will not provide recommendations based on the findings.

We would request that KHC and Mooton review the procedures and findings in our report and use the information to draw their own conclusions.

A key guide to the procedures that PHM would carry out would be related to the contractual terms of the licensing agreement. For example, the number of bags sold; the number of customer complaints about product quality; and the number of customer complaints about service quality.

The value of an AUP comes from PHM, as practitioners, objectively carrying out procedures and tests with relevant expertise thus avoiding the need for KHC to carry out the procedures and tests themselves and therefore it protects confidentiality for Mooton.

AUP are most effective in situations such as this where there is a clear matter to focus on in the form of the licensing contract.

The benefit to KHC of agreed-upon procedures is therefore that it provides evidence for the board that Mooton is complying with the terms of the licensing contract in identifying, measuring and attributing all sales of the Attitude range and is fully stating the royalty payments to KHC. This prevents understating of royalty payments by Mooton and the monitoring of other contractual terms in a manner that is inconsistent with the licence contract. Aspects of quality control could also be monitored (eg customer complaints) to restrict any reputational damage.

Mooton may be more likely to allow PHM to carry out this task as a professional accountant than perhaps they would with KHC staff, due to the commercial sensitivity of other information that may be obtained in the process. In this context ISRS 4400 requires compliance with the applicable requirements of the Code of Ethics for Professional Accountants.

(5) **Ethical matter**

Ethics pertains to whether a particular behaviour is deemed acceptable in the context under consideration. In short, it is 'doing the right thing'.

In making any ethical evaluation, it is first necessary to establish the facts. In this case, it would seem that the source of information is a casual conversation with a personal assistant. This relationship would need to be verified. Also there may be good reasons why Kiera is willing to pay more and this needs to be established.

If the relationship is substantiated, the ethical risk is that Kiera has been giving favourable treatment to Juno as a supplier (in terms of purchases above market price and acceptance of inferior quality) due to a personal relationship rather than on the basis of an arm's length commercial transaction.

Kiera may therefore have a conflict of interest between her role for KHC and her personal family relationship. This risk is that she has promoted self-interest, above the corporate interests of KHC.

A number of key issues arise:

- Although Kiera is the CEO and sole shareholder, KHC is a separate legal entity from Kiera. Moreover, Kiera has duties as a director towards the company. Ethically and legally she has a duty to other stakeholders (eg if suppliers are overpaid then there may be less cash available for debt holders in future and for employees). There is therefore a self-interest threat in this case.

- There is a governance issue in that Kiera is not permitting the board to discuss issues relating to Juno when they have a right to do so and, as a majority, Jeff and Rachel have the right to outvote Kiera at a board meeting. There may however be an intimidation threat in that Kiera, in her capacity as sole shareholder, can remove Jeff and Rachel from the board.

- There is an ethical issue of confidentiality in that disclosure to PHM staff by Jeff and Rachel may be a breach of confidentiality as this is a disclosure outside the company on a matter which is not directly relevant to the issue that PHM has been asked to advise on. It seems unlikely that this disclosure was authorised formally by the board, even though it was made by two members of that board who form a majority.

- Legality – it may be that this type of transaction by Kiera, if unauthorised by the KHC board, may be illegal. Legal advice should be obtained.

As a result, a number of business trust principles arise from the matter.

Transparency – would the parties be happy if the details of the transaction became more widely known, for instance to other suppliers?

Effect – whom does the issue affect? If the terms are unduly favourable then some stakeholders may lose out (eg debt holders may be at more risk) even though Kiera owns all the shares. An alternative, more worthy, supplier would also be affected by the continued use of Juno.

Fairness – would the arrangement be considered fair by those affected? Clearly if the commercial agreement is influenced by personal relations, then those adversely affected may regard this as unfair in not satisfying arm's length conditions. Competing suppliers to Juno who have not been offered such favourable terms will be disadvantaged.

Actions

As ICAEW Chartered Accountants, Jeff and Rachel are bound by the Ethical Code. If there is a belief that the transaction is illegal, they should obtain advice (eg ICAEW helpline). In this case, they should not speak to Kiera as this may be tipping off.

If advice is received that this is not an illegal transaction, but it may be unethical, then Jeff and Rachel should raise the issue formally at a board meeting and the response should be recorded in the minutes.

Jeff and Rachel are entitled to outvote Kiera in the best interests of the company if that is their view about removing Juno as a supplier.

41 Quinter plc

		Marks
(1)	Analyse financial and operating data to identify key factors that vary between quarter and thereby explain quarterly performance. Identify key operational weaknesses.	14
(2)	Identify and justify the additional data which should be made available at board level to assist decision making for: • Sales and and customer management • Inventory management	9
(3)	Explain the financial reporting issues for the valuation of Inventories. Recommend the information required to ensure that inventories are valued appropriately in the financial statements.	5
(4)	Identify and explain improvements in corporate goverance that would assist Quinter's management control and performance management.	5
(5)	Evaluate whether the sustainability policy suggested (in Exhibit 5) would: • Make a positive contribution to Quinter's public profile • Generate additional, useful management data	7
Total marks		40

(1) Analysis of quarterly performance and operational weakness

	£ Q1	£ Q2	£ Q3	£ Q4	£ Total
Units					
House	120,000	130,000	140,000	150,000	540,000
Garden	50,000	10,000	25,000	75,000	160,000
Total	170,000	140,000	165,000	225,000	700,000
Average price					
House	35	35	35	35	35
Garden	40	50	50	50	46.88
Revenue					
House	4,200,000	4,550,000	4,900,000	5,250,000	18,900,000
Garden	2,000,000	500,000	1,250,000	3,750,000	7,500,000
Total	6,200,000	5,050,000	6,150,000	9,000,000	26,400,000
Revenue					
Individual customers	4,805,000	3,913,750	4,766,250	6,975,000	20,460,000
Stores	1,395,000	1,136,250	1,383,750	2,025,000	5,940,000
Total	6,200,000	5,050,000	6,150,000	9,000,000	26,400,000

	£	£	£	£	£
	Q1	**Q2**	**Q3**	**Q4**	**Total**
Cost of sales					
House	2,940,000	3,185,000	3,430,000	3,675,000	13,230,000
Garden	1,200,000	300,000	750,000	2,250,000	4,500,000
Total	4,140,000	3,485,000	4,180,000	5,925,000	17,730,000
Gross profit					
House	1,260,000	1,365,000	1,470,000	1,575,000	5,670,000
Garden	800,000	200,000	500,000	1,500,000	3,000,000
Total	2,060,000	1,565,000	1,970,000	3,075,000	8,670,000
Number of product types	480	380	420	560	
Number of items returned by customers	8,500	7,000	8,250	11,250	35,000
Analysis					
Revenue per product type (£)	12,917	13,289	14,643	16,071	
% of items returned	5%	5%	5%	5%	
Gross profit %					
House	30%	30%	30%	30%	30%
Garden	40%	40%	40%	40%	40%
Total	33.2%	31.0%	32.0%	34.2%	32.8%
% revenue retail	77.5%	77.5%	77.5%	77.5%	77.5%
% revenue wholesale	22.5%	22.5%	22.5%	22.5%	22.5%
% revenue house	67.7%	90.1%	79.7%	58.3%	71.6%
% revenue garden	32.3%	9.9%	20.3%	41.7%	28.4%

Performance

Revenue

Revenue can be analysed according to type of customer or by product.

By **type of customer**, the retail market (ie individuals) is far more important than the wholesale market, comprising 77.5% and 22.5% of revenue respectively for the year as a whole. There is no quarterly variation in these % figures.

The dominance of the retail market is partly due to higher prices being generated from retail customers, as there is a 10% discount for stores. However given the dominance of retail sales this is only a small part of the explanation. Individual customers clearly buy in greater volumes than stores overall although, on average, the price and type of the goods may also vary between stores and individuals. There are quarterly variations over the year between stores and individuals, but no clear trend.

Analysis of costs would be useful by customer type to give a better indication of gross profit for each customer type.

Analysis of revenue by **product** shows household goods rising quarter by quarter over the year. This could be a variation within the year or an indication of a trend of growth. In contrast, garden goods are seasonal selling significantly better in summer.

The analysis of revenue by product shows household goods contributing most of the revenue, being 71.6% over the year as a whole. However, this is seasonal where in the winter months (Q2) few gardening items are sold so household goods contribute 90.1% of revenue; while in the summer months, when garden goods sell better, this falls to only 58.3% of revenue.

The average price of a garden product is higher than for household goods, but this is more than compensated for in larger volumes for household goods. There is some seasonality in garden good prices as well as volumes.

Gross profit

Costs are not provided by customer type. This analysis of costs would be useful to give a better indication of gross profit for each customer type.

In absolute terms, the gross profit generated by the household products is much greater than for garden products in most quarters. However in Q4 (the peak summer months), although the garden products only sell half of the volume of the household goods the gross profit is similar at £1.5m compared with £1.575m. The reason for this is the high average price and the higher gross profit % for garden products.

Overall, gross profit margins are around one third (32.8%). There is no data provided on other operating costs, which would show operating profit margins.

Areas of operational weakness

There are a significant number of product lines, but there is no further information to indicate whether these are all profitable or even whether they are mainly household products or garden products.

The returns of goods from customers, at 5% seems high and the costs of return and collection are likely to be high. However there is no information about whether these are faulty items or whether the customer has changed his/her mind within 14 days. It is important that data is collected on this in order to assess reliability overall and for each supplier.

(2) **Board level data**

The types of data made available to the board needs to be commensurate with the types of decisions being made at board level. This should be of sufficient detail and relevance to enable them to control the company and its operations.

Too much detailed data at board level may cause data overload and therefore the inability to comprehend and evaluate the key issues within that data. As it stands, however, (indicated by the data in Exhibit 3) the data appear to be too aggregated to be useful.

Sales and customer management

It would appear that data is held on a database of each customer's characteristics and transaction history. The comment by a member of staff that "there is just too much detailed data to be useful to us" needs to be treated with a degree of professional scepticism.

While this may be a large data set, companies are increasingly using Big Data analytics to analyse unstructured data to identify trends and extract insights to improve decisions. Identifying such patterns could enable target marketing by Quinter according to the type and frequency of historic purchases and customer characteristics, enabling flexible pricing and bespoke customer service.

Sales are only available by product type (household and garden) rather than by product line (where there are over 560 different types of individual product).

Showing revenue and gross profit for all 560 different items may be too much information for board level decisions. However, whether to discontinue a poorly selling product line or support further sales of a successful product line would be the type of decision appropriate to board level. Product line data could therefore be analysed (eg in order of size: best selling down to worst selling). Alternatively, management by exception could be used by reporting to the board only the outliers of the best and worst performing product lines.

Sales return information is also poor. The returns need to be analysed between faulty returns and 14 day returns from a change in the customer's mind. The faulty returns can then be identified with relevant suppliers so the board can decide whether contract terms have been fulfilled (ie do not pay the supplier) and whether Quinter wants to continue the supplier relationship in future.

Certain types of customer may also have a higher propensity to return goods within the 14 day period. Once identified, sales to these customers may not be encouraged by marketing staff.

Inventory management data

Better data, and better analysis of existing data, can help identify how much inventory is needed and when it is needed. Minimising inventory, while still having sufficient quantities to meet customer needs on a timely basis, can reduce inventory costs. These may include: storage costs; damage; obsolescence; insurance.

A key issue is predicting the timing of demand and ensuring that sufficient goods are ordered to arrive on time, after allowing for the lead time. Uncertainty of demand and uncertainty of lead time may mean a buffer inventory needs to be held to prevent shortages which could mean customer needs would not be satisfied on a timely basis.

Key factors would be analysing historic data to identify the timing of surges in demand or dropping off in demand (eg seasonality of garden goods). Other factors may not be captured in historic data such as an advertising campaign, a favourable review for a product in the press or a sudden spell of good weather to encourage garden purchases.

(Handwritten margin note: ⊛ Realtime ← information)

Data need to be constantly monitored, updated and analysed and compared to inventory levels which should be measured continually (continuous inventory measurement).

Relationships with suppliers also need to be part of the data management eg linking Quinter's IT systems with those of large key suppliers so forecast inventory shortages can be resupplied at the earliest opportunity.

(3) **Financial reporting – inventory**

A significant amount of inventory as suggested by Mike Fisher (Exhibit 4) creates the risk that there is scope for material misstatement in both the statement of financial position and the statement of profit or loss.

However, it is not merely the amount of the inventory that creates the risk of misstatement. It is also the nature of the goods and that the average inventory turnover is high, with some items likely to be held in inventory for far longer than the average turnover period.

IAS 2, *Inventories*, requires that inventories should be stated at the lower of cost and net realisable value. There is a risk that some electrical goods are likely to become obsolescent, (or at least only capable of being sold at reduced prices) if held in inventory for an extended period. This may be particularly the case with computer equipment, but may also apply to many other electrical items.

Poor information systems, or poor managerial controls in appropriately using these systems, means that old inventories or damaged inventories may not be readily identifiable (eg from the introduction of an ageing analysis of inventories) in order to be able to make the appropriate write down.

Inventories are non monetary assets in accordance with IAS 21, *The Effects of Changes in Foreign Exchange Rates*. As such, they will be translated at the exchange rate on the date of purchase and not normally retranslated thereafter. The fact of the inventories being purchased in a foreign currency is not therefore a major financial statement risk so long as the original purchase price is recorded.

However, where there is an impairment, or other fair value adjustment, the values of inventories are retranslated at the current date and therefore it is necessary to have detailed and reliable continuous inventory records in order to be able to do this.

(4) **Corporate Governance**

A number of aspects of corporate governance need to be reviewed.

Non-executive directors with the right skills and experience need to be appointed (eg IT skills as Quinter is an internet based company) to advise executive directors and to monitor and manage their performance at an operational level.

Subcommittees need to be set up.

Establishing an audit committee seems key to monitor internal performance and information flows (not just dealing with external auditors). Information flows and management controls would be enhanced by an internal audit function reporting to the audit committee. The audit committee would consist of non-executive directors who would monitor the performance of the company and its executive directors. As chairman, it may be suitable for Mike to also chair the audit committee.

A remuneration committee seems appropriate to ensure that, as part of performance management for the executive directors, they are motivated by their remuneration package for promoting the performance of the company. At the moment, without any non-executive directors other than the chairman, it is difficult to see who has been awarding the executive directors a 10% annual pay rise. If it was the directors themselves, then there may be a conflict of interest, a self-review threat and a self-interest threat.

New executive members of the board may be appropriate as, at four, the board is small and may not have the full spectrum of skills necessary. An appointment committee would be useful to do this.

(5) **Sustainability**

Sustainability is about ensuring that development meets the needs of the present without compromising the ability of future generations to meet their own needs.] *Def^n of sustainability*

The idea of recycling is consistent with sustainability, in that an organisation should only use resources at a rate that allows them to be replenished (in order to ensure that they will continue to be available). At the same time, waste should be confined to levels that do not exceed the capacity of the environment to absorb them. Quinter's proposed recycling policy attempts to reuse some resources and reduces waste.

However, recycling is only one aspect of sustainability. Wider social, environmental and economic issues also need to be addressed for Quinter to demonstrate corporate responsibility in promoting sustainability as a listed company acting in the public interest.

Sustainability reporting is an important issue. The ICAEW publication *Outside Insights: Beyond Accounting* highlights a number of issues that must be addressed for sustainability reporting to be effective and these are relevant to Quinter's decision to report its sustainability policy in the annual report in terms of the level of detail that should be indicated. These include the following:

- Who reports are for
- Links to corporate/business strategy
- Materiality of issues reported
- Validity of indicators
- Reliability of indicators
- Objectivity of reporting
- Transparency of information
- Comparability of information
- Balance of information
- Understandability of the report
- Audit/assurance of the report and performance
- External stakeholder engagement
- Integration with financial reporting
- Addressing true sustainability

Issues that must be addressed for sustainability reporting to be effective.

Tutorial note:

Some examples from this list would be sufficient for candidates to demonstrate the type of disclosures needed.

An integrated report should explain how the organisation creates value, using both quantitative and qualitative information.

One aspect of this is natural capital, including the impact of Quinter's activities are having on air, water, land, minerals and forests. Recycling would be one element addressing this.

The benefit to Quinter of such disclosures is that it presents the image of corporate responsibility in formal communication by indicating the proposed (if limited) sustainability policy.

In being part of integrated reporting the annual report it also makes environmental assurance more feasible to order to attest that the claimed policies are being implemented effectively.

Additional management data

While the primary purpose of Quinter's recycling is to demonstrate a policy of sustainability, and therefore corporate responsibility, it will also generate additional management information which may give rise to a range of business opportunities. These may include the following:

- Information that the customer will no longer be using the product previously purchased and therefore that there may be a sales opportunity to sell new goods to the customer. The purchase of new product is a necessary condition of the collection policy. This may be an opportunity to sell more goods. However it also casts doubt on the policy as being more about commerciality than sustainability.

- It provides a reason to contact customers periodically when it is possible that the average life of a past purchase has expired. Quinter sales staff can then market to them to recycle their old goods but also to persuade them buy a new item from the company.

- Provides general marketing data about the probable life cycle of Quinter products.

42 Wooster Ltd

		Marks
(1.1)	Compare and evaluate the German and Japanese supply contracts in terms of: • Financial appraisal (with supporting calculations) • Supply chain risks, foreign exchange risk, and risk management Provide a reasoned recommendation for the preferred supplier.	17
(1.2)	Recommend, and justify, two KPIs that could form part of the environmental impact and sustainability conditions in a service level agreement for Proposal 1. Set out and explain the assurance procedures that should be performed to provide evidence that the two KPIs are being achieved.	10
(1.3)	Describe and evaluate, with calculations, the potential benefits and risks of Proposal 2 in comparison to Proposal 1. Provide a reasoned recommendation for the most appropriate strategy.	11
(1.4)	Explain, for each proposal, the key financial reporting issues, and the appropriate treatment in the Wooster financial statements, for each of the financial years affected. Explain the financial reporting issues for both supplier contracts.	6
(1.5)	Analyse the financial and operating data in order to evaluate the performance of Wooster, and the Wooster management team, in the period since the acquisition by StockFin. Write an additional short paragraph summarising performance, which can be shown to the managers to support the redundancy policy.	12
(1.6)	Set out the ethical implications for Wooster, and for GW, arising from the matters noted by Harry Harris. Explain the actions GW should take.	6
Total marks		62

Draft response to Eric Edward's briefing document

Subject: Wooster's future car engine procurement – consideration of board proposals

1. **Proposal 1 - Outsourcing**

    1.1 **Financial appraisal**

    Method 1 – PV of engine costs method

    Gratz

	2017	2018	2019
Engines demand	3,800	4,100	4,400
Engines delivered	3,800	4,100	4,200
Cost per engine (euro)	14,000	15,400	16,800
Exchange rate	1.4	1.4	1.4
Cost per engine (£)	10,000	11,000	12,000
Total direct cost	38,000,000	45,100,000	50,400,000
Opportunity cost	–	–	9,000,000
Total cost (£)	38,000,000	45,100,000	59,400,000
DF at 6%	0.943	0.890	0.840
PV	35,849,057	40,138,839	49,873,385
NPV (£)	⟶ 125,861,281		

    Shensu

	2017	2018
Engines demand	3,800	4,100
Engines delivered	3,800	4,100
Cost per engine (yen)	1,540,000	1,540,000
Exchange rate	140	140
Cost per engine (£)	11,000	11,000
Total cost (£)	41,800,000	45,100,000
DF at 6%	0.943	0.890
PV	39,433,962	40,138,839
NPV (£)	79,572,801	

    Approach (a) – Annual equivalent

    Gratz

PV of engine costs (£)	125,861,281
AF 3 years 6%	2.673
Annual equivalent (£)	47,086,149

    Shensu

PV of engine costs (£)	79,572,801
AF 2 years 6%	1.833
Annual equivalent (£)	43,411,239

    Approach (b) - PV cost per engine

    Gratz

    PV per engine: £125,861,281/(3,800 + 4,100 + 4,200) = **£10,402**

    Shensu

    PV per engine: £79,572,801 /(3,800 + 4,100) = **£10,073**

Method 2 – Alternative NPV approach (using contribution)

Gratz

Contribution per car £	45,000	45,000	45,000
Lost sales (vehicles)			200
	2017	**2018**	**2019**
Engines demand	3,800	4,100	4,400
Engines delivered	3,800	4,100	4,200
Cost per engine (euro)	14,000	15,400	16,800
Exchange rate	1.4	1.4	1.4
Cost per engine (£)	10,000	11,000	12,000
Contribution (£)	171,000,000	184,500,000	189,000,000
Direct cost of engines (£)	38,000,000	45,100,000	50,400,000
Net contribution (£)	133,000,000	139,400,000	138,600,000
DF at 6%	0.943	0.890	0.840
PV (£)	125,471,698	124,065,504	116,371,233
NPV (£)	**365,908,434**		

Shensu

	2017	2018
Engines demand	3,800	4,100
Engines delivered	3,800	4,100
Cost per engine (yen)	1,540,000	1,540,000
Exchange rate	140	140
Cost per engine (£)	11,000	11,000
Contribution (£)	171,000,000	184,500,000
Direct cost of engines (£)	41,800,000	45,100,000
Net contribution (£)	129,200,000	139,400,000
DF at 6%	0.943	0.890
PV (£)	121,886,792	124,065,504
NPV (£)	**245,952,296**	

Approach (a) - Annual equivalent

Gratz

NPV	£365,908,434
AF 3 years 6%	2.673
Annual equivalent	**£136,890,548**

Shensu

NPV	£245,952,296
AF 2 years 6%	1.833
Annual equivalent	**£134,180,194**

because over different time periods.

Approach (b) - NPV per engine

Gratz

NPV per engine £365,908,434/(3,800 + 4,100 + 4,200) = **£30,240**

Shensu

NPV per engine £245,952,296/(3,800 + 4,100) = **£31,133**

Analysis

The analysis above (Method 1) determines the cost of supplying engines over the contractual periods for Gratz and Shensu, which are 3 years and 2 years respectively.

In addition, in 2019, although demand is for 4,400 engines the maximum capacity of Gratz is 4,200 engines. As a consequence, given that holding inventories at the beginning of 2019, by over-ordering in 2018, is not possible due to storage problems, there is a constraint on the number of cars that can be sold. There is therefore an opportunity cost on the Gratz contract in terms of lost contribution from lower sales of £9m (200 × £45,000). (NB Method 2 does not require the opportunity cost as the lost sales of 200 cars are built into the lower NPV).

It may be that the figure of £9m overstates the opportunity cost as it may be possible to increase price slightly, compared with the Shensu contract, in order to reduce demand to the available level of supply. Moreover, if the forecast demand for 2019 is over optimistic, then this will affect Shensu but, at the margin, will not affect Gratz and therefore the actual opportunity cost will be lower than expected.

A key comparability problem is the difference in the length of each contract. It is clear that the total cost of supplying engines over a 3-year period by Gratz (just over £125m in PV terms) will be greater than that for Shensu over 2 years (almost £80m in PV terms). Some method of averaging is therefore required.

Moreover, the Gratz contract has significant increases in price over the 3-year period so further averaging is needed.

The calculations show an annualised equivalent present value of approximately £47.09m for Gratz and £43.41m for Shensu. This would suggest that the Shensu contract is preferable. However, the figures are very close so a range of other financial and non-financial factors need to be considered. In particular, the annuity method adjusts for the differential time periods of the two contracts but does not adjust for the fact that the number of engines varies over the contract term and is largest in the final year.

An alternative method of adjustment is therefore to divide the PV of the costs by the number of engines produced which allows for the different contract periods and the variation in the annual number of engines over that period.

Beyond 2019

The above financial appraisal only goes up to the end of 2019. While there is no detailed data for 2020 and beyond, there are a number of indicators of future financial differences between the two contracts. If Wooster wishes to obtain continuity by continuing with the same supplier when the contract is renewed in 2020 then the data for 2019 for Gratz (and 2018 for Shensu) may be an indicator of what might be renegotiated.

A key factor is that the demand for Wooster cars is increasing and in 2019 is expected to be 4,400 which is greater than Gratz's capacity to supply Wooster. If the demand for Wooster cars continues to expand beyond 2019 then the opportunity cost of using Gratz, rather than Shensu, will continue to grow. It may be that, with the knowledge of a longer term supply relationship with Wooster, Gratz will invest to expand production from 2020 but, at current engine production capacity, it could become a major barrier to growth for Wooster.

Variation in pricing

Shensu is charging a fixed price of yen 1,540,000 per engine. This is £11,000 per engine at the assumed exchange rate of £1 = yen 140.

Over the term of the contract, Gratz is charging variable prices per engine in euro which in £s is as follows:

Year	euro	£	% increase
2017	€14,000	£10,000	–
2018	€15,400	£11,000	10.0%
2019	€16,800	£12,000	9.1%

The increases in price over the term of the Gratz contract gives a cash flow advantage to Wooster as the higher prices are at a later date. These are also discounted to a greater extent as they occur later.

If the contract is taken with Shensu in 2017 and then renewed with Shensu we do not know what price will be charged in 2019 under the new contract. However, the Gratz price for 2019 represents a significant increase of 9.1% on the Shensu price and on Gratz's own price for 2018.

If the Gratz contract is to be renewed in 2020, the highest price under the existing contract of £12,000 may form the basis of renewal negotiations and this would mitigate against renewal of the Gratz contract and therefore the possibility of supply continuity.

1.2 Supply chain

✓ Geographical distance

A key difference between the two contracts is geographical distance. Germany is relatively close to the UK, while the lead time to supply from Japan is many times longer, particularly as engines are large and are likely to be transported by ship, rather than by air.

If the costs of transport are to be incurred by the supplier, and deliveries are planned in advance, then this long lead time may not be a major issue. However, if there is uncertainty of demand or supply, then it could become a significant issue, which may result in temporary production closure at Wooster's assembly plant. This is particularly the case as there seems to be little capacity to store engines and thus hold a buffer inventory level to prevent shortages.

✓ Frequency of delivery

The frequency of delivery is different, with Gratz delivering weekly and Shensu only monthly.

The limited storage capability is placed under more strain with monthly deliveries, but would leave some spare storage capacity with weekly deliveries as each order is smaller.

The fact that orders are only monthly with Shensu means if there is a problem with fulfilling any order, there may be a significant delay before it can be rectified.

The even spread of sales over the year may imply there is stability of demand and this may reduce the uncertainty in the supply chain, enabling Shensu to provide a good service.

1.3 Foreign currency

Both supply contracts are in foreign currencies, but different foreign currencies.

A key issue is the correlation of each of the two currencies with the £, which appears to be Wooster's functional currency. This will depend on the relative growth rates, interest rates and monetary policies of the UK, Germany and Japan. Forward currency rates may give an indication of short-term market expectations of currency movements, but expert advice might be needed to assess longer term expectations of relative currency movements.

Foreign currency risk management needs to consider the wider picture of foreign currency flows for the company as a whole.

In 2017, predicted sales are 3,800 vehicles. Assuming the price per car remains at the 2016 level of £87,000, then this means total revenue in 2017 will be £330.6m. If the proportion of sales to eurozone countries remains at 30% then this will give euro revenues of £99.18m.

In 2017, the total direct cost of the Gratz contract is estimated to be £38m. The Gratz contract would therefore represent a direct natural hedge for over a third of euro revenues. As a consequence, rather than increasing foreign currency risk, it actually reduces this risk for the company as a whole.

There are currently minimal revenues (if any) in yen and hence there is no direct natural hedging in respect of the cost of the engines from Shensu. There may be an indirect hedge if movements in the yen are closely correlated with movements in the US$ or the euro but, at best, this is likely to be somewhat less than perfect.

Short term hedging of transactions is possible by using yen/£ forwards, futures and options. Given that contract prices are fixed and quantities required are stable then reasonably effective hedging should be possible, at a cost, over the contract term.

Recommendation

The Shensu contract has the lower annualised present value of £43.4 million compared with £47.1 million for the Gratz contract. On this pure financial basis the Shensu contract is to be preferred by a reasonable margin.

In addition however the Shensu contract is for two years compared with three years for the Gratz contract. This may enable renegotiation earlier but this may result in either a favourable or an adverse outcome.

The risk of the Gratz contract is lower in forex terms, minimum delivery and in reliability of supply chain terms.

In the longer term however the maximum quantities are greater for Shensu and along with the direct financial benefit this appears to be the best option but based on a close judgement.

2. KPIs and assurance

In order to deliver a successful outsourcing project, the relationship with the outsourcing company, the products and the service provided, all need to be monitored and controlled.

Outsourcing makes Wooster dependent on a third party supplier to provide a key element of the car at appropriate quality and time.

A service level agreement, with specific measures of performance required under contract, enables Wooster to maintain some control of the key features of the supply arrangement.

In this case the features highlighted include environmental impact and sustainability. Two KPIs could be:

(1) CO_2 emissions from the engines not to exceed an agreed maximum level
(2) Proportion of an engine that can be recycled to be specified at a minimum level

Assurance procedures

> ### Tutorial note
>
> The specific nature of the assurance procedures will vary according to the KPIs selected. The answers to this section are therefore illustrative.

CO_2 emissions from the engines not to exceed an agreed maximum level.

✓ Review the governance, culture and competence of Gratz/Shensu management for evidence of commitment to sustainability and controlling environmental impact. This may include a public pronouncement in their annual reports and the emissions levels achieved by their own cars.

✓ Review the design of the engine and the features that control CO_2 emissions within the engines. This may need the help of an expert who is familiar with emissions engineering. The purpose of this procedure is to ensure emissions controls are embedded within the engine's design.

Monitor the control procedures in the Gratz or Shensu factory to check for emissions of engines actually being produced. For example, are the checks independent of production line management; are they rigorous; are they on every car or on a sample.

Monitor any controls over emissions carried out at the Wooster factory eg as part of quality control checks.

Monitor compliance with environmental regulations in the UK and in Germany/Japan, investigating any breaches.

If Gratz/Shensu participates in the emissions trading scheme, ensure data processing and measurements comply with the scheme and appropriate disclosures are made in the annual report.

Proportion of an engine that can be recycled to be specified at a minimum level

Review the design of the engine in terms of the composition of parts that are made of materials which can be recycled. This may need to help of an expert who is familiar with engineering materials that can be recycled.

Review the procedures for reclaiming and recycling old vehicles and assess the cost of recycling relative to the likely benefits/revenues.

Test the Gratz or Shensu recycling arrangements for their own cars and ask for the historic evidence of the experience of implementing these procedures.

3. **Proposal 1 compared with Proposal 2**

Financial appraisal of Proposal 2

There is significant uncertainty over the useful life of the new engine factory equipment.

It would be unreasonable to compare directly the NPV of Proposal 2, re-equipping the engine factory, with the outsourcing options in Proposal 1, as the periods covered are different, as are the profiles of cash flows. Proposal 2 has a significant initial outlay, then a lower marginal cost. To compare the first two or three years' cash flows of Proposal 2 with the outsourcing options would be unreasonable, as the outlay of Proposal 2 would not expect to be recovered over this short time period.

One approach is therefore to compare the annualised equivalent PVs of Proposal 2 for a 7-year useful life and a 10-year useful life. This can then be compared with Proposal 1 annualised equivalent PVs. (NB. other approaches are acceptable)

Proposal 2 – PV of costs per engine

					2020 and
Cost per engine		6,000	6,000	6,000	6,000
Engines made (75% in 2017)		2,850	4,100	4,400	4,400
	2016	**2017**	**2018**	**2019**	**after**
Initial investment	40,000,000				
Production cost		17,100,000	24,600,000	26,400,000	26,400,000
Opportunity cost (£45k × 950 cars)		42,750,000			
Total variable cost	40,000,000	59,850,000	24,600,000	26,400,000	26,400,000
DF at 6%	1	0.943	0.890	0.840	0.84
Annuity factor 4yrs (ie 7 yr life)					3.465
Annuity factor 7yrs (ie 10 yr life)					5.582
PV 7 yr life	40,000,000	56,438,550	21,893,912	22,165,949	76,839,840
PV 10 yr life	40,000,000	56,438,550	21,893,912	22,165,949	123,786,432

Total PV 7 yr life	**£217,338,251**
Total PV 10 yr life	**£264,284,843**

Annual equiv PV 7 yr life
AF 5.582   **£38,935,552**
Annual equiv PV 10 year life
AF 7.36   **£35,908,267**

The above table shows that the PVs are sensitive to some key factors.

Useful life

The first of these is the useful life of the new equipment. If the new equipment lasts 7 years then the annual equivalent PV is approximately £38.9m, which is a lower cost than that for either of the outsourcing companies. On the other hand if the new equipment lasts 10 years then the annual equivalent PV is approximately £35.9m, which is even lower.

 The useful life of the new equipment is therefore a key risk and a key element in the decision that requires further investigation.

Three months' lost sales

Another key factor is that there will be three months of lost production when re-equipping the engine factory. The above table assumes that these sales will be lost and never recovered.

An alternative assumption is that customers are willing to defer their purchase and wait until the new factory and new engines are available. The factory has an annual capacity of 8,000 engines, so in the remaining nine months it can make 6,000 engines. Similarly, the assembly plant has an annual capacity of 5,200 cars so, in nine months, it could make 3,900 which is greater than the annual demand of 3,800 vehicles in 2017.

If the assumption that all sales in the 3 months can be recovered then the alternative calculation is:

Internal production without opportunity cost

		6,000	6,000	6,000	6,000
Cost per engine (£)					
Engines made		3,800	4,100	4,400	4,400

	2016	2017	2018	2019	2020 and after
Initial investment	40,000,000				
Production cost		22,800,000	24,600,000	26,400,000	26,400,000
Opportunity cost		–			
Total variable cost	40,000,000	22,800,000	24,600,000	26,400,000	26,400,000
DF at 6%	1	0.943	0.890	0.840	0.84
Annuity factor 4yrs (ie 7 yr life)					3.465
Annuity factor 7yrs (ie 10 yr life)					5.582
PV 7 yr life	40,000,000	21,509,434	21,893,912	22,165,949	76,839,840
PV 10 yr life	40,000,000	21,509,434	21,893,912	22,165,949	123,786,432

Total PV 7 yr life	**£182,409,135**
Total PV 10 yr life	**£229,355,727**

Annual equiv PV 7 yr life	
AF 5.582	**£32,678,095**
Annual equiv PV 10 year life	
AF 7.36	**£31,162,463**

Tutorial note

The NPV of the net contribution could also be used as in requirement 1.1 above.

In this scenario, if the new equipment lasts 7 years then the annual equivalent PV is approximately £32.7m, which is far lower than that for either of the outsourcing companies. On the other hand, if the new equipment lasts 10 years then the annual equivalent PV is approximately £31.2m, which is now a significantly lower annual cost than that for either of the outsourcing companies.

A balanced view might be that the useful life is somewhere between 7 and 10 years and that some, but not all, of the potential sales during the 3 months the engine factory is closed will be lost. A series of iterations on these assumptions would test the sensitivity of the outcomes.

PV of costs per engine

An alternative methodology is the PV of costs per engine (including opportunity costs) as follows.

Number of engines

7 year life	2,850 + 4,100 + (4,400 x 5) =	28,950 cars
10 year life	2,850 + 4,100 + (4,400 x 8) =	42,150 cars

PV of costs per car

7 year life	£217,338,251 / 28, 950 =	**£7,507**
10 year life	£264,284,843 / 42,150 =	**£6,270**

There are a number of other factors to consider in selecting between the two proposals:

Operating gearing

The two outsourcing options comprise entirely variable costs. However, the significant investment in the factory means that, while Proposal 2 has a lower variable cost per engine than outsourcing, there are greater fixed costs. As a result, operating gearing will be higher under Proposal 2. Therefore there is a risk if sales levels are lower than indicated by the forecasts.

However, the minimum quantities specified by the outsourcing companies are also a de facto fixed cost as, if future sales are low, then these minimum levels must still be ordered and paid for. This is a similar risk to Proposal 2 where the cost of the new equipment is paid irrespective of future demand.

In this respect, the Shensu contract is the greater risk as the minimum order is 3,800 which is equal to the 2017 level of demand. So any shortfall of sales volume against forecast would result in excess inventory on the Shensu contract. The Gratz contract is less risky as the minimum is of 3,500 engines per annum.

In both cases, as sales grow over time, the outsourcing company minima become less of a concern as there is more headroom on forecast sales.

Financial gearing

The costs of outsourcing are incurred gradually over time so no immediate borrowing is needed. Conversely, Proposal 2 requires £40m of immediate borrowing. This raises financial gearing and therefore financial risk in requiring future interest payments and capital to be repaid.

The life of the bond is 10 years, which is the maximum useful life of the new equipment. If the useful life is less than this, then replacement of this equipment may be needed with associated new finance within the life of the existing bond.

Wider benefits and risks of outsourcing engine production compared with internal manufacture

Benefits

Outsourcing enables Wooster to draw on the core competences of two market leaders. It is noted that Wooster engines have become inferior to competitors' engines in cost, efficiency and environmental impact. This may suggest that, unless the new engine is a significant improvement, the manufacture of engines is not a core competence of Wooster. Wooster's core competences may instead be in car assembly and brand development.

A further, and related, point is that both outsourcing companies are major multinational car manufacturing companies which benefit from economies of scale; particularly in comparison to Wooster, which is relatively small in the context of the industry. By outsourcing to these companies Wooster may benefit from their scale economies and from a lower price.

Risks

There are a number of key risks.

At the moment, the potential to continue internal manufacture of engines gives Wooster the choice to reject the outsourcing companies' offers. This may be helpful in negotiating price. However, if Proposal 1 is selected, the factory will be sold and key staff for engine manufacture made redundant. As a consequence, it would be extremely difficult for Wooster to resume internal manufacture in future by bringing production back in-house at the end of the current outsourcing contracts. While there may be competition amongst outsourcers on contract renewal, there is capacity for Wooster to be less well positioned in renewal negotiations without an in-house option than is currently the case.

Outsourcing may restrict future growth as, if sales increase, the capacity of the current two outsourcing companies appears to be significantly below that of the production capacity of 8,000 which could be achieved by a re-equipped engine factory.

Internal production would incur costs in £s sterling. This appears to reduce currency risk, as Wooster's functional currency is the £, compared to the outsourcing alternatives, which are denominated in foreign currencies. However, it could be argued that the Gratz contract actually gives lower currency risk than in-house production, as it gives some natural hedging to euro revenues.

One final issue is the supply chain where a UK engine factory located in the same location, a short distance from the assembly plant. It therefore has a short supply chain. It also probably benefits from a common internal information technology system. This may enable more reliable deliveries and appropriate conditions for just-in-time manufacturing.

4. Financial reporting

There are a number of financial reporting issues arising from the two proposals.

Factory closure

Factory closure relates only to Proposal 1 and is not applicable if Proposal 2 is decided upon.

Under Proposal 1, the engine factory assets would be disposed of to a rival company, Jadd Motors plc, collectively under a single contract. They therefore appear to form a 'disposal group' under IFRS 5 – defined as a group of assets to be disposed of, by sale or otherwise, together as a group in a single transaction.

Given the information about the planned sale, it seems clear that the disposal group would meet the definition of 'held for sale' as at 30 November 2016. (The disposal group would then be available for immediate sale in its present condition. It has been actively marketed at a reasonable price as evidenced by negotiations for a sale nearing conclusion. The sale would then appear to be virtually certain and will be completed within one year.)

Immediately before the classification of a disposal group as held for sale, the carrying amounts of the assets need to be reviewed (IFRS 5).

On this basis, evidence of impairment should be assessed on each individual asset (or CGU) immediately prior to the held for sale date. After classification as held for sale, any test for impairment will be based on the disposal group as a whole.

In the case of the engine factory, there is no apparent evidence of impairment on the assets but more information will be required to verify this, particularly if there is any evidence of uncertainty over the fair value of individual assets.

An adjustment that will need to be made prior to classification as held for sale is in respect of the depreciation charge for the 11 months to 30 November 2016. No further depreciation charge is made after the held for sale classification date.

The depreciation charge for 11 months to 30 November 2016 is: $(£600,000) \times 11/12 = £550,000$.

The overall adjustment to the financial statements immediately before reclassification as held for sale is therefore to reduce the depreciation charge to profit or loss to £550,000 million and increase the carrying amount of engine factory assets to £22.05m. (Increase is £600,000 – £550,000).

On re-classification as held for sale, IFRS 5 requires that a disposal group shall, at the date when reclassified as held for sale, measure the relevant assets at the lower of:

- Carrying amount
- Fair value less costs to sell

As the carrying amount is less than the fair value less costs to sell, there is no impairment charge required upon reclassification.

Based on the estimated amounts provided, a profit on the sale of the factory of £9.45m (£31.5 – £22.05m) would be recognised in the statement of profit or loss for the year ended 31 December 2017. The engine factory assets would be derecognised on sale. (Note that the £29m proceeds is net of closure costs whereas it should be gross at £31.5 without the closure costs deducted. These should be recognised as a provision in 2016 (see below).

Foreign currency movement and management

The functional currency is that of the primary economic environment in which the entity operates. This appears to be the £ for Wooster, as the UK is the largest revenue generator and most costs are currently incurred in £s.

Wooster should translate the foreign currency purchases from Gratz/Shensu at the spot exchange rate at the date on which the transaction took place. Given there are weekly or monthly deliveries this may be feasible.

However, if there are many transactions in each delivery, an average rate may be used. This appears reasonable as Wooster has sales evenly spread over the year.

These purchases give rise to:

- Assets (inventories in Proposal 1 and the new equipment in Proposal 2) – which are non-monetary items.

- Liabilities (ie payables to outsourcing companies in Proposal 1 or to Silvez Inc in Proposal 2) – which are monetary items.

Monetary items are translated on the date of the transaction and re-translated at the year end (ie if the foreign currency payable remains outstanding at the year end).

The exchange difference is the difference between initially recording the purchases of engines at the rate ruling at the date of the transaction and the subsequent retranslation of the monetary item to the rate ruling at the reporting date. Such exchange differences should be reported as part of Wooster's profit or loss for the year.

Non-monetary items (eg the inventories of engines) are carried at historical cost and are translated using the exchange rate at the date of the transaction when the asset or liability arose. They are not subsequently retranslated.

Gratz – cost recognition

The cash payment per engine changes over the life of the Gratz contract. However in terms of cost recognition in the financial statements it could be viewed as a single three-year contract where the engines being delivered are identical and therefore the cost per engine accrued should be constant, even though the cash payments are uneven.

On this basis the average cost per engine is:

Year	Cost per engine	Number of engines	Total cost €	Total cost in £ (£1 = €1.4)
2017	€14,000	3,800	€53.20m	£38.0m
2018	€15,400	4,100	€63.14m	£45.1m
2019	€16,800	4,200 (max)	€70.56m	£50.5m
Total		**12,100**		**£133.6m**

Average cost per engine = £133.6m/12,100 = £11,041

The costs recognised in the financial statements would therefore be:

Year	Cost per engine £	Number of engines	Total cost £
2017	£11,041	3,800	£41.957m
2018	£11,041	4,100	£45.269m
2019	£11,041	4,200 (max)	£46.374m
Total		12,100	£133.6m

Consideration should be given to using accrued amounts on a discounted basis and recognising the unwinding of the discount.

Provisions

Under Proposal 1 a provision of £2.5m would need to be made for closure costs of the factory in the year ended 31 December 2016. By 30 November 2016, the contract would be finalised and announced. There is therefore both a constructive and legal obligation to incur these costs from this date.

Request for advice from Harry Harris

To: Harry Harris: Wooster Chairman
From: Gieves & Wood LLP, Senior - Lisa Ling
Date: 8 November 2016
Subject: Share options and redundancies

1. **Evaluation of the performance of Wooster**

Introduction and context

This is an independent evaluation of the performance of Wooster, and its management since the acquisition by StockFin on 1 January 2014.

	2013	2014	2015	2016
Cars	3,000	3,300	3,600	3,600
Price per car (£'000)	80	82	86	87
• production cost per car	60	56	57	58
• Employees	1,500	1,350	1,200	1,200
Revenue	240,000	270,600	309,600	313,200
Cost of sales	180,000	184,800	205,200	208,800
Gross profit	60,000	85,800	104,400	104,400
Other operating cost	80,000	85,000	90,000	91,000
Operating profit	- 20,000	800	14,400	13,400
Finance costs	3,000	3,500	4,000	4,000
Profit before tax	- 23,000	- 2,700	10,400	9,400
Tax	4,600	540	- 2,080	- 1,880
Profit after tax	- 18,400	- 2,160	8,320	7,520
Property, plant and equipment	80,000	88,000	96,000	95,000
Net current assets	30,000	29,840	40,160	48,680
Non-current liabilities	60,000	70,000	80,000	80,000
Equity	50,000	47,840	56,160	63,680
• GP%	25.0%	31.7%	33.7%	33.3%
• Op profit %	-8.3%	0.3%	4.7%	4.3%
• PBT %	-9.6%	-1.0%	3.4%	3.0%
• PAT %	-7.7%	-0.8%	2.7%	2.4%
• ROCE	-18.2%	0.7%	10.6%	9.3%
• ROE	-36.8%	-4.5%	14.8%	11.8%

	2013	2014	2015	2016
Cars per employee	2	2.4	3.0	3.0
% changes				
Revenue %		12.8%	14.4%	1.2%
Gross profit %		43%	21.7%	0%
Operating profit %		-104.0%	1700.0%	-6.9%
Sales volume		10.0%	9.1%	0.0%
Sales price		2.5%	4.9%	1.2%
Cost of sales		2.7%	11.0%	1.8%

Revenue

There has been a clear increase in sales revenues over the period 2014 to 2016 represented by significant increases of 12.8% in 2014 and 14.4% in 2015, but a much smaller expected increase of only 1.2% for 2016.

Sales volumes and price are two possible causes of these increases in sales revenues.

Sales volumes have increased by 10% in 2014 and by 9.1% in 2015, so this was a significant cause of the increase in revenues. Sales volumes did not increase again in 2016, but by this stage there was a binding production capacity constraint from the engine factory which prevented further growth.

The average price increased by 2.5% in 2014 and by 4.9% in 2015, which are additional to the volume increases. Being able to sell more cars at a higher price is evidence of good performance by Wooster management.

In trying to identify underlying causal factors, it does not seem that the price increase reflects a quality increase as product costs have also fallen from a high in 2013 (see below) so this explanation may lack plausibility.

An alternative explanation is a change in the product mix being sold, with a higher proportion of higher priced cars being purchased by customers in 2014 and 2015 compared with 2013.

An additional explanation of the high price increase in 2015 could reflect the fact that the company is operating at productive capacity in 2015 and 2016 and management is increasing price to reduce effective demand to the level of available supply.

The price increase for 2016 is much smaller at 1.2%. This may be due to market conditions but it is also cumulative on top of significant price increases in 2014 and 2015 which are unlikely to be sustainable at this rate in the longer run.

Profit

Since 2013, the year before the acquisition, profit has improved from operating losses (also losses before and after tax) into profits.

Operating profits were achieved in 2014 and profits before and after tax by 2015. This was a rapid and significant turnaround achieved by management.

Percentage increases to turn a loss to a profit are not particularly instructive, so perhaps the best measure of the improvement in operating performance is seen in the improvement in gross profit. In particular, the increase in gross profit has outweighed the £11m increase in administration costs between 2013 and 2016 (compound average of 4.39% per annum).

The gross profit margin has increased from 25% in 2013; to 33.7% in 2015; before dropping back to an expected 33.3% in 2016.

This has meant a very significant increase in gross profit in 2014 of 43%; and a further significant increase in 2015 of 21.7%.

The main cause of the increase in gross profit has been revenue increases which have been discussed above. However, there has also been good control over production costs which have fallen from £60,000 per vehicle in 2013; to £56,000 per vehicle in 2014; before rising to £58,000 by 2016.

more cars per £'ee.

A key feature in <u>reducing production costs appears</u> to be <s>labour productivity</s>. Following the reduction of the labour force in 2014, and again in 2015, the annual number of cars produced per employee increased significantly from two to three.

There was no further increase in gross profit in 2016, compared with 2015, as although the price per vehicle increased by £1,000, the production cost per vehicle also increased by £1,000, with no change in sales volume.

Return on capital employed (ROCE)

↑ assets ∴
↑ profits
(in theory)

New capital assets, amounting to £10m, were added to the assembly plant in each of the years 2014 and 2015. Capital employed did not increase by this full amount, due to depreciation on existing assets, but nevertheless there was a significant increase in capital over this period. It would therefore be expected that profits, in absolute terms, should increase as the scale of the business has increased.

Due to operating losses being made in 2013, ROCE was negative (at minus 18.2%) in that year. Improving to near break-even (at ROCE = 0.7%) in 2014. There was a reasonable ROCE of 10.6% in 2015; before falling back to 9.3% in 2016. This represents a <u>significant improvement</u> in performance and a reasonable ROCE in absolute terms.

Return on equity

In terms of the investment performance for StockFin in 2013, return on equity (ROE) was significantly negative (at minus 13.8%) in that year. Improving in 2014, ROE was still negative at minus 4.5%. In 2015 it increased to 14.8%, before falling back to 11.8% in 2016. While this represents a significant improvement in investment performance, it could still be regarded as too low for this type of private equity investment; particularly with respect to the annual benchmark of 20% expected by StockFin.

The Wooster management performance

While the chief executive was changed on acquisition, the four other executive directors are the same as prior to the acquisition. The non-executives and the chairman are new. The change in performance may therefore be due to a partial change in the composition of the board.

It may also be due to the additional performance incentives given to management by the share options.

In attempting to distinguish management performance from company performance, the factors which management can control need to be considered compared with matters that are decided at a higher level (eg new investment by StockFin) or exogenous events which may affect Wooster's performance, but are beyond the control of management.

It is clear that performance has increased in 2014, and again in 2015, compared with 2013. Performance fell back a little in 2016. Issues such as pricing, sales volumes achieved and cost control in 2014 and 2015 have been favourable and largely attributable to actions within the control of management.

Production capacity was reached in 2015 and 2016 so further growth was difficult. New investment is required to sustain growth (which is now being considered – see above) but this is not directly within Wooster management's control.

2. **Summary**

In 2013, the year before StockFin acquired Wooster, performance was poor with significant operating losses being incurred. Performance improved significantly in 2014 and again in 2015 and began to turn the company around. Performance fell back a little in 2016, partly because the engine plant reached capacity output. New plans are in place to address this issue. Therefore the performance in the two years following the acquisition has been good but, for further improvements, and to prevent the stagnation of growth in 2016 reoccurring, there needs to be increased efficiency and further investment.

Ethical issues and implications

To: Alex Khan - Gieves & Wood LLP Manager
From: Lisa Ling - Gieves & Wood LLP, Senior
Date: 8 November 2016
Subject: Ethical issues – share options and redundancies

Ethical issues – redundancies and share options

Ethics pertains to whether a particular behaviour is deemed acceptable in the context under consideration. In short, it is 'doing the right thing'.

In making any ethical evaluation it is first necessary to establish the facts. In this case, it would seem that the facts are reasonably clear in terms of what Harry Harris and Wooster intend to do, although there may be some doubt about what it is legally able to do.

The issue of legality and compliance with employment law needs to be considered and legal advice taken by Wooster. If Wooster is acting contrary to employment law this is a strong indication of an unethical stance. This may prevent the redundancies/dismissals or, as a minimum, increase the cost to Wooster from legal actions against the company by the employees being dismissed or made redundant.

There is another issue of legality in that Harry, in his role as chairman, is not acting in the best interests of the company, or shareholders as a body, but for a section of shareholders. This could be a breach of his fiduciary duty as a director. Legal advice should be taken.

Separate legal advice is needed for the directors, who are officers of the company, and the senior managers, who are employees.

If the redundancies/dismissals are deemed, on the basis of legal advice, to be within the law then the ethical aspects still need to be considered.

In this respect, it is helpful to apply the Institute of Business Ethics three tests:

- Transparency
- Effect
- Fairness

Transparency – would StockFin mind people (existing customers, suppliers, employees) knowing that these redundancies/dismissals have taken place and the real reason for making them?

Moreover, was it made transparent to managers at the time of granting the options that it was possible that redundancies/dismissals could take place, which would prevent the options vesting?

At this stage, the redundancies/dismissals decision is confidential, but will become public knowledge on announcement. What will be less clear is that the underlying reason is to prevent share options vesting to the benefit of StockFin. The issue of poor performance in this respect appears more to reduce transparency with a false reason rather than increase transparency.

It is important that GW reports with objectivity on the performance of Wooster and not become subject to any intimidation threat to state that there has been poor performance, where it does not believe this to be the case.

The reason that there are now fewer people to manage so we need fewer managers is, at best, only partial, as the number of employees fell by 20% (1,500 to 1,200) from 2013 to 2015, but the number of managers is being reduced much more drastically by 60%. This indicates this is perhaps more of an excuse, than a genuine reason, for the redundancies/dismissals.

The ethical tests of openness and transparency do not therefore appear to have been met by StockFin.

Effect – whom does the decision to make redundancies/dismissals affect or hurt? There are substantial effects on the managers concerned who suffer in three ways:

- Their options will not vest on 31 December 2017 and there is therefore a significant potential loss of value in their investment

- They will lose their jobs and future income and they may suffer damage to their reputations

- The value of the 10% shareholding for which they subscribed may be adversely affected by this decision

The StockFin shareholders would be favourably affected, as their shareholding in Wooster will not be diluted and will therefore increase in value.

Value would therefore be transferred from Wooster managers to StockFin owners as a result of the redundancies/dismissals.

It may however be that the value of Wooster shares as a whole is largely unaffected if managers can be adequately replaced.

Fairness – would the redundancies/dismissals be considered fair by those affected?

Much would depend what was included in the option contract and the understanding that was given to managers at the time of granting about the possibility of redundancies or dismissals, which could prevent the options vesting.

If it was not made clear at the grant date, then managers may feel it unfair they have been incentivised by a possibility that is not now going to occur. In this respect StockFin owners would have gained significant and unfair benefits.

If it had always been intended from granting that redundancies/dismissals would occur to prevent the options vesting then this is a more extreme ethical case, amounting to deception by StockFin in order to make a gain. The ethical principles here are honesty and integrity but may also amount to a different type of fraudulent action. There is no suggestion of this in Harry's note, but if this turns out to be the case, then further legal advice would be needed.

Actions in response to ethical issues

GW's initial actions should be:

- Make clear that the report on performance will be an objective assessment and will be unaffected by any purpose that Harry would wish to use it for.

- Suggest that the company takes legal advice, as to whether Harry's intended actions would be illegal. If such advice deems they would be illegal, inform Harry that if they are implemented than GW will cease to act for Wooster and inform the Wooster board of the reasons.

43 Phantom West Airlines Plc

Marking guide

		Marks
(1)	Calculate the revenue per week which each of the two proposed seat configurations is expected to generate.	
	Provide a reasoned recommendation as to which seat configuration would be preferable.	9
(2)	Compare the two methods of financing the new aircraft, providing supporting calculations and explanations.	
	Provide a reasoned recommendation for how to finance the new aircraft.	
	State any further information that would be needed before making a final decision about financing.	8
(3)	For eah of the two finance methods (lease; buy) set out the financial reporting consequences of grouding one or both aircraft from 30 September 2020.	6

(4) Explain how fuel price changes and forward contracts on fuel prices have impacted PWA's profit and other comprehensive income in the year ended 30 September 2016.
(Explanation needs to focus on why the movements have been recognised in the financial statements shown in Exhibit 3, not just a a general explanation of what has occurred.) 7

(5) In relation to the hedging of fuel prices:
- Explain whether PWA should hedge or whether it should accept the risk of fuel price volatility
- If hedging is to take pace, provide reasoned advice to PWA on the most appropriate hedging strategies, and address the acting FD's concerns about hedging. 8

Total marks 38

Draft response to Kevin Gunn's request

(1) Seating configuration – revenue generation

80 Business Class (BC); 180 premium economy (PE)

Calculation

Business class = (80 × 3 days × £1,250) + (60 × 4 days × £1,250)
= £600,000

Premium economy = (180 × 3 days × £600) + (150 × 4 days × £600) + (20* × £600)
= £696,000

Revenue per week = **£1,296,000**

*: Upgrades of seats only occur on days when there is excess capacity in BC (ie demand = 60) and excess demand in PE (ie demand = 200). This only occurs on Saturday.

Alternative tabular approach

	Demand PE	Demand BC	Seats PE	Seats BC	PE pass	BC pass	Upgrades	PE price	BC price	PE rev	BC rev
M	150	120	180	80	150	80		600	1,250	90,000	10,0000
Tu	150	60	180	80	150	60		600	1,250	90,000	75,000
W	150	60	180	80	150	60		600	1,250	90,000	75,000
Th	150	60	180	80	150	60		600	1,250	90,000	75,000
F	200	120	180	80	180	80		600	1,250	108,000	100,000
Sa	200	60	180	80	180	60	20	600	1,250	120,000	75,000
Su	200	120	180	80	180	80		600	1,250	108,000	100,000
										696,000	600,000

Total revenue per week = **£1,296,000**

60 Business Class; 225 premium economy

Calculation

Business class = (60 × 7 days × £1,250)
= £525,000

Premium economy = (200 × 3 days × £600) + (150 × 4 days × £600)
= £720,000

Revenue per week = **£1,245,000**

*: Upgrades of seats only occur on days when there is excess capacity in BC (ie demand = 60) and excess demand in PE (ie demand = 200). This only occurs on Saturday.

Alternative tabular approach

	Demand PE	Demand BC	Seats PE	Seats BC	PE pass	BC pass	PE price	BC price	PE rev	BC rev
M	150	120	225	60	150	60	600	1,250	90,000	75,000
Tu	150	60	225	60	150	60	600	1,250	90,000	75,000
W	150	60	225	60	150	60	600	1,250	90,000	75,000
Th	150	60	225	60	150	60	600	1,250	90,000	75,000
F	200	120	225	60	200	60	600	1,250	120,000	75,000
Su	200	60	225	60	200	60	600	1,250	120,000	75,000
Su	200	120	225	60	200	60	600	1,250	120,000	75,000
									720,000	**525,000**

Total revenue per week = **£1,245,000**

Reasoned recommendation

Based on the estimates provided, the configuration of 80 Business Class; 180 premium economy generates revenue per week of £1,296,000 per week, which is £51,000 greater than the alternative configuration of 60 Business Class; 225 premium economy. Over a year this would generate £2.62m (£51,000 x 360/7) additional revenue, which is significant.

The passenger load is identical at 1,620 passenger per week, but with the first configuration there are 60 more BC customers and 60 fewer PE passengers. This might mean some additional costs (eg food, drinks) but this is likely to be small compared to the additional revenue.

Further, in the second option the BC is always full so if forecasts understate the business class demand there is no capacity to increase BC revenue.

There is more flexibility if forecasts understate the PE demand there is capacity to increase seat capacity by upgrading to BC if there is spare capacity there.

At full capacity the revenues generated would be very similar a follows:

$(80 \times £1,250) + (180 \times £600) = £208,000$
$(60 \times £1,250) + (225 \times £600) = £210,000$

Recommendation

The configuration of 80 Business Class; 180 premium economy generates more revenue per week but also has greater flexibility to take on more BC passengers. It may also enhance PWA's wider reputation.

(2) **Financing the new aircraft**

2.1 Lease-buy decision

Buying

	Cash flow	DF	PV
Outlay	(£40m)	1.0	(£40m)
Residual	£15m	$1/(1.07)^{10}$	7.625m
NPV			**(£32.375m)**

Leasing - no break clause

PV rentals (paid in advance) $= £5m \times (1 + (AF9yrs\ 7\%)) = £5m \times (1 + 6.515)$
NPV $= $ **(£37.575m)**

Leasing - break clause

PV rentals $= £5m \times (1 + (AF4yrs\ 7\%)) = £5m \times (1 + 3.387)$
$= £21.935m$

PV penalty $= £14m/(1.07)^5$
$= £9.982m$

NPV $= $ **(£31.917m)**

Comparison

The full lease term of 10 years is comparable with the expected useful life of the asset if it is purchased. Over this period using the assumed discount rate, purchasing is the lower NPV option and on this basis is to be accepted.

However the decision should not be taken on the basis of NPV alone. There are a range of other factors that should be taken into account, particularly as the difference in the two NPVs is relatively small and may be sensitive to changes (eg in the interest rate or in the tax rate).

Liquidity may be a key consideration. The purchase of aircraft requires an initial payment. This needs to be out of available cash or the £80m needs to be financed (eg by borrowing). If the company does not have the available cash and is near debt capacity then leasing may be the only available choice, notwithstanding the higher NPV.

Risk is also a key factor. If demand for the London to New Delhi route is not popular it may be possible to use the aircraft on other routes. If however the aircraft are particularly suitable for this route, or if there is a general fall in demand for PWA flights globally, then the costs of grounding the aircraft for substantial periods or disposing of the aircraft needs to be considered.

In this respect, the break clause offers an exit route after 5 years which gives a lower NPV than ownership. However, the penalty cost is substantial and the comparison of (a) ownership and (b) a 5-year lease using the break clause; assumes the aircraft are grounded for a full 5 years without use before being sold, which is unrealistic. So while the break clause offers some flexibility, it is limited in its application.

The interest rate should be the after tax rate once tax cash flows are included. More information is needed on the tax consequences of the various options.

Further information is also needed on how the interest rate is calculated and how sensitive the NPVs are to a change in interest rate. A significant rise in interest rates would make the leasing method more favourable as it reduces the PV of the lease rentals and also reduces the value of the residual receipt for the purchase method, while leaving the outlay PV unaffected.

Recommendation

There are benefits to both methods. Unless market research has a high degree of certainty for strong demand, the purchase of one aircraft and the leasing of the other may give some flexibility in that it is less likely, if both were leased, that demand would be so low that both aircraft would need to be grounded and the break-clause exercised on both contracts.

(3) Financial reporting consequences of grounding one or both aircraft

The lease arrangement appears to be an operating lease in accordance with IAS17 as substantially all the risks and rewards of ownership do not appear to have passed to PWA as lessee. This is indicated by the fact that there is a lessee option to cancel the lease after 5 years, albeit at a significant cost. Even if the lease contract runs the full term of 10 years the PV of the residual of £15m is a significant proportion of the fair value of the asset at 19% (£7.625m/£40m) suggesting that the lessor has a significant interest in the residual value. (However it should be noted that this is using the working assumption interest rate of 7% rather than the interest rate implicit in the lease).

The following calculations are for one aircraft.

Purchase

At 30 September 2020, the carrying amount would be:

Annual depreciation (£40m – £15m)/10   =   £2.5m

Carrying amount £40m – (£2.5m × 3)   =   £32.5m

If the aircraft is to be grounded permanently from 30 September 2020 then the value in use would be zero in respect of operating earnings.

The fair value less costs to sell would be the fair value at the date of impairment which is £25m. An impairment of £7.5m would therefore be recognised in profit or loss for the year ended 30 September 2020.

Leasing

If the aircraft are to be grounded permanently from 31 December 2019 then the lease agreement becomes an onerous lease in accordance with IAS37 and the PV of the future minimum lease rentals should be recognised as a provision in financial statements for the year ended 30 September 2020. This amounts to:

PV 2021 rental	=	£5m/1.07	=	£4.67m
PV 2022 penalty	=	£14m/$(1.07)^2$ =		£12.23m
Provision at 30 September 2020	=	**£16.9m**		

An expense of £16.9m would therefore be recognised in profit or loss for the year ended 30 September 2020.

Draft response to Zara Zhou's request (Exhibit 4)

(1) Financial reporting

The previous finance director has used forward contracts for fuel as a cash flow hedge for accounting purposes.

The purpose of cash flow hedging is to enter into a transaction (purchasing the forward contracts as a derivative) where the derivative's cash flows (the hedged instrument) are expected to move wholly or partly, in an inverse direction to the cash flow of the position being hedged (the hedged item) which is the future purchases of oil. The two elements of the hedge (the hedge item and the hedge instrument) are therefore matched and are interrelated with each other in economic terms.

The policy notes in PWA's accounts state that this matching has been highly effective in the year ended 30 September 2016.

Overall, the impact of hedge accounting is to reflect this underlying intention of the matched nature of the hedge agreement in the financial statements. Hedge accounting therefore aims to ensure that the two elements of the hedge are treated symmetrically and offsetting gains and losses (of the hedge item and the hedge instrument) are reported in profit or loss in the same periods. Normal accounting treatment rules of recognition and measurement may not achieve this and hence may result in an accounting mismatch and earnings volatility, which would not reflect the underlying commercial intention or effects of linking the two hedge elements which offset and mitigate risks. For example, typically, derivatives are measured at fair value through profit or loss; whereas the cash flows from fuel purchases that they are hedging are measured at cost or are not measured at all in the current period.

Hedge accounting rules are therefore required, subject to satisfying hedge accounting conditions.

If the hedge is for physical delivery of fuel (own use) then hedge accounting would not apply.

With hedging, but without hedge accounting, there would be a mismatch if the forward contract was taken out in the year ended 30 September 2016 for an anticipated fuel purchase in the year ending 30 September 2017. A gain (or loss) on a forward contract derivative would be recognised in the year ended 30 September 2016 but the fuel price change it was hedging would be recognised when the fuel is purchased in the year ending 30 September 2017.

Cash flow hedge accounting attempts to reflect the use the forward rate derivative to hedge against future cash flow movements from fuel price changes. To achieve this, movements in the derivative, in the year ended 30 September 2016, which would normally go through profit or loss, are recognised in other comprehensive income. The other comprehensive income balance (including further movements in the year ended 30 September 2016 in the forward exchange derivative) is restated/recycled to profit or loss in the same period in which the hedged highly probable transaction (fuel purchases) affects profit or loss which would mostly be for the year ending 30 September 2017.

The financial statements for the year ended 30 September 2016

Under OCI, the 'Fair value changes in cash-flow hedges in the year (fuel commodities)' of £85m represent a loss on forward rate derivative contracts taken out in the year ended 30 September 2016 to hedge fuel purchases after that date. This suggests that in hedging against fuel price increases, the price of fuel has fallen and a loss is therefore occurred on the forward contract as there is an obligation to deliver fuel at the contract price which is by 30 September 2016, now above the current market price of fuel.

Under OCI, the 'Fair value changes in cash flow hedges transferred to fuel costs' of £56m represent a loss on forward rate derivative contracts taken out in the year ended 30 September 2015 (or prior years) to hedge fuel purchases in the year ended 30 September 2016 (ie so gains and losses on the forward contracts can be recognised in profit or loss in the same period in which the hedged item (fuel purchases) affects profit or loss). As such, they are recycled to fuel costs in the statement of profit or loss in the year ended 30 September 2016. The figure of £56m is positive in OCI as a negative figure is being removed from OCI. The consequence is that fuel costs are increased to £942m. In the year ended 30 September 2016, the overall effect on total comprehensive income, of recycling the £56m is zero, as the extra cost under fuel is cancelled by the positive figure under OCI.

The underlying cost of fuel was £886m (£942m - £56m). This would reflect a lower than expected price of fuel purchases but with an added loss on a hedging arrangement that moved in the wrong direction for PDA. This loss on hedging increased underlying fuel costs by 6.3%.

(2) Hedging decision

2.1 Whether to hedge fuel costs

Fuel is a significant cost to PWA making up 42.5% of all operating costs for the year ended 30 September 2016.

The price of fuel is closely correlated with the price of oil which has been extremely volatile in recent years, particularly over the period 2014-16, when the price more than halved within 18 months.

There is therefore a possibility of significant fuel prices changes affecting profit if there is no hedging. Using the data for the year ended 30 September 2016, fuel costs were £942m. Thus, for example, a 20% increase in the fuel costs for this period would have cost an additional £188.4m which would have reduced profit before tax by about a third (33.4%).

PWA's core business is to operate airlines, not to speculate in oil price movements, where it does not have the relevant core competences. Without hedging, PWA's earnings stream could become volatile and investors may raise the cost of equity in light of this risk.

A hedging strategy to mitigate the impact of fuel price movements, if not remove it completely, therefore seems necessary.

The use of forwards or futures in this strategy means that, in protecting the company from upwards movements in fuel prices, it would also prevent the company from benefiting from downwards movements in fuel prices for the period of the contract.

2.2 Hedging arrangements

Forward contracts

A forward contract is a binding agreement to acquire a set amount of goods at a future date at a price agreed today.

A forward contract fixes the rate for a transaction, and these contracts must be settled regardless of whether or not the oil price at the settlement date is more favourable than the agreed forward price.

The hedge could be for aviation fuel itself, or for oil, which is very closely correlated to the price of aviation fuel.

While PWA uses fuel, it does not need to take physical delivery of the fuel. Instead it could use changes in the price of the forward contracts where the gains and losses would offset the movements in fuel purchase prices which are entirely separate contracts.

Thus, for example, PWA may arrange a forward contract with its bank. Subsequently, when it needs to purchase the fuel, the bank will close out the original forward contract, in effect by arranging another forward contract for the same settlement date, to cancel out the original contract. The close-out is then settled with a cash payment by one party to the other, depending on the difference between the forward prices in the contract and market prices.

Some advantages of forwards over futures are:

- They are transacted over the counter, and are not subject to the requirements of a trading exchange.

- They can, in theory, be for any amount.

- The length of time for the contract can be flexible, but contracts are generally for less than two years.

  Some disadvantages of forwards compared with futures are:

- PWA would not have the protection that trading on an exchange brings (see below).
- There is a risk of default by the counterparty to the contract.

Futures

A future would be an exchange-traded agreement to buy or sell a standard quantity of oil on a fixed future date at a price agreed today. They can be described as exchange-traded standardised forward contracts.

There are two parties to a futures contract – a buyer and a seller – whose obligations are as follows.

- The buyer of a future enters into an obligation to buy the specified asset on a specified date.

- The seller of a future is under an obligation to sell the specified asset on a future date.

Futures contracts are traded on an exchange with the contract terms clearly specified by the rules of the exchange.

The contracts are of a standardised size with standardised delivery dates (March, June, September and December). This means that it may not be possible to match the exact exposure that PWA requires for its fuel over the exact period for which fuel purchases are anticipated to be made.

Futures are traded on margin, meaning that the trader only has to spend a small amount of money, far below the value of the underlying commodity, to be exposed to the price rise or fall of that commodity. Margin is an amount of money deposited with the clearing house of the futures exchange, to cover any foreseeable losses on the futures position. Both buyers and sellers of futures deposit initial margin with the exchange when they make their transaction, and may subsequently be required to pay additional variation margin if they incur a loss on their futures position.

Recommendation

In general, the principle of both forward contracts and futures would be to lock PWA into a contractual price for fuel to be paid in the future. Gains or losses would offset changes in the underlying prices of fuel purchases, which is the item being hedged.

The key difference would be if PWA wished to hedge 18 months ahead like the previous FD did, then this would point towards forward contracts, as futures tend to be within 12 months, and possibly less.

It would be possible to extend hedging up to two years using forward contracts, but it would be difficult beyond that time frame.

Whether PWA wishes to hedge all of its fuel purchases or (say) 90% like the previous FD would depend on the risk appetite of the board. The advantage of not hedging 100% would be that the amount of fuel purchased next year may be below expectations and therefore result in over-hedging (ie >100% of actual fuel purchases are hedged), which would perversely expose PWA to increased risk rather than reduced risk.

In having a lower proportion of longer term fuel purchases hedged (say 60% like the previous FD) it leaves scope for top-up hedging at a later date and the flexibility to leave open positions while observing trends in fuel prices over time. Shorter term top up hedging at a later date would enable the use of futures if these had more favourable terms than forward contracts at this time.

ICAEW

ICAEW

REVIEW FORM – STRATEGIC BUSINESS MANAGEMENT: Question Bank

Your ratings, comments and suggestions would be appreciated on the following areas of this Question Bank

	Very useful	Useful	Not useful
Number of questions in each section	☐	☐	☐
Standard of answers	☐	☐	☐
Amount of guidance on exam technique	☐	☐	☐
Quality of marking guides	☐	☐	☐

	Excellent	Good	Adequate	Poor
Overall opinion of this Question Bank	☐	☐	☐	☐

Please return completed form to:

The Learning Team
Learning and Professional Department
ICAEW
Metropolitan House
321 Avebury Boulevard
Milton Keynes
MK9 2FZ
E learning@icaew.com

For space to add further comments please see overleaf.

REVIEW FORM (continued)

TELL US WHAT YOU THINK

Please note any further comments and suggestions/errors below.